Global Goods and the Country House

Global Goods and the Country House

Comparative perspectives, 1650–1800

Edited by Jon Stobart

First published in 2023 by
UCL Press
University College London
Gower Street
London WC1E 6BT

Available to download free: www.uclpress.co.uk

Collection © Editor, 2023
Text © Contributors, 2023
Images © Contributors and copyright holders named in captions, 2023

The authors have asserted their rights under the Copyright, Designs and Patents Act 1988 to be identified as the authors of this work.

A CIP catalogue record for this book is available from The British Library.

Any third-party material in this book is not covered by the book's Creative Commons licence. Details of the copyright ownership and permitted use of third-party material is given in the image (or extract) credit lines. If you would like to reuse any third-party material not covered by the book's Creative Commons licence, you will need to obtain permission directly from the copyright owner.

This book is published under a Creative Commons Attribution-Non-commercial Non-derivative 4.0 International licence (CC BY-NC-ND 4.0), https://creativecommons.org/licenses/by-nc-nd/4.0/. This licence allows you to share, copy, distribute and transmit the work for personal and non- commercial use provided author and publisher attribution is clearly stated. Attribution should include the following information:

Stobart, J. (ed.) 2023. *Global Goods and the Country House: Comparative perspectives, 1650–1800*. London: UCL Press. https://doi.org/10.14324/111.9781800083837

Further details about Creative Commons licences are available at https://creativecommons.org/licenses/

ISBN: 978-1-80008-385-1 (Hbk.)
ISBN: 978-1-80008-384-4 (Pbk.)
ISBN: 978-1-80008-383-7 (PDF)
ISBN: 978-1-80008-386-8 (epub)
DOI: https://doi.org/10.14324/111.9781800083837

Contents

List of figures	ix
List of tables	xv
List of contributors	xvii
Acknowledgements	xxv
Introduction: contexts and departures Jon Stobart	1

Part 1: Consuming global goods

1. Mahogany, sugar and porcelain: global goods for a Swedish aristocratic family in the eighteenth century — 27
   Gudrun Andersson and Göran Ulväng

2. Global goods and Imperial Knights: assemblages in country houses in south-western Germany, 1700–1820 — 53
   Daniel Menning, Anne Sophie Overkamp and Julietta Schulze

3. The global samurai: imports and daily life in isolated Japan — 77
   Martha Chaiklin

4. 'We are starving for want of Tea': Asian objects, domestic slavery and Caribbean sociability — 101
   Christine Walker

Object lessons 1: Traded goods

I. Statuette of Captain Jacob Beckmann — 125
   Mikkel Venborg Pedersen

II. Osnaburg: a study in global textile production and exploitation — 129
   Laura Johnson

III. Suite of ebony furniture inlaid with ivory, Charlecote Park — 133
   Annabelle Gilmore and Jon Stobart

IV. Newspaper advertisement for the English Depot. E. Grant & Comp., Bucharest — 137
   Nicoleta Roman

V *Histoire des deux Indes* by Guillaume Raynal, 1780   141
   Eleanor Matthews

Part 2: The global in the local

5 Power, friendship and delightfulness: global goods in the
   residences of an aristocratic family in the Kingdom of Naples   147
   Gaia Bruno

6 Luxury, international trade and consumption in three
   eighteenth-century Danish homes   169
   Mikkel Venborg Pedersen

7 Interiors as a visiting card: decoration, consumption and
   material culture in a mid-nineteenth-century Romanian
   country house   193
   Nicoleta Roman

8 An 'American bearskin merchant' in the 'wilds of
   Pennsylvania': trade and the British country house in North
   America   215
   Stephen G. Hague

Object lessons 2: Crafting global goods

VI Model of a Chinese pagoda by Elizabeth Ratcliffe, 1767   241
    Emile de Bruijn

VII The Barbados Monkey Jar   245
     Kevin Farmer and Tara Inniss

VIII Japanese red wool *jinbaori* (surcoat): East meets West   249
      Martha Chaiklin

IX Shellwork shadowbox grottoes as global goods   253
    Laura C. Keim

X Tobacco rolls, Württemberg   257
   Daniel Menning

Part 3: Domesticating the global

9 Second-hand empire? Global goods in English provincial
   auctions, *c.* 1760–1840   263
   Jon Stobart

10	Global houses of the Efik *Louis P. Nelson*	285
11	Negotiating cosmopolitan taste with local culture: porcelain rooms in Indian forts and palaces *Esther Schmidt*	307

Object lessons 3: Symbols and symbolism

XI	The new worlds' gate *Gaia Bruno*	333
XII	Two clubs, two perspectives: Haudenosaunee material culture at Audley End *Michael Galban (Wašiw & Kutzadika'a) and Peter Moore*	337
XIII	Design for pinery built for Sir Joseph Banks, 1807 *Katie Donington*	341
XIV	*Grosser Atlas über die Gantze Welt*, by Johann Baptist Homann *Mrinalini Venkateswaran*	345
XV	Frans Post's *View of Itamaracá Island*: rethinking a colonial past *Yme Kuiper*	349

Part 4: Imperial houses

12	Cartography, collecting and the construction of empire at Dyrham Park *Rupert Goulding and Louis P. Nelson*	355
13	Cultivating the world: English country house gardens, 'exotic' plants and elite women collectors, c. 1690–1800 *Katie Donington*	381
14	Colonial power and global gifts: the governorship of Johan Maurits, Count of Nassau-Siegen in Dutch Brazil (1637–44) *Yme Kuiper*	405

Conclusions 429
Jon Stobart

Index 433

List of figures

0.1	Mahogany chair by William Gomm, *c.* 1764. Stoneleigh Abbey	6
0.2	Powys Castle, home of the Clive family	7
0.3	Wilton House, Virginia	10
0.4	'Chinoiserie chair', Thomas Chippendale, *The Gentleman and Cabinet Maker's Director* (1754)	13
2.1	Porcelain teapot with lid, Ludwigsburg, 1758–70	60
2.2	Peter Jakob Horemans, 'Two Ladies Drinking Tea', 1772	63
2.3	Eight-piece *déjeuner* set with rococo decorations, Dresden, 1770–5	67
2.4	Coffee cup, Vienna, 1800	69
2.5	Peter Jakob Horemans, 'Spring (Johanna de Lasence Drinking Coffee in the Garden)', 1767	70
3.1	Modern reconstruction of Azuchi Castle	80
3.2	Daimyo's concubine and her maids in the garden. From Nishikawa Sukenobu, 'Hyakunin jorō shina sadame' [A Hundred Women by Rank], 1723	82
3.3	Lacquer *inrō* with hawk (front and back), nineteenth century	88
3.4	Tea Ceremony. From 'Ogasawara shorei taizen' [The Complete Ogasawara Etiquette], 1726.	90
3.5	Japanese Tea Ceremony 'Meibutsuki': Utensils (1600)	91
4.1	*A Midnight Modern Conversation* by William Hogarth, *c.* 1733	115
4.2	*The Strode Family* by William Hogarth, *c.* 1738	116
4.3	*Segar Smoking Society in Jamaica* by Abraham James, *c.* 1802	117
OL.I	Statuette of Jacob Beckmann, *c.* 1751	125
OL.II	Advertisements for osnaburgs in *The Pennsylvania Gazette*, 26 July 1753	129
OL.III	Two chairs in a set of ten pieces of seat furniture, of ebony inlaid with engraved ivory, comprising an open armchair, a daybed and eight standard chairs or backstools, Visakhapatnam, India, *c.* 1690–1720	133

OL.IV	English Depot. E Grant & Comp. advertisement in *Românul. Diariu politic, comercial, literar* [The Romanian. Political, commercial and literary journal]	137
OL.V	Guillaume Raynal, *Histoire des deux Indes* (1780), Brodsworth Hall, UK	141
5.1	Silver birds, chiselled on silvers, various sizes, nineteenth century	154
5.2	Chestnut bookcase with the Pignatelli coat of arms, nineteenth century. On the top: chinaware, eighteenth century	158
5.3	Cat with kitten, China, eighteenth century	159
5.4	M. Tolsà, Hernán Cortés, golden bronze on granite column and marble base, 1794	161
6.1	Dress in late empire style, made of Indian cotton with silver embroidery, c. 1810–20, and a Kashmir shawl from c. 1800	171
6.2	Two of 12 sets of chocolate cups bought in China in 1734 for the Danish king, Christian VI	173
6.3	Lacquer panelling *à la chinoise* from 1732 in King Christian VI's reception room in the Prince's Palais, Copenhagen, together with a cabinet in black and gold lacquer work	177
6.4	Two Chinese vases in Kangxi style, delivered to the Danish king's Artificial Chamber in 1701	181
6.5	Miss Justine van Hemert's bed chamber at Brede House decorated with English-made coton textiles, 1790s (reconstructed)	186
7.1	Constantin Daniel Rosenthal, *Nicolae Golescu*, 1848	205
7.2	Nicolae Grant, *Golești Konak*, 1898	207
7.3	Nicolae Grant, *Interior*	208
7.4	Nicolae Grant, *Interior*	209
7.5	Nicolae Grant, *Boyar Interior*	210
8.1	Stenton, near Philadelphia	216
8.2	The London-made Logan family tea service, 1720–4	220
8.3	Ceramics reconstructed from archaeology at Stenton display the range of china, stoneware and earthenware, including at least ten teapots	221
8.4	The fireplace wall of the 'Yellow Lodging Room' framed with English-made Delft or Dutch tiles	223

8.5	A Pennsylvania redware bowl with a slip-figure of a Native American, *c.* 1730–50	224
8.6	Desk and bookcase in Stenton's parlour with the Greek wine cup, or skyphos, and marble sample, all purportedly gifts from Royal Society member Peter Collinson to James Logan	231
OL.VI	Model of a Chinese pagoda in vellum, mica, mother-of-pearl, glass and stone, made by Elizabeth Ratcliffe (*c.* 1735–*c.* 1810), 1767	241
OL.VII	Barbadian Monkey Jar	245
OL.VIII	A typical *jinbaori* from early modern Japan	249
OL.IX	Shellwork shadowbox grotto by Anne Reckless Emlen (1721–1816), *c.* 1757	253
OL.X	Tobacco rolls, baked by the author	257
9.1	Thomas Rowland, *Christie's Auction Room*, 1808	264
9.2	Ecton rectory, Northamptonshire	268
9.3	Catalogue for the sale at Geddington House, Northamptonshire, 1823: front cover (detail)	278
9.4	Catalogue for the sale at Horton, Northamptonshire, 1781: library	280
10.1	'Iron Palace of King Eyembo', plans and view, *The Builder*, May 1843, 170–1	286
10.2	Gabriel Mathias, *Portrait of William Ansah Sessarakoo, son of Eno Baisie Kurentsi (John Currantee) of Anomabu*, 1749	293
10.3	'Design for a House in a Tropical Climate', Carl Wadström, *An Essay on Colonization* (London, 1794)	297
10.4	John Murray, *The First Day of the Yam Custom*, 1818	298
10.5	Thomas Parr House (Liverpool Royal Institution), *c.* 1799, Liverpool, England	301
11.1	The *Chini-ki-Chitrashali* with *jharokha* overlooking Manek Chowk, City Palace Udaipur	312
11.2	Dutch tiles, *c.* 1711, *chini-ki-chitrashali* or Chinese picture gallery, City Palace Udaipur, Rajasthan	314
11.3	Ornamental interior detail showing the *farangi* theme, *Chitram ki Burj*, City Palace Udaipur	316
11.4	Mural in the *Chitram ki Burj*, City Palace Udaipur, depicting Maharana Bhim Singh (r. 1778–1828) with gold nimbus depicted on a *jhula* (swing) in the *jharokha* of the *Chini ki Chitrashali* with several female attendants, City Palace Udaipur, no date	317

11.5	*Shiva, Maharana Ari Singh seated at night. On the terrace of the Chini ki Chitrashali* (1764), opaque watercolour heightened with gold on paper, 62 cm × 48 cm	318
11.6	*Bakhta, Maharana Ari Singh II in durbar* (1765), opaque watercolour and gold paint on paper, 58 cm × 46.2 cm	319
11.7	Porcelain room furnished with Staffordshire Blue Willow Pattern plates in the second part of the nineteenth century under Maharana Swarup Singh (1815, r. 1842–61), City Palace Udaipur, now called Fateh Prakash Palace	322
11.8	Blue Willow Pattern plates, detail of the *Chini Gokhada*, Juna Mahal, Dungarpur	323
OL.XI	Antonio Nicolini (?), the main entrance of La Floridiana, nineteenth century	333
OL.XII	Ball-headed war clubs, eastern woodlands – Haudenosaunee, *c.* 1775–83 and drawings of the clubs' etched iconography	337
OL.XIII	A pinery executed for the Right Honourable Sir Joseph Banks, Bart. at Spring Grove, Smallbury Green, Middlesex	341
OL.XIV	*Grosser Atlas über Die Gantze Welt*, Johann Baptist Homann (1663–1724), Nuremberg (detail)	345
OL.XV	Frans Post, *View of Itamaracá Island* (1637)	349
12.1	Dyrham Park east front with greenhouse	356
12.2	The Old [walnut] Stair Case, Dyrham Park	360
12.3	*A Cocoa Tree and Roasting Hut*, unknown artist, *c.* 1672	365
12.4	Stand, formed from enslaved African figure, late seventeenth century, English	366
12.5	Portrait of a family drinking tea in an interior, attributed to Roelof Koets (II), *c.* 1680	368
12.6	Johannes Kip, *Dyrham Park* (1712), showing the house and garden	371
13.1	*Mary Capel (1630–1715), Later Duchess of Beaufort, and Her Sister Elizabeth (1633–1678), Countess of Carnarvon* by Sir Peter Lely	386
13.2	Badminton from the south, attributed to Thomas Smith (*c.* 1708–10)	390
13.3	Beaufortia Decussata, Splendid Beaufortia in *Curtis's Botanical Magazine* 42.1726–1770 (1815): 1733	391

13.4	'Bulstrode, Buckinghamshire' engraved by Walker after a picture by Corbould, published in *The Copper Plate Magazine*, 1794	392
13.5	'Portlandia Grandiflora' by Mary Delany from an album Vol. VII, 91 (1782)	394
14.1	Map of Mauritsstad and Recife, *c.* 1645–47	407
14.2	Jan van Brosterhuyzen, after Frans Post, *Vrijburg*, *c.* 1645–7	408
14.3	Anon., *Boa Vista*, *c.* 1671	409
14.4	Frans Post, *Landscape in Brazil*, 1652, showing sugar plantation	417
14.5	Albert Eckhout, *Dancing Tupuyas*, 1643	422
14.6	Pieter Nason, *Johan Maurits, Count of Nassau-Siegen*, 1675	424

List of tables

1.1	Spens family assets in 1751 and 1802 in Riksdaler, deflated at constant prices (CPI, base year 1914)	31
1.2	Spens family's annual income and expenditure in 1727–30 and 1797–1800 (1810–15) in Riksdaler, and the totals at constant prices (CPI, base year 1914)	32
1.3	House contents in 1751 by category and origin, at constant prices (CPI, base year 1914)	35
1.4	Purchases in 1727–30 by origin and family residence, per year in Riksdaler, at constant prices (CPI, base year 1914)	38
1.5	House contents in 1802 by category and origin, in Riksdaler, at constant prices (CPI, base year 1914)	41
1.6	Purchases in 1797–1800 by origin and family residence, per year in Riksdaler, at constant prices (CPI, base year 1914)	43
1.7	Categorisation of goods as global, European or domestic	47
2.1	Tobacco paraphernalia (in brackets: items with silver content)	56
2.2	Paraphernalia for coffee consumption	57
2.3	Paraphernalia for tea consumption	58
2.4	Manufacture/place of origin of ceramics paraphernalia for coffee, tea and chocolate (1697–1811)	60
2.5	Paraphernalia for chocolate consumption	61
5.1	Exotic objects in the Pignatelli houses (1745, 1751, 1752)	151
9.1	Appearance of global goods in Northamptonshire house sales, *c.* 1760–1840	266

List of contributors

Gudrun Andersson is a Professor of History at Uppsala University. Her research interests include gender history, cultural history and material culture in seventeenth, eighteenth and early nineteenth-century Sweden. She has published extensively on early modern elite status and consumption (e.g. *Stadens dignitärer. Den lokala elitens status- och maktmaifestation i Arboga 1650–1770, 2009*) and is currently working on diaries by the middling sort, and on fashion magazines and the formation of the bourgeoisie.

Emile de Bruijn studied Japanese at Leiden University (The Netherlands) and museology at Essex University (United Kingdom). He worked in the Chinese and Japanese art departments of Sotheby's auctioneers in London before moving to the heritage charity the National Trust. He has published about various aspects of the material culture of orientalism, including his most recent book *Borrowed Landscapes: China and Japan in the Historic Houses and Gardens of Britain and Ireland* (Philip Wilson Publishers, 2023).

Gaia Bruno is a post-doctoral fellow at Ca' Foscari University of Venice in the project ERC-2018-Advanced Grants, Water-Cultures – The Water Cultures of Italy, 1500–1900 (PI Prof. David Gentilcore). Previously she was a post-doc at the University of Naples Federico II, where she obtained her PhD. Among others, she has published *Le ricchezze degli avi. Cultura materiale della società napoletana nel Settecento* (fedOA Press, 2022); 'Vivere a Napoli nel XVIII secolo: il Tribunale della Fortificazione, Acqua e Mattonata', *Società e Storia* 4 (2018); and 'Fronteggiare l'emergenza: le istituzioni del Regno di Napoli di fronte agli eventi sismici del XVII secolo', *Mediterranea* 51 (2021).

Martha Chaiklin is a historian of Japan and the East India Companies and independent curator, currently based in Maryland, USA. She obtained her PhD at Leiden University. Her major publications include *Cultural Commerce and Dutch Commercial Culture* (2003) and *Ivory and the Aesthetics of Modernity in Meiji Japan* (2014). She also translated C.T. Assendelft de Coningh's *A Pioneer in Yokohama* (2012) and edited

Asian Material Culture (2009), Mediated by Gifts (2017) and Animal Trade Histories in the Indian Ocean World (2020).

Katie Donington is a Senior Lecturer in Black, Caribbean and African history at the Open University. Her research focuses on the history and legacies of British transatlantic slavery. She is interested in how slavery impacted on the familial and cultural world of the planter-merchant elites. She worked on the Legacies of British Slave-ownership project at University College London between 2009 and 2015. She is author of The Bonds of Family: Slavery, Commerce and Culture in the British Atlantic World, 2019). She is interested in the representation of slavery in public history and was an historical advisor on the National Trust Colonial Countryside project.

Kevin Farmer is Deputy Director of the Barbados Museum and Historical Society (BMHS) and a member of the Barbados World Heritage Committee. His research interests include the creation of cultural identity in post-colonial states, the role of museums in national development, the management and curation of archaeological resources, and the role of heritage in national development. Farmer is co-editor of Pre-colonial and Post-colonial Contact Archaeology in Barbados (2019) and Plantation to Nation: Caribbean museums and national identity (2012) and author of articles on cultural resource management, historical archaeology and the future of heritage development.

Michael Galban is the Historic Site Manager of Ganondagan State Historic Site and the curator of the Seneca Art & Culture Center. Ganondagan is a seventeenth-century Seneca town site and nationally regarded as a centre for Iroquoian history, cultural and environmental preservation. His current research focuses on historic woodland arts and Indigenous/colonial history and he lectures on the subject extensively. He sits on the board of directors of the Museum Association of New York (MANY) and the editorial board of the New York History Journal and is currently working in the Indigenous Working Group component of REV WAR 250th NY commission.

Annabelle Gilmore is a PhD student at the University of Birmingham funded by AHRC Midlands4Cities. Her thesis is in collaboration with the National Trust and is analysing the hidden connections between slavery and imperialism and the country house of Charlecote Park in Warwickshire. She is also working on how to bring these histories to the public.

Rupert Goulding is a Senior Curator at the National Trust with responsibility for developing national research projects. As curator for Dyrham Park, he delivered several major projects to conserve, revive and interpret the house, including acquiring significant collections and publishing new research. His curatorial projects have included the transformation of Chedworth Roman Villa, the exhibition 'Prized Possessions' on Dutch seventeenth-century paintings and the re-presentation of the Bath Assembly Rooms. He studied archaeology at the universities of Durham and Reading and has worked for the National Trust for over 14 years.

Stephen G. Hague is Associate Professor of Modern European History at Rowan University in New Jersey, USA. He specialises in British and British imperial history with a particular interest in architecture and material culture. He researches and writes on the intersections of political, social, cultural and architectural history and is the author of *The Gentleman's House in the British Atlantic World, 1680–1780* (2015) and co-editor of *At Home in the Eighteenth Century: Interrogating domestic space* (2022). He holds a doctorate from Oxford University and is a Supernumerary Fellow of Linacre College, Oxford.

Tara A. Inniss is a Lecturer in the Department of History and Philosophy at the University of the West Indies (UWI), Cave Hill Campus and Director of the UWI/OAS Caribbean Heritage Network (CHN). The areas of focus for her teaching and research include history of medicine, history of social policy and heritage and social development. She holds a PhD in Caribbean History from the UWI, Cave Hill Campus, and a Master's in International Social Development from the University of New South Wales in Sydney, Australia.

Laura E. Johnson is the Linda Eaton Associate Curator of Textiles at Winterthur. Johnson received her PhD from the University of Delaware Program in American Civilization in 2011 and an MA in American Material Culture from the Winterthur Program. She has consistently focused on textiles, identity and Indigenous material culture in her academic and curatorial practice. She has curated exhibitions on jewellery, fashion and Indigenous trade items and has published in both academic and popular contexts about textiles and identity. Recent and current projects include *The Needle's I: Stitching identity*, researching early Spanish and Latin American textile production, and Philadelphia needlework instructors.

Laura C. Keim is Curator of Stenton, a historic house museum in Philadelphia, and is a Lecturer in Historic Preservation at the University of Pennsylvania. She studies architecture, decorative arts and material culture of the Atlantic World in the eighteenth and early nineteenth centuries, as well as the history of collecting and reinvention of the past in England and America in the twentieth century. Stenton recently received a Dean F. Failey grant from the Decorative Arts Trust to open, photograph, closely investigate and conserve the shellwork shadowbox grotto featured in this volume in summer 2023.

Yme Kuiper is an anthropologist and historian and Emeritus Professor of the University of Groningen where he had two endowed chairs: 'Historical Anthropology & Anthropology of Religion' and 'Historic Country Houses & Landed Estates'. He wrote a dissertation on the nobility and landed elite in Frisia during the eighteenth and nineteenth centuries and has written and edited books on topics such as country house culture, collective memory, hunting, urban identity and aristocracy in novels. With Nikolaj Bijleveld and Jaap Dronkers he edited and published *Nobilities in Europe in the Twentieth Century: Reconversion strategies, memory culture and elite formation* (2015).

Eleanor Matthews is a Curator of Collections and Interiors for English Heritage, covering sites across South Yorkshire and the North Midlands with a particular responsibility for Brodsworth Hall and Gardens. Her research interests include literary collections, the relationship between objects and people, and oral history. Matthews was the curator for the 'Liberty and Lottery' exhibition at Brodsworth, which focused on the site's links with the transatlantic slave trade. She has degrees from the University of Nottingham and the University of Oxford, and, prior to English Heritage, she worked for the National Trust and the Wordsworth Trust.

Daniel Menning is Associate Professor at the Institute of Modern History, University of Tübingen, Germany. He works on the history of the nobility and landed estates in Germany between the eighteenth and twentieth centuries. His current research project explores the economic history of Jebenhausen manor in the second half of the eighteenth century. Key publications include the monograph *Standesgemäße Ordnung in der Moderne: Adlige Familienstrategien und Gesellschaftsentwürfe in Deutschland 1840–1945* (2014) as well as the book chapter 'Nobility, peasantry and estates in southwestern Germany, from the eighteenth to the twentieth century' in *Estate Landscapes in Northern Europe*, ed. Finch et al. (2019).

Dr Peter Moore is an art historian and curator of collections and interiors for English Heritage, with primary responsibility for Audley End House in Essex and Wrest Park in Bedfordshire. He specialises in British art and material culture from the seventeenth to the nineteenth century. His current curatorial practice interrogates the diverse and eclectic nature of country house collections and the global narratives imbued in them. Prior to working for English Heritage, he held curatorial roles at the National Trust, the National Gallery and Gainsborough's House.

Louis P. Nelson is Professor of Architectural History and the Vice Provost for Academic Outreach at the University of Virginia. He is a specialist in the built environments of the early modern Atlantic World, with published work on the American South, the Caribbean and West Africa, and is a leading advocate for the reconstruction of place-based public history. An accomplished scholar, Nelson has authored two book-length monographs published by the University of North Carolina and Yale University presses, three edited collections of essays, dozens of articles and has served two terms as senior co-editor of *Buildings and Landscapes* – the leading English-language venue for scholarship on vernacular architecture.

Anne Sophie Overkamp is a postdoctoral researcher at the University of Tübingen. Her research covers a range of topics including business history, consumption preferences, fashion and shopping. She has published widely on economic and cultural history and is co-editor of the edited volume *Global Encounters in Early Modern Germany* (forthcoming). Currently she is working on a book project focusing on consumption in German country houses, 1780–1830.

Mikkel Venborg Pedersen, PhD and Dr Philos., is a curator and senior researcher at the National Museum of Denmark. He was trained as an ethnologist and cultural historian at Copenhagen University, Ludwig-Maximilian-Universität, Munich and Rice University in Houston, Texas. His doctoral thesis from 2000 explored the art of being a duke in Augustenborg, Schleswig, and his *Habitilation* from 2013 was on European and colonial consumption in early modern Denmark. Venborg Pedersen has worked broadly on both elite and popular culture in early modern and modern Europe and has published extensively on these subjects in articles, books and other formats.

Nicoleta Roman is Senior Researcher at the 'Nicolae Iorga' Institute of History (Romanian Academy). Her main research interests are social and economic history, gender and history of women, and childhood studies in (pre)modern Romania and South-Eastern Europe, in terms of the goods, mobility and material culture associated with them. She was Scientific Assistant in the ERC LuxFaSS project hosted by New Europe College and national coordinator for Romania in the European COST action *Women on the Move*. Her current research project within the Romanian Academy is entitled *Power, Memory, Education: Safta Castrisiu – A Merchant Woman in Nineteenth Century Wallachia*.

Esther Schmidt is director of the Centre for Historic Houses of India and Associate Professor of architectural history, design history and heritage at OP Jindal Global University. She received her PhD from the University of Oxford (John Lowell Osgood Prize), where she was Michael Wills Scholar and tutor. Her scholarship focuses on the role of objects and interiors and how the encounter of different cultural contexts informs design processes. She has received the Austin Award for services in Decorative Arts and an Ian Karten Award, and funding from Studienstiftung des deutschen Volkes, DAAD, and the Memorial Foundation for Jewish Culture.

Julietta Schulze studied history, German philology and musicology at the University of Tübingen. She wrote her Master's thesis on the connection between book ownership and consumption among imperial knights in the eighteenth century. Her current dissertation project examines the development of retail trade in towns of the Württemberg region in the eighteenth and early nineteenth centuries.

Jon Stobart is Professor of Social History at Manchester Metropolitan University. His research explores various aspects of retailing and consumption, mostly in eighteenth- and early nineteenth-century England. Recent work has focused on the country house as a site of consumption and on the ways in which it increasingly became a place of material and emotional comfort. This work has been published as *Consumption and the Country House* (2016) and *Comfort in the Eighteenth-Century Country House* (2022). He is currently researching the morality and materiality of consumption by Church of England clergy.

Göran Ulväng is Associate Professor in the Department of Economic History at Uppsala University. His research has focused on changes in agriculture, material culture, consumption, finances and insurance in eighteenth- and nineteenth-century Sweden, with a special emphasis on manors and manorial culture. He is the founder of the website Swedish manors, www.svenskaherrgardar.se, and former editor of *Bebyggelsehistorisk tidskrift/Nordic Journal of Settlement History and Built Heritage*, http://bebyggelsehistoria.org/en/bebyggelsehistorisk-tidskrift-english/.

Mrinalini Venkateswaran is a Leverhulme Early Career Fellow in History at Royal Holloway, University of London. Her research connects museums and modern South Asian history and has attracted prestigious grants and awards, including from the Cambridge Trust, Rajiv Gandhi Foundation and the J. N. Tata Endowment. She has worked in the Indian museum sector since 2006 in a wide range of roles. She served two terms on the Board of the Commonwealth Association of Museums and is a Fellow of the Royal Asiatic Society. She has been Museum Consultant to the MSMS II Museum Trust since 2016.

Christine Walker is an Assistant Professor of History at Yale-NUS College. She received a PhD from the University of Michigan (2014), an MA from the University of Connecticut (2007) and a BA from Yale University (2000). She specialises in the history of colonialism, gender and slavery in the Atlantic World. Her first book, *Jamaica Ladies: Female slaveholders and the creation of Britain's Atlantic empire* (University of North Carolina Press, 2020), examines the crucial roles played by women of European and African descent in making Jamaica the wealthiest and the largest slaveholding colony in the Anglo-Atlantic world.

Acknowledgements

This book grew out of a panel organised for the European Social Science History Conference in 2020 which, as COVID spread, ended up as an online meeting. The original contributors were joined by many more to provide the depth and breadth of coverage that marks this book. The decision to publish this as an open access book was made early on, but it has only been possible with the generous support of several institutions and organisations. I would like to thank the National Museum of Denmark; the 'Country Houses in Times of Change' project at the University of Tübingen, funded by the Irene und Sigurd Greven Stiftung; the Department of Architectural History, University of Virginia; the Department of Economic History, Uppsala University; and Manchester Metropolitan University.

Introduction: contexts and departures
Jon Stobart

When Sir Rowland Winn, fifth baronet, inherited Nostell Priory in Yorkshire in 1765, he promptly sacked James Paine, the architect employed by his father, and brought in Robert Adam to create fashionable neoclassical interiors. The rooms were filled with Chippendale furniture; paintings by the renowned Italian artist, Antonio Zucchi, adorned the walls; and busts of classical philosophers and poets topped the shelves in the library. Sir Rowland's wife, Sabine, busied herself corresponding with London mercers, looking to circumvent prohibitions and acquire French fashion items.[1] Nostell was thus suffused with British and European goods and influences – the epitome of an English country house. Yet Chippendale's furniture was made from mahogany, imported from the Caribbean; he supplied imported Chinese wallpaper for at least three rooms on the principal floor, and made matching green and gold chinoiserie furniture. Sabine, meanwhile, acquired exotic silks and chintzes. Fast forward to 2018 and the National Trust was engaged in a new interpretation that attempted to balance these two sides of Nostell's history. The visitor entered through an exhibition which examined the craftsmanship of Chippendale's furniture making (marking 300 years since his birth), then moved through rooms exploring his relationship with Sir Rowland and animating one of the Chinese wallpapers that he supplied. They were then confronted with text and video that highlighted the slavery and exploitation surrounding the harvesting of the Caribbean mahogany which surrounded them in the house. The visitor journey went from celebrating to unsettling.

These two episodes illustrate how this provincial British country house, owned by a largely unexceptional family, is filled with global goods and entangled with global connections but is also a product of its local, national and European context. Both aspects are important and must be understood in tandem, by the historian and the visitor alike. Nostell thus illustrates many of the issues addressed in this book. It is concerned with the acquisition, use and impact of global goods; their symbolism of and links with empire and the exotic; and their domestication within local material culture. It does so in a wide geographical and historical frame, exploring global goods in houses across Europe and the wider world between 1650 and 1850 – a period of profound commercial, cultural and political change that shaped the modern world. But it is also concerned with the local: how global goods impacted on and were shaped by the particularities of place.

The people studied in this book are the wealthy and often hereditary elite. This is not because we see other social groups as inconsequential or disengaged from global goods – far from it. Rather, it reflects the privileged position of this group: their wealth and power (both political and cultural) meant that they were the group best able to acquire global goods and use them to construct a material culture of their own making and in their own image.[2] This is not to say that these wealthy householders formed a homogeneous group. Within Europe and the Atlantic World, they came closest to sharing a common identity as a cosmopolitan and internationally networked elite. However, there were marked differences, for example in levels of wealth, religion, mobility, taste, connectedness and political ideology – empire, for example, might be critical in shaping the actions of some elites in Britain and the Dutch Republic, but had much less resonance in Sweden or Germany. These differences, of course, become more pronounced as we step beyond this Western world and compare European priorities with the tastes, desires and material cultures of indigenous elites: maharanas in Rajasthan, Efik chiefs in West Africa and samurai in Japan. What characterised them all was their social standing in their respective localities: these were people of consequence, at the apex of local, regional and sometimes national society.

Similar difficulties dog any attempt to define, in simple terms, the houses that these people occupied. They might be *schloss* in Germany, *kasteel* in the Dutch Republic, *slott* or *herrgård* in Sweden, *chateau* or *maison de plaisance* in France, *palazzo* or *villa* in Italy, big house in Ireland, plantation great house in the American south, *mahal* or *kila* in Rajasthan and *shiro* in Japan. The elites sometimes had houses in town (e.g. the Neapolitan *palazzi* or Parisian *hôtels*), but their main residences were generally in the countryside. Many were linked to the estates from which they drew both their political power and the bulk of their wealth – hence Girouard's designation of powerhouse – although income was often supplemented with earnings from public office, military service or commercial activities.[3] Referring to them collectively as country houses does not imply any British primacy; rather, it is adopted as a convenient shorthand for a wide array of palaces, castles, villas and mansions that together form the object of our study: the principal houses of the wealthy, generally landed, elite.

Finally, delineating global goods is both straightforward and complex: straightforward in that they are goods that are traded across the world and, from the perspective of a particular country, imported from overseas; complex because this means that they differ from place to place – as we shall see. Our focus is primarily on durable goods, but consumables such as tea and coffee are also discussed, as are plants and some unique objects sent across the world as gifts or trophies. In general, we are less concerned with quantities than with social, political and cultural contexts and consequences. By exploring the place of these goods in country houses across the world, we can see in this period the emergence of new power structures and sociocultural norms. Finding the same goods in different places helps us build a global story of consumption shaped by trade, wealth and empire, and mediated by local practices, preferences and politics.

Contexts

The shifting patterns of global trade in the long eighteenth century are very familiar as part of the so-called commercial revolution that opened up European markets to goods from across the world. This led to a significant, sometimes profound reorientation of trade, away from other parts of Europe and towards colonies and trading partners in the Atlantic World, India and the islands of South-East Asia, and China.[4] The focus has often fallen on the activities of the state-sponsored trading companies and international merchants responsible for bringing goods into Europe. Here attention has long centred on Britain, the Dutch Republic and France, whose East India Companies and merchants were key players in global trade; but there is growing awareness of the important role played by Danish and Swedish Companies, and by Hanseatic merchants, among others.[5] The overall quantities of goods being brought from the East may have been fairly modest, as Pieter Emmer notes, but their value was often immense, and their impact on European production and consumption was profound, if uneven.[6] Import-substitution and imitation played a large part in stimulating industrialisation; colonial groceries such as tea, coffee, sugar and tobacco transformed eating and drinking practices; and a raft of Chinese manufactures and Indian textiles shifted tastes and consumer aspirations.[7]

Many Europeans felt the impact of global goods most directly in their homes. A large body of work, much of it drawing on inventory evidence, has shown how caffeine drinks, cotton textiles and tropical woods transformed the homes of British artisans and landowners alike; others have argued that these material possessions and the rituals surrounding them were instrumental to the construction of social ideals such as politeness and respectability.[8] Furthermore, within the so-called core economies of north-west Europe, Anne McCants shows how tea, coffee and sugar found their way into even modest households in the Dutch Republic, and Jan Poukens demonstrates the presence of a similar equipage of grinders, kettles, pots and chinaware, plus a growing array of cottons in the houses of the middling sort of the Southern Netherlands from the late seventeenth century.[9] In other parts of Europe, this transformation of domestic material culture was less profound and occurred later, in the eighteenth and early nineteenth centuries – partly, Shelagh Ogilvie argues, because of the dampening effect of sumptuary laws and guild regulations.[10] To an extent her findings are borne out by recent studies in Sweden, Italy and Spain; but there is growing evidence that tea, coffee and sugar were more widely consumed than has been previously supposed,[11] and analyses of bourgeois homes across northern and southern Europe show a broad array of global goods appearing from the middle decades of the eighteenth century.[12] In the colonial houses of North America and the Caribbean, a similar set of changes was also apparent: a variety of new domestic items helped to transform the homes of the well-to-do but also those of other social groups, including Native Americans and enslaved Africans. Such developments tied these distant places and houses to a European model of domestic material culture, although race and ethnicity emerge as stronger motivations.[13]

Studies of country houses have traditionally taken an art historical perspective, focusing on architectural styles, collections of art, books or classical artefacts, and assemblages of luxurious furniture.[14] The concern is often with questions of provenance, aesthetics and changing systems of taste – the last often viewed as a linear progression which, in Britain, led from the baroque, through Palladianism and neoclassicism, to neogothic. Such studies privilege the architect, artist and master craftsman – men such as Jacques-François Blondel, Louis Laguerre and Thomas Chippendale – and emphasise the Grand Tour as key to honing taste and acquiring alluring artefacts.[15] Perspectives have been broadened more recently by growing interest in patterns and practices of consumption. Work by Amanda Vickery, Jon Stobart, Jennifer van Horn, Cary Carson and others has helped to bring a much wider range of goods and practices into focus.[16] As a consequence, more attention has been paid to the mundane and everyday, and to the routines of everyday life in the country house. We now know much more about how country house owners spent their days; how they arranged and rearranged their rooms to make them more comfortable and convenient; their spending on linen, groceries and candles (as well as paintings, furniture and stuccowork); and about the role of women and even servants in shaping the country house.[17] In short, the country house has been populated and animated as a place to live as well as a symbol of power. This has also enriched our understanding of the supply networks that serviced the country house. Adding grocers, chandlers, coal merchants and butchers into these networks embeds the country house more firmly into local and national economies; it also heightens awareness of the wider networks that connected these houses to the global trade in commodities such as tea, sugar and mahogany (widely used in English furniture: see Figure 0.1), as well as material artefacts such as Chinese porcelain, Japanese lacquerwork or Caribbean shells.

Underpinning such global modes of consumption was the expansion of European commercial and colonial power, first with Spain and Portugal and then the Dutch Republic rising to dominate the lucrative sea routes, especially to the east. Competition was fierce and fought out as much through military as commercial conflict; indeed, the series of wars between Britain and France that punctuated the eighteenth century were played out on a global stage. Crucial battles in the power struggle for commercial hegemony took place at sea or in distant lands rather than on European soil. Backing up Britain's military and naval triumphs were a complex array of regulations governing the nature of trade between the metropolis and its growing number of colonies. The nature and meaning of imperialism also changed: it remained largely focused on commercial influence and hegemony rather than formal control of territory, but the establishment of colonies in the Atlantic World and later in India increasingly pushed in the direction of formal empire.[18] France and the Dutch Republic also extended and formalised their colonies, and other European powers maintained a smaller-scale presence on the global stage. Denmark, for instance, had a new monopoly company from 1732 and later established trading stations in Ceylon (now Sri Lanka), West Africa and the Caribbean (see Chapter 6), while successful EICs had been launched in the Southern Netherlands (1715) and Sweden (1731).[19]

Figure 0.1 Mahogany chair by William Gomm, *c.* 1764. Stoneleigh Abbey. © Jon Stobart.

The cultural impact of these growing empires was profound. Global goods brought heightened awareness of cultures from across the globe, as DuPlessis, Riello and Eacott, among many others, have noted.[20] Distant luxuries spoke of the reach and knowledge of the consumer – an awareness of other places and cultures; chinoiserie designs appealed in terms of an exotic other, yet they also formed a 'critical visual and material language' that spoke of control and imperialism.[21] For some, these global goods represented personal and tangible links to empire. Stephanie Barczewski has traced the ownership of many British country estates by colonial merchants, Indian nabobs, West Indian planters, and military and naval officers.[22] She notes how some, but by no means all, displayed their colonial/imperial connections in their new houses through discourses of commodities, cosmopolitanism, conquest and collecting. These connections and their material footprint have been explored further by Margot Finn and Kate Smith. They traced the colonial, familial and material connections that linked British country houses with service in the East India Company (EIC), arguing that these connections endured as possessions, networks and family narratives passed down through generations – a set of practices most evident in Robert Clive and his family at Powys Castle (Figure 0.2).[23] Much the same is apparent in other colonial powers. Some VOC officials, like their British counterparts, made huge fortunes in the East (and more occasionally in the Americas) and returned home to purchase estates and build houses to display their treasures. They often brought with them objects and people that spoke of their colonial connections. In 1745, Jan Albert Sichterman returned to Groningen in the Dutch Republic with oriental porcelain (amounting to about 4,000 pieces, including several sets of armorial porcelain) as well as furniture, boxes and mirrors. Most visible, though, were his four black servants – probably slaves when he lived in Bengal and now serving as footmen and coachmen for this super-rich nabob.[24] Similarly, Baron von Schimmelmann used money from his extensive sugar plantations on St Croix in the Caribbean to buy land and build a substantial country house at Wandsbek in Schleswig-Holstein. He even had Caribbean slaves trained on the estate.[25] Others chose to mask the source of their wealth in the classical clothing of the European elite. Even so, it was often hard to escape the label of arriviste and the association with money quickly acquired in the colonies.[26] Some high-profile individuals were even the subject of public opprobrium as society became increasingly uneasy

Figure 0.2 Powys Castle, home of the Clive family. © Mike Peel (www.mikepeel.net), Available at https://commons.wikimedia.org/w/index.php?curid=51249783 and reproduced under the Creative Commons licence CC BY-SA 4.0.

about the means through which wealth was acquired. In Britain, Robert Clive was condemned for his rapacious greed and alleged brutality, and William Beckford, champion of the West Indian plantation owners, was similarly lambasted by a hostile press.[27]

Global goods and global connections were intensely political – in the past as much as the present. Of course, consumption is always in some senses a political act: much of the concern voiced in the luxury debate that rumbled on across Europe through the eighteenth century was to do with mercantilist ideas about the balance of trade, spiced up by nationalist sentiments that critiqued the debilitating and effeminising influence of foreign luxury.[28] Many European monarchs were thus engaged in sponsoring factories to produce luxuries such as porcelain, in an attempt to substitute imported goods.[29] To these long-standing concerns were added new ones driven by growing opposition to the slave trade and slave-based plantation economies. Abolitionists in Britain, the Dutch Republic and elsewhere drew a direct link between slavery and the consumption of sugar, and they mobilised large numbers of consumers – especially women – in a series of boycotts in the late eighteenth and early nineteenth centuries. Crucial to their argument was to forge a direct link in the minds of consumers between their actions and the fate of enslaved people in overseas colonies.[30] Ultimately, these boycotts were all relatively short-lived and they remained firmly focused on sugar rather than extending to other commodities produced using the labour of enslaved people, including mahogany and tobacco.

Tracing the colonial connections of country houses in the twenty-first century has proved just as political. The publication in 2020 of the National Trust report on colonialism, slavery and English country houses – a cautiously worded document that outlined some of the links that some of the properties in its care had with colonialism, plantation ownership and the slave trade – created an outcry,[31] especially in the Tory-leaning press in Britain. There were accusations of 'wokeism' and of the rewriting of history to serve politically correct ends, which tied into narratives of national pride and identity and debates about reparations and the repatriation of objects. Indeed, there is a growing literature that seeks to decolonise history, especially in terms of the legacies of slavery. In the UK, work by David Olusoga, Olive Otele and Ryan Hanley challenges traditional narratives by offering a decentred approach that gives voice to the subaltern and erases distinctions between black and 'mainstream' history.[32] This speaks directly to histories of the country house by reminding us of the manifold ways in which they are entangled with slave-based production systems, unequal trading relations and cultural appropriation. Such issues have long been buried, with Margot Finn noting that 'erasure and selective amnesia' were already being 'woven into the history of the stately home' in the eighteenth century – a process that involved hiding people (for example children of mixed race) as well as obscuring the origins of wealth.[33] The links identified in the National Trust report are thus the tip of the iceberg: nothing is said about the pervasive nature of global goods and commodities in these properties and pretty much every other house of the middling sort and above, both in Britain and across Europe and the Atlantic World.

Departures

Set in these various contexts, this book offers several important departures from the established historiography. The first is an obvious point, but one that is too easily overlooked: that the definition and character of global goods is contingent on location. Europe was far from a homogeneous unit in the eighteenth century: it was not an undifferentiated 'self' set against a global 'other'. Rather, Europe was a complex and shifting collage of regions, nations and empires with different levels of economic development, diverse cultural and political milieux, and varied cultures of consumption. These variations are often crystallised into a 'core' in north-west Europe and different levels of 'periphery' beyond this, often defined by their relative level of economic development.[34] Parts of Europe were familiar to contemporaries, while others were exotic (a distinction that often depended on relative location), and even the definition of what comprised Europe itself shifted, in part as the Ottoman Empire expanded/ retreated and Russia became a European power. What counted as 'global' might therefore be very different, depending on when and where in Europe we look. It was not, of course, a term that had any great currency at the time: goods were from particular and often specifically identified places, even if these were increasingly rolled up into notions of empire, at least in the British Atlantic World.[35] This contingency is even more evident when we shift our focus elsewhere in the world, but in ways that are complex and sometimes counterintuitive. As Eacott argues, Indian goods were global and culturally alien (at least initially) when found in the Caribbean and North America.[36] European goods were global in India, West Africa and Japan (to the extent they penetrated at all); but their 'otherness' depended on the identity of the consumer – Europeans living in Bengal or Batavia would have found them familiar reminders of home.[37] This was even more the case in the Atlantic World, where the houses of colonists and plantation owners, for example, Wilton House in Virginia, shared many characteristics with their European counterparts (Figure 0.3).[38] Global, then, was not a stable category but needs defining in each geographical and cultural setting.

This links to the second departure made by this book: that different local sociocultural milieux affected the use, meaning and significance of global goods. The interaction between the global and local has attracted considerable attention in recent years, driven by global history's emphasis on the interconnectedness of places, people and events, and a growing concern with micro-historical approaches which, *inter alia*, emphasise the importance of the local in mediating the global.[39] The consumption of imported or global goods was sometimes impacted by regional or national regulatory regimes: while formal sumptuary laws were increasingly rare and/or largely ineffective in eighteenth-century Europe, persistent guild regulation limited the spread of imported goods in rural areas of Sweden, southern Germany and elsewhere.[40] Mercantilist practices of imposing tariffs and prohibitions or encouraging import substitution created particular cultures of consumption, for example in the rising demand for domestically manufactured cotton linens in England following the ban on trading and later using imported Indian cottons.[41] Even among Europe's titled elite, marked differences in wealth

Figure 0.3 Wilton House, Virginia. © Stephen G. Hague.

could lead to very different engagement with the world of imported luxuries: the Imperial Knights of Württemberg, for instance, lacked the spending power of their counterparts in other parts of Germany, let alone France or Britain.[42] Equally, the urban-dominated culture of the Dutch Republic created a different cultural context from the quasi-feudal economies seen in parts of Eastern Europe.

Alongside these different spatial and behavioural contexts were differences in the ways in which global goods, and distant people and places, were conceived and represented, often in terms of the exotic.[43] Edward Said's work has been hugely influential in this regard, although the unity of an oriental 'other' has been challenged in the context of a web of global interactions, and it becomes highly problematic in parts of Europe that were under Ottoman rule and where the 'other' could more readily be conceived as the West.[44] Conceptions of distant places were dependent on knowledge, which for many people came second-hand through the growing body of travel literature.[45] This could shape demand for material objects from distant and exotic lands – from pagodas to palanquins to palampores – and even the texts themselves.[46]

Country houses formed particular sites of consumption: a spatial and cultural context unlike any other. They were, as we are increasingly aware, global places. Capital and goods from across the world flowed into the homes of the elite in an astonishing variety of forms, from armorial porcelain and ivory furniture, through tropical shells and plants, to coffee and spices.[47] These flows were underpinned by the economic and cultural reach of country house owners, which gave them unrivalled access to the exotic, costly and rare. Yet each householder engaged differently with the wider world, not only in an economic and cultural sense, but also politically. Imperial or EIC connections defined the identity and actions of some, but others – in Britain and especially elsewhere in Europe – were touched on lightly or indirectly by such concerns. The circumstances of the individual were important, and we should be wary of imagining the elite as an undifferentiated mass. More importantly, country houses were also local.

This localism had many dimensions, but three have particular significance for this book. Firstly, and most obviously, they were set within different national and regional contexts, a truism which had important political, cultural, commercial and environmental consequences. For example, the wealth and influence of many Imperial Knights in southern Germany was very different from that enjoyed by the English nobility or Indian maharajas; at a practical level, growing pineapples, for instance, was a very different prospect in Sweden and Italy, giving the fruit a different level of resonance as a symbol of exoticism. Secondly, country houses were almost invariably embedded firmly in their local economies. Supplies of fresh food; the services of blacksmiths, carpenters, tailors and the like; and young adults to act as servants all flowed into the country house from the surrounding area.[48] And ideas of a global consumer culture and even some global goods moved in the opposite direction, emanating from the country house into the surrounding countryside. Thirdly, as goods gained meaning from their context as well as their intrinsic qualities, the existing assemblages of goods and the way that new things were fitted into them is highly significant. Here, we might think of the so-called Diderot effect: the progressive transformation of the whole as a result of a single innovation.[49] However, the particular importance of heritance and pedigree to the titled elite – often embodied in the material culture of the country house – means that we need to be especially attentive to assemblages already present in order to fully understand the weight and meaning of global goods newly added into the country house.

The local and global frequently blended to create new material cultures and goods – our fourth departure. Eacott describes cultural blending in the adoption of certain Indian objects – for example in the use of hookahs in the late eighteenth and early nineteenth centuries – which led to English versions of the equipage, including basalt hookah bottoms made by Josiah Wedgwood.[50] Returning to Nostell, the wallpaper was a genuine Chinese product, yet such wallpapers were increasingly produced for export and incorporated European design elements. So too did many Indian textiles, the makers of which were also adept at drawing in Japanese and Chinese design elements.[51] While mahogany was self-evidently a global commodity, the furniture that it was used to make was the product of English workshops. Indeed, mahogany furniture became characteristically English, widely recognised and adopted as such by householders elsewhere in Europe.[52] But Chippendale incorporated design elements from across the world – cabriole legs originated in France, ball and claw feet were Chinese in inspiration – and his chinoiserie furniture was a fanciful concoction of imagined and real Chinese elements (Figure 0.4). More broadly, there are hundreds of examples of Chinese and Japanese porcelain augmented with silver handles, lids or stands, which changed their aesthetic and their use.[53] This created objects that were both Asian and European, or perhaps neither of these but instead a blended, even hybridised global object. The same might be argued for armorial dinner services which were made in Chinese workshops to designs sent by their European commissioners.

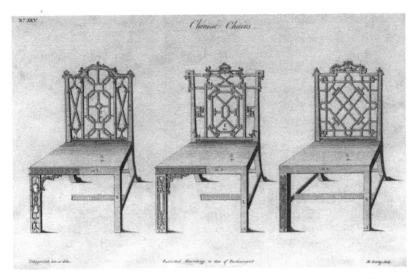

Figure 0.4 'Chinoiserie chair', Thomas Chippendale, *The Gentleman and Cabinet Maker's Director* (1754), public domain. Available at https://library.si.edu/digital-library/book/gentlemancabine00chip.

They sometimes included Chinese motifs alongside European coats of arms. The service at Shugborough in Staffordshire, England, was ordered by Admiral George Anson following his circumnavigation of the globe. It was decorated with traditional Chinese elements, plus symbols of family and others relating to Anson's famous journey, including a bread tree, the fruit of which was lauded as having saved his crew from starvation.[54] Whether these are truly hybrid objects – something genuinely new, created through melding existing objects – is perhaps less important than the way in which they were embodiments of layered aesthetics, practices and cultures.

The final departure made in this book is to pull together these local contexts into comparative perspective (see below). This has two key benefits. Firstly, it helps to redress an imbalance that focuses attention primarily on north-west Europe by including analyses centred on other parts of Europe and the wider world including Wallachia, Jamaica, West Africa and Japan. Secondly, and more importantly, it sets these different places alongside each other and explores how global goods were found everywhere yet had different meanings, uses and impacts in each setting. This helps us escape from narrow, national and Eurocentric viewpoints. For instance, empire is almost self-evidently an important part of British, Dutch and French engagement with the wider world; but how do we then understand motivations and practices in places such as Württemberg,

Naples and Sweden, which were marginal at best to European overseas imperialism, or in Japan and eighteenth-century Rajasthan, which were tied to other non-European empires? Equally, exoticism and orientalism might explain the allure of Eastern goods; but were similar reifications at play in the deployment of European goods in the palaces of Rajasthan and houses of the Efik in West Africa?

Key themes and structure of the book

The coverage of the book is geographically wide: 12 countries are discussed, including five outside Europe. There are gaps, of course, but this broad spread of case studies means that the chapters deal with very different places in terms of politics, socio-economic development (wealth), engagement with overseas trade and imperial ambition. They open many avenues of enquiry into the diverse ways in which global goods were defined, used and understood, and the variety of political, cultural and social meanings they carried.

There are many ideas that run through the book – not least issues of geographical diversity and connectivity, and the links between the global and the local – and the reader will find their own connections between chapters and the places, objects and connections they discuss. However, it is useful to identify some key themes that draw together the chapters and underpin the four sections into which the book is organised, remembering that they are by no means mutually exclusive and that individual chapters inevitably touch on more than one theme.

The first theme, covered in 'Consuming global goods', focuses on the global goods themselves: how they might be defined and identified among the myriad possessions of country house owners; how they were organised in groups or bundles, as Jan de Vries calls them; and how definitions, assemblages and uses varied across different times and places. These are deceptively simple questions which become analytically as well as conceptually challenging in the face of empirical evidence. Some of these difficulties are highlighted in Gudrun Andersson and Göran Ulväng's analysis of the possessions of two generations of the Spens family in Sweden: quantifying the proportion of objects that might be termed global, European or local, in order to assess changes over time, requires careful consideration of raw materials, craftsmanship, imitation and import substitution. Martha Chaiklin explores similar questions in the very different context of imperial Japan. In a society that was largely isolated from the outside world, imported goods came largely through Dutch merchants, which gave a European inflexion to global connections, reminding us of the contingent nature of global goods. In samurai castles, these European things included textiles and books. This bundling of global goods lies at the heart of the analyses of German Imperial Knights (Daniel Menning, Anne Sophie Overkamp and Julietta Schulze) and Jamaican women slaveholders (Christine Walker). In very different contexts, globally traded commodities such as tea and sugar were consumed using equipage assembled from across the world, from Chinese porcelain to tables made from Caribbean hardwoods. Quite apart from the complex international connections that these assemblages embodied, what is striking is the similarity of bundles and practices that characterised these very different social groups.

The second section focuses attention on 'The global in the local' and explores how global goods shaped local practices and identities in different parts of the world. There is an obvious connection here to the previous section, but the emphasis here is on how differently defined sets of global goods could create profoundly different effects on a locality. Gaia Bruno examines the location of global goods within and between the various houses of the Pignatelli family: the castle in their feudal lands, their Neapolitan palace and especially their villa near Vesuvius. She demonstrates how a range of objects, from exotic animals to oriental porcelain, were used to construct a cosmopolitan and noble rather than colonial identity, one articulated by the exchange of gifts between family and friends. A similar set of arguments is made by Mikkel Venborg Pedersen for the Danish aristocracy, although he focuses on three families with different levels of engagement with the Danish state and commerce. All three displayed an array of objects brought to Denmark from across the world, demonstrating their wealth, taste and cultural reach. Nicoleta Roman presents a very different picture in early nineteenth-century Wallachia where global might best be read as Western. Taking Goleşti Manor as a case study, she argues that oriental goods that spoke of centuries of Ottoman influence were increasingly layered with Western goods that reflected the political reorientation of the elite: goods marked a shift to a modern Western milieu. In some ways, a similar situation is seen in Stenton House, Pennsylvania. Again, as Stephen G. Hague demonstrates, global in part meant European, although here the owner's view went much further back, into classical civilisation and to the systems of learning that it inspired. Importantly, this was mixed with a more imperial perspective, born of James Logan's position as a merchant trading at the edge of the British Empire and reliant on enslaved labour.

Viewing the global–local relationship from the opposite side of the lens, the third theme, 'Domesticating the global', explores the ways in which global goods were drawn into assemblages, uses and cultures of consumption that were essentially local. This mostly created a variegated blending of local and global but occasionally produced distinctive hybrid objects and cultures. The mixing of global with European objects is explored by Jon Stobart. He argues that the imperial associations of objects that increasingly filled even modest English country houses were sometimes made apparent through placename associations, but they were also obscured by their association with English aesthetics and everyday practices. Their recirculation through house sales added further local associations in the form of the previous owner. More overt blending of objects and cultures is apparent in the houses of the Efik traders discussed by Louis P. Nelson. They purchased British goods and even whole houses and could readily navigate European dining practices and social norms, yet their material culture and social practices retained strong local elements, from food to clothing. As Nelson observes, the Efik were strategic and intentional participants in the global marketplace. Much the same was true of the Indian princes studied by Esther Schmidt. Focusing on the porcelain rooms installed by locals in the palaces of Rajasthan, she demonstrates how both Chinese and European ceramic tiles were used to create unique and innovative designs. This was a form of cosmopolitanism that became characteristic of the region, and like chinoiserie in Europe, the original meanings of motifs and designs were overwritten with a specific aesthetic that spoke of power and distinction.

The final key theme views global goods and cultural interchange through the lens of empire. We have already noted the importance of empire in the analyses offered by Hague, Walker, Stobart and others; but the chapters in 'Imperial houses' foreground the unequal power relations that lie at the heart of empire. These underpinned material and cultural exchange and are embodied in country houses, both in Europe and in the colonies. This is seen most clearly in Rupert Goulding and Louis P. Nelson's study of Dyrham Park in England – the home of William Blathwayt, the crown's senior colonial administrator. He used his connections with governors and merchants across the Atlantic World to acquire a range of raw materials and artefacts which shaped both the materiality and the meaning of his English home. Goulding and Nelson read the house as a statement of personal and national power over other people and places. Taking a similar approach, Katie Donington explores how the English country house garden became home to plants from across the imperial world. She builds on an understanding of the imperial basis of much botanical collecting by arguing that botany offered English landowners the opportunity to engage with the colonial world from a distance. Importantly, this was not an exclusively male world: aristocratic women also corresponded with collectors in the field, amassed collections and recreated empire in their gardens. Finally, Yme Kuiper demonstrates how this process could operate on both sides of the Atlantic. As governor of Dutch Brazil in the mid-seventeenth century, Johan Mauritz created two remarkable palaces which symbolised imperial and personal power, in part through the use of plants, foods and other goods brought from Europe. Returning home, Mauritz took with him an immense fortune, but also the fruits of wide-ranging ethnographic surveys in the form of paintings and artefacts – cultural capital that he was able to trade for social and political status. Global goods that he had created during his time in Brazil thus entered the houses of the European nobility.

The power of individual objects to tell stories that make connections and/or illustrate broader points is highlighted and explored through the inclusion of 15 short object lessons. These draw on aspects of thing theory by viewing objects as material and physical entities able to map out space 'as a network of relations involving a particular geography and human subjects'.[55] These geographies comprise the routes by which they came to their current location; the spaces of power, empire and coercion which they embody; and imagined places conjured by gazing at or handling the object. The humans include those involved in making, transporting and selling the objects as well as the eventual owner. In some instances, the present-day viewer is also drawn into the picture, as with the discussion of recent exhibitions held at the Mauritshuis in Den Haag. Each lesson focuses on a specific object or type of global good. They range from the individual and exquisite to the quotidian and commonplace: from the model of a pagoda made by a servant at Erddig in North Wales and a *jinbaori* surcoat made from European cloth and worn by Japanese samurai, to the osnaburg linens used to clothe enslaved people in North America and a recipe for tobacco rolls (a sweet pastry) in a German cookbook. What all these objects share is their ability to provide insights into the ways in which global goods both illustrate and articulate cultural, material and commercial connections. In this sense, they have a pedagogic as well as historiographical function. Again, they are divided into three groups: 'Traded goods', in which connections are revealed by tracing provenance or dispersal, and by recreating object biographies; 'Crafting global goods', where the focus is on the materiality of the object and the ways in which production processes reveal how systems of knowledge were spread, albeit sometimes partially; and

'Symbols and symbolism', in which the short essays examine the objects as representations of cultural practices and power relations, both in the past and in the present.

Above all, this book is about country houses as critical nodes of consumption and dissemination of global goods, and about the profound impact that these goods had on the material culture, domestic and consumption practices, and symbolism of country houses across the world. It is concerned with empires and power relations, but just as much with notions of utility, taste, knowledge and status, and with the ways in which all these influences became entangled in particular ways depending on the location of the house.

Notes

1. Bristol, 'Between exotic and everyday', 163–4, 169–71; Dyer, *Material Lives*, 127–31; de Bruijn et al., *Chinese Wallpaper*, 31–2.
2. See, for example, Hazzard, 'The Clives'; Kuiper, 'What about the Moorish footman?'; Finn and Smith, *East India Company at Home*.
3. Girouard, *English Country House*, 2–12. Notions of power inevitably invoke the more marginal and often exploited other, most obviously in the case of plantation houses.
4. The classic study remains Braudel, *Civilisation and Capitalism*.
5. Degryse and Parmentier, 'Maritime aspects'; Müller, 'Swedish East India trade', 2003; Weber, *Deutsche Kaufleute*; Hodacs, *Silk and Tea in the North*.
6. Emmer, 'Myth of early globalization'. See also Berg, *Goods from the East*.
7. On imitation, see Berg, 'From imitation to invention'. On social practices, see Smith, *Consumption*; Hochmuth, *Globale Güter*; McCants, 'Poor consumers as global consumers'; Ellis et al., *Empire of Tea*.
8. See, for example, Weatherill, *Consumer Behaviour*; Sear and Sneath, *Consumer Revolution*; Bowett, 'English mahogany trade'; Smith, *Consumption*.
9. McCants, 'Poor consumers as global consumers'; Poukens, 'Old and new luxuries'.
10. Ogilvie, 'Consumption'.
11. Moreno, 'Luxury, fashion and peasantry'; Ago, *Gusto for Things*. More positive results are found in Ulväng, 'Tea, coffee or printed cotton'; Jordan, 'Global goods'; Hodacs, *Silk and Tea*; Hochmuth, *Globale Güter*.
12. Berg, *Goods from the East*; Engelhardt Mathiassen et al., *Fashionable Encounters*; Calcagno, 'American colonial goods in the Mediterranean'.
13. See Martin, *Buying in the World of Goods*; White, *Wild Frenchmen*; Carson, *Face Value*; Falk, *Architecture and Artifacts*; Van Horn, *Power of Objects*.
14. See, for example, Harris, *Design of the English Country House*; Thornton, *Authentic Decor*; Hahn and Schütte, *Zeichen und Raum*.
15. But see also Sweet et al., *Beyond the Grand Tour*.
16. Vickery, *Behind Closed Doors*; Stobart and Rothery, *Consumption and the Country House*; Carson, *Face Value*; Van Horn, *Objects of Power*.
17. Girouard, *French Country House*, 163–96; Stobart and Rothery, *Consumption and the Country House*, 83–108; Whittle and Griffiths, *Consumption and Gender*, 26–49; Vickery, *Behind Closed Doors*, 231–90.
18. McAleer, *Britain's Maritime Empire*.
19. Degryse and Parmentier, 'Maritime aspects'; Müller, 'Swedish East India trade'.
20. *Inter alia*, Mintz, *Sweetness and Power*; Walvin, *Fruits of Empire*; Baghdiantz McCabe, *Global Consumption*; Niemeijer, *Batavia*. On cultural interchange, see Riello, *Cotton*; DuPlessis, *Material Atlantic*; Beckert, *Empire of Cotton*; Eacott, *Selling Empire*.

21 Sloboda, *Chinoiserie*. See also Barczewski, *Country Houses*; Finn and Smith, *East India Company at Home*; Phillips, *Everyday Luxuries*.
22 Barczewski, *Country Houses*.
23 Finn and Smith, *East India Company at Home*; Hazzard, 'The Clives'.
24 Kuiper, 'What about the Moorish footman?'.
25 Degn, *Die Schimmelmanns*.
26 Grass, 'House of a rich West Indian'; Nelson, *Architecture and Empire*, 235–67.
27 Hazzard, 'The Clives'; Gauci, *William Beckford*, esp. chapter 3. See also Gikandi, *Slavery and the Culture of Taste*.
28 For a useful summary, see Berg and Eger, 'The luxury debates'.
29 See, for example, Murhem and Ulväng, 'To buy a plate'; Lorenz, *Weißes Gold*.
30 Bickham, *Eating the Empire*, 221–9; Smith, 'Complications of the commonplace'; Davies, 'A moral purchase'; McCabe, *Global Consumption*, 261–4. On similar movements in Germany, see Lentz, 'Wer helfen kann'.
31 Huxtable et al., *Colonialism and Properties of the National Trust*.
32 Olusoga, *Black and British*; Otele, *African Europeans*; Hanley, *Beyond Slavery*.
33 Finn, 'Material turns', 2.
34 For a good summary of this, see De Vries, *European Urbanisation*. Italy is seen as slipping from core to peripheral status between 1600 and 1800.
35 See Bickham, *Eating the Empire*; Trentmann, *Empire of Things*, 119–73.
36 Eacott, *Selling Empire*.
37 See, for instance, Rasico, 'Making of the Nabob'.
38 Hague, *Gentleman's House*; Nelson, *Architecture and Empire*; Mooney, *Prodigy Houses*.
39 See, for example, Magnússon, 'Far-reaching microhistory'; Wimmler and Weber, *Globalized Peripheries*. The relationships for material goods are modelled by Riello, 'Global things'.
40 Ogilvie, 'Consumption'; Andersson, *Stadens dignitärer*.
41 Riello, *Cotton*, 117–26.
42 Godsey, *Nobles and Nation*, 72–106.
43 See, for example, Sloboda, *Chinoiserie*; Flüchter, 'Aus den fürnembsten Indianischen'.
44 For a recent critique of Said's arguments, see Akçetin and Faroqhi, *Living the Good Life*. For another perspective on East–West relations, see Muge Gocek, *East Encounters West*.
45 Brahm and Rosenhaft, *Slavery Hinterland*; Weiss, *Ports of Globalisation*; Flüchter, 'Aus den fürnembsten Indianischen'; de Bruijn, 'Virtual travel'.
46 Eacott, *Selling Empire*; de Bruijn, 'Virtual travel'.
47 Finn and Smith, *East India Company at Home*; Van Horn, *Power of Objects*; Hahn and Schütte, *Zeichen und Raum*.
48 See, for example, Whittle and Griffiths, *Consumption and Gender*, 72–84.
49 See McCracken, *Culture and Consumption*, 118–29.
50 Eacott, *Selling Empire*, 289–99.
51 De Bruijn et al., *Chinese Wallpaper*; Riello, *Cotton*, 127.
52 See, for example, Ijäs, 'English luxuries'.
53 Riello, 'Global things', 34–40.
54 McDowall, 'Shugborough dinner service', 2014.
55 Baird, 'Peregrine things', 3.

Bibliography

Ago, Renata. *Gusto for Things: A history of objects in seventeenth-century Rome*. Chicago: University of Chicago Press, 2013.

Akçtin, Elif, and Suraiya Faroqhi, eds. *Living the Good Life: Consumption in the Qing and Ottoman empires of the eighteenth century*. Leiden: Brill, 2018.

Andersson, Gudrun. *Stadens dignitärer: Den lokala elitens status- och maktmanifestation i Arboga 1650–1770*. Stockholm: Atlantis, 2009.

Baghdiantz McCabe, Ina. *A History of Global Consumption 1500–1800*. London and New York: Routledge, 2015.

Baird, Ileana. 'Introduction: peregrine things: rethinking the global in eighteenth-century studies'. In *Eighteenth-Century Thing Theory in Global Context*, edited by Ileana Baird and Christina Ionescu, 1–16. Farnham: Ashgate, 2013.

Barczewski, Stephanie. *Country Houses and the British Empire, 1700–1930*. Manchester: Manchester University Press, 2014.

Beckert, Sven. *Empire of Cotton: A global history*. New York: Penguin, 2015.

Berg, Maxine. 'From imitation to invention: creating commodities in 18th-century Britain', *Economic History Review* 45 (2002): 1–30.

Berg, Maxine, ed. *Goods from the East, 1600–1800: Trading Eurasia*. Basingstoke: Palgrave Macmillan, 2015.

Berg, Maxine, and Elizabeth Eger. 'The rise and fall of the luxury debates'. In *Luxury in the Eighteenth Century: Debates, desires and delectable goods*, edited by Maxine Berg and Elizabeth Eger, 7–27. Basingstoke: Palgrave Macmillan, 2003.

Bickham, Troy. *Eating the Empire: Food and society in eighteenth-century Britain*. London: Reaktion, 2020.

Bowett, Adam. 'The English mahogany trade, 1700–1793', PhD dissertation, Brunel University, 1996.

Brahm, Felix, and Eve Rosenhaft, eds. *Slavery Hinterland: Transatlantic slavery and continental Europe, 1680–1850*. Woodbridge: Boydell and Brewer, 2016.

Braudel, Fernand. *Civilisation and Capitalism, 15th–18th Century*, 3 vols. First published 1967; New York: Harper & Row, 1979.

Bristol, Kerry. 'Between the exotic and the everyday: Sabine Winn at home 1765–1798'. In *A Taste for Luxury in Early Modern Europe: Display, acquisition and boundaries*, edited by Johanna Ilmakunnas and Jon Stobart, 161–78. London: Bloomsbury, 2017.

Calcagno, P., ed. 'American colonial goods in the Mediterranean: major ports as centres of destination, consumption and redistribution', *RiME* special issue 8, no. 1 (2021).

Carson, Cary. *Face Value: The consumer revolution and the colonising of America*. Charlottesville: University of Virginia Press, 2017.

Davies, Kate. 'A moral purchase: femininity, commerce and abolition, 1788–1792'. In *Women, Writing and the Public Sphere, 1700–1830*, edited by Elizabeth Eger, Charlotte Grant, Cliona Ó Gallchoir and Penny Warburton, 133–59. Cambridge: Cambridge University Press, 2001.

de Bruijn, Emile. 'Virtual travel and virtuous objects: chinoiserie and the country house'. In *Travel and the British Country House*, edited by J. Stobart, 63–85. Manchester: Manchester University Press, 2017.

de Bruijn, Emile, Andrew Bush and Helen Clifford. *Chinese Wallpaper in National Trust Houses*. Swindon: National Trust, 2014.

de Vries, Jan. *European Urbanisation, 1500–1800*. London: Methuen, 1984.

Degn, Christian. *Die Schimmelmanns im atlantischen Dreieckshandel: Gewinn und Gewissen*. Neumünster: Wachholtz, 1974.

Degryse, Karol, and Jan Parmentier. 'Maritime aspects of the Ostend trade to Mocha, India and China (1715–1732)'. In *Ships, Sailors and Spices: East India Companies and their shipping*, edited by J. Bruyn and F. Gaastra, 139–75. Amsterdam: NEHA, 1993.

DuPlessis, Robert. *The Material Atlantic: Clothing, commerce and colonization in the Atlantic world, 1650–1800*. Cambridge: Cambridge University Press, 2015.

Dyer, Serena. *Material Lives: Women makers and consumer culture in the 18th century*. London: Bloomsbury, 2021.

Eacott, Jonathan. *Selling Empire: India in the making of Britain and America, 1600–1850*. Chapel Hill: University of North Carolina Press, 2016.

Ellis, Markman, Richard Coulton and Richard Mauger. *Empire of Tea: The Asian leaf that conquered the world*. London: Reaktion, 2015.

Emmer, Peter. 'The myth of early globalization: the Atlantic economy, 1500–1800', *European Review* 9, no. 1 (2003): 37–47.

Engelhardt Mathiassen, Tove, Marie-Louise Nosch, Maj Ringgard, Kirsten Toftegaard and Mikkel Venborg Pedersen, eds. *Fashionable Encounters: Perspectives and trends in textile and dress in the early modern Nordic world*. Oxford: Oxford University Press, 2014.

Falk, Cynthia. *Architecture and Artifacts of the Pennsylvania Germans: Constructing identity in early America*. University Park: Penn State University Press, 2008.

Finn, Margot. 'Material turns in British history: iv. Empire in India, cancel cultures and the country house', *Transactions of the Royal Historical Society* 31 (2021): 1–21.
Finn, Margot, and Kate Smith. *The East India Company at Home, 1757–1857*. London: UCL Press, 2017.
Flüchter, Antje. 'Aus den fürnembsten Indianischen Reisebe-schreibungen zusammengezogen'. In *The Dutch Trading Companies as Knowledge Networks*, edited by Siegfried Huigen, Jan L. de Jong and Elmer Kolfin, 337–59. Leiden: Brill, 2010.
Gauci, Perry. *William Beckford: First prime minister of the British Empire*. New Haven: Yale University Press, 2013.
Gikandi, Simon. *Slavery and the Culture of Taste*. Princeton: Princeton University Press, 2011.
Girouard, Mark. *Life in the English Country House*. New Haven and London: Yale University Press, 1978.
Girouard, Mark. *Life in the French Country House*. London: Cassell & Co., 2000.
Godsey, William. *Nobles and Nation in Central Europe: Free Imperial Knights in the age of revolution, 1750–1850*. Cambridge: Cambridge University Press, 2004.
Grass, Elisabeth. 'The house and estate of a rich West Indian: two slaveholders in eighteenth-century East Anglia'. In *Politics and the English Country House, 1688–1800*, edited by Joan Coutu, Jon Stobart and Peter Lindfield, 197–216. Montreal: McGill-Queen's University Press, 2022.
Hague, Stephen. *The Gentleman's House in the British Atlantic World, 1680–1780*. Basingstoke: Palgrave Macmillan, 2016.
Hahn, Peter-Michael, and Ulrich Schütte, eds. *Zeichen und Raum: Ausstattung und höfisches Zeremoniell in den deutschen Schlössern der Frühen Neuzeit*. Munich: Deutscher Kunstverlag, 2006.
Hanley, Ryan. *Beyond Slavery and Abolition: Black British writing, c.1770–1830*. Cambridge: Cambridge University Press, 2018.
Harris, John. *The Design of the English Country House*. London: Trefoil Publications, 1985.
Hazzard, Kieran. 'The Clives at home: self-fashioning, collecting, and British India'. In *Politics and the English Country House, 1688–1800*, edited by Joan Coutu, Jon Stobart and Peter Lindfield, 223–47. Montreal: McGill-Queen's University Press, 2022.
Hochmuth, Christian. *Globale Güter – lokale Aneignungen: Kaffee, Tee, Schokolade und Tabak im frühneuzeitlichen Dresden*. Konstanz: Universitätsverlag Konstanz, 2008.
Hodacs, Hanna. *Silk and Tea in the North: Scandinavian trade and the market for Asian goods in eighteenth-century Europe*. Basingstoke: Palgrave Macmillan, 2016.
Huxtable, Sally-Anne, Corinne Fowler, Cristo Hefalas and Emma Slocombe, eds. *Interim Report on the Connections between Colonialism and Properties now in the care of the National Trust*. Swindon: National Trust, 2020.
Ijäs, Ulla. 'English luxuries in nineteenth-century Viborg'. In *A Taste for Luxury in Early Modern Europe: Display, acquisition and boundaries*, edited by Johanna Ilmakunnas and Jon Stobart, 265–82. London: Bloomsbury, 2017.
Jordan, John. 'Global goods away from global trading points? Tea and coffee in early modern Bern', *History of Retailing and Consumption* 4, no. 3 (2018): 217–34.
Kuiper, Yme. 'What about the Moorish footman? Portrait of a Dutch nabob as a dedicated follower of fashion'. In *A Taste for Luxury in Early Modern Europe: Display, acquisition and boundaries*, edited by Johanna Ilmakunnas and Jon Stobart, 77–98. London: Bloomsbury, 2017.
Lentz, Sarah. *'Wer helfen kann, der helfe!' Deutsche SklavereigegnerInnen und die atlantische Abolitionsbewegung, 1780–1860*. Göttingen: Vandenhoeck & Ruprecht, 2020.
Lorenz, Angelika. *Weißes Gold aus Fürstenberg: Kulturgeschichte im Spiegel des Porzellans 1747–1830*. Braunschweig: Herzog Anton Ulrich-Museum, 1988.
Magnússon, S.G. 'Far-reaching microhistory: the use of microhistorical perspective in a globalized world', *Rethinking History* 21, no. 3 (2017): 312–41.
Martin, Ann Smart. *Buying in to the World of Goods: Early consumers in backcountry Virginia*. Baltimore: Johns Hopkins University Press, 2008.
McCants, Anne. 'Poor consumers as global consumers: the diffusion of tea and coffee drinking in the eighteenth century', *Economic History Review* 61 (2008): 172–200.
McDowall, Stephen. 'The Shugborough dinner service and its significance for Sino-British history', *Journal for Eighteenth-Century Studies* 37, no. 1 (2014): 1–17.
Mintz, Sidney. *Sweetness and Power: The place of sugar in modern history*. New York: Viking, 1985.

Mooney, Barbara. *Prodigy Houses of Virginia: Architecture and the native elite*. Charlottesville: University of Virginia Press, 2008.

Moreno, C. 'Luxury, fashion and peasantry: the introduction of new commodities in rural Catalonia, 1670–1790'. In *The Force of Fashion in Politics and Society: Global perspectives from early modern to contemporary times*, edited by Beverley Lemire, 67–93. Farnham: Ashgate, 2010.

Muge Gocek, Fatma. *East Encounters West: France and the Ottoman Empire in the eighteenth century*. Oxford: Oxford University Press, 1987.

Müller, Leos. 'The Swedish East India trade and international markets: re-exports of teas, 1731–1813', *Scandinavian Economic History Review* 51, no. 3 (2003): 28–44.

Murhem, Sophia, and Göran Ulväng. 'To buy a plate: retail and shopping for porcelain and faience in Stockholm during the eighteenth century'. In *A Taste for Luxury in Early Modern Europe: Display, acquisition and boundaries*, edited by Johanna Ilmakunnas and Jon Stobart, 197–215. London: Bloomsbury, 2017.

Nelson, Louis. *Architecture and Empire in Jamaica*. New Haven: Yale University Press, 2016.

Niemeijer, Hendrik. *Batavia: een koloniale sameleving in de zeventiende eeuw*. Amsterdam: Balans, 2005.

Ogilvie, Sheila. 'Consumption, social capital, and the "industrious revolution" in early modern Germany', *Journal of Economic History* 70 (2010): 287–325.

Olusoga, David. *Black and British: A forgotten history*. London: Palgrave Macmillan, 2016.

Otele, Olive. *African Europeans: An untold history*. London: Hurst & Co., 2020.

Phillips, Amanda. *Everyday Luxuries: Art and objects in Ottoman Constantinople, 1600–1800*. Dortmund: Verlag Kettler, 2018.

Poukens, Johan. 'Old and new luxuries in town and country in the eighteenth-century Habsburg Netherlands'. In *Reinventing the Economic History of Industrialisation*, edited by Kristine Bruland, Anne Gerritsen, Pat Hudson and Giorgio Riello, 213–28. Montreal: McGill-Queen's University Press, 2020.

Rasico, Patrick. 'Auctions and the making of the Nabob in late eighteenth-century Calcutta and London', *The Historical Journal* 65, no. 2 (2021): 1–22.

Riello, Giorgio. *Cotton: The fabric that made the modern world*. Cambridge: Cambridge University Press, 2013.

Riello, Giorgio. 'Global things: Europe's early modern material transformation'. In *The Routledge Handbook of Material Culture in Early Modern Europe*, edited by Catherine Richardson, Tara Hamling and David Gaimster, 29–45. New York and London: Routledge, 2017.

Sear, Jean, and Ken Sneath. *The Origins of the Consumer Revolution in England: From brass pots to clocks*. New York and London: Routledge, 2020.

Sloboda, Stacey. *Chinoiserie: Commerce and critical ornament in eighteenth-century Britain*. Manchester: Manchester University Press, 2014.

Smith, W. 'Complications of the commonplace: tea, sugar and imperialism', *Journal of Interdisciplinary History* 23 (1992): 259–78.

Smith, Woodruff. *Consumption and the Making of Respectability, 1600–1800*. London: Routledge, 2002.

Stobart, Jon, and Mark Rothery. *Consumption and the Country House*. Oxford: Oxford University Press, 2016.

Sweet, Rosemary, Gerrit Verhoeven and Sarah Goldsmith. *Beyond the Grand Tour: Northern metropolises and early modern travel behaviour*. London: Routledge, 2017.

Thornton, Peter. *Authentic Décor: The domestic interior, 1620–1920*. London: Weidenfeld & Nicolson, 1985.

Trentmann, Frank. *Empire of Things: How we became a world of consumers, from the fifteenth century to the twenty-first*. London: Allen Lane, 2016.

Ulväng, Marie. 'Tea, coffee or printed cotton? Farm households' consumption of goods in Northern Sweden, 1760–1820', *History of Retailing and Consumption* 7, no. 1 (2021): 137–61.

Van Horn, Jennifer. *The Power of Objects in Eighteenth-Century British America*. Chapel Hill: University of North Carolina Press, 2017.

Vickery, Amanda. *Behind Closed Doors: At home in Georgian England*. New Haven: Yale University Press, 2009.

Walvin, James. *Fruits of Empire: Exotic produce and British taste, 1660–1800*. Basingstoke: Macmillan, 1997.

Weatherill, Lorna. *Consumer Behaviour and Material Culture in Britain, 1660–1760*. London: Routledge, 1988.
Weber, Klaus. *Deutsche Kaufleute im Atlantikhandel 1680–1830: Unternehmen und Familien in Hamburg, Cadiz und Bordeaux*. Munich: Beck, 2004.
Weiss, Holger, ed. *Ports of Globalisation, Places of Creolisation: Nordic possessions in the Atlantic world during the era of the slave trade*. Leiden: Brill, 2015.
White, Sophie. *Wild Frenchmen and Frenchified Indians: Material culture and race in colonial Louisiana*. Philadelphia: University of Pennsylvania Press, 2014.
Whittle, Jane, and Elizabeth Griffiths. *Consumption and Gender in the Early Seventeenth-Century Household: The world of Alice Le Strange*. Oxford: Oxford University Press, 2012.
Wimmler, Jutta, and Klaus Weber. *Globalized Peripheries: Central Europe and the Atlantic world, 1680–1860*. Woodbridge: Boydell and Brewer, 2020.

Part 1
Consuming global goods

1
Mahogany, sugar and porcelain: global goods for a Swedish aristocratic family in the eighteenth century

Gudrun Andersson and Göran Ulväng

Countess Ulrika Eleonora Spens of Salnecke was in the habit of visiting Stockholm three times a year, in the spring, summer and autumn, to shop for herself, her husband Count Carl Gustaf and their two sons.[1] In July 1799, she spent a month in the capital. She spent 108 Riksdaler (Rd)during her stay, of which over a quarter went on salaries and other payments for serving women, lady's maids, footmen, maids-of-all-work, tailors, hairdressers and dentists; another quarter was spent on buying Swedish-made goods such as hats, gloves, scarves, paper, pounce, Epsom salts, spirit vinegar and radishes. However, nearly half her spending was on imported goods such as silk, sugar, tea, lemons and Seville oranges. In this chapter, we analyse consumption by the aristocratic Spens family, focusing on the quantity of global goods purchased compared with European and local (Swedish) goods. By analysing their probate inventories and household accounts, we can quantify the relative importance of these three categories of goods within the elite economy. Studying Swedish elite consumption gives a clearer picture of how deeply global goods penetrated elite houses – even outside the core colonial economies. The combination of a systematic quantitative analysis and a peripheral country – geographically and economically – nuances the picture of the dominance of global goods and emphasises the importance of applying broader perspectives to consumption and material culture.

There is extensive literature on eighteenth-century consumption, which has focused on the elite's luxury consumption in the major European cities, the role of women in the consumer society and the moral implications associated with it.² Sweden, with its harsh climate and comparatively small population, was in a different position from the major seafaring countries of Western Europe.³ Except for its successful iron exports and some exports of timber and herring, the economy was mainly agrarian and most of its towns were small, the exceptions being the capital Stockholm and Gothenburg on the west coast. Virtually all foreign trade came through these towns, including salt, textiles, sugar and fruit.⁴ Accordingly, this is where the wealthiest families, to which the Spens family belonged, went shopping, while the lower ranks of the elite living in the countryside depended on retailers in small towns and the secondary market.⁵

Colonial enterprises were few. The Swedish East India Company (SOIC), with its headquarters in Gothenburg, was founded by the Dutch in 1731 but re-exported most of its goods to Great Britain. The state attempted to gain a foothold in the Caribbean, eventually succeeding when it acquired the island of Saint-Barthélemy in 1784.⁶ The island gave Sweden access to the Atlantic trade, although the volume was negligible compared with England and the Dutch Republic. Domestic commerce, trade and crafts were strictly regulated by guilds, customs and excise duties, town customs, the ban on selling outside town markets and so forth. In practice, many exceptions were made to facilitate essential trade between Sweden's regions and to encourage domestic production. Greater integration into the global market, with its mass production of ever-cheaper goods, and the growth in iron exports and agriculture helped to fuel demand for goods and thus laid the foundations for an urban, industrial economy. However, total freedom of trade was not introduced until 1864.

Despite the influx of international trends, and the 'myriad' of merchants in Stockholm, the chances of increased consumption were poorer in Sweden than in many other European countries.⁷ For these reasons, analysing changes in consumer behaviour in eighteenth-century Sweden is an excellent way of testing how far engagement with the world of goods spread beyond the core and liberal economies of north-west Europe. What types of goods were owned or consumed in the 1720s and 1790s by a fairly typical aristocratic family (the Spens)? What proportion were of European or global origin? Where did they shop for these goods – in Stockholm, in county towns, or were they available in rural areas? We take a quantitative approach to these questions since it gives us detailed information on the total consumption of the households and allows us to compare the number of global goods to goods of different origins.

The Spens family

Our analysis starts from the probate inventories and household accounts of two women who married into the Spens family: Countess Beata Spens née Oxenstierna af Croneborg (1687–1735) and Countess Ulrika Eleonora Spens née Falkenberg af Bålby (1766–1802).[8] The former was the wife of Count Carl Gustaf Spens, Grand Master of the Hunt, whose main seat was Höja manor in Uppland. The latter married Carl Gustaf Spens, grandson of Beata and Carl Gustaf Spens, who was appointed to the judicial sinecure of *lagman* (lawman) but resigned to devote himself to running the family estates. In addition to Höja he bought the neighbouring manor Salnecke, which duly became the family's seat.

Two types of primary sources have been used in this study: probate inventories and household accounts. Unfortunately, the probate inventory for Countess Beata has not survived, but there is the one for her husband Carl Gustaf from 1751. It is probably an accurate picture of their belongings in the 1720s and 1730s, because he did not make any major alterations to his estates during his second marriage. The probate inventory for Countess Ulrika Eleonora from 1802 lists everything: personalty and realty, assets and liabilities, including her husband's entail, which was his private property.[9] In our analysis, we have used categories of items traditionally found in eighteenth- and nineteenth-century probate inventories. Items of clothing did not feature in probate inventories, as they were often considered personal belongings and distributed among the household servants. We have assessed the origin of each product listed in the inventories according to whether it was global, European or Swedish. This can be done with some certainty because many items are described as Dutch, English or East Indian, and others simply cannot have been produced or grown in Sweden – exotic woods, tea, spices, porcelain and certain types of luxury textiles (see Appendix). Caution is needed, though, as it was not unknown for national designations to become generic quality descriptions over the century.[10]

Surviving financial accounts from private individuals or households are far rarer than probate inventories, and even more so if they originate from the same family and estates. The Spens household accounts from 1720 to 1731 and 1789 to 1816 are unusually well documented. Since the number of purchases was huge in both households, we have limited the analysis to the periods 1727–30 and 1797–1800. The account books allow us to analyse a wider range of purchases because, unlike probate inventories, they contain information about consumables such as clothing, stationery, medicines and food. Some purchases were semi-finished goods where the final product or use is unknown. Thus the categories we have used are furnishings (furniture and the like for reception rooms), kitchenware (utensils and household goods), clothing, textiles and stationery, and foodstuffs – subdivided by meat, fish, fruit and vegetables, grain products, dairy products, beverages, colonial groceries and other.[11]

The two sets of accounts are rather different. Countess Beata was responsible for the family finances for the first set of accounts. She kept the running accounts of the family's and household's incomings and outgoings weekly. For the period 1789 to 1801, the accounts are more detailed but also less complete. Accounts were kept by both the count and the countess, but unfortunately most of his have been lost for the years up to 1810. Instead, we used the count's annual accounts of his and his family's income and expenditure from 1810 to 1815. There does not seem to have been any significant difference in their financial situation between the 1790s and the 1810s.[12] Countess Ulrika Eleonora took care of the household accounts from their marriage in 1789 until she died in 1802. Despite these differences, we argue that the Spens family accounts from 1727 to 1730 and 1797 to 1800 are comparable. In terms of the families' total spending, we can set Countess Beata's estate and household accounts from 1727 to 1730 against the count's accounts from 1810 to 1815. In terms of the breakdown of spending into different categories, Countess Ulrika Eleonora's household accounts for 1797–1800 are directly comparable to those for 1727–30 since they both included items bought for the household, and neither documented the counts' consumption in total: in 1727–30 because Countess Beata supplied her husband with cash for his spending, and in 1797–1800 because the count may have kept his accounts, which are now lost.

For our analysis, we have built two databases, one using Countess Beata's accounts for 1727–30 with 1,867 entries and the other using Countess Ulrika Eleonora's accounts for 1797–1800 with 2,419 entries. In addition, we have included the estate accounts for the same years for their country seat. Duplicate items found in the household and the estate accounts have been removed.

Income and outgoings

Whereas much research often focuses on either income or outgoings, we include both since they were decisive for the extent and nature of the Spens family's consumption.[13] Eighteenth-century Swedish household finances were complex affairs. A large part was based on an in-kind economy where goods were acquired and services done without cash changing hands, and without being put through the books. Still, work and goods had specific, accepted values at the time. Most of the work was done by agreement or under contract with tenant farmers, crofters, farmhands and farm women. They were always paid wages for any days' work beyond the agreed number of days' unpaid labour (corvée), and there were often cash bonuses for work well done.[14] This balance in the cash accounts was vital, as that was where any surplus from the count's salary, interest on loans and sales appeared, and it was this cash that was used to buy the goods and services that could not be produced on the family estates, or which they chose not to produce.

The Spens family's finances in the 1720s and 1790s were ostensibly similar because the family owned several country estates and town properties at both stages.[15] However, in practice, the differences were significant (Table 1.1). Reading from the probate inventories for Carl Gustaf Spens in 1751 and Countess Ulrika Eleonora in 1802, it appears they differed in three respects. In the 1720s, the count and countess inherited most of their properties and lent considerable sums to others. Consequently, in addition to their land holdings, they were debt-free with large amounts due and cash reserves at the time they died. At the end of the century, the younger generation also inherited significant land holdings; but they continued buying new estates,

Table 1.1 Spens family assets in 1751 and 1802 in Riksdaler, deflated at constant prices (CPI, base year 1914).

	1751		1802	
	Cash value	Distribution (%)	Cash value	Distribution (%)
House contents	84,699	15	17,127	2
Property	104,150	20	714,971*	90
Cash	49,460	9	961	0
Tools	3,480	1	9,336	1
Livestock	5,950	1	13,077	2
Grain	3,925	1	19,970	3
Debts due	275,081	53	15,401	2
Total assets	526,746	100	790,843	100
Debts	0		182,255	
Surplus	526,746		608,588	

Source: Riksarkivet (Swedish National Archives), Stockholm (RA), Svea hovrätt EXI:b 165 and 203.

* The property valuations for Höja, Salnecke and Grensholmen are taken from Carl Gustaf Spens's estate (1816) because they are omitted from Ulrika Eleonora's estate (1802). The valuations do not seem to have differed because the properties in question feature in both.

which they improved with land reclamation and construction work, putting them into debt. Their total assets (excluding debt) amounted to 790,843 Rd (deflated), but as much as 96 per cent of that was tied up in their country houses and contents, as compared with the 1720s, when the family assets were 526,746 Rd, of which only 20 per cent was property.[16]

The Spens family's income in the late 1720s came from several sources (Table 1.2). Their Höja and Ökna estates accounted for one-third, matched by the count's salary as Grand Master of the Hunt and his perks of office in charge of the royal parks and forests. An impressive 14 per cent of their income was interest payments from friends and relatives – although earlier in the decade it had amounted to almost 50 per cent. Aristocratic families in a position to do so were known to

Table 1.2 Spens family's annual income and expenditure in 1727–30 and 1797–1800 (1810–15) in Riksdaler, and the totals at constant prices (CPI, base year 1914).

	1727–30		1797–1800 (1810–15)	
	Amount	Distribution	Amount	Distribution
Income				
Balance	3,117	11	1,266	1
Family estates	9,263	32	39,751	43
Town house	0	0	1,405	2
Count's salary	4,884	17	0	0
Hunting grounds	3,473	12	0	0
Interests	4,208	14	46,804	51
Other income	3,919	14	2,440	3
Total	28,864	100	91,666	100
Expenditure				
Interest payments	598	2	71,879	78
Taxes	441	2	Unknown	
Surplus used for consumption	24,410	85	17,991	20
Balance to next year	3365	11	1796	2
Total	28,864	100	91,666	100
Expenditure (after taxes and interest payments)				
Salaries and wages	4,826	21	5,052	28
Estate investments	1,554	6	3,096	17
Furnishings/utensils	2,524	10	1,342	7
Clothing	4,508	18	348	2
Textiles	2,704	11	1,827	11
Foodstuffs	8,294	34	2,299	13
Other			4,034	22
Total	24,410	100	17,991	100

Source: Höja gårdsarkiv G1:1, Beata Oxenstiernas personliga räkenskaper; Höja gårdsarkiv K2:2, Carl Gustaf Spens personliga räkenskaper.

lend money at interest, one of the buffers against the cyclical fluctuations in agriculture and the social necessity of consumption.[17]

Compared with the 1720s, incomes in 1810–15 were about three times as high at about 99,000 Rd a year calculated at constant prices.[18] The most significant sources of income were interest on loans (51 per cent) and agriculture (43 per cent). The family's land holdings were now not only larger, but had also been improved by extensive land reclamation, land drainage and better farm equipment, resulting in a sharp rise in profits.[19] In the 1720s, the annual income from the Spens family estates was 10,000 Rd; in 1810–16 it averaged 43,000 Rd.

The Spenses had always sold grain from Höja and Salnecke to the Bergslagen mining district and Stockholm, but by 1800 it was being sold processed as flour and *brännvin* (aquavita). The grain concentration meant the estates' meadows and pastures were increasingly put to the plough, and the forests were used more intensively for grazing, which in the long run led to a reduction in livestock farming and a shortage of animal products. In other words, in the late eighteenth century, the family's country estates were less self-sufficient but, at the same time, better integrated into the market economy.[20]

Large incomes meant large expenditure. In the 1720s, only 4 per cent went to taxes and interest payments, 11 per cent was saved for the next year and 85 per cent was the family's surplus. Seventy-three per cent of this surplus was spent buying consumer goods, including clothing, textiles, food and other household expenditure and cash outlay to family members. Servants' wages accounted for 21 per cent and spending on the estates (building materials, etc.) 6 per cent. In the early nineteenth century, the family's outgoings were very different. Interest on loans and investments alone came to 78 per cent, and 2 per cent was saved for the next year, leaving only 20 per cent for consumption and wages. Even calculated at constant prices, the 17,991 Rd a year the family spent on consumption and wages in the 1790s was less than the average 24,410 Rd a year spent by the older generation in the 1720s. The breakdown of this expenditure had also changed: the wage bill and estate investment had risen to 28 and 17 per cent respectively. This reflected the Spens family's many investments in agriculture and the fact that the more intensive the farming operations, the more farmhands, farm women and day labourers were needed to work their estates in the 1790s. In other words, the amounts the two generations had left for personal consumption were very different. In the 1720s, the family could spend 22,605 Rd a year at constant prices, while in the 1790s, they only had 9,843 a year.

That wages were a relatively higher and consumption a lower proportion of costs in 1800 than in 1730 appears more than a little contradictory, given it was supposedly a period of market integration. Several possible explanations present themselves. One was that goods in the late eighteenth century were cheaper thanks to mass production and imports that characterised the period. Another was that the family at the end of the eighteenth century could exploit more fully the estates' residents and thus produce a range of consumer goods instead of buying them. In the 1720s, Countess Beata lived mainly in Stockholm, where she also did most of the family's shopping. In contrast, in the 1790s, Countess Ulrika Eleonora lived at Salnecke, controlling the estate's household and residents. Sweden's population growth in the eighteenth century meant reduced real wages and a sharp rise in rents for both tenant farmers and crofters, apparent in the days of unpaid labour they were expected to do.[21] Countess Ulrika Eleonora kept separate accounts for the textiles produced on the estates, from which it appears a large number of the womenfolk were involved in producing wool and linen cloth. One final explanation is tied to changing national priorities which involved propaganda against imports and encouraging people to buy Swedish goods.[22]

Possession and consumption of goods, 1727-30

The circumstances of the Spens family's consumption thus altered over the century in several respects regarding their finances and market developments. How did this affect the contents of the two houses and the Spenses' consumption? In the 1730s, most of the household's assets – some 15 per cent in all – were tied up in the family's possessions (Table 1.3). In the list of items of various sorts, the family silver dominated, accounting for almost half the total value. The fact that so much of their wealth was in precious metals reflected an older type of economy, where silver represented financial security. Still, silver items also had a substantial decorative value, not least when hosting a dinner party. Similarly, the family jewellery also accounted for a relatively large proportion – almost 20 per cent – which was comparable in size to the furnishings.

Just over a quarter of the items were global or European in origin, but this largely comprised three types of objects: almost all the jewels and jewellery were imported, as was half of the tableware and glassware, and only a slightly lower proportion of the furnishings. The probate inventory lists jewellery with diamonds and pearls, which explains their

Table 1.3 House contents in 1751 by category and origin, at constant prices (CPI, base year 1914).

Category	Amount	% of total	Global or European (%)				Total
			Global	Global or European	European	Possibly European	
Jewellery	14,874	18	87		1		88
Gold	4,436	5		Yes			
Silver	39,572	47		Yes			
Pewter	1,411	2					
Copper	1,215	1					
Brass	221	0					
Iron	304	0					
Tableware and glassware	1,032	1	21	26			47
Textiles	5,901	7			8		8
Furnishings*	14,052	17	1	6	42	7	56
Books	1,681	2			Yes		
Total house contents	84,699	100	17	1	8	1	27

Source: Riksarkivet (Swedish National Archives), Stockholm (RA), Svea hovrätt EXI:b 165 and 203.
* Includes bedding, wallcoverings and paintings.

high value and global origin. Among the pieces of jewellery was a one with 51 small and three large rose-cut diamonds, a crucifix with seven brilliant-cut diamonds and a pair of bracelets with no fewer than 822 pearls. In addition to the evident financial value, the family jewels would also have had a significant social value, to demonstrate the family's status, and emotional weight as heirlooms. That much of the glassware and tableware was also global or European is no great surprise since there was little domestic production. The furnishings were predominantly European and more precisely English and Dutch, including an English wall clock with a lacquered case, an English wicker chair and Dutch paintings. Materials could indicate foreign origin, for example a chiffonier in walnut with gilt fittings. Nonetheless, almost half of the furniture was made from wood grown in Sweden. This includes plain everyday items but also some more exclusive pieces in birch, maple and alder which were often manufactured in Stockholm and could act as substitutes for imported furniture.[23]

Evidently, the Spens family had a good selection of foreign possessions in their home in the 1730s. Thanks to their high monetary value and the exclusive (and exotic) materials, they were often regarded as status symbols and displayed as such. A visitor would immediately recognise their value and exclusiveness, and also their foreign origin.

If we then look at purchases for the Spens household in the 1720s, what jumps out is how active they were as consumers. There were many items purchased, as we noted earlier: 500–600 items a year on average, and many of them were several separate items listed together. Purchases were spread throughout the year, but there was substantial variation in the number of purchases and number of occasions, from just one purchase in June 1729 to 74 in May 1730. Countess Beata may have shopped only occasionally, but she often made up for it by the number of purchases. An illustrative example was the collection of entries for 10 June 1729, when she noted 24 transactions to pay for Seville oranges and lemons; nails, tobacco and bran; horse shoeing; a wig for the count; cotton and silk for the countess's quilted petticoat (and associated wages for 'Sybritta'); a fan for the countess; cash for the children in Uppsala; cash for the count; a gift towards the fabric of Gryta Church; Anders the foreman's salary; a salary given to Countess Beata's old wetnurse; Lidén's salary; a tip for Countess Beata's mother's cook; salaries for men from the province of Dalarna, temporarily employed at Höja; veal; French brandy for the Seville oranges; wine, including Pontac (French red wine);[24] Elström's for spices; Björnen the apothecary's; medicines for Countess Beata; linen fabric; and 'sundry' costs.[25] Most purchases included foreign items, such as oranges, lemons, tobacco, silk and spices, and only a few domestic ones, such as veal, nails and linen. On this occasion, the wine imported from Europe cost the most.

The large variety of disbursements, and not least the many small purchases, indicate demand-driven consumption. Goods were purchased, and services were engaged, when the need arose – provided, of course, the goods and services were available. It was perhaps the higher-status items that were most dependent on supply; Countess Beata's location would have dictated when she could buy them. When it came to the consumption of essentials, especially food and clothing items, the family's needs were continually met by purchases of varying sizes.

In moving from particular examples to general purchasing patterns, we focus on the product categories associated with the household's consumption – furnishings, clothing, textiles, stationery and food – rather than salaries, livestock, building materials and unrecognised costs, marked as 'cash' or 'outlay to the count'. To distinguish as much status-oriented consumption as possible, we have applied the two further subcategories of home and kitchen because the furnishings of the reception rooms would have been more status-driven than those of the kitchens. Concerning foodstuffs, we have aimed for categorisations that capture their origin, which would have affected both their price and status: meat, fish, fruit and vegetables, grain products, dairy products and colonial groceries.

Purchases in the 1720s were dominated by clothing and textiles, which between them accounted for 40 per cent of all spending (see Table 1.4). Next came beverages and colonial groceries, which at 11–13 per cent of all purchases predominated among foodstuffs. Stationery, fruit and vegetables, and dairy products comprised a tiny part. The number and cost of the purchases related to what the household could produce. Clothing and textiles were things they did not make themselves, while the opposite was true for many of the foodstuffs – colonial groceries excluded. This was underlined by the fact that, when the Spenses bought staple foodstuffs, it was primarily in Stockholm where their own produce was unavailable.

Goods of foreign origin made up a modest proportion of overall spending, and most were European. Textiles and certain types of foodstuffs stand out. It is difficult to judge the origin of textiles here, but we assess that just under half were made in Europe. Both textiles and clothing were primarily purchased in Stockholm, where the supply was more varied. The Spenses bought expensive silks such as satin,

Table 1.4 Purchases in 1727–30 by origin and family residence, per year in Riksdaler, at constant prices (CPI, base year 1914).

Category	Cost	% of total spend	Origin, where known (%)					Where purchased (%)		
			Total	Global	Global or European	European	Possibly European	Stockholm (65% of time)	Höja (26% of time)	Other (9% of time)
Furnishings	509	7	4	2		2	2	75	25	
Kitchen	302	4	6	–		2	4	39	61	
Clothing	1,753	25	3		2		1	100		
Textiles	1,081	15	42		1	12	29	85	15	
Stationery	143	2								
Foodstuffs: meat	315	4	2	–		2		100		
Foodstuffs: beverages	917	13	76	–		76		100		
Foodstuffs: fish	400	6	3	–		3		100		
Foodstuffs: fruit and vegetables	101	2	70		70	–		100		
Foodstuffs: colonial groceries	772	11	100		95	5		100		
Foodstuffs: dairy	151	2		–		–		100		
Foodstuffs: grain products	349	5	6	–		6		100		
Foodstuffs: other*	252	4	?							
Total	7,044	100								

Source: Riksarkivet (Swedish National Archives), Stockholm (RA), Svea hovrätt EXI:b 165 and 203.

* Includes medicines (673 daler kmt) and tobacco (61 daler kmt), but it is not clear how large a proportion of either was imported or made in Sweden.

damask and a silk-and-wool fabric called camlet, but also broadcloth, linen and chintz (the last of Indian origin). Again we see a mix of foreign (European) goods such as silk and camlet, and domestic goods such as broadcloth and linen. Individual items were noted separately in the accounts if they were expensive – including hats, gloves, stockings and shoes – and the indications are that the Spenses had relatively few, good-quality outfits rather than a wealth of clothing. They probably kept the foreign fabrics for exclusive items of clothing.

Foodstuffs and colonial goods such as spices, fruit and beverages were almost exclusively bought in Stockholm. The 'colonial groceries' category has been broadly defined for this study to include spices (never specified in the accounts), seasonings and preservatives (salt, sugar, oil and spirit vinegar) and hot drinks (tea, coffee and chocolate). Spices and loaf sugar were bought from two preferred spicers, often in large quantities: from a spicer named Hällström, for example, they purchased 20 sugar loaves for 214 daler kopparmynt (kmt) and unspecified spices for 316 daler kmt; from another spicer, Pasch, they bought spices to the tune of several hundred daler kmt. The Spens family had adopted some new fashionable habits and so regularly bought chocolate and tea of various kinds from a general merchant called Robert, but in contrast they purchased virtually no coffee beans. Many of these products depended on global trade and may have been difficult to source outside Stockholm and the other major ports. The same was true of the wines from France and Portugal, Seville oranges and a surprisingly large quantity of lemons – judging by the sums spent, Countess Beata bought a total of 975 lemons over four years.

In the 1720s, the Spenses had a great many items of foreign origin, even though they did not predominate among the family's possessions. Jewels and jewellery were naturally global in origin, while many of the furnishings and textiles originated in Europe. For several items – tableware and glassware, colonial groceries and fruit – it is impossible to determine whether their origin was European or global, but they were certainly imported. However, the preponderance of foreign items among the family's possessions was not echoed in their accounts. Jewels, jewellery and furnishings were major investments and therefore infrequent purchases and absent from this run of the accounts. Conversely, consumables brought in from overseas – textiles, colonial groceries, fruit and beverages – were not found in the probate inventory because foodstuffs were not included, and textiles were remade as clothing. Evidently, the family's consumption of foreign consumables would be rendered invisible if only their inventoried possessions were studied, and equally, some of their significant, long-term investments would be overlooked if only their accounts were analysed.

Possession and consumption of goods, 1797–1800

Turning to the 1790s, the family's household possessions comprised only a tiny proportion – 2 per cent – of their total assets. In terms of value, they were worth far less than before (Table 1.5). About 50 per cent were furnishings, and the other more significant categories were again jewels and jewellery (15 per cent) and a new frontrunner, textiles (another 15 per cent). The value of the family silver had fallen sharply and was now very low indeed, as was that of tableware and glassware. Silver items were probably no longer needed as economic insurance and many of the earlier items had been dispersed through inheritance.

Overall, foreign goods accounted for a quarter of all assets. As before, jewellery led among the global goods, predominantly diamonds and pearls. Glassware and tableware were now more certainly global or European, sometimes specified as East Indian and English china. One novelty was dinner services or matching sets of crockery, but unfortunately without their provenance being noted. Textiles are the hardest to pinpoint because references to their origins are so rare. We have not found anything that points to global imports, while the proportion of European textiles probably is underestimated. In contrast to earlier, a more significant proportion of furnishings were Swedish-made, pointing towards an increased tendency to spend money on Swedish substitutes. There are also examples of a mix of Swedish, European and global influences, including a state bed, made in Sweden but following the French model and from imported silk woven in Sweden.[26] At the same time, the global proportion had also increased since mahogany had replaced walnut as the valuable wood of choice. The Spenses had several mahogany commodes, cabinets, tea tables, sewing tables and card tables. The fact that most of their mahogany furniture was small meant it could be readily combined with their other furnishings or moved between rooms, and probably formed the key attraction of many pieces.

As already noted, the Spens household in the 1790s differed significantly from that of the 1720s, and they spent far less on consumables and wages than before. Again we have focused on the former. Their pattern of consumption had also changed. Textiles and items of clothing together accounted for the largest proportion of spending, but now textiles predominate over clothing (30 and 7 per cent respectively). Spending on

Table 1.5 House contents in 1802 by category and origin, in Riksdaler, at constant prices (CPI, base year 1914).

Category	Amount	% of total	Global	Global or European	European	Possibly European	Global or European total
Jewellery	2,772	16	73	27			100
Gold	1,005	6		Yes			
Silver	1,253	7		Yes			
Pewter	92	1					
Copper	181	1					
Brass	26	0					
Iron	92	1					
Tableware and glassware	547	3	23		20		43
Textiles	2,539	15			1	8	9
Furnishings	8,301	48	6	1	2	4	13
Books	318	2			Yes		
Total house contents	17,127	100	15	4	2	3	24

Source: Riksarkivet (Swedish National Archives), Stockholm (RA), Svea hovrätt EXI:b 165 and 203.

foodstuffs had fallen, except for colonial groceries, which had increased to 18 per cent of expenditure. The family also spent more on furnishings because they had a new residence in Uppsala to fit out.

A significant difference was that the younger generation shopped in more places. Thanks to increased geographical mobility, Stockholm was no longer the hub for the family's consumption (Table 1.6). They spent almost half of the year at Salnecke, their country estate, but only a fifth of their time in Stockholm; instead, they spent a similar amount of time in Uppsala, which was closer to Salnecke and more readily accessible by boat.[27] The proportion of foreign goods had also fallen overall, although the share of global goods had increased slightly. The accounts list a variety of textiles, including linen, silk, damask, taffeta, satin and others, and accessories such as feathers, fans and ribbons as well as large quantities of yarn and thread. The most significant purchases were of linens and silks, almost certainly intended to be made up into clothing. Although only a small proportion of the textiles were of foreign origin – 17 per cent – exclusive ones such as silk, taffeta and damask were imported, mainly from Europe. Some fans were labelled 'foreign', and it is likely that the others, especially those made of feathers, were foreign as well. Thus, imported goods were associated with being exclusive.

The Spenses now bought most of their expensive silks in Uppsala (68 per cent) rather than Stockholm (29 per cent); in Stockholm, they shopped for thread and ribbons and more unusual items such as feathers, fans and umbrellas, rather than large quantities of textiles. It seems very unlikely the Spens family would have settled for unfashionable or poor-quality materials; instead, the declining importance of Stockholm reflected the improved distribution of goods – and the significance of the Salnecke–Uppsala waterway. Stockholm continued to be the destination for more exclusive accessories. On the rare occasions when the Spenses bought eau de Cologne or other perfumes, it was always in the capital. The status value of such small items was not to be sneezed at, and they were an excellent opportunity to keep up with the fashions without spending a fortune.[28]

Spending on foreign consumer goods plummeted in some categories of goods: from 76 to 3 per cent for beverages and 70 to 39 per cent for fruit. The family's food was increasingly produced on their estates or bought locally. The family continued to bulk-buy lemons – in this period, about 760 – but otherwise, their estates grew far more fruit than before.[29] As for alcohol, it is not apparent what replaced the wine and sherry the older generation used to buy, as neither was produced in Sweden. Presumably, they drank beer or home-distilled spirits, or

Table 1.6 Purchases in 1797–1800 by origin and family residence, per year in Riksdaler, at constant prices (CPI, base year 1914).

Category	Cost	% of total spend	Origin, where known (%) Total	Global	Global or European	European	Possibly European	Where purchased Stockholm (19% of time)	Uppsala (20% of time)	Salnecke (42% of time)	Grensholmen (17% of time)	Other (2% of time)
Furnishings	613	14	21	8	4	6	3	6	75	10	9	0
Kitchen	326	8	1	–		1		87	0	0	13	0
Clothing	273	7	5		1		4	32	0	51	2	15
Textiles	1,281	30	17	1	1	1	14	33	59	7	1	0
Stationery	25	1	7			7		21	58	21		
Foodstuffs: meat	283	7						100				
Foodstuffs: beverages	32	1	3		3			65				
Foodstuffs: fish	161	4	9		9			65			35	
Foodstuffs: fruit and vegetables	85	2	39	39				34	0	34	1	
Foodstuffs: colonial groceries	777	18	100	21	71	8		34	25	21	19	1
Foodstuffs: dairy	79	2	1			1		100				
Foodstuffs: grain products	234	6	10	10				4	23	51	22	0
Total	4,170	100										

Source: Riksarkivet (Swedish National Archives), Stockholm (RA), Svea hovrätt EXI:b 165 and 203.

the wine they purchased was not recorded in the accounts. Conversely, the proportion of furnishings and colonial groceries which were global in origin was now more significant than before. With the former, the Spenses followed the new fashion for mahogany furniture, which had an impact in terms of both possessions and consumption. The family bought half a dozen mahogany chairs and mahogany wood for sofas and chairs for the house in Uppsala. There was also mahogany furniture at Salnecke, according to the probate inventory.

Shifts in the pattern of colonial groceries came down, in part, to the different ways they kept the books. Where Countess Beata only wrote 'spices', Countess Ulrika Eleonora detailed every purchase, thus making it possible to determine the spices' origin. The cinnamon, allspice, nutmeg, ginger, pepper, cloves and saffron they bought could only have been global. But there were also real changes in the consumption of other goods in this category. By the end of the century, spending on sugar had increased enormously, doubling as a proportion of the total expenditure. This was very much in line with the general increase in sugar consumption in Europe in the eighteenth century. In Sweden, average consumption quadrupled in the second half of the century, which, thanks to Kajsa Warg's and Anna Maria Rückerschöld's recipe books (published in 1755 and 1785), affected Swedish cuisine.[30] Some of the sugar was probably used to preserve berries and fruit, but the liking for sugar was also evident in cakes and pastries – gingerbread, ratafia biscuits, jumbles – which were a new element in the family's diet.

Coffee consumption increased significantly, and although spending on chocolate had virtually ceased, tea still seems to have been the most popular of the hot drinks. The fact that they were well established in the household is emphasised by purchases of the utensils needed to make and serve coffee and tea – objects that often had a high-status value.[31] Greater consumption presupposed greater availability, and, sure enough, imports of tea, coffee and other groceries rose markedly over the eighteenth century. Indeed, there was an explosive increase in coffee imports intended for the Swedish market in the second half of the century.[32] The consumption of colonial groceries of all kinds also shows that the Swedish market was growing and was no longer just about Stockholm. Spices and coffee could be bought at Salnecke (either delivered from elsewhere or bought from peddlers) and to some extent in Uppsala, though Stockholm was still the preferred place to buy tea and sugar. The varied supply at Salnecke was probably linked to better distribution, whether generally speaking from Stockholm to Uppsala or specifically from Uppsala to Salnecke by boat.

Conclusions: home comforts, foreign luxuries

Our analysis of purchases shows that, in both the 1720s and the 1790s, the Spens household actively participated in a consumer culture, shopping a great deal. They were engaged in continual consumption, whether for the household or individual family members, and they attached great importance to keeping records of their expenditure – like all aristocratic families. That this responsibility fell to the senior women in the family is not surprising but deserves to be underlined.

Despite significant changes in the Swedish economy, consumption did not increase during the century. On the contrary, the Spenses spent less money on household consumption in the 1790s than had their forebears. One explanation is that heavy spending was nothing new for aristocratic families who, because of their financial and social circumstances, already lived consumer lifestyles and were less affected by the burgeoning market economy. At the same time, there are noticeable differences in what they spent money on. Purchases of sugar and coffee replaced wine and chocolate, and textiles replaced clothing. Less foodstuff was bought, and they started buying mahogany furniture, and English and oriental porcelain. Focusing on the provenance of these things, the probate inventories and accounts show that both generations of Spenses owned imported global and European objects, but not in the quantities one might have expected from an aristocratic family. Nor was what they held incredibly flamboyant or luxurious, and there is nothing in their accounts to indicate excessive consumption.[33] However, we should bear in mind that simplicity was relative. The cost of the Spenses' sons' graduations and kitting them out as military officers was equivalent to 6,158 days' work by the crofters at Salnecke (1812). Moreover, Johanna Ilmakunnas points out that what Axel von Fersen thought was a 'necessary minimum of daily comfort' was unattainable for many nobles.[34] While wealthy burghers in Arboga, a town not so far away from the Spenses' house at Höja and Salnecke, had similar possessions and perhaps a shared consumer culture, their level of engagement with the world of goods was notably lower.[35]

By working with the two types of source material, thus analysing possessions as well as consumption, we have been able to outline a fuller picture of foreign influences in eighteenth-century Sweden. There was a mixing of local, European and global material cultures found among the Swedish nobility. Silks, printed cottons, Chinese porcelain, coffee and tea utensils, and mahogany furniture were found in all the better homes by the early eighteenth century, but alongside a high proportion of Swedish goods, made in imitation of expensive foreign originals.[36] It is well known that eighteenth-century Swedish culture was influenced by France, especially in royal and aristocratic circles. Yet a close study of the Spens family reveals few traces of French goods. Instead, we find numerous references to English (and Dutch) items during the second period. Thus, in the cultural battle between France and Britain, Britain emerged as the winner from the perspective of the European periphery. Still, the material culture of the elite was characterised by their national culture. Swedish products, often of high quality, predominated in elite homes and at their dinner tables, garnished with foreign luxuries.

Appendix: categorisation of goods as global, European or domestic

In general, the categorisation is made on the geographical origin of the items, based on knowledge of its definitive origin (e.g. East Indian porcelain), that the origin is mentioned (e.g. Dutch cloth, English clock), that they are very exclusive (e.g. fabrics of silk or damask) or that it could not possibly be manufactured or produced in Sweden (e.g. salt, rice, gilded leather). Furniture could consist of both imported and domestic materials and is classified as European or global based on the arguments mentioned above (an explicit provenance, costly fabrics for the hangings, furniture made of mahogany, walnut or lacquered). In some cases – for example for beds, where only the textiles were foreign in origin – items have been classified according to the origin of the most expensive material, that is, the textiles, since the bedsteads in most cases were made locally from Swedish wood. The items most difficult to categorise are textiles, as there were already considerable imports of expensive textiles such as silks and everyday ones such as burlap. From the mid-eighteenth century, there was also considerable domestic production. The most exclusive ones were most likely imported.

It is difficult to determine an object's origin based on its straightforward description. We have labelled them as 'global' or 'European' only when we are sure of their origin, and 'global or European' or 'possibly European' to convey a more uncertain foreign origin. Consequently, the amount of global or European goods might be on the low side.

Table 1.7 Categorisation of goods as global, European or domestic.

Goods	Category	Year	Consumption category	Comment
Jewels and jewellery	Jewels and jewellery	Both periods	Global	The valuation is often based on the number of diamonds and oriental pearls. Those with Swedish pearls are classified as domestic, and with corals probably coming from the Mediterranean
Gold	Gold	Both periods	Domestic	Only classified as European or global if the origin is mentioned, otherwise classified as domestic, even though there most probably were exceptions (e.g. with gold and silver, which mostly came from Sweden). Metals were, of course, reused to a great extent
Silver	Silver	Both periods	Domestic	
Pewter	Pewter	Both periods	Domestic	
Copper	Copper	Both periods	Domestic	
Brass	Brass	Both periods	Domestic	
Iron	Iron	Both periods	Domestic	
East Indian porcelain	Tableware and glassware	Both periods	Global	
English porcelain	Tableware and glassware	c. 1800	European	
Danziger stoneware	Tableware and glassware	Both periods	European	Imported from Poland
Stoneware, blue and white	Tableware and glassware	Both periods	Possibly European	Imported from the Dutch Republic or Germany, some domestic production
Exclusive glass	Tableware and glassware	Both periods	Possibly European	
Dutch cloth	Textiles	c. 1730	European	
Dutch cotton	Textiles	c. 1730	European	
High-quality fabrics of silk, damask, velvet and wool	Textiles	Both periods	European	
Printed cotton	Textiles	c. 1800	Possibly European	Huge imports but growing domestic manufacturing

Table 1.7 (continued)

Goods	Category	Year	Consumption category	Comment
Turkish tapestry	Textiles	c. 1730	European	Usually from Flanders
Cotton	Textiles	c. 1730	European	
Cotton	Textiles	c. 1800	Possibly European	Huge imports but growing domestic manufacturing
Gilded leather	Furnishings	c. 1730	European	Imported from Germany and France
Marble table tops	Furnishings	c. 1730	European	Imported
Marble table tops	Furnishings	c. 1800	Possibly European	Imported, but there were some domestic quarries
Walnut furniture	Furnishings	c. 1730	Global or European	
Mahogany furniture	Furnishings	Both periods	Global	
Lacquered furniture	Furnishings	Both periods	Global or European	Probably imported, even if there was some smaller domestic manufacturing
Dutch paintings	Furnishings	c. 1730	European	
Venetian soap	Kitchen	Both periods	European	
Wine	Foodstuffs: beverages	Both periods	European	Imported from France and Portugal
Lobsters, oysters	Foodstuffs: fish	Both periods	European	
Dutch herring	Foodstuffs: fish	Both periods	European	
Lemons, oranges	Foodstuffs: fruit and vegetables	Both periods	Global or European	
Salt	Foodstuffs: colonial groceries	Both periods	European	Imported from Portugal or Spain
Chocolate, coffee, tea	Foodstuffs: colonial groceries	Both periods	Global	
Sugar	Foodstuffs: colonial groceries	Both periods	Global or European	

Goods	Category	Year	Consumption category	Comment
Colonial groceries (nutmeg, ginger, allspice, almonds, cinnamon)	Foodstuffs: colonial groceries	Both periods	Global	
French mustard, vinegar	Foodstuffs: colonial groceries	Both periods	European	
Tobacco	Foodstuffs: other	Both periods	Global or European	To some extent imported, but difficult to estimate
Medicine	Foodstuffs: other	Both periods	Global or European	
English malt	Foodstuffs: grain products	c. 1730	European	
Rice flour, rice	Foodstuffs: grain products	c. 1800	Global	

Notes

1. This chapter was written within the project Manorial Housekeeping. Economy, Housekeeping and Material Culture on Swedish Manors 1700–1900, financed by Handelsbankens forskningsstiftelser, P2011-0239:1.
2. Fairchilds, 'The production and marketing of populuxe goods'; Coquery, 'The language of success'; Vickery, 'His and hers'; Whittle and Griffiths, *Consumption and Gender*.
3. By the mid-eighteenth century, the population amounted to a little less than two million, of which 400,000 lived in the eastern provinces (present-day Finland).
4. For an analysis of Swedish foreign trade in the eighteenth century, see Hodacs, *Silk and Tea*; Müller, *Sveriges första globala århundrade*.
5. Bailey, 'Squire, shopkeeper and staple food'. On the importance of the second-hand market, see van Damme and Vermoesen, 'Second-hand consumption as a way of life', 288–91; Ulväng et al., *Den glömda konsumtionen*, 119–27, 153–63.
6. Hodacs, *Silk and Tea*, 6–7; Müller, *Sveriges första globala århundrade*, 154–83; Thomasson, *Svarta Saint-Barthélemy*.
7. Söderlund, *Stockholms hantverkarklass 1720–1772*, 222–6, 298; Nyberg, 'The institutional setting of the luxury trades', 84 (quote).
8. For a brief history of the Spens family, see Ulväng, *Höja säteri*.
9. Swedish National Archives, Svea Hovrätts arkiv, EXIb: 40 and EXIb: 165.
10. Many thanks to Stina Odlinder-Haubo, Annika Tegnér and Marie Ulväng for identifying different types of furniture, porcelain and textiles in the inventories.
11. The categories Building material and Tools are excluded here since they consisted solely of Swedish-made goods.
12. He owned much the same in 1816 as in 1800, with the exception that he had sold his wife's part in Hasselfors ironwork and bought Ribbingsholm manor.
13. For a more detailed analysis of the account books, see Ulväng and Andersson, 'Grevinnorna Spens konsumtion under ett föränderligt 1700-tal'.
14. Magnusson, *Ty som ingenting angelägnare är än mina bönders conservation*; Ilmakunnas, *Ett ståndsmässigt liv*, 321–90.
15. Swedish National Archives, Svea Hovrätt, EXIb: 40 and 165.
16. All sums have been deflated, according to the Swedish Consumer Price Index (CPI), using 1914 as base year: https://web.archive.org/web/20150924114310/http://www.riksbank.se/upload/Dokument_riksbank/Monetar_hist/ConsumerPriceIndex1291_2006.xls.
17. As a comparison, the late seventeenth-century Count Stenbock had around 30 per cent of his income in interest payments; Kullberg, *Johan Gabriel Stenbock och reduktionen*, 25, 133. In the von Fersen family, the revenues from interest payments varied between 35 and 85 per cent in the late eighteenth century; Ilmakunnas, *Ett ståndsmässigt liv*, 333.
18. Ulväng and Andersson, 'Grevinnorna Spens konsumtion under ett föränderligt 1700-tal'.
19. Olsson, *Storgodsdrift*, 320–30; Ulväng, *Herrgårdarnas historia*, 113.
20. A more detailed analysis can be found in Ulväng, *Herrgårdarnas historia*, 68–75.
21. Olsson, *Storgodsdrift*, 320–30.
22. Runefelt, *Att hasta mot undergången*, 259–68.
23. Andersson, *Stadens dignitärer*; Brown, *Den bekväma vardagen*; Ulväng, 'Cabinetmakers and chairmakers'.
24. Pontac is a red wine produced in Bordeaux, originating from the town Pontacq. *Svenska Akademiens Ordbok*, 'Pontak'.
25. Accounts, 10 June 1729.
26. Lagerquist, 'Paradsängen från Höja'.
27. Both Höja and Salnecke were located by the Lake Mälaren, with access to Uppsala and Stockholm.
28. Ilmakunnas, *Ett ståndsmässigt liv*, 138–9.
29. Due to decreased prices for citrus fruits, the amount in the 1790s is lower than earlier. In the 1720s, the family could buy 975 lemons following the accounted cost, in the 1790s 766 lemons.
30. Rönnbäck, 'Socker och slavplantager i svensk historia', 109–12.
31. Andersson, *Stadens dignitärer*, 188–9.
32. Müller, 'Kolonialprodukter i Sveriges handel och konsumtionskultur, 1700–1800', 239–41.

33 Purchases of, for example, sewing materials suggest that they worked hard to make do and mend. Hamling and Richardson, 'Lifestyles and lifespans'.
34 Ilmakunnas, *Ett ståndsmässigt liv*, 140.
35 Andersson, *Stadens dignitärer*, 149–73.
36 Åström, 'Kolonialvaror och vardagsting i den europeiska margnalen'; Brown, *Den bekväma vardagen*; Ulväng, 'Cabinetmakers and chairmakers'.

Bibliography

Andersson, Gudrun. *Stadens dignitärer: Den lokala elitens status- och maktmanifestation i Arboga 1650–1770*. Stockholm: Atlantis, 2009.
Andersson, Gudrun. 'Too anxious to please: moralising gender in fashion magazines in the early nineteenth century', *History of Retailing and Consumption* 6 (2020): 216–44.
Åström, Anna-Maria. 'Kolonialvaror och vardagsting i den europeiska marginalen. Konsumtionsvägar, levnadssätt och varor på en herrgård i östra Finland under slutet av 1700-talet och början av 1800-talet', *Finskt museum* (2010–11): 6–28.
Bailey, Lucy A. 'Squire, shopkeeper and staple food: the reciprocal relationship between the country house and the village shop in the late Georgian period', *History of Retailing and Consumption* 1 (2015): 8–27.
Brown, Carolina. *Den bekväma vardagen: Kvinnor kring bord på 1700-talets Näs*. Stockholm: Carlsson bokförlag, 2020.
Coquery, Natacha. 'The language of success: marketing and distributing semi-luxury goods in eighteenth-century Paris', *Journal of Design History* 17 (2004): 71–89.
van Damme, Ilja, and Reinoud Vermoesen. 'Second-hand consumption as a way of life: public auctions in the surroundings of Alost in the late eighteenth century', *Continuity and Change* 24 (2009): 275–305.
Fairchilds, Cissie. 'The production and marketing of populuxe goods in eighteenth-century Paris'. In *Consumption and the World of Good*, edited by John Brewer and Roy Porter, 228–48. London: Routledge, 1993.
Hamling, Tara, and Catherine Richardson. 'Lifestyles and lifespans: domestic material culture and the temporalities of daily life in seventeenth-century England'. In *Daily Lives and Daily Routines in the Long Eighteenth Century*, edited by Gudrun Andersson and Jon Stobart, 19–40. New York: Routledge, 2021.
Hodacs, Hanna. *Silk and Tea in the North: Scandinavian trade and the market for Asian goods in eighteenth-century Europe*. London: Palgrave Macmillan, 2016.
Ilmakunnas, Johanna. *Ett ståndsmässigt liv: familjen von Fersens livsstil på 1700-talet*. Stockholm: Atlantis, 2012.
Kullberg, Anders. *Johan Gabriel Stenbock och reduktionen. Godspolitik och ekonomiförvaltning 1675–1705*. Uppsala: Studia Historica Upsaliensia, 1973.
Lagerquist, Marshall. 'Paradsängen från Höja', *Fataburen* (1959): 188–90.
Magnusson, Lars. *Ty som ingenting angelägnare är än mina bönders conservation – godsekonomi i östra Mellansverige vid mitten av 1700-talet*. Uppsala: Almqvist & Wiksell International, 1980.
Müller, Leos. 'Kolonialprodukter i Sveriges handel och konsumtionskultur, 1700–1800', *Historisk tidskrift* 124, no. 2 (2004): 225–48.
Müller, Leos. *Sveriges första globala århundrade: en 1700-talshistoria*. Stockholm: Dialogos, 2018.
Nyberg, Klas. 'The institutional setting of the luxury trades in eighteenth and early nineteenth-century Stockholm'. In *Luxury, Fashion and the Early Modern Idea of Credit*, edited by Klas Nyberg and Håkan Johansson, 79–96. New York: Routledge, 2021.
Olsson, Mats. *Storgodsdrift. Godsekonomi och arbetsorganisation i Skåne från dansk tid till mitten av 1800-talet*. Stockholm: Almqvist & Wiksell International, 2002.
Rönnbäck, Klas. 'Socker och slavplantager i svensk historia'. In *Global historia från periferin: Norden 1600–1850*, edited by Leos Müller, Göran Rydén and Holger Weiss, 98–115. Lund: Studentlitteratur, 2010.
Runefelt, Leif. *Att hasta mot undergången: anspråk, flyktighet, förställning i debatten om konsumtion i Sverige 1730–1830*. Lund: Nordic Academic Press, 2015.

Söderlund, Ernst. *Stockholms hantverkarklass 1720–1772: sociala och ekonomiska förhållanden*. Stockholm: Norstedts, 1943.

Thomasson, Fredrik. *Svarta Saint-Barthélemy. Människoöden i en svensk koloni 1785–1847*. Stockholm: Natur & Kultur, 2022.

Ulväng, Göran. *Herrgårdarnas historia: arbete, liv och bebyggelse på uppländska herrgårdar*. Uppsala: Hallgren & Björklund, 2008.

Ulväng, Göran. *Höja säteri. Fyra sekler, tre släkter*. Vänge: Göran Ulväng, 2015.

Ulväng, Göran. 'The Swedish manor 1750 to 1950: decline or continuity?' In *Estate Landscapes in Northern Europe*, edited by Jonathan Finch, Kristine Dyrmann and Mikael Frausing, 97–130. Aarhus: Aarhus University Press, 2019.

Ulväng, Göran. 'Cabinetmakers and chairmakers in Stockholm 1730–1850: production, market and economy in a regulated economy'. In *Luxury, Fashion and the Early Modern Idea of Credit*, edited by Klas Nyberg and Håkan Jakobsson, 151–69. London: Routledge, 2020.

Ulväng, Göran, and Gudrun Andersson. 'Grevinnorna Spens konsumtion under ett föränderligt 1700-tal'. In *Shopping i Stockholm 1700–1850: Sociala praktiker på gatunivå*, edited by My Hellsing and Johanna Ilmakunnas, 332–67. Stockholm: Stockholmia förlag, 2023.

Ulväng, Göran, Sofia Murhem and Kristina Lilja. *Den glömda konsumtionen. Auktionshandel i Sverige under 1700- och 1800-talen*. Gidlunds: Möklinta, 2013.

Vickery, Amanda. *The Gentleman's Daughter: Women's lives in Georgian England*. New Haven: Yale University Press, 1998.

Vickery, Amanda. 'His and hers: gender, consumption and household accounting in eighteenth-century England', *Past & Present* 1, no. 1 (2006): 12–38.

Whittle, Jane, and Elizabeth Griffiths. *Consumption and Gender in the Early Seventeenth-Century Household: The world of Alice Le Strange*. Oxford: Oxford University Press, 2012.

2
Global goods and Imperial Knights: assemblages in country houses in south-western Germany, 1700–1820

Daniel Menning, Anne Sophie Overkamp and Julietta Schulze

Even nowadays, a trip through rural south-western Germany can be arranged as a 'castle trail', moving from one stately house to the next. Most of these country houses are still found in small villages, sometimes right in the centre, sometimes at the edge of the settlement. Oftentimes these grand houses are very old, dating in some of their structures from late mediaeval times or the Renaissance. It is not always easy to identify them as homes of the nobility as some are only slightly larger than a substantial farmhouse and are constructed from timber-frame. It might need a second glance to detect, for example, the coat of arms above the entrance. In other instances, impressive structures of hewn sandstone still stand on rocks towering above the countryside. In yet other places, a private chapel with stucco features or a landscaped garden or even park attached to the country house speak of former grandeur. Overall, these remains tell a story of variable and widely fluctuating wealth.

A fair number of these country houses used to belong to Imperial Knights and can even be classed as palaces as the knights were independent rulers, albeit of tiny territories. Due to their legal status they can be defined as a group of their own among the variegated German nobility. Mostly they made their presence felt in south-western Germany, which, up to 1803/6, consisted of more than a hundred individual territories ranging from larger states such as Württemberg to ecclesiastical lands, independent cities and many village-sized principalities owned by the Imperial Knights. As their estates rarely raised enough revenue for a life in splendour, many Imperial Knights relied on opportunities to gain positions in the Imperial Church, in the administration of one of the larger states or in the army of a foreign power to finance their country houses and lifestyle.[1]

As is generally known, Germany did not belong to the early modern colonial powers. What is more, its south-western part remained quite remote from the dynamic centres of mercantile development in seventeenth- to nineteenth-century Europe. Yet in the early 1700s rooms in the aforementioned country houses were furnished with cotton textiles and contained the equipment necessary to enjoy a cup of tea, coffee or chocolate.[2] It can be argued that these country houses constituted spaces of global consumption. It would be too simple, though, to treat the fact that these German aristocrats also enjoyed the bounties of the world as a surprising revelation and to consequently focus on a timeline of diffusion – even though the history of consumption in early modern Germany still lags far behind its counterparts on Britain or the Netherlands.[3] After all, even a cursory search shows that novel foodstuffs penetrated central Europe in the seventeenth and eighteenth centuries, albeit at different speeds from other regions. Rather, there appears to be potential for fresh insights if we not only think about the world of goods, but also probe into practices of consumption. By studying how people in a particular region of continental Europe created assemblages of, with and around novel items, this chapter aims to shed new light on the domestication of the global.

Because a history of consumption of the Imperial Knights is still to be written, the following will necessarily remain somewhat sketchy. Firstly, the chapter analyses the manifold items that Imperial nobleman assembled for the consumption of global goods. What did they own, and were there particular patterns to their ownership? How did wealth, taste and fashion affect their acquisitions? Secondly, it studies assemblages of global goods in conjunction with other things. Concentrating on food items, the combination of global, European and local foods comes into view, raising the question of whether there was something that one might call a particular 'regional dialect' of consumption?[4] Thirdly, it looks at the role that items for the consumption of global goods played in assemblages of people. The Imperial Knights mingled with a wide range of people, among them the monarchs of larger territories, nobles of equal rank and status, as well as the knights' dependants and subjects – including peasants, artisans and day labourers. As part of enlightened society, the Imperial Knights also socialised with government administrators, professionals and literary elites.[5] How did the social setting influence the material culture of the Imperial Knights, and what role did global goods play in the creation of both splendour and comfort?

Our analysis relies primarily on probate inventories of the Imperial nobility, which are extant in significant numbers for men and women.[6] Our sample of 49 documents spans the years 1697 to 1811 and includes both married and unmarried persons. They range from the very rich who left estates close to 200,000 guilders (*fl.*) to impoverished nobles whose assets amounted to nothing more than several hundred guilders.[7] In our tables, we have only considered the inventories dated 1700 to 1799 to make our 25-year intervals coherent.

Assembling global items

As consumables, tobacco, coffee, tea and chocolate are hardly traceable through probate inventories. Rather, as Lorna Weatherill, Anne McCants and others have argued, a systematic understanding of their consumption can only be achieved by studying the material objects connected to these global goods: things such as snuff boxes, chocolate pots, coffee cups and tea urns.[8]

Among the global consumables in south-western German country houses, tobacco made its presence felt first. At his death in 1699, Philipp Wilhelm von Neuhausen owned, for example, a tobacco box, probably for snuff, made from gilded silver with an ivory inlay.[9] By the turn of the eighteenth century, taking snuff had generally eclipsed the practice of smoking tobacco among elite Europeans. The predominance of snuff boxes and utensils found in our inventories confirms this predilection among both men and women.[10] As tobacco pipes were usually made from earthenware and thus essentially disposable, they rarely make an appearance in the inventories – it is telling that in our sample the first mention occurs in the form of a small silver pipe.[11] Incidentally, smoking paraphernalia are only recorded in the inventories of males, testifying to a gender divide in tobacco consumption.[12] Snuff boxes are found in an astonishing variety of materials and a wide range of values (Table 2.1). The most widespread were made from silver, with values ranging from 1 to 17 *fl.* according to the metal's weight – at a time when a maid earned between 6 and 10 *fl.* a year. Snuff boxes with gold parts could be worth up to 150 *fl.*[13] Precious metals were combined with inset agate stones or other global materials such as tortoiseshell, ivory, shells, mother-of-pearl, or various rare materials such as petrified wood.

As the century progressed, new and less exclusive materials were introduced which also found their way into the Imperial Knights' hands and pockets. These included snuff boxes made from porcelain, faience

Table 2.1 Tobacco paraphernalia (in brackets: items with silver content).

	1700–1724	1725–1749	1750–1774	1775–1799	Entire period
Total number of inventories	8	10	14	11	43
Number of inventories with relevant objects	3	4	9	8	24
Tobacco box (*Tabakdose/Tabatiere*)	3 (3)	4 (4)	26 (23)	14 (6)	47 (36)
Tobacco pipe (*Tabakpfeife*)	0	4 (4)	1 (1)	3 (1)	8 (6)
Tobacco pipe bowl (*Tabakpfeifenkopf*)	0	0	28 (25)	9 (7)	37 (32)
Other accessories	0	0	3 (1)	3 (0)	6 (1)
Total number of objects	3 (3)	8 (8)	58 (50)	29 (14)	98 (75)

Sources: HStAS B 580, P10; StAL B 575 I, PL 9, 12, 18, 20

or serpentine, a greenish mineral, without metallic mounts. Boxes from tombac, an alloy similar to brass that looks like gold, also became increasingly popular.[14] These were priced rather low, ranging from 30 kreuzer (*xr.*) to 7 fl. 30 xr., and have been dismissed as a cheap product and indicative of the low economic status of the Imperial Knights.[15] Yet instead of seeing tombac snuff boxes exclusively as a sign of economic weakness, they might also be read as an attempt to engage with notions of taste and fashion which, according to Woodruff Smith and others, tempered conspicuous consumption.[16] The manufacturing process of tombac had only been transferred from Siam to Europe in the seventeenth century, so the material was still relatively new and possessed global implications, all of which might have added certain kudos to handling such a snuff box. Furthermore, made by toymakers in the Westphalian town of Iserlohn, these items constituted an internationally marketed consumer good, possibly adding to their appeal.[17] Finally, tombac had the advantage of being more durable and hard-wearing than gold, giving the former an edge over the latter when it came to the highly cherished embossed decorations.[18] Further inexpensive but fashionable items such as lacquered papier mâché boxes can also be found in some inventories; these speak of contemporaries' fascination with the Far East. Over the course of the century, both wealthy and poorer knights increasingly owned snuff boxes that ran the gamut from gold or silver to cheap ersatz materials (see Table 2.1), indicating that these accessories must have been deemed worthy of acquisition thanks to their fashionable nature rather than their intrinsic value. In short, semi-luxuries that are commonly associated with the middling ranks formed part of the Imperial Knights' material culture surrounding global goods, implying a certain domestication and increasing prosaicness of the latter's consumption.

Just like taking snuff, drinking tea and coffee was an important activity among the Imperial Knights and grew increasingly so over the course of the eighteenth century (Tables 2.2 and 2.3). Among our group, Ludwig Friedrich von Hallweyl was the first to own a coffee pot. Made from tin, it was rather inexpensive.[19] A teapot made its first appearance among the perused inventories in 1712, still declared 'new' at its owner's demise – so probably a recent addition to their material world of goods.[20] The Imperial Knights belonged to the vanguard of tea and coffee drinkers in southern Germany, a region much closer in its consumption trajectories to somewhat remote English counties such as Cornwall and Cumbria than to Kent or to metropoles such as London or Amsterdam.[21]

Table 2.2 Paraphernalia for coffee consumption.

	1700–1724	1725–1749	1750–1774	1775–1799	Entire period
Total number of inventories	8	10	14	11	43
Number of inventories with relevant objects	2	8	12	10	32
Coffee tin (*Kaffeedose*)	0	1	2	1	4
Coffee grinder (*Kaffeemühle*)	0	5	6	9	20
Coffee roaster/pan/burner (*Kaffeeröscher/-pfanne/-brenner*)	0	0	4	3	7
Coffee machine (*Kaffeemaschine*)	0	0	0	3	3
Coffee funnel (*Kaffeetrichter*)	0	0	1	0	1
Coffee kettle (*Kaffeekessel*)	0	0	1	1	2
Coffee table (*Kaffeetisch*)	0	0	1	5	6
Coffee tray (*Kaffeebrett*)	0	8	7	11	26
Coffee spoon (*Kaffeelöffel*)	1	0	19	42	62
Coffee pot (*Kaffeekanne*)	1	23	53	46	123
silver	0	2	11	8	
pewter	0	1	9	5	
brass	0	4	8	4	
copper	0	8	12	3	
sheet metal	1	4	1	2	
porcelain	0	4	6	23	
other materials	0	0	6	1	
Coffee bowl/cup/mug (*Kaffeeschale/-tasse/-becher*)	3	43	136	158	340
silver	0	8	0	0	
porcelain	0	24	125	156	
other materials	3	11	11	2	
Total number of objects	5	80	230	279	594

Sources: HStAS B 580, P10; StAL B 575 I, PL 9, 12, 18, 20

Table 2.3 Paraphernalia for tea consumption.

	1700–1724	1725–1749	1750–1774	1775–1799	Entire period
Total number of inventories	8	10	14	11	43
Number of inventories with relevant objects	1	8	12	8	29
Tea caddy (*Teedose*)	0	7	16	13	36
Tea kettle (*Teekessel*)	0	4	10	11	25
Tea urn (*Teemaschine*)	0	1	10	10	21
Tea strainer (*Teeseiher*)	0	1	1	4	6
Teaspoon (*Teelöffel*)	0	0	7	4	11
Teapot (*Teekanne*)	1	22	44	47	114
silver	0	2	11	10	
pewter	0	10	16	11	
brass	0	2	2	0	
copper	1	1	0	0	
sheet metal	0	0	0	0	
porcelain	0	3	8	23	
other materials	0	4	5	5	
Tea bowl/cup/mug (*Teeschale/-becher/-tasse*)	1	74	176	66	317
porcelain	0	28	166	66	
other materials	0	46	10	0	
Other accessories	0	0	2	1	3
Total number of objects	2	109	266	156	533

Sources: HStAS B 580, P10; StAL B 575 I, PL 9, 12, 18, 20

The knights' early forays into the world of hot beverages relied on tried and tested materials and demonstrated certain prudent strategies of investment: the 1712 teapot was made from copper, the traditional material for cooking equipment, but for coffee only a few copper kettles are listed – contemporaries warned about the harmfulness of boiling coffee in copper kettles tinned inside for corrosion protection.[22] The kettles were joined by coffee burners, roasters and pans as well as coffee grinders, the latter usually made from wood and iron but towards the end of the century also from brass, which proved more decorative if not as durable.

Beginning in the 1750s, showier items such as tea urns made from base metals also entered country houses. Further utensils popular among the Imperial Knights were tin tea caddies as well as pewter tea and coffee pots. The latter found usage both upstairs and downstairs into the nineteenth century.[23] Among the base metals, brass seems to have been appreciated the most, probably thanks to its decorative qualities and gold-like shine. Even though the metals did not differ significantly in price, copper, pewter and tin were more often referred to as 'old' in inventories. As this indication was used to justify a lower valuation, it probably refers to a worn-out appearance.

When serving tea or coffee in a polite setting, pride of place belonged to all kinds of silver paraphernalia. The metal was an established prestige material and thereby connected the drinking of an exotic beverage with existing elite practices. Accordingly, wealthy nobles such as Eberhard Maximilian vom Holtz (d. 1762) invested in numerous items, in his case five different coffee pots (two with stands and a tap), four different teapots, a set of silver coffee spoons, a tea caddy and even a tea kettle made from silver. Those drawing up the inventory described some of the items as 'newly fashioned', speaking of a recent investment or refashioning of existing silver.[24] His equally rich contemporary Ludwig Christoph Leutrum von Ertingen had purchased, among other things, a massive silver coffee tray, weighing 110 *lot* (c. 1.6 kg), and a silver tea urn, weighing 163 *lot* (c. 2.4 kg), both of them valued by their weight at 110 *fl.* and 163 *fl.* respectively. Eberhardine von Weiler had opted for a lighter showpiece of this 'icon of the eighteenth century'.[25] Most likely modelled in a more reduced neoclassical style, it was still valued at a respectable 48 *fl.* – more than twice as much as her kitchen maid's annual wages.[26] Not everyone among the Imperial nobility could afford such luxurious goods, though. Quite a few owned rather small tea and/or coffee pots, rarely weighing more than 25 *lot*, while others had to content themselves with a strainer made from silver or a set of six silver coffee spoons.[27] Anton Fidel von Freyberg even relied on a highly polished pewter teapot for some silver shine at his tea table, demonstrating once more the significant difference in levels of wealth among this group.[28]

Although highly breakable and thus prone to underrepresentation, porcelain constituted an important part of the tea and coffee culture among the Imperial Knights.[29] In addition to its aesthetic qualities and its function as a signifier of rank, porcelain had the advantage of being heat resistant and tasteless, unlike metal tableware.[30] Initially, Cologne stoneware was very popular, especially for teacups. It was much cheaper than Asian imports and exquisite European imitations. These purchases hint yet again at a certain prudent strategy of investment in connection to global goods in the initial phase. From the 1750s onwards, porcelain, often described as Japanese, Indian or Dutch, is steadily present (Table 2.4). Asian porcelain was usually accorded a higher value than delftware, but the most expensive items had been manufactured in Dresden (Meissen), Vienna and nearby Ludwigsburg (Figure 2.1). The last of these factories would have been well known to the knights

Figure 2.1 Porcelain teapot with lid, Ludwigsburg, 1758–70. Reproduced courtesy of Landesmuseum Württemberg.

Table 2.4 Manufacture/place of origin of ceramics paraphernalia for coffee, tea and chocolate (1697–1811).

Manufacture/origin name	Number of relevant inventories	Number of entries	Value range per item (in guilders)	Value range for six cups (in guilders)
Dresden (Meissen)	9	27	1–30 fl.	30 xr.–9 fl.
Vienna (Wien)	1	6	3–48 fl.	1 fl. 30 xr.–2 fl.
Ludwigsburg	1	1	1 fl. 15 xr.	1 fl. 15 xr.
Durlach (Faiences)	1	1	1 fl. 30 xr.	1 fl. 30 xr.
Cologne (kölnisch, stoneware)	2	5	1–20 xr.	6 xr.
Dutch (holländisch, delftware)	3	4	1–4 fl. 30 xr.	2 fl.–4 fl. 30 xr.
Indian (indianisch)	1	6	1–6 fl.	4–6 fl.
Japanese (japanisch)	1	2	not specified	not specified
Javanese (javanisch*)	2	2	6–8 fl.	6 fl.

* probably a spelling mistake for Japanese (japanisch)

who held offices at the court of Duke Carl Eugen of Württemberg as he regularly inspected the factory.[31] Buying local could in this instance also serve as a means to express political allegiance.

Considering the range of goods from expensive silver to cheap earthenware, it is striking that the inventories of even the richest members of the Imperial nobility list large quantities of porcelain at a few kreuzers or a couple of guilders. This indicates that the elite, just like the far better studied middling ranks, also appreciated the emerging market for inexpensive porcelain in the second half of the century – not unlike their appropriation of ersatz materials for snuff boxes.

Compared with tea and coffee, chocolate consumption left only limited traces in the material culture of country houses in southwestern Germany – only 13 out of 43 inventories contain chocolate paraphernalia (Table 2.5). This is somewhat surprising considering the Imperial nobles' close links to the Hapsburg monarchs in Vienna and the geographic proximity to Italy and Austria, where drinking chocolate was quite popular.[32] In comparison with tea and coffee, chocolate consumption seems to have been a personal preference rather than a widely shared one, albeit with a tendency to become more popular over the course of the century. Whereas just one individual owned most of the chocolate paraphernalia found in the period 1725–49 (a copper chocolate pot, 12 chocolate cups made from majolica and five such cups from porcelain), the second half of the eighteenth century saw a far more even spread of goods.[33] This is particularly true for the possession of chocolate cups, which can be found in all the inventories that contain items connected to the consumption of chocolate. Silver goods are only found in six of the inventories over the entire time span and these consist usually of one or several cups, the elaborate chocolate centrepiece for 32 *fl.* owned by Ludwig Christoph Leutrum von Ertingen in 1765 being a notable exception.[34] Considering the imbalance of chocolate cups and chocolate pots, the beverage seems to have been

Table 2.5 Paraphernalia for chocolate consumption.

	1700–1724	1725–1749	1750–1774	1775–1799	Entire period
Total number of inventories	8	10	14	11	43
Number of inventories with relevant objects	0	3	6	4	13
Chocolate pot (*Schokoladenkanne*)	0	2	1	1	4
Chocolate bowl/cup/mug (*Schokoladenbecher/-schalen/-tassen*) (thereof from porcelain)	0	26 (13)	58 (52)	69 (63)	153 (128)
Other accessories	0	0	2	0	2
Total number of objects	0	28	61	70	159

prepared mainly in the kitchen using utensils already at hand such as copper pots and wooden whisks, which can be found in virtually every inventory. The laborious preparation, which included making a chocolate paste and adding spices such as vanilla or cinnamon, was far more complex than the rather simple brewing of tea or coffee, which often happened at the table and was part of the ritual of imbibing them in polite society. In short, the material evidence certainly supports the notion of chocolate as a (noble) early morning indulgence rather than a promoter of sociability.[35]

To sum up, the Imperial Knights' consumption practices surrounding the new hot beverages incorporated both older notions of grandeur and exquisite refinement in the form of magnificent silver tea urns or coffee trays so heavy that they must have been difficult to handle as well as new ideas centring on comfort, pleasure and taste, expressed both in highly fashionable and exquisite porcelain sets and also in the drinking of hot chocolate in a private setting. Likewise, the widespread presence of cheap porcelain and the fact that many inventories contained odd numbers and broken pieces remind us further that consuming these global beverages was not exclusively a matter of old versus new luxury as a social statement but was also one of daily routines and everyday practices that catered to personal comfort and convenience.[36] That said, further research is needed to assess the different social functions of old and new luxury goods among the Imperial Knights and other elite families.

Assemblages of global and local goods

Tracing the appearance and subsequent consumption of global goods in country houses of the Imperial nobility in south-western Germany is no great challenge. However, the items themselves do not provide a comprehensive idea of how they were used in daily practices, and there is a danger of missing the interplay between local, European and global goods if we focus solely on the geographical origin of tobacco, tea, coffee or chocolate. In everyday life, people consumed local, European and global goods side by side or in combination – styles of consumption that also created specific regional food dialects. To trace these, one might imaginatively sit down at a table together with Imperial nobles.

The consumption of tea and coffee with slices of buttered bread (local products) is a well-documented elite practice;[37] but cookbooks and recipe collections also provide evidence for the appearance of specialised kinds of pastries. A recipe collection from the early nineteenth century, housed in the palace library of the von Liebensteins in Jebenhausen, contains directions for preparing a 'coffee cake' to be consumed alongside the beverage. It consisted of a shortbread crust strewn with sugar and cinnamon – yet another assemblage of global and local ingredients. In contrast, 'tea bread' – a kind of yeast pastry – called for flour, milk, yeast, butter and eggs (local goods), supplemented by raisins from southern Europe and sprinkled with sugar.[38] Once more, the purpose of the product was to accompany the drink. A very popular cookbook appearing first in the 1790s added almonds, lemon zest and candied lemon peel to a yeast-based 'coffee cake'.[39] Ingredients such as these Mediterranean delicacies were usually bought alongside coffee, tea and sugar at the local grocers.[40] Thus, hot drinks encouraged the consumption of foodstuffs that seamlessly connected the manor barns via local merchants to European as well as global commodity flows.

The connection of coffee and tea to another good, namely sugar, is a standard element in the narrative of global goods (seen prominently in Figure 2.2). Yet the inventories also point towards another way in which

Figure 2.2 Peter Jakob Horemans, 'Two Ladies Drinking Tea', 1772. Stadtmuseum München, public domain. Available at https://sammlungonline.muenchner-stadtmuseum.de/objekt/zwei-damen-beim-tee-10003659/ and reproduced under the Creative Commons licence CC BY 4.0.

GLOBAL GOODS AND IMPERIAL KNIGHTS

members of the Imperial nobility mixed their bitter caffeine drinks. Many coffee and tea sets came with a milk jug. These sets were often received as wedding gifts and can be found in several inventories. Wilhelmine von Woellwarth, for example, owned a matching silver coffee pot and milk jug worth 69 *fl.*; Eberhardine von Weiler's set was valued at 23 *fl.* though labelled 'very small'.[41] These combinations must have been popular as they also existed in pewter, brass, copper and tin, which reduced the price immensely; inventory appraisers estimated Maria Frederica von Liebenstein's coffee and milk set made from tin at 15 *xr.*, while Joseph Anselm von Adelmann possessed four pewter sets of various sizes which altogether were worth just 3 *fl.*[42]

Milk was probably the predominant regionally specific ingredient to coffee: Krünitz's *Oeconomische Encyclopädie* (economic encyclopaedia) identifies the combination as common in Germany and Sweden, though not in Western Europe. When it came to tea, Krünitz named both sugar and milk as important additives. While this difference to Western European standards might certainly be explained by a higher price of sugar or a taste preference, integrations of tea and coffee into medicinal thinking were also an issue. When Krünitz connected the additives to Galenic medicine, he drew on regionally specific traditions of integrating the foreign products and the effects of combining them into old-world consumption. According to him, milk made coffee acceptable for sanguine and choleric people, and he opined that those with a weak constitution should add a good quantity of it to their tea, to better tolerate it.[43] Global and local goods were thus fused with regional strands of knowledge, resulting in specific modes of consumption.

This is also true when turning the perspective around – from the local to the global. A common feature of country house shopping was grape shot and stones to ignite gunpowder.[44] These items point towards hunting, which not only constituted an element of noble self-fashioning but also provided game for the table. For a long time, such food had been dressed with Asian spices, particularly pepper, and recipes called for them repeatedly in the second half of the eighteenth century. A red deer roast in a 1749 cookbook from the region, however, also added raisins, lemon zest and peeled almonds to the meat's gravy and some extra syrup – most likely from sugar – to enhance the sweetness of the flavour.[45] Other game recipes demanded an ingredient for which quite a few of the Imperial nobles appear to have had a particular craving: capers. These needed to be imported from southern Europe, northern Africa or potentially even the Americas and were also used when preparing fish. Their growing consumption might reflect a transfer of modes of eating from one region to another. Capers were generally an important seasoning in the Mediterranean style of cooking. It seems that this became the leading type of cuisine not only in France but also among the German elite in the eighteenth and early nineteenth centuries, although it sometimes rivalled (incorrect) adaptations of British food such as *Rost Pfiff*.[46] Anchovies, olives and olive oil were further important elements of a new type of French cooking. All these ingredients are mentioned time and again in the various grocery bills found among the records of south-western German country houses in the second half of the eighteenth century.[47]

In short, the last examples might testify to the transfer of styles of cooking. Yet, as shown, there are also regional specialties. Global goods were fused with European and local ingredients as well as medical knowledge into dishes that sometimes appealed to consumers across various regions of the continent but at other times remained geographically distinct. One needs to be careful, though, when ascribing a particular 'food dialect' to the Imperial Knights: just because these noblemen drew their status from possessions in south-western Germany does not mean that their world did not extend beyond it. As William D. Godsey describes with respect to the emergence of nationalism in the eighteenth and nineteenth centuries, they also inhabited a 'geo-cultural landscape' that ranged from Paris to Vienna and from northern Germany to the southern outskirts of the Alps. This allowed them to partake in European fashions while at the same time there is some evidence that they retained regional specifics in their modes of consumption.

Assemblages of people around global goods

Global goods were rarely consumed in solitude or kept hidden in closets. Rather, they had meanings attributed to them in everyday settings and they interacted with their surroundings. Thus, practices of consumption and their social meaning varied according to location (townhouse versus country house), space (bedroom versus dining room) and social setting (family dinner versus (semi-)public event). The consumption of global goods in the country house was multi-layered and integrated various spatial dimensions and social strata. Thus, by scrutinising the spatial arrangement of goods in general and by highlighting the place of global goods within social settings, we can learn more about the lifestyle of the elite. While many of the probate inventories used here are, unfortunately, silent on the exact location of goods, they generally do record the location of porcelain, which therefore forms the centrepiece of the following analysis.

In the majority of south-western German country houses, porcelain used for the consumption of tea, coffee and chocolate was to be found in family rooms. It was kept either in bedrooms, which often doubled as sitting rooms and retained notions of the former 'great chamber', or, in more formal arrangements, in the antechamber of the master's or mistress's bedroom. Only in a few instances do we find porcelain placed in rooms used primarily for entertaining guests, such as the *Tafelzimmer* (dining room) or the *Wohnzimmer* (parlour). Here it might have been displayed for decorative purposes, but it was often stored alongside other tableware in a small cabinet adjacent to the dining room. In a few houses, towards the end of the century, some porcelain (usually that at the lower end of the price range) was kept in the kitchen or the pantry, where it joined the various utensils used for the preparation of the beverages. These included even the more decorative items such as lacquered tea caddies or tea urns made from base metals. Everyday goods, such as the copper set for making coffee owned by Gottfried vom Holtz in 1765 or the brass tea urn belonging to Joseph Anselm von Adelmann, might have been displayed in the kitchen to demonstrate with their polished sheen a well-managed household, serving a rather mundane, locally oriented function while at the same time still implying global connections.[48]

In contrast, selected items of porcelain served a double function as signifier of rank and status as well as utilitarian item. In some houses, entire rooms seem to have been arranged around china. Anna Elisabetha Philippina von Tessin, for example, at her death in 1780 had been the proud owner of an exquisitely furnished 'green room' at Schloss Kilchberg. This bedroom was hung with wallpaper made from oilcloth and decorated with two portraits showing unnamed princes as well as one each of the baroness and her husband. It was furnished with a bed with costly green hangings, an inlaid chest of drawers, two stools and three tables. The highlight of the room was the collection of china on display: a blue-and-white set of Dresden porcelain worth 10 *fl.* on the chest of drawers; seven Dresden chocolate cups on a corner table; half a dozen teacups with a rinsing bowl and figurines on a table under the first window; and a set comprising a teapot, rinsing bowl, twelve cups and four alabaster figurines on a table under the second window.[49] Arranged in clusters and with their colourful decorations, these ceramics certainly enhanced the aesthetic appeal of the room, which might have been shown to visitors and relatives but was most likely not put to practical use as the seating-accommodations were rather inadequate. Only a particularly exalted guest, such as the Duke of Württemberg, might have enjoyed this splendour hands-on.[50] In a highly formal room such as this, china seems

Figure 2.3 Eight-piece *déjeuner* set with rococo decorations, Dresden, 1770–5. Reproduced courtesy of Landesmuseum Württemberg.

to have played an important part in enhancing the principal message of splendour, rank and taste. Its practical properties were only rarely put to the test and only with choice company.

Even for the Tessins and other Imperial Knights, the potentially wide-ranging geographical implications of porcelain seem to have been a secondary consideration; it was rather valued as a key luxury object of its time. This explains the preference for more expensive European porcelain over Asian imports that emerges from our study of the inventories: while 'Indian' or 'Japanese' porcelains were sometimes accorded high value, the most valuable pieces and the most extensive sets were of European manufacture, Dresden in particular (see Table 2.4). Indeed, towards the end of the eighteenth century, Asian porcelain all but disappeared from the inventories, demonstrating how a former global luxury good had been superseded by local imitations which often corresponded closely to the artistic fashions of the day (Figure 2.3). A great deal of the porcelain was kept in bedrooms and their antechambers or in fairly informal drawing rooms. Other members of the Imperial nobility incorporated china into rather more personal settings directed at creating comfort. Eberhard Maximilian vom Holtz, for example, kept various sets of china consisting of matching chocolate, tea and coffee cups as well as the respective pots, including his finest pieces, in his bedroom. Some of the china was most likely put on display, but at least some of it must have been used to entertain guests as vom Holtz only kept a small quantity of china in a cabinet adjacent to the dining room.[51] Other families preferred their *Wohnzimmer* (parlour) as a site for partaking of tea and coffee in a polite but familiar setting. The Tessin family had, in addition to the sumptuously furnished state bedroom noted above, a parlour furnished more for personal well-being and comfort. It was decorated with nine family portraits to which two contemporary paintings showing the couple's children had been added as well as a miniature of the husband's mother. The furniture consisted of an inlaid desk, a sofa, a chaise longue, six armchairs, two stools and a variety of tables. An alcove was set into the room at one side, which housed a bed as well as a corner cupboard and a tiered shelf (called a pyramid). The latter two were filled with, according to their values, rather utilitarian chocolate and tea cups as well as a pewter teapot.[52] Here, the family could come together and drink tea or coffee with the usual round of guests consisting of relatives and neighbours, the latter normally being other country house owners, functional elites from nearby towns and, of course, the parish priest and his family.[53] As Jon Stobart and Mark Rothery have argued, these rooms are best interpreted as comfortable, personal and tasteful spaces in which their owners tried to make the country house feel more like a home.[54]

Quite a few families owned a townhouse in addition to their country abode(s). Urban sociability followed different trajectories than that in the countryside. Instead of hosting neighbours and relatives as well as, in some instances, officers stationed nearby, entertaining in town was far more geared towards (political) advancement and keeping up with one's peers and betters. Consequently, it called for a different kind of material culture. This becomes apparent in the case of the Adelmann family. Here, the head of the family lived alternately at Schloss Hohenstadt in the country and in Ellwangen, where the family owned a substantial townhouse. The third Adelmann place of residence, Schloss Schechingen, was usually reserved for one of the younger brothers. All these places were more or less substantially furnished and equipped for the consumption of global goods.[55] However, Joseph Anselm von Adelmann, head of the family until his death in 1805, kept the best china in Ellwangen. His dinner set there was manufactured in Vienna and comprised 184 gold-rimmed pieces. Each of the 24 coffee cups was valued at 2 *fl.* (see Figure 2.4).

Figure 2.4 Coffee cup, Vienna, 1800. Reproduced courtesy of Landesmuseum Württemberg.

At such, they cost 24 times more than the ones used at his country residence.

At their country house Schloss Hohenstadt, the Adelmanns relied rather on old-fashioned splendour and awe-inspiring grandeur when hosting dinners, including window hangings in red taffeta, an imposing chandelier and large mirrors. There seems to have been no need for porcelain in the latest taste when dining with the bailiff or entertaining one's doctor. Adelmann himself was content, it seems, to use pewter coffee pots when in the countryside, leaving his rather more fashionable brass tea urn in Ellwangen. Accordingly, the townhouse and its furnishings served as a material manifestation of the Adelmanns' elite cultural capital, whereas the country seat at Hohenstadt was geared to remind his subjects and dependants of the family's pre-eminence and status. As Mark Overton and his collaborators have demonstrated, genteel status relied on a mixture of lineage, landholding, wealth and office-holding, none of which were greatly influenced by the acquisition of new material goods.[56] While this also holds true for the Imperial Knights, the Adelmann example reminds us that the meaning and importance of material goods were dependent on their social setting (Figure 2.5). This circumstance affected established elites and their appropriation of global goods just as much as it did the middling ranks.

Conclusion

Notwithstanding the distance from major trade routes, the new global goods of the early modern period – tobacco, tea, coffee and chocolate – found a place in the country houses of the Imperial nobility of south-western Germany in the eighteenth century. This does not imply, however, that the meaning of these goods was straightforward. Rather, a multitude of associations were layered upon each other and absorbed consciously and subconsciously. The Imperial Knights acquired items that were appropriate to their wealth – such as silver teapots and gold snuff boxes – and others that reflected fashions and personal tastes, including porcelain. Money, of course, limited the number and quality of objects for the consumption of global goods that each individual could

Figure 2.5 Peter Jakob Horemans, 'Spring (Johanna de Lasence Drinking Coffee in the Garden)', 1767. Bayerische Staatsgemäldesammlungen.

afford; but both the multitude of objects owned by the richer members of this group and the individual pieces belonging to the poorer nobles testify to a situation that was not defined by money alone. Personal taste as well as ideas of polite sociability also informed consumer choices.

When actually consuming global foodstuffs, Imperial Knights combined them with or ingested them alongside European and local goods, the latter oftentimes procured directly at the country house. The hybrid consumption practices traced above mean that, by the turn of the nineteenth century, the exotic origin of tea, coffee and chocolate no longer played an important role: within the elite, at least, the process of appropriation seems to have been concluded.[57] Yet, if there was a geo-cultural landscape of allegiance destroyed by nationalism (as suggested by Godsey), there also existed a geo-cultural landscape of consumption of the Imperial nobility – one that was geographically much larger and tiered, and which intersected with other such landscapes. Central European dialects in the consumption of coffee and tea with milk existed alongside French-Mediterranean culinary influences, while global foodstuffs at the same time significantly transformed consumption habits.

Finally, it was not only the consumption of global goods and the combination with other items that mattered, but also the social settings in which they were consumed. These ranged from highly formal situations to more relaxed and familiar private settings. In the former, global goods took centre stage in the attempt to impress superiors and social equals, thereby translating cultural into social capital; in the latter, drinking tea in the living room or imbibing hot chocolate while still in bed were directed more towards creating personal comfort. The items studied here could fulfil all these functions by means of their appropriation, staging and usage. Some materials lent themselves to certain purposes better than others, which may partially explain the multitude of items as well as the retention of silver showpieces and the wide range of porcelain.

While further research is necessary, the results testify to a complex place of global goods in the country houses of south-western Germany in which the (exotic) point of origin, trade links, cultural allegiances and personal connections as well as experiences and imaginary worlds intermingled with other aims or were overshadowed by a preference for the products' taste or for personal comfort. In this context, the south-western German Imperial Knights present themselves as diverse consumers of newly emerging goods who should by no means be reduced by research to their economic situation but rather did their part in an increasingly inclusive consumer society.

Notes

1. For the most recent treatments see Godsey, *Nobles and Nation*; Menning, 'Nobility, peasantry and estates', 160–91.
2. Probate inventories of Johann Sebastian von Gaisberg (1713), Staatsarchiv Ludwigsburg (StAL) B 575 I Bü 215; Eberhardt Friedrich von Bouwinghausen-Wallmerode (1729), StAL B 575 I Bü 63.
3. For the most recent summary see Kleinschmidt and Logemann, *Konsum im 19. und 20. Jahrhundert*. More specifically on south-western Germany see Hirbodian et al., *Revolution des Fleißes*.
4. We are here drawing on a metaphor of Peter-Michael Hahn, 'Fürstliche Wahrnehmung', though applying it to the history of consumption specifically instead of court culture more generally.
5. Frie, 'Stand halten', 244–55; Kink, *Adelige Lebenswelt*; Spies, *Tagebuch der Caroline von Lindenfels*; Schraut, 'Reichsadelige Selbstbehauptung', 255–63.
6. Due to their status, the nobility living in Württemberg and the Imperial Knights were exempt from the inventory obligation, but they nevertheless used this practice to resolve inheritance matters. See Bidlingmaier, 'Inventuren und Teilungen', 71f.; Mannheims, *Wie wird ein Inventar erstellt*, 28f.
7. The records are drawn from the Baden-Württemberg State Archives in Stuttgart and Ludwigsburg, where they can be found among the records left by the knightly cantons (Ritterkantone) Neckar-Schwarzwald (HStAS B 580) and Kocher (StAL B 575). Individual family archives are also kept at the said archives. These have been consulted for the families Woellwarth (StAL PL 9/3), Adelmann (StAL PL 12), Liebenstein (StAL PL 18) and Varnbüler (HStAS P 10). The cited inventories calculate in the currency of the South German Gulden. 1 gulden (fl.) is divided into 60 kreuzer (xr.).
8. See Weatherill, *Consumer Behaviour*; McCants, 'Poor consumers as global consumers'. For a detailed discussion on using probate inventories as sources see Dean et al., *Production and Consumption*, 13–32.
9. Probate inventory of Philipp Wilhelm von Neuhausen (1699), HStAS B 580 Bü 1092.
10. See Menninger, *Genuss*, 277, 299, 312. The consumption of snuff is further suggested by two tobacco graters that were used to pulverise the tobacco purchased in the form of braids called carrots; see probate inventories Leutrum von Ertingen (1755) and Freyberg (1788), HStAS B 580 Bü 919 and 459.
11. Probate inventory Bouwinghausen-Wallmerode (1729), StAL B 575 I Bü 63. Spittoons and a rack for canaster tobacco, a smoking tobacco named after the baskets with which it was imported from America, also indicate the practice of tobacco smoking among the Imperial Knights. See inventory Kechler (1784), B 580 Bü 805 and probate inventory vom Holtz (1765), B 575 I Bü 468.
12. See also Sandgruber, 'Genußmittel', 85.
13. Probate inventories Woellwarth (1776), StAL PL 9/3 Bü 1462; Landsé (1787), HStAS B 580 Bü 864.
14. 'Tombac', 196.
15. Kollmer, *Die schwäbische Reichsritterschaft*, 48.
16. Smith, *Consumption and the Making of Respectability*, 81–2. See also Berg, *Luxury and Pleasure*, 21–6; Walter, 'Geschmack', 654–9.
17. See Reininghaus, *Die Stadt Iserlohn*, 151f.; Lockner, *Messing*, 135, 146.
18. 'Tombac', 198.
19. See probate inventory Hallweyl (1711), StAL B 575 I Bü 410. No values are given in the inventory.
20. Probate inventory Rheindorf (1712), HStAS B 580 Bü 835.
21. On the advent and spread of tea and coffee in Germany see Teuteberg, 'Kaffee', 81–8; Krieger, *Geschichte des Tees*, 161–6. Prior to 1720, no tea or coffee equipment (including among the gentry) was found in Cornish households. Dean et al., *Production and Consumption*, 106f. On regional variation see also Weatherill, *Consumer Behaviour*, 31f.
22. Bartels, 'Zinn', 489; 'Kaffe=Kanne', 266.
23. Even though porcelain pots for tea and coffee existed in great numbers alongside the pewter ones, they never outranked them completely.

24 Probate inventory Holtz (1762), StAL B 575 I Bü 468. The overall value of his estate was recorded at 188,000 fl., making him the richest person in our sample.
25 Berg, *Luxury and Pleasure*, 164.
26 Probate inventories Leutrum von Ertingen (1765), HStAS B 580 Bü 884; Weiler (1811), HStAS B 580 Bü 1962.
27 Probate inventories Barille (1753), HStAS B 580 Bü 68; Freyberg (1754), HStAS B 580 Bü 47; Liebenstein (1772), StAL PL 18 Bü 71; Kechler (1784), HStAS B 580 Bü 805.
28 Probate inventory Freyberg (1794), HStAS B 580 Bü 473.
29 The distinction between stoneware, real porcelain and its surrogates was not clearly defined in the linguistic usage of the early eighteenth century and probably was not easily recognised by the inventory writers, so the term porcelain may include all types of ceramics. See Pietsch, 'Die Erfindung', 12.
30 King, '"Asbestos fingers"', 168; Menninger, *Genuss*, 221, 408f.
31 Bouwinghausen von Wallmerode, *Tagebuch des Herzoglich Württembergischen Generaladjutanten*, 212. In addition, pieces of faience from the nearby factory in Durlach were also owned in individual cases.
32 On the regional differences of chocolate consumption in Central Europe see Wister, 'Chocolate consumption in Westphalia and Styria'.
33 Probate inventory of Frantz Joseph von Freyberg (1734), HStAS B 580 Bü 468.
34 Probate inventory of Ludwig Christoph Leutrum von Ertingen (1765), HStAS B 580 Bü 884.
35 The situation in Spain was, of course, quite the opposite. See Fattaciu, 'Exotic products'.
36 See Jan de Vries, *The Industrious Revolution*, 44–70.
37 Wiegelmann, *Alltags- und Festspeisen*; Czech, 'Reisen der Grafen', 180, 191.
38 StAL PL 18, Cookbook of Luisa von Liebenstein, née Weimer (1787–1865). As a recent acquisition, it does not yet have a call number.
39 Löffler, *Handbuch*, 496–7.
40 These local grocers make an intermittent appearance in the estate records as well as in private bills. See, for example, StAL PL 18 R183 (1762/63); StAL PL 12 II Bü 1912, collected bills (1780); StAL PL 12 II Bü 1927, collected bills (1797). For a detailed assessment of a grocer's stock see Selheim, *Inventare*.
41 Probate inventories Woellwarth (1806), StAL PL 9/3 Bü 1464; Weiler (1811), HStAS B 580 Bü 1962. For further sets see inventories Tessin (1780), HStAS B 580 Bü 1798; Landsé (1787), HStAS B 580 Bü 864.
42 Probate inventories Liebenstein (1772), StAL PL 18 Bü 71; Adelmann (1805), StAL PL 12 II Bü 829.
43 'Kaffe', 183–4 and 189–90; 'Thee', 30–1. On medical discussions in Germany see Menninger, *Genuss*, 237–76.
44 See Rösener, *Die Geschichte der Jagd*. For Jebenhausen in the second half of the eighteenth century see the account books in: StAL PL 18, R2–51.
45 *Aufrichtige und bewährte Nachrichten*, 301.
46 Flandrin, 'Der gute Geschmack'; Teuteberg, 'Von der Hausmutter zur Hausfrau'. See also Kink, *Adelige Lebenswelt*, 229f.; Spiegel, *Adliger Alltag*, 221, 240; Czech, 'Reisen der Grafen', 183, 195; Müllneritsch, 'The roast charade', 99–119.
47 The von Liebensteins purchased, for example, two pounds of capers over the 12 months between the summers of 1759 and 1760 in lots of a quarter pound, StAL PL 18 R183.
48 Probate inventories Holtz (1765), StAL B 575 I Bü 468; Adelmann (1805), StAL PL 12 II Bü 829.
49 Probate inventory Tessin (1780), HStAS B 580 Bü 1798.
50 Carl Eugen, the Duke of Württemberg, regularly visited some members of the Imperial Knighthood, such as the Leininger and Thumb families, in order to hunt with them or to inspect their horses, and stayed in this context for coffee meals. See Bouwinghausen von Wallmerode, *Tagebuch des Herzoglich Württembergischen Generaladjutanten*, 68, 124, 225, 232, 258, 269, 279.
51 Probate inventory Holtz (1762), StAL B 575 I Bü 468.
52 Probate inventory Tessin (1780), HStAS B 580 Bü 1798.
53 Czech, 'Reisen der Grafen', 216; Spies, *Tagebuch der Caroline von Lindenfels*, 134f.
54 Stobart and Rothery, *Consumption at the Country House*, 77f.; see also Lewis, 'When a house'.

55 Probate inventory Adelmann (1805), StAL PL 12 II Bü 829; Letters by Joseph Anselm von Adelmann to his son (1796–1805), StAL PL 12 Bü 784, 785; Treaty on the Adelmann succession (1803–5), StAL PL 12 Bü 1508.
56 Dean et al., *Production and Consumption*, 167.
57 Hochmuth, *Globale Güter*.

Bibliography

Aufrichtige und bewährte Nachrichten von Allem ersinnlichen Koch- und Backwerck. 2nd edition, Stuttgart, 1749.
Bartels, Christoph. 'Zinn'. In *Enzyklopädie der Neuzeit*, edited by Friedrich Jaeger, vol. 15, 488–91. Stuttgart and Weimar: Metzler, 2012.
Berg, Maxine. 'In pursuit of luxury: global history and British consumer goods in the eighteenth century', *Past & Present* 182, no. 1 (2004): 85–142.
Berg, Maxine. *Luxury and Pleasure in Eighteenth-Century Britain*. Oxford: Oxford University Press, 2005.
Bidlingmaier, Rolf. 'Inventuren und Teilungen: Entstehung und Auswertungsmöglichkeiten einer Quellengruppe in den württembergischen Stadt- und Gemeindearchiven'. In *Der furnehmbste Schatz. Ortsgeschichtliche Quellen in Archiven*, edited by Nicole Bickhoff and Volker Trugenberger, 71–81. Stuttgart: Kohlhammer, 2001.
Bouwinghausen von Wallmerode, [Alexander Maximilian Friedrich]. *Tagebuch des Herzoglich Württembergischen Generaladjutanten Freiherrn von Bouwinghausen-Wallmerode über die 'Land-Reisen' des Herzogs Karl Eugen von Württemberg in der Zeit von 1767 bis 1773*. Edited by Ernst von Ziegesar. Stuttgart: Bonz, 1911.
Czech, Vinzenz. 'Die Reisen der Grafen zu Lynar nach Prötzel: Adliges Landleben im 18. Jahrhundert in zeitgenössischen Berichten'. In *Pracht und Herrlichkeit. Adlig-fürstliche Lebensstile im 17. und 18. Jahrhundert*, edited by Peter-Michael Hahn and Hellmut Lorenz, 157–229. Potsdam: Verlag für Berlin-Brandenburg, 1998.
Dean, Darron, Andrew Hann, Mark Overton and Jean Whittle. *Production and Consumption in English Households, 1600–1750*. London and New York: Routledge, 2004.
De Vries, Jan. *The Industrious Revolution: Consumer behavior and the household economy, 1650 to the present*. Cambridge: Cambridge University Press, 2008.
Fattaciu, Irene. 'Exotic products, luxury and new forms of sociability: changing patterns of consumption in 18th-century Madrid'. In *Cultural Exchange and Consumption Patterns in the Age of Enlightenment: Europe and the Atlantic world*, edited by Veronika Hyden-Hanscho, Renate Pieper and Werner Stangl, 169–88. Bochum: Winkler, 2013.
Flandrin, Jean-Louis. 'Der gute Geschmack und die soziale Hierarchie'. In *Geschichte des privaten Lebens*, edited by Philippe Ariès and Roger Chartier, vol. 3: *Von der Renaissance zur Aufklärung*, 269–311. Augsburg: Weltbild Verlag, 1999.
Frie, Ewald. 'Stand halten: Adliges Handeln und Erleben in Preußen um 1800', *Journal of Modern European History* 19 (2021): 244–55.
Godsey, William D. *Nobles and Nation in Central Europe: Free Imperial Knights in the age of revolution, 1750–1850*. Cambridge: Cambridge University Press, 2004.
Hahn, Peter-Michael. 'Fürstliche Wahrnehmung höfischer Zeichensysteme und zeremonieller Handlungen im Ancien Régime'. In *Zeichen und Raum. Ausstattung und höfisches Zeremoniell in den deutschen Schlössern der Frühen Neuzeit*, edited by Peter-Michael Hahn and Ulrich Schütte, 9–38. Berlin: Deutscher Kunstverlag, 2006.
Hirbodian, Sigrid, Sheilagh Ogilvie and R. Johanna Regnath, eds. *Revolution des Fleißes, Revolution des Konsums? Leben und Wirtschaften im ländlichen Württemberg von 1650–1850*. Ostfildern: Thorbecke, 2015.
Hochmuth, Christian. *Globale Güter – lokale Aneignung: Kaffee, Tee, Schokolade und Tabak im frühneuzeitlichen Dresden*. Konstanz: UVK-Verlagsgesellschaft, 2008.
'Kaffe'. In *Krünitz Oeconomische Encyclopädie, oder allgemeines System der Land- Haus- und Staats-Wirthschaft in alphabetischer Ordnung …*, edited by Johann Georg Krünitz, vol. 32, 100–264. Berlin: Pauli, 1784.

'Kaffe=Kanne'. In *Krünitz Oeconomische Encyclopädie, oder allgemeines System der Land- Haus- und Staats-Wirthschaft in alphabetischer Ordnung ...*, edited by Johann Georg Krünitz, vol. 32, 266–72. Berlin: Pauli, 1784.

King, Rachel. '"Asbestos fingers" und "flaming lips": Metallgefäße für Heißgetränke und ihre Handhabung im 18. Jahrhundert'. In *Dinge im Kontext: Artefakt, Handhabung und Handlungsästhetik zwischen Mittelalter und Gegenwart*, edited by Thomas Pöpper, 163–74. Berlin and Boston: De Gruyter, 2015.

Kink, Barbara. *Adelige Lebenswelt in Bayern im 18. Jahrhundert: Die Tage- und Ausgabenbücher des Freiherrn Sebastian von Pemler von Hurlach und Leutstetten (1718–1772)*. Munich: Kommission für Bayerische Landesgeschichte, 2007.

Kleinschmidt, Christian, and Jan Logemann, eds. *Konsum im 19. und 20. Jahrhundert*. Berlin and Boston: De Gruyter Oldenbourg, 2021.

Kollmer, Gert. *Die schwäbische Reichsritterschaft zwischen Westfälischem Frieden und Reichsdeputationshauptschluß: Untersuchung zur wirtschaftlichen und sozialen Lage der Reichsritterschaft in den Ritterkantonen Neckar-Schwarzwald und Kocher*. Stuttgart: Müller & Gräff, 1979.

Krieger, Martin. *Geschichte des Tees: Anbau, Handel und globale Genusskulturen*. Vienna and Cologne: Böhlau Verlag, 2021.

Lewis, Judith S. 'When a house is not a home: elite English women and the eighteenth-century country house', *Journal of British Studies* 48, no. 2 (2009): 336–63.

Lockner, Hermann P. *Messing: Ein Handbuch über Messinggerät des 15.–17. Jahrhunderts*. Munich: Klinkhardt und Biermann, 1982.

Löffler, Friederike Luise. *Oekonomisches Handbuch für Frauenzimmer. Erster Band welcher das Kochbuch enthält*. Stuttgart: Steinkopf, 1795.

Mannheims, Hildegard. *Wie wird ein Inventar erstellt? Rechtskommentare als Quelle der volkskundlichen Forschung*. Münster: Coppenrath, 1991.

McCants, Anne E.C. 'Poor consumers as global consumers: the diffusion of tea and coffee drinking in the eighteenth century', *The Economic History Review* 61, no. 1 (2008): 172–200.

Menning, Daniel. 'Nobility, peasantry and estates in southwestern Germany, from the eighteenth to the twentieth century'. In *Estate Landscapes in Northern Europe*, edited by Jonathan Finch, Kristine Dyrmann and Mikael Frausing, 160–91. Aarhus: Aarhus University Press, 2019.

Menninger, Annerose. *Genuss im kulturellen Wandel: Tabak, Kaffee, Tee und Schokolade in Europa (16.–19. Jahrhundert)*. 2nd edition. Stuttgart: Steiner, 2008.

Müllneritsch, Helga. 'The roast charade: travelling recipes and their alteration in the long eighteenth century'. In *Traces of Transnational Relations in the Eighteenth Century*, edited by Tim Berndtsson, 99–119. Uppsala: Uppsala Universitet, 2015.

Pietsch, Ulrich. 'Die Erfindung des europäischen Hartporzellans 1708 in Dresden'. In *Mythos Meissen. Das erste Porzellan Europas*, edited by Ulrich Pietsch and Peter Ufer, 8–29. Dresden: Edition Sächsische Zeitung, 2008.

Reininghaus, Wilfried. *Die Stadt Iserlohn und ihre Kaufleute (1700–1815)*. Dortmund: Gesellschaft für Westfälische Wirtschaftsgeschichte, 1995.

Rösener, Werner. *Die Geschichte der Jagd: Kultur, Gesellschaft und Jagdwesen im Wandel der Zeit*. Düsseldorf: Artemis & Winkler, 2004.

Sandgruber, Roman. 'Genußmittel: Ihre reale und symbolische Bedeutung im neuzeitlichen Europa', *Jahrbuch für Wirtschaftsgeschichte* 35, no. 1 (1994): 73–88.

Schraut, Sylvia. 'Reichsadelige Selbstbehauptung zwischen standesgemäßer Lebensführung und reichskirchlichen Karrieren', *Zeitschrift für bayerische Landesgeschichte, Beiheft: Adel und Adelskultur in Bayern* 32 (2008): 251–68.

Selheim, Claudia. *Die Inventare eines süddeutschen Warenlagers 1778–1824: Beiträge zur Aufarbeitung einer Realienquelle*. Würzburg: Bayerische Blätter für Volkskunde, 1989.

Smith, Woodruff D. *Consumption and the Making of Respectability, 1600–1800*. New York: Routledge, 2002.

Spiegel, Beate. *Adliger Alltag auf dem Land: Eine Hofmarksherrin, ihre Familie und ihre Untertanen in Tutzing um 1740*. Münster: Waxmann, 1997.

Spies, Britta. *Das Tagebuch der Caroline von Lindenfels geb. von Flotow (1774–1850): Leben und Erleben einer oberfränkischen Adligen am Ende der ständischen Gesellschaft*. Münster: Waxmann, 2009.

Stobart, Jon, and Mark Rothery. *Consumption and the Country House*. Oxford: Oxford University Press, 2016.

Teuteberg, Hans Jürgen. 'Kaffee'. In *Genussmittel: Ein kulturgeschichtliches Handbuch*, edited by Thomas Hengartner and Christoph Maria Merki, 81–116. Frankfurt am Main: Campus-Verlag, 1999.

Teuteberg, Hans Jürgen. 'Von der Hausmutter zur Hausfrau: Küchenarbeit im 18./19. Jahrhundert in der zeitgenössischen Hauswirtschaftsliteratur'. In *Die Revolution am Esstisch: Neue Studien zur Nahrungskultur im 19./20. Jahrhundert*, edited by Hans Jürgen Teuteberg, 101–28. Stuttgart: Steiner, 2004.

'Thee'. In *Krünitz Oeconomisch-technologische Encyklopädie, oder allgemeines System der Staats- Stadt- Haus- und Landwirthschaft und der Kunstgeschichte ...*, edited by Johann Wilhelm David Korth, vol. 183, 1–35. Berlin: Pauli, 1844.

'Tombac'. In *Eröffnete Akademie der Kaufleute, oder vollständiges Kaufmanns-Lexicon ...*, edited by Carl Günther Ludovici, vol. 5, 196–8. Leipzig: Bernhard Christoph Breitkopf und Sohn, 1768.

Walter, Gerrith. 'Geschmack'. In *Enzyklopädie der Neuzeit*, edited by Friedrich Jaeger, vol. 4, 654–9. Stuttgart and Weimar: Metzler, 2006.

Weatherill, Lorna. *Consumer Behaviour and Material Culture in Britain: 1660–1760*. London: Routledge, 1996.

Wiegelmann, Günter. *Alltags- und Festspeisen in Mitteleuropa: Innovationen, Strukturen und Regionen vom späten Mittelalter bis zum 20. Jahrhundert*. 2nd edition. Münster: Waxmann, 2006.

Wister, Benita. 'Chocolate consumption in Westphalia and Styria during the 18th century'. In *Cultural Exchange and Consumption Patterns in the Age of Enlightenment: Europe and the Atlantic world*, edited by Veronika Hyden-Hanscho, Renate Pieper and Werner Stangl, 189–211. Bochum: Winkler, 2013.

Wittwer, Samuel. 'Ein Spiel zwischen Schein und Sein: Die Porzellankammer von Schloss Charlottenburg im Wandel', *Jahrbuch Preußische Schlösser und Gärten Berlin-Brandenburg* 7 (2005): 83–93.

3
The global samurai: imports and daily life in isolated Japan
Martha Chaiklin

In early modern Japan, there were no country houses exactly equivalent to those in Europe, but the regional castle is a close approximation. The quasi-feudal system established by Shogun Tokugawa Ieyasu (1543–1616) in 1603 was comprised of daimyo (lords) who swore fealty to him, the shogun being the largest and most powerful daimyo. For the purposes of this chapter, however, we will not look at Edo (Tokyo), where the Tokugawa shogun resided, or Kyoto, where the emperor lived, even though they contained castles because they functioned as capitals. Each daimyo had control over a domain (*han*) in which he had a castle, and that will be the focus of this chapter. The number of domains fluctuated throughout the Edo period (1603–1868) as they were absorbed, divided or consolidated, but they averaged around 260. While the shogun issued some blanket edicts, for the most part daimyo ruled autonomously within their domains.

The status of daimyo, like the lord of a country house or manor in Europe, was similarly based on land ownership. In fact, to be a daimyo, one had to receive at least 10,000 *koku* (approximately 1.8 million litres) in tax rice from one's lands. The largest, excluding the Tokugawa shogun who had much more, was the Maeda family of Kaga-han (present-day Ishikawa Prefecture) with some 1.2 million *koku*, but almost half were the lords of small domains of 10,000 to 30,000 *koku*.[1] Rice was the basis of the economy, but as the Edo period wore on, rice price fluctuations and rising standards of living forced daimyo to seek additional revenue streams such as small-scale manufacturing and timber. The latter was in constant high demand due to the frequency of fires. It was so important that it could replace tax rice in timber-producing areas.[2]

In 1635, a previously informal system known as *sankin kōtai* (alternate attendance) was made official, requiring daimyo to leave their families in Edo as hostages. The daimyo could only spend part of the year there with their families; the rest of the time they resided in their home provinces. In addition to Edo, daimyo often had residences in Osaka, where tax rice was sold, to oversee these vital commercial transactions, and in Kyoto, for political connections to the imperial house and the cultural life there. A system of highways was constructed to facilitate this travel, which required processions of soldiers that reflected their status – three thousand or more for the great daimyo. Lodgings along the route were reserved in advance so innkeepers could gather provisions and to avoid the conflict of two daimyo arriving at the same time.[3] A messenger could travel the 300 miles or so between Edo and Osaka in two and a half days, but these cumbersome processions would take about double that.

Since the daimyo kept houses in the shogunal capital, where they spent time each year and maintained their families, their home castles were effectively country houses, especially as generations were born and raised in Edo before ever seeing their ancestral homes. Because daimyo power relied on their ability to control the peasantry and their produce, the provincial castles of daimyo resemble the 'power houses' that Mark Girouard describes in his seminal *Life in the English Country House*.[4] *Sankin kōtai* also meant that even the smallest, most remote daimyo had access to the same goods as the richest ones because nearly all luxury goods, imported or otherwise, were available in Edo. The custom of bringing back souvenirs guaranteed that these goods circulated to the provinces. Castles were therefore places of collection, and daimyo were arbiters of taste.[5]

Early modern Japan was once thought of as closed because, in the 1630s, a series of shogunal edicts prohibited Japanese from travelling abroad, confined international trade to Nagasaki,[6] and ejected the Portuguese, making the Netherlands the only Western nation to maintain direct trade with Japan.[7] Trade prohibitions in Ming China also limited contact, which expanded somewhat after the foundation of the Qing dynasty in 1644. However, if examined closely, it is apparent that much of the material culture of this period flourished through foreign materials and objects. Even castle design was radically affected by the introduction of firearms, traditionally ascribed to the Portuguese in 1543. The remainder of this chapter will describe the regional castle and the importance of global connections for shaping this environment.

The regional castle

For much of Japan's history, castles had been functional fortifications for warfare. They came to resemble country houses after 1576 with the construction of Azuchi Castle for Oda Nobunaga (1534–82). After a hundred years of civil war, Nobunaga began a campaign for unification in 1560 that was completed by Toyotomi Hideyoshi (1537–98) in 1592 and culminated under Tokugawa Ieyasu in 1603 with the establishment of the Tokugawa Shogunate. Nobunaga was only halted by his assassination in 1582, but Azuchi Castle was the 'symbol and substance of his authority'.[8] It is significant for this discussion because it marked the transition from strategic utilitarian edifice to sumptuous residence, although it still remained a defensible structure. According to Jesuit missionary Luis Fróis (1532–97), 'Nobunaga does not believe in an afterlife or in anything he cannot see; as he is extremely wealthy, he will not allow himself to be outdone in anything by any other king but strives to surpass them all'.[9]

Located in what today is Shiga Prefecture on a hill about 30 miles from Kyoto overlooking Lake Biwa, construction of Azuchi Castle took three and a half years to complete. Its location would give him warning of aggression from his foes, and the lake gave him easy access to the emperor in Kyoto.[10] The seven-storey central tower (*tenshu*) had one subterranean level and an atrium to the fourth floor. The lower floors were of white plaster with black lacquer edging, over which was placed a vermillion-trimmed octagonal level roofed with blue tiles. The entire structure was surmounted by an observation deck topped with gilded tiles and mythical creatures called *shachihoko* that have a tiger face on a fish body (Figure 3.1). Believed to protect from fire, they subsequently became a common castle roof ornament. Often translated as keep or donjon, a *tenshu* was not fortified like these mediaeval structures but rather built from wood, which made them vulnerable. Therefore, these buildings had little military value besides the panoramic view at the top. Construction of a 'fragile extravagance' such as a *tenshu* was evidence of a ruler's prosperity, might and dominance.[11]

Not all castles had *tenshu*, but as Azuchi became a prototype, many castles built in the next two or three decades did. Daimyo who had been required to pay attendance to Nobunaga must have been impressed by the luxury of this new type of residential castle. The Azuchi *tenshu* contained an entrance hall, audience chambers, an office, private suites, a tea room and the personal residence of Nobunaga. The main audience chamber had a noh stage. Many of the sliding doors (*fusuma*) were

Figure 3.1 Modern reconstruction of Azuchi Castle. © Joakim Regnström.

covered with gold leaf and paintings made with bright colours and bold outlines by Kanō Eitoku (1543–90), the leading artist of his day.[12] Room fittings were gilded, and the tatami mats were edged with expensive imported Chinese brocades.[13] Inside the walls of the castle were gardens, a temple, vassals' houses and, according to Luis Fróis, stables that were 'so clean and well kept it seemed rather to be rather a fine place for the diversion of nobles than a place to lodge horses'.[14] After Nobunaga's assassination, Azuchi Castle was looted and burned. Today only parts of the stone foundations remain.

While there were many variations according to taste, wealth and topography, most castles built in Japan in the four decades after Azuchi were modelled after it. They had stone foundations and high plastered walls. In addition to common defensive measures including moats and gun ports, some castles had booby traps and other foils such as floors that purposely squeaked to warn of the ingress of intruders, secret tunnels or, like the castle at Kanazawa, a lead roof that could be melted down into bullets in an emergency.[15] But these castles now had multivalent functions, serving as a residence for the daimyo and his vassals, a place for leisure, and a place for bureaucratic activity and formal audiences.

In 1615, many castles were destroyed by order of the shogun, who imposed a limit of one per domain. Restrictions were also placed on new construction and repairs to prevent any fortification that would sustain a military uprising against the Tokugawa shogunate. Conversely, castles were supposed to be kept in good condition to ensure that daimyo could maintain control of their lands and to keep them from accumulating funds that might be used for rebellion. Nevertheless, as peace continued, the military need for castles diminished while alternate attendance shifted much of the focus of life to Edo. As a result, many castles fell into disrepair.[16] New castles were built after this date too, although the 40 or so that were permitted over the Edo period were only those deemed by the shogunate as absolutely necessary. Necessity included domains that bordered on those who had opposed Tokugawa Ieyasu. These daimyo, called *tozama*, were regarded with suspicion. Permission for reconstruction was granted in 1642, for example, when Ieyasu's grandson, Matsudaira Yorishige (1622–95), was made daimyo of Takamatsu in Sanuki (present-day Kagawa Prefecture) to replace the Igoma clan, who had been moved to a smaller domain as punishment for their inability to maintain peace within the domain.[17] This castle was nicknamed 'Seaweed Castle' (*Tamamo-jō*) because it faced the sea and its moats were filled with seawater.

Residential castles were built in *shoin-zukuri*, an architectural style that emphasised political function over military utility. Not all scholars agree on the precise definition of this form but generally it included tatami mats in all rooms, *fusuma* to divide the interior rooms, and *shōji* (paper-covered sliding doors) layered with sliding wooden doors (*mairado*), which acted as exterior walls. Literally, *shoin* means library or study – the naming derived from a desk built into the wall that had been used in temples to study sutras. In daimyo residences, writing implements were placed on it, often with an aspirational work of calligraphy hanging above. On the opposite wall was an alcove (*tokonoma*) which was used to display a scroll painting or calligraphy, and on its raised floor, an incense burner and seasonal floral arrangements. Adjacent to the *tokonoma* was a staggered shelf (*chigaidana*) for displaying treasures. For those who could afford it, these treasures and paintings were Chinese, a nod to the aesthetic of the Ashikaga shoguns, who acquired them through trade, gifts or acquisition by Buddhist monks who travelled to the continent. It is evidence of a long-standing appreciation for foreign things among Japan's elites.[18] This room was most frequently used to hold formal audiences with vassals and to receive guests. The *shoin-zukuri* architectural style was not exclusive to the warrior class and was widely used among the aristocracy, in temples and, by the end of the Edo period, in the houses of wealthy commoners.

Castles were laid out in zones in such a way to make it difficult for an enemy to overtake the entire structure at once.[19] There were three main sectors: formal, personal and service. The ostentatious formal rooms for audiences, meetings with vassals, ceremonial events and banquets usually had a separate entranceway and entrance hall.[20] Many aspects of local government were run from the castle. Unlike Azuchi, if a *tenshu* was present, the entertaining and residential areas were not usually in it. These non-formal areas were single-storied and connected by hallways, which could produce a maze-like result. There were several kitchens, including one for special occasions and one for day-to-day meals. The kitchens were usually rather distant from the dining room, so the lords were rarely able to eat anything hot.[21] The bathhouse, rather like a sauna, was a separate building. Other detached buildings included guard houses by the gates, roofed benches (*koshi kake*) that served as waiting areas for those who came to the castle on business, stables, tea ceremony huts, and numerous mud-walled fireproof storehouses, used for food, military equipment and treasures. The castle wall often had a parapet and turrets at the corners.

While the daimyo's proper wife and minor children lived in Edo as potential hostages, it was not expected that daimyo would be celibate while spending so much time away from them. Often, concubines would reside in the castle (Figure 3.2).[22] Concubinage was generally only practised by elites in Japan because having an official concubine, as opposed to a mistress, had a legal status that required the ability to

Figure 3.2 Daimyo's concubine and her maids in the garden. From Nishikawa Sukenobu, 'Hyakunin jorō shina sadame' [A Hundred Women by Rank], 1723. Reproduced courtesy of Special Collections, Waseda University Library.

support her within the household. Although the shogun generally had a number of concubines to ensure the continuity of the line, daimyo did not usually have many. The concubines and maids occupied a separate section of the castle (*okumuki*). Generally, all men, except the daimyo, were barred from this space, but there were exceptions such as male children and doctors.

Daimyo patronised various shrines and temples, but they also had religious spaces on the castle grounds, including repositories of deified ancestors. While the Tokugawa frowned on this, deification was one way to give both commoners and vassals a sense of membership in the ruling family. In order to circumvent shogunal proscriptions on castle construction, subterfuge was necessary to erect these religious spaces, such as adding them to repairs that had already been approved decades earlier. Additional construction could be added because the shogunate had not been notified that repairs had been completed.[23]

Castle grounds contained a variety of gardens. Some were designed for pleasure or contemplation, while others were to supply the kitchen. Many daimyo also kept medicinal gardens.[24] Often, these gardens would contain some sort of imported animal life, such as goldfish, peacocks or turkeys. Daimyo might also keep imported hunting or lap dogs, song birds or parrots. Trees and bamboo were often planted around the walls to screen the castle from outside eyes and provide material for arrows and pole arms in case of attack.[25] Resemblances to European country houses are striking but stem from similarities in social organisation and hierarchy rather than imitation.

Compared with the West, Japanese homes of all kinds traditionally had very little furniture. What there was consisted primarily of small, moveable pieces such as lacquered tables, writing desks and screens. Edward S. Morse (1838–1925), an American zoologist who taught at the Imperial University in Japan from 1877–80 and made several return visits, compared the traditional Japanese manner of furnishing with American homes of his day:

> If a foreigner is not satisfied with the severe simplicity, and what might at first strike him as a meagreness, in the appointments of a Japanese house, and is nevertheless a man of taste, he is compelled to admit that its paucity of furniture and carpets spares one the misery of certain painful feelings that incongruities always produce. He recalls with satisfaction certain works on household art, in which it is maintained that a table with carved cherubs beneath, against whose absurd contours one knocks his legs, is an abomination; and

that carpets which have depicted upon them winged angels, lions, or tigers, – or, worse still, a simpering and reddened maiden being made love to by an equally ruddy shepherd, – are hardly the proper surfaces to tread upon with comfort, though one may take a certain grim delight in wiping his soiled boots upon them.[26]

Morse admired the 'fresh air and broad flood of light, limited only by the dimensions of the room' that a Japanese house afforded.[27] A notable exception to portability were chests of drawers (*tansu*). Even some of these, however, were designed to be easily transportable, with bails on each end that could be slid up so that a pole could be inserted for carrying. These were outlawed in Edo in an attempt to avoid the clogging of the streets during fires but were made nonetheless. Paulownia and cedar, which are lightweight, and insect-, mould- and fire-resistant, were generally preferred but a variety of other hardwoods were also used. *Tansu* trickled up through the social hierarchy, first appearing in the late seventeenth century among the merchant class, who needed them as the spread of cotton made clothing cheaper and thus more abundant.[28] Daimyo *tansu* were usually qualitatively different from their merchant counterparts, with gilding on the fittings and makie (gold-sprinkled) lacquer.[29]

Naturally, daimyo castles had a wide range of quotidian objects – quotidian but not necessarily plain. Many things utilised extravagant, even imported, materials. Signature seals and pipe cases, for example, were often made of ivory or water buffalo horn imported to Nagasaki from South-East Asia. Women's hair ornaments could be made with ivory, tortoiseshell, red coral or exotic woods as could the ribs of fans or earwax cleaners. Game pieces for *go* or *shogi* (Japanese chess) were also often made of ivory.

Daimyo collecting

People form collections for a variety of psychological reasons including nostalgia, scientific interest, familial connection, as evidence of power and for pleasure, none of which are mutually exclusive. In times of active war, victory was celebrated with trophies, often of a gruesome kind such as the heads of defeated enemies. As an extreme example, in Kyoto there is a monument created in 1597 called the Mimizuka (Ear Mound) in which were interred more than 38,000 ears and noses from Koreans gathered in Toyotomi Hideyoshi's failed campaigns in 1592 and 1597.

When unification brought extended peace, such trophies were no longer readily available, and so the dominance that such prizes signified was expressed through the collection of other objects. These collections comprised what Pierre Bourdieu called symbolic capital, not just in terms of expressing power, but also of hierarchy and connection.[30] Because foreign objects were rare and expensive, they offered a homologous cache as war trophies and were included in many collections.

In substance, many collecting areas are very similar to those practised by the residents of European country houses. Antiquarian and Chinese paintings and calligraphy, especially from the Song (960–1279) and Yuan (1271–1368) dynasties, were highly valued. These ink works reflected the Zen aesthetic prized among elites and reflected in practices such as tea ceremony. Daimyo also patronised living artists: portraits were commissioned, especially of those who had been deified, and murals were painted on *fusuma*. Some daimyo were accomplished artists themselves, even in foreign styles. Mashiyama Sessai (1754–1819) of the Ise-Nagashima-han (present-day Mie Prefecture) was known for his Chinese-style landscape and bird-and-flower paintings. Satake Shozan (1748–85) of the Akita-han (present-day Akita Prefecture) was especially notable for pursuing Western painting techniques, authoring a book that outlined these techniques and founding a school based on Western painting principles.[31]

Because status was hereditary, things that connected the daimyo to their lineage or letters, calligraphy or objects that connected them to shoguns, emperors or other powerful men were carefully preserved. However, most artworks were kept in fire-proof *godowns*, the paintings and artworks rotated for season- or occasion-appropriate display. While collecting art was perhaps almost universal among elites, some daimyo collecting was more prototypically Japanese, yet these things often showed global connections.

Elite culture: swords and hunting

Armour, archery equipment and pole arms were not so much collected as kept. Even during extended peacetime, a level of military readiness had to be maintained. As a warrior class, however, military gear had great symbolic meaning, emphasising class, status and familial connections. Valued pieces were handed down for generations. Suits of armour were sometimes displayed in formal areas. Personal arms of powerful daimyo often had fine work and coverings from exotic animals imported from Asia, such as tigers and leopards. Besides the aesthetic appeal, these animals represented ferocity and had protective properties. Swords and sword furniture, however, had special meaning because they were markers of status – only those of the warrior class were allowed to wear both long and short swords. Although unquestionably deadly, their symbolic significance outweighed their actual utility in warfare.

Emblematic of warrior values, swords were treasured gifts within the feudal hierarchy. The shogun gave special blades to favoured daimyo, and daimyo gifted them to vassals. For example, the daimyo of the Owari han (present-day Aichi Prefecture), Tokugawa Yoshinao (1601–50), ninth son of Tokugawa Ieyasu, was given 39 swords by various shoguns between 1615 and 1650. He had so many swords he hired a curator for them in 1641.[32] Swords were handed out upon visiting or as gifts to wedding guests.[33] On significant birthdays blades inscribed with auspicious sayings such as 'long life' were gifted. In 1719, at the behest of the eighth Tokugawa shogun Yoshimune (1684–1751, r. 1716–45), a canon of sorts was created called the *Kyōhō meibutsuchō* (Kyōhō Record of Famous Things).[34]

Although swords would seem impervious to foreign influence and the blades were made in Japan, parts of the weapons were globalised. Sheaths of exotic animal hides such as leopard and tiger – real or ersatz (there were artisans in Kyoto who specialised in producing look-alikes) – were sometimes employed, but the uniquely Japanese katana sword had an even more integral foreign component: ray skins were used to cover the hilts to prevent the silk binding from slipping. Some kinds of rays swim off the coast of Japan but porcupine ray skins, valued for their large bumps, were only found in the Indian Ocean and other distant waters. Thousands of skins were imported each year for this purpose, brought to Japan by Dutch and Chinese merchants. Openings in the wrapping highlighted the ray skin texture, contributing to the overall aesthetic. To the frustration of the traders, skins that did not meet this aesthetic standard were rejected.

Hunting may seem an odd category for collecting, but it generated a great deal of material culture. There were professional hunters in early modern Japan but since very little meat was eaten in most regions, professional hunters pursued animals, such as wild boar, that damaged farmland. Like among the lords of manor houses, hunting was a popular pastime for daimyo. It was not just for food or the pleasure of it; hunting was seen as an important extension of their identity as warlords. It was a way to maintain martial skills and ensure detailed knowledge of local terrain, in the same way they were expected to have knowledge of *go* and *shogi* to heighten strategic ability.

Many kinds of hunting were practised, including with imported or domestic dogs, bows and firearms, but falconry was the most esteemed by far. This had been practised in Japan since ancient times, probably introduced from Mongolia or China through Korea. As a status symbol, it had been prohibited for commoners since 728, a ban that was reissued several times. Hawking (used here interchangeably with falconry) was once reserved for the imperial aristocracy, but as the upper echelons of the warrior class originated there, they also enjoyed it. By the sixteenth century, books on falconry proliferated. Nobunaga, Hideyoshi and Ieyasu all enjoyed this pastime. In 1627 it was made illegal for those of the imperial court to hawk as a way for the warrior class to assert dominance over the emperor, and the shogun would present the imperial court with cranes caught with his hawks annually as a reminder of his authority. Hunting with falcons was generally the realm of daimyo because of the great cost in keeping the birds. They required a range of special equipment, keepers, someone to catch sparrows and pigeons to feed them, and room to house them. Often, avid falconers would have more than one bird, each of which needed its own space as hoods were not commonly used in Japan. Moreover, it was the daimyo who controlled access to hunting grounds.

The main birds used in falconry were the goshawk (*Accipiter gentilisi*), sparrowhawk (*Accipiter nisus*) and peregrine falcon (*Falco peregrinus*), but in some areas the Japanese lesser sparrowhawk (*Accipiter gularis*) and Hodgson's (or mountain) hawk eagle (*Spizaetus nipalensis*) were also used. Aviculture was not practised with hawks and falcons; wild birds were trapped and trained, the younger the better. Although the raptors used for hunting were generally domestic, even those were occasionally imported, especially from Korea. For example, in 1607, some hawks were sent from Korea, along with tiger and leopard skins, as a gift to Tokugawa Hidetada (1581–1632) for becoming the second shogun (1605–23). Chinese ships would also sometimes bring hawks to sell.[35]

Hawking encouraged collecting, not just of the birds themselves and the things needed to care for and hunt with them but in terms of graphic representation. The esteem in which these birds were held can be seen in the numerous paintings, including portraits of individual birds and ornamentation of personal accoutrements such as *inrō* (decorative portable cases; see Figure 3.3). Hawks represented not just status but the properties that a warrior might want to emulate: fierceness, fearlessness and focus.

Figure 3.3 Lacquer *inrō* with hawk (front and back), nineteenth century. H.O. Havemeyer Collection, Bequest of Mrs H.O. Havemeyer, 1929. Public domain image available from the Metropolitan Museum of Art at https://www.metmuseum.org/art/collection/search/58657.

Japanese culture: Noh theatre and the tea ceremony

Noh theatre is almost the exception to the rule of globalisation but too important in castle life to omit from a grouping of daimyo collections. Noh was an outgrowth from earlier theatrical forms connected to Shintoism, but through the patronage of the third Muromachi shogun, Ashikaga Yoshimitsu (1358–1408), Kan'ami (1333–84) and his son Ze'ami (1363–1443) created a canon of plays performed in masks that emphasised music and dance, accompanied by flutes, drums and chanting. Although the stage and props were very simple, the costumes were made of the finest materials, including imported Chinese silks, and the masks were carved by specialised artisans.

Toyotomi Hideyoshi, who came from a very low-ranking family, always struggled to demonstrate his legitimacy. One way he did this was through noh theatre. He took it up late in life, after he had completed unification, in about 1592. He is reputed to have memorised ten plays in a month and had his life memorialised in songs that he had the actors he patronised perform.[36] When Tokugawa Ieyasu took power after

Hideyoshi's death, he continued the tradition, having noh performed at Nijo Castle when he received the title of shogun, which had to be bestowed by the emperor. Noh was made an official state ceremony in 1615 and was used to mark important occasions. Shogunal patronage and the long tradition of warrior participation made knowledge of noh necessary for all daimyo. Provincial castles had their own noh stages, usually placed in a garden facing the *shoin*.[37] Many daimyo patronised noh, maintaining their own troupes of performers.[38] In Kanazawa, noh chants were part of New Year's rituals when the daimyo was in residence and noh theatre was performed on the death anniversaries of his forefathers.[39] Most daimyo also practised it, and annual competitions of chanting and dancing (*utai-hajime*) were held. Costumes and masks were collected to perform these various rites, and because noh costumes and masks were valued both monetarily and as expressions of status and culture, the collections amassed in daimyo castles were carefully preserved for personal and ritual use. While the collections are not necessarily intact, many historical noh masks and costumes survive in museum collections.

The tea ceremony (*chanoyu*), although ostensibly a religious, meditative practice, was another important aspect of status, leisure and connoisseurship in premodern Japan. Introduced from China in the twelfth century, it was adopted by the warrior class as a secular practice in the fifteenth century through the patronage of the Ashikaga shoguns. The deep involvement by Oda Nobunaga, Toyotomi Hideyoshi and Tokugawa Ieyasu solidified it as a warrior pastime. In the Edo period, tea was seen as a way to practise discipline and an opportunity to make, extend or solidify political alliances. Although practised by other social classes, all daimyo were expected to have some familiarity with it as it was protocol when receiving important visitors. To teach tea to the shogun, the practitioner had to have a military rank.[40]

A number of schools developed, some by and for daimyo themselves. These schools are today referred to as 'daimyo tea' although the term was not used contemporaneously.[41] Not all authorities agree as to the attributes of daimyo tea, but besides the practitioner, the characteristics that made it specific included the use of a display stand called a *daisu* and a regard for tradition, authority and status, especially as laid out in the Ogasawara etiquette rule book for the military classes (Figure 3.4).[42] One of the founders of this style, Furuta Oribe (1544–1615), was daimyo of Fushimi in Kyoto who instructed Tokugawa Hidetada. Oribe departed from mainstream practices by using a larger, lighter space with more windows. He added a waiting area for the guests' attendants and

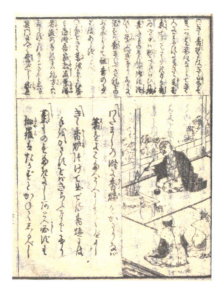

Figure 3.4 Tea Ceremony. From 'Ogasawara shorei taizen' [The Complete Ogasawara Etiquette], 1726. Center for Open Data in the Humanities, doi:10.20730/100249848. Image available at http://codh.rois.ac.jp/iiif/iiif-curation-viewer/index.html?pages=100249848&pos=25&lang=en reproduced under the Creative Commons licence CC BY-SA 4.0.

architectural adjustments that emphasised status. The banquet after the ceremony was performed in the *shoin* audience hall. Oribe also incorporated weapons into his designs, such as using arrows in the *daisu*, or tea bowls decorated with military fans.[43] The school (or one of its many offshoots) most widely practised among daimyo was called Sekishū. It was founded by the daimyo of the Koizumi-han (in present-day Nara Prefecture), Katagiri Sadamasa (1605–73), who used Sekishū as his tea name. Sekishū was inspired by older tea styles. From 1665, he instructed the fourth Tokugawa shogun, Ietsuna (1641–80, r. 1651–80). He transcribed the precepts of his practice in *Sekishū sanbyakujō* (Three Hundred Precepts of Sekishū), so it was possible for daimyo from across the country to apply his methods.[44]

The practice of tea required a wide variety of objects including tea bowls, water jars, tea containers and tea scoops. These objects were highly valued, collected and catalogued in volumes known as *Meibutsuki* (Record of famous objects) – Figure 3.5. While many distinctive forms of Japanese ceramics were developed specifically for tea such as raku, or the irregular pieces produced at the direction of Oribe,[45] many types of ceramics developed to imitate the highly valued pieces that came from abroad. In 1568, Oda Nobunaga began collecting these objects in a campaign known as *meibutsugari*, literally a hunt for famous treasures, making the equivalency with trophies more than metaphorical. He used the gifting of these objects to reward loyalty and cement alliances. This entrenched the place of the tea ceremony among the warrior class, who amassed collections as extensions of their power as much as for their utility or aesthetic sense.

As an originally Chinese practice, Chinese tea objects were always highly esteemed, especially in daimyo tea.[46] Many of these Chinese pieces had come to Japan in previous contacts with the continent; other were brought by traders. For instance, Francesco Carletti (1573–1632), an Italian merchant who was in Japan from 1597–8, noted a high demand for a certain kind of jar: 'They are not found today except as they were made many hundreds of years ago and are brought from the kingdoms of Cambodia and of Siam and Cochin China, and from the islands, Philippine and other, of that sea.' He claimed incoming ships were searched upon arrival so the 'King' could have first pick. Then, 'out of vainglory and for grandeur they make a contest of who possesses the larger quantity of them, displaying them to one another with the greatest satisfaction'.[47]

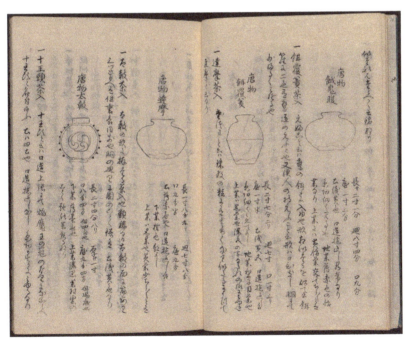

Figure 3.5 Japanese Tea Ceremony 'Meibutsuki': Utensils (1600). Smithsonian Institution. Public domain. Available at https://archive.org/details/meibutsuki00/page/19/mode/2up.

THE GLOBAL SAMURAI   91

Sen no Rikyū (1522–91), who is credited with the standardisation and formalisation of the tea ceremony as it is practised today, adopted Korean tea bowls (usually celadon), and they increased in popularity until the mid-eighteenth century. They may have been valued highly in part because in the sixteenth century there were no official trading relationships between Japan and Korea and they had to be smuggled in. Today some 660 heirloom Korean tea bowls, many named (an indicator of special reverence), exist in Japan.[48] Vietnamese, South-East Asian and occasionally even European objects were also put to use in tea ceremonies, and the careful combination of foreign and domestic elements was part of the aesthetic.[49] Many of these implements had cloth storage bags that were made from equally treasured textiles, often imported from China, South-East Asia or India. Furuta Oribe incorporated Western influences into his ceramic designs.[50] Additional connections to the outside world include ivory lids on tea containers, ivory tea scoops and boxes, and various incense components such as sandalwood and aloeswood – all brought to Japan from South-East Asia.

While all daimyo had collections of such objects, one particularly noted collector was Matsudaira Fumai (1751–1818), daimyo of Matsue-han (present-day Shimane Prefecture). His castle is one of the few extant Japanese castles that is not a reconstruction, although some buildings in the complex were torn down in the nineteenth century. He restored *han* finances, impoverished by a shogunal levy for repairs on Enryakuji Temple, by restructuring, opening new rice fields and encouraging the production of cash crops like ginseng and cotton. He used that surplus to amass a collection of over 800 tea objects, which by definition included objects from abroad, such as the famed Aburaya Katatsuki tea caddy, the tea bowl that had once belonged to Furuta Oribe, a Ming celadon vase from China and the Kizaemon tea bowl from Korea. He justified his expenditure by explaining that one needed utensils commensurate with the status of one's guests, and that such fine objects did not 'rain down from the sky or boil up from the earth'. He is significant not only for the act of collecting, but also for classifying and categorising tea implements, which he published in a series of volumes. He placed the highest value on ancient objects from China. His system is still used today to value relics associated with tea praxis.[51] Fumai specifically sought to claim tea as an activity for warriors.[52] He saw these objects as 'treasures of Japan' – almost a form of state business.[53]

Tea practice involved more than the ritual of production of tea. It was a curated environment that had its own building. The alcove included a seasonally appropriate painting complemented by a flower arrangement. As an example, 'Sekishiu [sic] once placed some waterplants in a flat receptacle to suggest the vegetation of lakes and marshes and on the wall above he hung a painting by Soami of wild ducks flying in the air'.[54] Thus, daimyo collected flower containers, scroll paintings, calligraphy, incense burners and other objects not directly connected to the making of tea but essential to its practice that were inspired by or directly from foreign sources.

Global influences: books and *ranpeki* (Dutch mania)

Another element that connects daimyo with the European landed elite was large personal libraries. Books were expensive, and literacy was a sign of status and culture. In wartime, not much value had been placed on book learning, but a peacetime daimyo was expected to have the ability to communicate in writing and literary ability that included reading and writing Chinese and poetry. Foreign books were usually brought by traders on personal account rather than as official trading goods, although requests were placed for specific books on topics such as medicine and warfare. Maeda Tsunanori of the Kaga domain (1643–1724) was reputed to be 'the best under the heavens' in book collecting, including Dutch and Chinese books – a practice which began in his teens. One year he supposedly bought every single book that came to Nagasaki on the Chinese ships. What he could not buy, he would borrow and have copied. Tsunanori's successors continued collecting so that by the end of the Edo period, their library contained tens of thousands of books.[55]

The library of Matsura Seizan (1760–1841) was also renowned. The ninth Matsura daimyo of Hirado (present-day Nagasaki Prefecture) also began collecting in his teens. His personal library, Rakusaidō, contained more than 5,000 Japanese and Chinese books, as well as 62 Western books, an enormous number considering their high cost. These included Dutch translations of Engelbert Kaempfer's *History of Japan* (1727) and Benjamin Martin's *Philosophical Grammar: Being a View of the Present State of Experimented Physiology or Natural Philosophy* (1735) as well as Dutch books on medicine, the history of the Netherlands and other topics.[56] Scholars were allowed access to this collection, notably including Shiba Kōkan (1747–1818), an astronomer and artist known for painting in the Western style. Any significant library of the day had Chinese and European books, and because many domains ran schools, most had substantial libraries.

The relationship with the Asian continent was ancient but contact with Europe only began in the 1540s. Initially, Westerners were welcomed. Oda Nobunaga, instrumental in unifying Japan, was enamoured of foreign things, even occasionally wearing capes, rosaries, ruffs and other Western accoutrements. Toyotomi Hideyoshi became suspicious of Christianity, however, and Tokugawa Ieyasu maintained these suspicions. Christianity was outlawed, and one corollary was a dampening of interest in all things Western because association with them might be construed as Christian. Even mathematical tomes in Chinese were forbidden because their translator was the Jesuit missionary Matteo Ricci (1552–1610). Nevertheless, certain things remained, even after the Portuguese were expelled in 1639. Tempura, for example, was originally brought in by the Portuguese – oil is not used much in traditional Japanese cooking. After Tokugawa Yoshimune personally pursued the study of Western things, there was increased interest through the eighteenth century, creating a subset of collecting called *ranpeki*, which translates literally as 'Dutch mania'. This term could refer to collecting knowledge about or objects from the West, both of which were common practices in the eighteenth century. Nearly all scholars of Western science, regardless of status, received patronage from a daimyo. While imported books were the basis for this study, a range of Western apparatus, including surgical instruments, microscopes and telescopes, were also brought on Dutch ships.

A few daimyo had the ability to directly make official requests for foreign objects from the Dutch East India Company (VOC) or its successor, the Nederlandsche Handel Maatschappij. Records only identify only four daimyo allowed this privilege: Matsura Sanenobu (1712–79) of Hirado (twice), Ōmura Sumihisa (1711–49) of Hizen, Matsudaira Tadami (1711–38) of Shimabara, and Shimazu Shigehide of Satsuma (1745–1833). All were from Kyushu and had connections with foreign trade. Shimazu Shigehide was also the shogun's father-in-law and made the most use of this privilege. He ordered an eclectic mixture of things including two red varnished European chairs, bottled caymans, ostrich eggs, live porcupines, monkeys with tails, glass flasks, an electrostatic generator and firearms.[57] He also amassed a large collection of clocks, glassware and other items such as books on Western astronomy and medicine. He studied Dutch and Chinese language using imported books.[58] Nabeshima Naomasa (1814–71) of Saga also learned to speak Dutch fluently, which he used to advance Western science and technology in his domain. Maeda Toshitsune of the Kaga domain similarly collected ceramics and textiles from the Asian continent.[59]

These special orders were the exception rather than the rule, and for the most part daimyo obtained their foreign objects through gifting or purchase at shops or through merchants who specialised in imports called *karamonoya* that evolved in the early seventeenth century. In some rare cases collections were built through personal relationships. For example, Kutsuki Masatsuna (1750–1802) of Tanba (now part of Kyoto and Hyōgo prefectures) had an enormous coin collection of some 9,000 coins partially acquired through his friendship with Opperhoofd (factory head) Isaac Titsingh (1745–1812), which included coins from China, Korea, Vietnam, various VOC outposts and Europe.[60] Masatsuna published four books on coins, including one just on Western coins. This fascination with coins, which began when he was 13, led to an interest in geography, and he published Japan's first atlas based on Western sources.[61] Less erudite were the occasional fads for Western things, such as the large numbers of buttons that circulated among daimyo in the early nineteenth century.[62]

Perhaps the most notorious *ranpeki* daimyo was Tanuma Okitsugu (1719–88). He was unusual in that in a society based largely on hereditary status, he came from a low-ranking family. Through sheer ability he worked his way up to the highest position in the shogunal government, chamberlain to Tokugawa Ieharu (1737–86, r. 1760–86), and received the appointment of daimyo of Sagara (in present-day Shizuoka Prefecture). Such a meteoric rise earned him enemies, who attacked him as soon as his protector died. His taste for luxury and support of commerce ran counter to the neo-Confucian ideas of his successor, Matsadaira Sadanobu (1759–1829), and for the last year of his life he was under house arrest. Although he did much to improve the economy, he also enjoyed and encouraged gifts, perhaps in excess of the gifting protocols of the day. To curry favour, many presented him with imported goods such as clocks and glassware, which he also actively collected. Because he was disgraced and his heir sent to a smaller northern domain, few specifics remain as to the content of his collections, but his enthusiasm spread, encouraging other daimyo to enjoy the fruits of foreign trade. Dutch plates, clocks, telescopes, binoculars, wine glasses and other Western goods proliferated in daimyo houses during the eighteenth century.

Conclusion

When the Tokugawa shogunate fell in 1868, many daimyo collections were dispersed, pawned or sold to raise cash. Some of these objects were acquired by industrialists such as Masuda Takeshi of the Mitsui zaibatsu.[63] Others went to Western collectors, especially after the surge of travellers in the 1890s brought by steamships. Eagerness to acquire Japanese goods was so great that there arose some 'auction-rooms where trashy stuff under the guise of "*daimyō* collections" is disposed of at stiff prices'.[64] However, a few have survived largely intact, such as that of the Ii of Hikone (present-day Shiga Prefecture); the Hosokawa of Higo (present-day Kumamoto Prefecture), which now forms the Eisei Bunko Museum; and the Owari Tokugawa, whose collection is the Tokugawa Art Museum, which can give us a sense of the material culture of the daimyo castle. Similarly, at the time of the Meiji Restoration, castles were seen as remnants of a shameful and barbaric past and many were torn down. As Edward Morse noted:

> Indeed, it is a question whether any of the old residences of the Daimios remain in the condition in which they were twenty years ago, or before the Revolution. Even where the buildings remain, as in the castles of Nagoya and Kumamoto, busy clerks and secretaries are seen sitting in chairs and writing at tables in foreign style.[65]

Even if they survived these purges or repurposing, bombing during the Second World War damaged or destroyed others.

Since Japan remained in a quasi-feudal state and did not fully embrace capitalism until after the Meiji Restoration in 1868 (the 'Revolution' Morse refers to), there was never an exact equivalent to the European country house during the eighteenth century. One could perhaps make a case for some structures from earlier periods before the imperial aristocracy was forced to submit to shogunal rule. Nevertheless, there are distinct similarities to Europe in the economic basis and collection patterns of daimyo castles. They shaped the areas over which they ruled, but they were integrated not only into a national market but also, through their collecting practices, into global trading systems.

The myth that Japan was 'closed' during the early modern period has been remarkably persistent despite the fact that scholars have rejected this characterisation at least since Donald Keene's *The Japanese Discovery of Europe* (1952). The daimyo and the material culture of their residences were by no means the only places where imported materials and goods proliferated in the consumerism of early modern Japan, but their ubiquity and importance in establishing status among daimyo show that even in the most remote regional castles, the material culture of both formal and leisure activities were shaped by global connections.

Notes

1. Fujino, 'Daimyo no keizai seikatsu', 79–80.
2. Totman, *The Lumber Industry*, 23.
3. Kaempfer, *Kaempfer's Japan*, 271.
4. Girouard, *Life in the English Country House*, 2.
5. Katz, 'Fools for Art', 75.
6. This was not strictly adhered to. For example, certain specific types of trade with Korea were conducted through Tsushima.
7. The English, unable to make a profit, left in 1623, while the Spanish were ejected in 1624.
8. Coaldrake, *Architect and Authority in Japan*, 107.
9. Cooper, *They Came to Japan*, 131–2.
10. Miura, *Nihon no shiro*, 22–3.
11. Bensch and Zwigenberg, *Japan's Castles*, 7–8.
12. The Kanō school was patronised by the warrior class. The imperial aristocracy patronised the Tosa school.
13. Ōta Gyūichi, *Chronicle of Lord Nobunaga*, 253–7, 423.
14. Cooper, *They Came to Japan*, 135.
15. Anonymous, 'The castles of Japan', 762.
16. Bensch and Zwigenberg, *Japan's Castles*, 24.
17. Miura, *Nihon no shiro*, 38.
18. Tokugawa, 'A daimyo's possessions', 27.
19. Schmorleiz, *Castles in Japan*, 59.
20. Hanley, 'Tokugawa lifestyles', 674.
21. Bushi seikatsu, *Kinsei bushi seikatsu*, 196.
22. Bushi seikatsu, *Kinsei bushi seikatsu*, 226.
23. Roberts, *Performing the Great Peace*, 139, 151–2, 156–7.
24. Tokugawa, 'A daimyo's possessions', 30.
25. Schmorleitz, *Castles in Japan*, 60.
26. Morse, *Japanese Homes*, 177.
27. Morse, *Japanese Homes*, 177.
28. Kozumi, *Dōgu to kurashi no edo jidai*, 12–33.
29. Bytheway, 'Nihon no tansu', 46–9.
30. First outlined in Bourdieu, 'Forms of capital', 241–58.
31. *Gahō kōryō* (1778).
32. Bolitho, 'Civilizing warriors', 38–9.
33. See, for example, Ogimachi, *In the Shelter of the Pines*. This memoir about Yangaisawa Yoshiyasu (1658–1719) by one of his concubines mentions numerous occasions when swords were exchanged.
34. Satō, *Japanese Sword*, 89, 177.
35. Kajishima, *Nihon dōbutsushi*, 81.
36. Kadowaki, 'Noh drama and the samurai', 108.
37. Tokugawa, 'A daimyo's possessions', 28.
38. Kadowaki, 'Noh drama and the samurai', 109.
39. McClain, *Kanazawa*, 139.
40. Nakano-Holmes, 'Furuta Oribe', xiii.
41. Landeck, 'Aesthetic authorities', 27.
42. Nakano-Holmes, 'Furuta Oribe', 50–2.
43. Nakano-Holmes, 'Furuta Oribe', 53–72.
44. Wilson, 'Tea ceremony', 71.
45. Landeck mentions that Oribe might have favoured domestic ceramics because he could not afford imported ones. Landeck, 'Aesthetic authority', 56.
46. Nakano-Holmes, 'Furuta Oribe', 50.
47. Carletti, *Voyage Around the World*, 99, 101–2.
48. Hur, 'Korean tea bowls', 1–22.
49. Katz, 'Fools for art', 78.
50. Varley, 'Chanoyu', 162.
51. Varley, 'Chanoyu', 177–80. Quote is originally from *Mudagoto* (1770).

52 Landeck, 'Aesthetic authorities', 13.
53 Landeck, 'Aesthetic authorities', 160–1.
54 Okakura, *Book of Tea*, 144–5. Soami (1472–1525) was a painter, poet, and landscape designer in the style of the Southern Song Chan painters who was patronised by the Ashikaga shogunate.
55 Nakae, *Edo daimyo no kokishin*, 130–1. The remnants of the library, which still exists today in Tokyo, is called Sonkeikaku bunko.
56 Kobe-shi hakubutsukan, *Nichiran kōryū no kakehashi*, 200.
57 Chaiklin, *Cultural Commerce*, 64–5.
58 Nakae, *Edo daimyo no kokishin*, 226–7.
59 Nakae, *Edo daimyo no kokishin*, 128.
60 The East Asian parts of this collection are now held at the British Museum and the Ashmolean.
61 The books on coins are *Shinzen zenpu*, Kaisei kōhō zukan, Seiyō senpu and Kokon senpu kagami. The atlas is Taisei yochi zusetsu. Nakae, Edo daimyo no kokishin, 220–3.
62 Nagasakishi shi vol. 4, 735.
63 Moslé, 'Sword Ornaments', 190–1.
64 Terry, *Terry's Japanese Empire*, cxviii.
65 Morse, *Japanese Homes*, 319.

Bibliography

Anonymous. 'The castles of Japan', *The Japan Magazine* 3, no. 12 (April 1913): 760–8.
Bensch, Oleg, and Ran Zwigenberg. *Japan's Castles: Citadels of modernity in war and peace*. Cambridge: Cambridge University Press, 2019.
Bolitho, Harold. 'Civilizing warriors'. In *The Japan of the Shoguns; Tokugawa Collection*. Exhibition Catalogue, 33–40. Montreal: The Montreal Museum of Fine Arts, 1989.
Bourdieu, Pierre. 'The forms of capital'. In *Handbook of Theory and Research for the Sociology of Education*, edited by J.G. Richardson, 241–58. New York: Greenwood Press, 1986.
Bushi seikatsu kenkyūkai. *Zuroku kinsei bushi seikatsu nyūmon jiten*. Tokyo: Kashiwa shobo, 1991.
Bytheway, Simon J. 'Nihon no tansu to sono rekishi ni kansuru ikkosatsu', *Tohoku kaihatsu kenkyū* 109 (1998):46–9.
Carletti, Francesco. *My Voyage Around the World: The chronicles of a 16th century Florentine merchant*. Translated by Herbert Weinstock. New York: Pantheon Books, 1964.
Chaiklin, Martha. *Cultural Commerce and Dutch Commercial Culture: The influence of European material culture on Japan, 1700–1850*. Leiden: CNWS, 2003.
Coaldrake, William H. *Architecture and Authority in Japan*. London and New York: Routledge, 1996.
Cooper, Michael, ed. *They Came to Japan: An anthology of European reports on Japan, 1543–1640*. Berkeley and Los Angeles: University of California Press, 1965.
Fieve, Nicholas, and Paul Waley, eds. *Japanese Capitals in Historical Perspective*. London: Routledge, 2013.
Fujino Tamotsu. 'Daimyo no keizai seikatsu'. In *Edo jidai bushi no seikatsu*, edited by Yoshimoto Shinji, 79–102. Tokyo: Yūzankaku, 1981.
Girouard, Mark. *Life in the English Country House: A social and architectural history*. New Haven and London: Yale University Press, 1978.
Hall, John W. 'Castle towns and modern urbanization. In *Studies in the Institutional History of Early Modern Japan*, edited by John W. Hall and Marius Jansen, 169–88. Princeton: Princeton University Press, 1968.
Hanley, Susan B. 'Tokugawa society: material culture, standard living and lifestyles'. In *Cambridge History of Japan*, vol. 4, edited by John Whitney Hall, 660–705. London: Cambridge University Press, 1991.
Hur, Nam-Lin. 'Korean tea bowls (Kōrai chawan) and Japanese wabicha: a story of acculturation in premodern Northeast Asia', *Korean Studies* 39 (2015): 1–22.
Kadowaki, Yukie. 'Noh drama and the samurai', *Bulletin of the Detroit Institute of the Arts* 88, no. 1/4 (2014): 104–13.

Kaempfer, Engelbert. *Kaempfer's Japan-Tokugawa Culture Observed*. Translated by Beatrice M. Bodart-Bailey. Honolulu: University of Hawaii Press, 1999.

Kajishima Takao. *Nihon dōbutsushi*. Tokyo: Yasaka shobō, 2002.

Katz, Janice. 'Fools for art: two Maeda daimyo as collectors in seventeenth century Japan'. In *Acquisition: Art and Ownership in Edo-Period Japan*, edited by Elizabeth Lillehoj, 74–90. Warren, CT: Floating World Editions, 2007.

Keene, Donald. *The Japanese Discovery of Europe*. London: Routledge and Kegan Paul, 1952.

Kobe-shi Hakubutsukan, ed. *Nichiran kōryū no kakehashi*. Exhibition Catalogue. Kobe: Kobe City Museum, 1998.

Kozumi Kazuko. *Dōgu to kurashi no edo jidai*. Tokyo: Yoshikawa kobunkan, 1999.

Landeck, Melinda. 'Aesthetic authorities: the socio-political dimensions of warlord tea praxis in early modern Japan, 1573–1860', PhD dissertation, University of Kansas, 2015.

McClain, James L. *Kanazawa: A seventeenth-century Japanese castle town*. New Haven and London: Yale University Press, 1982.

Miura Masayuki, ed. *Sugu wakaru nihon no shiro*. Tokyo: Tokyo Bijutsu, 2009.

Morse, Edward S. *Japanese Homes and Their Surroundings*. 2nd edition. Salem, MA: Tichnor, 1886.

Moslé, Alexander G. 'Sword ornaments of the Gotō Shirobe family', *Transactions and Proceedings of the Japan Society, London* 8, no. 2 (1908): 188–208.

Nagasaki shiyakusho, ed. *Nagasaki shishi*, vol. 4. Nagasaki: Nagasaki shiyakusho, 1925.

Nakae Katsumi. *Edo daimyo no kokishin*. Tokyo: Daisan bunmeisha, 2022.

Nakano-Holmes, Julia R. 'Furuta Oribe: iconoclastic guardian of chanoyu tradition', PhD dissertation, University of Hawaii, 1995.

Ogimachi Machiko. *In the Shelter of the Pine: A memoir of Yanagisawa Yoshiyasu and Tokugawa Japan*. translated by G.G. Rowley. New York: Columbia University Press, 2021.

Okakura Kakuzo. *The Book of Tea*. New York: G.P. Putnam's Sons, 1906.

Ōta Gyūichi. *The Chronicle of Lord Nobunaga*. Translated and edited by J.S.A. Elisonas and J.P. Lamers. Leiden and Boston: Brill, 2011.

Roberts, Luke S. *Performing the Great Peace: Political space and open secrets in Tokugawa Japan*. Honolulu: University of Hawaii Press, 2012.

Rozman, Gilbert. 'Castle towns in transition'. In *Japan in Transition: From Tokugawa to Meiji*, edited by Marius Jansen and Gilbert Rozman, 318–46. Princeton: Princeton University Press, 1986.

Satake Yoshiatsu. *Gahō kōryō*. 1778.

Satō Kanzan. *The Japanese Sword: A comprehensive guide*. Translated by Joe Earle. Tokyo and New York: Kodansha, 1983.

Schmorleitz, Morton. *Castles in Japan*. Rutland, VT and Tokyo: Charles Tuttle, 1974.

Terry, T. Philip. *Terry's Japanese Empire with Formosa and Korea*. Boston and New York: Houghton Mifflin, 1919.

Tokugawa Yoshinobu. 'A daimyo's possessions'. In *The Japan of the Shoguns; Tokugawa Collection*. Exhibition Catalogue, 25–32. Montreal: The Montreal Museum of Fine Arts, 1989.

Totman, Conrad. *The Lumber Industry in Early Modern Japan*. Honolulu: University of Hawaii Press, 1995.

Varley, Paul. 'Chanoyu from Genroku to modern times'. In *Tea in Japan: Essays in the history of chanoyu*, edited by Paul Varley and Kumakura Isao, 161–94. Honolulu: University of Hawaii Press, 1995.

Wilson, Richard. 'Tea ceremony: art and etiquette for the Tokugawa era'. In *The Japan of the Shoguns; Tokugawa Collection*. Exhibition Catalogue, 63–74. Montreal: The Montreal Museum of Fine Arts, 1989.

Yoshimoto Shinji, ed. *Edo jidai bushi no seikatsu*. Tokyo: Yūzankaku, 1981.

4
'We are starving for want of Tea': Asian objects, domestic slavery and Caribbean sociability

Christine Walker

In 1752, Samuel Martin, one of Antigua's wealthiest planters, sent a polite reminder to his children who lived in England, writing: 'I hope my girls will not fail to send me Tea.'[1] Seven months later, after his daughters had ignored his request, Martin turned to his eldest son, Samuel Junior, who acted as the family head in London, to obtain his beloved beverage. Expressing indignation, he exclaimed, 'your sisters not having sent me an ounce of tea for above a year past thoughtful girls of their old father!'. Invoking both sibling rivalry and guilt, the injured father sought to contrast the errant daughters with the dutiful son: 'if they will so neglect me I hope you will remember to send me 3 pounds of very good Hyson tea'. In December 1753, the father wrote to Martin Junior, 'pray send me with all expedition the necessaries I wrote for, particularly my tea'.[2] As Martin awaited shipments of his favourite beverage, politeness gave way to hostility. He implored his daughter to send the leaves, writing, 'Sal and you have forgotten, for we are starving for want of Tea'.[3]

As his letters show, Chinese tea was more than a drink for Samuel Martin. Its arrival in the Caribbean signalled the strength of the bonds of affection and obligation that tied the family together. Through its consumption, tea drinking materialised these invisible links, inviting the father to imagine a shared domesticity across the Atlantic, or reminding him of the vast distance that separated them. Tea's absence signified painful separation and emotional neglect. In making requests for 'one pound of Hyson extraordinary' or 'plain' green tea,[4] Martin also performed his role as a sophisticated consumer in the Anglo-Atlantic market for Asian goods. This knowledge, in turn, bolstered Martin's status among the colonial elite. Martin wrote in one letter of his debt to another colonist for an earlier shipment of tea, indicating that the good was so prized in Antigua that islanders used it as a form of social and monetary currency. Once it arrived in the Caribbean, tea's perishability further enhanced its value, leading Martin to instruct his son to send him shipments 'twice a year' because it 'soon spoils here'.[5]

Had Martin resided in Boston or Philadelphia, his devotion to tea would be unremarkable. By the middle of the eighteenth century, tea drinking was a well-established ritual throughout the Anglo-Atlantic World. Martin's residency in Antigua, however, makes his desire for tea unexpected and surprising. Largely omitted, and occasionally caricatured, Caribbean consumers such as Samuel Martin do not figure in scholarship on early modern consumption, global trade and material culture. Stereotypes originating in the late eighteenth century continue to influence historical studies, making illustrations of cosy family gatherings around tea tables seem anathema to scenes of planters sadistically torturing enslaved people. The region's inhabitants are typically associated with the debauchery and excess of the rum punch bowl, not the polite sociability of tea drinking.[6] By highlighting the consumption of Asian goods by colonists such as Samuel Martin, this chapter seeks to challenge the dichotomy between British refinement and West Indian savagery. Generated by antislavery activists who sought to condemn plantation slavery, careworn tropes obscure more than they reveal, overlooking a shared Anglo-Atlantic culture and even downplaying British complicity in slavery and colonialism.[7]

Here, I pair selections from the Martin family papers with a detailed sample of 179 probated inventories of female-owned estates in Jamaica, recorded between 1674 and 1770.[8] It is important to recognise the geographic and demographic differences between the two islands where these sources were produced. Geographically, Jamaica is 40 times larger than Antigua. The demographics were also varied. By the 1770s, 37,500 enslaved people were held in captivity by fewer than 3,000 white people in Antigua. During the same era, 12,000 white colonists commanded more than 200,000 enslaved people in Jamaica. Nevertheless, the places shared social and economic similarities. They were sites of intensive wealth production, where minorities practised brutal forms of exploitation to command the labour of majority populations of captives of African descent. Integrating material from the two colonies thus allows for a shared regional material culture to emerge. This subject is ripe for further inquiry, and future scholars who adopt a comparative approach may consider the similarities and the divergences between the islands.

There are limitations to relying on textual evidence in a study of material culture. Specifically, historians have expressed concerns about probate inventories. Writing about early modern Europe, Giorgio Riello observes that the act of 'inventorying' was poorly defined. Inventories are deceptive, appearing to be formulaic documents when, in fact, they are idiosyncratic, reflecting the individual goals, skills and knowledge of appraisers.[9] Inventories recorded in Jamaica share similar traits. Devoid of thick description, they reveal very little about the owners of the objects, the places where objects were made or how owners obtained them. Most colonial appraisers used a simple set of adjectives to describe material goods. They were especially concerned with identifying the age of items. The term 'old' appeared the most frequently, 364 times in the sample of 179 inventories. In contrast, appraisers only identified 24 artefacts as 'new'. Size was also a notable marker, with 'small' used 95 times and 'large' 40 times.[10]

Despite all these potential conceptual and methodological flaws, surviving evidence from the eighteenth-century Caribbean – a region where environmental conditions and the economic and social depredations of colonialism and slavery have whittled away material – is precious. Inventories may be sparse, but they do capture the practices and tastes of a diverse range of consumers. The probate records used here centre women's possessions, offering a counterbalance and a point of comparison with male-authored texts from the Martin collection. Read together, this evidence shows that colonists throughout the Lesser and the Greater Antilles appropriated the labour of enslaved people to keep pace with and even anticipate British fashions. Collectively, free and unfree residents transformed imported luxuries into everyday necessities.

Silk and slavery

Slaveholding was not an oppositional practice that deviated from metropolitan norms. On the contrary, the wealth generated by slavery enabled West Indian colonists to participate more fully in Anglo-imperial material and social practices. Their households were laboratories of material experimentation, where polite sociability merged with brutal exploitation, creating an alternative form of domesticity. Sarah Golding, for instance, established a separate estate from her husband, laying claim to nearly one hundred enslaved people who cultivated sugar on her plantation. This wealth, in turn, enabled Golding to buy a tea table, a mahogany chest and a mahogany press. When she died, her appraisers used similar terminology to classify her captives as they did to describe her clothing and home goods. Assessing captives' health, age, physical condition and skills, appraisers sorted people into the categories of 'best', 'old and ordinary' and 'ordinary'.[11] Caribbean enslavers were on the front line of global commerce, commodifying both artefacts and people. They used Asian goods and African captives interchangeably as props to bolster their refinement, gentility and taste.

Golding's exploitation of enslaved labourers to produce the sugar that she then used to finance the purchase of genteel furnishings is not surprising. An expansive literature has been produced that explores the connections between slavery and capitalism. Yet this vast body of work focuses almost exclusively on plantation slavery. Far less attention has been paid to domestic captives. It was an army of servants, cooks, laundresses, seamstresses and coach drivers, though, who fashioned Caribbean performances of politeness, taste and refinement.

The influx of new goods into the colonies generated new forms of labour. For instance, three enslaved women, Pathena, Easter and Nanny, and a child, Betty, worked in Elizabeth Bishop's household, facilitating the polite Christianity conveyed by her Bible prayer book and writing desk. As domestic servants, Bishop's captives may have been employed in brewing and serving tea and chocolate. While Bishop herself could have taken centre stage in orchestrating these rituals of consumption, making the tea herself and handing it to her guests, it is also plausible that the women used and cared for the array of objects these customs required, including Bishop's tea tongs, kettle, chocolate cups, saucers, half-pint basins, teapot, milk pot and sugar dish.[12] Whether they steeped the tea and made the chocolate themselves, or just cleared tables, cleaned and stored the porcelain, these women played critical roles in integrating novel objects, including Asian manufactures, into local households.

We need look no further than the Martin family to uncover the comingling of violence and polite consumption. As children, Samuel and Josiah Martin witnessed the brutal demise of their father, who was hacked to death in 1701 by the people he enslaved for allegedly refusing to give them Christmas Day off. Samuel Martin's predilection for tea, then, was informed by his need to distance himself from the ruthlessness of the plantation slavery that his habit depended upon. Describing himself as a 'weak drinker', Martin used tea to project a brand of sober and restrained masculinity that contributed to his reputation as an enlightened and benevolent enslaver among locals and metropolitan visitors to Antigua.[13] Few would have interpreted Martin's position as an enslaver negatively. Before the 1770s, the trafficking of African people across the Atlantic and the profits produced by their labour were viewed as essential strands of imperial business. In this context, Martin was viewed as benevolent. Not a trace of irony tinged his portrayal of himself as 'starving' without tea during a time of severe drought on the island that left thousands of enslaved people starving and dehydrated.

Silk's popularity in the region offers another entrée into colonists' complex uses of Asian and European manufactured goods to both contribute to imperially oriented fashions and enforce their status as enslavers. Colonists expressed their wealth, status and taste by dressing in silk.[14] There were 34 references to silk in the inventory sample of women's estates in Jamaica, making it the most popular textile in their possession. Appraisers did not specify whether the silk in female households was made in China or Europe, suggesting that locals prized other qualities in the material. Josiah Martin's repeated requests for silk offer more insight into the material and intangible elements that made colonists seek out silk.

Silk was an especially critical signifier for his family, who travelled frequently between Antigua and North America before permanently relocating to New York. The Martins used fashionable clothing tailored from the expensive fabric to visually convey their rank and fortune when they arrived in places such as New York, Philadelphia and Boston – communities where they had fewer social connections than they did in Antigua. Before sailing for New York in 1731, Martin ordered three pairs of deep blue and deep green silk stockings of a small size for his wife, together with two pairs of silk stockings for his five-and-a-half-year-old daughter. Martin claimed that the women in his family needed to wear these striking and royal colours to protect their legs from cold weather, which was 'much severer' in New York.[15] But their desire to appear fashionable, rather than practical concerns, drove the Martins to make costly purchases.

Josiah Martin and his wife, Mary, were financially and culturally invested in appearing fashionable. In one letter, Martin asked for a 'handsome' suit of nightclothes for his wife that was 'fashionable dressed' with lace. Though seemingly generic, the Martins assumed a shared understanding with their correspondents in Britain and North America about the qualities that made items fashionable and handsome. Rather than diminish their taste, the Martins' status as Caribbean colonists amplified their fashion sensibilities. Mary, for example, asserted her superior awareness of novel styles. At the end of her husband's letter to Stephen Bayard, a wealthy merchant in New York, Josiah Martin noted that Mary was sending 'some of the highest fashion ribbon' to

Bayard's wife.[16] It was Mary Martin, not a British relative, or her New York acquaintance, who shared her knowledge of the latest modes.

In addition to enhancing their own prestige, the Martins imposed their fashion sensibilities and access to imported luxury textiles such as silk upon the people whom they enslaved. In 1730, Josiah Martin ordered three coats made of 'deep blue silk coat' and black *pattisway*, a rich, heavy silk, requesting that they be lined with 'silk of their respective colors', for the enslaved driver and postillions who attended his coach – itself the foremost status symbol of the eighteenth century. Covering the bodies of these men in liveries made of silk and emblazoned with his initials, J.M., Martin advertised his family's fortune while also claiming ownership of them through dress. Some servants may have resented wearing livery in Britain, but the garb took on different meanings in the Caribbean, where people of African descent were legally classified as moveable goods.[17]

In this context, it is likely that the women in the Martin family relied on the domestic labour of captives, and specifically their skills with the needle and thread. It is plausible that enslaved women assisted Martin's wife and daughter in using the sewing silk ordered by Josiah in 1729 to turn a 'handsome piece of silk' into a 'suit of cloathes' for Mary.[18] Enslaved people may have been involved in turning the silk that Martin ordered into two waistcoats and breeches, together with a suit of superfine broadcloth lined with silk of the same colour.[19] Research needs to be done to determine whether English enslavers devised the kinds of formal apprenticeships of the sort established by French colonists who sent enslaved women to France to be trained as seamstresses.[20] Given the presence of enslaved labourers in nearly every industry in Antigua and Jamaica, it is reasonable to assume that colonists relied, at least informally, upon the skills of captive seamstresses and tailors to produce fashionable clothing.

For all the tea and china

Tea drinking was the most popular practice that connected Caribbean colonists to an emergent Anglo-imperial culture that was developed, in part, through trading ties with Asia.[21] Appraisers began cataloguing objects made for tea in Jamaican households as early as the 1720s. Similar wares did not proliferate in Britain until the 1740s.[22] In Jamaica, appraisers made 95 references to the term tea to describe objects in the sample of 179 inventories. In contrast, they only identified

22 items related to coffee drinking, and 15 artefacts for chocolate and cocoa combined. On an island where cocoa had been cultivated since the seventeenth century and coffee plantations flourished in the cool mountains by the late eighteenth century, women's strong preference for tea over the other two stimulant beverages is especially striking.[23] Cocoa and later coffee would have been more readily available and affordable for local consumers. As Samuel Martin's letters show, tea was, in contrast, difficult to obtain and preserve in a tropical environment. Like English appraisers, appraisers in Jamaica rarely identified perishable goods such as tea. Only two of the inventories contain explicit references to tea leaves, including one to an 'old cannister of musty tea'.

More durable objects offer evidence of tea's popularity in the region. Between the 1720s and 1730s, women in Jamaica began amassing a diverse collection of teapots, tea kettles, tea tables and tea chests. More than 20 per cent of the households in the sample owned items categorised as china. Normally grouped with other cooking utensils in inventories, the catch-all term china included high-end porcelain and lower-quality 'old' earthenware.[24] Many of these china objects were designed specifically for brewing, serving and drinking tea.[25] Mary Hutchinson, for instance, owned a 'china plate, 26 blue and white saucers … 15 tea cups, 1 tea pot and tea cannister all china' when she died in 1740.[26] Upon her death in 1750, widow Elizabeth Cadogan had collected '11 china plates, 1 china tea pot, 3 cups and saucers, 1 sugar dish, and 3 chocolate cups'.[27] Women purchased china in sets or parcels, rather than individual pieces, and these sets became more elaborate and extensive over the eighteenth century.

Unlike coffee or chocolate, tea artfully combined objects that Europeans associated with the ancient East and novel Western appurtenances, such as tea tongs, teaspoons and tea kettles. When the merchant Dorothy Matson died in 1734, the 'tea table and tea boards' in her Kingston home were set with a 'china bowl, china dishes … 1 doz chocolate cups unsold' and a 'parcel of china'.[28] Similarly, the tea table owned by Rachel Beach, who died in 1741, was set with an assortment of porcelain saucers, cups, teapots, coffeepots, milk pitchers, bowls and plates.[29] Matson and Beach likely acquired these objects in the 1720s and 1730s, making them early adopters of tea drinking. Their tea tables were what Maxine Berg has called 'British new consumer goods'.[30] However, these objects were not just of British origin. Likely made from mahogany trees that grew in Jamaica, the tables materialised Caribbean, as much as they did British, sensibilities. While much of the island's mahogany was harvested and shipped to Britain, it would have been easier and cheaper for local cabinetmakers to transform the wood into the tea tables found in Matson's and Beach's homes. If the tables were made in Jamaica, then it is also plausible that enslaved men, who were frequently apprenticed to skilled artisans, aided in their creation.[31]

By 1770, Ann Bennett, a wealthy widow, was able to acquire a dizzying array of highly specialised porcelain, including 12 china plates, six large china cup saucers, china mugs, a china pickle stand and pickle plates, a blue and white china tureen, two dozen shallow plates, two dozen soup plates, five 'scallop oyster china shells', six cups and saucers made of 'dragon china', a large china bowl, china coffee cups and a china sauce boat. While Bennett bought separate dishes for pickles, soups, sauces and coffee, much of her china was dedicated to tea drinking. She owned a 'complete set' of red and white 'tea table china' and stored her tea in a mahogany tea chest. Using the tea chest, a bespoke piece of furniture, women such as Bennett treated tea as a uniquely special and precious good that required specific and careful handling. Women stored coffee in cannisters and kept grinding stones for cocoa in their kitchens. Tea was the only beverage to be kept in a treasure chest made specifically for its preservation. Bennett relied upon the labour of an enslaved woman, Lucy, to maintain this massive assortment of tableware.[32]

Bennett's enthusiasm for such a bewildering collection of porcelain may have marked her as the type of frivolous female consumer lampooned by satirists and critics. There, chinoiserie was denigrated for embodying feminine fragility, superficiality and vanity. Yet scholars have increasingly recognised chinoiserie as a unique and important cultural trend. Porcelain decorated in Chinese and pseudo-Chinese styles invoked imperial power, antiquity and sophistication, thereby combining legitimate art with fashion and offering consumers an alternative to the restrained and masculinised aesthetics of neoclassicism.[33]

The Caribbean stood at the centre, not on the periphery, of global trade. The diverse constellation of territories claimed by European imperial regimes connected Atlantic and Pacific trade routes. This geographic position afforded inhabitants ready access to a variety of Asian and South Asian goods. While brief inventories offer few clues about how Chinese- and European-made porcelain transited to the Caribbean, the Martin Papers reveal the existence of complex trading networks made up of family, friends and business associates. Samuel Martin, as we have seen, pled with his children to send him tea. His son, Samuel Junior, responded to his requests. He recorded multiple purchases of tea from Daniel Twining, Britain's tea innovator, for his father in his receipt book, paying 18 shillings for a pound of Twining's 'best Hyson' in August 1752, and buying three pounds of Hyson and two pounds of 'plain' green tea 'for the use of my father' in 1753, and again in 1754. Samuel Junior's purchases of chinoiserie objects including 'small figures of Vauxhall China' from an early local porcelain producer, a Mr Crispe of Bow Church yard, and a set of 'blueish color' cups and saucers for a woman named Dame Levitt from the china man's shop on the Strand, offer clues about where colonists obtained their porcelain.[34] Josiah Martin, who was estranged from his elder brother Samuel's branch of the family, purchased tea and china on credit from London merchants, rather than relatives.

Relying on a combination of kin, business partners and members who occupied both roles, elite colonists such as the Martins obtained Chinese tea and porcelain through legal channels. On paper, at least, they bought items that had been shipped to Britain by the East India Company and then had them transported to Antigua and New York. Yet the Martins, who commanded considerable fortunes and maintained strong ties to London, are not necessarily representative of middling consumers. The Caribbean was a hotbed for illicit trade well into the eighteenth century. Colonists who were well versed in the arts of smuggling, privateering and even piracy undoubtedly sought out desirable imports via legal and extra-legal means.

If trade from Britain to the islands was slow and expensive, they may have turned to other outlets. Much to the chagrin of South Sea Company employees, Jamaica's colonists engaged in a buoyant contraband trade with Spanish territories. Scholars have exposed the scale of human trafficking conducted by British slavers, who used Jamaica as a base for trans-shipping African captives to Spanish customers. Little attention has been paid, however, to the illegal flow of objects between these imperial regimes. It is plausible that Jamaica's consumers bypassed Atlantic trading routes altogether, opting instead to obtain Asian wares from Spanish merchants who travelled on Pacific routes to America. One of a constellation of small islands under French, Dutch and Danish control, Antigua's inhabitants were close to European territories that allowed free trade. Indeed, Samuel Martin complained about 'illicit trade' and 'clandestine trade' between 'foreigners' in the Caribbean and British colonies in North America, underscoring the rampancy of smuggling that his neighbours undoubtedly participated in.[35]

Furnishings and clothing hint at these complex and overlapping trade routes, which were circular and dynamic rather than one-directional. Some items travelled along officially sanctioned paths from East to West, with Britain serving as the trans-shipment point.

Other objects traversed circum-Caribbean routes that were often in violation of imperial rules and thus intentionally hidden. Women in Jamaica collected an array of objects that appraisers categorised as Spanish. The inventory sample contains 25 references to 'Spanish chests', 'Spanish chairs', 'Spanish mats' and 'Spanish jars' identified in Jamaican households. Whether the descriptor referred to the origin of manufacture (either Spain or a Spanish colony), an aesthetic style or a combination of both, these artefacts materialise otherwise invisible and likely illicit commerce. In their usage of Spanish chests, mats and jars to decorate households, women embraced local connections and objects, eliding or ignoring imperial restrictions and military rivalries. These artefacts ensured the continuance of Spanish cultural influence on the island long after Britain's seizure of the territory in 1655, just as colonists preserved the Spanish buildings and layout of Jamaica's capital: Spanish Town.[36] These regional influences lent a distinctive quality to material culture on the islands, distinguishing colonial spaces from British exteriors and interiors.[37]

Living on islands that frequently changed hands and in a theatre of nearly constant inter-imperial warfare, inhabitants amassed an assortment of artefacts from a variety of vendors. Women's households in Jamaica reflected the hybridity of the Caribbean. They integrated Spanish chests and chairs with homeware and textiles from India. Though the term 'India' was only used to describe ten items, 54 references to cotton, calico, muslin and chintz reveal a much wider dispersal of Indian manufactures on the island. When Rachel Beach's household was inventoried in 1741, for instance, her appraiser found an assortment of Indian textiles, including muslin towelettes, nine chintz gowns, a calico wrapper and a muslin hood.[38] Appraisers found both calico and material they labelled as 'Indian calico' in the home of merchant Dorothy Matson. These lightweight and colourful cottons were both fashionable and practical, ideally suited for tropical humidity. Inventories also show a growing material literacy among appraisers, who displayed expertise in Eastern wares through their differentiation between Indian textiles.[39]

Overall, Caribbean consumers exhibited a strong appetite for goods and the rituals associated with the East Indies – a confused amalgam of China and India. They draped their bodies and homes in South Asian cottons and mixed a variety of objects associated with the East that may have been made locally, in Europe or in Asia. Anna Lewis combined a tea table, kettle stand, copper tea kettle, tea equipage and a parcel of old chinaware with a cane-bottom couch and calico counterpane. Elizabeth Cadogan decorated her domicile with '12 printed pictures in frames and glasses' from India and six larger ones that were listed as 'India factorys'. The additional details about Cadogan's artwork suggest that the prints were either commissioned by the East India Company in India or, more likely, the kind of wallpaper that was trans-shipped from China to company factories in India and then sold in Britain.[40] These prints were customised to appeal to Western taste, just as the motifs on porcelain and textiles were adapted for European consumers. Like Cadogan, several other women exhibited 'India prints' on their walls. Mary Skipp owned India prints, as did Rachel Beach, who hung six 'large Indian pictures' in her home. Some underscored the cultural and financial value of this artwork by having it framed in protective glass.

Tropical libraries

Displaying globally sourced goods in their homes, women such as Skipp and Beach affirmed their material sophistication. In addition to collecting Eastern objects, they exhibited their erudition by participating in an Anglo-Atlantic world of letters. More than 30 per cent of the female householders in the sample of Jamaica inventories owned books. The tropical climate was harsh on ephemeral texts, just as it was on tea. Few copies of volumes owned by the island's inhabitants have survived. No known libraries remain intact. When appraisers inventoried women's estates, they recognised the material decay wrought by humidity, heat and insects on paper. Most collections, classified in a distinctive category for books, were described as parcels of old books that were rarely worth much from a monetary perspective. The dearth of surviving texts amplifies the significance of references to books and book titles in inventories and letters, offering rare glimpses of the literary tastes of Caribbean women.

Female colonists exhibited intellectually capacious interests, importing, collecting and borrowing works on law, politics, religion and travel. Some women owned only a Bible or prayer book, but the majority acquired more varied texts and several women owned between ten and 30 books. Rachel Beach amassed a small library of 27 books. Widow Mary Hutchinson, who died in 1740, was rich enough to maintain a 'parcel of good reading books' in her bureau, including 'the laws of Jamaica'.[41] It is possible that Hutchinson had inherited this text from her deceased husband, but it is equally likely that she herself acquired it. As I discuss in my book *Jamaica Ladies: Female slaveholders and the creation of Britain's Atlantic empire,* free and freed women displayed an impressive degree of legal savvy in a variety of contexts, from the courtroom to last wills and testaments. And, whether she or her husband purchased the tract, Hutchinson could have read it herself. The inventory of Hutchinson's estate offers important evidence of the diffusion of legal knowledge in the colony. More broadly, the prevalence of books among women's possessions reveals their participation in an Atlantic world of letters that typically focuses on North America and excludes the Caribbean. Elizabeth Cadogan left behind a two-volume set of *The History of England* by French Whig writer Paul de Rapin when she died in 1750, highlighting her interest in politics.[42]

While inventories offer evidence of women in Jamaica owning books outright, female colonists obtained literature in more informal ways. Josiah Martin's first wife, Mary Martin, for instance, borrowed books from her father-in-law and brother-in-law who lived in Antigua, including a text entitled 'Frirers Voyages' and several volumes of the 'Atalans'. Far from an armchair explorer, Mary herself engaged in overseas travel. When she and Josiah moved temporarily to New York in 1731, Mary carried these books with her.[43] Recognising the value of these texts to his family and perhaps responding to a request for their return, Josiah Martin explained to his mother that his wife had simply forgotten to return the books to her male kin before their departure from the island. He promised that they would be returned. Scholars have neglected the subject of education, especially female education, in the eighteenth-century Caribbean.[44] Shreds of evidence gleaned from inventories and correspondence, however, disclose a high level of interest among female inhabitants in buying and borrowing books. Through their engagement in Anglo-Atlantic reading and writing practices, free and freed women mastered another key element of genteel refinement.

Rum punch sociability

Caribbean consumers did much more than emulate British cultural and intellectual trends. They brought enslaved people of African descent and objects made in the region, in Europe and in Asia into their households, creating hybridised spaces of captivity and material efflorescence. The prominence of rum punch bowls in the homes of women in Jamaica offers tangible evidence of local improvisations. When Martha Rose, a Kingston widow, died in 1770, she had compiled 16 teaspoons, sugar tongs, a tea strainer and an 'old tea chest'. She also kept a punch ladle, a 'china punch bowl' and an 'old rum case with 8 bottles'.[45] Rose kept a mahogany tea table and a small tea table in her home, suggesting that she arranged large gatherings as well as more intimate meetings. Rose likely offered both rum and tea to her guests since a 'china punch bowl' would be unnecessary for individual drinking. In doing so, she contributed to a specifically Caribbean form of domestic hospitality.

Samuel Martin offered a more descriptive account of his understanding of hospitality, which he presented as a duty and a pleasure. Martin portrayed himself as a consummate host. While he claimed to prefer sober Chinese tea, he regularly imported expensive European wine for the men and women he entertained, writing in one letter, 'I love to please my friends, as well as strangers who happen to come here, whom I think it a duty to treat with all hospitality, tho' that virtue is quite out of fashion'.[46] For Martin, hospitality meant offering all his visitors costly wine, though he asked his son to buy cheaper 'Rhinish' wine to 'treat' the 'ladies', suggesting their inferior palates or their taste for sweeter white wines.[47] Martin's elite status and wealth enabled his importation of European wine.[48] Women's inventories indicate that this alcoholic beverage was either out of reach or less desirable to ordinary colonists. They were willing to spend on Chinese tea as a stimulant beverage, preferring this global import to regionally grown cocoa and coffee. But locally made rum was their alcohol of choice.

Women acquired far more rum punch wares than they did wine paraphernalia. Wine and wine-related artefacts were recorded 14 times by appraisers, whereas punch-related objects appeared 24 times. Perhaps the disparity in these items reveals different types of consumption in the home. Colonists may have served rum that was distilled locally, perhaps even on their own plantations, more frequently and for a wider variety of occasions while reserving imported wine for formal gatherings. Whatever the case, the presence of rum punch bowls in the domiciles of women in Jamaica indicates the emergence of a multifaceted form of domestic sociability that melded tea and punch drinking. This comingling of tea and rum in colonial households departed from British practice.

During the eighteenth century, the tea table and the punch bowl took on highly gendered and divergent associations. Men, women and children drank tea together in intimate domestic settings. It was socially acceptable for men to display occasional politeness, however, moving from the tea table at home to the punch bowl in the tavern without tarnishing their reputations. Women, in contrast, were confined to the tea table. They governed the ritual, brewing and serving the beverage and orchestrating the conversations that took place during its consumption. As notions of masculinity and femininity changed, women assumed responsibility for refining male behaviour through polite practices such as tea drinking. Consumed in the homosocial spaces of the tavern and the punch house, rum punch acted as a foil to Chinese tea, undoing the genteel polish of the stimulant beverage and encouraging men to become reckless, debauched and uncivilised.[49]

Differences in ritualised consumption practices, the material objects and the consumables themselves reinforced the divergent meanings of tea and rum punch. Porcelain tea sets facilitated an ancient ritual associated with an advanced civilisation. The objects encouraged a carefully choreographed event that emphasised hierarchy, with one person, normally a woman, controlling the teapot and pouring tea into individual cups. This order seemed to break down at the rum punch bowl. More communal in nature, the bowl encouraged a promiscuous, chaotic and egalitarian form of sociability where each drinker decided when to serve themselves and all participants handled the punch ladle. The punch bowl itself was an entirely novel object created to hold a new beverage. Simultaneously durable and delicate, sometimes covered in irreverent chinoiserie motifs, it merged Chinese manufacturing technology with Caribbean plantation slavery.[50] In contrast to ageless tea, rum punch was also a hybrid product, made from rum and sugar cultivated and distilled by enslaved people in America and combined with citrus fruits that originated in Asia that were then transplanted to Europe and the Caribbean. Even Chinese tea was added to this concoction, muddling East and West with old and new.

Visual media produced by British artists and critics aided in turning these consumption disparities into recognisable tropes. Two images by William Hogarth, the era's most famous satirist, showcase the dissimilar gendered meanings attached to rum punch and tea. Printed in 1733, Hogarth's *A Midnight Modern Conversation* depicts a group of inebriated, wealthy men, including a clergyman, gathered around a bowl of rum punch (Figure 4.1). Filled to the brim, with citrus peels hanging on the sides and decorated in recognisably Eastern motifs, the rum punch bowl takes centre stage. Punch consumption has caused a scene of chaos that is the opposite of modern civility. Too intoxicated to hold a polite conversation, some of the men totter on their seats, while others stumble; one has already fallen off his chair, showing where the rest will end up – on the floor. One man is setting his coat sleeve on fire instead of lighting his pipe. Coats and shirts are unbuttoned, and wigs are tilted askew or falling off completely – their slovenly appearances reflect the disarray of their minds.

The men's incapacitation renders them ridiculous. Yet, as Hogarth writes underneath the illustration, 'Think not to find one meant

Figure 4.1 *A Midnight Modern Conversation* by William Hogarth, c. 1733. Public domain image available from the Metropolitan Museum of Art at https://images.metmuseum.org/CRDImages/dp/original/DP827009.jpg.

resemblance there, we lash the vices but the persons spare'. Hogarth critiques his viewers, as much as the subjects of the illustration, for blaming consumables such as tobacco and rum rather than critiquing the moral failings of specific individuals. While Hogarth maintains notoriety today for his satirical prints, he was also an accomplished painter. Made in 1738, Hogarth's *The Strode Family* (Figure 4.2), commissioned by a wealthy family (William Strode, Lady Anne Cecil, Col. Strode and Dr Arthur Smyth), contrasts in genre and composition with *A Midnight Modern Conversation*. Presented in the everyday act of drinking tea, the subjects naturalise their fortune and polite refinement through the genre of the conversation piece. The male members of the Strode family are dressed in coats embroidered with gold and silver embellishments, while the tutor and the servant wear plain coats.

Tea drinking is central to the family's claim to taste and gentility. Hogarth captures the ritual of the tea table, freezing a male servant in the act of pouring heated water from a silver tea kettle into a blue and white porcelain teapot to steep. Clad in striking red breeches, Strode asserts his virility and patriarchal authority, resting his elbow on his wife's chair and gripping a phallic gold-tipped cane. It is Lady Cecil, however, the sole woman in the portrait, who captures the viewer's attention.

Figure 4.2 *The Strode Family* by William Hogarth, *c.* 1738. Courtesy of the National Gallery and available at https://commons.wikimedia.org/wiki/File:William_Hogarth_(1697-1764)_-_The_Strode_Family_-_N01153_-_National_Gallery.jpg.

Clothed in lustrous pink silk garnished with lace, her dress shimmers. Cecil's figure merges with the spotless white tablecloth, signifying her unblemished character and sexual virtue. The men, outfitted in darker colours, contrast with Cecil and fade into the brown background. Most strongly associated with the tea service, Lady Cecil claims authority over the ritual. The porcelain teapot is placed nearest to her, suggesting that she will pour it for the male guests after it finishes steeping. A mahogany tea chest rests near her feet. Holding a dainty porcelain saucer and teacup, Cecil is also the only one who is depicted drinking tea.

Of course, the Strodes and other wealthy families paid artists such as Hogarth to devise idealised versions of their polite respectability. Nevertheless, the immense popularity of Hogarth's work aided in coding novel objects such as the tea table and the rum punch bowl with deeply gendered moral meanings. When Abraham James's satirical print

Segar Smoking Society in Jamaica (1802) was published decades later, the symbols would have been obvious to viewers fed on a diet of Hogarthian caricatures (Figure 4.3). The crudely drawn illustration depicts a gathering of drunken people around a table littered with large decanters of wine and gargantuan wine goblets. The hurricane lamps, plates of citrus fruits and pineapples on the table belie its tropical location. The figures in the image are portrayed in a state of disarray. Aside from two of the people who have their legs up on the table, most are seated with their backs to it and facing the walls of the house, with their legs splayed out and resting on its exterior. This is not a scene of polite conversation. They are all too busy smoking cigars to talk to each other.

Segar Smoking Society in Jamaica draws upon the conventions established in earlier prints such as *A Midnight Conversation* with one major difference: it includes women. Viewers raised on a diet of Hogarthian visual cues would have immediately recognised the mixed-gender nature of the scene of drunken revelry as a violation of the gendered norms that governed British sociability. While the public might have snickered at military officials adopting ridiculous and unrespectable poses, scenes of young and even old women with their legs open in an era when people did not wear underwear had stronger implications. Airing their nether regions in the tropical climate, the women signalled to the men, and the viewers, their sexual availability.[51] Colonists forsook

Figure 4.3 *Segar Smoking Society in Jamaica* by Abraham James, c. 1802. Reproduced courtesy Lewis Walpole Library, 802.11.12.01+.

the tea table for the pleasures of wine and punch, turning domestic spaces into dens of inequity. Wives and mothers acted as bawds who tempted British military officers into excessive consumer and sexual behaviour. Cast as both masculine and sexually alluring, these women epitomised West Indian degeneracy, excess and brutality, underscoring their incompatibility with polite codes of conduct.

Conclusions

Segar Smoking Society in Jamaica does capture certain differences between British and Caribbean sociability. Colonists responded to the geographic, environmental and social realities of the region. They built houses where the boundary between indoor and outdoor spaces was more porous. They drank locally made rum in social gatherings. Consuming this beverage did not diminish a woman's respectability. On the contrary, the presence of punch bowls and punch ladles in women's homes indicates that hosts were expected to offer and partake of punch. But James's illustration also effaces key elements of Caribbean material culture that connected the region to the wider Anglo-Atlantic World.

As the Martin letters and the probated inventories show, colonists painstakingly imported, served and showcased a range of objects and consumables that manifested cosmopolitan taste. West Indian subjects successfully embraced props and practices of polite sociability. They also used material artefacts to reinforce the boundaries between slavery and freedom. It is no coincidence that the sole enslaved person in James's illustration, standing and holding a huge empty wine glass, is depicted as shirtless, wearing only a pair of white trousers. James's illustration may have been more oblique than the media generated by British antislavery activists, but its messaging was not trivial. Published during the Haitian Revolution, *Segar Smoking Society in Jamaica* aided in portraying the Caribbean as a foreign space of gendered and racialised disorder. Thus, all the blame for the brutality and violence of slavery could be displaced from Britons themselves.

Over time, these tropes have come to dominate our perception of Caribbean colonists. It is difficult for modern readers to perceive of violent enslavers as cosmopolitan consumers and adept performers of politeness. Contemporaries did not experience this conceptual challenge, however. Subjects living throughout the empire accepted the commodified legal status of enslaved people while unquestioningly enjoying the direct and indirect benefits of their labour.[52] West Indians were not treated as social outcasts. On the contrary, they manoeuvred in the upper echelons of British society, wielding immense fortunes and considerable political influence in the capital and overseas. In the eighteenth century, consumption, trade, slavery and sociability went hand in hand.

Notes

1. British Library, Samuel Martin Senior to Samuel Martin Junior, 4 August 1753, Add. MS 41346, vol. 1. For further information about Samuel Martin see Zacek, '"Banes of society"'; Samuel Martin, *Oxford Dictionary of National Biography*, Oxford, 2004. Accessed 20 May 2022. https://doi-org.libproxy1.nus.edu.sg/10.1093/ref:odnb/64973.
2. British Library, Samuel Martin Senior to Samuel Martin Junior, 8 December 1753, Add. MS 41346, vol. 1.
3. British Library, Samuel Martin Senior to Samuel Martin Junior, 25 May 1754, Add. MS 41346, vol. 1.
4. British Library, Samuel Martin Senior to Samuel Martin Junior, 30 November 1752, Add. MS 41346, vol. 1.
5. British Library, Samuel Martin Senior to Samuel Martin Junior, 7 June 1753, Add. MS 41346, vol. 1.
6. A small but growing body of scholarship has been produced that examines the material lives of free and enslaved inhabitants in the colonial Caribbean. Titles include Burnard, 'Tropical hospitality'; DuPlessis, 'What did slaves wear?'; DuPlessis, *The Material Atlantic*; Zacek and Brown, 'Unsettled houses'; Petley, 'Plantations and homes'; Mann, 'Becoming Creole'; Burton, *Afro-Creole*.
7. See, for instance, Holcomb, 'Blood-stained sugar'; Katz-Hyman, 'Doing good while doing well'.
8. This chapter uses a sample of 179 probated inventories of women's estates that I recorded while conducting research for my book *Jamacia Ladies*. However, I was unable to use this evidence in the book. The inventories I use here were recorded between 1674 and 1770 and they are held in the Jamaica Archives. I transcribed inventories for the following years: 1674, 1675, 1676, 1677, 1678, 1684, 1685, 1686, 1700, 1701, 1702, 1703, 1704, 1705, 1716, 1717, 1718, 1719, 1720, 1721, 1731, 1732, 1733, 1734, 1740, 1741, 1749, 1750, 1760, 1769, 1770. Trevor Burnard has compiled a database of more than 10,000 Jamaican inventories but it does not record detailed descriptions of objects. Burnard's database has been integrated into the Centre for the Study of the Legacies of British Slavery database. Accessed 10 August 2022. https://www.ucl.ac.uk/lbs/search/.
9. Riello, '"Things seen and unseen"'.
10. Riello, '"Things seen and unseen"'.
11. Jamaica Archives, probated inventory of Sarah Golding (1741), Jamaica Inventories, vol. 21, fol. 80.
12. Jamaica Archives, probated inventory of Elizabeth Bishop (1740), Jamaica Inventories, vol. 29, fol. 28.
13. Zacek, '"Banes of society"', 117.
14. For more on the manufacture, circulation and cultural significance of silk in the Atlantic World see Anishanslin, *Portrait of a Woman in Silk*; Marsh, *Unravelled Dreams*.
15. The parents left their daughter Elizabeth Martin in Antigua. Mary then gave birth to another child during their first stay in New York. British Library, Josiah Martin to William Gerrish, 25 June 1731, Add. MS 41352.
16. British Library, Josiah Martin to William Gerrish, 25 June 1731; Josiah Martin to Stephen Bayard, 12 March 1732, Add. MS 41352.
17. British Library, Josiah Martin to Charles MacNeily, 30 July 1730, Add. MS 41352. For more on the meaning of the livery in Britain see Styles, *The Dress of the People*.
18. British Library, Josiah Martin to Slingsby Bothel, 11 August 1729, Add. MS 41352.
19. British Library, Josiah Martin to William Gerrish, 3 November 1730, Add. MS 41352.

20 For more on enslaved seamstresses in the francophone Atlantic see Weaver, 'Fashioning freedom'.
21 Scholarship on the growth of British involvement in the tea trade is considerable. See Chaudhuri, *The Trading World of Asia*; Macfarlane and Macfarlane, *Green Gold*; Lawson, *A Taste for Empire and Glory*; Smith, 'Complications of the commonplace'; Forrest, *Tea for the British*; Norwood, *Trading Freedom*. This body of work does not investigate trade between China and the Caribbean, however.
22 Weatherhill, *Consumer Behaviour*; Dean et al., *Production and Consumption*; Sear and Sneath, *Origins of the Consumer Revolution*.
23 For more on the rise of coffee and chocolate consumption in the early modern era see Norton, 'Tasting empire'; Cowan, *Social Life of Coffee*; Pincus, '"Coffee politicians does create"'.
24 By the 1730s and 1740s, colonists increasingly distinguished between porcelain and cheaper, cruder European earthenware in Jamaican probated inventories.
25 There are 38 references to china in the sample of 179 probated inventories. Jamaica Archives, Jamaica Inventories.
26 Jamaica Archives, probated inventory of Mary Hutchinson (1740), Jamaica Inventories, vol. 21, fol. 42.
27 Jamaica Archives, probated inventory of Elizabeth Cadogan (1750), Jamaica Inventories, vol. 29, fol. 127.
28 Jamaica Archives, probated inventory of Dorothy Matson (1734), Jamaica Inventories, vol. 16, fol. 135.
29 Jamaica Archives, probated inventory of Rachel Beach (1741), Jamaica Inventories, vol. 21, fol. 203.
30 Maxine Berg observes that Britons imported the goods but not the technologies for manufacturing them from Asia. Rather, they developed alternative techniques for making items such as porcelain and developed a variety of novel objects that facilitated tea consumption. Berg, 'In pursuit of luxury'.
31 See Anderson, *Mahogany*.
32 Jamaica Archives, probated inventory of Ann Bennett (1770), Jamaica Inventories, vol. 50, fol. 162.
33 Alayrac-Fielding uses the term 'pseudo-Chinese'. Alayrac-Fielding, '"Frailty thy name is china"', 660–3. See also Porter, 'Monstrous beauty', 398–401.
34 British Library, Receipt-book of Samuel Martin Junior, entries for 21 August 1752; 24 March 1753; 7 July 1754; 3 May 1755, Add. MS 41358, vol. 13.
35 British Library, Samuel Martin Senior to Samuel Martin Junior, 22 August 1751; 15 September 1752, Add. MS 41346, vol. 1.
36 The sample of probated inventories includes 25 references to 'Spanish' items. For more on the contraband trade between British and Spanish territories in the Caribbean see Finucane, *Temptations of Trade*; Palmer, *Human Cargoes*; O'Malley, *Final Passages*.
37 For more on domestic material culture in Britain see Weatherhill, *Consumer Behaviour*; Dean et al., *Production and Consumption*; Sear and Sneath, *Origins of the Consumer Revolution*.
38 Jamaica Archives, probated inventory of Rachel Beach (1741), Jamaica Inventories, vol. 21, fol. 203.
39 Serena Dyer uses the term material literacy in Dyer, *Material Lives*.
40 For more on Chinese wallpaper see Clifford, 'Chinese wallpaper'; Bruijn, *Chinese Wallpaper in Britain and Ireland*. Madeline Dobie discusses the influence of Indian designs on French furniture. See Dobie, 'Orientalism, colonialism and furniture'.
41 Jamaica Archives, probated inventory of Mary Hutchinson (1740), Jamaica Inventories, vol. 21, fol. 42.
42 Jamaica Archives, probated inventory of Elizabeth Cadogan (1750), Jamaica Inventories, vol. 29, fol. 127.
43 Josiah Martin to Lydia Byam, 22 November 1731, Add. MS 41352.
44 Kamau Brathwaite offers a short overview of boys' schools in eighteenth-century Jamaica. See Brathwaite, *Development of Creole Society*, 268–77.
45 Jamaica Archives, probated inventory of Martha Rose (1770), Jamaica Inventories, vol. 50, fol. 159.
46 British Library, Samuel Martin Senior to Samuel Martin Junior, 20 February 1754, Add. MS 41346, vol. 1.

47 British Library, Samuel Martin Senior to Samuel Martin Junior, 31 August 1753, Add. MS 41346, vol. 1.
48 For a comprehensive study of wine-drinking culture in the eighteenth century, see Hancock, *Oceans of Wine*.
49 For more on rum drinking and tavern culture see Harvey, 'Barbarity in a teacup?'; Thompson, *Rum, Punch and Revolution*; Goodall, 'Tippling houses'.
50 Porter, 'Monstrous beauty', 403.
51 Kay Dian Kriz offers a detailed analysis of satirical illustrations of Jamaica. See Kriz, *Slavery, Sugar, and the Culture of Refinement*.
52 See Wilson, *Bonds of Empire*.

Bibliography

Alayrac-Fielding, Vanessa. '"Frailty thy name is china": women, chinoiserie and the treatment of low culture in eighteenth-century England', *Women's History Review* 18, no. 4 (2009): 660–3.
Anderson, Jennifer. *Mahogany: The costs of luxury in early America*. Cambridge: Cambridge University Press, 2015.
Anishanslin, Zara. *Portrait of a Woman in Silk: Hidden histories of the British Atlantic world*. New Haven: Yale University Press, 2016.
Berg, Maxine. 'In pursuit of luxury: global history and British consumer goods in the eighteenth century', *Past and Present* 182 (2004): 85–142.
Brathwaite, Kamau. *The Development of Creole Society in Jamaica, 1770–1820*. Kingston: Ian Randle Publishers, 2005.
de Bruijn, Emile. *Chinese Wallpaper in Britain and Ireland*. London: Philip Wilson Publishers, 2019.
Burnard, Trevor. 'Tropical hospitality, British masculinity, and drink in late eighteenth-century Jamaica', *The Historical Journal* 65, no. 1 (2022): 202–23.
Burton, Richard. *Afro-Creole: Power, opposition, and play in the Caribbean*. Ithaca, NY: Cornell University Press, 1997.
Chaudhuri, K.N. *The Trading World of Asia and the English East India Company: 1660–1760*. Cambridge: Cambridge University Press, 2006.
Clifford, Helen. 'Chinese wallpaper: from Canton to country house'. In *The East India Company at Home, 1757–1857*, edited by Margot Finn and Kate Smith, 39–67. London: UCL Press, 2018.
Cowan, Bryan. *The Social Life of Coffee: The emergence of the British coffeehouse*. New Haven: Yale University Press, 2005.
Dean, Darron, Andrew Hann, Mark Overton and Jane Whittle, eds. *Production and Consumption in English Households 1600–1750*. London and New York: Routledge, 2012.
Dobie, Madeline. 'Orientalism, colonialism and furniture in eighteenth-century France'. In *Furnishing the Eighteenth Century: What furniture can tell us about the European and American past*, edited by Dena Goodman and Kathryn Norberg, 13–36. London and New York: Routledge, 2010.
DuPlessis, Robert. 'What did slaves wear? Textile regimes in the French Caribbean', *Monde(s)* 1, no. 1 (2012): 175–91.
DuPlessis, Robert. *The Material Atlantic: Clothing, commerce, and colonization in the Atlantic world, 1650–1800*. New York: Cambridge: Cambridge University Press, 2015.
Dyer, Serena. *Material Lives: Women makers and consumer culture in the 18th century*. London: Bloomsbury, 2021.
Finucane, Adrian. *The Temptations of Trade: Britain, Spain, and the struggle for empire*. Philadelphia: University of Pennsylvania Press, 2016.
Forrest, Denys Mostyn. *Tea for the British: The social and economic history of a famous trade*. London: Chatto and Windus, 1973.
Goodall, Jamie. 'Tippling houses, rum shops, and taverns: how alcohol fuelled informal commercial networks and knowledge exchange in the West Indies', *Journal For Maritime Research* 18, no. 2 (2016): 97–121.
Hancock, David. *Oceans of Wine: Madeira and the emergence of American trade and taste*. New Haven: Yale University Press, 2009.

Harvey, Karen. 'Barbarity in a teacup? Punch, domesticity and gender in the eighteenth century', *Journal of Design History* 21, no. 3 (2008): 205–21.

Holcomb, Julie. 'Blood-stained sugar: gender, commerce and the British slave-trade debates', *Slavery & Abolition* 35, no. 4 (2014): 611–28.

Katz-Hyman, Martha. 'Doing good while doing well: the decision to manufacture products that supported the abolition of the slave trade and slavery in Great Britain', *Slavery and Abolition* 29, no. 2 (2008): 219–31.

Kriz, Kay Dian. *Slavery, Sugar, and the Culture of Refinement*. New Haven: Yale University Press, 2008.

Lawson, Philip. *A Taste for Empire and Glory: Studies in British overseas expansion, 1660–1800*. London and New York: Routledge, 1997.

Macfarlane, Alan, and Iris Macfarlane. *Green Gold: The empire of tea*. London: Ebury Press, 2003.

Mann, Douglas. 'Becoming Creole: material life and society in eighteenth-century Kingston, Jamaica', PhD dissertation, University of Georgia, 2005.

Marsh, Ben. *Unravelled Dreams: Silk and the Atlantic world, 1500–1840*. Cambridge: Cambridge University Press, 2020.

Norton, Marcy. 'Tasting empire: chocolate and the European internalization of Mesoamerican aesthetics', *American Historical Review* 111, no. 3 (2006): 660–91.

Norwood, Dale. *Trading Freedom: How trade with China defined early America*. Chicago: University of Chicago Press, 2022.

O'Malley, Gregory. *Final Passages: The intercolonial slave trade of British America, 1619–1807*. Chapel Hill: University of North Carolina Press, 2014.

Palmer, Colin. *Human Cargoes: The British slave trade to Spanish America, 1700–1739*. Urbana: University of Illinois Press, 1981.

Petley, Christer. 'Plantations and homes: the material culture of the early nineteenth-century Jamaican elite', *Slavery & Abolition* 35, no. 3 (2014): 437–57.

Pincus, Steve. '"Coffee politicians does create": coffeehouses and Restoration political culture', *Journal of Modern History* 67, no. 4 (1995): 807–34.

Porter, David. 'Monstrous beauty: eighteenth-century fashion and the aesthetics of the Chinese taste', *Eighteenth-Century Studies* 35, no. 3 (2002): 395–411.

Riello, Giorgio. '"Things seen and unseen": the material culture of early modern inventories and their representation of domestic interiors'. In *Early Modern Things: Objects and their histories, 1500–1800*, edited by Paula Findlen, 124–50. London and New York: Routledge, 2021.

Sear, Joanne, and Ken Sneath. *The Origins of the Consumer Revolution in England: From brass pots to clocks*. London and New York: Routledge, 2020.

Smith, Woodruff. 'Complications of the commonplace: tea, sugar, and imperialism', *Journal of Interdisciplinary History* 23 (1992): 259–78.

Styles, John. *The Dress of the People: Everyday fashion in eighteenth-century England*. New Haven: Yale University Press, 2008.

Thompson, Peter. *Rum, Punch and Revolution: Taverngoing and public life in eighteenth-century Philadelphia*. Philadelphia: University of Pennsylvania Press, 1998.

Walker, Christine. *Jamaica Ladies: Female slaveholders and Britain's Atlantic empire*. Chapel Hill: University of North Carolina Press, 2020.

Weatherhill, Lorna. *Consumer Behaviour and Material Culture in Britain, 1660–1760*. London and New York: Routledge, 1996.

Weaver, Karol. 'Fashioning freedom: slave seamstresses in the Atlantic world', *Journal of Women's History* 24, no. 1 (2012): 44–59.

Wilson, Lee B. *Bonds of Empire: The English origins of slave law in South Carolina and British plantation America, 1660–1783*. New York: Cambridge University Press, 2021.

Zacek, Natalie. '"Banes of society" and "gentlemen of strong natural parts": attacking and defending West Indian Creole masculinity'. In *New Men: Manliness in early America*, edited by Thomas Foster, 116–33. New York: New York University Press, 2011.

Zacek, Natalie, and Laurence Brown. 'Unsettled houses: the material culture of the missionary project in Jamaica in the era of emancipation', *Slavery & Abolition* 35, no. 3 (2014): 493–507.

Object lessons 1
Traded goods

I
Statuette of Captain Jacob Beckmann
Mikkel Venborg Pedersen

Figure OI.I Statuette of Jacob Beckmann, *c.* 1751. National Museum of Denmark. Photo: National Museum of Denmark, Arnold Mikkelsen.

In 1732, a new Royal Chartered Danish Asiatic Company was founded. It replaced several ill-fated predecessors, but with this new company Danish trade east of the Cape was placed in secure and monopolised hands.[1] The company sent ships to both India – the colonies of Tranquebar in

Tamil and later Frederiksnagore in Bengal – and to the Danish factory, that is, the trade office, in China, located in Canton together with the other European factories. From this site at the mouth of the Pearl River, European trade was commissioned via Chinese merchants acting as brokers, a system that kept control of trade in Chinese hands.[2]

Tea, silk, furniture and porcelain from China and Japan were at the top of the list of goods requested by the company's shareholders and customers back in Copenhagen. Profits were high, especially for tea, which was traded in large quantities by Copenhagen merchants; about 80 per cent of all imported tea was re-exported, turning the capital of Denmark–Norway into a north-east European hub.[3] The Asiatic Company became the biggest civilian enterprise of the realm, and many people found their daily living in its service, either at home or at sea. The ships were by far the largest of the merchant navy, many being converted naval vessels, and the sailors received good wages, sometimes supplemented with the profits on importing goods in their own hands.

Jacob Beckmann was one man who benefited from such dealings.[4] He had begun his service with the Company as a seaman and worked his way up to become mate in 1742. It is his statuette, now in the National Museum of Denmark, which is shown here.[5] It was made in Canton by a Chinese so-called face-maker and shows Beckmann in his prime. Most likely he had it made to commemorate being made a captain in 1751–3 at the age of 33, a dating supported by his clothes with wig, coat with broad sleeves and other details pointing to a time around 1750. Missing is a long cane for the figurine's right hand.

Such an artefact combines East and West. The statuettes were very popular among the Company's officers and supercargoes, that is, the Company merchants concerned with the trade in China. A European fascination with high-quality Chinese craftsmanship was important in enabling the Chinese to do business – fulfilling the market wants of Europeans coming to Canton by applying traditional Chinese art techniques to new purposes. Europeans used such goods within their own cultural horizons: the statuettes served as markers for important events, as was most likely the case for the newly promoted Captain Beckmann, and they were kept afterwards to decorate the home and demonstrate pride in their long world journeys and good fortune in life.

After his return home in 1753, Beckmann bought a house in Copenhagen. In tax records a few years later he is mentioned as living there with his wife Christine Dorothea and six children. In 1767 he sold the house and moved to another one, where he lived till his death in 1771, aged 52 years. The cause of death was probably tuberculosis, perhaps acquired on one of his long journeys around the world; but Beckmann was one of the lucky ones. Between 1732 and 1753, the Company sent 60 ships to Tranquebar and Canton: only 43 returned home.[6] Among these was *Kongen af Danmark*, which left Copenhagen in 1751 under the command of Captain Holman. Bad weather damaged the ship and he soon had to seek port in Norway's Bergen for repairs. Shortly after emptying the ship of movables, Bergen and its warehouses burnt down, and it took half a year before the ship was re-equipped to continue its journey to China. During this voyage, Captain Holman died, and it was the first mate Jacob Beckmann who took over as captain for the journey back home. His success was proven to contemporaries and to posterity by the statuette, made in China!

Notes

1. See Chapter 6 for discussion of the Kingdom of Denmark–Norway and its colonies.
2. Asmussen, *Kinafarerne*, provides the general information on the Asiatic Company for this object lesson.
3. Venborg Pedersen, *Luksus*, 42–55.
4. Clemmensen and Mackeprang, *Kina og Danmark*, 185–8, describes the figurine and tells the tale of Jacob Beckmann.
5. National Museum No. H.233.
6. Clemmensen and Mackeprang, *Kina og Danmark*, 185.

Bibliography

Asmussen, Benjamin: *Kinafarerne. Mellem kejserens Kina og kongens København*. Copenhagen: Gads Forlag & Maritime Museum of Denmark, 2019.

Clemmensen, Tove, and Mogens B. Mackeprang. *Kina og Danmark 1600–1950. Kinafart og kinamode*. Copenhagen: National Museum of Denmark, 1980.

Venborg Pedersen, Mikkel. *Luksus. Forbrug og kolonier i Danmark i det 18. århundrede*. Copenhagen: Museum Tusculanum Press, 2013.

II
Osnaburg: a study in global textile production and exploitation
Laura Johnson

Figure OL.II Advertisements for osnaburgs in *The Pennsylvania Gazette*, 26 July 1753.

The cloth known as osnaburg or osnaburgs is named after its purported town of origin, Osnabrück, in the present-day north-west German state of Lower Saxony.[1] Also called ozenbrigs or osnabrigs, it was an inexpensive, coarse linen or hempen cloth that could be unbleached grey or brown, bleached, or dyed. In the absence of any documented examples of osnaburgs in museum collections (with the exception of a cotton fragment in the American Civil War Museum dated from 1861 to 1865), understanding of this textile is based largely on archival evidence.[2]

As early as 1655 Jacob Alrichs wrote to Amsterdam from the Dutch colony of New Amstel for 'grey Osnaburgs' as they were among the goods 'most in demand here'.[3] By the early 1700s, as a supplement to domestic American linen production, it was used for wrapping bundles and for inexpensive clothing.[4] Trader Evert Wendell offered indigenous customers osnaburg shirts in the 1730s, as did traders working for James Logan in Pennsylvania (see Chapter 8).[5] Osnaburgs appeared in colonial American merchant advertisements and in descriptions of indentured servants fleeing their contracts, often on the same page (Figure OL.II):

Elizabeth Humphreys ran away wearing her 'ozenbrigs' petticoat with a calico border in the summer of 1752, while merchant William Fisher offered 'ozenbrigs' newly imported from London.

Unrest in German lands affected supply in the 1740s, helping drive a British-made version. In 1745 Parliament passed the linen bounty to encourage domestic manufacturers in Ireland and Scotland. Scottish weavers, with the help of French cambric weavers and Dutch bleachers, began producing osnaburgs using Russian flax in imitation of German goods.[6] By 1758 osnaburg accounted for approximately one-third of total Scottish linen production.[7] Planters in the British West Indies preferred Scottish osnaburg, often dyed to help identify those who chose to self-emancipate.[8] Many Southern planters in America made the switch from German to Scottish osnaburg. In 1768 Virginian Robert Beverley ordered 1,000 ells of German osnaburg, but in 1772 he requested both British and German osnaburg. Such changes reinforce Lord Sheffield's claim that 'formerly the planters used almost entirely the German Osnaburghs for their slaves, until the bounty'.[9]

By the late eighteenth century cotton overtook linen in price and popularity, but osnaburgs remained an inexpensive, increasingly racialized, material for packing and worker's garments.[10] Often confused with so-called 'negro cloth' today, the two were distinctive, coarse textiles. In 1766 a Georgia man who self-emancipated wore 'osnaburg' breeches and a white 'negroe cloth' jacket.[11] George Washington noted that his shipment of 'Negro cloaths' had not yet arrived in 1757, so he purchased 250 yards of osnaburg from a local supplier.[12] In the 1930s, previously enslaved individuals noted that osnaburg was a coarse, heavy cotton cloth often woven on the plantation or bought once a year and used for summer clothing, while 'negro cloth' could describe a wide range of coarse goods. Mills also offered 'negro cloth' and osnaburg, marketed specifically to enslavers.[13] Osnaburg was a product of not only global commerce but also global exploitation of bodies and materials.

Notes

1 Montgomery, *Textiles in America*, 312.
2 See Knowles, 'Fashioning slavery', figs 2.1 and 2.2, fragment woven by enslaved persons from the Mitchell King plantation, Witherspoon Island, SC, object 0985.10.00085.
3 'Letter to Burgomaster De Graaff from Vice Director Alrichs September 21, 1659'.
4 Hood, *The Weaver's Craft*, 117–19.
5 Beverley cited in Baumgarten, 'Clothes for the people'; Johnson, 'Goods to clothe themselves', 115–40; Waterman and Michelson, *'To do justice to him & myself'*.

6   Collins and Ollerenshaw, 'European linen industry', 1–42.
7   Durie, 'Imitation in Scottish eighteenth-century textiles', 71.
8   Truxes, *Irish–American Trade*, 187.
9   Cited in Truxes, *Irish–American Trade*, 177–8.
10 Lemire, 'Transforming consumer custom', 187–208.
11 *Georgia Gazette*, 7 November 1766.
12 Baumgarten, 'Clothes for the people', 41.
13 Knowles, 'Fashioning slavery', 47–61; Shaw, 'Slave clothing', 75–133; Foster, 'Constructing cloth and clothing', 75–133; White and White, 'Slave clothing'.

Bibliography

Baumgarten, Linda. 'Clothes for the people: slave clothing in early Virginia', *Journal of the Museum of Southern Decorative Arts*, no. 15 (November 1988): 26–70.

Collins, Brenda, and Philip Ollerenshaw. 'The European linen industry since the Middle Ages'. In *The European Linen Industry in Historical Perspective*, edited by Brenda Collins and Philip Ollerenshaw, 1–42. Oxford: Oxford University Press, 2003.

Du Plessis, Robert S. *The Material Atlantic: Clothing, commerce, and colonization in the Atlantic World, 1650–1800*. Cambridge: Cambridge University Press, 2016.

Durie, Alastair J. 'Imitation in Scottish eighteenth-century textiles: the drive to establish the manufacture of osnaburg linen', *Journal of Design History* 6, no. 2 (1993): 71–6.

Foster, Helen Bradley. 'Constructing Cloth and Clothing in the antebellum South'. In *New Raiments of Self: African American clothing in the antebellum South*, edited by Helen Bradley Foster, 75–133. Oxford: Berg Publishers, 1997.

Hood, Adrienne D. *The Weaver's Craft: Cloth, commerce, and industry in early Pennsylvania*. Philadelphia: University of Pennsylvania Press, 2003.

Johnson, Laura E. 'Goods to clothe themselves: Native consumers and Native images on the Pennsylvania trading frontier, 1712–1760', *Winterthur Portfolio* 43, no. 1 (2009): 115–40.

Knowles, Katie. 'Fashioning slavery: slaves and clothing in the U.S. South, 1830–1865'. PhD Dissertation, Rice University, 2014.

Lemire, Beverly. 'Transforming consumer custom: linens, cottons, and the English market, 1660–1800'. In *The European Linen Industry in Historical Perspective*, edited by Brenda Collins and Philip Ollerenshaw, 187–208. Oxford: Oxford University Press, 2003.

'Letter to Burgomaster de Graaff from Vice Director Alrichs, September 21, 1659', *Documents Related to the Colonial History of New York*, volume 2. Edited by John Romeyn Brodhead, Berthold Fernow and E.B. O'Callaghan, 77. Albany, NY: Weed, Parsons and Co., 1853.

Montgomery, Florence M. *Textiles in America, 1650–1870*. New York: W. W. Norton, 2007.

Shaw, Madelyn. 'Slave clothing and clothing slaves: craftsmanship, commerce, and industry', *Journal of the Museum of Southern Decorative Arts* 33 (2012): 161–95.

Truxes, Thomas M. *Irish–American Trade, 1660–1783*. Cambridge: Cambridge University Press, 1988.

Waterman, Kees-Jan, and Gunther Michelson, eds. *'To do justice to him & myself': Evert Wendell's account book of the fur trade with Indians in Albany, New York, 1695–1726*. Philadelphia: American Philosophical Society, 2008.

White, Shane, and Graham White. 'Slave Clothing and African-American Culture in the Eighteenth and Nineteenth Centuries', *Past & Present*, no. 148 (August 1995): 149–86.

III
Suite of ebony furniture inlaid with ivory, Charlecote Park

Annabelle Gilmore and Jon Stobart

Figure OL.III Two chairs in a set of ten pieces of seat furniture, of ebony inlaid with engraved ivory, comprising an open armchair, a daybed and eight standard chairs or backstools, Visakhapatnam, India, *c.* 1690–1720. © Jon Stobart.

George Hammond Lucy was, in many ways, a man of his times: he re-edified Charlecote in the early nineteenth century in a way that underlined the Tudor credentials of the house and his family's long residence there.[1] While much of the original interior was changed and the house considerably extended, he sought to retain the feel of 'old England', engaging Thomas Willement to provide a wealth of heraldic stained glass and acquiring a range of period furniture, including a hugely impressive *pietra dura* table, said to have come from the Borghese Palace in Rome and bought at William Beckford's 1823 sale at Fonthill.

Lucy's interest in the past is epitomised by a different purchase, made 14 years later. He had just bought a Dutch marquetry cabinet from the London furniture dealer Samuel Isaacs, in a deal brokered by William Buchanan, who supplied Lucy with paintings. Buchanan then wrote with great excitement: 'But now for a chance! Which has never occurred to you in all probability and never may occur again.' Isaacs had shown him a 'set of 8 chairs, armchair couch and pair of cabinets which were made a present of by Queen Elizabeth to the Earl of Leicester, and were formerly at Kenilworth … They are massive solid ebony and richly inlaid with the tooth of sea horse [ivory].'[2] Lucy quickly bought the pieces, no doubt excited by their apparent provenance and age, especially as Queen Elizabeth had come to Charlecote when visiting Leicester at Kenilworth Castle in 1572. New needlework upholstery was designed by Willement, including the monogram ER. It was sewn by Mary Elizabeth Lucy – George Hammond's wife – so family was literally stitched into the furniture. However, the suite of furniture was not sixteenth century and not English. In fact, it was made *c.* 1690–1710 in Vizagapatam on the Coromandel Coast, India. These objects were made in an English style and may have been intended for export, like many of the products brought to Britain by the East India Company.

In the late seventeenth century, Dutch East India Company men were already noting the production of ebony chairs and furniture on the Coromandel Coast. They detail the fine quality of the craftsmanship and the movement of the items to other parts of India, China, England and the Dutch Republic.[3] Furniture from Vizagapatam was made into recognisable European shapes which relied on the work of skilled artisans and the local availability of hardwoods, in this instance ebony, although teak was also often used.[4] Local craftsmen used ivory inlay techniques to create delicate motifs and images in the dark ebony wood. This, in combination with European style shapes, produced furniture that was simultaneously recognisable while having the 'exotic' style that was desired by Europeans in India.

British country house residents whose wealth derived from imperialism presented ebony and ivory furniture as Indian rather than drawing on the erroneous and widespread belief that this sort of ebony and ivory furniture was old English; examples include Balls Park, Daylesford and Powys Castle.[5] This highlights the different networks of knowledge in Britain surrounding ebony and ivory furniture, and the diverse imperatives of different country house owners. While families with imperial connections proudly presented the furniture as Indian, people such as George Hammond Lucy, in the early nineteenth century, were more concerned with recapturing a (mythical) past and desired the supposed connection to a more local history. It is possible that Samuel Isaacs knew of the real provenance of the furniture, as Buchanan mentions that he refused to specify from which 'old mansion' they had come. In George Hammond's oversight, the imperial connection embodied in the furniture was never considered when displaying the suite. Its origin was further erased by the delicate needlework by Mary Elizabeth displacing the expressive and fine Indian craftsmanship in favour of what was imagined as a greater Tudor past for Charlecote Park.

This suite of ebony furniture was complex in its materiality and its storied nature. It was an Indian product, made of exotic materials and relying on highly skilled craftsmen in Vizagapatam, yet it was a hybrid of Indian and Western styles. More importantly, it was not acquired because of these exotic connections, but rather because it was thought to be a link to England's past and to a particular episode in the history of the country, monarch and house. This makes us (re)think the connection between provenance, knowledge, motivation and meaning. Products and symbols of empire can be present even when unintentional, a presence which underlines the extensive reach of imperialism within Britain.

Notes

1 For a fuller discussion see Wainwright, *Romantic Interior*, 215–35.
2 Warwickshire Record Office, L6/1118: letter from John Buchanan to George Hammond Lucy.
3 Jaffer, *Furniture from British India*, 132.
4 Um, 'Chairs, writing tables, and chests', 720.
5 Smith, 'Production, purchase, dispossession, recirculation', 69–70.

Bibliography

Jaffer, Amin. *Furniture from British India and Ceylon: A catalogue of the collections from the Victoria and Albert Museum and the Peabody Essex Museum*. Salem, MA: Peabody Essex Museum, 2001.

Smith, Kate. 'Production, purchase, dispossession, recirculation: Anglo-Indian ivory furniture in the British country house'. In *The East India Company at Home, 1757–1857*, edited by Margot Finn and Kate Smith, 68–87. London: UCL Press, 2018.

Um, Nancy. 'Chairs, writing tables, and chests: Indian Ocean furniture and the postures of commercial documentation in coastal Yemen', *Art History* 38, no. 4 (2015): 718–31.

Wainwright, Clive. *The Romantic Interior: The British collector at home, 1750–1850*. New Haven: Yale University Press, 2009.

IV
Newspaper advertisement for the English Depot. E. Grant & Comp., Bucharest

Nicoleta Roman

Figure OL.IV English Depot. E. Grant & Comp. advertisement in *Românul. Diariu politic, comercial, literar* [The Romanian. Political, commercial and literary journal]. © 'Carol I' Central University Library, Bucharest, Romania.

Advertisements for various commercial products started to appear in the Romanian Principalities of Wallachia and Moldova during the 1840s. This innovation was linked with the commercial openness gained by these regions through the Treaty of Adrianople (1829), which favoured a mobility of people and goods between Eastern and Western Europe, and specifically the emergence of a national press. This object lesson – an advertisement placed in a national newspaper – highlights part of Effingham Grant's (1820–92) businesses in Wallachia. As secretary to the British consul in Bucharest, his intertwined activities between politics and economy had an important impact on the development of the country. Grant imported Western and especially English goods through his newly established depot in the capital, Bucharest.

The first advertisements to appear in 1857 presented the merchandise that Grant brought over from England separately: Havana cigarettes, clothing, hunting items, English weaponry and even cement. For cloth he collaborated with factories in Belfast and for weaponry with Deane brothers in London. Grant sold a huge variety of products and gave his contact address as Bossel House on the prestigious Mogosoaiei Street, a building which comprised first-floor rooms rented to tourists and commercial space on the ground floor, occupied by Grant's business. By the end of 1857, Grant had changed strategy and began to 'institutionalise' his business, and his advertisements refer to the 'English Depot: E. Grant & Comp.'. New goods arrived (from money chests by Mordean & Co. to English pale ale to cheap soaps) and the depot became specialised in merchandise that matched the Romantic ideal of masculinity. This ideal followed the practices of the English elite and implies the development of similar tastes within the local, incipient Romanian bourgeoisie. Through its goods, the English Depot encouraged leisure activities such as hunting and the decoration of home interiors with Western items.

In an 1858 advertisement (Figure OL.IV), under the name *Magazie englezească. E. Grant & Comp. Casă de Comision și de vânzare cu ridicata și cu amănuntu(l)* [English Depot. E. Grant & Comp. Commissions House and selling house *en gros and en detail*], the Depot is promoted as having 'acquired in a short time a great name both through the specialisation of its English products and its moderate prices'. It goes on to list a range of merchandise:

Irish cotton	*Iron beds and gilded copper*
Tableware sets, damask	*Coloured paper, for the walls*
Towels	*Oilcloth*
Napkins	*Porcelains, tableware sets, white*

Tartans, shawls
Fine cutlery
Plated items, English, first quality

Papier-mâché items
Necessaires for the toilette
Leather
Harness

Decorated tableware
Tea and coffee sets
Tea and coffee sets, white
Tea and coffee sets, decorated

Powder sets
Crystals, glassware

The advertisement also announces a 'Bazaar for hunting' including rifles, carabines, revolvers and hunting knives. There is an association between this hunting paraphernalia, travel accessories and gourmet items such as Havana cigarettes, teas, wines, liquors and tins. As an encouragement, the last sentence of the advertisement specifies that the prices are fixed. This is relevant as a sign of modern retail practice, especially in a country that had just came out of the Crimean War and sought economic stability, while the elite and the bourgeoisie looked for material comforts that tied them more closely to the West.

The English Depot closed in 1865. It was no longer profitable as new shops selling Western goods appeared and the market became increasingly competitive. Effingham Grant acknowledged the fact to his brother-in-law Constantin A. Rosetti and expressed a desire to start new businesses. These included selling orchids, but more notably the establishment of a pioneering and highly successful Western style tobacco manufactory in Bucharest. Today his heritage is recognised through the preservation of his urban mansion (Golescu-Grant mansion or Belvedere), while two quarters in the capital bear his family name.

Bibliography

Bucur, Marin, ed. *C.A. Rosetti către Maria Rosetti. Corespondență*, vol 1. Bucharest: Minerva, 1988.
Crutzescu, Gheorghe. *Podul Mogoșoaei Povestea unei străzi*. Bucharest: Meridiane, 1987.
Hilton, Marjorie. 'Retailing in Russia and Eastern Europe'. In *The Routledge Companion to the History of Retailing*, edited by Jon Stobart and Vicki Howard, 396–412. London and New York: Routledge, 2019.
Roman, Nicoleta. 'Nineteenth-century magazines and consumption'. In *Luxury, Fashion and Other Political Bagatelles in Southeastern Europe, 16th–19th Centuries*, edited by Constanța Vintilă, Giulia Calvi, Mária Pakucs-Willcocks, Nicoleta Roman and Michał Wasiucionek, 69–74. Bucharest: Humanitas, 2022.
Românul. Diariu politic, comercial, literar, 1857–1864.

V
Histoire des deux Indes by Guillaume Raynal, 1780

Eleanor Matthews

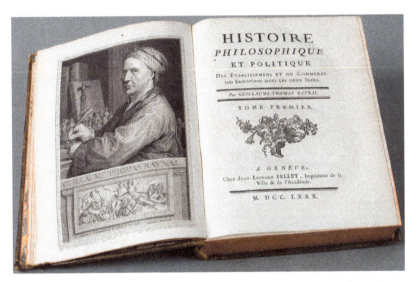

Figure OL.V Guillaume Raynal, *Histoire des deux Indes* (1780), Brodsworth Hall, UK. EH Inventory No. 90013671 © English Heritage Trust. Originally published anonymously, Raynal announced authorship of the work in the 1780 edition, accompanied by his engraved portrait opposite the title page.

The relatively compact library of Brodsworth Hall contains over six hundred volumes bearing the bookplate 'Mr Thellusson', understood to be merchant banker and financier Peter Thellusson (1735–97), who purchased the Brodsworth estate in South Yorkshire in 1791.[1] Within Thellusson's collection is a five-volume set of *Histoire Philosophique et Politique des Établissemens et du Commerce des Européens dans les deux Indes* by Guillaume Thomas François Raynal (1731–96).

Translated into multiple languages and capturing attention across Europe, Raynal's influential text – commonly known as *Histoire des deux Indes* – was first published in 1770 and explores the history of European settlement, commerce and trade in the Caribbean, South-East Asia and the Americas. Produced in collaboration with other writers including Denis Diderot, it is viewed as a key Enlightenment text which draws directly upon the work and contributions of others.[2] By the time Thellusson's copy was printed in Geneva (1780), the book had gone through multiple editions in France and in other countries, and an English translation was published in 1783. Raynal's works were among the first to consider European colonisation, often critically. *Histoire des deux Indes* discusses enslavement and the transatlantic slave trade: while it condemns enslavement and criticises seizing land, it also considers the slave trade to be essential for economic progress. Such inconsistencies are thought to arise from its multiple authors and Raynal's own varied religious, literary and political career.[3]

Owned by Thellusson at a time when he already had large investments in the Caribbean, the book would have been of great interest, combining practical information with philosophical reflection. Born in Paris of Huguenot descent, living in England and marrying an English woman, and with business interests in Europe, the Caribbean and the East Indies, Peter Thellusson's own life mirrors the geographical scope and reach of his near-contemporary Raynal's publication. Taken in the context of his own global connections, Thellusson's ownership of this book enables us to appreciate its global reach. Thellusson amassed a considerable fortune through his financial dealings, a substantial part of which was derived from his involvement with the transatlantic slave economy. This included, amongst other activities, lending money to plantation owners, insuring and owning slaving ships, and involvement in the production and trading of raw materials and goods used in the slave trade.[4] Raynal's book usefully illustrates the immense amount of European trade with the West Indies, in enslaved people as well as in produce such as textiles, pigments, exotic hardwoods and sugar. *Histoire des deux Indes* is itself a traded object: Raynal used his own and others' ideas and words to create a product bought and sold throughout Europe.

Thellusson's main residence was Plaistow Lodge on the outskirts of London, but following his retirement he spent increasing amounts of time at Brodsworth and requested to be buried in the local church.[5] It has been suggested that the act of purchasing the Brodsworth estate reflected his ambitions to create a dynastic residence for his descendants.[6] Thellusson's desire for permanence contrasts with Raynal's life experience, with the latter being exiled in 1781 with his publication deemed radical and subsequently banned. Raynal was later allowed to return to France in 1790, but not to Paris. Although the carefully pasted-in bookplates of Thellusson's library indicate he certainly looked at each volume, we will never know whether he actively read the books to inform his world view, or whether their presence instead acted as a visible reflection of how Thellusson wanted to be perceived: perhaps as a global citizen who was economically successful whilst understanding the moral implications of and arguments against enslavement.

The library collection remaining at the present-day Brodsworth Hall is one of very few tangible heirlooms linked with Peter Thellusson. The presence of *Histoire des deux Indes* within it acts as a gateway through which we can share and interpret broader stories of the earlier Brodsworth Hall and its owners for modern visitors.[7] Without books such as Raynal's, the intangible connections between Peter Thellusson, the transatlantic slave trade, global economics and Brodsworth Hall might have remained hidden from public view.

Notes

1 Griffiths, 'Libraries project final report', 6.
2 See, for example, Courtney and Mander, *Raynal's* Histoire des deux Indes.
3 Thomson, 'Colonialism, race and slavery'.
4 See Seymour and Haggerty, 'Slavery connections', 19–36; Polden, *Peter Thellusson's Will*.
5 TNA PROB 11/1294, f. 574, 'The Will of Peter Thellusson dated 2nd Day of April 1796'.
6 Seymour and Haggerty, 'Slavery connections', 70–4.
7 Brodsworth's copy was displayed in the exhibition *Liberty and Lottery: Exploring the legacy of the transatlantic slave trade at Brodsworth Hall and Gardens* (September 2021–November 2022).

Bibliography

Courtney, Cecil, and Jenny Mander, eds. *Raynal's* Histoire des deux Indes: *Colonialism, networks and global exchange*. Oxford: Voltaire Foundation/Oxford University Studies in the Enlightenment, 2015.
Griffiths, David. 'Yorkshire country house partnership libraries project final report', University of York Library, 2006.
Polden, Patrick. *Peter Thellusson's Will of 1797 and Its Consequences on Chancery Law*. Lampeter: The Edwin Mellen Press, 2002.
Seymour, Susanne, and Sheryllynne Haggerty. 'Slavery connections of Brodsworth Hall (1600–c.1830): Final report for English Heritage', 2010. https://www.english-heritage.org.uk/learn/research/slavery/.
Thomson, Ann. 'Colonialism, race and slavery in Raynal's *Histoire des deux Indes*', *Global Intellectual History* 2, no. 3 (2017): 251–67.

Part 2
The global in the local

5
Power, friendship and delightfulness: global goods in the residences of an aristocratic family in the Kingdom of Naples

Gaia Bruno

On 9 October 1760, Empress Maria Teresa of Austria wrote to Duchess Margherita Pignatelli: 'I really appreciate your kind expressions, demonstrating a clear proof of your feelings for me, as for the present [you sent me]: I am much obliged to you, assuring you that I always keep it in mind'.[1] Friendship between the two women was regularly marked through the exchange of gifts, as we understand by another letter sent on 1 April 1772: 'the expressions with which you manifest your satisfaction with the porcelain I sent you correspond to your feelings that I know very well'.[2] Even if written in an archaic and quite uncertain Italian, these two letters reflect the personal link that connected Margherita Pignatelli with the Austrian court – royal connections which characterised all the main members of the Pignatelli di Monteleone in the eighteenth century. The Pignatelli possessed feudal estates in the Kingdom of Naples and also in the Kingdom of Sicily. In addition, this side of the family descended from the famous Hernán Cortés, a circumstance that made them owners of lands in the Mexican Oaxaca valley.[3] Their deep entanglement in the political web of the times, as well as the vast size of their possessions, makes them an ideal case study to analyse the diffusion of global goods into the houses of the eighteenth-century Neapolitan aristocracy.

The presence of global goods in the houses of the English upper classes has been read as material evidence of their participation in colonialism and empire.[4] But here the question is: are we able to apply this model to a rather different context – the Neapolitan one? Does the presence of similar global goods imply the same engagement with colonial power? The question is important because the diffusion of global goods into high-ranking estates is well documented by Neapolitan inventories, yet the Kingdom of Naples and its aristocracy did not directly participate in the colonial expansion of European countries in the Far East or the Americas. Thus, one key question is: why do we find such goods in Neapolitan aristocratic houses and what was their actual meaning?

Another issue concerns the importance of the different houses. Although most British aristocratic families had large London houses which contained many of their most treasured artistic possessions, Stobart points to the importance of the country house in the life of the English upper classes. The great house in the countryside was a sort of headquarters from which landowners controlled their estates and where they concentrated a great deal of resources, with the aim of materialising their wealth and power.[5] In contrast, as Labrot has shown, the Neapolitan aristocracy lived a more itinerant life, moving between three houses at least: one in the capital, one on the feudal estate and another in the countryside near Vesuvius.[6] Their respective importance in the life of their owners changed according to personal taste and the political scenery of the time. Apart from some dissident voices,[7] Italian historians of the eighteenth century agree in attributing the main importance to the house in Naples;[8] but this does not mean the country houses were insignificant. The location of global goods should be taken into consideration as an additional factor to understand the relative importance of the different houses in the Neapolitan aristocratic context. Indeed, thanks to their high value, they were central to the materialisation of power.

These questions are all related to the main aim of this chapter, which is to understand the meaning of global goods in Neapolitan aristocratic houses. To do so I use probate inventories from the private archive of the Pignatelli, drawn up in the 1740s and 1750s and today stored in the Naples State Archive. They refer to the family's three most important houses in the Kingdom of Naples, without considering those in the Kingdom of Sicily. Two of the documents are about the family's goods in their palace in Naples, another two list goods at the feudal castle of Monteleone in the province of Calabria Ultra, and the final two are about their villa near the capital, in a place called Barra.[9]

As Jules Prown has shown, in order to understand fully the features of household possessions, a comparison between written documents and museum objects would be ideal.[10] In this specific case a collection of family objects still exists, but it comes from the property of the Sicilian Princess Rosa Fici di Amalfi (1869–1955), wife of Diego Pignatelli (1862–1930) and niece-in-law of the eighteenth-century members of the family mentioned in this chapter. Fewer, but nonetheless relevant, objects came from the property of her daughter, Princess Anna Maria.[11] The collection is set in the Principe Diego Aragona Pignatelli Cortes Museum in Naples, the nineteenth-century house of the family, which displays its objects to recreate interiors as lived spaces.[12] In the absence of a complete and updated catalogue, we cannot be sure whether the various examples of eighteenth-century Chinese and Japanese objects found in the museum are the same as those mentioned in the inventories. Nevertheless, these objects are an important source that can enrich the analysis of the simple written documents by giving additional information on the material features of the goods.

Based on written sources and partly also on material ones, this chapter analyses the presence of global goods in some of the main houses of the Pignatelli of Monteleone in the Kingdom of Naples during the first half of the eighteenth century. After a brief survey of the diffusion of global goods in the three houses, I focus my attention on the villa in Barra and the palace in Naples in order to identify any difference between the kinds of objects in the two houses and their respective meanings. The reference period for this analysis is the life of the Duke Diego Pignatelli Aragona Cortés (1687–1750): ninth Duke of Monteleone and Terranova, prince of Castelvetrano, Duke of Bellosguardo, prince of the Holy Roman Empire, marquis of the Oaxaca Valley, knight of the Toson d'or.[13] The other key names mentioned in the text are his father Nicolò, first viceroy of the Kingdom of Sicily, his second wife Margherita, and their son and heir Fabrizio.

The delight of exoticism

The Pignatelli needed to manage their lands and to participate in the social and political life of the courts in Madrid, Vienna, Naples and Palermo. This implies that they, like other aristocratic families, conducted an itinerant existence, moving among the residences they had in these various places, with a lifestyle that is reminiscent, in some senses, of a Renaissance court. Such a lifestyle carried two implications. The first is that objects circulated among houses with their owners. The second is that political relationships were often fundamental to the presence of global goods in the Pignatelli houses.

Let us begin with the castle. The poor road network and transport infrastructure meant that reaching the feudal lands was neither easy nor fast.[14] Living far from the capital could mean being isolated from the centre of power; for a great many families in the eighteenth century, therefore, their houses in the provinces were largely neglected, as revealed by inventories and confirmed by the existing literature.[15] If we look at the Pignatelli, their feudal castle in Monteleone (Calabria) was no exception: it contained neglected belongings and no exotic objects.[16] Landlords traditionally devoted the period of residence in their feudal possessions to the management of lands, but in the eighteenth century many visited only occasionally, preferring to delegate this activity to reliable deputies.[17] Neapolitan men of letters accused landlords of absenteeism and argued that the neglect of their lands by some aristocrats was the cause of backwardness in the southern provinces.[18] The aristocrats' physical absence from their feudal estates did not exactly coincide with the accusation, but it nevertheless shows a decreased interest in life in the countryside, while living in the urban context of the capital became increasingly important.

Overall, the importance attributed to the different kinds of houses changed with the passing of time. Accordingly, owners moved from a house to another and objects circulated with them, as is clearly shown in the case of the Pignatelli. Between December 1723 and September 1724, Duke Nicolò ordered the transfer of some goods from Naples to Monteleone, as specified in an inventory.[19] This is the last moment of enrichment of furniture for the castle. Later, the trajectory of the objects reveals a shift in the investments in the houses. The villa in Barra was the chief beneficiary: constructed between 1728 and 1766, it received pieces from all the properties belonging to the Pignatelli. Some things were transported from Monteleone, including a collection of paintings noted as 'Quadri che vennero da Calabria' and a six-piece dining table made in Monteleone. This movement of goods suggests that some pieces of furniture were more useful to the duke in Barra than in Monteleone. Indeed, to furnish the villa, goods also came from Spain, the birthplace of Diego (the furniture for the private chapel) and from the Sicilian houses of the family (a living bird and some worked stones).[20] After the death of Duke Diego (1750), the attention of the family seemed to switch to the palace in Naples. This is the reason why in the same inventory we find some annotations indicating that some things were missing because they had been transported to Naples in 1757 and in 1760. Specifically, these were two curtains and two beds, useful for the celebration of the day of the Madonna di Piedigrotta.[21] The presence of the new royal court in Naples (definitive from 1744) was probably the key reason for the new central importance of the urban palace. This is attested firstly by its renovation in the middle of the 1720s,[22] secondly by the arrival of a collection of books from Calabria,[23] and finally by a high concentration of luxury goods, including exotic items.

As is apparent from these examples, for the Pignatelli the placement of objects followed in some measure the fortune of their houses – fortune that depended on the personal inclination of the owners, but also on the political context in which they lived. Exotic objects were particularly important in this respect as they were key indicators of the importance attributed to the different houses. Table 5.1 shows that the majority of exotic goods were in the palace in Naples, with Chinese objects being especially evident – in line with the taste of the first half of the century. As for the Indian pieces, it is hard to say whether they came from the East or West, or what their import channel might have been, as the adjective 'Indian' could refer to objects from the Americas, India or elsewhere in Asia, as is apparent from a comparison of the seventeenth-century Medici and Habsburgian collections.[24] This was because the term used by the writers of the inventories recalled the original idea of India as a land of marvels and so the adjective came to identify all unusual, exotic and wonderful objects.[25] The table also provides evidence of the Pignatelli passion for animals, birds in particular, which has its material footprint even in the castle, although exotic animals were most evident in the villa at Barra.

Table 5.1 Exotic objects in the Pignatelli houses (1745, 1751, 1752).

	Exotic objects		
	Chinese	**Others**	**Animals**
Naples	The duke's bed Five pieces of furniture Sixteen vases Three mirrors Twelve paintings One clock The duchess's porcelain	Three pieces of Indian earthenware Eight Indian paintings The duchess's Japanese porcelain	Several birdcages Fourteen ostrich eggs
Barra	Six paintings Seven chairs Some pieces of porcelain	Two Greek paintings One peacock fan Two portraits of slaves	One lion Three Turkish ducks Two bears Two ostriches One peacock
Monteleone			Two parrot cages

Source: Naples State Archive, Archivi privati, Pignatelli Aragona Cortés, serie Napoli, busta LIX, Inventario del palazzo del duca di Terranova e Monteleone, 17 June 1751; Inventario delle robbe del ducal castello in custodia del guardarobba Gio Battista Petitto, 23 May 1745; Inventario del palazzo della Barra di tutto ciò che stava in consegna di Fortunato Camerino, 15 September 1752.

Exploring the villa in more detail, this would generally be the ideal place to spend the summer months, away from the heat of the city and engaged in amusing activities. Neapolitan aristocrats owned country villas from at least the sixteenth century. At that time, the favourite places were Posillipo and Chiaia, but both became less popular with the passing of time because of the difficulty of reaching them.[26] In contrast, the plain below Vesuvius gained favour because of the fertility of the soils and the ease of access. In the seventeenth and eighteenth centuries, therefore, a great many villas were constructed in the area: most had agricultural land attached and were built around a rustic courtyard.[27] With the construction of the Royal Palace in Portici (1738–42), the area experienced a new wave of popularity. An impressive number of villas were built, side by side, on the route from Naples to Portici, which became known as the 'golden mile'. These houses were different from earlier villas because they did not have productive lands but were instead built primarily as a place of sociability. Their main doors and balconies were on the street, then a courtyard gave access to the garden, separated by real agricultural spaces.[28] This setting was described as 'delightfulness', something that united the Latin concept of *otium* with a high sense of lavish pleasures in which aristocrats spent their spare time. In Barra, the Pignatelli constructed their own villa.[29] Historians have pointed out the contrast between the original keen interest of the owners in building the villa and its present state of neglect.[30] Indeed, while the building still exists, it is unfortunately not an historical house but rather is subdivided and inhabited by different families, part of the densely populated environment of the Vesuvian towns.[31]

The villa Pignatelli in its golden age was depicted on the famous 1775 map made by Duke Giovanni Carafa di Noja and was one of the first villas designed based on modern design criteria.[32] Actually, the building was never entirely completed, so this representation is partly fictional, but the incomplete nature of the house was not so exceptional at the time for Neapolitan aristocrats, who frequently preferred to start new works instead of completing ongoing projects.[33] Particularly important was the large external space (still existing, with its café and pavilions, even if largely abandoned).[34] At the time of the Pignatelli, the garden was used for leisure activities such as parties and balls. A contemporary engraving (1732) depicts a serenade to celebrate Duke Diego's investment in the Toson d'or.[35] Even if it is not clearly specified which place is depicted, the set with its ephemeral apparatus seems to correspond to the famous French garden of the villa in Barra. Beyond the garden was a rural estate that was used for hunting.

The Neapolitan upper class of the eighteenth century took the idea of building a quiet place from the Roman model, in which the villa should be immersed in nature but well distinguished from wilderness through the cultivation of the garden. Here spaces should be articulated to host fruit trees, evergreen plants, medicinal herbs, mazes of flowers and flowerbeds and fountains.[36] Flora and fauna were often enriched with exotic species. All was set around the concept of delightfulness. In concrete terms, this meant creating an environment which rested and delighted the spirit of the owner and the guests. Exoticism was important in achieving this. The 1750 inventory listed 'the animals, quadrupeds and birds, in the country house in Barra' (unfortunately, we are not so lucky to have a similar inventory of the plants):

> a female lion, two bears, one male and the other female, a porcupine, two ostriches one male and the other female, fifteen fallow deer, four of them white, fifteen deer, four [sic] female and a male, twelve boars plus nine born in 1750, eighteen ducks, three of them property of the marquis, two Turkish duckling, four guinea fowl, a peacock, seventeen chicken including four rooster, two partridge, twelve pheasant, a cage with canaries, another cage with grey doves, two big fishes.[37]

This list comprises an interesting mix of global and local beasts. Some of them (particularly the fallow deer, boars and ducks) were part of the duke's hunting reserve. Hunting was one of the favourite activities performed in the context of the country villa and was particularly important among the aristocracies of all Europe for its impact in strengthening sociability.[38] Moreover, the passion of the first Bourbon kings and their Neapolitan court for hunting is well known.[39]

Then there were the exotic animals, first a female lion. As studies of the collections of the Medici courts have revealed, the lion was the core of the collection of exotic animals because it symbolised the authority of the prince.[40] Other animals, such as peacocks and ostriches, were also used for their secondary products, such as feathers and eggs.[41] Indeed, the Pignatelli also had a large peacock fan in the villa and two ostrich eggs, displayed in the duke's bedroom at the palace in Naples.[42] While ostriches were rarer, and therefore held a certain cachet, the cultural value of the peacocks is more complicated to define. In Neapolitan gardens such birds have been seen as one of the oldest symbols of exoticism, being among the delights of villas since Roman times.[43] By the eighteenth century, the blue peacock was widespread in Europe, making it less prestigious than the white variety imported from India from the Renaissance, for example, into the Medici aviaries.[44]

In the eighteenth century, living animals had a high aesthetic value, being among the delights of the house. Unfortunately, we do not have any contemporary representation of the Pignatelli menagerie. In order to visualise the aesthetic value of animals we can look to the Pignatelli Museum, where there is a collection of 21 different birds, including a peacock, made in chased silver (Figure 5.1). There are bigger and smaller birds represented; some are exotic and others local; all are represented in a natural attitude to simulate the actions of walking or pecking. But living animals had meanings beyond the aesthetic. Possessing them was a matter of magnificence, a central concept in aristocratic ideology.[45] Due to the high cost of acquiring and keeping exotic beasts, their presence was proof of the family's wealth.[46] In aristocratic culture, of course, being rich did not mean accumulating a fortune, but rather spending it in order to support a lifestyle characterised by liberality and magnificence – behaviours which often created problems of indebtedness.[47] Indeed, while the Pignatelli lands below Vesuvius and in the other places were productive, family expenses were always higher than their incomes. This was rather common among noble families of the Kingdom of Naples because of the different kinds of expenses they had, but it was by no means unusual among the other aristocrats in Europe.[48] Having said that, Diego Pignatelli was particularly indebted.[49]

Animals were also an important part of the gift economy that, on a global scale, interconnected different courts. Popes and princes were

Figure 5.1 Silver birds, chiselled on silvers, various sizes, nineteenth century. Reproduced courtesy of Museo Principe Diego Aragona Cortés, Naples.

honoured with such precious gifts, most of them coming from countries around the Indian Ocean.[50] The first monarchies to possess exotic animals were those which had power over colonies in Asia, Africa and India: the Ming and Qing Chinese dynasties, the Indian Mughal and the Ottoman emperors. Then there were the European powers which controlled the routes to exotic lands: Portugal and Spain first, then the Low Countries and England.[51] If a family did not live in a country which either ruled colonies or controlled trading routes, the possession of exotic beasts was probably due to its relationship with one of the more powerful dynasties. Most of the animals listed in the Pignatelli villa were with all probability brought from the Indian Ocean via the intermediation of the Ottoman Empire. There is a lack of documents on the provenance of such animals, and the adjectives used in the inventories are often generic. Nevertheless, we can determine their provenance partly from the species – the lion and the peacock, in particular – and partly from place name adjectives: a *pecorone* (sheep) from Barbaria and two 'Turkish' ducks. These animals, destined only to be admired, were clearly distinguished from the more local beasts.

The Pignatelli menagerie had multiple functions. Keeping a collection of exotic beasts certainly testifies to the wealth of the family, who could afford such a lavish hobby; but it was also the result of diplomatic relationships with the Near East. In the villa, the animals were displayed not only for their aesthetic value, but also as a symbol of familial and economic power. We do not have any explicit evidence on why the collection was in the villa and not in the palace of Naples. Probably, it was a matter of space: the palace had its own internal garden, but it was much smaller than that at the villa. More deeply, we can guess that the animals were a leisure attraction for the Pignatelli guests, one of the delights used to facilitate aristocratic sociability in the countryside.

Global porcelain in the palace

Given their provenance, these animals could be called exotic. For other goods, we are able to recognise more clearly a global trajectory. Perhaps the most renowned category of exotic object in the eighteenth century was porcelain from China and Japan. Actually, the Pignatelli inventories list both Chinese objects – that is, original, truly imported – and objects in a Chinese style, but probably manufactured in Europe. The villa at Barra held a few examples of such goods: the duke's bedroom was furnished with some pieces in a Chinese style, including two paintings in the antechamber and seven chairs of red and yellow velvet with Chinese motifs (Table 5.1).[52] As for the porcelain, a final annotation to the 1752 inventory noted that in one room there was 'all the Marsiglia porcelain together with the Chinese one and a few others from Vienna', although the inventory went on to specify that 'some of these pieces of porcelain have been found broken'.[53] Although the villa was built during the golden years of the taste for chinoiserie, the influence of this fashion does not seem to have had a fundamental impact on the house interiors. Even more interesting is the damage apparently suffered by such goods. Although the inventory does not include values for the objects, we know that pieces of porcelain from China, Vienna and Marsiglia were valuable because here and in other aristocratic houses we notice a difference between imported porcelain and earthenware of local production called 'faenza', which was for daily use.[54]

In truth, however, these pieces in Barra were secondary to the main part of the Pignatelli collection in the palace in Naples. The first feature to reflect on is their collocation within the house. There were pieces in several rooms, but the most interesting spaces were the duke's bedroom and the duchess's cabinet, where Chinese objects were concentrated. Helen Clifford, among others, has shown how precious Chinese wallpaper was predominantly used in the private spaces of houses.[55] Conversely, we are often inclined to think that luxury objects were positioned in 'front-stage' rooms frequented by guests.[56] Of course, the concept of privacy in the aristocratic house was not completely comparable to that pertaining today. The birth of a sense of intimacy has been a matter of debate,[57] but it is known that the aristocratic house was similar to a court: it required many servants with different duties, organised in a hierarchical order, as well as spaces with different ceremonial and social purposes.[58] This means that private and public spaces were tightly connected. Thus, the rooms of the duchess's apartment had the two functions of displaying precious objects for guests invited to this side of the palace and of delighting the eyes of their owner.

Apart from their position in the house, it is interesting to analyse the different kinds of objects which formed the collection. Firstly, the 1763 inventory of the palace listed 26 pieces of chinaware of different sizes.[59] We know that some of them were a gift from Empress Marie Therese to Duchess Margherita Pignatelli, as is documented by the 12 letters stored in the Naples State Archive. One of these contains references made by the empress to the reciprocal exchange of porcelain and the long-standing nature of their relationship. On 30 November 1770 she wrote: 'with this letter I give you another sign [of esteem] due to the memories that I always keep of people I met during my youth'.[60] Apart from the biographical information, the documents are important because they give meaning to the collection of exotic objects. In this sense, the 26 pieces of chinaware belonging to the duchess were global objects because they came from the Far East; they were then passed on by the court of Vienna where, according to the logic of the gift economy, they became a tool to strengthen a personal and political relationship. As noted earlier, the link between the Habsburgs and the Pignatelli of Monteleone was not restricted to the friendship between these two women but was larger and stronger. After the Spanish War of Succession (1700–14), when the Austrian Habsburgs ruled the Kingdom of Naples and the Kingdom of Sicily, the Pignatelli were among their favourite families. Duke Nicolò was invested as first viceroy of Sicily; his son Diego received the important collar of the Toson d'Or in appreciation of his fidelity. Later, when Carlo di Borbone attacked the kingdom, Diego tried to organise a defensive army but was defeated (1744).[61] Thus, the 26 Chinese vases were also a clear sign of belonging to a political group, much like the sleigh brought from Vienna and the portraits of the emperors, still stored in Barra ten years after the final victory of the Bourbons.[62]

The duchess's porcelain collection was not limited to these gifts from the empress; they included a great many other pieces imported from China and Japan. The 1763 inventory lists in a separate room 'five small statues, three representing women and two representing men' ('5 statuette, tre di donne, due di uomini'), which were Chinese and part of the collection of gifts from the empress, and 'a showcase with small statues of Chinese porcelain, depicting two shepherds and a little dog' ('uno scarabattolo con statuette di porcellana della China rappresentanti due pastori e un cagnolino'), a typical European subject and probably made for export.[63] These appear to have been genuine Chinese objects, but there was a growing range of European porcelain also available. The development of imitation techniques has been studied with particular attention, from the first attempt of imitation in the Meissen factories, established in 1710–13, to the latter case of Josiah Wedgwood.[64] Scholars in Britain have underlined how the desire among middle-ranking people to acquire imitation products could have driven the production of novelty, so-called import substitutions and therefore served as an important stimulus for the consumer revolution.[65] Similarly, in the Netherlands, historians have demonstrated that imported items were present in noticeable quantities even in the houses of middle-status people and migrants.[66] Such a study in the context of the Kingdom of Naples does not yet exist, so we are not able to understand fully the diffusion of exotic goods and imitations among the Neapolitan middle rankings of the eighteenth century. However, the products of the Capodimonte workshop, created following a mercantilist logic to reduce imports of goods,[67] quickly became luxury items to be collected by elites along with other prestigious European productions, such as Meissen and Sèvres. Nevertheless, exotic goods retained great importance for Neapolitan aristocrats well into the nineteenth century. We can see this in the collections of the Pignatelli Museum. These include many examples of Chinese porcelain very similar to the ones mentioned in the inventories, with the advantage that we can see rather than simply imagine their physical qualities. These include an animal with its offspring, variously identified as a cat or a dog, made in majolica, white with black and brown spots and 25 centimetres tall (Figure 5.2). There is also a group of three priests which was probably displayed on a table or desk. Details of their faces have vanished, but it is still possible to see the brilliant colours fixed through the original Chinese technique: green, yellow and purple.

One particularly important set of oriental porcelain is the set of four Japanese cups with the family coat of arms painted on them.[68] Such armorial china was widespread in Europe at the time.[69] In the British context, sets could be imported through the East India Company and, as Katie Smith has pointed out, used by men in particular as symbols

Figure 5.2 Chestnut bookcase with the Pignatelli coat of arms, nineteenth century. On the top: chinaware, eighteenth century. Reproduced courtesy of Museo Principe Diego Aragona Cortés, Naples.

of autonomy, honour, reputation and self-control.[70] They form part of a wider practice of emblazoning goods with symbols of noble title. The 1751 inventory notes the family arms on some pieces of furniture – namely the chests at the entrance – as well as silverware and the servants' livery.[71] These were all goods with a high level of visibility in and beyond the house. The museum also contains a great many surviving objects marked with the coat of arms, again allowing us to see the extent and impact of this practice. In the dining room, for example, they appear on the chairs, the cutlery and the glasses, all produced during the nineteenth century. In the library, a chestnut bookcase, carved with figures on its sides, has in the centre the coat of arms with the three *pignatte* (jars), the symbol of the family. Arranged on the bookcase are three interesting eighteenth-century examples of pieces of Chinese porcelain (Figure 5.3).

The 1750 and 1763 inventories make clear the predominance of the Chinese style in the interiors of the Naples palace. Different pieces of furniture labelled as in the 'Chinese style' were set in the duchess's and the duke's bedrooms. This was in accordance with the prevailing taste in the first half of the eighteenth century, but they were accompanied by some pieces of furniture in ebony wood that, with its dark appearance, was very common in the houses of the upper classes during the period of the Spanish vice-kingdom (1504–1707).[72] In the duchess's bedroom, for example, various pieces of furniture decorated with Chinese motifs ('stipi dipinti alla chinese') were placed near two small ebony commodes ('due piccoli commò di legno d'Ebano').[73] In the duke's room, the main pavilion bed was hung with green damask decorated with Chinese figures.[74]

Figure 5.3 Cat with kitten, China, eighteenth century. Reproduced courtesy of Museo Principe Diego Aragona Cortés, Naples.

On a purely aesthetic note, the exotic motifs seem to match well with a dark background, as is clear from some other objects, including a black Chinese bureau chiselled in gold and a Chinese pendulum clock, black and gold, with golden pomes.[75]

These are the main kinds of goods from the Far East which appeared in the Pignatelli palace in Naples: Chinese and Japanese porcelain gifted by the empress of Austria – luxury goods that materialised and consolidated a political and personal friendship – as well as pieces of chinoiserie and porcelain, probably manufactured in Europe, that signalled the wealth of the family, who could afford to refurbish the palace interiors according to the current taste of the time. However, there were other exotic goods that reflected the family's connections with Mexico.

In the duke's bedroom there were two earthenware jars described as 'Indian'.[76] We know that the adjective is generic and could be used to refer to goods from the East or West, so it is impossible to determine their provenance from the inventory alone. Nevertheless, these objects are an interesting example of the process of 'domesticating goods from overseas'.[77] Anne Gerritsen has shown for the Netherlands that objects from faraway lands acquired multiple meanings during their route to the European homes.[78] Her theorisation of hybrid objects is based on the case of imported Asian goods that acquired the status of Dutch things by their use and circulation in Dutch society. The Pignatelli earthenware jars show a different process: the global creation of an object. The raw material – a sort of clay, 'varro, ovvero creta delle Indie' – was Indian,[79] but the manufacturing was commissioned by the family, as is apparent from the coat of arms carved into the surface of the earthenware. The origin of the two jars remains unknown, even if by carving their symbol on an Indian piece of clay the Pignatelli created a hybrid object and a symbol of their global power. The practice of imprinting the coat of arms on earthenware was quite rare, while commissioning armorial chinaware was quite common. Indeed, in the British context, sets could be imported through the East India Company and, as Katie Smith has pointed out, used particularly by men as symbols of autonomy, honour, reputation and self-control.[80]

The only object in the palace inventory which unequivocally recalled the New World was the portrait of Hernán Cortés, part of a collection of six paintings of family ancestors located in the gallery.[81] However, the museum holds another object that reflects the family connection with the New World: a bust of Cortés in the ballroom. The bust was donated to the museum in 1960 by Princess Anna;[82] it is made of gilded bronze

Figure 5.4 M. Tolsà, Hernán Cortés, golden bronze on granite column and marble base, 1794. Reproduced courtesy of Museo Principe Diego Aragona Cortés, Naples.

and displayed on a granite column with a white marble base which again includes a plaque of the family coat of arms (Figure 5.4). According to the existing literature, the bust was created in 1794 by Manuel Tolsà, a Spanish artist who emigrated to New Spain to decorate the Cortéses' tomb. The statue remained in Mexico until the first half of the nineteenth century, when it disappeared during the War of Independence and mysteriously arrived in Naples.[83] The object was created by a Spanish artist but made in Mexico, and by unknown means arrived at the Pignatelli house in Italy. In this sense the bust might be considered a global object, for it connected Spanish imperialism and craftsmanship, exotic Mexican raw materials and a European destination. Its acquisition in the Pignatelli collection makes clear that its function was to materialise the genealogy and, with this, legitimise the right of the descendant to rule on those lands, so that it can be considered more properly a sign of the global power of the family.

Conclusion

The Pignatelli family, with all its lands and possessions, offers important examples that are useful for understanding the meaning of the presence of global goods in Neapolitan aristocratic houses. These goods' presence was primarily the result of global political links rather than the result of a direct form of colonialism. Although the Pignatelli was one of the few families in the Kingdom of Naples to possess land overseas, there is little evidence that they imported objects or animals from their possessions in Mexico. The painting and the bust of Cortés are the most concrete examples, and the earthenware jars might reflect a link to Mexico; but it is impossible to determine, based on the inventories, if other commodities, such as objects in silver for example, also came from Mexico.

The location of global goods also says something interesting about the importance attributed to the different houses. Neapolitan aristocrats maintained an itinerant lifestyle but put their main attention on the urban palace in the capital, where, not surprisingly, the most precious collections of exotica were located. The Pignatelli gained some of their Chinese objects through their friendship with the Habsburg dynasty; others, imported and not produced as an imitation, demonstrated the degree of wealth of the family and allowed them to refurbish the houses' interiors according to the current taste of fashion. Wealth was strictly connected with power and reflected the ability of the Pignatelli to insert themselves into the global channels of politics. This power was physically expressed through engraving the family coat of arms on different commodities, a common practice among European nobilities. One final explanation of the presence of global, exotic objects in their houses is that such goods were acquired and displayed as part of an aristocratic ideology that required families to spend economic resources in pursuit of a lifestyle of magnificence and delightfulness, a concept materialised most clearly in the menagerie at their suburban villa. In conclusion, the meaning of global goods appears to be multiple: a sign of power, a material footprint of personal and political friendship, and a means of conducting a lavish and delightful lifestyle.

Notes

1 '… ben grate mi sono le di lei cortesi espressioni, ricavandone, come anche dal Regallo, mandatomi, un contrassegno evidente dei suoi sentimenti a Mio riguardo: gliene sono molto obligata, asicurandola, che sempre ne conservo la memoria …', Naples State Archive (NSA),

Archivi Privati, Pignatelli Aragona Cortés, busta II, letter of Maria Teresa of Austria, Vienna, 9 October 1760.
2 '… corrispondono le espressioni colle quali palesa le sue soddisfazioni sulla porcellana mandatale ai sentimenti che sempre le conosco …', NSA, Archivi Privati, Pignatelli Aragona Cortés, busta II, letter of Maria Teresa of Austria, Vienna, 1 April 1772.
3 Calcagno, *Notizie genealogico-storiche*.
4 Finn and Smith, 'Introduction'.
5 Stobart, 'Introduction'.
6 Labrot, *Il barone in città*, 27–9.
7 Musi, 'Introduzione', 7; Sodano, 'Tra localismo, impegno internazionale e corte', 160.
8 Labrot, *Il barone in città*.
9 NSA, Archivi Privati, Pignatelli Aragona Cortés, serie Napoli, busta LIX: Inventario del palazzo del duca di Terranova e Monteleone, 17 June 1751; Inventario dell'Eccellentissima casa di Terranova Pignatelli formato sotto li 28 April 1763; Notamenti di robbe del Guardarobbe di S.E., December 1723–September 1724; Inventario delle robbe del ducal castello in custodia del guardarobba Gio Battista Petitto, 23 May 1745; Inventario del palazzo della Barra, May 1750; Inventario del palazzo della Barra di tutto ciò che stava in consegna di Fortunato Camerino, 15 September 1752.
10 Prown, 'Mind in matter'.
11 Museo Principe Diego Aragona Pignatelli Cortés, Inventario completo (con opere e libri) sempre descritte, 1960.
12 Molajoli, *Il Museo*; Spinosa, *Il Museo di Villa Pignatelli*; Tecce, *Il Museo Pignatelli*.
13 Cancila, 'Pignatelli Aragona Cortés e Mendoza, Diego', 637–9.
14 On the street system of the time see Bulgarelli Lukacs, 'Le comunicazioni nel Mezzogiorno'.
15 Galasso, 'Il barone in città', 297.
16 Bruno, 'Le residenze dell'aristocrazia', 64–7.
17 Covino, 'La gemma preziosa', 234.
18 On the feudal question in the Kingdom of Naples see Rao, *L'amaro della feudalità*.
19 NSA, Archivi privati, Pignatelli Aragona Cortés, serie Napoli, busta LIX, Notamenti di robbe (1723–4).
20 NSA, Archivi privati, Pignatelli Aragona Cortés, serie Napoli, busta LIX, Inventario del palazzo della Barra (1752).
21 NSA, Archivi privati, Pignatelli Aragona Cortés, serie Napoli, busta LIX, Inventario del palazzo della Barra (1752).
22 Bisogno, *Nicolò Tagliacozzi Canale*, 155–6, 174–5.
23 NSA, Archivi privati, Pignatelli Aragona Cortés, serie Napoli, busta LIX, Inventario del palazzo (1751).
24 Keating and Markey, '"Indian" objects'.
25 Keating and Markey, '"Indian" objects', 286, 297.
26 De Seta, 'Il sistema residenziale', 11–12.
27 De Seta, 'Il sistema residenziale', 22.
28 De Seta, 'Il sistema residenziale', 25–6.
29 Trombetti, 'La villa Pignatelli'; additional information is also available in Rizzo, *Il presepe*.
30 di Mauro, 'Villa Pignatelli di Monteleone', 213.
31 De Seta, *Ville vesuviane*, 360–6, reported a survey of the destination of 143 Vesuvian villas.
32 *Mappa topografica*, table 20. All the tables of the map are visible on the website of the Biblioteca Nazionale di Napoli, http://digitale.bnnonline.it/index.php?it/149/ricerca-contenuti-digitali/show/85/.
33 Pane, 'Introduzione'.
34 di Mauro, 'La villa Pignatelli di Monteleone', 215.
35 Bisogno, *Nicolò Tagliacozzi Canale*, 171.
36 Giannetti, *Il giardino napoletano*, 12.
37 'Nota degli animali quadrupedi e volatili sistentino nel detto casino della Barra: una leonessa, due orsi uno maschio e l'altro femina, un'estrice, due struzzi uno maschio e l'altro femina, numero 15 daini, quattro d'essi bianchi, numero 15 cervi quattro femmine ed uno maschio, cinghiali di corpo numero dodici e n 9 piccoli nati nel 1750, n 18 anatrelle cioè tre di esse dell'ecc. marchese, due papare turchesche, quattro galline faraone, uno paone, n 17 galline incluso 4 galli, 2 pernici e 12 faggiani, uno gabbione con razza di canari, un altro

gabbione dentro il giardino di tortore, due mafroni', NSA, Archivi privati, Pignatelli Aragona Cortés, serie Napoli, busta LIX, Inventario del palazzo della Barra (1750).
38 Stone, *An Open Elite?*, 214–15.
39 *Un elefante a corte*.
40 Cockram, 'Interspecies understanding', 277.
41 Cockram, 'Interspecies understanding', 280.
42 NSA, Archivi privati, Pignatelli Aragona Cortés, serie Napoli, busta LIX, Inventario del palazzo (1751).
43 Giannetti, *Il giardino napoletano*, 21.
44 Groom, *Exotic Animals*, 93.
45 Cockram, 'Interspecies understanding', 279.
46 Cockram, 'Interspecies understanding', 284–9.
47 Montroni, 'L'indebitamento dell'aristocrazia'.
48 Rao, 'La questione feudale nell'età tanucciana', 84–90; Labatut, *Le nobiltà europee*, 147.
49 Cancila, 'Pignatelli Aragona Cortés e Mendoza, Diego', 639.
50 Cockram, 'Interspecies understanding', 281.
51 Groom, *Exotic Animals*, 7–12.
52 NSA, Archivi privati, Pignatelli Aragona Cortés, serie Napoli, busta LIX, Inventario del palazzo della Barra (1752).
53 '… tutta la porcellana di Marsiglia unitamente alla porcellana della china ed altra poco da Vienna …'; 'nota bene detta porcellana si è trovata più pezzi rotti', NSA, Archivi privati, Pignatelli Aragona Cortés, serie Napoli, busta LIX, Inventario del palazzo della Barra (1752).
54 NSA, Archivi privati, Pignatelli Aragona Cortés, serie Napoli, busta LIX, Inventario di tutti li mobili, suppellettili, et altre robbe di S.E. sig. duca di Monteleone, nel casino della Barra quali si consegnano a Monsieur Giovanni Enrico Hermans suo giardiniero e guardarobba in detto casino, 25 October 1765. Other examples come from the Carafa di Ielsi castle in Molise: NSA, Processi Antichi, Sacro Regio Consiglio, Ordinamento Zeni, fascio 239, Atti di annotazione dei beni mobili ritrovati nel palazzo di Ielsi, carte 4–7. For a brief discussion of the difference between porcelain and faenza see Bruno, 'Civiltà materiale', 6–9.
55 Clifford, 'Chinese wallpaper', 64.
56 Weatherill, 'The meaning of consumer behavior', 213.
57 Pardaille Galabrun, *La naissance de l'intime*.
58 Muto, 'Il segretario a corte', 593–6.
59 NSA, Archivi privati, Pignatelli Aragona Cortés, serie Napoli, busta LIX, Inventario dell'Eccellentissima casa (1763).
60 '… non posso [fare] a meno di accompagnarlo di questa lettera per darle un nuovo contrassegno per essere immancabile la rimembranza che sempre conservo di quelli che ho conosciuto fino dalla mia gioventù …', NSA, Archivi Privati, Pignatelli Aragona Cortés, busta II, letter of Maria Teresa of Austria to Margherita Pignatelli, Vienna, 30 November 1770.
61 Carignani, 'Il partito austriaco', 54.
62 NSA, Archivi privati, Pignatelli Aragona Cortés, serie Napoli, busta LIX, Inventario del palazzo della Barra (1752).
63 NSA, Archivi privati, Pignatelli Aragona Cortés, serie Napoli, busta LIX, Inventario dell'Eccellentissima casa (1763).
64 Berg and Clifford, 'Global objects', 104; Haggar, *The Concise Encyclopedia*, 306–13; McKendrick, 'Josiah Wedgwood'.
65 Berg, 'New commodities'; Berg, 'From imitation to invention'; Berg, 'In pursuit of luxury'. On the consumer revolution see Trentmann, *Empire of Things*, 43–71 (from the Italian edition).
66 McCants, 'Asiatic goods'.
67 Clemente, 'Innovation in the capital city'.
68 NSA, Archivi privati, Pignatelli Aragona Cortés, serie Napoli, busta LIX, Inventario dell'Eccellentissima casa (1763).
69 Smith, 'Manly objects?'.
70 Smith, 'Manly objects?', 114, 117.
71 NSA, Archivi privati, Pignatelli Aragona Cortés, serie Napoli, busta LIX, Inventario del palazzo (1751).
72 De Fusco, *Storia dell'arredamento*.

73 NSA, Archivi privati, Pignatelli Aragona Cortés, serie Napoli, busta LIX, Inventario dell'Eccellentissima casa (1763).
74 NSA, Archivi privati, Pignatelli Aragona Cortés, serie Napoli, busta LIX, Inventario del palazzo (1751).
75 'Un burò alla chinese di nero storiato d'oro'; 'un orologio a Pendolo con sua cassa lunga di pianta alla chinese nero ed oro con pomi dorati', NSA, Archivi privati, Pignatelli Aragona Cortés, serie Napoli, busta LIX, Inventario del palazzo (1751).
76 NSA, Archivi privati, Pignatelli Aragona Cortés, serie Napoli, busta LIX, Inventario del palazzo (1751).
77 Gerritsen, 'Domesticating goods from overseas'.
78 Gerritsen, 'Domesticating goods from overseas', 228.
79 NSA, Archivi privati, Pignatelli Aragona Cortés, serie Napoli, busta LIX, Inventario del palazzo (1751).
80 Smith, 'Manly objects?', 114, 117.
81 NSA, Archivi privati, Pignatelli Aragona Cortés, serie Napoli, busta LIX, Inventario del palazzo (1751).
82 Inventario completo (1960).
83 Causa, 'Il busto di Cortéz dal Messico a Napoli', 30.

Bibliography

Berg, Maxine. 'New commodities, luxuries and their consumers in eighteenth-century England'. In *Consumers and Luxury: Consumer culture in Europe 1650–1850*, edited by Maxine Berg and Helen Clifford, 63–85. Manchester: Manchester University Press, 1999.

Berg, Maxine. 'From imitation to invention: creating commodities in eighteenth-century Britain', *Economic History Review* 55 (2002): 1–30.

Berg, Maxine. 'In pursuit of luxury: global history and British consumer goods in the eighteenth century', *Past and Present* 182 (2004): 85–142.

Berg, Maxine, and Helen Clifford. 'Global objects'. In *Treasured Possessions from the Renaissance to the Enlightenment*, edited by Victoria Avery, Melissa Calaresu and Mary Laven, 103–111. London: PWP, 2015.

Biblioteca Nazionale di Napoli. *Mappa Topographica delle cita di Napoli*. http://digitale.bnnonline.it/index.php?it/149/ricerca-contenuti-digitali/show/85/.

Bisogno, Serena. *Nicolò Tagliacozzi Canale: architettura, decorazione, scenografia dell'ultimo rococò napoletano*. Naples: Fridericiana editrice universitaria, 2013.

Bruno, Gaia. 'Civiltà materiale del XVIII secolo nelle voci dell'Encyclopédie', *Laboratorio dell'ISPF* 17 (2020): 2–15.

Bruno, Gaia. 'Le residenze dell'aristocrazia napoletana. Indagine sugli inventari dei Pignatelli di Monteleone', *Napoli Nobilissima* 7 (2021): 63–74.

Bulgarelli Lukacs, Alessandra. 'Le comunicazioni nel Mezzogiorno dall'arrivo di Carlo di Borbone al 1815: strade e poste', *Archivio Storico per le Province Napoletane* 15 (1976): 283–309.

Calcagno, Antonio. *Notizie genealogico-storiche dell'antichissima ed illustrissima famiglia Pignatelli-Aragona-Cortes, dei duchi di Monteleone e Terranova in Sicilia*. Milan: dalla Tip. di C. Wilmant, 1847.

Cancila, Rossella. 'Pignatelli Aragona Cortés e Mendoza, Diego'. In *Dizionario Biografico degli Italiani*, 637–639. Turin: Istituto dell'Enciclopedia Italiana, 2015.

Carignani, Giuseppe. 'Il partito austriaco nel Regno di Napoli al 1744', *Archivio storico per le province napoletane* 7 (1881): 37–73.

Catello, Elio and Corrado Catello. *Cineserie e turcherie nel Settecento napoletano*. Naples: Sergio Civita editore, 1992.

Causa, Raffaello. 'Il busto di Cortéz dal Messico a Napoli', *Napoli Nobilissima* 7 (1968): 29–30.

Causa, Raffaello, and Nicola Spinosa, eds. *Civiltà del Settecento a Napoli*. Florence: Centro DI, 1980.

Clemente, Alida. 'Innovation in the capital city: central policies, markets, and migrant skills in Neapolitan ceramic manufacturing in the eighteenth century.' In *Cities and Innovation in Early Modern Europe*, edited by Karel Davids and Bert De Munck, 315–35. Aldershot: Ashgate, 2014.

Clifford, Helen. 'Chinese wallpaper: from Canton to country house'. In *The East India Company at Home, 1757–1857*, edited by Margot Finn and Kate Smith, 39–67. London: UCL Press, 2018.

Cockram, Sara. 'Interspecies understanding: exotic animals and their handlers at the Italian Renaissance court', *Renaissance Studies* 31 (2017): 277–96.

Covino, Luca. '"La gemma preziosa de' Baroni": Giurisdizione e amministrazione del feudo nella Calabria del tardo Settecento'. In *Baroni e vassalli: storie moderne*, edited by Elisa Novi Chavarria and Vittoria Fiorelli, 228–58. Milan: Franco Angeli, 2011.

De Fusco, Renato. *Storia dell'arredamento*, vol. 2. Turin: UTET, 1985.

De Seta, Cesare. 'Il sistema residenziale e produttivo delle ville vesuviane: dall'ancien régime alla decadenza'. In *Ville Vesuviane*, edited by Cesare De Seta, Leonardo di Mauro and Maria Perone, 11–33. Milan: Rusconi, 1980.

De Seta, Cesare, Leonardo di Mauro and Maria Perone, eds. *Ville vesuviane*. Milan: Rusconi, 1980.

di Mauro, Leonardo. 'Villa Pignatelli di Monteleone'. In *Ville Vesuviane*, edited by Cesare De Seta, Leonardo di Mauro and Maria Perone, 213–16. Milan: Rusconi, 1980.

Finn, Margot, and Kate Smith. 'Introduction'. In *The East India Company at Home, 1757–1857*, edited by Margot Finn and Kate Smith, 1–23. London: UCL Press, 2018.

Galasso, Giuseppe. 'Il barone in città: residenza e status antropologico'. In *L'altra Europa. Per un'antropologia storica del Mezzogiorno d'Italia*, edited by Giuseppe Galasso, 293–308. Naples: Guida, 2009.

Gerritsen, Anne. 'Domesticating goods from overseas: global material culture in the early modern Netherlands', *Journal of Design History* 29, no. 3 (2016): 228–44.

Gerritsen, Anne, and Giorgio Riello, eds. *The Global Lives of Things: The material culture of connections in the early modern world*. London: Routledge, 2016.

Giannetti, Anna. *Il giardino napoletano. Dal quattrocento al Settecento*. Naples: Electa, 1994.

Groom, Angelica. *Exotic Animals in the Art and Culture of the Medici Court in Florence*. Leiden and Boston: Brill, 2018.

Haggar, Reginald George. *The Concise Encyclopedia of Continental Pottery and Porcelain*. London: Andre Deutsch, 1960.

Keating, Jessica, and Lia Markey. '"Indian" objects in Medici and Austrian-Habsburg inventories: a case-study of the sixteenth-century term', *Journal of the History of Collections* 23 (2011): 283–300.

Labatut, Jean-Pierre. *Le nobiltà europee dal XV al XVIII secolo*. Bologna: Il Mulino, 1982 (original edition Paris, 1978).

Labrot, Gerard. *Baroni in città: residenze e comportamenti dell'aristocrazia napoletana, 1530–1734*. Naples: Società editrice napoletana, 1979.

McCants, Anne. 'Asiatic goods in migrant and native-born middling households'. In *Goods from the East, 1600–1800: Trading Eurasia*, edited by Maxine Berg, Felicia Gottmann, Hanna Hodacs and Chris Nierstrasz, 197–215. Basingstoke: Palgrave Macmillan, 2015.

McKendrick, Neil. 'Josiah Wedgwood and cost accounting in the Industrial Revolution', *The Economic History Review* 23 (1970): 45–67.

Molajoli, Bruno. *Il Museo principe Diego Aragona Pignatelli Cortes*. Naples: Arte Tipografica, 1960.

Montroni, Giovanni. 'L'indebitamento dell'aristocrazia'. In *Fra storia e storiografia: scritti in onore di Pasquale Villani*, edited by Paolo Macry and Angelo Massafra, 443–52. Bologna: Il Mulino, 1995.

Musi, Aurelio. 'Introduzione'. In *Feudalità laica e feudalità ecclesiastica nell'Italia meridionale*, edited by Aurelio Musi and Maria Anna Noto, 5–12. Palermo: Associazione Mediterranea, 2011.

Muto, Giovanni. 'Il segretario a corte'. In *Hacer historia desde Simancas. Homenaje a José Luis Rodriguez de Diego*, edited by A. Marcos Martin, 588–606. Valladolid: Junta de Castilla y Léon, 2011.

Pane, Giulio. 'Introduzione'. In *Mappa topografica della città di Napoli e de' suoi contorni, VII–XVIII*. Naples: Gremaldi & Co., 2003.

Pane, Roberto, Giancarlo Alisio and Paolo di Monda, eds. *Ville vesuviane del Settecento*. Naples: Edizioni scientifiche italiane, 1959.

Pardaille Galabrun, Annike. *La naissance de l'intime (3000 foyers parisiens XVIIe-XVIIIe)*. Paris: PUF, 1988.

Prown, Jules. 'Mind in matter: an introduction to material culture theory and method', *Winterthur Portfolio* 17 (1982): 1–19.

Rao, Anna Maria. *L'amaro della feudalità. La devoluzione di Arnone e la questione feudale a Napoli alla fine del '700*. Naples: Guida, 1984.
Rao, Anna Maria. 'La questione feudale nell'età tanucciana', *Archivio Storico per la Sicilia Orientale* 84 (1988): 77–162.
Rizzo, Vincenzo. *Il presepe, il palazzo e la villa vesuviana dei Pignatelli di Monteleone*. Naples: Natale, 1987.
Scalisi, Lina. 'Al di là dei mari. I possedimenti messicani degli Aragona Pingatelli Cortés'. In *Studi storici dedicati a Orazio Cancila*, edited by Antonio Giuffrida and Fabrizio D'Avenia, 393–412. Palermo: Associazione Mediterranea, 2011.
Smith, Katie. 'Manly objects? Gendering armorial porcelain wares'. In *The East India Company at Home, 1757–1857*, edited by Margot Finn and Kate Smith, 113–30. London: UCL Press, 2018.
Sodano, Giulio. 'Tra localismo, impegno internazionale e corte: il caso degli Acquaviva d'Atri'. In *Feudalità laica e feudalità ecclesiastica nell'Italia meridionale*, edited by Aurelio Musi and Maria Anna Noto, 157–80. Palermo: Associazione Mediterranea, 2011.
Spinosa, Nicola, ed. *Il Museo di Villa Pignatelli*. Naples: Electa, 2000.
Stobart, Jon. 'Introduction: travel and the British country house'. In *Travel and the British Country House: Cultures, critiques and consumption in the long eighteenth century*, edited by Jon Stobart, 1–18. Manchester: Manchester University Press, 2017.
Stone, Lowrence, and Jeanne C. Fawtier Stone. *An Open Elite? England 1540–1880*. Oxford and New York: Oxford University Press, 1986.
Tecce, Angela. *Il Museo Pignatelli di Napoli*. Naples: Electa, 1994.
Trentmann, Frank. *Empire of Things: How we become a world of consumers, from the fifteenth century to the twenty-first*. London: Penguin, 2016 (cited from the Italian edition).
Trombetti, Elena. 'La villa Pignatelli di Monteleone a Barra', *Napoli Nobilissima* 9 (1970): 61–70.
Un elefante a corte. Allevamenti, cacce ed esotismi alla Reggia di Caserta. Naples: F. Fiorentino, 1992.
Weatherill, Lorna. 'The meaning of consumer behavior in late seventeenth and early eighteenth-century England'. In *Consumption and the World of Goods*, edited by Jonh Brewer and Roy Porter, 206–27. London and New York: Routledge, 1993.

6
Luxury, international trade and consumption in three eighteenth-century Danish homes
Mikkel Venborg Pedersen

In 1618, 'Our first Indian Fleet' sailed out from the port of Copenhagen, King Christian IV of Denmark–Norway noted in his diary.[1] Two years later, the small fleet arrived at Ceylon, present-day Sri Lanka, negotiated with the local Prince Raghunatha, and obtained the right against tribute to trade from a strong point on the Indian mainland, soon to be founded as the colony Tranquebar. The Kingdom of Denmark–Norway, with the Duchies Slesvig and Holsten,[2] entered a new era of partaking in the general European expansion across the world.

Protected by Fort Dansborg, trade began in pepper, cotton textiles, dye-wood and other local produce. Much trade was taken along the Indian East Coast, and in 1755 Tranquebar was followed by the settlement Frederiksnagore, today Serampore, close to Calcutta. The Chinese (and Japanese) trade was extensive too, and in 1732 a new company was founded covering all Danish trade with the Far East, the Royal Chartered Danish Asiatic Company, which quickly developed into the largest enterprise of the realm.[3] Next to porcelain, tea, furniture and silks were the most important goods being taken back to Europe from China. Danish trade houses also took part in the Atlantic trade, including forts at the Gold Coast, in present-day Ghana, and eventually three islands in the Caribbean – St Thomas, St John and St Croix – mainly producing sugar to go with various trade goods. In relation to furnishing and luxury in eighteenth-century stately homes in Denmark, the Asiatic trade was, of course, more important than trade with the Americas.

Trade was one thing. For a young Danish or Norwegian lad with an adventurous mind, the colonial possessions also meant that he could avail himself of many new possibilities for seeing the world. Navigating rough northern waters hardened Danish and Norwegian sailors, who were much in demand in other countries as well and were paid high wages.[4] For most of the population, however, the colonies were and remained places one may have heard of, not places one had visited. But through consumption of foreign goods the new world came closer to everyday life.

International goods in Danish homes

As research over the last couple of decades has made clear, the expansion of oceangoing commerce is one of the more important aspects in the development of the (early) modern world. This was a process, as seen above, in which Denmark took part, with the capital Copenhagen as its epicentre.[5] Colonial influence on everyday life was broad and multi-faceted; however, it was perhaps most visible in new consumer possibilities and the pursuit of novelties. Europe, including Scandinavia, imported manufactured goods on a wider scale than ever before. The appearance of these goods coincided with a new civility in middle- and upper-class society, for instance in new ways of eating, drinking, furnishing, socialising and dressing (Figure 6.1); in reality it covered most of life. The import and logistics of international goods stimulated a consumer society, technical innovations, new products, marketing strategies and commercial institutions, as well as philosophical thought.[6]

This chapter looks at such influences in the furnishing and household goods in three Danish elite homes in the eighteenth century. Although this period witnessed consumption in the streets, shops and elsewhere, it was mostly in the homes that things, artefacts, were gathered. The home is at the heart of public and private life. Here, cultural values encounter technology as well as economic and ecological conditions. Here, one can see compromises between personal choices and the traditions and boundaries that constitute a given reality of life. The home both provides shelter and, especially in elite settings, offers a scene for social life – and it must not be forgotten that the family was only part of an extended household. In the home, life is lived and possessions are accumulated and utilised, framing daily and formal routines. Public meets private, and it is in the home that the most important arena for status consumption is situated.[7]

The play between public and private in a home also reveals that households were complex social institutions through which people's different needs were met, including a mix of comfort and cultural significance. There is no easy way to analyse such crossings of

Figure 6.1 World trade goods conquered dressing too. This dress in late empire style, of Indian cotton with silver embroidery in *boteh* pattern, dates from 1810–20. It was made for a Danish factory owner's wife, Mrs Kjerulf in Tranquebar. With it a Kashmir shawl from around 1800. Photo: National Museum of Denmark, John Lee.

sociocultural wants with artefacts or descriptions of them. However, as with everything else of human creation, artefacts can be seen as indicators of cultural values, choices and conceptions. We might usefully conceive this at three levels: being made for a purpose (a cupboard is used for storage); signifying a fixed value (the cupboard is of a certain style or place in time or economic value); and as a cultural symbol, which is more open-ended than a sign. This might lead the cupboard to be analysed as a token of cultural values,[8] for instance of belonging to a certain social group or cultural horizon shared with a select group of others, which may include a desire to consume foreign goods. In this chapter, these different social and cultural qualities will be kept in mind simultaneously.

The empirical basis is information from inventories, mixed with empirical knowledge of artefacts themselves and their uses. The places are a) Augustenborg Castle in 1725, situated in the Duchy of Slesvig and belonging to cousins of the Danish Royal House, of growing political importance; b) the noble seat of a widowed countess, Lille Hesbjerg Manor in Funen, in the 1790s, representing old nobility on the decline; and c) the *maison de plaisance* of a large-scale merchant and industrialist – and man of the new era of international trade and bourgeois ambition – Brede House, north of Copenhagen, in 1805. The second two are part of the National Museum of Denmark,[9] while the old Augustenborg Castle was replaced by a new castle finished in the 1770s. These three houses provide the basis for analysis of both change over time and the impact of differing social contexts: from old and uncontested princely and noble elites to a rising, money-based upper class with inherent social aspirations and uncertainties. Central to the discussion is not only the idea that people acquired more things, but also that these were increasingly differentiated in material, design and use as they went from being rare luxuries to almost everyday goods – at least for these elites. This went together with a general increase in wealth during the century.[10]

Luxury and civilised manners

In Denmark the new wealth that increasingly characterised societies across Europe became important from sometime around the middle of the eighteenth century. Coupled with global trade and (early) industrial development, this prompted higher levels and new patterns of consumption. A hitherto unknown demand for goods and services arose, stemming from a new civility in middle- and upper-class society, famously noted by the German historian Norbert Elias, whose work has given rise to a multitude of studies in the history of civilisation.[11] Exotic drinks form the classical example, bringing with them not only the use of cups and saucers (Figure 6.2), tea and coffee pots and sugar tongs, but also new types of furniture suitable for polite conversation over and following these (often non-alcoholic) drinks. According to the Norwegian-born Danish playwright and enlightened thinker Baron Ludvig Holberg, this was a blessing: he often used the new drinks in his plays, writing in his epistle 91, from the 1740s, that coffee had the great virtue of enabling women to make numerous visits during the day and yet stay sober.[12]

Figure 6.2 Two of 12 sets of chocolate cups bought in China in 1734 for King Christian VI. The cups' double walls provide insulation and enable the exquisite, penetrated sides and high-quality porcelain painting. Photo: National Museum of Denmark, Roberto Fortuna.

New imported goods also fitted nicely into an all-embracing conspicuous consumption. Eighteenth-century society was (still) preoccupied with rank and social status, and consumption was therefore not just about obtaining goods and/or services or following fashions; it also aimed to fulfil social norms and to maintain social standing or to help one climb to a higher place in the social hierarchy. This, of course, lay at the heart of the American Thorstein Veblen's celebrated yet contested notion of conspicuous consumption.[13] Equally, consumption is often used to present oneself in a positive light, but in reality it is not just conspicuous consumption that has this effect. 'Inconspicuous consumption transmits its own message and so does conspicuous refraining from consuming', as the British cultural historian Peter Burke points out when emphasising the importance of understanding context.[14] In the narrow meaning of conspicuous consumption, people acquire objects in order to compete with others. In a broader, looser, less reductionist meaning, conspicuous artefacts are acquired because of what they symbolise in both the society and the culture of the possessors.

Such a broad understanding of artefacts, conspicuous consumption and the civilisation of manners is followed in this chapter.[15] The theme is viewed through a cultural lens and weight is given to selected items of consumption directly connected to international trade and to their place in the cultural horizon of people living with them. This means, in some ways, to be focused on detail; but looking closely is not the same thing as being narrow sighted. Micro-history is not defined by studying the small and insignificant, but by looking in a minor scale, as the Italian historian Giovanni Levi has argued regarding this scholarly tradition and method.[16] Such well-proven ways of both reading sources in a hermeneutical interpretive light and analysing them in context will be applied here too. Hence, this analysis brings another understanding to a field often dominated by structurally guided economic, trade or world history and results in a fruitful combination of a broad view and attention to glimpses of real lived lives.[17]

When it comes to consumption of the goods that started to pour into Denmark from Europe and the world in these centuries, luxury was an important motivation. Luxury might be understood as something which (at first) can be done without, so that luxuries were most appropriate to demonstrate status through conspicuous consumption. But luxury is both a concept and a cultural phenomenon, and in both capacities in early eighteenth-century Europe it already provided the focus for hundreds of political and satirical pamphlets dealing with luxury as either an economic trigger or a vice, the conceptualisation reflecting either liberal or conservative opinion makers' ideals for society.[18] This goes hand in hand with the fact that, during this century, luxury became more widespread in society – to some extent found in everyday goods – and appeared in new forms.

As mentioned above, the availability of luxury goods coincided with a new civility in eating habits, interior designs and ways of socialising, forming a distinct civilisation process.[19] Much of the new consumption befitting this development featured goods from the colonies and/or world trade. Europeans increasingly brought the world into their living rooms: tea, dye-wood, lacquer work and shawls from the East; ivory, gold and exotic woods from Africa; and sugar, rum, mahogany wood and cotton from the West Indies and Americas eventually became well-known features of Danish homes. The centre for it all was the capital, Copenhagen. It was here that most of the companies had their warehouses and offices, and already by the beginning of the eighteenth century all imaginable goods could be bought in Copenhagen and from there resold in towns all over the realm.

Augustenborg Castle, 1725

The Dukes of Augustenborg's official title was Duke of Slesvig-Holsten-Sønderborg,[20] and their main seat was Augustenborg Castle, named after the first duchess of this particular line, Duchess Augusta. The Dukes of Augustenborg were royal siblings, heirs to Norway and the Duchies, and later married into the Danish Royal House. This importance of the family in Danish history continued until 1848 when the duke and his brother broke the old ties with Denmark and headed the Schleswig-Holstein rebellion, leading to a three-year war over the Duchies and, after Danish victory, the expulsion of the duke and his family from the realm. Thereafter the family took up residence in Prussia.

Not much is known of the old Augustenborg Castle, but in old topographies it is described as having a four-wing layout, well equipped and fairly stately with a beautiful garden and behind this a forest with avenues cut through it.[21] Fortunately, an inventory of one apartment in the year 1725 has survived, connected to a complicated legal case after the death of a ducal mother-in-law who lived there, Countess Marie Elisabeth Ahlefeldt, née Leiningen-Dachsburg-Hartenburg.[22] Her apartment covered five rooms, which was a standard size in castles for private chambers of princely persons, and it seems to have been well furbished and (surprisingly) modern for an elderly woman – she was born in 1648. She brought the furniture to Augustenborg Castle from her former residence at her late husband's Gråsten Castle,[23] which was much more splendid than the old Augustenborg Castle before it was partially destroyed by fire in 1757. Given her considerable wealth and the fact that she appears to have been a strong-willed woman,[24] it is plausible that she herself played a major role in the selection of how to equip her apartment at Augustenborg Castle.

The walls of her antechamber were covered with new and expensive hangings.[25] Perhaps, we might guess, they showed landscapes or allegories of Roman history, then the highest fashion. Two windows were covered with sets of yellow curtains, probably silk and most likely of French origin, although Chinese silks were also found in Denmark at this time. On the wall hung a gilded mirror which both expressed wealth and played the practical role of reflecting light and thus saving on expensive candle wax. There were seven portraits hanging on the walls, depicting Duke Frederik Vilhelm (the countess's son-in-law) and her daughter Sophie Amalie, Count Ahlefeldt (her deceased son), Countess Ahlefeldt (her deceased daughter-in-law), the countess to Gråsten Castle (her unmarried granddaughter) and two others. In other words, the closest and highest-ranking family members were displayed in the antechamber where every guest could see them. They would understand what these meant and hence appreciate the rank and status of the countess, and her family's background and connections. Guests could then deduce whether or not they had sufficient rank and status to enter the next room.

In the same room stood 12 'English chairs', probably indicating that they were of polished rather than painted or gilded wood, two of them with armrests. There was a bench and a green armchair, perhaps the very one the countess would use if she was ever to find herself in her antechamber. To go with the sitting furniture there were two tables with 'stone tops', presumably marble, an old 'Chinese' table – that is, lacquerwork, perhaps an import from the East or perhaps of humbler European origin – and a tabletop without legs, which in fact was a kind of big tray. No fireplace is mentioned, which is unsurprising as an antechamber was not for long stays but for arriving, small talk, to see and be seen – hence the family portraits.

In a 'hidden room' – entered through a jib door – we find what must be understood as the countess's library and daily room. Here too the walls were covered with hangings and the door was hidden behind yellow curtains, as were the two windows. These curtains were not only for embellishing the room; they also served to reduce drafts, something that was only too necessary in the splendid but mostly inconvenient and, in winter, bitterly cold rooms of old castles. There were well-stuffed armchairs for the countess's use; along the walls stood four gilded bookshelves, and the inventory mentions valuable ornamental porcelain on the mantelpiece, telling us both of Eastern imports and the fact that the room could be heated. In general, the impression is of a cosy and warm room to which the countess could withdraw together with friends, neighbours and trusted servants. Together with the armchairs there were a lacquered bureau and several *l'hombre* tables for such purposes. Six chairs and two other armchairs with 'gilded feet' – perhaps brass? – and upholstery in yellow moiré silk were followed by two stools of the same calibre. It was important to have furniture of different status value, suiting the rank of various guests; one might have the right to a stool but not a chair, to a chair but not an armchair or, for most, no right to sit at all. Supporting the countess's high rank was a huge portrait of her highest-ranking relative, her son-in-law, the Duke of Augustenborg, boasting a gilded frame.

No fewer than 35 books seem to have been in the countess's possession and kept in this hidden room. They were mostly of a religious nature but there were also five French *romans de coeur* and a copy of *Ulysses*. How she used them is impossible to say, though if they were there only for display, then why were they placed here in the 'hidden room' and not in a more public space? Did they send subtle signals of piety to some and amusement reading to others, referring to the different nature of the books? Did she read them and discuss them with friends? The sources are silent.

In the adjoining red room, the countess could entertain guests and fully display her status; it was a public arena. The walls were covered with red hangings of moiré silk alternating with lanes of embroidered ones, described in the inventory as old. The doors and windows had red moiré silk curtains and most likely between the (then) three windows were placed two gilded consoles with mirrors. Most of the furniture was of red Chinese lacquerwork (Figure 6.3), perhaps of European extraction, comprising two round tables, two bureaus, a red and golden canapé with 'silver feet', six chairs and two armchairs, all with red moiré silk upholstery. In addition, there was a very big green armchair – probably for the countess's own use – and next to it a reading desk with a large book on it, perhaps not for reading but rather for showing the intellectual standard of the house. Lighting was provided by four bracket

Figure 6.3 The lacquer panelling *à la chinoise* from 1732 in King Christian VI's reception room in the Prince's Palais, now the National Museum of Denmark, gives an impression of a 'red salon'. The cabinet in black and gold lacquerwork is a European product; under it is a vase of blue and white porcelain and on top is a night clock. Photo: National Museum of Denmark, Niels Elswing.

lamps and the fireplace was equipped with elegant tools. Had one entered through the antechamber into the red room, one would by now know the countess's background, rank and status as well as her civilised manners in the choice of furniture and decorations.

The civility of her room and socialising can also be discerned from smaller items in the room. On four shelves above the mantelpiece different copper and brass kettles found a home; many more were located in cupboards, together with her silverware. Above the three doors of the room was more of the countess's porcelain: a coffee set for 28, a tea set for 22 and a chocolate set for 16 persons. In 1725, this was a modern trait pointing directly to international trade, regarding both the drinks themselves and their containers, but the countess seems to have taken them to heart and her porcelain services also show her refined manners. Chocolate was somewhat better known in 1725 than tea and especially coffee and was often consumed for breakfast, although this was not to the liking of doctors, who argued that the hot drink would cause the blood to flow too fast in the veins.[26] Not that this stopped anyone from drinking chocolate. Tea and coffee also became, in that order, highly fashionable.

The countess's bed chamber could not live up to the splendour of the red room; in fact, it appears a bit shabby. It was decorated in white and blue, but the curtains were old and apparently did not function properly. Whilst it was still common to use one's bedroom as a sitting room in this period, the state of the room makes it likely that this was not the case here, though there were indeed both chairs and tables and even a small tea tray in the room. The bed is not mentioned, but from the inventory's list of linen it can be deduced to have been well equipped with pillows, eiderdowns and linen sheets. It was made of simple wood draped with green silk, probably of French origin. Maybe the countess had brought the bed with her from Gråsten Castle and the rest of the furniture was not her own choice? Perhaps it is just a case of private rooms being more relaxed than public ones.

For our theme of international consumption, it is perhaps most striking that, although the countess possessed a number of items apparently linked to trade with the Far East, most were probably European pieces in the taste of *chinoiseries*, using French silks or Danish or European lacquerwork. The porcelain, by contrast, was more likely to have been of Chinese extraction; it was only in 1708 that European porcelain was first produced in Meissen and the sources would usually mention this origin if it were the case. But whether directly or just in taste, many of the inventoried items in the 1725 apartment of an elderly woman of the highest standing in society were deeply embedded in or inspired by the trade in exotic luxuries. They were practical; they could show wealth, *savoir-faire* and knowledge of fashionable style in furnishings; and they were suited to both her particular situation and her need to display her status as a countess and mother-in-law to a duke. These global objects thus fulfilled the theoretical triad outlined earlier: they had a function or purpose, signified a specific value and symbolised broader cultural values.

Lille Hesbjerg Manor, 1790s

At Lille Hesbjerg Manor in Funen, things were not at all as they ought to have been in the 1790s. In fact, it was home to a divorced countess, Birgitte Eleonora Rantzau, who had just inherited her deceased mother's furniture from the neighbouring Kragsbjerg Manor. The divorce was a theme for society gossip and highly disreputable:[27] her husband of only a few months, Count Niels Krag Levetzau, was close to the king, and the wedding had been celebrated with pomp; the countess was now pregnant, yet fierce accusations soon arose between the spouses and a divorce was permitted by the king. Moreover, after some years, in 1795, the king granted the countess the rank of a widow, enabling her to act legally in her own right. At the time of the divorce, a relative had provided her suitable accommodation at Lille Hesbjerg Manor, which was a modest three-wing, half-timbered house with relatively small estate lands. Thus, even though the inhabitant was of high rank, it is not a ducal residence such as Augustenburg Castle. However, it was two generations later and, as shall be seen, the direct influence of global trade had grown considerably and was demonstrated much more clearly in this home.

The household was small: by the general census of 1801 the countess, aged 41, and her son of 15 years lived together with a lady's companion, only 16 years old. The household was governed by a house master leading a staff of indoor servants comprising a house maid, a female cook, a kitchen maid and 'a fragile old servant'. This is not impressive when compared with similar manor houses in Denmark at the time,[28] and it might be ascribed to the countess's peculiar position which meant that she did not engage in much socialising. The countess resided at Lille Hesbjerg Manor from 1793 to 1809; in 1797, inventories both for her mother's Kragsbjerg Manor and for her own Lille Hesbjerg Manor were made.[29] In the inventories for the two places, many fully equipped rooms are listed, but here, and in line with the first example, we shall restrict ourselves to those which seem to have served as the daily dwelling for the Countess Rantzau at Lille Hesbjerg Manor. They were in part decorated and furbished before her time, in part equipped with the furniture bequeathed by her mother.

One of the rooms, perhaps used by the young count, served as a sleeping chamber with three windows. In this room the commission of the estate, which drew up the inventory, found two gilded mirrors with consoles and a mahogany chest of drawers. In the drawers were curtains of nettle, a thin flax fabric,[30] several textiles for upholstery and quite a bit of equipment for beds, including two 'yellow striped English bed curtains', probably meaning cotton with yellow stripes. An ottoman upholstered with yellow embroidered silk fabric and with a red and white cover of French linen indicates the period's interest not only in the Far East but also in the Near East. Two chairs with round backs and three other simpler chairs painted white were equipped with chintz upholstery, and there was a brown tea table with drawers containing porcelain sugar bowls, a tea caddy of tinplate and two small plates. The windows were covered with white linen roller blinds – another inspiration from the East – and in front of them stood what seems to be a Chinese painted folding screen.

In the next room there were huge quantities of linen and tableware. According to the inventories this was the case in all rooms: drawers and cupboards, chests and other storage furniture were bursting with linen tablecloths and napkins of the best quality, such as German Bielefeld or French Chambray, as well as almost uncountable numbers of bed sheets and so forth of linen or cotton fabric, the latter perhaps of Indian or more likely English or Danish origin, using Eastern and American materials.

For laying the table the countess was just as well equipped. A set of Copenhagen porcelain was laid out for display; more mundane were 12 chamber pots of stoneware and four in blue and white faience to go with ten sets for washstands, indicating the late eighteenth century's new-found concern with hygiene. For the equally new fashion of placing flowering plants in the windows, the house possessed 11 stoneware flowerpots. At the table, rum punch, the colonial drink above all others, could be served in a punch bowl of Chinese porcelain and another of stoneware. No fewer than 171 plates of white faience, two of blue faience and 50 of porcelain – nine of them Chinese, five Japanese and the rest from Copenhagen – were also at hand. Soup could be served from 67 dishes, and for dessert there were 29 faience or six porcelain plates to choose from, two of them Chinese. Although relatively small in number, the presence of this Chinese and Japanese porcelain is significant in expressing a cultural desire for consuming the exotic. Coffee, meanwhile, was mostly served in Chinese cups with a handle, specially made for the European market, and teapots were of Chinese, Meissen or Copenhagen porcelain as well as different forms of faience, probably mostly Danish or Dutch. The countess's tableware was thus replete with global meaning (Figure 6.4).

Heating stoves were mostly of fine and expensive Swedish faience, with some of Norwegian iron. A striking feature in these inventories are bird cages – one for parrots and one for turtle doves; keeping birds in cages was in all likelihood an inspiration from more exotic shores. The countess could also call on Eastern inspiration and carry a parasol on a lacquered stick while waking in the garden, and in her rooms, just as at Augustenborg Castle though more in the style of the rococo than the

Figure 6.4 These two slender porcelain vases in Kangxi style were part of a larger set delivered to the King's Artificial Chamber in 1701. They show the high-quality porcelain that Europeans at last learned how to produce some ten years later in Meissen. Photo: National Museum of Denmark, Arnold Mikkelsen.

baroque, she had furniture upholstered with silks and cotton fabrics, such as chintz. Of older extraction were her gilded furniture and mirrors; more modern were her mahogany card tables and several cupboards and chests of drawers of the same noble wood. Even wallpapers of Chinese origin were to be found in her storerooms, and the windows were embellished with curtains of silk, French or English linen and cotton fabric, the latter of a colourful kind based on patterns from India.

The theme continued in the room that seems to have been the countess's own boudoir, where white curtains with fringe supplemented by green silk taffeta roller blinds were hung in the windows. Most likely at the windows stood two small, white-painted tables with 'green edges and green, rifled feet' (that is: fluted legs) and on each was a white stoneware flowerpot. On a small, oblong, brown-painted wooden table was a blue and white faience sugar bowl together with a wooden bowl containing ammonium carbonate, praised as a laxative. Perhaps the countess would have appreciated the powder, which she could take with water from the source in Pyrmont, two bottles of which were also present in the room.

Apart from a mahogany toilet table with mirror, drawers and a crystalware toilet set and a number of smaller pieces, including tables with porcelain tea sets, the room was dominated by the countess's modern, iron four-post bed, probably imported from Great Britain. It boasted elegant curtains; the same went for another, somewhat more modest bed next to the countess's own. In front of them there was a fashionable and modern oak wood oblong table with a waxed green tablecloth. To go with it were six chairs with blue linen upholstery. The countess's own chair may have been the wing chair with two cushions and yellow linen upholstery, in front of which was placed a small copper brazier to keep her feet warm. Another comfortable brown chair with wooden stool was ideal for keeping one's feet from the drafts which crept along the floors. The whole room was lit by a brass chandelier and on the wall were, among other things, a barometer and a thermometer, indicating a knowledge of the new scientific instruments so important for international trade – though one might suspect the countess, in another bid in status competition, possessed these instruments more for display than for actual use.

The list of items in this very rich interior goes on; however, this should suffice to make it clear that, at Lille Hesbjerg Manor in the 1790s, the global world of consumption had made a deep impression on the home, both in artefacts themselves and in cultural habits such as roller blinds or the use of tea sets. The cultural importance of consuming exotic food and drink had shifted, of course: things that had once been very exotic – such as tea, coffee and chocolate, cotton and silk fabric, lacquer and mahogany wood furniture – had now begun to enter the sphere of everyday goods to a degree that the once exotic may not have been perceived as such anymore. Yet such an argument should not be stretched too far: there were more goods from the East (and West) than could be seen at Augustenborg Castle two generations earlier, along with a range of Oriental-inspired European goods produced in Germany, France and increasingly Britain. The countess was not rich or of princely status – in contrast with her counterpart at Augustenborg Castle – and her consumption does not seem to suggest the same keen concern about displaying status. Nevertheless, time had passed, and she possessed a greater variety of exotic goods and European replicas than were present at Augustenborg Castle. This is especially evident in terms of the equipage for eating and drinking: Countess Rantzau lived an eighteenth-century life of civilised manners at Lille Hesbjerg Manor.

Brede House, 1805

During the eighteenth century a number of *maisons de plaisance* were built north of Copenhagen, in some cases by old elites but mostly by tradesmen of bourgeois extraction rising in society and gaining their fortunes from trade and early industry. Indeed, following the example of the old elite, many of them ended up as estate owners, some with noble titles. Danish–Norwegian neutral trade benefitted greatly from the outbreak of the American War of Independence in 1776, and in Danish historiography the decades up to the English Wars of 1801 and 1807–14, the Danish part of the Napoleonic Wars, are often labelled *den florissante periode* – the blooming period. Not least among those who prospered were these merchants whose base was in the old, fortified, fairly small, dirty and cramped Copenhagen. In the summer, and increasingly for most of the year, they sought fresh air and tranquillity in the countryside, away from though near to the capital.

One of these merchants was Peter van Hemert. He had interests in the Asiatic Company (of which he was one of the directors from 1776 to 1783), trade with the West Indies, various parts of Europe and within Denmark–Norway, and much more besides. He owed much to his father Joost and his grandfather, the Dutch immigrant Peter van Hemert, from whom he inherited a copper mill in Brede, some 15 kilometres north of Copenhagen in the beautiful Mill Stream Valley. Here, a house was erected by his predecessors, but in the 1790s he decided to have a new one built to the highest standards of the day. That this decision went together with his businesses being in financial difficulty is our luck as he went bankrupt in 1805, leaving posterity an inventory of the new house.[31] It is hence possible to examine some of the most important rooms, though not in such meticulous detail as the two other houses, mainly because the inventory was made in January 1806 when the house was not in use and all the smaller personal items had been removed. That said, more long lists of belongings are unnecessary and would be too repetitious. For let it be said straight away, the global imprint on this house is immediately evident in the huge amounts of silverware, porcelain from both the Far East and Europe, Indian textiles and European copies of them, silks of different extraction, and food and drink of exotic or foreign origin. All these tell of cosmopolitan living in a rich and civilised house of the 1790s which lived up to all standards for elite living of the day in Denmark as in Europe more generally.

Back in 1795, the new house had been erected as a neoclassical building with an elegant park behind it. The factory huts were a bit too close, but they needed the water from the Mill Stream and could not be moved. As interior decorator, Peter van Hemert chose the Royal carpenter, Joseph Christian Lilje, who not only was the best of his day but also worked in both the French and English traditions. What could be more suitable for the family van Hemert? It had to be a large house, both for status reasons and because the Copenhagen household in 1787 numbered no fewer than 27 persons. Van Hemert himself and his second wife Agatha Hooglandt (also of Dutch extraction) had five daughters, though the two eldest had left home before Brede House was finished. Thus, Brede House needed to accommodate their daughters Justine, Petronella and Maria Agatha as well as their son Joost. The servants in these years of – on paper – staggering profits for van Hemert's business included both a butler and a housekeeper, cooks and kitchen maids, chamber maids, house maids and two male servants, while the children had private teachers. In winter they lived in Copenhagen and, from 1795–1805, spent the summer in Brede House.

Brede House has three storeys: the cellar housing the kitchens and storage facilities, and the ground floor with highly elegant entertaining rooms comprising entrance hall, dining hall, grand hall, the mistress's entertaining room and the grand salon, as well as the family's daily dining room and sitting room. On the first floor there was a guest room, Miss Justine's chamber, a shared chamber for the two younger daughters, a two-room apartment for the son, storage, a master bedroom, a tea (or morning) room and the daughters' living room, as well as van Hemert's huge library. Following the pattern of the two previous examples, we shall look into just a few of these rooms.

The dining room was a Pompeian decorated hall with four windows hung with cotton curtains and with cupboards below. A dining table of no fewer than eight parts was at hand and scalable for the number of guests. With it went 12 lacquered chairs with chintz seats, which could hardly be more exotic, and along the walls were four serving tables. Twenty chairs of lesser refinement were tucked away in the adjoining storage rooms, while the dining room itself also contained a tea table and two grand chandeliers with glass drops together with three wall brackets that could create an enchanted atmosphere. For setting the table, full sets of porcelain, faience, silver and linen were at the ready, even during winter.

Upstairs and turning to the right, guests would be accommodated in the green guest room, itself a display case of Eastern trade. The green theme was everywhere: the interior decorator, Lilje, had green silk upholstery put both on a sofa and on nine chairs (all of which were probably lacquered), and he used it for curtains à la Sheraton and to cover an iron four-post bed, probably of English provenance. On the walls, rice paper sheets imported from China in green with exotic flowers and scenery were glued to linen frames above the panelling. A gilded mirror with a painting of rabbits underneath – a personal favourite of J.C. Lilje – was accompanied by huge mirrors and a clock. The room was completed with a washstand with toilet set and mirror; a tea table and a basket with a probably European-made porcelain tea set was at hand for the use of guests.

On the other side of the staircase was Miss Justine's chamber (Figure 6.5). Her four-post bed was hung with chintz curtains and had a cover blanket embellished with floral motifs. The bed curtains and cover were most likely imported from England, woven and perhaps painted with Indian-inspired designs. Next to this room was the living room used by all three daughters for writing, needlework or playing music on the *Klausumball*, a type of small harpsicord. Teapots of porcelain and brass with six teacups were found in the room, and on the walls flowery wallpaper provided a desirable feminine impression, underlined by very light cotton window curtains. Dressed according to the current fashion (Figure 6.1),[32] as they surely were, their dresses would resemble the curtains and be of cotton in classical style, somewhat cold in the north, but then they would have had woollen shawls from Kashmir or, perhaps more likely, from Paisley in Scotland – inspired by Indian designs.

Figure 6.5 Miss Justine van Hemert had her bed chamber at Brede House decorated with modern English cotton window and bed curtains à l'Indie, here remade at Brede House. The mirrors are original to the room. Through the window, a glimpse of the factory buildings. Photo: National Museum of Denmark, Woldbye & Klemp.

At Brede House, these few indications once again show how a mix of domestic, European and global, mostly Far Eastern, goods had filtered into every aspect of daily living and every room in an elite house of the late eighteenth century. Other than mahogany, Caribbean goods were more evident in food items, above all chocolate, coffee and sugar – although tobacco should not be forgotten. Well-known insecurities of new money aside, things went according to the standards of the day at Brede House – as long as it lasted. This brief insight into the home gained from the bankruptcy proceedings tells of a bourgeois environment around 1800 living up to ideals and partaking in the pleasures (and curses) of consumer society to a degree probably higher than the old elite. Even in January, when the house was not fully equipped, there were many more global items at Brede, especially in comparison with Augustenborg Castle, and they pointed to full-scale, globally engaged consumption. Compared with Lille Hesbjerg Manor, perhaps the most striking change is the quality of the Brede House furniture and general household possessions. Moreover, the building, decorating and furnishing of the new Brede House – placed in the hands of the highly professional J.C. Lilje – was above all a token of a new elite seeking to take steps up the social ladder through the use of both modern consumption strategies and old, well-proven elite symbols, such as a country house.

Conclusions: with the world in the living room

In this chapter, we have followed three inventories from three different elite houses in Denmark, covering the decades from 1725 to 1805. They show that international trade, often but not exclusively connected to European colonialism, deeply permeated all three homes, especially in the pursuit of what were initially luxuries in furniture and nutrition. Weight has been laid on both the presence of things and their meaning in the particular cultural setting. A general trait was the presence of more and more things; another was that international consumption was a mix of exotic goods themselves and European replicas – in fact, the latter outnumbered the former in the first two examples and probably even in the third. Returning to the three analytical levels of the cultural meaning of things, it is apparent that they expressed functionality, a certain period of style, and a cultural wish for owning them and using them according to developing ideas of refined and civilised life. This demanded, for example, the presence of teacups and elegant salon furniture, or Chinese lacquerwork and silks. At best they would be brought home on Asiatic Company ships; more often, however, they were of European origin but still of high craftsmanship and expressing the cultural values of possessing and using exotics.

The particular context of the three houses was also important, not least the different social situations they represented. The apartment at Augustenborg Castle was probably furbished by the Countess Ahlefeldt herself, using furniture chosen from her splendid former home, whereas the Countess Rantzau at Lille Hesbjerg Manor lived with a mix of what was in the house provided to her and what she had inherited from her mother. At Brede House, van Hemert turned to a professional, making it difficult to assess the degree to which his and his wife's tastes and preferences were being expressed in the house; for the formal rooms, it was probably not much. It is an old truth in elite studies that elite lives were, in many ways, mediated by others,[33] be they servants or a hired decorator who knew the fashionable styles of the day. The result was a house of high quality, especially compared with the situation at Lille Hesbjerg Manor, one which contested the absolute reign of the old elites' dwellings such as Augustenborg Castle, itself rebuilt in the 1760s and 1770s to fit modern standards of comfort and take a step upwards in scale to meet status concerns.[34] It is also telling that what was once exotic was now so well known that it could form the basis for fashionable, professional interior decorating – very different from the expression of social or personal wants and tastes through single pieces of furniture, porcelain and the like.

Another contextual difference was that the manifestation of rank and princely status was at the forefront at the ducal Augustenborg Castle, and the new goods fitted this traditional purpose very nicely. At Lille Hesbjerg Manor, we visited nobility on the decline, and the new goods perhaps mostly filled new needs of comfort and ideas of civilised living, which (with origins back in the Renaissance) rapidly developed during the eighteenth century. At Brede House, a display of new money (perhaps to stiffen creditors' belief in the merchant house) and consumption of the best objects of the day created a mix of international goods in one of Denmark's elegant *maisons de plaisance* around 1800. Ironically, this was around the same time as the great catastrophe of Danish trade in 1807 – domestic, European and global alike – when the English Wars broke out again and previous Danish neutrality experienced a seven-year intermission. In the same year, Copenhagen was bombarded and the Royal Danish Navy was subjugated by the British; the Danish colonies were occupied, merchants could not sell their goods and went into bankruptcy, and merchant ships were captured. In 1813 Denmark–Norway itself went bankrupt, followed by the ceding of Norway to Sweden in 1814 as the price for peace.

With the new century, the prosperous 'flourishing days' had ended and, even though Denmark continued as a colonial power after the English Wars, it never returned to the same level. After the wars, colonial trade never really regained power; new ideas of liberal trade versus the old mercantilism also worked against the various royal chartered companies and favoured factories. In 1843, the Asiatic Company was dissolved and two years later the Indian possessions were sold to Britain; the African forts went to the same buyer in 1850, and the West Indian islands to the United States of America in 1917. However, international consumption persisted and swiftly spread into society at large during the nineteenth century.[35] Today, it is so intertwined with everyday life that we can hardly tell it apart from other kinds of consumption when simultaneously shopping in the supermarket for Danish flour and Indian tea, Persian almonds and French wine. In the general discussion, the globalised world is often seen as something new, a token perhaps of the world after the Second World War. At least for the elite and even at the Nordic fringe of Europe, already in the eighteenth century the world's goods were present in their homes, food and everyday life, in their cultural practices and desires.

Notes

1. Feldbæk and Justesen, *Kolonierne i Asien og Afrika*, 41; Hornby, *Kolonierne i Vestindien*; Brimnes et al., *Danmark og Kolonierne*, vol. 1–5, especially the volume *Indien*, 34ff.
2. In the eighteenth century, the Danish Realm proper covered the Kingdoms Denmark and Norway, the Duchies Slesvig and Holsten as well as the Faroe Isles, Iceland and Greenland. In this chapter, Denmark is used as a cover term for all parts. The Duchies were governed in German, hence the sources use Schleswig and Holstein.
3. The Royal Danish Ministry of Foreign Affairs, *Asiatisk Plads*.
4. Shown by Asger Nørlund Christensen in Guldberg et al., 'Handel og vandel', 36–60.
5. Venborg Pedersen, 'At the Nordic fringe of global consumption', 141–56.
6. Many references could be made, but two newer British studies have been very inspirational: Berg and Clifford (eds.), *Consumers and Luxury*; Berg and Eger, *Luxury in the Eighteenth Century*. On Danish material, first and foremost Venborg Pedersen, *Luksus*.
7. Roche, *A History of Everyday Things*, 8.
8. Venborg Pedersen, 'At the Nordic fringe of global consumption', 145–7; Gerndt, *Kultur als Forschungsfeld*, 117–31.
9. The reconstruction of Brede House is described in Clemmensen and Raabyemagle, *Brede Hovedbygning 1795–1806*.
10. A point made by economic historian Jan de Vries as well in *The Industrious Revolution*.
11. Elias, *Über den Prozess der Zivilisation*.
12. Holberg, 'Epistola 91'.
13. Veblen, *The Theory of the Leisure Class*.
14. Burke, 'Res et verba'.
15. Venborg Pedersen, 'At the Nordic fringe of global consumption', 145–7; Gerndt, *Kultur als Forschungsfeld*, 117–31.
16. Levi, 'On micro-history', 93–113. In cultural anthropology and European ethnology, which have provided so much inspiration to cultural history, this would imply a meticulous description, attention to detail and open-ended analysis. Geertz, 'Thick description'.
17. Venborg Pedersen, 'Etnologi og ny kulturhistorie'; Venborg Pedersen, *Luksus*.
18. Berg and Eger, *Luxury in the Eighteenth Century*; Venborg Pedersen, *Luksus*.
19. Elias, *Über den Prozess der Zivilisation*.
20. In German, Schleswig-Holstein-Sonderburg(-Augustenburg). They were usually referred to as Dukes of Augustenborg in order to distinguish them from other dukes of Slesvig-Holsten(-Sønderborg); there were always several such, including the Danish king as duke.
21. Pontoppidan, *Den Danske Atlas*, 493; Paulsen, *Augustenborgerne*.
22. Danish State Archives (DSA), Landsarkivet for Sønderjylland: Det augustenborgske Godsarkiv, pk. 145: 1724–1818: Testamenter og arvesager; Venborg Pedersen, *Hertuger*, 111–19.
23. Gravenstein in German. With the countess's daughter's marriage to the Duke of Augustenborg, Gråsten Castle came into Augustenborg possession, in part as inheritance, in part as a settlement of the deceased count Ahlefeldt's monetary debt to the Duke. It served thereafter as summer castle and hunting seat for the dukes.
24. Venborg Pedersen, *Hertuger*.
25. DSA, Landsarkivet for Sønderjylland: Det augustenborgske Godsarkiv, pk. 145: 1724–1818: Testamenter og arvesager.
26. Venborg Pedersen, *Luksus*, 218.
27. Leilund and Boritz, 'Herregården Lille Hesbjerg og Birgitte Eleonora Rantzau'.
28. Erichsen and Venborg Pedersen, *The Danish Country House*.
29. DSA, Landsarkivet for Fyn: Folketælling 1801. Odense Amt. Odense Herred. Ubberud Sogn. QB 007. Brahesborg Gods. Pk 29/9. 1797. Skiftedokumenter mv. efter grevinde Rantzau.

30 The sources use the word nettle, which by this point in time was not the original from the nettle plant but made of flax. In the latter part of the nineteenth century it became a thin cotton fabric, which the word still means in modern Danish.
31 DSA, Landsarkivet for Sjælland mv.: Folketælling 1787. København. Rosenborgs Kvarter. Store Købmagergade. Københavns Rytterdistrikts Birk. 1800–1809. Forseglings- og registrerings-protokol nr 1.
32 Melchior and Venborg Pedersen, *Moden i Danmark gennem 400 år*, vol. 1, 90–133.
33 Venborg Pedersen, *Hertuger*, 51–92.
34 Venborg Pedersen, *Hertuger*, 119–28.
35 This happened from the late eighteenth century onwards, as demonstrated in Venborg Pedersen, *Luksus*, where not only elite consumption but also peasant and middle-class examples are analysed.

Bibliography

Berg, Maxine, and Helen Clifford, eds. *Consumers and Luxury: Consumer culture in Europe 1650–1850*. Manchester and New York: Manchester University Press, 1999.
Berg, Maxine, and Elisabeth Eger, eds. *Luxury in the Eighteenth Century: Debates, desires, and delectable goods*. Basingstoke: Palgrave Macmillan, 2003.
Brimnes, Niels, Hans Christian Gulløv, Erik Gøbel, Per Oluf Hernæs, Poul Erik Olsen and Mikkel Venborg Pedersen, eds. *Danmark og Kolonierne*, vols 1–5. Copenhagen: Gad, 2017.
Burke, Peter. 'Res et Verba: conspicuous consumption in the early modern world'. In *Consumption and the World of Goods*, edited by John Brewer and Roy Porter, 148–61. London and New York: Routledge, 2000.
Clemmensen, Tove, and Mogens B. Mackeprang. *Kina og Danmark 1600–1950. Kinafart og Kinamode*. Copenhagen: Nationalmuseet, 1980.
Clemmensen, Tove, and Hanne Raabyemagle. *Brede Hovedbygning 1795–1806*. Copenhagen: Nationalmuseet, 1996.
Elias, Norbert. *Über den Prozess der Zivilisation. Soziogenetische und psychogenetische Untersuchungen*. Frankfurt am Main: Suhrkamp Verlag 1980 (original 1939).
Erichsen, John, and Mikkel Venborg Pedersen. *The Danish Country House*. Copenhagen: Historismus, 2014.
Feldbæk, Ole, and Ole Justesen. *Kolonierne i Asien og Afrika*. Copenhagen: Politiken, 1980.
Geertz, Clifford. 'Thick description: towards an interpretive theory of culture'. In *The Interpretation of Cultures: Selected essays*, by Clifford Geertz, 3–30. New York: Basic Books, 1993 (original 1973).
Gerndt, Helge. *Kultur als Forschungsfeld. Über volkskundliches Denken und Arbeiten*. Munich: Münchener Verein für Volkskunde, 1986.
Guldberg, Mette, Asger Nørlund Christensen, Max Pedersen, Christina Folke Ax, Martin Rheinheimer and Elsemarie Dam-Jensen: 'Handel og vandel – dansk-hollandske kontakter i 1600–1700-tallet', *Temp – Tidsskrift for historie* 10 (2020): 36–60.
Holberg, Ludvig. 'Epistola 91'. In *Ludvig Holbergs Epistler*, edited by F.J. Billeskov Jansen, vol. 2, 47–50. Copenhagen: Gyldendal, 1944–54.
Hornby, Ove. *Kolonierne i Vestindien*. Copenhagen: Gyldendal, 1980.
Leilund, Helle, and Mette Boritz. 'Herregården Lille Hesbjerg og Birgitte Eleonora Rantzau – historien om en usædvanlig komtesse og hendes stuer'. *Nationalmuseets Arbejdsmark* 2003: 177–96.
Levi, Giovanni. 'On micro-history'. In *New Perspectives on Historical Writing*, edited by Peter Burke, 93–113. Cambridge: Polity Press, 1991.
Melchior, Marie Riegels, and Mikkel Venborg Pedersen. *Moden i Danmark gennem 400 år*, vols 1–2. Copenhagen: Gad, 2022.
Paulsen, Jørgen. *Augustenborgerne. Slottet – Flækken – Fyrstehuset*. Copenhagen: Gad, 1981.
Pontoppidan, Erich. *Den danske Atlas*. Copenhagen, 1781.
Roche, Daniel. *A History of Everyday Things: The birth of consumption in France 1600–1800*. Cambridge: Cambridge University Press, 2000.

The Royal Danish Ministry of Foreign Affairs. *Asiatisk Plads. The Danish Foreign Service's new Headquarters in Copenhagen*. Copenhagen: The Royal Danish Ministry of Foreign Affairs, 1980.
Veblen, Thorstein. *The Theory of the Leisure Class*. New York: Dover Publications, 1994 (1899).
Venborg Pedersen, Mikkel. 'Etnologi og ny kulturhistorie'. In *Norden og Europa. Fagtradisjioner i nordisk etnologi og folkloristik*, edited by Bjarne Rogan and Bente Gullveig Alver. Oslo: Novus, 2000, 249–53.
Venborg Pedersen, Mikkel. *Hertuger. At synes og at være i Augustenborg 1700–1850*. Copenhagen: Museum Tusculanum Press, 2005.
Venborg Pedersen, Mikkel. *Luksus. Forbrug og kolonier i Danmark i det 18. århundrede*. Copenhagen: Museum Tusculanum Press, 2013.
Venborg Pedersen, Mikkel. 'At the Nordic fringe of global consumption: a Copenhagen bourgeois' home and the use of new goods in the mid-18th century'. In *Fashionable Encounters: Perspectives and trends in textile and dress in the early modern Nordic world*, edited by Tove Mathiassen, Marie-Louise Nosch, Maj Ringgaard, Kirsten Toftegaard and Mikkel Venborg Pedersen, 141–56. Oxford and Philadelphia: Oxbow Books, 2014.
Vries, Jan de. *The Industrious Revolution: Consumer behaviour and the household economy, 1650 to the present*. Cambridge: Cambridge University Press, 2008.

7
Interiors as a visiting card: decoration, consumption and material culture in a mid-nineteenth-century Romanian country house

Nicoleta Roman

1853, the year in which the Crimean War broke out, saw the publication in London of a book signed by 'a British resident of twenty years in the East' and suggestively entitled *The Frontier Lands of the Christian and the Turk*. Later republished with the revised title *The Danubian Principalities*, it offers subjective glimpses of the social history of the Romanian Principalities of Wallachia and Moldavia.[1] Its Scottish-born author, James Henry Skene, compares almost all he sees with his native land. On his travels, he is received by boyars (nobles) and invited to their country residences, having been forewarned that 'everything is in a very different style'. East and West are, in his opinion, still quite distinct cultural spaces in this respect in the mid-nineteenth century. As a general characteristic, Skene observes that:

> They have a strange notion of a country house in Wallachia. They build a splendid mansion, not on the banks of the river which winds through the fields there, nor on the borders of that old oak wood, nor on the rising ground which must command so fine a view towards the south; but in the centre of their poor, squalid, filthy, assemblage of huts, which they call a village.[2]

He argues that the space around the Romanian country house 'does not form a picturesque object in the science of landscape gardening'. It thus lacks an aesthetic harmony with its surroundings and does not foster meditation or recreation: 'and not a seat nor rustic arbour to go with a book'. In the mid-nineteenth century, the Romanian country house was seen by the elite not as a unit that included a park, a garden or places for outdoor sociability ('neither walks, nor rides, nor drives'), but merely as a building that had to be lavish to legitimise and impose their social status.

Skene indirectly grasps the difference between an economy influenced by industrialisation and one which remained profoundly agrarian and was only starting to be open to change following the Treaty of Adrianople (1829). Free trade treaties made with the Ottoman Porte by Western European powers and Russia brought new areas of economic interest into contact, although throughout the nineteenth century the Porte's alliances remained, as Kasaba points out, 'kaleidoscopic in character'.[3] The Crimean War and the 'Eastern Question' gave the public, via diplomacy, the perception of a weak and fragile Ottoman Empire,[4] the economy and market of which was ready to be explored and 'conquered' by Western powers (France, England, Austria, Germany). The ambition to colonise such a vast territory through economic hegemony brought these powers into competition with one another and with the Russian Empire. Borderland territories experienced the impact of the clash of these economic interests. The inter-imperialist rivalry over the Ottoman market was doubled by poor infrastructure, a local tendency to hold economic monopolies and tight centralisation, all factors that made it difficult for foreign investment and goods to infiltrate before the mid-nineteenth century.[5] As a response, efforts intensified and the involvement of Western powers in the regulation of the trade, industry and steam navigation through the Danube and the Black Sea ports should be seen as a strategy to assure an economic presence and facilitate the circulation of goods. Prior to the 1830s trade intermediaries, mostly Balkan Orthodox merchants, were dominant, buying Western goods from fairs such as those in Leipzig.[6] Even though they paid more for French and English merchandise, it was still profitable for them when selling the goods in the Romanian lands – goods that were afterwards reported as being either Austrian or simply European.[7]

Goods that came from Britain through the port cities of Moldavia (Galaţi) and Wallachia (Brăila) were divided into four categories (manufactured goods and cotton, sugar, iron and coal), but before the mid-nineteenth century the British commercial presence remained modest in comparison with that of Turkey, France, Austria, Russia and even the newly independent Greece.[8] The first commercial house of the British Empire established in Wallachia (1834), Bell & Anderson, had the political support of London and the ambition to counterbalance Austrian imports in the principality.[9] It was short-lived, but it showed the potential of the Romanian market, the significance of the trade routes and the competition between old (Austria) and new (Britain) economic partners of the Principalities. In the 1850s, Britain ranked third after Austria and Turkey in the commerce with these territories;[10] it then had a slight ascendancy in the 1860s, but by the end of the nineteenth century its involvement had decreased.

The Union of the Romanian Principalities (1859), their recognition (1861), the independence of the Ottoman Empire (1878) and the declaration of Romania as a kingdom under the house of Hohenzollern-Sigmaringen rule (1881) made this territory fully enter a global market. Step by step, political barriers to a direct economic foreign presence in this European peripheral market faded.[11] This economic integration connects with two other factors (political and cultural) in a period that lasted from the Treaty of Adrianople to the end of the First World War.[12] The break from Turkish or 'Oriental' taste was gradual and enthusiastically embraced by the young generation, as 'Turkish trousers were replaced by German clothes, the Turkish divan by the French couch, and the hookah by cigars'.[13] Europeanisation was instrumentalised by the young Romanian elite to emancipate themselves from the Porte. After independence they shaped and promoted a national identity for the country in terms of architectural style, manufactured goods, industry and sociocultural policies. These shifts were in their infancy when James Skene made his observations about the country houses and the region's specificity and disconnectedness from Western Europe. His visits to the Romanian elite were intermediated by the secretary of the British consul in Bucharest, Effingham Grant. Afterwards, Skene himself became the British consul in Aleppo.

The aim of this chapter is to observe the place and significance of global goods in a peripheral European country house, namely that of the Golescu family in present-day Romania. I consider global goods as means by which the local elites experienced and achieved Westernisation and their presence in the country house as an effect of a cultural encounter. In a *longue durée* approach, the country house's interior inevitably changes and with it the importance of items depending on availability, the tastes of the owner and the trends in art and display. The interior is considered as an ephemeral assemblage meant to transmit the personal experiences of the owner/family and their status, prestige and cultural belonging. Thus, while we consider the house as an 'architectural and socio-political statement', both its exterior and its interior were intimate declarations of the identity of its owners.[14]

Elite country houses in the Romanian provincial setting

Subject to Ottoman suzerainty, on a periphery of the empire, in a region with an ethnically and confessionally diverse population, predominantly Christian but open to various cultural influences, the Principalities offered a contradictory spectacle to the foreign visitor. The pre-modern period saw 'a luxuriousness in the adornment of interiors with mural paintings – of religious or historical themes – in the Byzantine tradition, Oriental-style floral painting and stucco-work, and furniture, carpets, embroideries, silk, and silverware produced in local workshops or brought either from the Western world (Venice, Florence, Nuremberg, Augsburg, etc.) or the Near East'.[15] Anca Brătuleanu discusses the notion of the ensemble for the residences of the Romanian elite, 'understood as a grouping of buildings/architectural elements with a relative autonomy' and a spatial organisation similar to that of Western Europe but incorporating 'a certain traditionalism that meets innovation and the new brought from other regions'.[16] In short, traditional large mansions specific to the Balkan region – named, with an Oriental accent, *konak*, and comprising enclosed ensembles of brick structures – were already starting to change their functionality in the eighteenth century.

The direction of influence on residential seats in the country was from the ruling prince named by the Porte to the noble elite (boyars). Brătuleanu remarks that Constantin Brâncoveanu, ruler of Wallachia, borrowed and adapted elements already in circulation from *The Four Books of Architecture* by Andrea Palladio (1508–80).[17] In the second part of his book, Palladio defines the connection between the owner and his country house, the place where he spends his time in 'seeing and adorning his own possessions, and by industry, and the art of agriculture, improving his estate'.[18] The country house had the role of restoring one to a healthy balance, lost in the tumult of administrative and state affairs in the capital, of being the setting for relaxation alongside family and friends, but also for study and contemplation. The site chosen for the house should be in the middle of the estate. It might be near a source of water but nevertheless should be protected from the weather; and special attention should be given to the organisation of the interior in relation to household activities.[19]

By the middle of the nineteenth century, then, the Oriental type of residence was losing its appeal, falling into disuse or being completely transformed. James Henry Skene, the Scottish traveller with whom we began this exploration, notes that one exception to the rule of the Oriental-style *konak*, and one that marks the cultural transition, is the country house of the Golescu boyar family, which he describes as follows:

> The house is spacious and comfortable, and its interior differs little from the style of such residences in England; indeed, the inmates too are more like honest Britons than members of the corrupt society of Bucharest. That, I also understood to be the reason for their preferring to live in the country, for they are a family forming an exception to the general Wallachian rule, and consequently incapable of devoting themselves to the frivolous and dissipated mode of life prevalent in the chief town of the province. ... The objects surrounding this country mansion reminded one of the past vicissitudes of Wallachia: an extensive court-yard and garden, in which the dwelling-house stood, was still enclosed by a thick and high wall; the gate was flanked by hollow projections, and surmounted by an open platform, which was now fitted up as a kiosk, where the family often sat in the evening, but which had evidently been constructed for the purpose of firing on assailants; while the whole range of the wall was loopholed at regular distances.[20]

The somewhat Europeanised interior of the Golescu country house (which, according to Skene, 'differs little from the style of such residences in England') may have been an exception in the first part of the nineteenth century, but turned out to be the harbinger of a modernising trend that would affect almost all boyar residences in the Romanian lands.[21] The liberal families of Wallachia, such as the Golescus, the Brătianus and the Rosettis, were close to the centre of power and gave meaning to the notion of *patrie* (homeland, country) by adapting their European experiences to Romanian realities. It might be said that they promoted an enlightened patriotism.

Members of these boyar families were leaders of the Romanian revolution of 1848 in Wallachia, a nationalist uprising against the presence of Russia as a protective power. Having studied in the capitals of Europe (Paris, London, Vienna), they sought a regeneration of the country through the application of certain reforms (equal political rights, abolition of noble ranks and Roma slavery, freedom of the press, etc.) which were aimed at integrating this territory into Europe despite the fact that the suzerain power was the Porte. Recent research argues that these young men considered themselves to be 'part of multiple and interconnected communities',[22] believing that a Romanian could be at the same time a subject of the Porte and also a European. While the revolution failed and they went into exile, their beliefs remained. Thus, their homes should be seen at the intersection of nation-building ideals and cosmopolitanism, a place that hosted the local tradition of being a Romanian in the Ottoman Empire, colloquially seen as Oriental, while also incorporating the features of becoming a European.

The country house in Goleşti: construction and transformation

Evidence for what the country house was like before James Skene's visit in 1851 can be found in diverse but complementary sources: documents, travel narratives and archaeological investigations. Together, they recreate the atmosphere that characterised it at the time. In one of the earliest sources, Paul of Aleppo, a well-known traveller in the Ottoman Empire who passed through Wallachia in the seventeenth century, explains that the boyars were accustomed to founding monasteries and churches close to their *konak*s and residences on their estates and endowing them with the proceeds of taxes.

On the road linking the capital of Wallachia, Bucharest, with that of the suzerain power, Constantinople, lies the estate of Goleşti (Argeș county), where our traveller discovered a similar church beside what he considered a palace, a building defended by many towers and surrounded by a village.[23] The *konak*, founded in 1640, appeared to Paul of Aleppo on his journey in 1657 as a new building, only recently erected. It conformed to the architectural norms of the period, combining different defining functions: defence, authority and prestige, and comfort. The defensive walls, provided with a parapet, buttresses and brick corner towers, were for protection against attack by rebels against the Porte from across the Danube. The church and the frames of the cellar windows preserve the names of the founding couple and the master builder, a common commemorative practice in Romania and the Balkans. The interior of the building is characterised by a local variation on Oriental comfort, adapted to the history of the region and to the sorts of goods in circulation at the time.

The most important intervention after the initial construction of the house took place in the eighteenth century, when a village primary school was added to the estate buildings and the existing park was extended and improved along Western lines. In the nineteenth century, the period that concerns us here, the ensemble of buildings on the Goleşti estate comprised the *konak* itself (also called 'the big house', 1640), the Holy Trinity Church (1646) and various annexes (kitchen, washhouse, infirmary, Turkish bath, stables, guest rooms and servants' quarters), surrounded by the defensive walls mentioned above.[24] The rearrangements had involved enlarging or changing the function of some rooms: a porch was replaced by a larger space; a reception room with an annex was created on the upper floor. The process of spatial and cultural adaptation thus continued with each generation of the Golescu family.

The present entrance to the courtyard of the house dates from the eighteenth century. It is guarded by two fountains in the form of lions' heads, through whose mouths water flowed. Over each fountain is a marble plaque inscribed in Greek:

> My origin lies in the clouds above,
> But Golescu's renown brought me here.
> A man of many gifts, I found on my arrival,
> A lover of his country, delighting in his guests.
>
> A fine place he gave me, for my crystal wave
> To share its pure nectar with every traveller.
> His word is my law, from which I do not swerve,
> So the Fountain of Golescu is the name I bear.
> [the left-hand fountain]
>
> A man of great renown, and with mercy for the weak,
> Golescu Radu the vornic set me in this place.
> That his kind heart towards guests I may delight,
> To the traveller I give water that gushes from the earth.
>
> If you should be hungry, eat here and drink your fill
> From the Fountain of Golescu, and it will give your rest.
> And if you wish to come back, for friends may help themselves,
> Because it is as though the house of Abraham were here.
> [the right-hand fountain][25]

The visitor is thus alerted from the beginning to the fact that the residence has as its founding guides the spirit of hospitality, philanthropy and love of art, and that it is open to strangers.

The Golescu family were heavily involved in the politics, administration and cultural activities of their day. The most well-known of them, Constantin (Dinicu) Golescu (1777–1830), made a series of journeys across Europe, in a sort of semi-Grand Tour, passing through Austria, Hungary, Italy and Switzerland. The impressions he published in Romanian literature's first travel journal became a reference point in the nineteenth century.[26] He admired 'the happy and fortunate social life' he saw in the West and commented particularly on the country estates of the Austrian Empire, which were much to his taste: Avrig (the property of Baron Samuel Brukenthal) in Transylvania, Dornbach (the property of Prince Karl Philipp of Schwarzenberg), Kalenberg and Leopoldberg. The elite of Vienna had bought and built very comfortable country houses on the heights of Kalenberg, a select area which the Prince de Ligne (himself one of the owners) considered a colony, where the houses were similar in form but differed in their gardens, terraces, landscaping and decoration. Discussing his own house in his memoirs towards the end of the eighteenth century, Charles-Joseph Lamoral (1735–1814), Prince de Ligne and Marshal of the Holy Roman Empire, described it, in a passage that was borrowed by the travel guidebooks of the period, as a refuge:

> I have a Gothic hall and an Egyptian room, and a Turkish salon where, at the platform, stepped, attractively painted balustrades, precious divans, of the most beautiful oriental cloth, rich ceiling with gilded borders and painted in the style of this country, quotes from the Quran in gold letters, and pyramidal and colourful fireplaces, I picked up and overshadowed what I saw as the most beautiful thing in Turkey and from the Tatars' land, where I've been. The name [of my country-house] is My Refuge ... I did not renounce them; they are all that were left to me in the world.[27]

The interior of such country houses in the vicinity of Vienna, a cultural and diplomatic centre of great interest to the Romanian elite, was a panoply reconstructing the travels, passions and interests of their owners, and at the same time a way of connecting to the local and European trends of the age.

This is the type of country house owned by the European elite with whom Dinicu Golescu began to mix in the years 1824–6, and whom he admired. At Avrig he remarked on the pond and the landscaping, and at Dornbach he was delighted by the pheasants and the 'carriage roads, such as I had [also] happened to see at [the houses of] others'. Kalenberg and Leopoldberg had the same constant feature of interest: the park and gardens. In the middle of the nineteenth century, these two houses still featured in Murray's travel guides, though they no longer aroused the enthusiasm of earlier times.[28]

In spite of changing tourist fashions, however, it is clear that Dinicu Golescu was influenced by what he saw. At home, on his old estate at Golești, he introduced new plants and landscaping arrangements. In the mid-nineteenth century, access to the house was by way of a vaulted gate in the wall. The *konak* had a 'little garden' in front with flowers and, to the right as you looked at it, was the 'large garden' with 'diverse fruit trees'. The imported, global goods in this context were the flowers barely known here at the time: magnolias, philadelphus, azaleas and laurels. In the salon of the house were two divans and an oval table with tall-backed chairs around it, upholstered in bright red Utrecht velvet. On the walls were portraits of the Golescus, while in the courtyard an Oriental touch was still present in the form of a Turkish bath.[29] This reconstruction, by the historian George Fotino, is based on archaeological discoveries and oral history interviews with the last occupants. It shows how the Europeanisation of the interior was accentuated by the mid-nineteenth century, but without putting aside references to the family and to tradition. It appears to be an amalgamation of Westernisation and a process of building a family and a national identity, the objects intermediating the encounter.

The new Golescu generation was committed to the revolution of 1848, seeking alignment with a Europe that they knew from their student years in Paris, where they and their fellow 'forty-eighters' had listened to the lectures of Jules Michelet and Edgar Quinet. This 'circle of friends', as Jianu called them, comprised Romanian revolutionaries living in exile in the cities of France and Italy, centred around the Golescu brothers.[30] They remained in exile until around 1857, but their correspondence with their mother, Zinca, reveals the transformation of the *konak* into a veritable ad hoc republic. The partial confiscation of their wealth by the state, in addition to the general difficulties of the situation and the desire to maintain the revolutionaries in exile, led to a depletion of the family's resources and successive sales of property.[31] Although she was herself in exile for a short time, Zinca Golescu returned to her estate and, together with the ladies who had stayed there, transformed the *konak* into 'our promised land' and 'a fresh, green oasis'; the occupying troops during the Crimean War 'did not manage to bring legal order to the republic of Golești'.[32] Inevitably, alongside the rugs and divans, new objects began to appear in the rooms, brought by her sons from abroad. For over seven years, from 1849, the interior of the house was turned into a place of nostalgia and longing, embodying sentiments and looking forward to the moment of reunion. In this way, the distinctiveness that Skene noted in 1851 was accentuated: despite the traditional appearance of the house, its interior became Europeanised and came to signify silent resistance to the regime that had led to the exile of the Golescu brothers.

Material culture and decoration at Golești

The Romanian elite was already subscribing to foreign newspapers in the first half of the nineteenth century, especially those from France, Austria and the German lands. Zinca Golescu herself was an educated boyaress and even progressive for her time: she read French journals such as *Charivari* and *Europe démocratique*. The family library was quite large, and the ground floor salon was a meeting place for the remaining occupants; from there, they could walk to the park of the *konak*, which had been reconstructed on the model of those seen by Dinicu Golescu on his travels.

At that time, Romanian industry was almost non-existent, with just a few factories having been established, and handicrafts only produced objects for mass consumption, from pots to thick peasant fabrics. The body and the house constituted the general focus of dealers in luxury goods, but with a tendency towards increasing specialisation in their shops. Imported luxury items were not limited to perfumes, jewellery and clothes but also included food, furniture and interior decorations. In the capital, the number of shops grew from one year to the next, and announcements in newspapers of the goods they had brought appeared more and more frequently. Alongside stores selling a diverse mixture of goods, there also appeared outlets specialising in products of a particular territory (British, French or the German lands) or in products of a specific type (furniture, clothing, foodstuffs, etc.). Specialisation was slow to develop, but it can be seen by the 1850s and 1860s, with gazettes alerting buyers to the local suppliers of foreign goods to suit their specific wishes. It was no longer necessary to order from Paris, Vienna or London: they could find what they wanted in Bucharest. Furnishing and decorating one's house in a Western style became an increasingly accessible option for the urban population, while among the wealthy, interest shifted towards country houses. The liberal newspaper *The Romanian* [Românul] advocated for 'Europeanisation' through the announcements it promoted, mostly related to the sale of furniture and books.

At the same time, bonds of family and friendship gave privileged access to such consumer goods. The Golescu family was related by marriage to Effingham Grant, secretary of the British Consulate in

Bucharest and the owner of a store supplying British products advertised in *The Romanian*. Through him, Zinca sent letters to her exiled sons and obtained goods for her house and family. James Skene was introduced to the Golescu family by Grant, and he also was invited to the nearby mansion of Grant's father-in-law.[33]

In reconstructing the appearance of the *konak* at this time, we may imagine that it would have contained some of the goods brought by Effingham Grant from Britain through the Magasin Anglais E. Grant & Comp. on Podul Mogoșoaiei (today's Calea Victoriei) (see Object Lesson 4). In 1858 alone, it stocked a wide range of *meubles de fantaisie*, carpets, iron frames for greenhouses and gardens, and *cheminées calorifères*. Here one could also find candelabra, iron and gilded bronze bed frames, fabrics for upholstery, and 'very wide oilcloths, thick and durable, imitation of parquet, marble'.[34] Effingham Grant's store was among the first in Wallachia that encouraged a rearrangement of the home with products widely used in Western Europe and especially of British manufacture. More than that, Grant knew the houses and leisure pursuits of the Romanian elite, and his shop had a sub-specialty in hunting equipment. In 1858, his company brought 'to the attention of amateurs of hunting weapons that they have received a new delivery of weapons from one of the best factories in England'. To make use of them, however, one needed the right suit and footwear, and Grant's store also had 'English boots, of different sorts' and 'English fabrics, various – for trousers, for waistcoats'.[35] In a natural extension of his professional duties at the Consulate, Grant, as the owner of a store, was 'selling' a lifestyle, the items in his stock representing a form of globalisation of British-made goods.

Little by little, other shops which sold furniture and decorative items opened up in Bucharest. *The Romanian* included from the summer of 1858 a large advertisement for a Great Store of Furniture and Pianos of Paris, which considered itself to be the only store to have 'a large quantity of merchandise, on special prices, to fully furnish a house'. This meant not only chairs, sofas, carpets and mirrors, but also special cloth and decorative items such as porcelain, paintings and engravings. It also sold money chests 'with a double insurance against fire and thieves, modern machines and different systems', which came from 'prestigious factories'. Furthermore, this Great Magasin stated that it could receive orders for 'any other French furniture and (decorative) goods' the customer wanted and was able to deliver in the Romanian counties.[36] While Effingham Grant's store specialised in British goods for the house, with a sub-specialisation in hunting, this one was more or less its French counterpart. It enlarged the consumer audience to the well-to-do to the counties and a less mobile wealthy population.

The readership of *The Romanian* and other gazettes that promoted Western goods was restricted to subscribers, a mainly urban elite and the bourgeoisie.[37] Those boyars who lived in the capital or large cities also had residences on their estates, and their attention was no doubt caught by announcements for goods that would embellish their homes, making them more comfortable and in keeping with the latest novelties. For stores such as those mentioned above, selling to a mainly urban market also implied the possibility of reaching the provincial market as well since many owners of urban residences also had a country house. For the Golescus and other families who experienced exile and transformed their country houses into a space of safety and conviviality among themselves, this was even more relevant.[38]

Today, little is left of the original nineteenth-century furnishings of the Golescu country house.[39] Important items come from the second half of the nineteenth century, although the provenance and the route of purchase are not always clear. Masculine goods include a duelling kit with two pistols (German workshop: Louis Adami) and a bowler hat (Viennese workshop). These match with other items that refer to hunting and the sociability around it: a serving platter for wild game (French workshop: Christofle), platters and plates (English workshops: F. Primavesi & Sons of Cardiff, Kannreuther, Frauer & Co. of Birmingham). An eighteenth-century davenport, made in a Dutch workshop, belonged to one of the young Golescus and could have been either an inherited item or bought from abroad. The travelling case of another young Golescu, Nicolae, does not have its identification details. However, his travels connect him with the West and especially London and Paris, therefore it would be safe to assume this provenance, even more so if we take into account his 1848 portrait that depicts him in a hunting costume, considered to be an echo of his travels in England (Figure 7.1). Meanwhile, feminine goods refer especially to Zinca Golescu, the matriarch of the house: a sweet jar, a silver watch, an umbrella, an ivory and silk fan, a jewellery box and her wedding veil. All these goods, together with local items such as rugs and pottery, created an assemblage that defined the boyar interior of the country house. Even though there was a particular cultural tendency predominant in this synthetic display, the variety of goods and their provenance suggest the owners' experiences and personal taste. As a more general note, it also argues for the use of furnishings and decoration in the construction of Europeanness within national boundaries.

Figure 7.1 Constantin Daniel Rosenthal, *Nicolae Golescu*, 1848. Reproduced courtesy of National Museum of Art of Romania, Bucharest.

Nicolae Grant and the memorialisation of the family country house(s)

We might wonder how representative the so-called boyar interior (*interior boieresc*) was by the end of the nineteenth century. While Europeanness became a prominent feature of Romanian elite houses, following independence (1878) and after Romania became a kingdom under the rule of a German dynasty (1881, Hohenzollern-Sigmaringen), another aspect started to take shape. The monarchy and the liberal elite (of which the Golescu family and their 1848 revolutionary friends were part) made a return to local heritage to create a national identity and (neo-Romanian) architectural style and to distinguish Romania on the map of Europe and among other countries of the region. This meant recognising the 'Oriental' veil of the Ottoman Empire, but also the importance of vernacular culture.[40] Encouraging national industry, crafts and an idealisation of the rural environment were at the core

INTERIORS AS A VISITING CARD   205

of this new policy. The interior of elite residences became a conscious expression of what it meant to be both a European and a Romanian. Under the monarchy's patronage, art associations flourished and young artists became the promoters of this new ideology. Thus, Romania was seeking to make up for an economic lag in relation to the West, but also to find a cultural equilibrium whereby 'the progressive Westernisation of Romanian society was counterbalanced by a more and more profound examination of its own history and culture'.[41]

The Golescu family had its own connections to art and culture that interfered with this new shift in context. Two factors were key to enforcing this aspect: matrimonial alliances and entanglements between politics and the economy. Effingham Grant and his sister Marie were instrumental in this sense. As noted above, Effingham had one of the first shops in the capital to sell British-made goods, while Marie, although a foreigner in Wallachia, became the symbol of revolutionary, modern Romania through Constantin D. Rosenthal's painting of her as *Revolutionary Romania*, dressed in Romanian folk costume and holding the Romanian flag in her left hand and a Turkish dagger in her right.[42] Both Effingham and Marie married into liberal, 1848 revolutionary families linked to the Golescus by kin: Effingham with Zoe Racoviță, the niece of Zinca and Dinicu Golescu, and Marie with Constantin A. Rosetti. Furthermore, as secretary to the British Consulate, Effingham Grant helped the Golescu family and used his contacts to enter the Romanian retail and later industrial market (see Object Lesson 4).

Two of Effingham Grant's four sons, Eduard and Nicolae, were painters and participated in national exhibitions at the turn of the twentieth century: Eduard as a member of the Romanian committee on the domestic industry section (furnishings and carpets) in 1889, while Nicolae (1868–1950) displayed four of his works in 1900. After studying painting in France, Nicolae had travelled frequently between Romania and the West, finding inspiration in both. He was a member of various artistic associations and worked on advertisements for businesses (Chocolat Meunier, the A. Bord piano factory), but also for the Romanian royal family. He belonged within the artistic tendencies of the time, having a particular fascination with interiors. His first work depicted his childhood home in Bucharest and was entitled *The Belvedere Mansion* (1884), and the first painting that he exhibited at an international level, at the French Artists' Salon in Paris (1886), *Interior with Lamplight Effect*, was of the salon of his aunt, Marie Grant-Rosetti.[43] In 1910, he returned permanently to Romania, and after the First World War he settled in the provincial town of Câmpulung-Muscel, not far from Golești.[44] The boyar *konak* was a recurrent theme in his work as he depicted the country houses of family members. This choice of theme was not simply a matter of his affective response to the subject; it should also be seen in the context of the recovery of cultural identity characteristic of the period and of the reactivation of collective memory. In Charles Rice's approach, the interior as a construct can be tackled 'as it travels' through time, idealising and conceptualising 'a particular emerging and developing consciousness' in relation to a person's cultural belonging.[45]

Of particular importance is Nicolae Grant's interest in the reactivation and re-formulation of identity focused on the country residence of the Golescu family, which he explored from both exterior and interior perspectives. In an 1898 oil painting, he rendered Golești in full colour, its entrance covered with greenery and its park dominating the composition, suggesting a relaxing and refreshing space on a torrid summer day. In his works showing the exterior at Golești, Grant focused particularly on the park, the kiosk and some of the annexes. These are the elements that link the Europeanisation of the interior to the rural surroundings (Figure 7. 2).

The three untitled boyar interiors show either the *konak* at Golești or the artist's own house in Câmpulung-Muscel; the interiors are hard to distinguish and the location is not stated. They continue the train of

Figure 7.2   Nicolae Grant, *Golești Konak*, 1898. Reproduced courtesy of Golești Museum, Argeș, Romania.

evocations and gravitate around an armchair with red striped upholstery. It is this armchair that carries us through the three watercolours depicting three different spaces. In two of them, it stands by the window of what might be a ground floor salon or dining room, while in the third it is in a more intimate space, close to a sofa with cushions. In Figure 7.3, the light and greenery from outside seem to burst through the window and spread over the walls with a relaxed and playful enthusiasm. In Figure 7.4, we contemplate a noontide restfulness, with the greenery barely visible through the window, while the armchair is accompanied only by a simple table bearing a coffee cup and a book.

In Figure 7.5, the window has gone, but the interior is shown in more detail: a chest of drawers with gilt ornament and a mirror in Belle Époque style dominate the corner of a room. The same red-striped armchair stands to one side of the chest of drawers, and on the other is a sofa with black floral cushions. On top of the chest of drawers can be seen a vase of flowers, a china ornament, photographs and two jugs; below them, two garments hang negligently out of an open drawer. On the sofa, an illustrated magazine lies open, waiting for its reader's return, while the crimson walls are occupied by a painting of flowers, a mirror flanked by

Figure 7.3 Nicolae Grant, *Interior*. Reproduced courtesy of Goleşti Museum, Argeş, Romania.

Figure 7.4 Nicolae Grant, *Interior*. Reproduced courtesy of Goleşti Museum, Argeş, Romania.

two small family portraits, and a little display cabinet containing twelve jugs which are most likely folk products. The carpet, which appears to be Oriental, brings together the colours of the furniture, the garments and the flowers. If we look back to Figure 7.3, we can see the same recurrent feature – objects created locally: the plates arranged in a circle around a simple square mirror, whose shapes and colours suggest that they may be from the potteries of Hurez; a rug on the floor with just enough detail visible to suggest that it is a traditional piece woven in Oltenia. However, the striking accents of colour come from the European furniture with its rounded edges and from the picture frames, whose contents are depicted in a muted manner in comparison.

The three pictures are, to a greater or lesser degree, an evocation and a reflection of the family's interiors as they remained at the end of the nineteenth century in the memory of those who had known them. Their inspiration is filtered through the artist's sensibility, but we may get a glimpse of it from the photographs made by the same Nicolae Grant,[46] and the objects his family owned. The art critic Tudor Octavian has

Figure 7.5 Nicolae Grant, *Boyar Interior*. Reproduced courtesy of Goleşti Museum, Argeş, Romania.

noted that Grant 'became more and more British as he grew older, in a world becoming more and more French, and his watercolours supremely preserve the scent of the 1900s'.[47] In a way, Nicolae Grant retraces in these interiors the cultural encounter between his family roots, part Romanian through the Golescus, part British through the Grants. The paintings are nostalgic for a nineteenth century when Europeanisation reached Romania and local objects and global goods were part of a negotiated, imaginary invention of the personal habitus, characteristic of an elite with noble, boyar origins.

Conclusions

The Romanian case study shows that a single habitus can be immersed in what appear to be competing visions of self-identity. This is to be expected for a province of a declining empire, for which other empires were involved in an (in)formal rivalry for economic and political influence and hegemony. In reality, however, this competition is illusory because the goods observed in visual and literary documents represent complementary lines of action and dialogue in the emancipation and formation of the Romanian nation during the nineteenth century. Europeanisation through global goods (from furniture to garden plants) gave the owner of the country house a sense of a broader cultural belonging while also incorporating the local. The interior and exterior of the house gradually became a coherent aesthetic unit, in harmony with one another. The individual boyar or family selected and formed their own habitus in response to changes in politics and the economy that enabled new personal experiences and gave direct access to new products. Global goods of British, French or German manufacture were, by the mid-nineteenth century, advertised in the Romanian lands as part of two interrelated processes: Europeanisation and economic development.

The taste displayed in assembling the interior of the Goleşti family country house was shaped by family reactions to shifting political regimes, by their connectedness with Western Europe and their claim to Romanian roots and heritage. It is an implicit selective agency in the face of global trends in furnishing and taste, but also proof of the diversity of routes the goods took to reach their owner. At the end of the nineteenth century this type of interior became representative of a reforming Romanian elite that drew its power from an ability to balance the past with the present, tradition with progress, and to transform the assemblage into a sort of visiting card. There is something of a neutralisation effect in this aesthetic of the interior as global goods did not surpass or eliminate indigenous ones, and vice versa. Instead, they cohabitated and shaped an identification and representational process across generational lines. Larger political events thus left a trace on the dynamic beyond the embrace of goods and how this relationship takes place.

Acknowledgements

This study was conducted within the framework of the UEFISCDI PN-III-P3-3.6-H2020-2020-0035 Prize for Excellence in Research awarded to New Europe College–Institute for Advanced Study, Bucharest. I thank James Christian Brown for help with the translation and Jon Stobart for his understanding, patience and kindness.

Notes

1 Skene, *Frontier Lands*. Republished in 1854 as *Danubian Principalities*. For details, see Brown, 'Representation of the Romanian space', and the biographical sketch by Adrian-Silvan Ionescu in vol. 5 of the series *Călători străini despre țările române în secolul al XIX-lea*.
2 Skene, *Frontier Lands*, vol. 1, 219–20.
3 Kasaba, *Ottoman Empire and the World Economy*, 34.
4 For the expression 'the sick man of Europe' in reference to the Ottoman Empire see Badem, *Ottoman Crimean War*, 68–9.
5 Pamuk, *Ottoman Empire and European Capitalism*, 130–47.
6 Paul Cernovodeanu, *England's Trade Policy in the Levant*, 48, 107.
7 Marinescu, 'Aspects of economic relations', 776.
8 The products England imported from the Principalities were cereals, wool, flax and tallow; see Cernovodeanu, *Relațiile comerciale româno-engleze*, 89–90, 147; Cernovodeanu and Marinescu, 'British trade in the Danubian ports'.
9 Cernovodeanu, *Relațiile comerciale româno-engleze*, 67–8; Tappe, 'Bell and Anderson'.
10 Marinescu, 'Economic relations', 278. The main items imported were manufactured goods, iron and colonial goods (coffee, pepper, sugar, rum, etc.).
11 Georgescu, *The Romanians*, 128. With a German monarchy, by 1913, Romania's foreign commerce ranked Germany (23%), Austria-Hungary (19%), Belgium (16%), England (8%), France (8%) and Russia (1%). The rest of the percentage is completed by other countries.
12 Georgescu, *The Romanians*, 122–88.
13 Georgescu, *The Romanians*, 172.
14 Stobart and Rothery, *Consumption and the Country House*, 1.
15 Nicolescu, *Case, conace și palate*, 93–4.
16 Brătuleanu, *Curți domnești și boierești*, 7, 9.
17 Brătuleanu, *Curți domnești și boierești*, 53. For Western Europe see Stobart and Rothery, *Consumption and the Country House*, 4.
18 Palladio, *The Four Books*, 171.
19 Palladio, *The Four Books*, 175.
20 Skene, *Frontier Lands*, vol. 2, 59–60.
21 Ion, *Elitele și arhitectura rezidențială*; Marinache, *Reședințele Știrbey*, 207.
22 Morris, 'Locating the Wallachian Revolution of 1848', 625.
23 *Călători străini*, serie veche, vol. 6, 1976, 149–50.
24 Popescu and Iliescu, *Golești*, 20; Spirescu, *De la Orient la Occident*, 43–4.
25 Rendering based on George Fotino's verse translation in the appendix to his *Casa din Golești*, n.p.
26 Golescu, *Însemnare a călătoriei*.
27 'J'ai une salle gothique et une chambre égyptienne, et un salon turc ou, en estrade, gradins, balustrades joliment peintes, divans précieux, cousins des plus belles étoffes orientales, riches plafonds, bordure dorée et peinte a la manière de ce pays, passages tires de l'Alcoran en lettres d'or, et cheminées pyramidales et bariolées, j'ai ramassé et surpasse ce que j'ai vu de plus beau dans le peu de Turquie et Tatarie ou j'ai été. Le nom de Mon Refuge … je ne l'ai point donne au hasard; c'est tout ce qui me reste au monde': *Annales des Voyages, de la Géographie et de l'Histoire*, 52.
28 *Handbook for Travellers in Southern Germany*, 165.
29 Fotino, *Casa din Golești*, 12–13.
30 Jianu, *A Circle of Friends*.
31 Pally, *Documente inedite din colecțiile Muzeului Golești*, 193.
32 Fotino, *Din vremea renașterii*, vol. 3, 29.
33 Skene, *Frontier Lands*, vol. 1, 214, and vol. 2, 58.
34 *The Romanian*: advertisements were repeated through 1857.
35 *The Romanian*: advertisements appeared throughout 1858.
36 *The Romanian*, vol. 2, no. 49, 23 June/5 July 1858.
37 Drace-Francis, *The Making of Modern Romanian Culture*.
38 Liberal families such as Brătianu or Kretzulescu, who had estates close to Golesti.
39 Some are in the permanent display at Golesti Museum, while others were presented in the temporary exhibition *Golescu: The memory of an old boyar family* (Bucharest, June 2022).
40 Blakesley, *The Arts and Crafts Movement*, 157.

41 Teacă, 'Istoria artei în context identitar românesc', 154.
42 Marie briefly established and ran the first Romanain journal on puericulture, *Mother and Child* [Mama și copilul].
43 Călin and Boțoghină, *Nicolae Grant*, 4–5.
44 Boțoghină, 'Pictorul Nicolae Grant', 331.
45 Rice, *The Emergence of the Interior*, 75–6, 2–3.
46 Călin and Boțoghină, *Nicolae Grant*, 48; the second photograph with the same title, 'Boyar interior', is located in the provincial town of Câmpulung Mușcel.
47 Boțoghină, 'Pictorul Nicolae Grant', 333; Octavian, *Pictori români uitați*, 78.

Bibliography

Alexandrescu-Dersca Bulgaru, M.M., and Mustafa Ali Mehmed, eds. *Călători străini despre țările române*, serie veche, vol. 6. Bucharest: Editura Academiei Române, 1976.

Anghel, Costina, and Mariana Vida, eds. *Repertoriul picturii românești moderne: secolul al XIX-lea*, vol. 3. Bucharest: Muzeul Național de Artă al României, 2018.

Ardeleanu, Constantin. *Evoluția intereselor economice și politice britanice la gurile Dunării (1829–1914)*. Brăila: Istros, 2008.

Ardeleanu, Constantin. *The European Commission of the Danube, 1856–1948: An experiment in international administration*. Leiden: Brill, 2020.

Badem, Candan. *The Ottoman Crimean War, 1853–1856*. Leiden: Brill, 2010.

Berindei, Dan, ed. *Istoria românilor*, vol. 7, tome 1. Bucharest: Editura Enciclopedică, 2003.

Blakesley, Rosalind. *The Arts and Crafts Movement*. London: Phaidon, 2006.

Boțoghină, Cristina. 'Pictorul Nicolae Grant (1868–1950) – Vlăstar din neamul 'Goleștilor', *Analele Dobrogei* 1, no. 3 (2019): 327–34.

Brătuleanu, Anca. *Curți domnești și boierești în România. Valahia veacurilor al XVII-lea și al XVIII-lea*. Bucharest: Simetria, 1997.

Brown, James. 'The representation of the Romanian space in the writings of British travellers in the nineteenth century', PhD dissertation, University of Bucharest, 2007.

Călin, Gerard, and Cristina Boțoghină. *Nicolae Grant, un pictor aproape uitat. Catalog de pictură*, 2nd edition. Ștefănești: Muzeul Golești, 2020.

Cernovodeanu, Paul. *Relațiile comerciale româno-engleze în contextul politicii orientale a Marii Britanii (1803–1878)*. Dacia: Cluj-Napoca, 1986.

Cernovodeanu, Paul, and Beatrice Marinescu. 'British trade in the Danubian ports of Galatz and Brăila between 1837 and 1853', *Journal of European Economic History* (Rome), 3 (1979): 707–41.

Cernovodeanu, Paul. *England's Trade Policy in the Levant and the Exchange of Goods with the Romanian Lands under the Latter Stuarts (1660–1714)*. Translated by Mary Lăzărescu. Bucharest: Editura Academiei, 1972.

Coman, Roxana. 'Ottoman residential architecture of the 18th and 19th centuries and the Romanian provinces: from cosmopolitanism to nationalism', *Revue des Etudes Sud-Est Européennes* 59 (2021): 217–44.

Drace-Francis, Alex. *The Making of Modern Romanian Culture: Literacy and the development of national identity*, London: I.B. Tauris, 2005.

Drace-Francis, Alex. *The Traditions of Invention: Romanian ethnic and social stereotypes in historical context*. Leiden: Brill, 2013.

Fotino, George, ed. *Din vremea renașterii naționale a Țării Românești: boierii Golești*, 4 vols. Bucharest: Imprimeria Națională, 1939.

Fotino, George. *Casa din Golești*. Bucharest: Institutul Național al Cooperației, 1943.

Georgescu, Vlad. *The Romanians: A history*. Edited by Matei Călinescu, translated by Alexandra Bley-Vroman. Columbus: Ohio State University Press, 1991.

Golescu, Dinicu. *Însemnare a călătoriei mele, Constantin Radovici din Golești: făcută în anul 1824, 1825, 1826*. Critical edition by Panaitescu-Perpessicius. Bucharest: Editura de Stat pentru Literatură și Artă, 1952.

Handbook for Travellers in Southern Germany; being a guide to Bavaria, Austria, Tyrol, Salzburg, Styria & c, the Austrian and Bavarian Alps, and the Danube from Ulm to the Black Sea. London: John Murray & Son, 1837.

Ion, Narcis-Dorin. *Elitele și arhitectura rezidențială în țările române (secolul XIX–XX)*. Bucharest: Oscar Print, 2011.

Jianu, Angela. *A Circle of Friends: Political exile and the creation of modern Romania, 1840–1859*. Leiden: Brill, 2011.

Kasaba, Reşat. *The Ottoman Empire and the World Economy: The nineteenth century*. Albany: State University of New York, 1988.

Malte-Brun, M., ed. *Annales des Voyages, de la Géographie et de l'Histoire; ou Collection des Voyages nouveaux les plus estimes, traduits de toutes les langues européennes; Des relations originales inédites, communiquées par des voyageurs Français et Etrangers*. Paris: Chez F. Buisson, tome IV (VIII), 1809.

Marinache, Oana. *Reședințele Știrbey din București și Buftea: arhitectura și decorația interioară*. Bucharest: ACS, 2013.

Marinescu, Beatrice. 'Economic relations between the Romanian Principalities and Great Britain (1848–1859)', *Revue Roumaine d'Histoire* 2 (1969): 271–81.

Marinescu, Beatrice. 'Aspects of economic relations between Romania and Great Britain (1862–1866)', *Revue Roumaine d'Histoire* 4 (1979): 773–84.

Morris, James. 'Locating the Wallachian Revolution of 1848', *The Historical Journal* 64, no. 3 (2021): 606–25.

Nicolescu, Corina. *Case, conace și palate vechi românești*. Bucharest: Meridiane, 1979.

Octavian, Tudor. *Pictori români uitați*. Bucharest: Noi Media Print, 2008.

Palladio, Andrea. *The Four Books of Architecture*. With a new introduction by Adolf K. Placzek. New York: Dover, 1965.

Pally, Filofteia, ed. *Documente inedite din colecțiile Muzeului Golești*. Argeș: Asociația Română pentru Educație Individual Adaptată, [2012].

Pamuk, Şevket. *The Ottoman Empire and European Capitalism, 1820–1913: Trade, investment and production*. Cambridge: Cambridge University Press, 1987.

Popescu, M., and C. Iliescu. *Golești*. Bucharest: Meridiane, 1966.

Rice, Charles. *The Emergence of the Interior: Architecture, modernity, domesticity*. London and New York: Routledge, 2007.

The Romanian, 1857–64.

Skene, James. *The Frontier Lands of the Christian and the Turk; comprising travels in the regions of the Lower Danube, in 1850 and 1851. By a British Resident of Twenty Years in the East*. 2 vols. London: Richard Bentley, 1853.

Spirescu, Irina. *De la Orient la Occident. Decorația interioară în reședințele domnești și boierești (1774–1914)*. Bucharest: Noi Media Print, 2010.

Stobart, Jon, and Mark Rothery, eds. *Consumption and the Country House*. Oxford: Oxford University Press, 2016.

Tappe, E.D. 'Bell and Anderson: a Scottish partnership in Wallachia', *Balkan Studies* 2 (1971): 479–84.

Teacă, Corina. 'Istoria artei în context identitar românesc (a doua jumătate a secolului XIX și începutul secolului XX)'. In *150 de ani de învățământ artistic național*, edited by Adrian-Silvan Ionescu, 154–9. Bucharest: UNArte, 2014.

8
An 'American bearskin merchant' in the 'wilds of Pennsylvania': trade and the British country house in North America

Stephen G. Hague

In 1751, Benjamin Franklin penned an obituary for an old friend and distinguished scholar named James Logan. Logan had spent his career as the agent for the Penn family, proprietors of the Pennsylvania colony in British North America. After many years of labour in colonial administration, Franklin wrote, Logan had 'retir'd from publick Affairs to Stenton, his Country Seat, where he enjoy'd among his Books that Leisure which Men of Letters so earnestly desire'.[1] After a young Franklin arrived in Philadelphia from Boston, Logan had served as something of a mentor, schooling him in Pennsylvania politics, engaging him in intellectual discussions and welcoming him to peruse the books in Stenton's extraordinary library. Logan's web of influence in 'publick Affairs' extended in many directions, as he made a fortune in the fur trade with Native America, imported manufactured products, invested in property and ultimately built Stenton as a substantial gentleman's house that highlighted his leading role in the colony (Figure 8.1).

Logan was among Pennsylvania's most influential citizens in the early eighteenth century and his move to a 'Country Seat' had been a long time in the making. Nearly four decades earlier, he first expressed a desire to purchase 'a Plantation to retire to', and he often talked about 'trading the town for the country' and wanting to 'retire with my family into the countrey'.[2] The countryside for which Logan yearned was 5 miles from Philadelphia, eighteenth-century British North America's largest port city. Situated at the conjunction of two major roads, the 500-acre Stenton estate was at the centre of political and economic networks in America closely tied into extensive transatlantic and global connections.

Figure 8.1 Stenton, near Philadelphia. Reproduced courtesy of the National Society of the Colonial Dames of America in the Commonwealth of Pennsylvania at Stenton, Philadelphia.

James Logan was many things: an important colonial official, a leading merchant, an enslaver and a gifted scholar. But his voluminous correspondence records his ambivalence about his position in Atlantic World society. He described himself to one European correspondent as an 'American bearskin merchant' writing 'from the wilds of Pennsylvania', an indication that his ambiguous status as an American chafed against his intellectual and social standing as an erudite, genteel Briton.[3] But he used such self-effacing language both to acknowledge ideas about Americans and to disarm them. Establishing Stenton as a country seat was a critical way that Logan confirmed his position as an influential agent of the British Empire.

As a crossroads of trade and empire, Stenton illustrates the role of the country house in the acquisition, use and display of global goods. It was a locally inflected example of genteel domestic architecture awash with material objects and peoples from across the world. Reconsidering Stenton as a British country house located in North America positions colonial domestic space as part of greater Britain's cultural and material geographies in ways that historians have undertaken for other building types.[4] Although initially Logan referred to his property as a plantation, and accounts reference it as thus into the 1750s, Stenton was a modest estate that did not by itself generate adequate income to support the house and its inhabitants. Stenton served Logan as a small country house or, in line with many other houses built for genteel families around the Atlantic World, as a house in the country.[5] The term Franklin used, 'Country Seat', captured this essence. Interpreting James Logan's country seat as British – which it was – and as a form of country house – which it functioned as – reveals the house's multiple roles as a site of empire, as a transatlantic symbol of gentility, as a location for the widespread circulation of goods, and as a place of consumption with significant influence on the material lives and culture of colonial settlers and indigenous and enslaved peoples.

Logan's country seat was simultaneously prototypical and singular. Stenton typified the domestic space of a leading eighteenth-century colonial figure.[6] Like many of his colonial cohorts – merchants, colonial administrators, government officials and a burgeoning professional class – Logan established a comfortable home filled with regional and global commodities, reliant on indentured and enslaved labour from around the Atlantic basin to sustain it. Even in purported retirement, he maintained an expansive variety of activities, managing political affairs in the colony, conducting diplomacy with Native Americans and importing goods from Britain. Sprinkled around the periphery of Britain's empire, houses like Stenton played critical roles in global trade and imperial expansion. At the same time, Stenton was a highly unusual space, where Logan housed an enormous classical library acquired from the booksellers of Europe and displayed some of the earliest antiquities in British North America. He enjoyed leisure time with his books as a deeply knowledgeable and respected scholar.

This chapter focuses on the array of furnishings at Logan's house in 'the wilds of Pennsylvania', but it is part of the larger story told in this volume about the extensive networks that circulated commodities from all over the world, in this case to one corner of the eighteenth-century British Empire.[7] The first section traces Logan's consumption practices by considering the geographic reach of Stenton's furnishings, highlighting the range and typicality of those possessions. The second half of the chapter turns to discuss the unique nature of Logan's classical collections, which connected eighteenth-century Pennsylvania with the intellectual and commercial life of Britain and Europe as well as the ancient worlds of Greece and Rome. The copious documentation and largely extant collections related to Stenton and the Logan family – ledgers, account books, journals, inventories, letters, books and material goods – illustrate that colonial houses like Stenton were important sites of consumption in networks that stretched from the borderlands of Native America to every other continent. Examining the intersection of trade and this British country house in North America charts how objects drew a colonial outpost into the vast web of Atlantic and global commerce.

Consumption in the colonial country seat

From the earliest days of European settlement, global trade played a significant role in shaping the nascent American colonies.[8] Atlantic World commercial networks have been well mapped, demonstrating how quickly the North American colonies became integrated into a vast economic system with a worldwide reach.[9] The presence of global goods in domestic settings reveals the character of this expansive trade, and studies dealing with domestic consumption have highlighted the flow of goods in numerous directions around the Atlantic World.[10] Recent work has also yielded rich insights into the intersection between imperialism, colonialism and the British country house.[11] But despite these growing bodies of literature, the crucial role of North American country houses as sites of consumption on the periphery of Britain's eighteenth-century empire is less well understood. Some of this inattention may be the result of definitional issues. While the term 'country house' has purchase in Britain, early American scholarship has often associated great houses of the Chesapeake or the South Carolina low country with plantations and slave-driven plantation economies.[12] But the vast estates and great houses of upstate New York, the seats of Quaker merchants in the Delaware Valley, and mansions in Massachusetts, Virginia, South Carolina and elsewhere served much the same purpose as the country house in Britain, even if their social and economic organisation was somewhat different.[13] Like the British country house, these houses in the colonies were considerable engines for the demand, circulation and consumption of goods from around the world.[14]

As Britons established colonies in the landscape of North America, settling lands appropriated from indigenous peoples, they imposed structures that simulated those found in the British Isles but adapted to local conditions. Such was the case with their organisation of domestic spaces. Pennsylvania was a hub for Quaker religious, personal and commercial relationships vital to Atlantic World trade networks and proved fertile ground for colonial development.[15] Between his arrival in the colony in 1699 and his death in 1751, James Logan amassed a fortune through trade in manufactured goods and cloth, export of furs and skins to Britain, and property speculation aided by his role as proprietary agent for the Penn family and a Commissioner of Property.[16] Logan's activities left him a rich man, which permitted him to join the ranks of provincial gentlemen, colonial merchants and officials, and minor gentry in Britain and the American colonies who acquired modest estates and built small country houses.[17] By 1730, Logan and his family had left urban Philadelphia and removed to the rural environment of Stenton.

The Logan family's participation in the commercial and knowledge economies of the eighteenth century reveal the panoply of goods available to elite colonial Americans. These objects demonstrated that global goods were widespread and carried cultural meaning even on the periphery of the British Empire. As historian Cary Carson noted, 'the veneer of genteel culture was necessarily thinner' in the American colonies than in Britain, but nevertheless the colonial gentry of America 'were no more rustic than large parts of rural England'.[18] In Pennsylvania, they staked out the Logans as leading members of the colonial elite.

With every step through Stenton's halls and rooms, visitors engaged in a sort of journey, as the objects they encountered evoked distant lands and dim pasts. Take, for example, John Smith, a Quaker from Burlington County, New Jersey, who regularly visited Stenton in the last decade of James Logan's life. Smith came to woo Logan's daughter, Hannah; as his intimacy with the family grew, he spent time talking, dining, taking tea and staying in the house, and he became a familiar guest with inside knowledge of the house and its inhabitants.[19] John Smith possessed a capacious mental world map. Although born in the colonies, his diary mentioned places near and far that were part of his frame of reference: Antigua, Barbados, Jamaica, Martinique, Ireland, Dublin, Liverpool, Bristol, London and the new colony of Georgia, from whence came '2 Live Allegators' sent to a friend.[20] Smith had knowledge of the world and, as a merchant, a ready appreciation for the value and quality of goods. As a result, specific objects that he saw prominently displayed at Stenton communicated the Logan family's worldwide connections.

John Smith knew Stenton during the 1740s, years that marked its high point as a centre of consumption. The finished house was brimming with furnishings, and objects accumulated over James Logan's lifetime crowded its spaces. Everywhere Smith turned, each room he entered, nearly every object he saw or touched or sat on, created an association with somewhere beyond the mid-Atlantic region of the American colonies. These ran the gamut from furniture inspired by Asian cultures, to spices and tea, to enslaved African people. The parlour, the most highly finished room, stood ready to impress and entertain guests such as Smith. On numerous occasions, tea drinking comprised a main activity with the family in this well-furnished space.[21] On such sociable occasions, sat around a tea table, the Logans used a London-made tea service, which descended in the Smith line of the family (Figure 8.2). James Logan likely acquired the set on his last voyage to England in the mid-1720s. The service comprised pieces from different silversmiths, each enumerated on a 1754 inventory, and included a 'Teapot, Lamp and Stand with Cream Pot' and a 'Pair of Canasters and Sugar Dish', as the service was described.[22] The tea service is one example of colonial elite consumption, an object of precious metal made in the metropole for the preparation and service of a fashionable foreign commodity. Used with regularity, it highlighted connections with the shops and makers of the British Empire's capital city, the genteel world of sociability and the tea-producing areas on the far side of the globe.

The white inhabitants at Stenton regularly consumed meals off a range of metal and ceramic objects originating in various parts of the world. Dozens of pewter plates and serving dishes carried London makers' marks. Stenton's archaeological collection shows the diversity

Figure 8.2 The London-made Logan family tea service, 1720–4. Reproduced courtesy of the Philadelphia Museum of Art.

of the Logans' possessions. Numerous ceramics excavated from a cistern behind the house are dated between about 1720 and 1760 and included no fewer than ten teapots from the middle of the eighteenth century. Mostly made of various kinds of stoneware from England, the range of forms and types is expansive.[23] Included among them were a Chinese porcelain teapot and an English salt-glazed stoneware teapot with decorative designs taken from a seventeenth-century treatise on japanning (Figure 8.3).[24]

Nearly every room contained objects that reinforced the Logans' involvement in global trade networks. The furnishings included local Philadelphia wares, numerous English products and many goods from beyond the British Isles. Until the late 1720s, most of the chairs, chests and looking glasses came from England, but as Philadelphia's cabinetmaking

Figure 8.3 Ceramics reconstructed from archaeology at Stenton display the range of china, stoneware and earthenware, including at least ten teapots. Reproduced courtesy of the National Society of the Colonial Dames of America in the Commonwealth of Pennsylvania at Stenton, Philadelphia.

and joinery sector developed, Logan increasingly purchased locally made furniture and other objects.[25] Logan's correspondence in the late 1710s and 1720s contains frequent orders for different goods from his contacts in Bristol and London. On one occasion he ordered a clock with a 'black Japann'd oak case'.[26] Like porcelain from China, japanned furniture sprinkled throughout the house hinted at parts of the world that European colonists thought of as exotic. Despite such goods increasingly being made in Britain in imitation of Asian products, the association reinforced the connections across myriad geographies. Household accounts also listed a 'Japan'd oval table', a 'Sett of 5 maps' and a 'pair of Globes', further indicators of cosmopolitan sensibilities at Stenton.[27]

As John Smith made the gentle climb up a broad staircase that led from the ground to the more private first floor, he found that Stenton concealed privileged treasures, spaces and global goods above. Curators and conservators have devoted much energy to reconstructing the grandest bed chamber at Stenton, where additional hints of foreign lands were plentiful. An impressive display of yellow worsted damask fabric woven in England hung as bed and window curtains and upholstered the slip-seat bottoms of 12 American-made maple chairs. The bed displayed a half-canopy, or flying tester, an English form rare in the American colonies. Recent research has identified the dye of a Logan family quilt as old fustic, a reddish-gold yellow colour produced from a mulberry family tree in South America. This colour is consistent with the description of 'yellow worsted damask' in this chamber.[28] Further circumstantial textile evidence of the same colour comes from a mid-eighteenth-century settee that likely stood in this room and passed to John and Hannah Smith's descendants. The settee displays pronounced Irish characteristics, as did other furniture at Stenton, drawing links with James Logan's Irish birthplace.[29] Although most likely produced in England, contemporaries knew the tin-glazed earthenware tiles that framed the fireplace as Delft or Dutch tiles based on the association of this type of ceramic with the Netherlands (Figure 8.4).[30] As in the parlour, a tea table arrayed with Chinese porcelain evoked the faraway exotic lands of East Asia. In one grand room, then, John Smith confronted a bevy of objects, colours and stylistic forms that transcended the 'wilds of Pennsylvania' and conjured up a decidedly cosmopolitan temple of consumption.

In addition to the many material goods Smith encountered, however, there were living indicators of the sprawling economic system that enabled not only the acquisition of material goods but also the ability to put them into action. Furnishings from around the globe shaped domestic space and how it was used, but it was the people associated

Figure 8.4 The fireplace wall of the 'Yellow Lodging Room' framed with English-made Delft or Dutch tiles. Reproduced courtesy of the National Society of the Colonial Dames of America in the Commonwealth of Pennsylvania at Stenton, Philadelphia.

with the Stenton household who provided the animating energy of Logan's country seat. Recent scholarship has exposed the extent to which wealth derived from colonialism and the institution of slavery fuelled colonial and metropolitan consumption in country houses throughout the British world, as well as developing the inextricable connection between the seeming opposites of slavery and eighteenth-century taste and civilisation.[31] Like many colonial elite houses, Stenton owed its existence to the exploitation of native inhabitants and to the Atlantic slave trade. Stenton signalled Logan as a key interlocutor with indigenous people and implicated the Logan family in the enslavement of Africans.

Native Americans were vital to the political life of Pennsylvania, and the murky and complex boundary between Native America and regions of European settlement were areas of intense interaction.[32] For Logan, deeply entangled in Pennsylvania geopolitics, relations between Native Americans and European colonisers were critical to the colony's survival and prosperity. Although there is no record that he noticed such an object, John Smith might have seen a redware bowl with a slip-figure image of an Iroquois sachem that marked the presence of native people in the spaces of this European encroachment on native lands (Figure 8.5).[33] Nothing is known about how this bowl came to Stenton or how it might have been used. By the 1760s the bowl had been broken and discarded and archaeologists only unearthed it during excavations in the 1980s. But this singular representation of a Native American on a commonplace piece of Pennsylvania pottery is a tangible indication of James Logan's deep political and economic involvement with Native inhabitants. Logan was simultaneously a leading and respected negotiator, occasionally hosting native encampments on the Stenton estate, and notorious for manipulative and exploitative dealings with native peoples, particularly the infamous 'Walking Purchase', a massive land grab in 1737 that

Figure 8.5 A Pennsylvania redware bowl with a slip-figure of a Native American, *c.* 1730–50. Reproduced courtesy of the National Society of the Colonial Dames of America in the Commonwealth of Pennsylvania at Stenton, Philadelphia.

effectively swindled the local Lenape, or Delaware, nation out of over one million acres of land.[34]

The economic relationships Logan established with native inhabitants were especially lucrative. The complicated and nuanced interchange of goods with Native Americans on the Pennsylvania frontier extended Stenton's economy in multiple directions and underpinned Logan's wealth, fuelling his acquisitive efforts in other areas. The trade in furs and skins with Native Americans especially profited Logan.[35] Not long after his arrival in Pennsylvania to act on behalf of the Penn family, Logan looked to participate in the growing market in furs and skins provided by Native Americans in exchange for manufactured European cloth and other goods.[36] In 1720, he mentioned 'ten Chests of Deer skins' being shipped to England, and he regularly sent deer, bear, beaver, fox and raccoon skins.[37] Textiles comprised a key good of exchange and were central to these economic arrangements. Curator Laura Johnson has noted that cloth, clothing and items of personal adornment made up nearly 60 per cent of James Logan's trade going to Native Americans, whereas less than 25 per cent was weapons, tools and other manufactured goods.[38] Cloth originating or associated with various other countries constituted many of Logan's imports, including orders for several varieties of linen, such as oznabrigs (Germany), 'Irish' linen and 'Holland' linen, while Stroud cloth from the west of England comprised the largest recorded mentions of imported cloth in Logan's account books.[39]

Although Logan sustained a varied portfolio of investments – land, mercantile activities, colonial administration and some early industrial efforts – the Native American trade contributed significantly to his ability to maintain Stenton's large household, which included hired servants, indentured people contractually tied to the Logans for a set period and enslaved Africans.[40] James Logan's account book, his ledger, and the journals of his son William provide the names and, in some cases, the responsibilities of servants on the property. The Stenton plantation stood on a little over 500 acres of contiguous property 5 miles north and west of Philadelphia, with barns, a chaise house, a cider mill and a dairy.[41] Logan acquired the acreage over time, and the house was not completed until 1730. In the meantime, it was a working farm, with a plantation manager, John Steers, supervising indentured and hired white servants to accomplish most of the plantation's work. Two tenants farmed the property, growing grains, maize, tobacco and fruit, as well as raising cows, pigs and horses.[42] Accounts often recorded labourers only by their country of origin, for example a 'Palatine Servant man', 'Dutch Philip' and 'A Dutch Boy'. An 'Irish Servant Lad' later ran away and ended up in gaol, after which Logan sold the balance of his indenture.[43] By 1720 Logan had purchased enslaved Africans to bolster the Stenton workforce and was active in buying and selling people of African descent.[44] In other words, trafficking in human bodies made James Logan's trade in and enjoyment of other global goods possible. Sometimes textiles that Logan imported from England became the currency of exchange for human beings, as when Logan paid for the labour of a 'negro girl' with 'borlap and garlix' cloth.[45]

In the early 1720s Logan, with an eye on retirement to country life, decided to build a brick mansion on the estate for his growing family.[46] During the construction of the house, a host of labourers worked to erect the structure, including carpenters, masons, brickmakers, lime-burners and blacksmiths, while lumber merchant Charles Read provided materials.[47] Often free and unfree labour overlapped, as in the case of Logan's hire of Clement Plumstead's 'Negroes' to assist in building the house.[48] In the four decades after Stenton's completion in 1730, a bevy of servants accomplished the work of the household. In 1748, Phebe Dickenson was the indentured 'housekeeper', and accounts listed hired workers as including a spinner, a farmer, a servant maid and two wet nurses. During the middle years of the eighteenth century, there were perhaps ten free and unfree workers at any given time working in and around the house, fairly typical for a house its size.

Enslaved people are mostly known as names alone, such as Diana, Roger Rowe, Thomas, Robert Southam, Hannibal (or Annibal), Mingoe, 'a negro boy Larry' and a 'Negro Girl Arimina'.[49] One enslaved woman, Menah or Mina, comprised heritable property for Hannah Logan Smith, although John Smith, an opponent of slavery, insisted that Menah remain at Stenton with his brother-in-law William; as Smith said of enslaved Africans, 'I do no chuse either to buy or sell them'.[50] John Smith may never have entered into the spaces at Stenton associated with service – attics, garrets, outbuildings, basements – yet these simply furnished rooms, often with only 'a Servant bed' or a chair, contained people commodified as a form of global goods.[51]

Some evidence indicated that, although racial distinctions existed, there was considerable interaction between black and white workers at Stenton. On one occasion, Logan wrote to agents in South Carolina 'to consign to you a Negro boy of mine' who had provided 'very good service'. Although it is unclear what the boy's primary tasks were, it is likely he worked in the household, as Logan noted that 'The Lad really deserves a good price being strong and ambitious' and even having 'some knowledge of his Letters'. But the boy had crossed racial and gender lines and run afoul of his master and other servants.[52] As Logan recounted, 'his manhood rousing upon him he has happened unluckily to direct his Inclination to the wrong colour and Servants at the Plantation where he lived being generally of the fairer sort his company was no longer tolerable there nor did I think fitt to keep him anywhere in the Province'.[53] The young man's seeming attention to white female servants necessitated that the enslaver Logan effect his removal from Pennsylvania. Logan admired the young man's hard work and abilities but nevertheless hoped to reap an ample profit from his sale.

Like many of his contemporaries, Logan's acquisition of silver, tables, chairs, cloth, furs and people demonstrated a truly global reach. His wide-ranging networks reveal the sinews that connected this country house in America to the Atlantic World and beyond. In the way that he purchased and displayed goods, Logan set himself up as a leading affluent colonial with a gentleman's house and the trappings of genteel Atlantic World culture. In this way, Stenton typified efforts by elites on the periphery of the British Empire to participate in what Timothy Breen has called an 'empire of goods'.[54]

Collecting and classicism at Stenton

At Stenton, John Smith encountered a building and objects that would have been immediately familiar to people of similar social standing across Anglo-America. Yet despite its typicality, James Logan's country seat housed goods that made it highly unusual in Pennsylvania and distinguished it even by comparison with other country houses throughout the Atlantic World. Logan had long cultivated a love of classical culture, and his voracious book buying, which occupied much of his time in the 1730 and 1740s, and ownership of a few rare classical artefacts illustrate another aspect of trade in the North American country house.[55]

For Logan and the intelligentsia of early America, knowledge of the ancient world transcended their colonial environment and tied them to the cultural patrimony of Europe. As historian Caroline Winterer has noted, 'transplanted Europeans maintained a lively interest in the old, especially the ancient classical world. Seen by few but known by many, Greece and Rome were ancient places as fascinating to both Europeans and Americans as the Western Hemisphere was to homebound Europeans.'[56] Although classicism in America later became closely allied with the republican ideals of the new United States, some of the earliest manifestations of classical influence in the colonies were seen in their country houses.[57]

As Smith traversed the house, in room after room he confronted a staggering collection of a valuable but comparatively uncommon object: books.[58] In 1718, Logan told London bookseller Josiah Martin, 'I confess, as I advance in years, the ancients still gain upon me'.[59] Logan knew books, and a signal achievement was the acquisition of an enormous library at Stenton of several thousand volumes.[60] His expansive collection had a particular concentration in the Greek and Roman classics. Logan recounted that he had 'above one hundred volumes of authors, in folio, all in Greek, with mostly their versions; all the Roman classics without exception; all the Greek mathematicians … besides there are many of the most valuable Latin authors'.[61] One vast room on the first floor initially housed this library, although most likely the library had migrated to the ground floor by the 1740s. There were so many books that they were likely scattered throughout the house. Their accumulation was an effort to stake out genteel and civilised behaviour, an important act to gainsay his status as a simple American bearskin merchant operating in the 'wilds of Pennsylvania'.

Although Logan was enormously proud of his collection, it was not simply for show. Benjamin Franklin called him 'A Gentleman of universal Learning and the best Judge of Books in these Parts'.[62] Logan was a scholar of an exceptional calibre who saw his country seat as a key transmitter of classical culture in eighteenth-century North America.[63] By looking to the ancient world of Greece and Rome, Logan established Stenton as an intellectual hub. There were several considerable libraries in the American colonies, although Logan's was certainly the richest in classical literature, comparable to country house libraries in Britain.[64] His letters to booksellers and some of the leading scientific and intellectual figures of Britain and Europe make clear that these books formed part of the fabric of Logan's being. One correspondent told a friend that Logan 'is a Great man in Every Capacity'.[65] He had a rare knowledge of the value of books and a capacity to recall the details of various editions. His polymath interests meant that he read and annotated the works and carried on extensive debates about the ideas they raised.

Another correspondent was the German classicist Johann Albrecht Fabricius. Logan wrote to this eminent scholar to dispute a point raised in the professor's *Bibliotheca Graeca*, his massive bibliography of Greek texts. 'Allow me', asked Logan politely, 'since what is strange and distant wins esteem not on account of its worth but because it is unusual, to address you from the wilds of Pennsylvania.'[66] Despite the modesty, his letter to Fabricius, written politely in Latin, the lingua franca of the Western intellectual world, demonstrated Logan's intellectual agility and attention to detail, noting an error in Fabricius's bibliographic work. Fabricius was a leading intellectual light and the two men established a cordial correspondence. Nonetheless, Logan was a sharp critic who had grumbled to a London bookseller that he hoped that Fabricius 'may at length have thought fitt to putt an end to ye tedious and overswoln Work'.[67]

Because of his political power and intellectual reputation, he drew visitors to Stenton from throughout the colonies and beyond to admire his library and seek his advice. John Smith was cognisant of the role that knowledge, scholarship and classicism played at Stenton, and the library with its carefully curated collection in numerous languages from all around Europe was a further form of global goods. On one visit, Smith recorded, Logan ushered him 'into his Library, and took a great deal of pains to Entertain me there'.[68] Another visitor commented in 1744 that 'it appeared we must first view his library', which for Logan was customary 'to any persons of account. He had really a very fine collection of books, both ancient and modern.'[69]

Benjamin Franklin's obituary of Logan noted that 'His life was for the most part a life of business, tho' he was passionately fond of study'.[70] The promise of Logan's library abetted efforts to establish higher education in Pennsylvania, when it formed a substantial selling point for Franklin's plan for an academy in Philadelphia, later to become the University of Pennsylvania. 'We may expect', Franklin wrote, 'the benefit of another [library] much more valuable in the Learned Languages, which has been many Years collecting with the greatest Care.'[71] Yet despite having a library unsurpassed in America and equal to many of the finest in Europe, Logan admitted to his agent in Hamburg, 'It may appear strange to thee perhaps to find an American bearskin merchant troubling himself with such books'.[72] On the periphery of the Atlantic World, Logan's country house library empowered him to contribute significantly to the circulation of knowledge while also demonstrating his wealth, connections and cultural reach.

A handful of material objects further reinforced his country seat as a centre of classicism in early America. Through the 1730s and 1740s Logan frequently exchanged letters with Peter Collinson, a Quaker from a family of London cloth merchants that had extensive trade with America. Collinson was a close friend of Sir Hans Sloane, founder of the British Museum, and other eminent figures in natural philosophy, including Linnaeus. Interested in a host of subjects, Collinson took a special interest in scientific investigation emanating from the American colonies.[73]

Their exchange of occasional packages also included several classical objects. In one intriguing letter Collinson mentioned, 'I retained fragments of a ancient skiphus for my own cabinet. The glories of such ancients are clear in the smallest of their accomplishments.' It seems that Collinson kept fragments of a skyphos, or Greek wine cup, while sending along a similar object – the 'smallest of their accomplishments' to which Collinson referred – that descended in the Logan family and is now on loan to the Stenton Museum.[74] The Logan skyphos is typical of red-figured pottery produced between 440 BCE and 300 BCE by Greek colonists who had settled in southern Italy and Sicily. Not until the later eighteenth and nineteenth centuries did some of this pottery emerge 'at various sites in Apulia and Campania', where it 'was highly prized because of the interest of its subject-matter'.[75]

In 1738, then, an object such as the skyphos was a rare treasure. Accordingly, it is probably the first documented piece of classical pottery to arrive in the American colonies.[76] Collinson followed this singular gift with another parcel early the next year: 'Symonds conveyed', Collinson wrote to Logan, 'your receipt and thanks for the books and marbles, and I today forwarded another parcel by him to you'.[77] As always, books were of great interest to Logan, but the marbles were a special gift worthy of particular mention: 21 pieces of marble of different types wrapped in eighteenth-century paper and carefully labelled, in different hands, on the front of each (Figure 8.6).

There is no reference to how Logan used or displayed these objects. The fully panelled parlour's dramatic shell buffet cupboard contained the family's most prized and costly possessions, such as silver plate and perhaps the skyphos. Logan may have housed them in his handsome desk and bookcase that also stood in the parlour, or in his library as a sort of cabinet at Stenton, to be shown only to those privileged to be invited into Logan's most intellectually intimate world. Stenton's archaeological collection contains not a single piece of classical material, and the absence of archaeological evidence likely constitutes a statement about the value of these rarities. Whereas even the finest pieces of chinaware might be discarded when broken, classical artefacts such as the skyphos held a treasured place among Logan's many valuable possessions. In whatever way they were housed, these 'glories of the ancients' conveyed messages of elite status, of classical learning, and of connection with the culture of the metropole and the ancient past. They were objects worthy

Figure 8.6 Desk and bookcase in Stenton's parlour with the Greek wine cup, or skyphos, and marble sample, all purportedly gifts from Royal Society member Peter Collinson to James Logan. Reproduced courtesy of the National Society of the Colonial Dames of America in the Commonwealth of Pennsylvania at Stenton, Philadelphia and the Fairmount Park Historic Resource Archive, Loudoun Collection.

of the Grand Tour and a significant watershed in the dissemination of classical learning in America.

Logan's large and qualitatively outstanding library and his few classical artefacts were rare, but colonial gentry at other country houses in America picked up on these classical cues. Isaac Norris, Jr, who married Logan's intellectual daughter Sarah, amassed a substantial library at his house Fairhill and helped Logan to compile the first catalogue of Stenton's library. Several other mansions housed significant book collections, if not as large or scholarly as the one at Stenton.[78] Moreover, to link the classical world with the eighteenth century, and the old world with the new, James Logan donated his entire library to benefit of the citizens of Philadelphia. He meant this philanthropic gift to expand interest in and access to classical learning and to encourage a more active intellectual community in the 'wilds of Pennsylvania'.

David Hancock has noted that this sort of collecting often served as 'social camouflage by which the merchant instructed others and reminded himself of the legitimacy of new wealth in polite society'.[79] Although Logan's bibliophilia and classical acquisitions may have served in part as social camouflage, they certainly demonstrated a deep commitment to learning, antiquity and intellectual discourse. They were evidence of an expansive participation in the global world of goods as well as ideas. Stenton and its contents stood as an eighteenth-century representation of classical influences in America.

Conclusion

By taking us to the shores of North America, this chapter has explored the trading activities, domestic furnishings and collecting passions of James Logan at his country seat on the fringes of Britain's eighteenth-century empire. There Logan experienced the global reach of commodities that linked colony to mother country and to networks of trade touching virtually every continent. Stenton is a particularly compelling case study of goods in the country house context beyond Europe because it illustrates both commonplace consumption for eighteenth-century elites and exceptional collections almost unparalleled in America.

Like so many other eighteenth-century British country houses, Stenton was a significant site of consumption.[80] By the standards of the American colonies or provincial Britain, Stenton was a commodious mansion appropriate to a member of the Atlantic World gentry. Although awash in objects from many corners of the earth, the Logan family was not significantly more materially blessed than others of similar social standing. Their possessions put into motion the complex human drama acted out in the domestic space of the country house between free and unfree peoples. Cross-cultural trade in goods, including human bodies, underpinned these material and human interactions. Houses such as Stenton were local models to the extent that by the end of the eighteenth century, teeming consumption meant that even modest Americans furnished their houses with goods from various parts of the world.[81]

Yet this country seat in America filled with the Logan family's assemblage was, by comparison with everyday Pennsylvanians and colonial Americans, also quite remarkable. As a demonstration of Logan's collecting penchant, Stenton, with its vast library and sprinkling of classical objects, gave the lie to James Logan's claim to be a 'simple bearskin merchant' scraping for survival out in the 'wilds of Pennsylvania'. An array of global goods made their way to Stenton from the porous and contested borderlands between Native America and British-settled Pennsylvania, from African shores, London booksellers and silversmiths, the leading intellectual centres of Europe, and the distant, exotic lands of Asia, all to be used, displayed or recirculated at this crossroads of the British Empire.

Notes

1. Obituary of James Logan, *The Pennsylvania Gazette*, 7 November 1751. *Papers of Benjamin Franklin*, vol. 4, 207. https://franklinpapers.org/framedVolumes.jsp.
2. James Logan to Thomas Story, 26 June 1714, *James Logan Letterbook 1717–1731*, Historical Society of Pennsylvania, 199; Tolles, *James Logan and the Culture of Provincial America*, 186; James Logan to Thomas Penn, *Penn Manuscripts: Official Correspondence*, vol. 2, 41.
3. Tolles, *James Logan and the Culture of Provincial America*, 95; James Logan to Johann Fabricius, 11 November 1721, *James Logan Letterbook*, vol. 3, 20–2.
4. Maudlin and Herman, *Building the British Atlantic World*. See also Upton, *Holy Things and Profane*; Herman and Guillery, 'Negotiating classicism in eighteenth-century Deptford and Philadelphia'; Crowley, *The Invention of Comfort*; Herman, *Town House*; Nelson, *Architecture and Empire in Jamaica*.
5. Hague, *The Gentleman's House*, 57–8.
6. Hague, *The Gentleman's House*; Hood, *The Governor's Palace*; Reinberger and McLean, *The Philadelphia Country House*.
7. Gerritsen and Riello, *The Global Lives of Things*.
8. Horn, *A Land as God Made It*; Kelso, *Jamestown*. On the first importation of enslaved people, see Horn, *1619*.
9. One approach has focused on specific types of goods and material objects, for example, Anderson, *Mahogany*; Peck, *Interwoven Globe*; Beckert, *Empire of Cotton*; and DuPlessis, *The Material Atlantic*. Zahediah, *The Capital and the Colonies*, looks at London's role in shaping transatlantic trade. Other studies examine specific colonies or regions, such as Matson, *Merchants & Empire*. Martin, *Buying into the World of Goods*, developed the consumer connections in one borderland. Hart, *Trading Spaces*, assessed the interaction between space and capitalism in early America. Anishanslin, *Portrait of a Woman in Silk*, innovatively mines a single object to map Atlantic World trade and culture. A landmark volume was Lindsey, *Worldly Goods*.
10. Styles and Vickery, *Gender, Taste, and Material Culture*; Martin, *Buying into the World of Goods*. Carson, *Face Value*, highlights demand for goods over their supply. See also Van Horn, *The Power of Objects*; Boudreau and Lovell, eds., *A Material World*; Hague and Lipsedge, eds., *At Home in the Eighteenth Century*.
11. Barczewski, *Country Houses and the British Empire*; Dresser and Hann, *Slavery and the British Country House*; Finn and Smith, eds., *The East India Company at Home*; Huxtable et al., *Interim Report*.
12. Walsh, *Motives of Honor, Pleasure, and Profit*; Edelson, *Plantation Enterprise*. Mooney, *Prodigy Houses*, 3, draws 'a social, though not stylistic, parallel between England's prodigy houses and those constructed later in Virginia'.
13. Kim, *Landlord and Tenant*; Reinberger and McLean, *The Philadelphia Country House*; Sweeney, 'Mansion people'; Mooney, *Prodigy Houses*.
14. Stobart and Rothery, *Consumption and the Country House*.
15. Sahle, *Quakers in the British Atlantic World*. On Pennsylvania, see Tolles, *Meeting House and Counting House*; Lemon, *The Best Poor Man's Country*; Smolenski, *Friends and Strangers*.
16. Tolles, *James Logan and the Culture of Provincial America*, 86–91.
17. Much of Logan's accumulated wealth was invested in land, although he began to divest himself of some of this to buy English securities. He had sent nearly £1,000 to his brother in Bristol for this purpose by September 1733. His will of 1749 suggests that he owned nearly 18,000 acres in Pennsylvania and New Jersey and had an estate valued at £8,500. *James Logan Will*, 1749, transcript on file at Stenton.
18. Carson, *Face Value*, 17.
19. Smith's many visits to Stenton are recounted in his diary, published as *Hannah Logan's Courtship*. The original of the diary is at the Historical Society of Pennsylvania.
20. *Hannah Logan's Courtship*. The alligator reference is on 102.
21. *Hannah Logan's Courtship*, e.g., 114, 158, 208.
22. Shepherd, 'James Logan's Stenton', 39–40, 177, 192. Sarah Read Logan inventory, 1754, on file at Stenton. This inventory is likely of a townhouse in Philadelphia, with the objects moved from Stenton after her husband's death in 1751. The tea service is now in the Philadelphia Museum of Art, 1959.151.9-12 and 1975.49.1.2.

23 Archaeologist Barbara Liggett, who excavated the site, noted that the archaeological materials at Stenton constitute one of the most significant assemblages from a colonial North American house. 'Archaeological Notes on Stenton' (1983, on file at Stenton). An important contribution is Miller, '"Just imported from London"'. On stoneware, see Edwards and Hampson, *White Salt-Glazed Stoneware of the British Isles*; Skerry and Hood, *Salt-Glazed Stoneware in Early America*.
24 Grigsby, 'John Stalker and George Parker's *Treatise*'.
25 Shepherd, 'James Logan's Stenton', 36. On developments in early Philadelphia furniture production, see Stiefel, *The Cabinetmaker's Account*, especially 23–8.
26 *James Logan Letterbook 1717–1731*, 95: 18 November 1719.
27 Shepherd, 'James Logan's Stenton', 175, 179.
28 Keim, '"Ochre, old fustic, and maple', 116.
29 Glin and Peill, *Irish Furniture*, 152–4; Keim, 'Stenton room furnishings study', 45.
30 *Dutch Tiles in the Philadelphia Museum of Art*.
31 Dresser and Hann, *Slavery and the British Country House*; Barczewski, *Country Houses and the British Empire*; Huxtable et al., *Interim Report*; Gikandi, *Slavery and the Culture of Taste*.
32 Richter, *Facing East from Indian Country*; Merritt, *At the Crossroads*; Spero, *Frontier Country*.
33 Keim and Orr, 'Redware Native American bowl'.
34 Merrell, *Into the American Woods*; Harpur, *Promised Land*; Newman, *On Records*, especially chapter 4.
35 Johnson, '"Goods to clothe themselves"', 64–5.
36 Johnson highlights how Native Americans 'acquired and utilized European trade cloth to create their own identity and cultural vocabulary', Johnson, '"Goods to clothe themselves"', 16.
37 *James Logan Letterbook 1717–1731*, 156: 3 August 1720, James Logan to Henry Goldney. Numerous entries in the *James Logan Ledger, 1720–1727* and *James Logan Account Book, 1712–1720* (both Historical Society of Pennsylvania) record other furs.
38 Johnson, '"Goods to clothe themselves"', 15, 88 Fig. 21, 95 Table 1.
39 Johnson, '"Goods to clothe themselves"', 23, 91 Fig. 24.
40 Keim, 'Acco't of negroes'; Dickey and Engle, *Stenton Historic Structure Report*, 319–20, Tables 7 and 8.
41 Dickey and Engle, *Stenton Historic Structure Report*, 4, 7.
42 Dickey and Engle, *Stenton Historic Structure Report*, 7, 319.
43 Dickey and Engle, *Stenton Historic Structure Report*, 319–20, Tables 7 and 8. For the Irish lad, see Keim, 'Acco't of negroes', 13.
44 Keim, 'Acco't of negroes', 4–6.
45 Keim, 'Acco't of negroes', 5.
46 On the construction of Stenton, see Dickey and Engle, *Stenton Historic Structure Report*, chapter 2. 'A handsome house' is in *Penn Manuscripts: Official Correspondence*, vol. 2, 41.
47 Dickey and Engle, *Stenton Historic Structure Report*, 11, Table 2.
48 *James Logan Ledger, 1720–1727*, 26 September 1723. See also Dickey and Engle, *Stenton Historic Structure Report*, 9.
49 Keim, 'Acco't of negroes'; Dickey and Engle, *Stenton Historic Structure Report*, 319–20, Tables 7 and 8.
50 *Hannah Logan's Courtship*, 350.
51 For comparison, see the description of servants' furniture in England in Stobart, 'Servants' furniture'.
52 Kendi, *Stamped from the Beginning*.
53 *James Logan Letterbook 1717–1731*, 333: 31 August 1723.
54 Breen, 'An empire of goods'.
55 Wolf, *The Library of James Logan*.
56 Winterer, 'From royal to republican', 1264.
57 Onuf and Cole, eds., *Thomas Jefferson*. See also Maudlin and Herman, *Building the British Atlantic World*, 5–7.
58 Hague, *The Gentleman's House*, 133, Tables 6.2 and 6.3.
59 James Logan to Josiah Martin, 26 October 1718, in Wolf, *James Logan, Bookman Extraordinary*, 16.
60 Wolf, *The Library of James Logan*.
61 Quoted in Hornor, *Blue Book of Philadelphia Furniture*, 54.

62 Quoted in Wolf, *The Library of James Logan*, xvii.
63 Tolles, 'Quaker humanist'.
64 Purcell, *The Country House Library*.
65 Collinson, *'Forget not Mee & My Garden'*, 49.
66 James Logan to Johann Fabricius, 11 November 1721, *James Logan Letterbook*, vol. 3, 20–2.
67 James Logan to William Innys, 30 November 1719, in Wolf, *The Library of James Logan*, 166.
68 *Hannah Logan's Courtship*, 154.
69 Black, 'The journal of William Black', 407.
70 Obituary of James Logan.
71 Franklin, *Proposals Relating to the Education of Youth*.
72 Tolles, *James Logan and the Culture of Provincial America*, 95.
73 Collinson, *'Forget not Mee & My Garden'*; O'Neill and McLean, *Peter Collinson and the Eighteenth-Century Natural History Exchange*.
74 Peter Collinson to James Logan, 7 August 1738, Transcription from Pennsylvania Museum of Art Archives/*Worldly Goods* exhibit files/Box 5/Item 46. The history and documentation of the skyphos is somewhat problematic. According to family tradition, the skyphos belonged to James Logan and was in the collection at Loudoun, another Logan family house near Stenton. The quotes appear in a letter of 17 October 1998 in the *Worldly Goods* file, transcribed from two 1738 Collinson–Logan letters. These letters were noted as from the Royal Society in London, but the original manuscript letters are not presently at the Royal Society and their whereabouts are unknown.
75 Trendall, *Red Figure Vases of South Italy and Sicily*, 7.
76 Oakley, 'Greek vases in early America'.
77 Peter Collinson to James Logan, 4 March 1738/[1739?], Pennsylvania Museum of Art Archives/*Worldly Goods* exhibit files/Box 5/Item 46.
78 Korey, *The Books of Isaac Norris*; Hayes, *The Library of William Byrd of Westover*; Hamilton, 'The library of Sir William Johnson'.
79 Hancock, *Citizens of the World*, 360.
80 Stobart and Rothery, *Consumption and the Country House*.
81 Miller, *'Great* earthly riches'.

Bibliography

Anderson, Jennifer L. *Mahogany: The costs of luxury in early America*. Cambridge and London: Harvard University Press, 2012.
Anishanslin, Zara. *Portrait of a Woman in Silk: Hidden histories of the British Atlantic World*. New Haven and London: Yale University Press, 2016.
Barczewski, Stephanie. *Country Houses and the British Empire, 1700–1930*. Manchester: Manchester University Press, 2014.
Beckert, Sven. *Empire of Cotton: A global history*. New York: Alfred A. Knopf, 2015.
Black, William. 'The journal of William Black', *Pennsylvania Magazine of History and Biography* 1, no. 4 (1877): 404–19.
Boudreau, George W., and Margaretta Markle Lovell, eds. *A Material World: Culture, society, and the life of things in early Anglo-America*. University Park: Pennsylvania University Press, 2019.
Breen, T.H. 'An empire of goods: the anglicization of colonial America, 1690–1776', *Journal of British Studies* 25 (October 1986): 467–99.
Carson, Cary. *Face Value: The consumer revolution and the colonizing of America*. Charlottesville: University of Virginia Press, 2017.
Collinson, Peter. *'Forget not Mee & My Garden …': Selected letters 1725–1768 of Peter Collinson*. Edited by Alan W. Armstrong. Philadelphia: American Philosophical Society, 2002.
Cook Myers, Albert, ed. *Hannah Logan's Courtship*. Philadelphia: Ferris & Leach, 1904.
Crowley, John. *The Invention of Comfort: Sensibilities and design in early modern Britain and America*. Baltimore: Johns Hopkins University Press, 2001.
Dickey, John M., and Reed Engle. *Stenton Historic Structure Report*. Unpublished report, 1982.
Dresser, Madge, and Andrew Hann, eds. *Slavery and the British Country House*. Swindon: English Heritage, 2013.

DuPlessis, Robert S. *The Material Atlantic: Clothing, commerce, and colonization in the Atlantic World, 1650–1800*. Cambridge: Cambridge University Press, 2016.

Dutch Tiles in the Philadelphia Museum of Art. Philadelphia: Philadelphia Museum of Art, 1984.

Edelson, Max. *Plantation Enterprise in Colonial South Carolina*. Cambridge and London: Harvard University Press, 2006.

Edwards, Diana, and Rodney Hampson. *White Salt-Glazed Stoneware of the British Isles*. Woodbridge: Antique Collector's Club, 2005.

Finn, Margot, and Kate Smith, eds. *The East India Company at Home, 1757–1857*. London: UCL Press, 2017.

Franklin, Benjamin. *Proposals Relating to the Education of Youth in Pensilvania*. Philadelphia, 1749.

Gerritsen, Anne, and Giorgio Riello, eds. *The Global Lives of Things: The material culture of connections in the early modern world*. London and New York: Routledge, 2016.

Gikandi, Simon. *Slavery and the Culture of Taste*. Princeton: Princeton University Press, 2011.

Glin, The Knight of, and James Peill. *Irish Furniture: Woodwork and carving in Ireland from the earliest times to the Act of Union*. New Haven and London: Yale University Press, 2007.

Grigsby, Leslie. 'John Stalker and George Parker's *Treatise*: an inspiration for relief decoration on English stoneware and earthenware', *Antiques* (June 1993): 886–93.

Hague, Stephen. *The Gentleman's House in the British Atlantic World, 1680–1780*. Basingstoke: Palgrave Macmillan, 2015.

Hague, Stephen, and Karen Lipsedge, eds. *At Home in the Eighteenth Century: Interrogating domestic space*. New York and London: Routledge, 2022.

Hamilton, Milton W. 'The library of Sir William Johnson', *New York Historical Society Quarterly* 40, no. 3 (July 1956): 209–51.

Hancock, David. *Citizens of the World: London merchants and the integration of the British Atlantic community, 1735–1783*. Cambridge: Cambridge University Press, 1995.

Harpur, Steven Craig. *Promised Land: Penn's holy experiment, the walking purchase, and the dispossession of Delawares, 1600–1763*. Bethlehem, PA: Lehigh University Press, 2006.

Hart, Emma. *Trading Spaces: The colonial marketplace and the foundation of American capitalism*. Chicago and London: University of Chicago Press, 2019.

Hayes, Kevin J. *The Library of William Byrd of Westover*. Madison, WI: Madison House, 1997.

Herman, Bernard L. *Town House: Architecture and material life in the early American city, 1780–1830*. Chapel Hill: University of North Carolina Press, 2005.

Herman, Bernard L., and Peter Guillery. 'Negotiating classicism in eighteenth-century Deptford and Philadelphia'. In *Articulating British Classicism: New approaches to eighteenth-century architecture*, edited by Barbara Arciszewska and Elizabeth McKellar, 187–225. Aldershot: Ashgate, 2004.

Hood, Graham. *The Governor's Palace in Williamsburg: A Cultural History*. Williamsburg, VA: The Colonial Williamsburg Foundation, 1991.

Horn, James. *A Land as God Made It: Jamestown and the birth of America*. New York: Basic Books, 2006.

Horn, James. *1619: Jamestown and the Forging of American Democracy*. New York: Basic Books, 2018.

Hornor, William MacPherson. *Blue Book of Philadelphia Furniture: William Penn to George Washington*. Alexandria, VA: Highland House, 1935.

Huxtable, Sally-Anne, Corinne Fowler, Christo Kefalas and Emma Slocombe, eds. *Interim Report on the Connections between Colonialism and Properties now in the Care of the National Trust, Including Links with Historic Slavery*. Swindon: National Trust, 2020.

Johnson, Laura. '"Goods to clothe themselves": native consumers, native images on the Pennsylvania trading frontier, 1712–1730', MA thesis, University of Delaware, 2004.

Keim, Laura C. 'Stenton room furnishings study'. Unpublished report, 2010, on file at Stenton.

Keim, Laura C. 'Ochre, old fustic, and maple: Stenton's yellow lodging room restored', *Antiques & Fine Art* (Winter 2017): 112–17.

Keim, Laura C. '"Acco't of negroes": The labor force at a merchant's mid-Atlantic plantation'. Paper delivered at the Mid-Atlantic Plantation conference, 2019.

Keim, Laura C., and David Orr. 'Redware Native American bowl'. In *Ceramics in America*, edited by Laura C. Keim and David Orr, 294–300. Milwaukee, WI: The Chipstone Foundation, 2008).

Kelso, William M. *Jamestown: The truth revealed*. Charlottesville: University of Virginia Press, 2018.

Kendi, Ibram X. *Stamped from the Beginning: The definitive history of racist ideas in America*. New York: Bold Type Books, 2016.

Kim, Sung Bok. *Landlord and Tenant in Colonial New York: Manorial society 1664–1775*. Chapel Hill: University of North Carolina Press, 1978.

Korey, Marie Elena. *The Books of Isaac Norris (1701–1766) at Dickinson College*. Carlisle, PA: Dickinson College, 1976.

Lemon, James T. *The Best Poor Man's Country: Early southeastern Pennsylvania*. Baltimore: Johns Hopkins University Press, 2002.

Liggett, Barbara. 'Archaeological notes on Stenton'. On file at Stenton, 1983.

Lindsey, Jack, ed. *Worldly Goods: The art of early Pennsylvania, 1680–1758*. Philadelphia: Philadelphia Museum of Art, 1999.

Martin, Ann Smart. *Buying into the World of Goods: Early consumers in backcountry Virginia*. Baltimore: Johns Hopkins University Press, 2008.

Matson, Cathy. *Merchants & Empire: Trading in colonial New York*. Baltimore: Johns Hopkins University Press, 1998.

Maudlin, Daniel, and Bernard L. Herman, eds. *Building the British Atlantic World: Spaces, places, and material culture, 1600–1850*. Chapel Hill: University of North Carolina Press, 2016.

Merrell, James H. *Into the American Woods: Negotiators on the Pennsylvania frontier*. New York: W. W. Norton, 1999.

Merritt, Jane T. *At the Crossroads: Indians & empires on a mid-Atlantic frontier, 1700–1763*. Chapel Hill: University of North Carolina Press, 2003.

Miller, Deborah L. '"Just imported from London": the archaeology and material culture of Stenton's feature 14', MA thesis, Pennsylvania State University – Harrisburg, 2006.

Miller, Deborah L. '"Great earthly riches are no real advantage to our posterity …": space, archaeology, and the Philadelphia home'. In *At Home in the Eighteenth Century: Interrogating domestic space*, edited by Stephen G. Hague and Karen Lipsedge, 174–98. New York and London: Routledge, 2022.

Mooney, Barbara Burlison. *Prodigy Houses of Virginia: Architecture and the native elite*. Charlottesville and London: University of Virginia Press, 2008.

Nelson, Louis P. *Architecture and Empire in Jamaica*. New Haven and London: Yale University Press, 2016.

Newman, Andrew. *On Records: Delaware Indians, colonists, and the media of history and memory*. Lincoln and London: University of Nebraska Press, 2012.

Oakley, John H. 'Greek vases in early America', *Studi Miscellanei Di Ceramografia Greca* (2018): 93–104.

O'Neill, Jean, and Elizabeth P. McLean. *Peter Collinson and the Eighteenth-Century Natural History Exchange*. Philadelphia: American Philosophical Society, 2008.

Onuf, Peter S., and Nicholas P. Cole, eds. *Thomas Jefferson, the Classical World, and Early America*. Charlottesville: University of Virginia Press, 2013.

Peck, Amelia, ed. *Interwoven Globe: The worldwide textile trade, 1500–1800*. New Haven: Yale University for the Metropolitan Museum of Art, 2013.

Penn Manuscripts: Official Correspondence, 1728–1734. Historical Society of Pennsylvania.

Purcell, Mark. *The Country House Library*. New Haven and London: Yale University Press, 2017.

Reinberger, Mark, and Elizabeth McLean. *The Philadelphia Country House*. Baltimore: Johns Hopkins University Press, 2016.

Richter, Daniel K. *Facing East from Indian Country: A native history of early America*. Cambridge and London: Harvard University Press, 2001.

Sahle, Esther. *Quakers in the British Atlantic World, c. 1660–1800*. Woodbridge: Boydell & Brewer, 2021.

Shepherd, Raymond V. 'James Logan's Stenton: grand simplicity in Quaker Philadelphia', MA thesis, Winterthur/University of Delaware, 1968.

Skerry, Janine E., and Suzanne Findlen Hood. *Salt-Glazed Stoneware in Early America*. Hanover, NH and London: Colonial Williamsburg and University Press of New England, 2009.

Smolenski, John. *Friends and Strangers: The making of a Creole culture in colonial Pennsylvania*. Philadelphia: University of Pennsylvania Press, 2010.

Spero, Patrick. *Frontier Country: The politics of war in early Pennsylvania*. Philadelphia: University of Pennsylvania Press, 2016.

Stiefel, Jay Robert. *The Cabinetmaker's Account: John Head's record of craft & commerce in colonial Philadelphia, 1718–1753*. Philadelphia: American Philosophical Society Press, 2019.

Stobart, Jon. 'Servants' furniture: hierarchies and identities in the English country house'. In *At Home in the Eighteenth Century: Interrogating domestic space*, edited by Stephen G. Hague and Karen Lipsedge, 245–65. New York and London: Routledge, 2022.

Stobart, Jon, and Mark Rothery. *Consumption and the Country House*. Oxford: Oxford University Press, 2016.

Styles, John, and Amanda Vickery, eds. *Gender, Taste, and Material Culture in Britain and North America 1700–1830*. New Haven and London: Yale University Press, 2006.

Sweeney, Kevin. 'Mansion people: kinship, class, and architecture in western Massachusetts in the mid eighteenth century', *Winterthur Portfolio* 19, no. 4 (Winter 1984): 231–55.

Tolles, Frederick. *Meeting House and Counting House: The Quaker merchants of colonial Philadelphia, 1682–1763*. Chapel Hill: University of North Carolina Press, 1948.

Tolles, Frederick. 'Quaker humanist: James Logan as classical scholar', *PMHB* 75, no. 4 (October 1955): 415–38.

Tolles, Frederick. *James Logan and the Culture of Provincial America*. Boston: Little, Brown, 1957.

Trendall, A.D. *Red Figure Vases of South Italy and Sicily: A handbook*. London: Thames and Hudson, 1989.

Upton, Dell. *Holy Things and Profane: Anglican parish churches in colonial Virginia*. New Haven and London: Yale University Press, 1997.

Van Horn, Jennifer. *The Power of Objects in Eighteenth-Century British America*. Chapel Hill: University of North Carolina Press, 2017.

Walsh, Lorena. *Motives of Honor, Pleasure, and Profit: Plantation management in the colonial Chesapeake, 1607–1763*. Chapel Hill: University of North Caroline Press, 2010.

Winterer, Caroline. 'From royal to republican: the classical image in early America', *The Journal of American History* 91, no. 4 (March 2005): 1264–90.

Wolf, Edwin. *James Logan, 1674–1751, Bookman Extraordinary*. Philadelphia: Library Company of Philadelphia, 1971.

Wolf, Edwin. *The Library of James Logan of Philadelphia, 1674–1751*. Philadelphia: Library Company of Philadelphia, 1974.

Zahediah, Nuala. *The Capital and the Colonies: London and the Atlantic economy, 1660–1700*. Cambridge: Cambridge University Press, 2010.

Object lessons 2
Crafting global goods

VI
Model of a Chinese pagoda by Elizabeth Ratcliffe, 1767

Emile de Bruijn

Figure OL.VI Model of a Chinese pagoda in vellum, mica, mother-of-pearl, glass and stone, made by Elizabeth Ratcliffe (c. 1735–c. 1810), 1767. © Emile de Bruijn.

Erddig, near Wrexham in Wales, is a 'sleeping beauty' country house. When it was donated to the National Trust in 1973, successive generations of the Yorke family had been living there since 1733, accumulating many layers of possessions.[1] Among the family portraits and furniture in the Gallery at Erddig stands a model of a Chinese pagoda (Figure OL.VI). It has been at Erddig since about 1767, when it was created by the artist Elizabeth Ratcliffe, who also worked in the household as a lady's maid. Although made in Britain, this model is also a global object, embodying the increasing awareness of things Chinese among the British in the eighteenth century.

The European public was introduced to the pagoda in the seventeenth century, in particular through the illustrations in Johan Nieuhof's book about a Dutch diplomatic mission to China, published in Amsterdam in 1665 and quickly translated into several other languages.[2] Every Chinese city illustrated by Nieuhof featured one or more pagodas, and in addition there was a large plate of the so-called Porcelain Pagoda of Nanjing. Soon pagodas became a staple of European representations of East Asia, as seen on tin-glazed earthenware imitating Chinese and Japanese porcelain, imitation lacquer furniture, chased silver, painted panelling and tapestries.

Pagodas began to appear in English gardens in the mid-eighteenth century, for instance at Marybone House, Gloucester, *c.* 1748, and at Shugborough Hall, Staffordshire, *c.* 1752.[3] When William Chambers published *Designs of Chinese Buildings* in 1757, it included an elevation and plan of a pagoda he had observed on the banks of the Pearl River near Guangzhou when working as a supercargo for the Swedish East India Company.[4] In 1762 Chambers built an actual pagoda at Kew, on the western outskirts of London, for Augusta, Dowager Princess of Wales, which is still extant. As Chambers had visited China, he could claim that his designs were authentic representations of Chinese architecture, although in retrospect they appear to be seen through a European, classical lens.

The pagoda model at Erddig, made in about 1767, was previously thought to have been inspired by Chambers's pagodas, but its appearance is actually closer to the model pagodas in ivory and mother-of-pearl that began to be produced by Chinese artisans for the European market during the second half of the eighteenth century.[5] Most of the surviving Chinese pagoda models appear to date from the late eighteenth and early nineteenth centuries, but some may be earlier – for instance the pair of carved ivory models at Blickling Hall, Norfolk, which are thought to have been owned by Henrietta Howard, Countess of Suffolk, who died in 1767.[6]

Both the Chinese-made pagoda models and Ratcliffe's version can be described as forms of orientalism, or the cultural expression of the

European perspective on Asia and the Middle East.[7] The models made in China can be defined as a form of self-orientalism, that is, the production by Asian artisans of objects designed to appeal to European preconceptions of Asia. Ratcliffe's model, in turn, demonstrates the circularity of orientalism, being an object made by a British artist who was inspired by a Chinese product which was made in response to a European enthusiasm for a Chinese type of building.

As a decorative object, moreover, Ratcliffe's pagoda is an example of how the exotic was being domesticated in eighteenth-century British interiors. It is the embodiment of the notions of politeness and civilisation which were increasingly valued in Britain at that time: having been made by a servant whose artistic accomplishments were being encouraged by the Yorke family, it was also an emblem of a distant culture that was considered to be particularly civilised.[8] Significantly, another model created by Ratcliffe (and also on display in the Gallery at Erddig) represents the ruins of the Temple of the Sun at Palmyra, showing how classical antiquity and modern China were both considered to be exemplary: models in both senses of the word.

Notes

1. Garnett, *Erddig*, 12–29.
2. See Nieuhof, *An Embassy*, for the English translation.
3. Both now lost. For the Marybone pagoda see Spence, *Nature's Favourite Child*, 69–71; for the Shugborough pagoda see Robinson, *Shugborough*, 21.
4. Chambers, *Designs of Chinese Buildings*, pl. 5 and p. 6.
5. For the suggestion that it was inspired by Chambers see Garnett, *Erddig*, 68.
6. Inv. no. NT 356415.
7. Somewhat expanding on Edward Said's definition, which was focused on Western perceptions of the Middle East and North Africa, for which see Said, *Orientalism*.
8. For the emergence of the notion of a polite and civilised society in eighteenth-century Europe see Taylor, *A Secular Age*, 235–7.

Bibliography

Chambers, William. *Designs of Chinese Buildings, Furniture, Dresses, Machines, and Utensils*. London: published by the author, 1757.
Garnett, Oliver. *Erddig, Wrexham*. London: National Trust, 1995 (revised 2002).
Nieuhof, Johan. *An Embassy Sent by the East India Company of the United Provinces to the Grand Tartar Cham or Emperor of China*. London: John Ogilby, 1669.
Robinson, John Martin. *Shugborough*. London: National Trust, 1989 (revised 1996).
Said, Edward W. *Orientalism*. London: Penguin Books, 1978.
Spence, Cathryn. *Nature's Favourite Child: Thomas Robins and the art of the Georgian garden*. Bradford on Avon: Stephen Morris, 2021.
Taylor, Charles. *A Secular Age*. Cambridge and London: Harvard University Press, 2007.

VII
The Barbados Monkey Jar
Kevin Farmer and Tara Inniss

Figure OL.VII Barbadian Monkey Jar. Barbados Museum and Historical Society.

Water pitchers used to carry or store water are found in many cultures throughout the world. This object lesson discusses the origin and importance of the ceramic Barbadian water pitcher or as it is popularly known the 'Monkey Jar', which has an additional function beyond a water carrier – the porosity of the locally mined clay, once fired, allows the water to remain cool in the tropical heat. Born out of slavery, colonial ideation, reversal of gender roles and the exchange of ideas brought by transatlantic slavery into the mid-Atlantic island of Barbados, the Monkey Jar has been a fixture in the households of all classes of Barbadians for well over a century. Early forms, called 'goglets' or 'gurglets', were observed and documented on the island as early as the 1820s, and similar jars – also known as 'Monkeys' – have been manufactured and documented across the Caribbean, including in Jamaica.[1]

Ceramic manufacture has a long history on the island of Barbados, starting with the various indigenous cultures which resided on the island from 1600 BCE. However, the introduction of industrial-style pottery manufacturing into Barbados began in the late seventeenth century owing to the need for wares for the production of the colonial export staple, sugar.[2] These potters were free or indentured English, Scots and Irish, hired to produce European wares utilising locally sourced clay from well-known deposits found on the east coast of Barbados in the Scotland District. As the demand for sugar and the wares needed for its production and distribution increased, so did the need for labour. This need was met with enslaved Africans, who provided almost all general labour requirements in Barbados by the mid- to late seventeenth century. Some of this labour was apprenticed to learn a new trade because a skilled artisanal enslaved labour force was needed to supply all manner of ceramic products for industrial production. In most West African societies, however, ceramic traditions were largely the preserve of women, using a coil and build technique to create ceramic vessels.[3] In Barbados, pottery was manufactured on a wheel and fired in a kiln; it evolved to become a largely local industry in which men were employed as artisans. The use of kick-wheel technology from Britain was the work of male potters. The wares produced were primarily for industrial use – clay drippers, molasses drip jars, tiles and guttering. It is believed some wares for cooking and eating were made as an adjunct. Over time, with the increase in new technology for sugar production, these pottery manufactories ceased to exist. The persons trained were reallocated or made a subsistence living producing domestic wares for a domestic market. Women marketed these items in town and along roadsides.[4] In this evolution, the Barbadian Monkey Jar was created.

Typically manufactured in two sizes, the Monkey Jar resembles a large tea kettle: either 12–14 inches or 8–10 inches high, it is about 8–12 inches at its maximum width. Its spout is constructed separately and is wheel thrown and then fixed when wet on to the sundried monkey.

The handles are kneaded by hand and fixed onto the vessel in a similar manner. The lid is also wheel thrown. Traditionally, the vessel is not decorated but is hand trimmed and burnished. It is an item of domestic use, informed by European ceramic technology in its formation but created by market needs by African hands drawing on a tradition of remembered African forms. It was used to hold and cool water: as it was not glazed, the vessel allowed for evaporation to take place for whatever liquid it held.[5]

The Monkey Jar has become an iconic part of Barbados's material culture. It was a long-standing fixture in the so-called Great Houses belonging to wealthy Barbadian planter-merchants as well as the humble working-class dwellings of urban and rural wage labourers – a reflection of its important function of storing and cooling water. This continued into the mid-twentieth century, when it was still being used among lower socio-economic groups whose means did not stretch to refrigeration.[6] Some might have found their way into British or European households where owners had connections to Barbados or the Caribbean. It had certainly become a popular item for tourist consumption by the mid-twentieth century and made its way to Europe via this route.

Notes

1 Heath, 'Yabbas, monkeys, jugs and jars'.
2 Farmer et al., 'Are they local or foreign?', 253.
3 Farmer, 'Women potters'.
4 Hauser, *Archaeology of Black Markets*.
5 Handler, 'Pottery making in rural Barbados'.
6 Handler, 'Pottery making in rural Barbados'; Scheid, 'Ceramic production in Barbados'.

Bibliography

Farmer, Kevin. 'Women potters? A preliminary examination of documentary and material culture evidence from Barbados', *History in Action* 2, no. 1 (2011): 1–8.

Farmer, Kevin, Jeffrey Ferguson and Michael Glascock. '"Are they local or foreign?": an examination of some Barbadian potteries and market networks'. In *Pre-Colonial and Post-Contact Archaeology in Barbados*, edited by Maaike De Waal, Niall Finnernan and Matthew C. Reilly, 253–68. Leiden: Sidestone, 2019.

Handler, Jerome. 'Pottery making in rural Barbados', *Southwestern Journal of Anthropology* 19, no. 3 (1963): 314–34.

Hauser, Mark. *An Archaeology of Black Markets: Local ceramics and economies in eighteenth-century Jamaica*. Gainesville: University Press of Florida, 2008.

Heath, Barbara. 'Yabbas, monkeys, jugs, and jars: an historical context for African–Caribbean pottery on St. Eustatius'. In *African Sites Archaeology in the Caribbean*, edited by Jay Haviser, 196–220. Princeton: Markus Wiener, 1999.

Scheid, Dwayne. 'The political economy of ceramic production in Barbados: from plantation industry to crafts production', PhD dissertation, Syracuse University, 2015.

VIII
Japanese red wool *jinbaori* (surcoat): East meets West
Martha Chaiklin

Figure OL.VIII A typical *jinbaori* from early modern Japan. Metropolitan Museum of Art, 10.187.71.

Although quintessentially Japanese, this samurai's *jinbaori*, or armour surcoat, only existed through global trade. *Jinbaori* is sometimes translated literally as camp or campaign coat, but it was not necessarily worn in battle or even in times of warfare. Armour existed in Japan from ancient times, but the *jinbaori*'s origins only date from the second half of the fifteenth century, mostly likely evolving from garb worn over underclothes when the armour was removed (*dōfuku*). Unlike the medieval surcoat, *jinbaori* were short, to be worn on horseback, but could have a huge variety of shapes – with or without sleeves or pleats, or even cape-like, showing Portuguese influence. According to one eighteenth-century source, the *jinbaori* was 'worn when beginning a march, retreating to rest, at inspections, when triumphantly returning, when calling on anyone of higher rank than oneself, at the assembly of officers, when sent out as an Ambassador, &c. Anyone holding an important position must wear it always.'[1] Although often highly individualised, when issued as a uniform (resembling a livery) they demonstrated the power of the lord and clan that issued them and conformity for the wearer. Thus, a *jinbaori* was a statement of economic strength and dominance as well as of clan identity and personal expression.

Warriors had been the main political force in Japan since 1185, but during unification (1560–1600) they enjoyed exceptional extravagance bolstered by the expanded mining of precious metals and the enormous profits garnered by trade with Iberians. The use of luxurious imported materials for what was ostensibly a utilitarian article of war was not mere excess but a naked demonstration of power. The most exotic – and often imported – materials possible were employed, including yak hair, Chinese damasks, Persian tapestry, velvet, shearling, and even bird feathers such as pheasant and peacock. The *jinbaori* pictured here was typical rather than extraordinary, although it is not without its unique aspects. The red wool fabric was laken, woven in Leiden and imported to Japan by the Dutch East India Company. Wool had to be imported because sheep are not indigenous to Japan. Laken was made from fulled merino that was napped on one side and smooth on the other. This process made it warmer and more durable than felt as well as water-resistant. These properties made it especially desirable for use as a surcoat. Its bright scarlet was produced with cochineal from Mexico fixed with tin mordant, and the velvet details and glass beads were probably imported too. Besides being beautiful, the colour and composition of this *jinbaori* made it a very conspicuous form of consumption.

This specific colour, *shōjōhi*, was so named for a mythological Chinese animal that lived in the sea, drank alcohol, could understand humans and had red hair. Red was a popular colour for *jinbaori*. It is auspicious in Japanese culture and was believed to protect the wearer from evil. It was so common, playwright Kinoshita Junji (1914–2006) entitled a historical farce 'Akai Jinbaori' (Red Jinbaori, 1947), which was made into a film, kabuki play, puppet play, opera and ballet. The story, a comment on social classes, revolves around a local magistrate (*daikan*) whose pride in his red *jinbaori* is his downfall.

Like most *jinbaori*, this one has a large crest (*mon*) of the owner, or the person he served, on the back in a stylised lozenge (*hishi*) shape.

Originally marks of status, by the time this *jinbaori* was produced, *mon* were used outside the warrior class, even by low-status groups such as actors. The comma-shaped mark called a *tomoe* was a shape of ancient religious import. It had dual militaristic symbolism in that it was associated with the god of war, Hachiman, possibly because it resembled the leather band that archers wore on their wrists to cushion the recoil of the bowstring. It also represented water and thunder and was thought to avert evil. The *tomoe* was a popular *mon*, used by at least eight daimyo families.[2] Underneath the *mon* is embroidered a ferocious *kimenjishi*, literally devil-faced lion, to keep the wearer from harm. This protective spirit was popular on military gear such as helmets and sword guards (*tsuba*). In Japan, the lion was a mythical creature, the knowledge of which was transmitted from China or Korea. No living lion arrived in Japan until 1866. Through material and design, the *jinbaori*-wearing samurai, who never left Japan, nevertheless carried the world on his back.

Notes

1 Quoted in Garbutt, 'Japanese armour', 153–4.
2 Allen, *Japanese Art Motives*, 164–5.

Bibliography

Allen, Maude Rex. *Japanese Art Motives*. Chicago: A.C. McClurg, 1917.
Garbutt, Matthew. 'Japanese armour from the inside', *Transactions and Proceedings of the Japan Society* 11 (1912–13): 134–86.

IX
Shellwork shadowbox grottoes as global goods

Laura C. Keim

Figure OL.IX Shellwork shadowbox grotto by Anne Reckless Emlen (1721–1816), c. 1757. Reproduced courtesy of The National Society of The Colonial Dames of America in the Commonwealth of Pennsylvania at Stenton, Philadelphia.

Crafted by an elite Quaker woman in the American colonies for delight and display, this shellwork composition depicts an idealised classical house and fanciful garden. The setting represents genteel domestic life, anchored in a global mercantile culture that privileged colourful, exotic, worldly objects to communicate membership in the polite classes. Such objects also circulated goods and ideas that inculcated Enlightenment values such as ownership, collecting, organised display and hierarchy.[1] Philadelphian Anne Emlen's grotto box conjured layers of association, both personal and universal. Secured behind a large piece of crown glass, this female inner world likely followed a prescribed design.[2] Emlen's gilded initials and the year in the shell house pediment mark the space as her own. Three female figures inhabit the miniature landscape. A small press-moulded figurine is possibly a servant, while two wax-headed dolls represent genteel women. Emlen may have sewn and pinned the green plain-woven silk, sack-back gown and velvet stomacher worn by the smaller doll from imported, probably European, textiles she owned.[3]

Shells have 'inspired pleasure, curiosity, introspection, and wonder' since ancient times.[4] While learned male collectors frequently stored shells in specimen cabinets, ladies of taste and leisure adopted shellwork to create small-scale decorative objects such as grottoes in cases. The shadowbox grotto reflects decorative themes seen in female-produced textiles. Needlework often displayed floral and faunal images and houses set in garden landscapes.[5] Urns-of-flowers motifs were common to Philadelphia Quaker whole cloth quilts, evoking Asian tree-of-life designs translated from the cotton chintzes of India.

The grotto's scenery is reminiscent of country house landscapes, shell-decorated rooms, and Grand Tour Italian Renaissance gardens. The five-bay, pedimented house takes centre stage, situated inside a fenced-in courtyard perched on a cliff of shells overlooking an English-style park. Terracing and a wainscoted stair, key aspects of eighteenth-century English garden design that allowed for changing elevations and vantage points, descend to a formal garden with a folly, populated by ducks in a stream of mirrored glass, birds and stone animal figurines.[6] Emlen's creation displays shells from around the Caribbean basin, the Carolina coast and South America. Pink tellin shells from tropical waters comprise the house, while the cliffside foregrounds a large tent olive (*Oliva porphyria*) shell from the western coast of South America. C-scroll-handled urns with emerald nerite shell 'stems' crowned by shell flowers decorate the side walls. Shells and coral (or red-dipped threads) dangle from the ceiling and walls, like stalactites in a natural cave.

This complex grotto box was an intricate, time-consuming and tedious object to assemble, suggesting its maker's wealth and leisure. Anne Emlen was in her late thirties when she created the grotto and relied on servants and enslaved labourers to look after everyday chores and concerns.[7] To craft this striking object, she had access to imported goods, such as silk, wax doll parts, stone figures and most especially shells. This assemblage of global goods and ideas embodied her family's genteel social status and represented literal connections and visual allusions to locations around the world.

Notes

1. MacGregor, *Curiosity and Enlightenment*, chapter 2.
2. Rebecca Evans created a similar, shallower shellwork box in a maple frame (Colonial Williamsburg). The overall composition, particularly the house on a cliff, is remarkably similar to Emlen's, suggesting that at least some of the design elements may have come from a kit or common source.
3. Dyer, *Material Lives*, 169–70.
4. Goldgar, 'Introduction', 1.
5. Beck, *Gardening with Silk and Gold*.
6. Hunt, *Garden and Grove*, 131, 141.
7. 1757 is the same year that the Philadelphia Yearly Meeting investigated its members who continued to trade in human beings as 'global goods'.

Bibliography

Beck, Thomasina. *Gardening with Silk and Gold: A history of gardens in embroidery*. Newton Abbot: Brunel House, David and Charles, 1997.

Dyer, Serena. *Material Lives: Women makers and consumer culture in the 18th century*. London: Bloomsbury Visual Arts, 2021.

Goldgar, Anne. 'Introduction: for the love of shells'. In *Conchophilia: Shells, art, and curiosity in early modern Europe*, edited by Marisa Bass, Anne Goldgar, Hanneke Grootenboer and Claudia Swan, 1–17. Princeton and Oxford: Princeton University Press, 2021.

Hunt, John Dixon. *Garden and Grove: The Italian Renaissance garden in the English imagination, 1600–1750*. Philadelphia: University of Pennsylvania Press, 1986.

MacGregor, Arthur. *Curiosity and Enlightenment: Collectors and collections from the sixteenth to the nineteenth century*. New Haven and London: Yale University Press, 2007.

X
Tobacco rolls, Württemberg
Daniel Menning

Figure OL.X   Tobacco rolls, baked by the author. Photo: author.

Tobacco is one of the iconic global goods that shaped European consumption by the eighteenth century and constituted a regular item in country houses of south-western Germany as evidenced from inventoried snuff boxes and pipes.[1] In contrast to the British Empire, where tobacco remained a colonial good as laws prohibited its cultivation in Britain itself,[2] it had been acclimatised in Germany by the seventeenth century and was grown in large areas of the Middle-Rhine region by the eighteenth century, although product names for different varieties reminded consumers of its global origins.[3] Even so, the following recipe, which can be found in various forms in cookbooks from country houses and those of village artisans in south-western Germany in the second half of the eighteenth century, is at first sight a riddle:

> Tobacco rolls filled with almonds: Make a firm dough from 1 lb. of fine flour, 4 spoons of sour cream, 4 spoons of rosewater and an egg, roll it out, roll ¼ lb. of butter into it and cut it into square pieces so that they fit around a small piece of wood designated for the purpose and overlap a little bit, now mix finely pounded almonds, sugar, cinnamon, thinly sliced lemon peel, egg-white and lemon juice and spread it onto the dough not too thinly, but also not to the edges and also add a few raisins, now roll the dough on the covered side around the wood and tie a piece of yarn around it so that the roll is wound around like a screw, bake them nicely brown in lard, untie the yarn again, brush them of the wood and while they are still warm sprinkle them well with sugar and cinnamon.[4]

It might be expected that the baked goods described were meant to resemble a cigar. These emerged in Europe over the course of the second half of the eighteenth century but had not really gained wide popularity prior to 1800, implying that the origin of the name derives from another source. Studying tobacco production and further cookbooks, the connotation becomes clearer. Although much tobacco left America in casks, which provided the imagery for some British advertisements,[5] Brazilian and Dutch producers also shipped tobacco in rolls covered with thin leather or reeds on the outside to protect the leaves from the elements and prevent them from drying out. At their centre these cylinders contained a wooden stick that was utilised in rolling up the tobacco but also must have been quite useful when handling the spools, which sometimes weighed up to 200 lbs, though lighter ones came in at 10 lbs.[6] This transportation method appears to be the reason why the recipe did not simply suggest rolling the dough up tight but instead called for a wooden stick to be placed at the centre. It resembled the analogue more closely that way, and a Göppingen cookbook even suggested that the wood used for baking could be the recycled tobacco roll sticks – perhaps adding extra flavour to the biscuit.[7] The layering texture of the puff pastry further supported the visual correspondence between smokable and baked good.

Not only global goods had made their way into country houses of south-western Germany; their forms of handling had also inspired replica dishes in the region. Tobacco rolls provide evidence for the metaphorisation and transmutation from a foreign commodity to be smoked or sniffed into a domestic digestible good that resulted from frequent encounters. But it is significant that this domestication involved further global ingredients such as sugar and cinnamon as well as items from across the Alps such as almonds, raisins and lemons. Cooks in country house kitchens fused the global, European and local for the residents to admire visually and digest physically in one piece.

Notes

1 See Chapter 2 in this volume.
2 Jonsson, 'Natural history and improvement'.
3 Hochmuth, *Globale Güter – lokale Aneignung*.
4 Cookbook of Luisa von Liebenstein, née Weimer (1787–1865), StAL PL 18, 129–30. As a recent acquisition, it does not yet have a call number.
5 Bickham, 'Eating the Empire', 2008, 86.
6 Halle, *Die Tabaksmanufactur*, 48–50.
7 *Göppinger Kochbuch*, 191.

Bibliography

Bickham, Troy. 'Eating the empire: intersections of food, cookery and imperialism in eighteenth-century Britain', *Past & Present* 198 (2008): 71–109.
Göppinger Kochbuch. Zweyter Teil oder Neue Sammlung vieler Vorschriften von Fastenspeisen und allerley Koch- und Backwerk […]. Stuttgart: Erhard und Löflund, 1790.
Halle, Johann Samuel. *Die Tabaksmanufactur, oder die vollständige Oekonomie des Tabaksbaues nach allen seinen Zweigen*. Berlin: Pauli, 1788.
Hochmuth, Christian. *Globale Güter – lokale Aneignung: Kaffee, Tee, Schokolade und Tabak im frühneuzeitlichen Dresden*. Konstanz: UVK-Verlagsgesellschaft, 2008.
Jonsson, Fredrik Albritton. 'Natural history and improvement: the case of tobacco'. In *Mercantilism Reimagined: Political economy in early modern Britain and its empire*, edited by Philip J. Stern and Carl Wennerlind, 117–33. Oxford: Oxford University Press, 2014.

Part 3
Domesticating the global

9
Second-hand empire? Global goods in English provincial auctions, c. 1760–1840
Jon Stobart

In January 1742, the genteel Mrs Elizabeth Purefoy visited a sale at Biddlesden Park just a few miles from her own house at Shalstone in Buckinghamshire. On the first day of the sale she acquired a 'Buroy with glasse doors', two tablecloths, a tea table, a card table and a pair of sconces for herself, and a mahogany chest of drawers, a hearth and fire irons, and a 'pewter soup cradle' for her adult son. She returned on the next day of the sale and bought a chimney glass and another pair of sconces, paying £22 16s. in total.[1] Elizabeth Purefoy was a wealthy and exacting customer who patronised London retailers as well as those in local towns; she often wrote lengthy letters detailing her particular requirements or complaining about the goods supplied. It is particularly telling, therefore, that she was happy to buy furniture and household goods second-hand – a choice that highlights the importance of auctions as a route through which a variety of goods, some with global connections, could be acquired by householders in Georgian England.

House sales have caught the eye of historians over the years but remain a relatively neglected form of exchange. Fashionable London sales are perhaps the most familiar, with the activities and auction rooms of John Sotheby, Harry Philips and especially James Christie receiving the most attention (Figure 9.1).[2] These formed part of the social round for both Hannah Greig's Beau Monde and Fanny Burney's fictional Cecilia, who visited the sale at Lord Belgrade's house to see and be seen rather than to buy.[3] Also important as social occasions were big sales organised at the country houses of prominent social figures, the sales of William Beckford's belongings at Fonthill, for example, drawing such crowds that the roads around the house were blocked with carriages.[4]

Alongside these spectacular events, which were reported in the national press, were the numerous auctions of goods belonging to gentlemen, professionals, shopkeepers and the like – the kind of sale visited by Elizabeth Purefoy. These have received less attention yet were far more significant in the (re)circulation of global goods.[5] They were generally occasioned by the death of the previous owner, providing an opportunity to raise money to meet debts or pay legacies, to finance redevelopment or to clear things prior to refurbishment.

Country house sales almost invariably took place at the house of the previous owner: the goods were available for viewing on several days prior to the sale, which itself lasted anything up to a week depending on the number of lots to be cleared.[6] By the second half of the eighteenth century, they were being organised by professional auctioneers, most of them locally based, who would advertise the sale in local and sometimes in London newspapers. From 1777 they were obliged by an Act of Parliament to produce catalogues listing the goods available (generally organised room by room) and informing potential buyers about the conditions of sale, themselves pretty much standardised by this time.[7] These catalogues provide us with a vivid picture of what was present in

Figure 9.1 Thomas Rowland, *Christie's Auction Room*, 1808. Reproduced courtesy Lewis Walpole Library, Quarto 646 808 M58 v.1.

the house, the location and setting of the goods, and the ways in which they were promoted to potential buyers.

This chapter draws on a set of 51 auction catalogues for the English county of Northamptonshire. They include three titled individuals but mostly comprise houses of the county gentry and wealthy clergymen – a group hitherto under-researched in terms of their ownership of global goods.[8] My analysis traces changes in the nature of global goods present in these houses and made available at sales between 1760 and 1840. The dataset is not large enough to allow for detailed temporal analysis but is broken down into three periods, each with a similar number of sales. I focus on four types of durable goods and say little about consumables such as tea, sugar and spices – not because these were unimportant, but rather because they left only an indirect material footprint in the catalogues. The chapter begins by charting the changing frequency with which these global goods appear in the catalogues to give an idea of their relative importance as consumer goods. Here I draw on Stephanie Barczewski's argument that, according to one's perspective, it is possible to see empire everywhere or nowhere in the country house.[9] The focus then narrows to descriptions of goods to assess the ways in which placenames were used to indicate provenance but also highlight the desirability of certain goods, particularly in terms of their authenticity. I end by exploring what their availability second-hand might tell us about the motivations underpinning their ownership, the spread of knowledge about such things and the colonial/imperial associations that came with them. Overall, I argue that a range of sometimes surprising global goods were increasingly commonplace in the houses of the Georgian gentry and that their easy availability at house sales widened access both to the goods themselves and to knowledge of their material qualities and cultural associations.

Seeing empire everywhere or nowhere: the availability of global goods

Among the array of household goods available at these Northamptonshire sales was a broad range and sometimes large quantity of global goods. By far the most widespread was mahogany furniture which, following the removal of import duties on timber from the Caribbean and American colonies in 1721, had quickly grown in popularity for furniture making in Britain.[10] It was found in all the sale catalogues, with the number of lots rising considerably from the late eighteenth to the early nineteenth century (Table 9.1). At some houses, the amount of mahogany furniture being sold was considerable – 58 lots at Brixworth Hall (1797), 71 lots at Laxton Hall (1801) and 92 lots at Crick rectory (1836)[11] – and only in the aristocratic mansions at Horton and Kirby were mahogany pieces outnumbered by those of oak and/or walnut wood. This is telling: oak and walnut were characteristic of an earlier aesthetic, one based on woods sourced within Britain and occasionally from neighbouring European countries. Oak furniture remained widespread into the nineteenth century, although the number of lots decreased, but walnut declined precipitately and became marginal to an aesthetic dominated by mahogany.[12]

Dominance and marginality can be seen in spatial as well as numerical terms. Mahogany furniture was found throughout the house, dominating in drawing rooms, dining rooms and libraries as well as bedchambers, and even making its way into the rooms of senior servants – for example, at Rollaston Hall (1802) and Geddington House (1823).[13] By contrast, oak was increasingly relegated to service and servants' rooms, where it was deployed in functional and sturdy pieces. Various pieces of walnut furniture remained in the principal rooms, perhaps as a symbol of inheritance and pedigree, whereas other pieces shared the fate as oak, being sold off from the servants' rooms to which they had

Table 9.1 Appearance of global goods in Northamptonshire house sales, c. 1760–1840.

	1761–1800		1801–24		1824–40	
	Sales (n=15)	Lots	Sales (n=18)	Lots	Sales (n=18)	Lots
Mahogany	15	439	18	688	18	649
Spanish mahogany	0	0	2	18	5	46
Rosewood	2	2	5	7	7	13
Satinwood	4	6	5	7	7	13
Oak	14	133	17	115	17	103
Walnut	14	105	10	39	5	18
Chintz	8	18	15	68	15	48
Damask	8	28	5	6	4	7
Ivory	3	6	6	24	7	25
Pianos	0	0	8	10	7	7
Animal products/ Shells	1	1	2	4	3	3
Indian/Chinese	7	31	11	28	11	38

Source: Northamptonshire Central Library, collection of auction catalogues.

Note: The three periods are chosen to give roughly similar numbers of sales in each; different periodisations do not affect the overall trends.

been carried when no longer fashionable. At Thorp Malsor (1815), for example, one of the servants' attics contained six walnut chairs with stuffed seats.[14]

This replacement of native woods by a product of the British colonies would suggest that empire was everywhere in these English houses. Yet this simple narrative is complicated by four related developments. Firstly, walnut was not always of European origin: four sales noted that particular pieces were made from Virginia walnut, a wood quite often seen in inventories for gentry houses. It was recognisable to the auctioneers and worth highlighting to potential customers, retaining its place in family rooms, as at Hazlebeach Hall (1802) where there was a 'handsome Virginia Walnut-Cabinet' with gilt brass pillars situated in one of the main bedchambers.[15] Even within a declining wood type, then, there was a small-scale shift to colonial supplies.

Secondly, supplies of mahogany were similarly diverse. Spanish mahogany (from Santo Domingo) appeared in a growing number of sale catalogues in the early nineteenth century – a development made possible by the 1766 Free Ports Act and encouraged by the higher quality of this wood. This is reflected in the labelling of items as being Spanish mahogany: a geographical descriptor deployed to highlight that these pieces were more worthy of the buyer's attention and would be expected to sell at a higher price. It is also apparent from the concentration of this wood in the principal rooms, as at Crick rectory (1836), where the dining room in particular was mostly furnished in Spanish mahogany.[16] The placename highlighted the quality and price differences but also layered British with Spanish (and, given the complex political history of the region, French) colonialism.

Thirdly, mahogany was joined by a growing array of other tropical woods (Table 9.1). These first appeared as one-off pieces in a small number of sales in the 1790s but became widespread, both in the number of sales and the number of lots, by the 1820s. The most prevalent were rosewood and satinwood, sourced from both the East and West Indies in the eighteenth century and increasingly from Brazil in the nineteenth century. More occasionally, the catalogues also list pieces made from brazilwood, zebrawood and kingwood, all of which were being sourced from Brazil by the time they appeared in the sale catalogues in the early nineteenth century. These woods were all costly and were often used in smaller or special items, such as the satinwood card table being sold at Stanford Hall in 1792 or the rosewood escritoire in the drawing room at Geddington House (1823).[17] Again, these were global goods but increasingly from areas beyond the formal bounds of the British

Empire. Their presence in these gentry houses is all the more significant because they were primarily located in the principal rooms. Usually, they were eye-catching islands in a sea of mahogany, as at St Martin's (1823), where a satinwood Pembroke table is listed in the dining room alongside a mahogany sideboard, table, chairs, knife box, commode and bookshelves.[18] Occasionally they defined the aesthetic. At Crick rectory, for example, the 1836 catalogue lists 11 pieces of rosewood furniture in the drawing room, including commodes, screens, writing desks and loo tables; four years later at Ecton rectory, the drawing room contained all eight pieces of kingwood furniture being sold from the house (Figure 9.2).[19]

Finally, and cutting across these colonial connections, mahogany furniture was viewed as particularly English. It was far more widespread in England than elsewhere in the Europe and its material qualities were central to the characteristic aesthetics of furniture throughout the Georgian era and beyond: finer pieces with clean lines that spoke of modernity.[20] The mediation and workmanship of British furniture makers meant that the linguistic (and mental) associations were usually with them rather than the colonial origins of the raw material: furniture was in the style of Chippendale or from the workshops of Gillows, not of Honduran mahogany.

The global origins of furnishing textiles are less easy to trace, in part because European manufacturers adopted Indian names for their products. The rise of chintz – that is, painted or printed Indian

Figure 9.2 Ecton rectory, Northamptonshire. Author's own postcard.

268   GLOBAL GOODS AND THE COUNTRY HOUSE

cottons – within British homes was noted with dismay by Daniel Defoe right at the start of the eighteenth century. He viewed its adoption as a sign and cause of the decline of traditional English textiles: 'almost everything that used to be made of wool or silk', he complained, 'was supplied by the Indian trade'.[21] By the period covered here, chintz was thus well established, although it initially shared primacy as a textile for hangings and curtains with damask (Table 9.1). Into the early nineteenth century, chintz became all but ubiquitous and it formed the most common drapery textile in these genteel houses – perhaps not the height of fashion, but a widespread marker of respectable good taste. As the furniture designer George Smith advised in the early 1800s, 'printed calicos may answer extremely well for secondary apartments, or for those in houses of persons of small fortune; but they are not at all suitable for persons of rank and splendid income'.[22] By this time, chintzes were almost certainly British textiles, woven in northern mills in imitation of patterns previously imported from India – themselves often designs created for Western markets. The global nature of the goods was thus layered and in many ways undermined firstly by aggressive import substitution and later by the eclipse of Indian textile manufacturing by mechanised production in Britain.[23]

Animal products could strike a more overtly global or exotic note. These genteel houses were not the place to find ostrich feathers adorning bedsteads or menageries of African or Asian animals, but there were some surprisingly exotic items available. The most widespread commodity of this type was ivory, the presence and availability of which increased markedly from the late eighteenth to the early nineteenth century (Table 9.1). Much as we might expect from Kate Smith's discussion of ivory furniture, the catalogues list a small number of decorative pieces made from or incorporating ivory, including a pair of boxes at St Martin's (1823) and a puzzle at Crick rectory (1836).[24] However, the kinds of things noted by Smith were comparatively rare: most ivory appeared in the form of handles on silver cutlery, first listed in the 1790 sale at Broughton rectory and found in considerable quantities at Rollaston Hall (1801) and Geddington Hall (1828).[25] This application of ivory to a practical and everyday use served to familiarise and normalise its presence in these houses and make it an object of desire for those bidding for lots. This almost surreptitious appearance of ivory was carried further in the shape of piano keys, ivory being used alongside ebony, another colonial import, in what remained a key mark of gentility in late Georgian Britain. In both these uses – as with mahogany – it is uncertain how much the colonial connections or even exotic nature of these materials was evident to the householder or potential buyer at the auction. Knife handles made from bone had a similar appearance and feel, while pianos were almost invariably promoted in the catalogues by noting the manufacturer.

More self-evidently exotic were shells and animal skins, listed in the catalogues for a small number of house sales. Collections of shells, especially those brought from tropical waters, were particularly fashionable in the middle decades of the eighteenth century. Katherine Sharpe argues that this popularity reflected European influences in the form of classical mythology, a vogue for rococo and an Enlightenment-inspired interest in natural science (see also the object lesson by Laura C. Keim in this volume, see p. 253). The wider availability of shells and a proliferation of handbooks for shellwork served to spread such activities down through the social hierarchy and undercut their ultra-fashionable credentials, but they remained an important pursuit for genteel and elite women in particular.[26] Indeed, they received something of a boost following the excitement generated by James Cook's voyages in the Pacific. These heightened awareness and knowledge about distant lands and opened up new and exotic sources of shells; they also linked domestic craft and decoration with discovery and empire.

The shells listed in the auction catalogues were displayed in two ways. At Horton (1781), there were two sets of 'curious sea-shells on the chimney-piece' in the saloon – a prominent location in a key public space that suggests that these were objects of desire, but also that they were displayed individually. A similar arrangement was seen three years later in the catalogue for the sale at Barton Hall and at Hazlebeach Hall (1802), where there were three shells on a bedroom chimney piece along with a pair of bottles, three small flower jars and two pairs of cut-glass candlesticks.[27] Rather more in keeping with the earlier taste for shellwork, the 1823 sale at St Martin's included a 'curious French dog, made of shells' and two shell snuff boxes, mounted in silver. These were listed as part of a 'Cabinet of Miscellaneous Articles' which also included an agate tea caddy, carved ivory boxes, watch cases and miniatures, a piece of lapis lazuli, an Indian beetle and various Chinese figures and vases.[28] In all, this was a cornucopia of exotic and curious items; but it is telling that – just like the shells set on the chimney pieces – this exotica was intermixed with distinctly European pieces: silver and gold filigree scent cases, a 'curious Head of Henry 4th of France, of silver', 'two pieces of very curious petrifaction', various spar vases and a silver snuff box apparently taken from Napoleon's carriage at Waterloo. The overall effect of this cabinet is hard to assess, but its contents were available as distinct lots and would thus be dispersed through the sale – a point to which we return later.

Exotic animal skins were listed in just three sale catalogues, making them particularly significant in the houses where they do appear. At Rushton Hall (1826), there was a leopard skin and a bear skin, at Castle Ashby (1836) another leopard skin, and at Ecton rectory (1840) a tiger skin. The placement and function of these objects were very different, but all spoke of global trade, colonialism or empire. The two skins at Rushton Hall are listed right at the end of a catalogue which, unusually, does not itemise goods by room. It does, however, make the use of these skins clear enough: 'bear skin and leopard skin for saddle'.[29] In reality, the skin would have been placed under the saddle, but the impact was still striking and carried associations of the military and royalty (Marie Antoinette was famously pictured riding a horse with a leopard skin under-saddle). In contrast, the 'very handsome tiger skin' at Ecton was a decorative piece, set in a drawing room that also contained large quantities of mahogany, rosewood and especially kingwood furniture, upholstered in chintz to match the large and impressive window curtains.[30] Together, these would have given the room an opulent feel, to which the tiger skin would have added a more specific statement of exoticism and empire. And yet other explicitly global goods were dispersed across the house – a 'Turks head' on the stairs, and ivory candlesticks and an Indian box in a bedroom – rather than being grouped in a conscious statement of cosmopolitanism.

Declaring global goods: placenames and provenance

Placenames were important in marking the global and exotic nature of objects, especially when it was possible for auctioneers to declare pieces as Chinese or Indian, the latter often being used as a catch-all for Eastern goods and referring to items from China, or at least in a broadly Chinese style.[31] Such placenames were used quite widely in the late eighteenth century but more sparingly in the early nineteenth century (Table 9.1). In terms of furniture, Indian and Chinese were most frequently used to describe cabinets (probably lacquered or japanned), screens, boxes and paintings. These included the 'India japan'd cabinet on a frame' sold from Cottingham (1761), the 'Five raised Figures of India Birds, in Four rich Japan Frames' at Broughton rectory (1790) and the 'handsome six-leaf India screen of the scarce old black and gold japan, 8 feet 6 high' in the dining room at Wollaston Hall (1830).[32] On occasions, auctioneers also noted the Asian provenance of textiles, labelling them as 'Indian chintz' (Ecton, 1840) or of a 'real Indian pattern' (Thorp Malsor, 1815). Whether these really were genuine Indian textiles matters less than the desire of the auctioneer to label them so. So far as the auctioneers were concerned, tangible links to India were a selling point – a way of distinguishing them from what were, quite literally, run-of-the-mill British products.

The vast majority of porcelain listed in the sale catalogues was either not given a provenance or attributed to British manufacturers, most commonly Wedgwood (named in around 40 per cent of catalogues). This places additional emphasis on those cases where the auctioneer specifically identified porcelain as oriental or nankeen. This was generally a label applied to one or two pieces, which suggests that there was some validity to the claim. The biggest assemblage was available at the 1831 Kirby Hall sale where there was a 'set of real nankeen china' comprising a teapot, cream jug, sugar and slop bowls, tea and coffee cups, and a tea canister.[33] If genuine, then this was certainly made for the Western market; but what matters more is the desire to distinguish sale lots by emphasising their colonial or exotic character. Drinking tea from these 'authentic' products may have allowed consumers to feel themselves engaged in a similarly authentic set of practices. This is something that grocers and tea dealers emphasised on their trade cards in the early decades of the nineteenth century, along with the colonial and especially the commercial links that tea drinking implied.[34] That said, the sets of porcelain listed in the catalogues invariably reflected British rather than Chinese practices; their impact on the character of a room was limited by the fact that they were generally listed in china cupboards, probably in the housekeeper's room where most of this useful ware would have been stored when not in use. The material footprint of tea drinking is thus extensive yet elusive, particularly in the way that it linked the consumer to the exotic point of origin of both commodity and utensils.

A more direct global link was apparent in descriptions of ornamental pieces, with jars and figures occasionally being described as Indian (i.e. Chinese), as at Stanwick (1788) and Ecton rectory (1840).[35] These were widely available items, increasingly being copied by British manufacturers, so some caution is needed in taking these descriptions as genuine; but again the desire on the part of auctioneers to make this link shows the currency of genuine Chinese porcelain, both in cultural and in economic terms. Yet the best example of porcelain being used to make global connections was seen at Horton and was a European product. Listed under the menagerie and following the sale of the books from the library, auction goers could bid for 'four vases bronz'd with trophies of the four quarters of the globe, executed by that ingenius Italian La Mott'.[36]

Even where they were most numerous, these overt references to the Orient rarely numbered more than a handful of pieces: eight different lots at the 1781 Horton sale were labelled as Indian and 11 at Ecton rectory (1840) were either Indian or Chinese, the latter referring exclusively to porcelain.[37] Despite these modest numbers, the impact of these pieces could be enhanced within the house, on the page of the catalogue and in the mind of the potential buyer when they were grouped together. Having particular rooms decorated with chinoiserie was not unusual in aristocratic houses, but it was much less widespread in the genteel houses covered here. Much the same was true of the gentlemen's houses analysed by Stephen Hague, but he argues that the portability of smaller pieces meant that they could add a touch of exoticism to a variety of rooms.[38] Moreover, even a small number of 'Indian' pieces could combine to create a cosmopolitan feel. The drawing room at Sudborough House (1836), for instance, was furnished in mahogany but contained an antique Indian quadrille table, a large Indian scent jar, a range of 'Indian china vases', a 'china japanned cabinet of Ladies dressing boxes' and a pair of 'Indian glasscases and flowers'.[39] The overall tone was rendered cosmopolitan rather than overtly imperial by the presence of Dresden porcelain, ormolu candlesticks and a brussels carpet. In the breakfast room at Hazlebeach Hall (1802), a similar backdrop of mahogany was complemented by an Indian screen, a 'blue and white China essence jar', six pictures of Indian birds in japanned frames and a set of ten chairs with 'India cane' frames. These objects were given additional meaning by the prints listed in the room. Among the views of country houses and scripture pieces were two prints showing 'those grand and brilliant victories, Admiral Boscawen's defeat of Mons. de la Clue, off Cape Lagos' (lot 337) and 'Lord Hawke's defeat of Mons. de Conflans, off Belle Isle' (lot 338) and another of 'Sir W. Penn's Treaty with the Indians'.[40] These pieces might tip our perspective and perhaps that of those reading the catalogue and visiting the sale: the Indian (Chinese) prints, screens and jars might then be read not simply as decorative, but also as redolent of Britain's increasingly hegemonic commercial empire.

The significance of second-hand

The catalogues analysed here reveal that a world of goods could be accessed via country house sales; but why would wealthy householders choose to buy these things second-hand, and how does the availability of such an array of global goods at country house sales impact on their colonial/imperial associations? There are two ways of addressing this question. The first is to examine the motivations of people buying second-hand things per se, and how global goods might fit into these; the second is to think about how the format of marketing and selling at house sales may have impacted on buyers' awareness of and attitudes towards global goods.

Many historical studies emphasise financial necessity as the primary reason for buying second-hand, but this is an argument that fits best with clothing: household goods were bought by a much wider range of people, from the aristocracy down.[41] Drawing on the work of the geographers Nicola Gregson and Louise Crewe provides a broader explanatory framework in which necessity sits alongside the desire to capture value through 'a set of practices which reveal and display heightened consumption knowledge/s and skills', and to capture difference by acquiring goods that mark out a distinct identity.[42] Stana Nenadic, in her study of the buying practices of Glasgow merchants at house sales in the city, noted that many sought out useful items – kitchenware, linen, tableware and the like – which could be had for well below their price when new.[43] The global goods listed in the Northamptonshire catalogues probably appealed for similar reasons: they represented good value. For example, the ready availability of large quantities of porcelain provided auction goers with an opportunity to upgrade their tea sets or dinner services, or to add a breakfast set to their array of tableware. The attraction might have come in terms of quality or the completeness of a set, both of which were highlighted in the catalogues. At Stanford Hall (1792), for instance, the catalogue listed a 'beautiful dessert service, and tea and coffee equipage, of Sevres porcelain', and at Broughton rectory (1790) the auctioneer waxed lyrical about a 'table set of the neat much-improved Staffordshire ware with the greatly admired Blue-tinged edges which give it all the genteel effect of a service of china' and then listed a total of 95 pieces.[44] Indeed, it is striking that tableware was almost invariably sold in sets, although this also reflected the practicalities of clearing huge quantities of porcelain in an efficient manner. It might also have dissuaded some potential buyers because not every householder had the space, need and desire for such large assemblages of porcelain.

Much the same was true of assemblages of furniture. House sales provided an opportunity to buy *en-suite* the furnishings of an entire room at a fraction of the cost of buying new. The catalogue for the 1761 sale at Cottingham includes what were, in effect, reserve prices;

adding together the lots in the well-furnished parlour gives a total of about £35, for which the canny buyer would get pier glasses, a writing table, sideboard, card table, sofa, six chairs, fire screen, curtains and an eight-day clock.[45] Yet there is very little evidence of buyers purchasing whole rooms of furniture. Kerry Bristol notes that the Winn Williams of Nostell Priory bought up much of the furniture already in situ in their new London house in 1766, including almost the entire contents of the grand drawing room; but this was exceptional and reflected a willingness to accept the taste of the previous (aristocratic) owners.[46] Most householders acquired just a few pieces at a time, probably as availability met need or desire. We can see this in the pattern of purchases at the 1801 Fonthill sale, where the numerous buyers, from tenants to neighbouring peers, each purchased small numbers of lots.[47] It comes into sharper focus in the behaviour of the Purefoys, whom we met right at the start of the chapter buying a variety of individual pieces which were probably destined for the drawing room and a bedchamber at Shalstone. This appears to have been their usual practice: at an earlier sale at Maids Moreton, they acquired a similar variety of pieces, including stools for the servants' hall and six wrought worked chairs.[48] A generation later, Parson Woodforde combined purchases of new and used furniture, noting in his diary on 13 November 1789 that he had just bought '2 large second hand double-flapped Mohogany Tables, also one second hand Mohogony dressing Table with Drawers, also one new Mohogany Washing-Stand, for all which paid 4. 14. 6'. He added, 'I think the whole of it to be very cheap'.[49]

Woodforde clearly felt that he had got a bargain, an evaluation which involved balancing two aspects: price and quality. The latter is hard to measure with any accuracy from the sale catalogues, but auctioneers were certainly anxious to persuade potential buyers that the goods were worthy of their attention. Advertising an auction in 1780, one assured his readers that 'There are no Scraps or Scrapings of Time, to be met with in this House'.[50] Individual lots were regularly singled out for particular attention with superlatives such as handsome, elegant and capital.[51] This was persuasive rhetoric, of course, and was applied to a wide range of items, including global goods; but it was used sparingly enough to draw attention to particular pieces. Of the items listed for sale from the dining room at Stanford Hall (1792), for instance, the mahogany chairs were excellent, the set of dining tables was handsome, as was a gilt-leather screen, and a pier glass had a 'fine clear plate'; but the mahogany card table, dumb waiter, cellarette and Pembroke table went without adjectives, as did the fireplace.[52]

Quality was also communicated through material descriptions which noted the type and sometimes variety of wood: kingwood, Spanish mahogany or Nova Scotia birch. Such descriptions depended on the buyer having at least some knowledge about the physical and aesthetic qualities of different woods, a material literacy that was needed across all manner of purchases in order to assess their quality, suitability and worth.[53] The last of these meant knowing something of the cost of an item when new and using this to assess what should be paid for it second-hand. Direct price comparisons are difficult to make from the evidence in the sale catalogues, but the reserve prices noted for the sale at Cottingham (1761) are a helpful guide. A mahogany oval table was expected to fetch at least £1 5s. 6d., a pillar table 12s. and a close stool 10s. In comparison, when refurnishing Stoneleigh Abbey in the early 1760s, Lord Leigh paid the London chairmaker William Gomm £3 15s. for a Pembroke table, £3 10s. for a small oblong table and £2 2s. apiece for close stools.[54] There may have been differences in quality, but the auctioned items were likely to cost perhaps a quarter to a third of those bought new.

The goods available at house sales were desirable because they fulfilled a need, could be had relatively cheaply and were available to carry away there and then. We should not underestimate the attraction of seeing the finished products and taking them home, especially if they were made of rare or sought-after materials. The satinwood table available at the 1792 Stanford Hall sale or the suite of kingwood furniture listed at Ecton rectory (1840) would have been very difficult to source elsewhere unless the householder had very deep pockets. More broadly, the growing availability of mahogany at these Northamptonshire sales brought it into the reach of many more householders in the county. By the 1820s and 1830s, my set of sales provided an average of 43 lots of mahogany each year, compared with just ten lots per annum in the late eighteenth century. This widened and deepened the opportunity to buy mahogany furniture – and an array of other global goods – thus helping to normalise these things as standard furnishings for a respectable home. Owning these things was more important than the route by which they were acquired.

Overlain on these motivations were those centred on capturing difference and marking distinction. To an extent, this could be achieved through positional goods. Kingwood and Spanish mahogany distinguished the owner as wealthy, as did the pianos, carriages and ormolu ornaments which were also available at the sales. Personal identity (or difference) was more readily built around objects that were unusual or rare such as medals, paintings and old books, or (more exotically) ivory boxes and shellwork ornaments, or through the acquisition of individual items that took something from their previous owner and bestowed it on the buyer. Cynthia Wall makes much of this, arguing that acquiring goods at auction allowed the buyer to 'share in another's "genuine" world'.[55] It is possible to see this as a motivation driving some of the buyers at Fonthill and perhaps at Horton and Kirby, where something of the kudos of the Earl of Halifax or Sir Christopher Hatton might rub off on the new owner. At most sales, however, the identity of the owner was important for other reasons. It was invariably printed in large letters on the cover the auction catalogue, primarily to give reassurance about the provenance, authenticity and quality of the goods being offered.[56] This was underlined in the headline on catalogues and the accompanying newspaper advertisements: they were declared as the 'genuine' household goods of a named and genteel or titled individual. This added a further layer to the associations carried by global goods. Thus, at the 1823 sale at Geddington House, the large quantities of mahogany furniture were promoted on the cover of the catalogue as, first, the 'property of R.J. Tibbets, Esq., deceased', and second, 'principally supplied by Messrs Gillows, within these three years' (Figure 9.3).[57] The colonial origin of the timber remained unmentioned.

To what extent, then, did the exotic or imperial provenance of an object motivate the buyer because it might mark them out as different? The cabinet of miscellaneous articles at St Martin's certainly suggested an eclectic taste on the part of Henry Fryer, but the collection was being broken up by the sale, each item a different lot and available to a different buyer. As separate objects, their importance in the marking of difference and the creation of a specific identity would be far less. Placename associations might allow the auction goer to identify genuinely exotic objects that could then speak of their cultural and social capital: the 'real Indian pattern' chintz at Thorp Malsor (1815), for example, or the 'real nankeen china' at Kirby Hall (1831). In this respect, it is notable that Henry Purefoy described two of his purchases at Maids Moreton (1737) as 'an Indian screen' and 'an Indian Tea board', though whether it was their oriental qualities or provenance that made him choose to buy them is not recorded.[58] Of most potential importance in this regard were things that were self-evidently exotic. Shells from tropical seas held this possibility, but their kudos declined as supplies increased and there is nothing in the catalogues to highlight the intercultural importance of ivory or animal skins. It is the workmanship that is important in the former, while the latter are passed over without comment in the catalogues or labelled with the generic 'very handsome' – the superlative afforded to

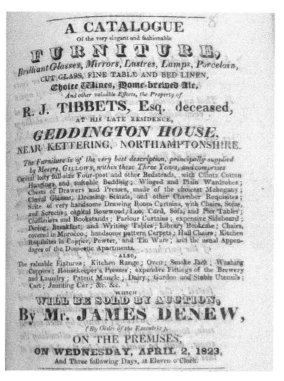

Figure 9.3 Catalogue for the sale at Geddington House, Northamptonshire, 1823: front cover (detail). Reproduced courtesy of Northamptonshire Central Library.

a rosewood teapoy, a pair of flower pots, a French candelabra and a hall lamp situated in other rooms at Ecton rectory.[59] But this tiger skin was more than simply handsome; it must surely have attracted its original owner and potential buyers because of its cultural associations as well as its aesthetic qualities. Did it speak of a mastery of nature, a fascination with the oriental or an identification with India and empire? All are possible motivations, but we cannot know for certain.

We can be more certain about the ways in which the availability of these global or colonial objects at auctions helped to shape broader consumer practices and cultures, primarily through the familiarity and knowledge gained by reading sale catalogues, going to pre-auction viewings and attending the auction itself. These three linked activities would quickly reveal the ubiquity of chintz hangings, porcelain tea sets and especially mahogany. For the middling sorts, at least, global goods were everywhere and were therefore unremarkable; by extension, the same might be argued for empire: it was hiding in plain sight in this proliferation of colonial imports and their related equipage. At the same time, seeing novel items such as rosewood or kingwood furniture appear in the catalogues heightened awareness of their existence and their attraction as objects of desire: they were new, different and exotic. Over the months and years, studying auction catalogues and viewing the lots before the sale allowed householders to understand better what could be had at most sales and what came up only occasionally; what was everyday, what were the necessary markers of respectability or gentility, and what might add distinction to their homes.

In this way, familiarity with objects linked to knowledge about their aesthetic and especially their material qualities. Auctions were particularly important in this regard because they allowed householders to view, touch and assess things as part of a process that might or might not end up with a purchase. In this sense, auction goers were very much like people browsing in shops: inspecting goods was about acquiring knowledge as well as possessions. For example, catalogues informed householders or heightened their awareness of the different qualities of mahogany; attending the viewings allowed them to see and feel these distinctions, to appreciate what made Spanish mahogany superior and to assess whether the difference was worth the likely extra cost. Equally, one could see and maybe feel what made 'real' nankeen china different and more desirable or appreciate the different appearance and feel of ivory rather than bone handles on cutlery. This kind of experiential learning was central to material literacy and made the householder better able to assess the quality of pieces they encountered at other auctions or in shops and showrooms: shopping was an iterative process that involved the accretion of knowledge.[60]

Crucially, attending auctions also provided knowledge about price, against which the attraction of a piece might be weighed. There were many warnings about the unwary being lured into bidding beyond what they intended by unscrupulous auctioneers so that any notion of a bargain evaporated. As one early nineteenth-century pamphleteer put it: 'men who are for ever hunting for bargains, are for ever being cheated'.[61] Knowing a realistic price for a variety of second-hand goods was therefore important in redressing the information imbalance between buyer and seller.[62] We can see this in action through the annotations added to the lists of books sold in many of the catalogues. At the Horton sale, for example, an unknown hand has written in the price at which each book was sold, plus more occasional notes on their condition (bad, gilt, neat, 'wants 1 vol') and the identity of the successful bidder (Afflick, Lacy, Dash and Burnham appear most frequently) (Figure 9.4).[63] Making such notes and retaining the catalogues allowed this individual to track prices against quality and identify likely competitors at future auctions. In my set of catalogues, this is only done for books – no doubt reflecting the particular interests of whoever assembled the collection – but exactly the same process would apply for porcelain, curtains, furniture or decorative items. Knowing what a mahogany desk or a set of chintz curtains usually fetched empowered the householder. Woodforde needed this kind of knowledge to be able to declare his purchases 'cheap' (or a bargain) and it probably informed his actions when attending an auction in April 1793. He noted in his diary that he had bid for 'a very handsome Mohogany Side-board, a very good and large Wilton Carpet, and a Mohogany Cellaret', but also that he was only successful with the first two because 'the last was carried too high great deal' – beyond what he was happy to pay.[64]

Conclusions

Colonial goods were important in shaping the houses and lives of country gentlemen and rectors just as they were for their aristocratic neighbours and urban counterparts. Indeed, it would be extraordinary to

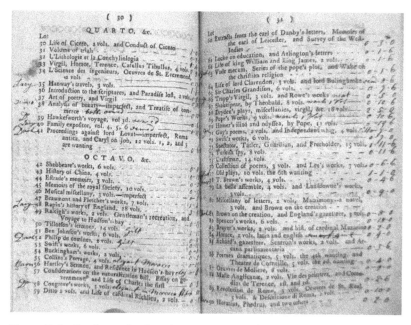

Figure 9.4 Catalogue for the sale at Horton, Northamptonshire, 1781: library. Reproduced courtesy Northamptonshire Central Library.

find any respectable home or household not profoundly touched by the products of global trade. This analysis of auction catalogues confirms the widespread nature of many mundane colonial commodities, such as tea, coffee and sugar (seen through their equipage) and mahogany; the steady rise of others, including rosewood and ivory; and the occasional appearance of special objects, such as the tiger skin at Ecton rectory. The catalogues reveal the distribution of these things through the house and their concentration in certain key spaces, most notably drawing rooms and chimney pieces. They also show how these global goods were frequently grouped with those of local or European origin in a way that served either to domesticate the global and imperial or to globalise the domestic. Much depends on perspective: whether empire can be seen everywhere – in the mahogany furniture, china tea cups, chintz curtains, ivory handles and piano keys – or nowhere, as these things blended into a familiar domestic material culture that was first and foremost British. The identity and personal connections of the householder might prove to be crucial here and is an area requiring further research, not least to uncover potential East India Company ties among these Northamptonshire householders.

The fact that global goods were being sold off and could be acquired second-hand from modest country houses in an unremarkable corner of the English Midlands complicates our perspective on the provenance of these things. It made them accessible to a wider array of social groups, through lower prices and greater local availability, and normalised acquisition and ownership. It was unremarkable to own mahogany furniture, increasingly common to have rosewood and even possible to have a tiger skin in one's drawing room. It is impossible to know from the catalogues what motivated buyers or to what extent they connected these global goods to their place of origin or to ideas of empire. There is little in them that highlights the colonial origins or exotic nature of these goods. The same lexicon of descriptors was applied to pier glasses, dining tables and tiger skins (handsome, elegant, capital, etc.), and placenames were used most often to emphasise material qualities or the scarcity and thus the value of the object. It seems likely that considerations of quality and price – of getting a bargain – were more important than those of identity and distinction. Yet the format of auctions was important in shaping the spread of these things by making them familiar and knowable. Catalogues and viewings allowed people to view and touch global goods and thus gain a better understanding of their material qualities as well as their setting and use. In this way, auctions allowed for the recirculation of global goods, but also the (re)circulation of knowledge about global goods.

Notes

1. Eland, *Purefoy Letters*, 110.
2. Learmount, *History of the Auction*, 101–26; Wall, 'English auction'; Rascio, 'Auctions and the making of the nabob'.
3. Greig, *Beau Monde*; Burney, *Cecilia*.
4. Gemmett, 'Tinsel of fashion'; Richter, 'Spectacle, exoticism, and display'.
5. See Nenadic, 'Middle-rank consumers'; Stobart, 'Luxury and country house sales'; Stobart, 'Domestic textiles'.
6. For fuller discussion, see MacArthur and Stobart, 'Going for a song'.
7. Ohashi, 'Auctioneers in provincial towns'.
8. But see Hague, *The Gentleman's House*; Stobart, 'Genteel or respectable?'.
9. Barczewski, *Country Houses and the British Empire*, 13.
10. Bowett, 'Commercial introduction of mahogany'.
11. Lots might comprise individual items but sometimes grouped sets of chairs, for example, so the overall number of pieces of mahogany furniture being sold ran to thousands over the period as a whole.
12. See also Bowett, 'After the Naval Stores Act'.
13. Northamptonshire Central Library (NCL), M0005647NL/2, Rolleston Hall (1801), 2; M0005644NL/8, Geddington House (1823), 10.
14. NCL, M000564NL/14, Thorp Malsor (1815), 6.
15. NCL, M0005647NL/7, Hazlebeach Hall (1802), 5.
16. NCL, M0005644NL/19, Crick rectory (1836), 10–11.
17. NCL, M0005646NL/11, Stanford Hall (1792), 5; M0005644NL/8, Geddington House (1823), 16.
18. NCL, M0005644NL/9, St Martin's, Stamford Baron (1823), 54–5.
19. NCL, M0005644NL/19, Crick rectory (1836), 16–17; M0005644NL/24, Ecton rectory (1840), 20–1.
20. See, for example, Bowett and Lomax, *Thomas Chippendale*.
21. *Weekly Review*, 31 January 1708.
22. Smith, *Collection of Designs*, xii–xiii.
23. See Riello, "Globalization of cotton textiles'.
24. NCL, M0005644NL/9, St Martin's, Stamford Baron (1823), 49; M0005644NL/19, Crick rectory (1836), 17; Smith, 'Production, purchase, dispossession, recirculation'.
25. NCL, M0005646NL/10, Broughton rectory (1790), 5; M0005647NL/2, Rollaston Hall (1801), 5; M0005644NL/8, Geddington House (1823), 19.
26. Sharpe, 'Conchology and creativity'; Vickery, *Behind Closed Doors*, 242.
27. NCL, M0005647NL/6, Horton (1781), 19; M0005646NL/5, Barton Hall (1784), 7; M0005647NL/7, Hazlebeach Hall (1802), 21.
28. NCL, M0005644NL/9, St Martin's, Stamford Baron (1823), 49–50.
29. NCL, M0005646NL/17, Rushton Hall (1826), 16.
30. NCL, M0005644NL/24, Ecton rectory (1840), 20–1.
31. On Chinoiserie, see Sloboda, *Chinoiserie*; de Bruijn, *Chinese Wallpaper*.
32. NCL, M0005644NL/2 Cottingham (1761), 6; M0005646NL/10, Broughton rectory (1790), 9; MM0005644NL/5, Wollaston Hall (1805), 6.
33. NCL, M0005644NL/? Kirby Hall (1831), 6.
34. Stobart, *Sugar and Spice*, 165–89.
35. NCL, M0005646NL/9, Stanwick Hall (1788), 9; M0005644NL/24, Ecton rectory (1840), 17.
36. NCL, M0005647NL/6, Horton (1781), 32.
37. NCL, M0005647NL/6, Horton (1781); M0005644NL/19, Crick rectory (1836).
38. Hague, *Gentleman's House*, 92, 102.
39. NCL, M0005645NL/22, Sudborough House (1836), 7–8.
40. M0005647NL/7, Hazlebeach Hall (1802), 17–18.
41. Lemire, 'Secondhand clothing trade'; Nenadic, 'Middle-rank consumers'; Gemmett, 'Tinsel of fashion'.
42. Gregson and Crewe, *Second Hand Cultures*, 11.
43. Nenadic, 'Middle-rank consumers'.

44 NCL, M0005646NL/11, Stanford Hall (1792), 12; M0005646NL/10, Broughton rectory (1790), 10–11.
45 NCL, M0005644NL/2 Cottingham (1761), 8. See also Stobart, 'Luxury and country house sales', 30. Unfortunately, there is no indication of the actual selling price of the goods and contemporary reports differ widely: some warned against paying over the odds at auctions and others remarked that lots went for remarkably low prices – see Learmount, *History of the Auction*; Gemmett, 'Tinsel of fashion'.
46 Bristol, 'Tale of two sales'.
47 Gemmett, 'Tinsel of fashion'.
48 Eland, *Purefoy Letters*, 110.
49 Woodforde, *Diary of a Country Parson*, vol. 3, 151: 13 November 1789.
50 *Northampton Mercury*, 3 January 1780.
51 For further analysis of the language deployed in auction catalogues, see Stobart, 'Language of luxury goods'.
52 NCL, M0005646NL/11, Stanford Hall (1792), 6.
53 Dyer and Wigston-Smith, *Material Literacy*. On the appeal of different woods, see Bowett, *Woods in British Furniture Making*.
54 Shakespeare Centre Library and Archive, DR18/5/4408 bill from William Gomm, 1764.
55 Wall, 'English auction', 20.
56 Stobart, 'Luxury and country house sales'.
57 NCL, M0005644NL/8, Geddington House (1823), cover.
58 Eland, *Purefoy Letters*, 110.
59 M0005644NL/24, Ecton rectory (1840), *passim*.
60 See the various contributions to Dyer and Wigston-Smith, *Material Literacies*.
61 Anonymous, *Ruinous Tendency of Auctioneering*.
62 See Blondé and Van Damme, 'Retail growth'.
63 NCL, M0005647NL/6, Horton (1781), 29–32.
64 Woodforde, *Diary of a Country Parson*, vol. 4, 18: 2 April 1793.

Bibliography

Anonymous, *Ruinous Tendency of Auctioneering*. London, 1828.
Barczewski, Stephanie. *Country Houses and the British Empire, 1700–1930*. Manchester: Manchester University Press, 2014.
Blondé, Bruno, and Ilja Van Damme. 'Retail growth and consumer changes in a declining urban economy: Antwerp (1650–1750)', *Economic History Review* 63, no. 3 (2010): 638–63.
Bowett, Adam. 'The commercial introduction of mahogany and the Naval Stores Act of 1721', *Furniture History* 30 (1994): 43–57.
Bowett, Adam. 'After the Naval Stores Act: some implications for English walnut furniture', *Furniture History* 31 (1995): 116–23.
Bowett, Adam. *Woods in British Furniture Making, 1400–1900*. London: Oblong Creative, 2012.
Bowett, Adam, and James Lomax. *Thomas Chippendale 1718–1779: A celebration of British craftsmanship and design*. Bradford: The Chippendale Society, 2018.
Bristol, Kerry. 'A tale of two sales: Sir Rowland Winn and no. 11 St James's Square, London, 1766–1787', *History of Retailing and Consumption* 2, no. 1 (2016): 9–24.
Burney, Fanny. *Cecilia: Memoirs of an heiress*, London, 1782.
de Bruijn, Emile. *Chinese Wallpaper in Britain and Ireland*. London: Philip Wilson, 2017.
Dyer, Serena, and Chloe Wigston-Smith, eds. *Material Literacy in Eighteenth-Century Britain: A nation of makers*. London: Bloomsbury, 2020.
Eland, G., ed. *Purefoy Letters, 1735–53*. London: Sidgwick & Jackson, 1931.
Gemmett, Robert. '"The tinsel of fashion and the gewgaws of luxury": the Fonthill sale of 1801', *The Burlington Magazine* 150 (2008): 381–8.
Gregson, Nicola, and Louise Crewe. *Second Hand Cultures*. London: Berg, 2003.
Greig, Hannah. *The Beau Monde: Fashionable society in Georgian London*. Oxford: Oxford University Press, 2013.

Hague, Stephen. *The Gentleman's House in the British Atlantic World, 1680–1780*. Basingstoke: Palgrave Macmillan, 2015.

Learmount, Brian. *A History of the Auction*. London: Barnard and Learmount, 1985.

Lemire, Beverley. 'The secondhand clothing trade in Europe and beyond: stages of development and enterprise in a changing material world, c.1600–1850', *Textile* 10 (2012): 144–63.

MacArthur, Rosie, and Jon Stobart. 'Going for a song? Country house sales in Georgian England'. In *Modernity and the Second-Hand Trade: European consumption cultures and practices, 1700–1900*, edited by Jon Stobart and Ilja Van Damme, 175–95. Basingstoke: Palgrave Macmillan, 2011.

Nenadic, Stana. 'Middle-rank consumers and domestic culture in Edinburgh and Glasgow 1720–1840', *Past and Present* 145 (1994): 122–56.

Ohashi, Satomi. 'Auctioneers in provincial towns in England and Wales at the end of the eighteenth century', *Shi'en* 73, no. 2 (2013): 174–98.

Rascio, Patrick. 'Auctions and the making of the nabob in late eighteenth-century Calcutta and London', *The Historical Journal* 65, no. 2 (2022): 349–70.

Richter, Anne. 'Spectacle, exoticism, and display in the gentleman's house: the Fonthill auction of 1822', *Eighteenth Century Studies* 41 (2008): 643–64.

Riello, Giorgio. 'The globalization of cotton textiles: Indian cottons, Europe and the Atlantic world, 1600–1850'. In *The Spinning World: A global history of cotton textiles, 1200–1850*, edited by Prassanan Parthasarathi and Giorgio Riello, 261–87. Oxford: Oxford University Press, 2009.

Sharpe, Katherine. 'Conchology and creativity: the rise of shellwork in eighteenth-century England', MA thesis, V&A/RCA, 1995.

Sloboda, Stacey. *Chinoiserie: Commerce and critical ornament in eighteenth-century Britain*. Manchester: Manchester University Press, 2014.

Smith, George. *A Collection of Designs for Household Furniture and Interior Decoration*. London: J. Taylor, 1808.

Smith, Kate. 'Production, purchase, dispossession, recirculation: Anglo-India ivory furniture in the British country house'. In *The East India Company at Home, 1757–1857*, edited by Margot Finn and Kate Smith, 68–87. London: UCL Press, 2016.

Stobart, Jon. 'The language of luxury goods: consumption and the English country house, c.1760–1830', *Virtus* 18 (2011): 89–104.

Stobart, Jon. *Sugar and Spice: Grocers and groceries in provincial England, 1650–1830*. Oxford: Oxford University Press, 2013.

Stobart, Jon. 'Luxury and country house sales in England, c.1760–1830'. In *The Afterlife of Used Things: Recycling in the long eighteenth century*, edited by Ariane Fennetaux, Amélie Junqua, and Sophie Vasset, 25–36. Abingdon: Routledge, 2015.

Stobart, Jon. 'Domestic textiles and country house sales in Georgian England', *Business History*, 61, no. 1 (2019): 17–37.

Stobart, Jon. 'Genteel or respectable? The material culture of rural clergy in late Georgian England', *Journal of Religious History, Literature and Culture* 6, no. 2 (2021): 95–120.

Vickery, Amanda. *Behind Closed Doors: At home in Georgian England*. New Haven: Yale University Press, 2009.

Wall, Cynthia. 'The English auction: narratives of dismantlings', *Eighteenth-Century Studies* 31 (1997): 1–25.

Weekly Review, 31 January 1708.

Woodforde, James. *The Diary of a Country Parson*. Edited by John Beresford, 5 vols. Oxford: Oxford University Press, 1968.

10
Global houses of the Efik
Louis P. Nelson

In May 1843, the *Liverpool Times* announced the opening of a spectacular exhibition in the yard near the post office: a prefabricated iron palace intended for Old Calabar, West Africa (Figure 10.1).[1] Built by a local iron merchant, the palace was two storeys over a raised basement, the whole surrounded by a two-storey veranda. Its exterior was to be painted a light stone colour 'to resist the solar heat', according to the local reporter. The ground floor chambers boasted ten-foot ceilings, and the 12-foot-tall upper storey was dominated by a single 'extremely airy and handsome' state room richly ornamented with 'splendid pictures ... [and] papier maché'. Open to visitors through the summer as its ornamentation was being completed, the spectacular iron palace was a 'great curiosity'.[2] Surely part of the curiosity of British visitors was that this building had been ordered from Liverpool by an Efik king in West Africa; the international purchase of such an enormous luxury good as a house challenged British preconceptions of both African agency and African taste.[3]

Just three years later, in 1846, missionary Hope Masterton Waddell visited the same building then re-erected in Duke Town in Old Calabar, along the banks of the Calabar River (now in south-eastern Nigeria). One of the most intensive slaving communities in the Bight of Biafra, Old Calabar was a series of Efik trading towns in the estuaries of the Cross River Delta.[4] Visiting decades after the British abolished the legal slave trade, Waddell noted the continuing wealth of Calabar elites who had pivoted from trading in enslaved Africans to trading in palm oil. Having paid his respects to various leaders of the region, Waddell made his way to Duke Town, which was filled with houses he described as 'low, mud-plastered, and palm-thatched, without windows, but each with a capacious door, leading into a small court-yard'. He did note

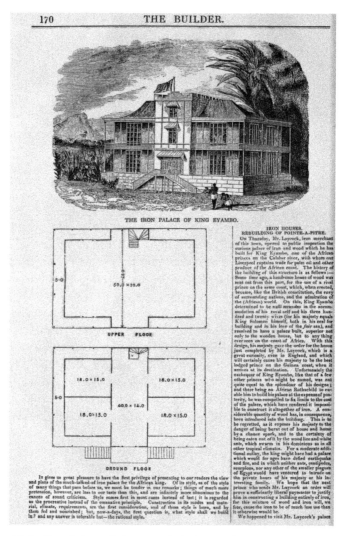

Figure 10.1 'Iron Palace of King Eyembo', plans and view, *The Builder,* May 1843, 170–1.

from the ship's deck that there were 'several two-story wooden-framed houses ... and the king's iron house in the centre of the town'. Arriving at the *obong's* (king's) palace, 'covered and roofed with galvanized plates, and handsomely furnished', he was disappointed at the lack of prospect because the palace was 'shut in by means of native houses, some of them even built up against it', reminding us of his inevitable British bias.[5] Eventually admitted to the 'handsomely furnished' stateroom, he met Obong Edem Ekpenyong Offiong Okoho Efiom Ekpo 'in black hat and feathers, with waistcloth, according to country fashion, and loads of beads and brass rings'. Obong Eyemba, an elderly man, 'paraded before the large mirrors, turning and admiring himself in every attitude'.[6] The *obong*'s manner was echoed by his two pet peacocks, which wandered freely through the house. After admiring himself for some time, Eyemba eventually sat 'in an arm-chair of solid brass, under a handsome canopy, meant for a throne. Four sofas were wheeled around in front of the company, and a small table placed in the centre for the gift Bible' brought by Waddell. A few days later, Waddell was summoned by Obong Eyemba to a dinner in this same stateroom. Eyemba was 'dressed in his best style – broad silk waist coat, hat and feathers, a profusion of beads, but neither shirt nor shoe ... In the dining room a long table was laid out, and properly furnished. Eyamba took the head, his white guests sat all on his right, the black on his left.' Although seated at a long dining table in the European manner, the meal was in regional West African tradition, including a pepper stew with yam, fish stew with palm oil, and a yam and goat stew, each served in a hollowed calabash. Pounded yams, or *fufu*, were served in a locally fired earthenware pot.[7] Just a few days after his dinner in the famous iron palace, Waddell 'began to prepare for erecting the wooden frame-house we had brought with us from Liverpool'.[8]

Obong Eyemba's Iron Palace was a global house filled with global goods, one born of African incentives and embedded in a local cultural context that speaks to the deep material and economic connections between Efik elites in Calabar, who controlled the lower Calabar and Cross Rivers and their adjacent rivers and tributaries through the period in question, and merchants of the British port of Liverpool. Eyemba assembled his material world to his own liking, certainly intended to signal status to both locals and international visitors, but more importantly experienced by the patron and his immediate circle as an integrated whole. While Waddell and earlier visitors made a point of differentiating between African and European material and cultural modes, this chapter seeks to understand Obong Eyemba's palace and its predecessors as sites of intentional curation by patrons who were active consumers of and contributors to the making of the Atlantic World. This house, and many others that preceded it, was literally a trans-Atlantic product, one whose story opens a window into the under-examined context of elite Africans in Calabar as strategic consumers of English and European goods and builders of global houses.[9]

Critical to understanding the story of this extraordinary iron palace is the fact that this was the most spectacular example of a very long practice of Africans importing English- and European-made goods for the fashioning by Africans of West African port cities. By at least the 1790s, leading Efik traders were importing whole house frames from Liverpool.[10] This connection was so well established that Ebo Young's house in Duke Town was even called Liverpool Hall.[11] Writing back to London during a three-month stay in Calabar, Henry Nicholls described a typical trader's house in 1805:

> The principal traders' houses are built of wood, brought out by the different captains from Liverpool, oblong, and thatched with bamboo leaves, which last very well two years. The house I reside in was brought out by Mr. Patrick Fairweather; was built in the year 1785, and still remains very good. A description of mine will suffice for all the rest, as they are all built upon the same principle; the house is about twenty yards long and thirty feet high, with a ground floor, a first floor, and a kind of cock-loft: the first floor contains two rooms, one I occupy, and the other my attendants, and two small rooms in each wing for bedrooms. My room is about forty feet long, twenty-five feet wide, and fifteen feet high, and has been very handsomely finished. A covered gallery surrounds the house.

Nicholls noted that the interior of his guesthouse

> put me in mind of a drawing room in England. I have two large pier-glasses, seven feet by four, elegantly gilt and ornamented; twenty five ditto, from two and a half to four feet; three large sophas, twelve chairs, two handsome escrutoire desks, six tables ... one handsome marble side-board, and an immense quantity of glasses, china, and earthen ware; six paintings, and twenty large engravings, five clocks, and two musical ditto; and a pretty jumble of furniture it is.[12]

These houses were certainly intended by their builders to signal their status and wealth to their local community and to signal their fluency with the structures of the trans-Atlantic trade to their international interlocutors. These houses were commonly the sites of dinners hosted by African traders for ship captains and other British agents. But these material practices are rightly understood as part of the integrated materiality of the Atlantic World.[13] The interpretive potential of this material integration is to see the larger project of elite self-fashioning, the participation in the circum-Atlantic project by elite Efik to gain strategic advantage in the exploding marketplace of commodification and consumption.[14] Put simply, powerful Africans were strategic and intentional participants in the rapidly expanding marketplace of the long eighteenth century. *The Builder* magazine, in its description of the iron palace, makes this point clear. Obong Eyemba had been in conversation with Liverpool correspondents about ordering a house that would be grander than any of the others that had been previously ordered by other regional African elites. But when the cost of a fully iron house was returned to Eyemba, he pivoted and chose a more economical wood frame palace with iron cladding, so the external appearance would remain largely unchanged. Once the detailed negotiations were finalised, 'his majesty gave the order for the house'.[15] Although manufactured in Liverpool, this iron palace was ordered by an African chief who intended it to signal his pre-eminence and worldliness to both local and international audiences.[16]

That Obong Eyemba had business correspondents in Liverpool should come as no surprise. As David Imbua and other historians have documented, the Calabar region of West Africa had traded with British and European ships for generations. For various reasons the Efik had risen to regional prominence and economic advantage a century before their economic interactions with Europeans began to expand. Exploiting the natural advantages of the delta, the Efik shifted towards a trade economy, depending far less on farming, fishing and hunting. In so doing, they embraced currency and fixed prices, practices that easily transferred to their interactions with the British ship captains who frequented Calabar by the late seventeenth century.[17] The Efik were involved in the trans-Atlantic slave trade as early as the 1660s, and the growing wealth generated by that trade secured their regional dominance.[18] Over the eighteenth century, individual Efik traders forged relationships with preferred merchants in Liverpool, born primarily of the extraordinary financial interdependence between the two places after the 1750s. Liverpool was Britain's leading port for the export of African captives into the Atlantic slave trade by the 1750s; three decades later, the port commanded 90 per cent of the British trade.[19] And Calabar merchants reserved the majority of their trade (85 per cent) for British ships.[20] But the African traders shaped this relationship to their advantage in a distinctive way. In contrast to their counterparts elsewhere along the African coast, chiefs in the Bight of Biafra, which included the regions of the Calabar River, never granted Europeans the right to build trading posts, which over time became trading forts or castles, on their soil. African traders in Biafra understood from their interactions with trading partners along the Gold Coast (now Ghana) that the construction of a European fort could certainly serve as a catalyst for local African economic development. But they also knew that allowing such a fort ceded too much leverage – and wealth – to Europeans. Upon meeting Egbo Young Eyambo, an Efik king, in 1805, Henry Nicholls reported back to his readers in London that the chief was unhappy at his arrival; he was 'very badly received'. Eyambo wished to know if Nicholls intended to bring either of two great economic threats, the rhetoric of English abolitionist Wilberforce or the intent to build a fort.[21] The result of this policy of forbidding European forts was the growth of entirely African-controlled trading towns along the banks of various rivers, centres that were connected to vast trading networks into the African interior. These trading towns were the seats of African merchants who engaged in regular correspondence with merchants in England: London in the seventeenth century, Bristol in the early eighteenth century and Liverpool at the height of the trade in the later eighteenth century.[22] These ships, waiting sometimes for only a few weeks but often up to a year in the safe haven of the Niger and Cross River Deltas, collected almost one-third of all captive peoples taken from Africa in British and American slaver ships, a higher percentage than any other region. Those business relationships pivoted after 1807 to traffic primarily in palm oil rather than people, but many of the business relationships remained intact.[23]

West African traders were savvy businessmen.[24] They actively limited European access to the interior, for example, preserving for themselves the role of middleman between the demand for and supply of captive people.[25] In his deeply researched and compelling examination of the African port of Annamaboe (now in modern Ghana), Randy Sparks devotes an entire chapter to the story of John Corrantee, the leading African trader of that town in the early eighteenth century. Sparks reveals Corrantee's strategy for forging social and economic alliances by sending one son to Paris and the other to London for their education. In doing so, these young men were gathering strategic information and equipping their father to play European powers off one another for personal gain. Corrantee, and many other African agents, were hardly pawns.[26] Sparks argues that '[t]he successful, capable, and wily merchants of Annamaboe were as integral to Atlantic commerce as those of Liverpool, London, Cadiz, Nantes, Charleston, New York, or Kingston'.[27] We can and should assume the same of the merchants of Calabar. Obong Eyemba, for example, was familiar enough with Liverpool merchants to find an iron merchant willing to prefabricate his house. But in the light of the decline in the British slave trade, he also was interested in the transition to a plantation economy based on cotton, coffee or sugar cane. He wished to ensure his control over such a prospect; in 1846, within a decade of the termination of slavery in the British Caribbean, he reported to Waddell, 'I hear your countryman done spoil West Indies. I think he want to come spoil we country all same.'[28] These elite traders were also quite familiar with London and Liverpool as many of them – like John Corrantee in Annamaboe – sent their sons to be educated there. 'It has always been the Practice of Merchants and Commanders of Ships trading to Africa', a group of Liverpool slave traders reported, 'to encourage the Natives to send their Children to England, as it not only consolidates their Friendships and softens their Manners, but adds greatly to the Security of the Trade, which answers the Purposes both of Interest and Humanity'.[29] The education in England of favoured sons was an advantage not only for the traders but also for Liverpool merchants who wished to secure the trust and favour of these soon-to-be-powerful men.

The Efik had been trading with English slaver ships since their first sustained contact in Old Calabar in the 1660s.[30] Most historians agree that Efik traders in Old Calabar were in direct contact with Liverpool business correspondents and partners by the 1760s, by which point 'there is rarely a period that there are not at Liverpool, Calabar Negroes sent there expressly to learn English'.[31] In 1805, Henry Nicholls, as he prepared for his never-taken expedition into the African interior, was called upon by Otto Ephraim, an Efik man 'who had received his education in Liverpool'.[32] By the end of the eighteenth century, Old Calabar's elite had built a clear and intentional relationship with the merchants of Liverpool.

Duke Town was the leading town of Old Calabar, a community of about 2,000 residents at the beginning of the nineteenth century.[33] The Duke family founded their own trading centre in 1748, first called New Town but soon thereafter known as Duke Town, which rose in prominence among the various trading towns in the later decades of the eighteenth century. This was especially the case after the massacre of 1767 in which leading traders of Duke Town successfully conspired with British traders to massacre 300 leading men from Old Town, one of Duke Town's leading competitors. As a result, Duke Town and neighbouring Henshaw Town were the major centres of the British slave trade in later eighteenth-century Calabar.[34] Though he believed the traders held 'all of the power' and were in his eyes of greater importance, Nicholls included a visit to the king during his engagements in Old Calabar in 1805.[35] Slaving expeditions sent by Efik traders into the African interior were not usually launched until a ship had anchored in the river and an agreement had been reached between its captain and a local merchant.[36] Enslaved Africans arrived in Calabar in great canoes, which usually belonged to a trader's canoe house, the major organisational framework for trading among the Efik. Usually headed by a trader of great charisma and talent in trade, these canoe houses functioned as trading companies connecting numerous households, which generally shared kinship ties, in different locations along a river system.[37]

After a long journey, captives were distributed among the houses of a town where they were washed and fed in preparation for sale to a ship captain.[38] English trading records provide ample evidence for the purchase by Efik traders of iron manillas, often inscribed with the merchant's name, suggesting that the captives were in fact shackled whilst awaiting purchase.[39] In 1773, for example, Efik trader Robin John ordered from Liverpool agent Ambrose Lace 'large leg manillas with locks, and large iron manillas' for his 'Room of irons', suggesting that John had a small prison in his courtyard house compound.[40] As a result, Duke Town and other smaller trading towns in the region were filled with houses that functioned as small-scale centres of containment and processing of those people intended for sale to British captains.

If Efik elites were *trading* with British captains for common and luxury goods throughout the eighteenth century, they began *ordering* luxury goods and specialty items – including whole houses – by the closing decades of the century.[41] One especially lengthy 1773 order sent by Efik trader Robin John and received by Liverpool agent Ambrose Lace included materials to fit out his slaving canoes, trade goods and items for personal use. To keep his operations running, he ordered 'new canvas to make sails for his canoes, large leg manillas with locks, and large iron manillas'. Trade goods to purchase captive Africans at inland markets included hats, hand mirrors, pewter and brass drinking containers and basins, flintlock muskets, butter, sugar, drinking horns, caps, canes and nails. But beyond these items a substantial portion of the items on John's list were for his personal consumption. He also requested furniture for his house including one hundred yards of chintz, a large mirror, one table, six chairs, two armchairs, two small writing desks and a stool. For dining he ordered 12 pewter plates, four dishes, 12 knives, 12 forks, two large tablespoons, a trowel and one pair of balances. John was also aware of the various personal items that signalled status and refinement to his British business partners. He ordered a long, gold-mounted walking cane and two coats with gold lace, one red and one blue, 'to fit a Large man', and one case of shaving razors. This commitment to personal consumption extended even to monogramming: 'Please to have my name put on Everything that you send for me.'[42] But maybe most importantly, John understood that this substantial order bought him leverage for future trading. He wrote to Lace that if these items were all to John's satisfaction, then upon its arrival in the region Lace's ship would 'no stand long' in the river, meaning that John would ensure a speedy supply of enslaved cargo on Lace's ship and a shorter, cost-saving wait along the West African coast.[43] Given the substantial morbidity among the enslaved, the longer the wait the greater the loss of life, and thereby investment. Both John and Lace understood that goods – especially luxury goods – were critical vehicles for the construction of African and English wealth and, by extension, elite identity in the machinery of the Atlantic market.

This access to the Atlantic market meant that wealthy African traders were deeply enmeshed in the trans-Atlantic practice of elite self-fashioning. John Corrantee's son returned to Annamaboe from London in 'a full-dress scarlet suit, with gold lace a la Bourgogne, point d'Espagne hat, handsome white feather, diamond solitaire buttons, etc.' He even had his portrait painted in London (Figure 10.2). Familiar with British comportment and fashion, elite Efik traders typically dressed in English

Figure 10.2 Gabriel Mathias, *Portrait of William Ansah Sessarakoo, son of Eno Baisie Kurentsi (John Currantee) of Anomabu*, 1749. Reproduced courtesy of The Menil Collection, Houston, TX.

clothing when entertained on a slaver ship by its captain.[44] And these traders reciprocated by inviting the captains to dine in their houses as well. This practice was not unique to the Efik. As early as the 1750s, Nicholas Owen reported a mulatto trader on the Windward Coast who 'lives after the manner of the English, having his house well furnish'd with English goods and his table tolerably well furnish'd with the country produce. He dresses gayley and commonly makes use of silver at his table, having a good side board of plate.'[45] Efik traders expressed discernment and preferences in their selection of luxury goods.[46]

We might at first be tempted to filter these objects into two material categories: African and European. But when European goods were purchased by African consumers, they were experienced as an integrated whole. Efik elites often painted their houses in bright colours in geometric patterns, purchased and used English made furniture, and dined on Efik cuisine using English silver and wearing West African clothing. These material choices reflected intentional consumption choices as elites curated their own experience of the Atlantic World. After generations of consumption, European goods – even luxury goods – were neither surprising nor alien in African port towns. While Efik traders could don English clothing when dining onboard a ship, they could just as easily integrate Efik and English modes there and elsewhere. The Efik had been consumers of European manufactured luxury goods for a long time and that inflow of materials and objects inevitably changed Efik modes of material expression, and their reception, over time. Duke Ephraim, another Efik trader, generally dressed very simply, 'consisting of a paan or mantle, with a sash formed of a white handkerchief or piece of cloth'. But on occasion his dress was 'more gaudy and imposing', including 'a sort of robe or mantle reaching to the knee, and composed of several colours, with a silk sash thrown over the shoulder' and 'a gold-laced round hat, like those worn by gentlemen's servants, which is sometimes set off with plumes of feathers'.[47] Duke Ephraim knew that his attire depended on European materials, forms and manufacture – they were likely ordered from Liverpool factors – but the assemblage was entirely his own. He was an elite man self-fashioning from the goods made available by his participation in the Atlantic market. That same strategy was apparent in the importation of Western furniture and household goods. In his 1846 description of the house of chief Willy Tom Robins, Waddell indicated that 'the house was of native structure, surrounding a quadrangular court-yard with an inner court, for his private use, painted in Calabar style, and containing English furniture and trade goods'. Robins had imported English manufactured furniture but had not yet chosen to import a Liverpool house frame. Importantly this material integration still accommodated traditional religious practices. Waddell noticed 'two human skulls in the ground at his door-step, skulls of enemies', which he writes 'were deemed of use for keeping out enemies. Such things were seen at every door at that time except one in Creek Town.'[48]

European objects might also have been enlisted into long-standing Efik political hierarchies. While communities were long organised by family-affiliated, multi-generational houses, all the houses of a community, and all the communities of a district, were subject to laws imposed by the Epke Society, a hierarchical organisation that oversaw legislative, executive and judicial functions across a network of towns. While the number of ranks in the Epke changed over time – there were five reported in 1828 and 11 almost two decades later – the mechanism for populating those ranks was quite stable: membership fees. Membership in a rank depended on payment: the higher the rank, the dearer the price. While it was more commonly men, membership was also open to wealthy women. Oral tradition even records a few Liverpool ship captains and merchants who purchased membership in Epke Society ranks.[49] But it was also clear that once membership was purchased into a rank, objects and adornment signalled that rank; ostrich feathers, for example, were sumptuary goods reserved for membership in the highest rank. Historian David Imbua argues that the Epke Society created a stability that made trade with the Efik all the more appealing among British captains. It increased the centrality of economic exchange in everyday life and grew in its own power in the eighteenth century, eventually overriding other stabilising social structures.[50] While the historical record does not capture this evidence, it seems fair to assume that European luxury goods – including imported houses – might well have found their way into the material expressions of this severely hierarchical, wealth-dependent fraternity.[51] Thus, in sum, elite Efik traders were savvy businessmen, seasoned by generations of trade with Europeans and often acting on information and relationships built while educated abroad. They were voracious consumers of British and European manufactures, ranging from mahogany furniture, richly carved mirrors and spectacular chandeliers to silk and gold-laced coats and plumed hats, goods which they imported and integrated into their own material worlds. And for a few of the wealthiest, these items were exhibited in a Liverpool-manufactured house.

The idea of a prefabricated house disassembled and shipped to West Africa in the hull of a British ship might seem surprising, but it should not. Shipping prefabricated house frames from established ports to the tropical periphery of the British Empire had been happening through the eighteenth century. In a brief study of the customs records of the Piscataqua region of Maine and New Hampshire, for example, James Garvin uncovered 147 building frames shipped out between 1770 and 1775 alone. He recounts that these ranged from planters' houses to stores and shops and 'Negro Hutts'. Most of these buildings were destined for Grenada, Tobago, Dominica or St Vincent, all newly acquired by Britain from France in the 1763 Treaty of Paris.[52] As was common for houses built by British colonials across the tropical reaches of their empire, these pre-manufactured houses were often described as including a 'gallery', which was referred to as a piazza or a veranda in the West and East Indies respectively.[53] In 1794, economist and abolitionist Carl Bernard Wadström published a treatise arguing for the colonisation and development of plantations in West Africa, primarily to incentivise the abolition of the slave trade. Amid his extensive discussion of plantation economy, he offered advice on houses designed to preserve settlers' heath and comfort, arguing that the high mortality rate of the British in Africa was 'owing to the want of good houses'.[54] Illustrated with an architectural section, his treatise urged colonists to build a single-storey house raised on piers 'to a proper elevation above the ground in order to give free circulation of air underneath to carry off the vapors' (Figure 10.3). And, importantly, the whole should be encircled by a 'gallery covered by the projecting roof of the house all round in order to keep off the Sunshine'. And to erect these buildings more quickly, he suggested that they be pre-manufactured in England and shipped to Africa as a kit of parts.[55] Just two years earlier, the Sierra Leone Company had erected a church, a warehouse, a range of shops, two hospitals and several dwellings in Freetown, all of which arrived as pre-manufactured building frames. The governor's house, one of those several dwellings, was very much like Wadström's model, including elevated single-floor living surrounded by shaded galleries.[56] Unlike those intended for Sierra Leone, the shipments to Duke Town were driven not by British supply but by local demand. Prefabricated houses had been produced by Liverpool housebuilders for African traders since at least the 1780s. Each of those two-storey houses observed by Waddell in 1846, for example, were likely prefabricated in Liverpool.

The importation of these Liverpool prefabricated two-storey frame houses corresponds closely to the rise of Calabar's mercantile households. As described by Okon Edet Uya, traditional Efik households were comprised of several compounds, each dominated by internal courtyards called *esit ebiet* or *esit esa*.[57] These courtyards included deep verandahs that accommodated everyday activities of cooking and childcare.

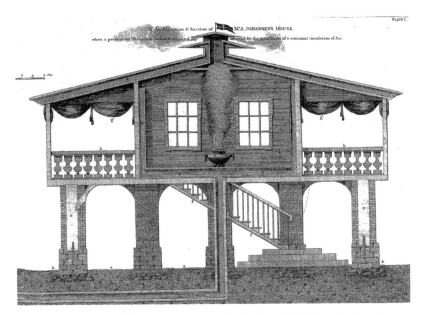

Figure 10.3 'Design for a House in a Tropical Climate', Carl Wadström, *An Essay on Colonization* (London, 1794). Public access. Courtesy of the Beinecke Rare Books and Manuscript Library. Available at https://collections.library.yale.edu/catalog/16166139.

The house of the head of the family stood at the centre of each compound, surrounded by those of his wives and relatives. The head of the household would usually receive visitors on verandah benches.[58] Whereas earlier households were comprised almost entirely of individuals from the same family, the increased labour demands on the houses participating in the Atlantic market meant the incorporation of non-relatives, resulting in the adoption of a new word, 'Ufok', for household, a word that broke the earlier alignment of household and family.[59] While scholars have often presumed to see the rise of the West African slave trade and the growth of the Atlantic market of global goods through the lens of British ports and American plantations, elite Africans also benefited from the slave trade, and the rapid expansion of their wealth through the eighteenth century had a profound impact on their social and political structures. African elites used this new world of goods to navigate the world of business and to secure their social and political standing in their communities. Items of personal adornment, portable luxury objects, rich furniture and even whole houses were purchased and became the building blocks of new strategies for cementing the local power of elites under their growing wealth through the later eighteenth century.

Figure 10.4 John Murray, *The First Day of the Yam Custom*, 1818. © National Maritime Museum, Greenwich, London. Michael Graham-Stewart Slavery Collection. Acquired with the assistance of the Heritage Lottery Fund.

Just as with personal costume, the elite of Calabar folded their new architectural solutions into existing material and social structures. Even Obong Eyemba's Iron Palace, once rebuilt along the Calabar River, was literally enmeshed in long-standing social and spatial practices. Waddell described the palace as surrounded by eight or nine courtyards for his wives, domestics and trade goods, each comprised of low thatched rooms, one opening into the other. The public courtyards were 'tastefully painted in gay and bold native patterns, by native pigments – his women being the artists'. Waddell also noted that along the street in front of the iron palace 'was a long sofa-like seat, made of beaten clay, well shaped and painted', the traditional space for the reception of local visitors. The importation of the iron palace was not the adoption of an entirely new material practice but the incorporation of a new material expression into the evolving social structures of power and wealth in that community.[60]

In his 1805 visit to and account of Calabar, Nicholls recorded the delivery of an umbrella to the king.[61] Gifts of large and brilliantly coloured umbrellas had long been given as tribute to Africans from European and British ship captains and agents. An extraordinary 1818 sketch of the first day of the Yam Custom is probably the most striking visualisation of this practice (Figure 10.4). Located in Kumasi, now in modern Ghana, this festival celebrated the arrival of annual tribute to the king of Asante, who in the sketch is seated on a throne under a central elephant-crested crimson umbrella surrounded by flags representing the various European countries that he counted among his trading partners. In the 1840s, Waddell described the arrival of Obong Eyo Honesty of Creek Town in Calabar by great canoe 'covered by an immense and handsome umbrella of various colors'. The canoe also boasted 'an English ensign, with his name thereon in large capitals'.[62] In the same narrative, Waddell recounted the great canoe of Eyemba, the occupant of the iron palace:

His great canoe was gaily decked out with several ensigns streaming in the wind, British ensigns, with his name thereon in large letters. The little house amidships was brilliantly painted red and yellow. Astride the roof thereof sat two men beating drums with might and main. Before it stood Eyamba, shaded by his grand umbrella, dressed as usual, except in having a gold laced cocked hat under his arm, and a splendid sword, a present from the Dutch Government, at his side.[63]

Kings and chiefs across West Africa deployed colourful tribute umbrellas and ensign flags to signal their status and authority. This function is made explicit in their choice to order objects emblazoned with their names. They also incorporated objects of British and European manufacture among their personal accoutrements – feathered hats, walking canes, swords and so forth – to these same ends. Eyemba's extraordinary iron palace functioned in much the same way. But how did the earlier, simpler, two-storey frame houses function? Were they also bold declarations of power? Certainly the very first imported frame house functioned to set one trader apart from his competitors. But as others of very similar form arrived, these houses functioned more to cohere the community of traders in Duke Town, to set Duke Town apart from other potential trading communities, especially after the massacre of 1767. Certainly, these two-storey houses functioned to set their elite owners apart from others in their immediate community, most of whom lived in one-storey earthen-walled courtyard houses. But since the Efik and others along the Calabar River never allowed their partners in trade to build fortifications, these houses were not only the residences of the traders and their families, but also centres of business and accommodations for clients. They were also commonly used to entertain or even house ship captains and other English and European agents. They might also have functioned as gaols for newly arrived captives. In this way, these buildings communicated to both locals and international business partners that this class of men understood that objects and spaces were used to convey status, but more importantly were also used to signal their status as savvy consumers. These houses might even have been filled with objects that announced the international agency of the trader. Antera Duke, an Efik trader, for example, ordered in one shipment 12 brass basins engraved with his name.[64] These houses clearly communicated that the elite traders of Calabar were seasoned participants in the Atlantic market, one shaped profoundly by a world of goods.

This incorporation of manufactures in traditional practices continued even into death. Near the end of his account, Waddell describes Eyemba's internment:

> A great pit was dug, wide and deep inside a house and at one side of it, a chamber was excavated, in which were placed two sofas. On these the body was laid dressed in its ornaments, and a crown on its head. Then his umbrella, sword, snuff box bearers, and other personal attendants were suddenly killed, and thrown in with the insignia of their offices; and living virgins also, it was said, according to old custom. Great quantities of food and trade goods, and coppers were added; after which the pit was filled, and the ground trampled and beaten that no trace of the grave might remain. Lest they should be violated whether through revenge or cupidity, such precautions are always used to conceal the graves of the nobles.[65]

The consumption of European manufactures by elite Efik traders opens the possibility of various interpretations. But the most direct is to simply understand these consumption practices as the expansion of African material worlds to include European manufactures – even houses – as elements in the slowly changing practices of costly signalling, status performance and social control that elites practiced in all the spaces of exchange that shaped the trans-Atlantic marketplace.

This trans-Atlantic trade, of course, also had implications for architecture in Liverpool. By the time of the exhibition of Obong Eyemba's Iron Palace in the square by the post office, the legal trans-Atlantic slave trade was long over. But as David Pope's and Jane Longmore's research has shown, the wealth derived from the trade with Calabar's elite had reshaped the city in important ways, even if the rapid suburban expansion of the mid-twentieth century means that few of these buildings still stand. Pope initially identified 39 country houses and suburban villas surrounding Liverpool occupied by merchants deeply involved in the slave trade. Longmore, focusing more specifically on those houses actually built in the eighteenth century by merchants involved in the slave trade and therefore presumably funded by that trade, found 24 such country houses and villas, ten of which were built in the 1770s alone. One of those was the country house at Spekelands, built by Thomas Earle, whose family undertook 174 slaving voyages between 1699 and 1804.[66] Thomas invested in 16 voyages to Calabar. John Tarleton, an investor in 25 different voyages from Liverpool to Calabar, lived in Finch House.[67] The Parr family, builders of both a country house called Elm House

Figure 10.5 Thomas Parr House (Liverpool Royal Institution), *c.* 1799, Liverpool, England. © Louis P. Nelson.

in 1770 and a grand townhouse on Colquitt Street, were also deeply involved in the slave trade, investing in 13 voyages between Liverpool and Calabar from the 1750s to the 1800s (Figure 10.5). The large warehouse that still rises behind the Parr house is a stunning reminder of the vast volumes of trade goods and personal items shipped from Liverpool to Calabar and many other African ports. And participating in this trade generated wealth enough for families to buy into or build one of the most important signals of status in British culture: the country house. Thus, as Efik traders were ordering two-storey wood-framed houses, their Liverpool counterparts were investing in country houses. But may we never forget the cost. The Voyages Database records 469 voyages disembarking from Liverpool to either Calabar or New Calabar over the course of the entire slave trade – 469 voyages deporting almost 150,000 people out of Africa to the forced labour camps that were the plantations of the Americas.

Notes

1 The Iron Palace of Obong Eyemba has been briefly discussed in Imbua, *Intercourse and Crosscurrents*, 70. It is also mentioned in Edet Uya, *Architecture of Old Calabar* and Hutchinson, *Impressions*, 116.
2 Anonymous, 'Iron houses', 170–1.

3   This chapter builds on the excellent scholarship by Cécile Fromont on the consumption of luxury goods by early modern elites in West Central Africa, namely the Kongo. See Fromont, *The Art of Conversion*.
4   On the Efik and Old Calabar, see Imbua, *Intercourse and Crosscurrents*; Behrendt et al., *Diary of Antera Duke*; Sparks, *Two Princes*; Behrendt and Graham, 'African merchants'; Oku, *Kings & Chiefs*; Nair, *Politics and Society*; and Forde, *Efik Traders*. For a comprehensive discussion of the structure of the slave trade in Angola, see Miller, 'Commercial organization of slaving'. For a careful study of a slave port in the Bight of Benin, see Law, *Ouidah*.
5   Recognising the variable motivations for the consumption of things is essential in scholarship that seeks to understand the motivations of early modern African consumers. This point is beautifully argued in Fromont, 'Taste of others', 273–92.
6   For more on Obong Eyemba, see Oku, *Kings & Chiefs*.
7   Waddell, *Twenty-Nine Years*, 243–7.
8   Waddell, *Twenty-Nine Years*, 253.
9   The iron palace lasted little more than a decade. It was demolished by his successor soon after Eyemba's death in 1847. Hutchinson, *Impressions*, 116.
10 The earliest example thus far is Egbo Young's Liverpool Hall, so named by Antera Duke, in 1785. Forde, *Efik Traders*, 28. See also Waddell, *Twenty-Nine Years*, 244; and Simmons, 'Ethnographic sketch', 9. Such exportation of house frames was also presumed among the English. In his discourse advocating for the English colonisation of West Africa, Wadström recommends that all colonists bring a house frame with them. See Wadström, *Essay on Colonization* I, 49.
11 Imbua, *Intercourse and Crosscurrents*, 69.
12 Hallett, *Records of the African Association*, 207–8.
13 In concert with Cécile Fromont, I understand the early modern Atlantic World as a social and economic system shaped by trade in both luxury goods and enslaved people. She argues that 'the circulation of elite objects and the parallel traffic in enslaved people emerged as cornerstones of the Atlantic system'. See Fromont, 'Taste of others'. Her insistence on including the trans-Atlantic trade in enslaved people builds on a larger body of scholarship that amplifies the importance of the circulation of luxury goods as central to the making of the Atlantic World, including work by T.H. Breen, Cary Carson and Jennifer Van Horn, among many others. See Breen, *Marketplace of Revolution*; Carson, *Face Value*; and Van Horn, *Power of Objects*.
14 Amplifying the agency of the African consumer is an important thread of Fromont's scholarship, cited above. There are also some useful comparisons of this context with what Richard White has called a 'middle ground', a space of social and cultural accommodation and negotiation between two communities experiencing a general balance of power. See White, *Middle Ground*.
15 Anonymous, 'Iron houses', 170.
16 Obong Eyemba's importation of this iron palace marked a shift in the profile of imported architecture. Whereas all previous buildings were timber framed, the importation of major iron pre-manufactured buildings would persist throughout the nineteenth century and many of these later nineteenth-century buildings survive. For more on these later buildings, see Imbua, *Intercourse and Crosscurrents*, 70–4. This importation preceded the more famous importation of the House of Wonders in Stone Town, Zanzibar. For more on that extraordinary building, see chapter 3 of Meier, *Swahili Port Cities*, 102–39.
17 Imbua, *Intercourse and Crosscurrents*, 12–18.
18 Imbua, *Intercourse and Crosscurrents*, 40.
19 Drescher, *Econocide*, 65–76.
20 Imbua, *Intercourse and Crosscurrents*, 34; Behrendt and Graham, 'African merchants', 52.
21 Nicholls was an intended explorer of the African interior sent by the Africa Association. He died three months after arriving in Calabar. Letter from Nicholls to the Association written in Calabar, 15 February 1805, cited in Hallett, *Records of the African Association*, 198; on the power of a fort to generate local wealth, see Sparks, *Where the Negroes Are Masters*, 17, 34, 64.
22 The complexity of these commercial centres is discussed in detail in the introductory essays in Behrendt et al., *Diary of Antera Duke*. On the importance of Liverpool, see Behrendt et al., *Diary of Antera Duke*, 76–7.

23 On the continuing trade after 1807, see Lynn, 'Liverpool and Africa'.
24 This assumption is in line with a growing body of historical research that finds its origins in the work of John Thornton and Paul Gilroy.
25 Imbua, *Intercourse and Crosscurrents*, 43.
26 See Sparks, *Where the Negroes Are Masters*.
27 Sparks, *Where the Negroes Are Masters*, 3. See Axtell, 'First consumer revolution', 132.
28 Waddell, *Twenty-Nine Years*, 663–4.
29 Sparks, *Where the Negroes Are Masters*, 196.
30 Behrendt et al., *Diary of Antera Duke*, 49.
31 Robin Hallett as quoted in Imbua, 'Old Calabar merchants', 67.
32 Letter from Nicholls to the Association written in Calabar, 15 February 1805, cited in Hallett, *Records of the African Association*, 203.
33 Behrendt and Graham, 'African merchants', 206.
34 Imbua, *Intercourse and Crosscurrents*, 39.
35 Letter from Nicholls to the Association written in Calabar, 15 February 1805, cited in Hallett, *Records of the African Association*, 200.
36 Domingues da Silva, 'Atlantic slave trade from Angola', 116–21.
37 Northrup, *Trade without Rulers*, 89, 100.
38 Lambert, *House of Commons Sessional Papers*, 126.
39 Behrendt et al., *Diary of Antera Duke*, 57; Park, *Travels in the Interior*, 18.
40 Behrendt et al., *Diary of Antera Duke*, 56–7.
41 Ume, *Rise of British Colonialism*, 82.
42 Cited in Behrendt et al., *Diary of Antera Duke*, 56.
43 Behrendt et al., *Diary of Antera Duke*, 56–7.
44 Behrendt et al., *Diary of Antera Duke*, 57.
45 Owen and Martin, *Journal of a Slave-Dealer*, 76.
46 For a comparable assessment of personal choice and discernment among Native Americans, see Axtell, 'First consumer revolution', 134–44.
47 Quote by H. Crow, cited in Forde, *Efik Traders*, 9.
48 Waddell, *Twenty-Nine Years*, 251.
49 Hart, *Report of Inquiry*, 167.
50 Imbua, *Intercourse and Crosscurrents*, 43.
51 Imbua, *Intercourse and Crosscurrents*, 19–25.
52 Garvin, *Building Frames*.
53 See Nelson, 'Anglo-tropical architecture'. See also John Crowley's important work on the intersection of health and comfort in Crowley, 'Inventing comfort', 277–316.
54 Although Swedish, Wadström was a central figure in the British debates around abolition. The model for this house was designed by Swiss architect A. Johansen. Wadström, *Essay on Colonization* I, 50. His treatise was translated into German in 1796 and French in 1798.
55 Wadström, *Essay on Colonization* II, 37. On the early use of galleries or verandahs in West Africa as sites of cross-cultural engagement and trade, see Mark, *'Portuguese' Style*, 46–9.
56 Kubler, 'Machine for living', 31–2.
57 Edet Uya, *Architecture of Old Calabar*.
58 Bassey, 'Architecture of Old Calabar', 4.
59 Bassey, 'Architecture of Old Calabar', 6; for more on the rise of the mercantile household in Calabar, see Nair, *Politics and Society*.
60 Waddell, *Twenty-Nine Years*, 249.
61 Letter from Nicholls to the Association written in Calabar, 15 February 1805, cited in Hallett, *Records of the African Association*, 203.
62 Waddell, *Twenty-Nine Years*, 242.
63 Waddell, *Twenty-Nine Years*, 247–8.
64 Behrendt et al., *Diary of Antera Duke*, 43.
65 Waddell, *Twenty-Nine Years*, 336–7.
66 Longmore, 'Rural retreats', 44. For Spekelands, house of Thomas Earle, see Barczewski, *Country Houses and the British Empire*, 36. Earle is identified as one of the leading Calabar traders in Imbua, *Intercourse and Crosscurrents*, 39.
67 Behrendt et al., *Diary of Antera*, 71; Longmore, 'Rural retreats', 44.

Bibliography

Anonymous. 'Iron houses: rebuilding of Pointe-A-Pitre', *The Builder* (May 1843): 170–1.

Axtell, James. 'The First Consumer Revolution'. In *Beyond 1492: Encounters in Colonial North America*, 125–51. New York: Oxford University Press, 1992.

Barczewski, Stephanie. *Country Houses and the British Empire, 1700–1930*. Manchester: Manchester University Press, 2014.

Bassey, Nnimmo. 'The architecture of Old Calabar'. In *International Seminar on the Story of Old Calabar*. National Museum at the Old Residency, 1986. https://www.si.edu/object/siris_sil_437343

Behrendt, Stephen D., and Eric J. Graham. 'African merchants, notables and the slave trade at Old Calabar, 1720: evidence from the National Archives of Scotland', *History in Africa* 30 (2003): 37–61.

Behrendt, Stephen, A.J.H. Latham and David Northrup. *The Diary of Antera Duke, an Eighteenth-Century African Slave Trader*. New York: Oxford University Press, 2010.

Breen, T.H. *Marketplace of Revolution: How consumer politics shaped American independence*. Oxford: Oxford University Press, 2005.

Carson, Cary. *Face Value: The consumer revolution and the colonizing of America*. Charlottesville: University of Virginia Press, 2017.

Crowley, John. 'Inventing comfort: the piazza'. In *American Material Culture: The shape of the field*, edited by Ann Smart Martin and J. Richie Garrison, 277–315. Knoxville: University of Tennessee Press, 1997.

Domingues da Silva, Daniel B. 'Atlantic slave trade from Angola: a port-by-port estimate of slaves embarked, 1701–1867', *International Journal of African Historical Studies* 46, no. 1 (2013): 116–21.

Drescher, Seymour. *Econocide: British slavery in the era of abolition*. Pittsburgh: University of Pittsburgh Press, 1977.

Edet Uya, Okon. *The Architecture of Old Calabar*. Unpublished manuscript. University of Calabar, 1986.

Forde, Daryll, ed. *Efik Traders of Old Calabar: Containing the diary of Antera Duke together with an ethnographic sketch and notes and an essay on the political organization of Old Calabar*. London: Dawsons of Pall Mall for the International African Institute, 1968.

Fromont, Cécile. *The Art of Conversion: Christian visual culture in the Kingdom of Kongo*. Chapel Hill: University of North Carolina Press, 2014.

Fromont, Cécile. 'The taste of others: finery, the slave trade and Africa's place in the traffic in early modern things'. In *Early Modern Things: Objects and their histories, 1500–1800*, edited by Paula Finden, 2nd ed., 273–93. Abingdon: Routledge, 2021.

Garvin, James. *Building frames for the West Indies*. Unpublished manuscript, 2007.

Hallett, Robin. *Records of the African Association, 1788–1831*. Edinburgh: Thomas Nelson and Sons, 1964.

Hart, K. *Report of Inquiry into the Dispute Over the Obongship of Calabar*. Enugu: Government Printers, 1964.

Hutchinson, Thomas. *Impressions of Western Africa*. London: Longman, Brown, Green, Longmans & Roberts, 1858.

Imbua, David Lishilinimle. *Intercourse and Crosscurrents in the Atlantic World: Calabar–British experiences, 17th–20th centuries*. Durham: Carolina Academic Press, 2012.

Imbua, David Lishilinimle. 'Old Calabar merchants and the off-shore British community, 1650–1750', *Paideuma: Mitteilungen zur Kulturkunde* 59 (2013): 51–75.

Kubler, George. 'The machine for living in eighteenth-century West Africa', *Journal of the Society of Architectural Historians* 3 (April 1944): 30–3.

Lambert, Sheila, ed. *House of Commons Sessional Papers of the Eighteenth Century 73*. Wilmington: Scholarly Resources, 1975.

Law, Robin. *Ouidah: The social history of a West African slaving port, 1727–1892*. Athens: Ohio University Press, 2004.

Longmore, Jane. 'Rural retreats: Liverpool slave traders and their country houses'. In *Slavery and the British Country House*, edited by Madge Dresser and Andrew Hann, 43–53. Swindon: English Heritage, 2013.

Lynn, Martin. 'Liverpool and Africa in the nineteenth century: the continuing connection'. 1998. Accessed 15 August 2021. https://www.hslc.org.uk/wp-content/uploads/2017/05/147-3-Lynn.pdf.

Mark, Peter. *'Portuguese' Style and the Luso-African Identity: Precolonial Senegambia, sixteenth-nineteenth centuries*. Bloomington: Indiana University Press, 2003.

Meier, Prita. *Swahili Port Cities: The architecture of elsewhere*. Bloomington: Indiana University Press, 2016.

Miller, Joseph. 'Some aspects of the commercial organization of slaving at Luanda, Angola – 1730–1830'. In *The Uncommon Market: Essays in the economic history of the Atlantic slave trade*, edited by Henry Gemery and Jan Hogendorn, 77–106. New York: Academic Press, 1979.

Nair, Kannan. *Politics and Society in South Eastern Nigeria, 1841–1906: A study of power, diplomacy and commerce in Old Calabar*. London: Frank Cass, 1972.

Nelson, Louis P. 'Anglo-tropical architecture of Empire'. In *Architectures of Power*, edited by Edward Gillin and Harry Mace. Forthcoming.

Northrup, David. *Trade without Rulers: Pre-colonial economic development in south-eastern Nigeria*. Oxford: Clarendon Press, 1978.

Oku, Ekei Essien. *The Kings & Chiefs of Old Calabar (1785–1925)*. Calabar: Glad Tidings Press, 1989.

Owen, Nicholas, and Eveline Martin, eds. *Journal of a Slave-Dealer: A living history of the slave trade*. London: Routledge, 1930.

Park, Mungo. *Travels in the Interior Districts of Africa*. London, 1799; reprint New York, 1971.

Simmons, Donald. 'An ethnographic sketch of the Efik people'. In *Efik Traders of Old Calabar: Containing the diary of Antera Duke together with an ethnographic sketch and notes and an essay on the political organization of Old Calabar*, edited by Daryll Forde. London: Dawsons of Pall Mall for the International African Institute, 1968.

Sparks, Randy J. *Two Princes of Calabar*. Cambridge: Harvard University Press, 2009.

Sparks, Randy J. *Where the Negroes Are Masters: An African port in the era of the slave trade*. Cambridge: Harvard University Press, 2014.

Ume, K.E. *The Rise of British Colonialism in Southern Nigeria, 1700–1900*. New York: Exposition Press, 1980.

Van Horn, Jennifer. *The Power of Objects in Eighteenth-Century British America*. Chapel Hill: University of North Carolina Press, 2017.

Waddell, Hope Masterton. *Twenty-Nine Years in the West Indies and Central Africa*. London: T. Nelson & Sons, 1863.

Wadström, Carl Bernhard. *Essay on Colonization, Particularly Applied to the West Coast of Africa, With Some Free Thoughts on Cultivation and Commerce Also Brief Descriptions of the Colonies Already Formed, Or Attempted, in Africa, Including Those of Sierra Leona and Bulama I*. London: Darton and Harvey, 1794.

White, Richard. *The Middle Ground: Indians, empires, and republics in the Great Lakes Region, 1650–1815*, 2nd ed. Cambridge: Cambridge University Press, 2012.

11
Negotiating cosmopolitan taste with local culture: porcelain rooms in Indian forts and palaces
Esther Schmidt

The focus of this chapter is the phenomenon of the porcelain room in Rajput palaces, understood as a specific room typology in its larger context of global trade, Indian courtly life and diplomatic gift-giving, and as an indication of cosmopolitanism in the historic interior. Aesthetic cosmopolitanism in interiors implies engagement with the world through global objects and transregional design principles. Their integration into local design schemes and domestic practices provides important insights on the analysis of the historic interior in Indian palaces.[1]

Porcelain rooms in Rajput palaces, combining Chinese export porcelain and European ceramics, emerged in the early eighteenth century and were inspired by the *Chini khana* (China house or room) that originated in Islamic courtly culture and flourished on the subcontinent under the Mughals in the sixteenth and particularly the seventeenth century. Even geographically more isolated palaces in Rajasthan reinterpreted global objects and designs from different cultures, religions and aesthetic traditions. This resulted in interwoven design practices that challenge notions of a linear process of imitation and suggest multi-directional artistic exchange. Porcelain rooms can be found in the City Palace of Udaipur, Junagarh Fort in Bikaner, Juna Mahal in Dungarpur, Jaisalmer Fort in Kishangarh and the now demolished Diwan Dewdi at Hyderabad in the Deccan.[2] The ceramics used in Indian porcelain rooms were Chinese export porcelain, blue and white Dutch tiles and, by the nineteenth century, plates or fragments of dinnerware from various European porcelain manufactories. The appreciation of the exotic and 'foreignness' was the invisible thread behind the porcelain room connected with the *farangi* theme. Derived from 'Franks', 'farangi motifs imply the depiction of foreigners in art and interiors in response to encounters with Europeans and European art.[3]

Ceramics and glass were mainly associated with Islamic courts in India and were avoided in Hindu households due to religious concerns about materials regarded as porous and unsuitable for food consumption.[4] The fact that such objects were nevertheless integrated into rooms in Rajput palaces by the early eighteenth century points to a transformation of more orthodox religious life towards secularism and cosmopolitan artistic innovation. Inspired by Timurid and Persian examples, the Mughal *Chini khana* was originally a room or wall with niches to display Chinese porcelain, often found in garden pavilions and garden tombs. One of the earliest-known references to a *Chini khana* is found in the Baburnama, the memoirs and historical accounts of the first Mughal emperor Babur (r. 1526–30): a garden pavilion in Samarqand decorated with imported Chinese hexagonal and square tiles to house a porcelain collection built by his ancestor Ulugh Beg (r. 1447–9), grandson of Timur and patron of art, architecture and science.[5] The example illustrates the mediation of foreign luxury goods with local culture as indicated by the hexagonal shape of the tiles, which was not a Chinese tradition.[6]

Mehreen Chida-Razvi has shown that the *Chini khana*, understood as a building in the 'Timurid' context in the fifteenth century, underwent significant developments over time until it became a decorative element.[7] The design could range from wall niches to display porcelain to an ornamental relief during the reign of Jahangir (1605–27), when 'the favourite motif of wall decoration, regardless of the technique, was the *Chini khana*'.[8]

There is ample evidence that large quantities of Chinese porcelain were exported to India by the ninth century.[9] Blue and white Chinese porcelain was used at banquets and receptions during the Tughlaq Sultanate (1320–1414), which coincided with the large-scale production of blue and white porcelain in the Yuan period.[10] Popular in the context of pleasure, the erotic and the exotic, blue and white porcelain featured in books on food, perfume and aphrodisiacs, such as the Ni'matnama (c. 1495–1505) created for the Malwa Sultanate.[11] The discovery in 1961 of Yuan period blue and white porcelain shards at the Tughlaq palace of Firuz Shah (r. 1351–88) in New Delhi represents one of the largest known collections of Yuan porcelain with over 70 pieces, rivalled only by collections at the Topkapi Palace and the Ardebil Shrine in Persia.[12] The latter was established in 1611 when Shah Abbas (r. 1588–1629) had the royal porcelain collection of about 1,126 pieces transferred to the shrine as a *waqf* or charitable endowment.[13] Another example is the music room at the Ali Qapu palace, installed around 1614 in Isfahan, where the ornate, honeycomb-like niches, or *muqarnas*, were made of plaster with cut-outs in the form of arches or vessels in a vaulted ceiling.[14] In 1618 the Mughal Emperor Jahangir sent ambassadors to Isfahan where they would have likely seen the recently completed music room. During this visit Shah Abbas was presented with a Chinese porcelain cup from the emperor, underlining the importance of porcelain in diplomatic gift-giving.[15]

These porcelain displays in early seventeenth-century Persia are comparable to the European porcelain cabinets which appeared by the mid-seventeenth century, for example Amalia von Solm's *groote porceleyn cabinet* of 1648–9 at Oude Hof in the Netherlands, which comprised 500 pieces of porcelain.[16] The fascination with porcelain, well recognised at the time as *maladie de porcelaine*, resulted in huge collections: August the Strong (1670–1733) accumulated the largest porcelain collection in Europe, with 50,000–60,000 pieces intended for the interiors at his Japanisches Palais.[17] That massed porcelain displays in early modern Europe were associated with a Dutch interior design practice is indicated by the 1641 inventory of Countess Arundel's (c. 1582–1654) 'Dutch Pranketing Room' at Tart Hall.[18] At Santos Palace in Lisbon (1680–5), 261 pieces of blue and white Ming porcelain were integrated into a pyramidal ceiling.[19] By the early eighteenth century, porcelain rooms with movable collections were turned into elaborate interior design schemes, such as the porcelain cabinet in Castle Charlottenburg in Berlin, designed by Johann Friedrich Eosander von Göthe (1706).[20] At the time it contained 400 pieces of Chinese porcelain and 80 pieces of delftware.[21] This combination of Chinese export porcelain and Chinese-inspired Dutch ceramics also characterised early eighteenth-century porcelain cabinets in Udaipur Rajasthan.

Porcelain cabinets at City Palace, Udaipur

The city of Udaipur, named after Maharana Udai Singh II (r. 1540–72) of the Sisodia Rajputs, is located in Rajasthan and surrounded by hills and several artificial lakes. It was founded as the new capital of the Mewar kingdom after the Mughal Emperor Akbar's siege of their former capital Chittorgarh in 1567–8.[22] The Mewar kingdom was the largest of the Rajput kingdoms and the last to form an alliance with the Mughals under Emperor Jahangir in 1615. The Udaipur City Palace is an example of water architecture with a concern for the picturesque and the aesthetic rather than fortification. Overlooking Lake Picchola and framed in the distance by the Aravalli hills, the white palace is part of an enchanting water landscape where the aesthetic, the sacred and the utilitarian coalesce: the artificial lakes functioned as reservoirs, social space for religious festivals and a world of pleasure, with white lake palaces and boat rides reserved for the ruler and his household.

The lake palace is a specific Indian architectural genre characterised by the aesthetic phenomenon of appearing to float on water; it utilises the water surface as a mirror to enhance the visual effect. While lake palaces were built as early as the sixteenth century, they proliferated in the eighteenth century, coinciding with the ascendancy of the *maison de plaisance* in Europe. The artificial waterscape also influenced the interior design of porcelain rooms at City Palace with a focus on the colour scheme and reflective quality of the materials replicating the surface of the lake. Built in several stages with each ruler adding sections, City Palace is typical of Rajput palace architecture with its asymmetrical plan incorporating several mahals (royal apartments or specific room types, such as the *sheesh mahal* or mirror cabinet). Mirror or glass elements were typically combined with ceramics, probably in recognition of their reflective quality and their exotic and luxurious character. The *sheesh mahal* became a popular feature of palace architecture by the seventeenth century, as described by the political agent James Tod:

> The court and the household economy of a great chieftain is a miniature representation of the sovereign's: ... He must have his *sheesh-mahall* [mirror cabinet], his *bari-mahall* [terrace garden within the palace], and his mandir [temple], like his prince. He enters the *dari-sala*, or carpet hall, the minstrel preceding him rehearsing the praises of his family; and he takes his seat on his throne.[23]

The travel guide *Handbook of Mewar* (1888) describes the curiosities, depictions of Europeans and important *mahals* within the City Palace complex, placing particular emphasis on the porcelain cabinet.[24] The poetic names of the apartments allude to the display of exotic and foreign materials of European and Chinese origin. The integration of such global objects into interiors may be attributed to the establishment of the porcelain cabinet in the *mardana* or male section of the palace under Maharana Sangram Singh (r. 1710–34). Inaugurated in 1723 and possibly established as early as 1711, the porcelain cabinet marks a time of major transformation in the art, architecture and lifestyle of the palace towards an aesthetic of pleasure – away from fortification and a religiously inspired art of manuscript illumination to the depiction of courtly life.[25] Referred to as *Chini chitra shala* (Chinese picture hall), the former 'China house' evolved into a gallery space suggesting connoisseurship, prestige and a sophisticated place of leisure.[26] As Goetz notes:

> In most old palaces in India one or several richly decorated corner rooms abundant with murals and glass mosaics are reserved for the private life of the ruler, where he also receives the women of his harem. At times it is a small hall, often a courtyard with gallery, a formal hall and two intimate rooms (hence the term Chitrasala). Scenes often depict the life of women, heavenly and earthly love and musical moods. In their midst other rare art works can be found such as European prints, convex mirrors etc.[27]

The porcelain room conceived as a *Chitrashala* ensemble of interior and exterior spaces embodies the cosmopolitan character of the rooms, furnished with foreign art works associated with the exotic and the erotic.[28] Daily records in Udaipur reveal that the *Chitrashala* fulfilled specific ceremonial purposes and was part of semi-public viewings where courtiers were asked to present and later inscribe art works in the presence of the ruler.[29] Wall decorations were particularly important because interiors in Indian palaces had few pieces of furniture: most attention was focused on surface decoration and soft furnishings, such as bolsters on the floor, carpets and curtains; some of the room dividers or screens (*chik*) were made of bamboo interwoven with silk threads to create elaborate patterns.

Designed as a pavilion, the porcelain room is part of an ensemble consisting of a balcony on one side and a courtyard on the other, with two smaller adjacent rooms. The pavilion is covered with over 1,700 blue and white Chinese export porcelain tiles on the interior and exterior. The Kangxi porcelain tiles measure 18 × 18 cm, with an underglaze cobalt blue design dating to *c*. 1690–1710. They are decorated with flower buds in the centre and an ornamental border with a basket of flowers and scrolling foliage with gilded accents. Similar tiles can be found at the Topkapi Palace Museum and in the palace interior at Jaisalmer fort, suggesting a common source and a wider, diverse market.[30]

Designed with five cusped arches in the form of a colonnade or loggia, the porcelain cabinet allows for fluidity between the exterior and the interior and the public and the private, incorporating bioclimatic, ceremonial and gender considerations (Figure 11.1). The reflective quality of the tiles is combined with mirror elements on the upper interior part of the cusped arches mirroring the surface of the lake and adding extra light. The porcelain cabinet is located in the *mardana* (male section), which allowed for views of the surrounding landscape, whereas the female *zenana* was inward-looking. The pavilion opens towards a *jharokha* (balcony or protruding window) on the exterior framed extravagantly by coloured glass panels on either side and overlooking the *Manek Chowk,* the largest courtyard on the ground floor. Constructed under Maharana Karan Singh I (r. 1620–8), it was used for official processions, festivities and animal fights.[31]

The balcony allowed the ruler to be viewed from below and enabled him to view events from above – a reciprocity of viewing and being viewed which is closely related to the Hindu concept of *darshan* (vision or gaze) which implied the beneficial aspects of those present at the ceremony, endowing the ruler with the significance of a divinity.[32] The blue and

Figure 11.1   The *Chini-ki-Chitrashali* with *jharokha* overlooking the *Manek Chowk*, City Palace Udaipur. Photograph: Dr Joachim K. Bautze, Berlin.

white Chinese porcelain tiles on the exterior of the balcony make the porcelain cabinet clearly visible and stand out from afar, highlighting the splendour of the Mewar dynasty and their embrace of the world.

The exclusive use of tiles instead of niches to display porcelain or reliefs with similar motifs shows the introduction of a novel design element in the porcelain cabinet. There are only a few examples of glazed tiles on the exterior of Rajput buildings before 1800, such as the Man Singh Mahal (1486–1517) in Gwalior and small sections of the Patta Palace (c. 1560), Chittorgarh of the Mewar dynasty. From the early eighteenth century onwards foreign tiles were installed in niches, around arches, on walls, ceilings and on *jharokhas* in Rajasthan. These examples are similar to *Hollandse tegelkamers* (tile rooms) found in European residences by the second half of the seventeenth century. In Europe, Dutch tiles were often found in five room types, as Cordula Bischoff has pointed out – chinoiserie cabinets, display kitchens, formal bathrooms, garden pavilions and porcelain grottoes – but can also be found as accent decoration in other parts of buildings. Examples of seventeenth-century tile rooms with Dutch tiles in European residences are the Sala dos Paineis in the Palace of the Marquess de Fronteira in Lisbon (1678) or the tile cabinet in Wilanow Palace, Poland. Dutch tiles were exported all over Europe, Russia, South America, North Africa and India, including Udaipur.

The interior of the porcelain pavilion at City Palace has four small niches, placed on either side of a door leading into another small chamber. The niches are lined with Dutch blue and white ceramic tiles with biblical scenes, such as Jacob's Ladder or Mary and Joseph's Flight into Egypt – effectively turning the niches into windows into an imaginary world (Figure 11.2). The meaning of these tiles was unlikely to be understood, as the same motifs are repeated and combined in a seemingly arbitrary fashion. In the Netherlands, biblical scenes on tiles would not be repeated but were instead used for religious edification. The Dutch tiles were part of the Chinese porcelain cabinet and do not necessarily express an interest in Dutch culture. It was the merchants who were mobile: they selected goods, responding to consumer wishes and the world around them, interpreting and shaping tastes, experimenting with novel cultural contexts and customs, and experiencing a world beyond the familiar. Those on the receiving end, whether in the East or the West, did not share the same mobility and experienced the world around them through novel objects presented to them; their interpretations and misinterpretations were at the bottom of the chinoiserie movement. Hence, both Dutch and Chinese tiles in the *chini ki chitrashali* fulfilled the function of exoticism and cosmopolitanism regardless of their iconography.

Figure 11.2 Dutch tiles, c. 1711, *chini-ki-chitrashali* or Chinese picture gallery. City Palace Udaipur. Photograph: Maharana of Mewar Charitable Foundation.

The porcelain room also relates to the visit of the Dutch East India Company (VOC) under Johan Josua Ketelaar (1659–1718), who may have delivered the Dutch tiles. Ketelaar was the son of a bookbinder from Elbing, East Prussia, who joined the VOC in 1683. Like many other Europeans of humble origin, service in India – either with the European trading companies or with Indian rulers – offered career opportunities and upward social mobility. As newly appointed ambassador and director of the factory in the port city of Surat, Ketelaar embarked on an overland journey in 1711 to meet the Mughal Emperor Bahadur Shah I. (r. 1707–12) in Lahore to secure favourable trade rights. Such journeys were long, dangerous and expensive, not least because, according to Ketelaar's journal, 'the petty rajas of Malwa made it their business to levy blackmail from the caravans passing through their territories'.[33] Good relationships with influential Rajput rulers such as the Maharana of Udaipur were important, and the Dutch envoys stayed in Udaipur for several weeks in March 1711.[34] Various contemporary accounts of Ketelaar's embassy depict the importance of diplomatic gift-giving and underlying cultural expectations.[35] For instance, a contemporary describes how the traditional black Dutch costume was exchanged with a red, yellow and blue attire to avoid offending the colour sense of the locals.[36] A list of over 178 pages of expenses and gifts associated with Ketelaar's visit includes East Asian and European luxury goods.[37] His journal reveals consultation with local Europeans in navigating different taste cultures: the Portuguese Donna Juliana Dias da Costa, referred to as 'governess of the Royal Seraglio' in Ketelaar's journal,[38] presented olfactory gifts and dishes from the emperor and 'expressed delight at the curiosities inspected'.[39] Among the gifts for the emperor were 'several articles of Chinese and Japanese workmanship', 'fine cloths' and large mirrors.[40] Those for the Maharana and his household included 'Japanese lacquer, swords and other arms, nails, mirrors, spectacles, velvets and a gold flower'.[41]

This encounter with foreigners was captured in several art works, ranging from paintings on cloth to miniature paintings, murals and wooden doors carved in relief, which have been identified as a *farangi* genre.[42] A large painting on cloth made at around the same time depicts the visit of the Dutch envoy to City Palace.[43] In the painting some of the Dutch men are shown with dark faces as opposed to the pale faces of the Indian courtiers, possibly to exoticise the foreigners. This trend of satirical depiction of foreigners is also shown in an opaque watercolour depicting a winged Dutchman riding a composite camel.[44] Several depictions of Europeans incorporate 'signals' to convey foreignness or the exotic. While the turban in European art, such as in Rembrandt's *Man in Oriental Clothing* (1635), conveyed the exotic, it was the wig or the hat (such as the tricorne or 'cocked hat') that fulfilled a similar function in the *farangi*-themed art works in India.[45] That European clothes were regarded as entertaining can be seen in the example of a mid-eighteenth-century miniature painting showing Indian female performers dressed up in European costumes as part of a court entertainment.[46] *Farangi*-themed images and foreign objects could also have erotic or sexual undertones: European couples were depicted with intimate gestures and European women were shown with suggestive cleavages or black spots on their face, suggesting the contraction of syphilis.[47] Murals at City Palace dating to the time of Maharana Sangram Singh, whose reign (1710–34) coincided with the visit of the Dutch embassy, explicitly depict a European couple having sexual intercourse (Figure 11.3).[48] The integration of foreign motifs is manifold, but there five distinct variations (or manifestations) of how the *firangi theme* in the historic interior was applied: firstly as decorative elements in interiors ranging from foreign

Figure 11.3 Ornamental interior detail showing the *farangi* theme, *Chitram ki Burj*, City Palace Udaipur. Photograph: Dr Joachim K. Bautze, Berlin.

objects and materials to depictions of Europeans in the form of murals, inlay of ornamental details or in relief on doors; secondly in the form of art works as a caricature or the fantastic; thirdly in the form of reportage involving foreigners and the recording of specific events, receptions and the like; fourthly as a specific genre of the erotic associated with either global objects or materials; and fifthly in the application of global objects and materials to accentuate status and cosmopolitanism.

Highly sought-after European mirrors feature prominently in erotic paintings, such as that of Maharana Bhim Singh (r. 1778–1828) in a love scene with a woman on a swing with two large mirrors on either side.[49] Swings were particularly popular in monsoon times and are associated with love-making. A photograph of the *Chini-ki-chitrashali* taken in 1882 shows rings in the ceilings of the porcelain cabinet, which were typically used to attach *jhulas* (swings). A mural in the adjacent *chitram-ki-burj* (picture tower) depicts a night view of the porcelain cabinet with Maharana Bhim Singh seated on a swing in the presence of several female attendants.[50] The mural shows that the porcelain cabinet was used by the ruler for private meetings with women of the *zenana* and accentuates a time of passion, serenity, intimacy and leisure at night. Carpets and blinds add texture, warmth and richness to the room (Figure 11.4).

That these global objects and materials were primarily valued for their exotic and foreign quality can also be seen by the decoration of the *chowk* (inner courtyard) that the *Chini ki chitrashali* overlooks: the murals

Figure 11.4 Mural in the *Chitram ki Burj*, City Palace Udaipur, depicting Maharana Bhim Singh (r. 1778–1828) with gold nimbus depicted on a *jhula* (swing) in the *jharokha* of the *Chini ki Chitrashali* with several female attendants, City Palace Udaipur, no date. Photograph: Dr Joachim K. Bautze, Berlin.

of the courtyard walls – probably established in the nineteenth century – are adorned with glass mosaics depicting Europeans and Indian-looking females carrying Dutch green gin bottles, which connects the *farangi* theme with the porcelain room.[51] Boxes of gin bottles were typical diplomatic gifts given by Dutch traders. The murals with the *farangi* theme are interrupted by windows offering a view of the lake and the *Jag niwas* lake palace, allowing the unique water landscape to be carried over into the interiors and blending the local with the wider world.

Contemporary use of porcelain rooms

Murals and miniature paintings offer important insights into the use and role of porcelain cabinets depicting small durbar scenes with courtiers, musical performances, *nautch* dances and games at night, suggesting an intimate, private use. The porcelain cabinet was used for special occasions, such as the birthday celebrations of a male child, where the Maharana was seated in the *jarokha*, to be viewed by the public from the *Manek Chowk* below.[52] The actual porcelain pavilion was reserved for the Maharana and his most important courtiers or ladies while others were located in the adjacent courtyard, part of the architectural ensemble of the porcelain cabinet. The painter's interpretation of the scenes allows the viewer to catch a glimpse of the mood and atmosphere there.

In a miniature created by the painter Shiva in 1764, Maharana Ari Sing (r. 1761–73) is seated with a hookah in front of a porcelain cabinet above the *Surya Mahal* (Sun apartment) that prominently displays a solar symbol (Figure 11.5). Referred to as *Bari Chitrasali*, or 'great porcelain hall', the second porcelain cabinet was established under Maharana Jagat Singh II (r. 1734–51) and shows the evolution of this specific room type. This porcelain cabinet is shown on a terrace in the

Figure 11.5 *Shiva, Maharana Ari Singh seated at night. On the terrace of* the *Chini ki Chitrashali* (1764), opaque watercolour heightened with gold on paper, 62 cm × 48 cm. Simon Ray, Gateway Gallery, London, UK.

miniature painting, which was later incorporated into the *Pitam Niwas* Apartments (Abode of Delight). The Chinese tiles are identical to those used in the earlier eighteenth-century porcelain cabinet. They are still depicted in several paintings in the nineteenth century and mentioned in Fateh Lal Mehta's *Handbook* of 1888 but were removed at a later date.[53]

In this painting, as in similar paintings where the porcelain cabinet features as the background for social gatherings, the Maharana is shown in front of the porcelain pavilion, accentuating its significance. Molly Emma Aitken summarises the underlying design strategies poignantly in reference to a similar scene of 1765 (Figure 11.6): 'the tiles Dutch and Chinese were in reality a statement of the maharana's worldly connection and cosmopolitan sophistication and they repeat their message here'.[54] The more scenic rendering of some of the tiles in the 1765 miniature painting might be an artistic liberty rather than an indication of actual Dutch tiles because in the 1755, 1762, 1764 and 1829 images of the porcelain cabinet only Chinese tiles are shown.[55]

Figure 11.6 *Bakhta, Maharana Ari Singh II in durbar* (1765), opaque watercolour and gold paint on paper, 58 cm × 46.2 cm. Accession no: AS183-1980, National Gallery of Victoria, Melbourne, Australia.

The discrepancy in several architectural details could indicate that some parts of the paintings were made from memory and that the focus was on the Maharana, his courtiers and the actual event being depicted. In the 1764 and 1765 miniatures we see a more formal durbar arrangement with courtiers, whereas in the earlier 1762 painting we see the Maharana inside the porcelain cabinet playing *Chaupar* (an earlier version of pachisi) in a more informal setting. In all cases the porcelain cabinet and Surya Mahal seem to be part of a stand-alone scene: no other parts of the palace are visible. In all three paintings showing Maharana Ari Singh (r. 1761–73) in the *bari chitrashala* the events take place at night. In 1762 the scene takes place at dusk indicated by pink clouds; in 1764 we see a monsoon scene with clouds and lightning, and in 1765 there is a black sky. The 1761 scene of Maharana Ari Singh attending a *nautch* (dance) at the *chini-ki-chitrashali* is also set at night.[56] The overall effect of the night views is to bring the focus onto the interior world of the porcelain cabinet where the Maharana and his courtiers, in intimate settings, become the centre of attention. Interior and architectural details are highlighted by bright and brilliant colours, in contrast to the darkness of the night. Red and gold are used for carpets, the balustrade of the porcelain cabinet and other architectural details, just as orange is used for the turban or part of the garments of the courtiers, or the *nautch* or dancing girls (usually courtesans). The bright lacquer red of the interior scene is continued in the frame, typical of Udaipur miniature paintings.[57]

The monsoon setting in the 1764 painting, with its bursting clouds and snail-like flashes of lightning, embodies a time of powerful emotions. Feelings could oscillate between the joyful time of fulfilled love, united lovers and abundance – often personified by depictions of Radha and Krishna – and *ashta nayika* scenes (referring to the eight different heroines which represent different female lovers based on several Sanskrit texts) of loneliness, separation from the lover, neglect, disappointed love or longing for the lover. The dialectic of monsoon feelings is accompanied by a rich history of monsoon poetry, music and paintings. Images of lovers, dancing peacocks, bursting clouds, black skies, cascades of white rain drops and love scenes with empty beds and swings are used as stimulants to evoke specific emotions in the viewer.[58] The connection between the emotions and eroticism of the monsoon on the one hand, and porcelain rooms on the other, is further accentuated by miniature paintings of porcelain rooms on monsoon terraces or during the monsoon. The Chinese porcelain cabinet in the miniature painting of 1764 can also be identified as a monsoon terrace, which was typically used to celebrate and view the monsoon. Given the complex underlying cultural meanings of the monsoon, we can further associate the blue and white Chinese tiles with the water world of Udaipur. The clouds in the painting add drama to what might otherwise be regarded as a glimpse into courtly life. On the right-hand side of the painting, an arched movable structure is shown, reminiscent of a similar object in another painting from *c.* 1761 described as a 'golden chamber with drawn curtains for privacy' used for love-making.[59] Although we cannot know for certain, it is possible that the object is a portable chamber allowing a glimpse inside showing an empty bed, which would also make it a stimulant for a monsoon scene. There are no female figures depicted in the scene, except for two women in the form of a striking gold relief on the doors in the background of the porcelain pavilion.

The connection between porcelain rooms and the sensual experience of water and the monsoon can also be seen in other Rajput palaces such as the Badal Mahal (Cloud Palace) at Junagarh Fort in Bikaner. Decorated with paintings of clouds and lightning, it is also embellished with fragments of Blue Willow Pattern porcelain tiles cut from English transfer ware.[60] This tableware was possibly purchased by Maharaja Ratan Singh (r. 1828–51) of Bikaner as the interior decoration of the 'porcelain rooms' was completed between 1872 and 1887.[61]

The transformation of porcelain rooms in the nineteenth century

In the second half of the nineteenth century, several other porcelain rooms adorned with Blue Willow Pattern plates emerge. The most prominent example of a room furnished entirely with European porcelain plates is Fateh Prakash Palace within the City Palace complex in Udaipur (Figure 11.7). The room is covered with 378 Staffordshire Willow Pattern plates, installed under Maharana Swarup Singh (r. 1842–61).[62] Decorated in a symmetrical pattern, the space between the plates is embellished with an ornamental floral glass mural in an Indian *sheesh mahal* aesthetic. A border of Kangxi Chinese export tiles applied throughout the room is identical with the tiles used in the earlier eighteenth century *chini-ki-chitra-shali* and establishes a direct connection and revival of this design principle. A bright lacquer red border adds a visual surprise reminiscent of the borders of eighteenth-century miniature paintings from the palace atelier which captured courtly life, palace interiors and the general mood and atmosphere.

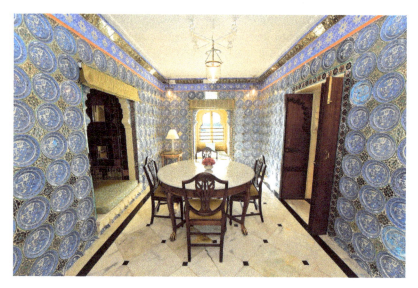

Figure 11.7 Porcelain room furnished with Staffordshire Blue Willow Pattern plates in the second part of the nineteenth century under Maharana Swarup Singh (1815, r. 1842–61), City Palace Udaipur. Photograph December 2022, reproduced with thanks to Mohanchandran Kottarapurath Taj Fateh Prakash Palace Hotel.

These nineteenth-century global objects and materials in the porcelain rooms at City Palace again correlate with the encounters of specific visitors. Just as the Dutch embassy reception was connected with Dutch and Chinese export tiles, the increasing presence of the British in the nineteenth century resulted in the incorporation of objects from Britain. Blue Willow Pattern became the most ubiquitous design in the West and was industrially produced in large quantities. In 1852, Charles Dickens captured its ubiquity in 'A Plated Article', written for his weekly *Household Words*: 'that amusing blue landscape, which has, in deference to our revered ancestors of the Cerulean Empire and in defiance of every known law of perspective adorned millions of our family since the days of the platters'.[63] Yet while Dickens asserts how the formerly exotic design has now become familiar and popular, the plates were unfamiliar and novel in India. The fact that plates associated with European dining practices were used in place of tiles adds another novel dimension to the interior as Indian palaces increasingly introduced European-style dining rooms and dinnerware to entertain European visitors. The nineteenth-century porcelain rooms in Rajput palaces are thus examples of a larger transformation of lifestyles and more interactions with foreigners, foreign products, travel, art, books and newspapers.

As the largest palace in Rajasthan, City Palace Udaipur had an impact on other palaces, and the Blue Willow Pattern plates found their way to the *Diwan-i-Khas* (private audience chamber) at the Juna Mahal in Dungarpur. Artisans from City Palace Udaipur were at times employed at Juna Mahal, which accounts for the similarities. In Dungarpur the porcelain cabinet was part of the enclosed upper balcony of the private audience chamber introduced by the ruler of Dungarpur Mahrawal Udai Singh II (r. 1846–98) in the second half of the nineteenth century – possibly between 1883 and 1886.[64] The fact that this rather small section of the room had its own designation, *Chini Gokhada* (Chinese balcony), accentuates its important role in the eyes of the ruler. A total of 144 Staffordshire Blue Willow Pattern plates were embedded in four interior walls of the *gokhada* and embellished with additional murals and mirror work. The European artistic imagination of Chinese porcelain was 'Indianised' by adding stylised painted floral ornamental features between the plates and mirror elements reminiscent of a *sheesh mahal* or mirror cabinet inspired by Udaipur (Figure 11.8). A complementary colour scheme is used, with ornamental painted details in red and green. The painted and inlaid plate incorporates an Indian miniature painting under glass, changing the narrative of the Blue Willow Pattern. It is not the pagoda, willow tree, bridge or lovers that are at the centre of the narrative but the ruler himself, seated at leisure in an idyllic garden and

Figure 11.8 Blue Willow Pattern plates, detail of the *Chini Gokhada*, Juna Mahal, Dungarpur. © Paulus Veltman and Anja Brunt.

revered by visitors. The exoticism of the object adds to the distinction of the ruler but is reinterpreted: the unfamiliar narrative is changed by shifting the focus onto the ruler of Dungarpur, accentuating the audience character and role of diplomacy of the room. Other murals at Juna Mahal depict blue and white Chinese porcelain vessels that appear to be Chinese from a distance yet portray Indian architecture – establishing an Indian type of chinoiserie.

The audience hall and *Chini gokhada* were reserved for meetings with distinguished guests such as Maharao Shatrusal (r. 1886–9) of Kota.[65] It was consequently one of the most richly decorated rooms, with various murals including glass work. Murals of important visitors, including foreigners, add worldliness to the interior and underline the function of the room. In Dungapur, the *Chini gokhada* was still used as a private durbar hall in the late nineteenth century: overlooking the *Kothar Chowk* (storage area), where the general public was invited and public spectacles were performed, Maharawal Udai Singh II would view the performance from the *Chini Gokhada* above.[66]

A description of the daily routine of the ruler Maharawal Udai Singh II (r. 1846–98) sheds further light on its use:

> Having refreshed himself, he attended to court matters in the *Diwan-e-Aam* [public audience hall] from 1pm to 4pm, where all his eight ministers reported through the Prime Minister about their work. This was also the time when poets, scholars, artists, etc. met him. Traders from outside, including far off places like Kabul and Nepal, offered their wares, which included their animals and birds … At this time of the day sometimes music was played in the palace. … He gave audiences to people and heard their complaints after returning in the evening and then again attended to court work in the *Diwan-e-Khaas* [private audience hall], where he heard discussion or discourses on scriptures. Newspapers from different places were read out to him through officers in the English Office and correspondence received from British Officers and Rulers of other States was dealt with.[67]

Conclusion

The world came into the audience hall and porcelain cabinet in the form of newspapers, letters, visitors (including foreigners) and, last but not least, global objects. Porcelain rooms in Rajput palaces from the early eighteenth century to the second half of the nineteenth century reflect global contact and cross-cultural exchange. From imagination to caricature and design innovation to status, cosmopolitan aesthetics in Rajput interiors reveal a willingness to engage with difference and the world at large. Porcelain rooms in Rajput palaces could provide settings for diplomacy, celebrations, games, music, dances and other night-time entertainments, as well as spaces for intimate and erotic meetings. The multiple worlds associated with porcelain cabinets combined familiar and local environs with the novel and the world at large, the past and the present. Despite their novelty, they reflect their topography and the cultural associations of their locality and of the seasons. At times the cultural memory of the aesthetic associated with porcelain rooms in Central Asia and Mughal Asia found its way into the porcelain cabinet almost unconsciously, where it coalesced with the tribute to past rulers or powerful courts.

Chinese export porcelain and European ceramics with a chinoiserie motif were reinterpreted and integrated into a new context and an Indian aesthetic sensibility. They were no longer consumer goods but were integrated into both the interior world of buildings and the domestic life of their inhabitants. Not their original meaning but their rarity, novelty and decorative exotic quality stood in the foreground – as it did with chinoiserie designs in Europe. Exotic objects were paired with other global objects and materials and combined with a *farangi* theme depicting the very foreigners that were associated with the trade, production and use of these objects. Foreigners were considered just as interesting in their exoticness as the objects themselves and became part of elaborate decorative design schemes over an extended period of time. Porcelain rooms sparked creativity and innovation in the art and interiors of Rajput courtly life and are examples of negotiating cosmopolitan taste with local culture.

Notes

1 Publications on the built environment in India have favoured surveys of architecture as opposed to comprehensive publications dedicated to the historic interior. See Reuther, *Indische Paläste*; Tillotson, *Rajput Palaces*; Michell and Martinelli, *Royal Palaces of India*; Nossov, *Indian Castles*. On Mughal architecture see Asher, *Architecture of Mughal India*; Koch, *Mughal Architecture*; Fergusson, *History of Indian and Eastern Architecture*.
2 I am grateful to Joachim Bautze for drawing my attention to Kishangarh.
3 Topsfield, 'Ketelaar's embassy'; Bautze, 'Maharana Sangram Singh'. See also Bautze, 'Representation of Europeans'.
4 Chaudhuri, *Asia before Europe*, 332–3.
5 Chida-Razvi, 'From function to form', 82. See also an entry on mid-fifteenth-century tiles produced at Jingdezhen, now at the British Museum: https://www.britishmuseum.org/

collection/object/A_1993-1027-1-2, accessed 9 February 2022. For further information on Ulugh Begh's *Chini khana* see Golombek, 'Paysage as funerary imagery'.
6 Golombek, 'Paysage as funerary imagery', 251.
7 Chida-Razvi, 'From function to form'.
8 Koch, *Mughal Architecture*, 70. On the *Chini khana* in Mughal architecture see Koch, 'Painted and sculptured decoration'.
9 Guy, 'China in India', 49f.
10 Guy, 'China in India', 61.
11 Titley, *Ni'matnama Manuscript*, 25.
12 Guy, 'China in India', 61.
13 Morton, 'Ardabīl Shrine', 36, 32f; Pope, *Chinese Porcelains*, 7 and 49f.
14 On the description of the Ali Qapu music room, the materiality and acoustics see Azad, 'Ali Qapu'.
15 Robinson, 'Shāh 'Abbās', 58–63.
16 Friedrich Sarre, *Denkmäler persischer Baukunst*, vol. 2, (Berlin, 1919), 41, quoted in Pope, *Chinese Porcelains*, 17; Treanor, 'Amalia van Solms', 144.
17 Monti, *Der Preis des "weißen Goldes"*, 69. Bischoff, 'Japanese Palace', 134, gives the total number of 50,000–60,000.
18 Claxton, 'Countess of Arundel's Dutch pranketing room', 190. This is confirmed by Bischoff, 'Japanese Palace', 136.
19 Burchmore, 'Maladie de Porcelaine', 264f.
20 Reidemeister, 'Die Porzellankabinette', 55 and 46; Wittwer, 'Ein Spiel zwischen Schein und Sein', 84.
21 Reidemeister, 'Die Porzellankabinette', 55.
22 The dates are based on Topsfield, *Museums of India*, 14.
23 Tod, *Annals and Antiquities of Rajasthan*, 172.
24 Mehta, *Handbook of Mewar*, 16–19.
25 The date 1716 is mentioned in Cole, *First Report*, 23. The same year is mentioned in Goetz, 'Holländische Wandfliesen', 240; 1723 is mentioned in Topsfield, *Museums of India*, 355.
26 Note that the name or designation of rooms or apartments could change: the porcelain cabinet also had other designations such as '*Badi Chatur Shala*' or *Choti Chitrashali* (small picture hall) when it was compared with the second porcelain cabinet installed above the Surya Mahal.
27 Goetz, 'Holländische Wandfliesen' 239: 'In den meisten alten Palästen Vorder-Indiens sind im obersten Stockwerk ein order mehrere reichverzierte Eckzimmer dem Privatleben des Herrschers reserviert, wo er auch die Frauen seines Harems zu empfangen pflegte. Manchmal nur ein kleiner Saal, meister aber ein Hof mit Gallerie, Festsaal und zwei intimen Zimmerchen, sind diese üppigen Räume jedes Palastes über und über mit Glasmosaik und Malereien bedeckt (daher Chitrasala genannt), welche meist Szenen aus dem Frauenleben, der irdischen and himmlischen Liebe, sowie musikalische Stimmungen darstellten. Dazwischen mischen sich aber auch andere Raritäten, europäische Stiche, konvexe Spiegel usw' (translation by author).
28 Bautze, 'Depiction of Europeans'.
29 Diamond and Khera, *Splendid Land*, 30.
30 Krahl and Ayers, *Chinese Ceramics*. The same tile can also be found in an art gallery in the UK: https://www.chinese-porcelain-art.com/item/Q691/blue-and-white-tile-18th-century/ (accessed on 26 April 2022). Their origin is unclear: Purohit, *Mewar History*, 13, suggests that they were bought through the Portuguese, but no source is mentioned.
31 Asher, 'Sub-imperial palaces', 282f.; Zaweed, 'Rajput architecture', 400.
32 Vidal 'Darshan'. In the courtly context of applying the concept of *darshan* to a ruler see Aitken, *Intelligence of Tradition*, 135f.
33 Vogel, *Journaal van Ketelaar*, 2.
34 For dates of the actual time spent in Udaipur, see Topsfield, 'Ketelaar's embassy', 365.
35 On gift-giving and diplomacy in the context of the Dutch East India Company see Swan, *Rareties of These Lands*.
36 Gottlieb Worm and Weise, *Ost-Indian-und Persianische Reisen*, 251.
37 Kopie-staats van de uitgaven op de hofreis naar de groot-mogol in 1710–1713 voor Joan Josua Ketelaar en van de geschenken van de VOC aan dit hof 1716, National Archives, Netherlands, https://www.nationaalarchief.nl/en/research/archive/1.04.02/invnr/%40Deel%20II~Deel%20II%7C%7CI~Deel%20II%7C%7CI.2~Deel%20

II%7C%7CI.2.1~Deel%20II%7C%7CI.2.1.23~11321 (accessed 23 February 2022). On the reception of European glass at Mughal courts see Markel, 'Western imports'; on East Asian gifts presented by the British to the Mughal emperor in 1618 see Foster, *Embassy of Sir Thomas Roe*, 459.
38 Vogel, *Journaal van Ketelaar*, 6. On Donna Juliana see also Zaman, 'Visions of Juliana'; and Irvine and d'Eremao, 'Note on Bibi Juliana'.
39 Vogel, *Journaal van Ketelaar*, 10.
40 Vogel, *Journaal van Ketelaar*, 10.
41 Vogel, *Journaal van Ketelaar*, 387; cf. Topsfield, 'Ketelaar's embassy', 352.
42 Topsfield, 'Ketelaar's embassy', 350–67; Bautze, 'Maharana Sangram Singh'.
43 *Maharana Sangram Singh receives the Embassy of Johan Josua Ketelaar, c.* 1711, painting on cloth, 161.3 cm × 120 cm, Udaipur, Victoria & Albert Museum, London.
44 *Winged Dutchman riding a Composite Camel, Mewar India, c.* 1725, 2006AG1925, Victoria & Albert Museum, London.
45 On the significance of the turban in Dutch visual culture in the context of diplomacy and trade see Swan, *Rareties of These Lands*, 128f.
46 *Queen being Entertained by Ladies in European Costumes*, Mughal, 1742, Collection of Edwin Binney, San Diego.
47 Painting of a European couple with black dots in the face (*c.* 1720), Udaipur, British Museum, museum number 1956,0714,0.27.
48 Bischoff, 'Women collectors, 171. I am grateful to Joachim Bautze for drawing my attention to this mural and for providing images and translating the inscription.
49 See Maharana Bhim Singh with a rani (queen) or pasawan (high-ranking mistress), inscribed to Chokha, dated 1803, Udaipur, Mewar. Opaque watercolour and gold on paper, dimensions unavailable. Faculty of Fine Arts, Baroda; and Maharana Bhim Singh with a rani or pasawan, attributed to Chokha, *c.* 1800–10, Udaipur, Opaque watercolour and gold on paper, Francesca Galloway Ltd., London.
50 The date and name of the Maharana is unclear. It is most likely Maharana Bhim Singh (r. 1778–1828) based on other portraits.
51 The gin bottles have also been identified by Topsfield, 'Ketelaar's embassy', 355. It is possible that some of these glass bottles were produced in Dutch factories in Gujarat: see Markel, 'Western imports', 55. On a discussion of glass bottles in India at the time see Um, 'Nested containers'.
52 In a painting at City Palace Museum Udaipur, Maharana Sangram Singh is celebrating the birth of Prince Pratap Singh in the *Chini ki Chitrashali, c.* 1724. See Topsfield, *Museums of India*, 30f.
53 Mehta, *Handbook of Mewar*, 16–19. Depictions of the tiles can be seen in *Maharana Bhim Sing of Mewar ties his Turban*, attributed to Chokha, *c.* 1810, Harvard Art Museum, Cambridge, MA, accession no 1999.03.
54 Aitken, *Intelligence of Tradition*, 151.
55 See Ragunath, son of Maluk Chand, 'Maharana Raj Singh II (1754–1761) receiving Maharao Durjan Sal of Kotah in Durbar in December 1755', Udaipur, 1756, in: *Indian Miniatures: The Property of the British Rail Pension Fund* (London: Sotheby's, 1994): Lot 39. 'Maharana Ari Singh at Leisure with his Nobles in the Palace' (1762) *Simon Ray Indian & Islamic Works of Art* catalogue, 2015, 110–15, cat. no. 48. Shiva, Maharana Ari Singh seated at night. On the terrace of the Chini ki chitrasali (1764, opaque watercolour heightened with gold on paper, 62 cm × 48 cm, Simon Ray, Gateway Gallery, London, UK). *Bakhta, Maharana Ari Singh II in durbar,* (1765, opaque watercolour and gold paint on paper, 58 cm × 46.2 cm, accession no: AS183–1980, National Gallery of Victoria, Melbourne, Australia. Maharana Bhim Singh receiving British officers in the Mor Chowk, Udaipur, *c.* 1827, in Topsfield, *Museums of India*, 73.
56 Maharana Ari Singh (1761–73) attending a *nautch* in the Chini-ki-chitrashali by Bhima, 1761, in *Sotheby's London, Persian and Indian Manuscripts and Miniatures: From the Collection formed by the British Rail Pension Fund* (London, Sotheby's, auction catalogue, 1996), lot 49. I am indebted to Joachim Bautze, who brought this painting to my attention.
57 I am grateful to Joachim Bautze, who pointed out that the same red frame can be found in Kotah miniatures and has been analysed and found to have also been used for the practical reason to repel insects.
58 See Orsini, 'Clouds, cuckoos and an empty bed', 100.

59 Maharana Ari Singh II of Mewar (r. 1761–73) with his Consort on a terrace, gum tempera and gold on paper, *c.* 1761, The Cleveland Museum of Art.
60 See Goetz, *Art and Architecture*; Hoexter and Siddall, 'English transfer printed earthenware'.
61 Hoexter and Siddall, 'English transfer printed earthenware', 21.
62 Topsfield, *Court Painting at Udaipur*, 254–5; Ray, *Indian and Islamic Art*, 60.
63 Lanone, '"Toujours la porcelaine"'.
64 This information is based on research of the late archivist Mahesh Purohit. See also Imig and Purohit, *Juna Mahal Dungarpur*, 129.
65 See Purohit, *History of Juna Mahal Dungarpur*, 33.
66 Purohit, *History of Juna Mahal Dungarpur*, 24.
67 No direct source is mentioned for this description, but the book is based on research at Maharawal Bijay Singh Research Archives, Udai Bilas Palace, Dungarpur. See Purohit, *History of Juna Mahal Dungarpur*, 64f.

Bibliography

Aitken, Emma. *The Intelligence of Tradition in Rajput Court Painting.* New Haven: Yale University Press, 2010.
Asher, Catherine. *Architecture of Mughal India.* Cambridge: Cambridge University Press, 1992.
Asher, Catherine. 'Sub-imperial palaces: power and authority in Mughal India', *Ars Orientalis* 23 (1993): 281–302.
Azad, Hassan. 'Ali Qapu: Persian historical music room', *Akutek, Proceedings of the Institute of Acoustics*, University of Teheran, https://www.akutek.info/Papers/HA_Persian.pdf, accessed on 11 February 2022.
Bautze, Joachim. 'Maharana Sangram Singh of Udaipur entertaining members of the Dutch East India Company led by Johan Josua Ketelaar', *Bulletin van Het Rijksmuseum* 36, no. 2 (1988): 117–32.
Bautze, Joachim. 'Representation of Europeans in Rajasthani murals', presentation at the *Centre for Historic Houses of India* on 16 November 2021. Available at https://youtu.be/-jP5xy9NtKo.
Bischoff, Cordula. 'Women collectors and the rise of the porcelain cabinet'. In *Chinese and Japanese porcelain for the Dutch Golden Age*. Edited by: Jan van Campen and Titus Eliëens, 171–89. Zwolle: Waanders, 2014.
Bischoff, Cordula. 'The Japanese Palace in Dresden: a highlight of European 18th century craze for East Asia', *Ritsumeikan Studies in Language and Culture*, 30, no. 3 (2019): 133–48.
Burchmore, Alex. 'La Maladie de Porcelaine: Liu Jianhua Regular/Fragile (2007) at Oxburgh Hall and the history of massed porcelain display in English aristocratic interiors', *Oxford Art Journal* 42, no. 3 (2019): 253–81.
Chaudhuri, K.N. *Asia before Europe: Economy and civilisation in the Indian Ocean from the rise of Islam to 1750.* Cambridge: Cambridge University Press, 1990.
Chida-Razvi, Mehreen. 'From function to form: Chini khana in Safavid and Mughal architecture', *South Asian Studies* 35, no. 1 (2019): 82–106.
Claxton, Juliet. 'The Countess of Arundel's Dutch pranketing room', *Journal of the History of Collections* 22, no. 2 (2010): 187–96.
Cole, H.H. *First Report of the Curator of Ancient Monuments in India for the Year 1881–82.* Simla: Government Central Branch Press, 1888.
Diamond, Debra, and Dipti Khera, eds. *A Splendid Land: Paintings from royal Udaipur.* Munich: Hirmer Verlag, 2022.
Koch, Ebba. *Mughal Architecture: An outline of its history and development 1526–1858.* Delhi: Primus Books, 2014.
Fergusson, James. *History of Indian and Eastern Architecture.* London: John Murray, 1891.
Foster, W., ed. *The Embassy of Sir Thomas Roe to the Court of the Great Mogul (1615–1619).* London: Hakluyt Society, 1899.
Galdieri, Eugenio. *Esfahan, Ali Qapu: An architectural survey.* Rome: Ismeo, 1979.
Gill, Maninder. 'Glazed tiles from Lodhi and Mughal northern India: a technological appraisal', PhD dissertation, UCL Qatar, 2015.
Goetz, Hermann. *Art and Architecture of Bikaner State.* Oxford: Bruno Cassirer, 1950.

Goetz, Hermann. 'Holländische Wandfliesen in einem altindischen Königspalast', *Oud Holland* 66 (1951): 239–40.
Golombek, Lisa. 'The paysage as funerary imagery in the Timurid', *Muqarnas Online* 10, no. 1 (1992): 241–52.
Gottlieb Worm, Johann, and Crispin Weise, eds. *Ost-Indian-und Persianische Reisen: Oder Zehenjährige auf Groß Java, Bengala und in Gefolge Herrn Joann Josuä Kotelär geleistete Kriegsdienste.* Frankfurt and Leipzig, 1745.
Guy, John. 'China in India: porcelain trade and attitudes to collecting in early Islamic India'. In *China and Southeast Asia: Historical interactions*, edited by Geoff Wade and James K. Chin, 44–84. Abingdon and New York: Routledge, 2019.
Hoexter, David, and Judie Siddall. 'English transfer printed earthenware at Junagarh Fort, Bikaner, Rajasthan, India: an extraordinary occurrence', *TCC Bulletin* 21, no. 3 (2020): 11–28.
Imig, Klaus, and Mahesh Purohit. *Juna Mahal Dungarpur: Ein Rajputen-Palast in Rajasthan*. Zurich: Museum Rietberg, 2006.
Irvine, William, and P. Val d'Eremao. 'Note on Bibi Juliana and the Christians at Agrah', *Journal of the Royal Asiatic Society of Great Britain and Ireland* (April 1903): 355–8.
Jonge, J. de. 'Hollandse Tegelkamers in: Duitse En Franse Kastelen', *Nederlands Kunsthistorisch Jaarboek Online* 10 (1959): 125–209.
Kamermans, Johan. 'Dutch tiles, the beginning of an export: new findings with reference to the tile works of Jan Van Oort'. In *Azulejaria Na Região Centro. Cadernos Municipais, Figueira Da Foz, Património*, edited by Maria De Lurdes Craveiro and Inês Maria Jordão, 45–61. Figuera: Cadernos Muncipais, 2019.
Koch, Ebba. 'Notes on the painted and sculptured decoration of Nur Jahan's pavilions in the Ram Bagh (Bagh-I Nur Afshan) at Agra'. In *Facets of Indian Art*, edited by Robert Skelton, Andrew Topsfield, Susan Stronge and Rosemary Crill, 51–65. London: Victoria & Albert Museum, 1986.
Krahl, Regina, and John Ayers. *Chinese Ceramics in the Topkapi Saray Museum, Istanbul*. London and New York: Harper and Row, 1986.
Lanone, Catherine. '"Toujours la porcelain": George Meredith and the Willow Pattern', *Miranda* [Online], https://journals.openedition.org/miranda/4450, accessed on 13 April 2022.
Markel, Stephen. 'Western imports and the nature of later Indian glassware', *Asian Arts* 6 (Fall 1993): 34–59.
Markel, Stephen. 'Once the capital of India: the great fort of Daulatabad', *Orientations* 25, no. 2 (1994): 47–52.
Mehta, Fateh Lal. *The Handbook of Mewar and Guide to Its Principal Objects of Interest*. Bombay, 1888, second edition 1902.
Michell, George, and Antonio Martinelli. *The Royal Palaces of India*. New York and London: Thames and Hudson, 1994.
Monti, Alessandro. *Der Preis des "weißen Goldes": Preispolitik und -strategie im Merkantilsystem am Beispiel der Porzellanmanufactur Meissen 1710–1830*. Munich and Oldenburg: Wissenschaftsverlag, 2011.
Morton, A.H. 'The Ardabīl Shrine in the reign of Shāh Ṭahmāsp I', *Iran* 12 (1974): 31–64.
Nossov, Konstantin. *Indian Castles: The rise and fall of the Delhi sultanate*. Oxford: Osprey, 2006.
Orsini, Francesca. 'Clouds, cuckoos and an empty bed: emotions in Hindi–Urdu Barahmasas'. In *Monsoon Feelings: A history of emotions in the rain*, edited by Imke Rajmani, Margit Pernau and Katherine Butler, 97–137. New Delhi: Nyogi, 2016.
Pope, John. *Chinese Porcelains from the Ardebil Shrine*. Smithsonian Institution Freer Gallery of Art. Washington, DC: The Lord Baltimore Press, 1956.
Purohit, Dev Nath. *Mewar History: Guide to Udaipur*. Bombay: The Times of India Press, 1938.
Purohit, Mahesh. *History of Juna Mahal Dungarpur*. Atharva: Dungarpur, 2019.
Ray, Simon. *Indian and Islamic Art*. London: Simon Ray Gallery, 2016.
Reidemeister, L. 'Die Porzellankabinette der brandenburgisch-preußischen Schlösser'. *Jahrbuch Der Preuszichen Kunstsammlungen*, 55 (1934): 42–56.
Reuther, Oscar. *Indische Paläste und Wohnhäuser*. Berlin: Leonhard Preiss, 1925.
Robinson, B.W. 'Shāh 'Abbās and the Mughal Ambassador Khān 'Ālam: the pictorial record', *The Burlington Magazine* 114, no. 827 (1972): 58–63.
Sarre, Friedrich, *Denkmäler persischer Baukunst*. Berlin: Wasmuth, 1919.
Smith, Edmund W. *Moghul Colour Decoration of Agra*. Allahabad, Supdt.: Government Press, 1901.
Swan, Claudia. *Rareties of These Lands*. Princeton: Princeton University Press, 2021.

Tillotson, Giles. *Rajput Palaces: the Development of an Architectural Style, 1450–1750*. Oxford: Oxford University Press, 1999.

Titley, Norah. *The Ni'matnama Manuscript of the Sultans of Mandu: The Sultan's Book of Delights*. London: Routledge, 2004.

Tod, James. *Annals and Antiquities of Rajasthan: or the Central and Western Rajput States of India*. London: Smith, 1829.

Topsfield, Andrew. 'Ketelaar's embassy and the farangi theme in the art of Udaipur', *Oriental Art*, NS 30, no. 4 (1984/85): 350–67.

Topsfield, Andrew. *Museums of India: The City Palace Museum Udaipur: Paintings of Mewar court life*. Ahmedabad: Mapin, 2009.

Topsfield, Andrew. *Court Painting at Udaipur: Art under the patronage of the Maharanas of Mewar*. Ahmedabad: Mapin, 2002.

Treanor, Virginia C. 'Amalia van Solms and the formation of the Stadhouder's Art Collection, 1625–1675', PhD dissertation, University of Maryland, 2012.

Um, Nancy. 'Nested containers for maritime journeys: tools of aromatic diplomacy around the late 17th and early 18th century Indian Ocean', *West 86th* 25, no. 2 (2018), https://www.west86th.bgc.bard.edu/articles/nested-containers/.

Vidal, Denis. 'Darshan'. In *Key Concepts in Modern Indian Studies*, edited by Gita Dharampal-Frick, Monika Kirloskar-Steinbach, Rachel Dwyer and Jahnavi Phalkey. New York: New York University Press, 2015.

Vogel, J.P., ed. 'Embassy of Mr. Johan Josua Ketelaar, Ambassador of the Dutch East India Company to the Great Moguls – Shah Alam Bahadur Shah', translated by D. Kuenen-Wicksteed, *Journal of the Panjab Historical Society*, 10:L (1929): 1–95.

Wittwer, Samuel. 'Ein Spiel zwischen Schein und Sein – Die Porzellankammer von Schloss Charlottenburg im Wandel', *Jahrbuch Stiftung preussischer Schlösser und Gärten Berlin Brandenburg* 7 (2005): 83–93.

Zaman, Taymiya. 'Visions of Juliana: a Portuguese woman at the court of the Mughals', *Journal of World History* 23, no. 4 (2012): 761–91.

Zaweed, Salim. 'Rajput architecture of the Mewar from the 13th to the 18th centuries', *Proceedings of the Indian History Congress* 73 (2012): 400–7.

Object lessons 3
Symbols and symbolism

XI
The new worlds' gate
Gaia Bruno

Figure OL.XI Antonio Niccolini (?), the main entrance of La Floridiana, nineteenth century, pencil and charcoal. Naples, Certosa e Museo Nazionale di S. Martino

On the hill of Vomero in Naples there is a park famous from the beginning of nineteenth century for its collection of exotic plants from all around the world. Between 1816 and 1817, King Ferdinando I Borbone, restored on his throne after ten years of Napoleonic domination, bought the estate for his second wife, Lucia Migliaccio, Duchess of Floridia. The villa was reorganised by the Tuscan architect Antonio Niccolini,[1] who was very active in Naples at the time, working on other important projects such as the renovation of the opera theatre San Carlo. Initially employed as scenographer, Niccolini designed the building in neoclassical style. For the park, he looked to the English landscape garden, trying to combine two kinds of spaces: the first picturesque, where wild nature could bloom, accompanied by statues, mock ruins and benches; the second one with a more structured articulation, open to the breath-taking scenery of the gulf of Naples. He sought to create a dialogue with nature. The most distinctive feature of the park was its collection of exotic plants. The new owners, the king and the duchess, enriched the exotic collection with 150 new specimens. The main route to the house, for example, was lined by two avenues of *Robinia pseudoacacia*, a north American tree, while in the greenhouse pineapples were cultivated at least until 1825, when the duchess died.

In order to symbolise the exoticism of the park, Niccolini designed an iron gate surmounted by two gold pineapples to be put at the main entrance. Between the two exotic fruits, made of gilded wrought iron, stood the name of the villa: 'La Floridiana'. The gate, which still exists, is depicted in Nicolini's original sketch made with pencil and charcoal on paper (Figure OL.XI).[2] In the sketch, two agave plants – themselves natives of Central America and the Caribbean, and today replaced by two stone panthers – were placed beyond the pineapples. They have the optical function of making the exotic fruits appear bigger and more visible, an effect achieved by repeating their shapes.

According to some scholars, the pineapples on the gate had the purpose of wishing good luck,[3] but the meaning is actually more complicated. Indeed, the pineapple was a complex symbol of globalisation in the early modern world.[4] It was known in Europe from the conquest of the New World in the sixteenth century, one of the first references to the so-called Mexican Treasure coming in a collection of observations on South America's flora and fauna written by Francisco Hernández, the main focus of which was medical.[5] In the Italian compendium by Nardo Antonio Recchi, the pineapple is listed as a plant originally from Haiti with the *tolteca* name *Matzalti*, translated into Latin as *Pinea Indica*.[6] In this Renaissance context the fruit symbolised the power of the conquerors over the New World; for example, in the marriage ceremony of Eleonora de Toledo with Cosimo I Medici (1539), the bride was followed by a pineapple and a llama.[7] In the eighteenth century, the fruit became a gift to be exchanged in new practices of sociability. Like other lavish global goods, it was considered precious because of the difficulties of transportation from overseas and the unsuccessful efforts to acclimatise it in the European soils, at least until 1723, when a first specimen appeared in the botanical garden of Pisa.[8]

More than two centuries had passed from the first appearance of the fruit in Europe to the beginning of the nineteenth century when Niccolini chose it for the gate decoration. Yet pineapples were still considered the best symbol to depict a garden where exoticism was displayed as the highest expression of private luxury. Today, the plants of the park have changed, but the place keeps its original character. Trees come from Japan, the Americas and Australia, while the golden pineapples remain on the top of the gate, as unchanging tracks of the unchanged exotic connotation of the park.[9]

Notes

1 Venditti, *Architettura Neoclassica a Napoli*, 235–320.
2 The sketch is the work of Niccolini, even if the lack of his original signature has caused some doubt in the attribution.
3 Giannetti et al., *Parco di Villa Floridiana*, 7.
4 The topic has been discussed in the conference *Power, Promise, Politics: The pineapple from Columbus to Del Monte*, Cambridge, UK, 20–21 February 2020.
5 Hernández, *Rerum medicarum novae Hispaniae thesaurus*.
6 Hernández, *Rerum medicarum novae Hispaniae thesaurus*, 313.
7 Groom, *Exotic Animals*, 52.
8 Maddaluno, 'Box of fresh pineapples'.
9 A list of the exotic trees can be found in Giannetti et al., *Parco di villa Floridiana*, 7–10.

Bibliography

Giannetti, Anna, Vincenzo Campolo and Enrico Ferranti. *Parco di Villa Floridiana*. Naples: Electa, 1999.
Groom, Angelica. *Exotic Animals in the Art and Culture of the Medici Court in Florence*. Leiden and Boston: Brill, 2018.
Hernández, Francisco. *Rerum medicarum novae Hispaniae thesaurus, seu Plantarum animalium mineralium Mexicanorum historia ex Francisci Hernández novi orbis medici primarij relationibus in ipsa Mexicana urbe conscriptis; a Nardo Antonio Reccho … collecta ac in ordinem digesta; a Ioanne Terrentio … notis illustrata*. Rome: Istituto poligrafico e Zecca dello Stato, Libreria dello Stato, 1992 [Romae: ex typographeio V. Mascardi, 1649].
Maddaluno, Lavinia. '"A box of fresh pineapples to the Holy Father"': pineapples and the worlds of sociability and science in eighteenth-century Rome'. In *The Pineapple from Domestication to Commodification: Re-presenting a Global Fruit*, edited by Melissa Calaresu and Victoria Avery. Oxford: Oxford University Press, forthcoming 2023.
Venditti, Arnaldo. *Architettura Neoclassica a Napoli*. Naples: Edizioni scientifiche italiane, 1961.

XII
Two clubs, two perspectives: Haudenosaunee material culture at Audley End

Michael Galban (Wašiw & Kutzadika'a) and Peter Moore

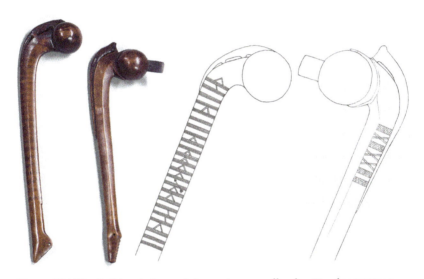

Figure OL.XII Ball-headed war clubs, eastern woodlands – Haudenosaunee, c. 1775–83. On loan to English Heritage from a private collection for display at Audley End House and Gardens, Essex. Drawings of the clubs' etched iconography: left, EH Inventory No. 81031676; right, EH Inventory No. 81031677 © English Heritage.

Summer was the season for war among the Haudenosaunee (or Iroquois) people during the eighteenth century. Young warriors sought recognition and status by joining and eventually leading war parties into battle. They carried a small bedroll of personal belongings, a musket, powder horn, small bag of ammunition, a knife in a sheath that hung from the neck, and a tomahawk or ball-headed war club. The war club was the symbol of the warrior's identity. Carved with specific motifs and designs, it could be 'read' by other Native peoples and, as a result, it became a warrior's calling card, recording his clan or war crest, a record of the battles in which he had fought, and even the number of enemies he had slain or captured.

The two ball-headed war clubs at Audley End are of exceptional quality and history. Charles, 1st Marquess Cornwallis (1738–1805), who fought for the British crown during the American War of Independence, brought home war-related objects that he acquired from his closest allies, the Haudenosaunee. The club on the left (81031676), which has an otter carved as a crest invoking the power and protection of that spirit, is the more storied of the two. According to the markings, it was taken into battle 23 times, represented by rectangular 'War Mats'. Once, the owner fought in three separate campaigns without going home and was even wounded, as can be seen by the broken arrow. On the obverse, the X symbols represent his enemies: six captured (four men, two women) and five slain, drawn without 'heads'. The other club (81031677) has an iron blade fixed to the ball, increasing its lethality. It reveals four war mats or campaigns and three defeated enemies, and no captives.

It is likely that these clubs were given to Charles Cornwallis as personal gifts of friendship from specific Haudenosaunee allies, a common practice during the colonial wars in North America.[1] They are the physical embodiment of shared experience between warriors and represent a bond forged in battle but also a global and cultural connection. In 1823 the clubs were inherited by Charles Cornwallis's granddaughter, Lady Jane Cornwallis (1798–1856), heiress to the family's Suffolk estates. She had recently married Richard Neville (1783–1858) and moved to Audley End. The Cornwallis properties were sold but the majority of their collections, including the ball-headed clubs, went to Audley End. As early as the 1840s, the clubs were displayed prominently above a stone doorway in the Great Hall, where they remain today. Jostling for attention with a large pair of postilion boots, funerary helmets, gauntlets, swords and nearby cabinets filled with taxidermy, geological specimens and other curiosities, they contribute to an overwhelming impression of Audley End as a microcosm of the world. Jane and Richard were renowned antiquarians, and it was clearly their intention to create a visual and intellectual feast for the eye through the interiors of their home.

Divorced form the indigenous culture in which they were created, it seems likely that the clubs were predominantly understood through the lens of imperial nostalgia and military achievement. Although Charles Cornwallis effectively ended the War of Independence by surrendering at Yorktown in October 1781, he continued to enjoy a successful career in colonial administration and warfare, leading British forces in India during the Third Anglo-Mysore War and defeating Tipu Sultan in 1792.[2] He was, at least to his granddaughter Jane, a man whose contribution to the empire could be signified through the display of artefacts relating to the campaigns in which he served. Looking more broadly across the house, this meaning was reinforced by Benjamin West's portrait of Sir John Griffin Griffin, a previous owner of Audley End, which shows him dressed in uniform, thus recalling his involvement as a general in the Seven Years War. It was subsequently augmented by an assortment of artefacts relating to the Sebastopol campaign, displayed in the Saloon following the untimely deaths of Henry and Grey Neville in the Crimean War in 1854.

Understood in this wider collective context of military commemoration at Audley End, the clubs play a vital role in communicating a multi-generational narrative of global warfare, seen through the eyes of elite British society. For over 200 years the Haudenosaunee culture from which they came has merely been a footnote in the story. By giving voice to indigenous perspectives, we now hope to redress this imbalance.

Notes

1 Carpenter, *Two Essays*, 95–100.
2 Cornwallis, *Memoirs*.

Bibliography

Carpenter, Edmund. *Two Essays: Chief and greed*. North Andover: Persimmon Press, 2005.
Cornwallis, Charles. *Memoirs of the Life of the Most Noble Marquis and Earl Cornwallis*. London: J. Marshall, 1806.

XIII
Design for pinery built for Sir Joseph Banks, 1807
Katie Donington

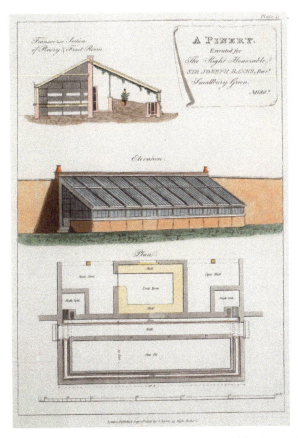

Figure OL.XIII A pinery executed for the Right Honourable Sir Joseph Banks, Bart. at Spring Grove, Smallbury Green, Middlesex, in George Tod, *Plans, elevations and sections, of hot-houses, green-houses, an aquarium, conservatories*, Plate XI. Digitised by the University of Wisconsin-Madison. Public domain, available at https://search.library.wisc.edu/digital/ASF3KWXYVBCBFV9B.

The eighteenth-century taste for possessing 'exotic' plants led to material changes to the design of the country house garden. Orangeries, forcing houses, greenhouses, peacheries, vineries, pineries and hothouses were built to accommodate specimens which relied on controlled conditions to survive. In 1807, George Tod published *Plans, elevations and sections, of hot-houses, green-houses, an aquarium, conservatories*. He noted in his preface that 'Botany, an elegant and interesting study, has lately become a favourite pursuit among the higher classes of the community'.[1] The publication included descriptions and plates of 26 of the finest examples drawn from the homes of royalty, the aristocracy and wealthy merchants including the greenhouse of the Marquis of Blandford at Whiteknights in Berkshire, the conservatory of Lord Viscount Courtenay at Powderham Castle in Devon, the hothouse of the Duke of Bedford at Woburn Abbey in Bedfordshire, and the greenhouse and hothouse of Queen Caroline at Frogmore in Berkshire. Readers could peruse the impressive structures which offered an insight into how the fashionable classes lived and leisured, while also improving their own knowledge and finding inspiration for the modelling of their own gardens.

Figure OL.XIII depicts the pinery built for Sir Joseph Banks (1743–1820) at his country estate Spring Grove, Middlesex. Banks's life and home exemplified the entanglement of the natural sciences, collecting and colonialism. His career as a naturalist and botanist enabled him to travel the world collecting specimens. He eventually became advisor at the Royal Botanic Gardens at Kew and president of the Royal Society. Both his town house in Soho Square and Spring Grove were shaped by global botanical culture. They were domestic dwellings and sites of scholarly learning. Spring Grove was located close to Kew Gardens and consisted of 49 acres split into four fields. There was an extensive botanical garden where both 'native' and 'exotic' plants were cultivated. The garden was also home to Lady Dorothea Banks's (1758–1828) dairy, which housed her extensive collection of Chinese porcelain. The pinery was designed by William Townsend Aiton (1766–1849), superintendent of the Royal Gardens at Kew and founder of the Horticultural Society of London. It was a predominantly glass structure with a 40-foot by 14-foot pine pit heated by two fires at each end. There was a fruit room behind the pine house fitted with shelves, drawers and compartments to display the pineapples.

The garden blurred the boundaries between the public and the private; it was both a place of leisure for the Banks family and a space in which they received distinguished visitors to discuss the latest scientific ideas. The Danish zoologist Johann Christian Fabricius visited Spring

Grove in 1782 and remarked on the hothouse in his letters, noting that 'As soon as we arrived in the evening we visited the little Greenhouse, where besides a large quantity of pineapples there is also a cactus grandiflorus which was in full bloom'.[2]

The pinery allowed Banks to perfect the art of cultivating pineapples. Originally found in South America and spread to the Caribbean through indigenous travel, this fruit was a rare commodity. Increasingly wealthy botanical collectors were able to grow them in Europe thanks to the development of the hothouse. The Banks household was well stocked according to the French volcanologist Barthélemy Faujas de Saint-Fond (1741–1819), who marvelled at the 'abundance of pineapples' on display at a dinner party there in 1784.[3] After her husband's death, Lady Dorothea continued to use the pinery to grow the fruit. In 1821 she gifted a Russian Globe pineapple to the Horticultural Society which had been nurtured from a plant sent from St Petersburg in 1819.[4] The pinery formed part of the Banks's desire to make their home into a productive site of sociable scientific endeavour.

Notes

1   Tod, *Plans, elevations and sections*, 5.
2   Johann Christian Fabricius quoted in Addison, 'Spring Grove', 96.
3   Barthélemy Faujas de Saint-Fond quoted in Beauman, *The Pineapple*, 106.
4   Addison, 'Spring Grove', 95.

Bibliography

Addison, R.E. 'Spring Grove, the country house of Sir Joseph Banks, Bart, P.R.S', *Notes and Records of the Royal Society of London* 11, no 1 (1954): 91–9.
Beauman, Francesca. *The Pineapple: King of fruits*. London: Chatto & Windus, 2005.
Leis, A.'"A little old-China mad": Lady Dorothea Banks (1758–1828) and her dairy at Spring Grove', *Journal for Eighteenth-Century Studies* 40, no. 2 (2017): 199–221.
Tod, George. *Plans, elevations and sections, of hot-houses, green-houses, an aquarium, conservatories, &c., recently built in different parts of England, for various noblemen and gentlemen: including a hot-house and green-house in Her Majesty's gardens at Frogmore*. London: J. Taylor, 1807.

XIV
Grosser Atlas über die Gantze Welt, by Johann Baptist Homann

Mrinalini Venkateswaran

Figure OL.XIV *Grosser Atlas über Die Gantze Welt,* Johann Baptist Homann (1663–1724), Nuremberg (detail). MSMSII Museum Library 4427.

The *Grosser Atlas* at Jaipur is a well-thumbed copy. Today, it is held in the collection of the Maharaja Sawai Man Singh II Museum at the City Palace. When it first arrived, Jaipur's grid plan had just been laid out, and its principal buildings (such as the City Palace) were under construction. The city was founded in 1727 by Maharaja Sawai Jai Singh II (r. 1699–1743),[1] before which the capital of the kingdom over which he ruled was at Amber. His life exemplifies the global connections embodied in the *Atlas*.

Sawai Jai Singh was a seasoned diplomat, administrator and military commander of the Mughal court who saw service under successive emperors. As a patron of distinction on a well-travelled international route, he drew an array of artists, intellectuals and collectible objects to his new court at Jaipur; the *Grosser Atlas* was among them. It is a compendium not only of European geographic and cartographic knowledge of its time, but also includes city and garden plans, and elevations of buildings. There is even a folio dedicated to ship design, and another to cannons and fortifications. A large section at the outset is devoted to astronomy and the cosmos, including tables listing the positions of major stars and constellations as recorded from observatories located in Europe. Sometime in the mid-1730s, Sawai Jai Singh, who was a noted astronomer, completed the *Zij-i-Muhammad Shahi*, which comprised his revisions and corrections to the astronomical tables then in use and was dedicated to his overlord, Emperor Muhammad Shah. Such treatises would have been used to calculate important dates and occasions in both the imperial and Jaipur calendars, and Sawai Jai Singh's *Zij* was widely used across the empire after its publication. He had spent significant time and resources on this enterprise and collected books from the European, Indic and Islamic mathematical and astronomical traditions, commissioning translations locally where these were not already available. The best-known testament to his efforts is the string of five observatories that he built across what is now north India: in Delhi, Varanasi, Mathura, Ujjain and of course Jaipur.[2] They are known as Jantar Mantar (a vernacular rendition of the Sanskrit *yantra* and *mantra*, loosely meaning mathematical diagrams and formulae), and the Jaipur observatory is now a World Heritage site.

The *Grosser Atlas*, first published in 1716,[3] was widely available in Europe by the time this particular edition, published in 1725, made its way to Jaipur. It was likely gifted by the local Jesuit community sometime after 1731.[4] They were familiar with Sawai Jai Singh's research (indeed, they shared his interests)[5] and had been recruited for assistance in 1729, when he took advantage of an official Mughal embassy to send the rector of the Agra Jesuit mission to Lisbon, accompanied by multilingual scholars. Their task was to collect books and instruments to further his research.[6] Other maps from his collection detail the division of the Americas among European colonial powers, summarise the cities and characters of the 'nations' involved, and show the Levant divided among the tribes of Israel. They represent the 'current affairs' and 'international politics' of his day. At a time when Europe and the Americas were still marginal to the politics of Asia, they point to a ruler and a court that were embedded in, open to and active agents in global knowledge networks. This was no 'provincial' backwater.

The *Atlas*'s career did not end with Sawai Jai Singh's reign. This particular volume has been rebound locally, with remnants of marbled paper on the leather cover and printed endpapers that date from the nineteenth century. Some of the hand colouring is different from editions in other collections.[7] The aerial views of European cities likely provoked a creative response among the artists at court in later centuries.[8] Tucked into individual folios are slips, translating or transliterating either titles or the contents within into the local language and script. The notes are scrawled on newer paper, probably from the nineteenth century, when colonial politics prompted another ruler of Jaipur to refer to the *Atlas*, in anticipation of charting his own course.[9]

Notes

1 For more on the city see Sachdev and Tillotson, *Building Jaipur*.
2 The Mathura observatory no longer exists.
3 'Homann, Johann Baptist'.
4 Sachdev and Tillotson, *Building Jaipur*, fn. 27, 181.
5 Sachdev and Tillotson, *Building Jaipur*, fn. 67, 182.
6 Delire, 'Elevation of the Samrat Yantra'.
7 For example: 'Grosser Atlas über die Gantze Welt'.
8 Tillotson, 'Education of the Yadav children', 100.
9 Most likely Maharaja Sawai Ram Singh II (b. 1833, r. 1835–80).

Bibliography

Delire, Jean Michel. 'Elevation of the Samrat Yantra', 'Folio from a manuscript of *Rekha Ganitam*' and 'Manuscript of *Graamadhayamakriya*'. In *Masterpieces at the Jaipur Court*, edited by Mrinalini Venkateswaran and Giles Tillotson, 56–7, 70–3. New Delhi: Niyogi Books, 2022.
'Grosser Atlas über die Gantze Welt'. Royal Collection Trust. https://www.rct.uk/collection/1046735/grosser-atlas-uber-die-gantze-welt-von-joann-baptist-homann, accessed 6 February 2022.
'Homann, Johann Baptist (1663–1724)'. Christie's. https://www.christies.com/en/lot/lot-598 3190, accessed 6 February 2022.
Sachdev, Vibhuti, and Giles Tillotson. *Building Jaipur: The making of an Indian city*. London: Reaktion Books, 2002.
Tillotson, G. 'The education of the Yadav children'. In *Masterpieces at the Jaipur Court*, edited by Mrinalini Venkateswaran and Giles Tillotson, 100–1. New Delhi: Niyogi Books, 2022.

XV
Frans Post's *View of Itamaracá Island*: rethinking a colonial past

Yme Kuiper

Figure OL.XV Frans Post, *View of Itamaracá Island* (1637). Reproduced courtesy of Rijksmuseum. Public domain. Available at https://commons.wikimedia.org/wiki/File:Gezicht_op_het_eiland_Itamarac%C3%A1,_Brazili%C3%AB_Rijksmuseum_SK-A-4271.jpeg.

Since 1822 the Mauritshuis has housed the Royal Cabinet of Paintings, mostly of famous seventeenth-century Dutch masters such as Rembrandt, Vermeer and Hals. Originally, it was the town residence of Johan Maurits, count and later prince of Nassau-Siegen (1604–79). The house was built during his governorship of Dutch Brazil (1636–44). Today, the original Dutch classicist exterior of the building remains as it was in Maurits's day, but the interior has changed drastically due to a fire in 1704. In his time rooms were decorated with Frans Post's Brazilian landscapes or Albert Eckhout's portraits from Amerindians or African men and women; the large room on the top floor was filled with treasures that he had collected in the New World: weaponry, headdresses, feathers, shells, stuffed animals and jewels.

Contemporaries of Johan Maurits gave his Dutch residence a telling name: 'the Sugar House', referring to the wealth he had earned as governor in Brazil. Recent research reveals that Maurits was also engaged in an illicit, private trade of enslaved Africans, a practice hidden even from the board of his employer, the Dutch West India Company. After the 2014 reopening of the Mauritshuis, a public debate started on its colonial legacy, which reached its peak three years later when the museum removed a replica bust (made in 1979) of Johan Maurits from its foyer, later placing it in a new exhibition room with objects referring to his governorship.[1] Yet 15 years earlier, in 2004, another replica (in bronze) of this bust was unveiled in the town of Recife. This representation of a colonial governor was a present from the German ambassador and, to date, has not been contested by the general public in Brazil.

Growing public antipathy in the Netherlands is mirrored by changes in academia. Since the nineteenth century Johan Maurits had been praised as a patron of arts and science, and the contents of his collection of Brasiliana were valued as representations of indigenous culture and processes of acculturation. The 1979 collection of essays on Maurits's legacy, subtitled 'A humanist prince in Europe and Brazil', is a clear expression of this positive reputation. Nowadays, a new generation of (young) researchers criticises this historiographic tradition and pleads for a deconstruction of the mythification of Dutch Brazil, highlighting the dark side of Maurits's governorship. They argue that the romanticised view of this short colonial period was kept alive by the prevailing Eurocentric view of peoples and cultures in the New World, based on the dichotomies of barbaric versus civilised people or a land of abundance and natural beauty versus one of wild and dangerous animals. These dichotomies can be interpreted as another way of legitimising occupation and exploration.[2]

Triggered by public debate, the Mauritshuis developed a 2019 exhibition which presented a more comprehensive view of Maurits and his role in the transatlantic slave trade, entitled *Shifting Image: In search of Johan Maurits*. In total, 11 art works of the Mauritshuis permanent collection which had direct and indirect ties to Dutch Brazil were exhibited. They were analysed by more than 40 people, including scholars, museum professionals, politicians, artists and writers. An important object of the exhibition, Frans Post's *View of Itamaracá Island* (1637), was analysed by five different scholars. Monteiro noted that 'this was the first time this painting has been displayed presenting a narrative that does not purely emphasize its natural scenery, Post's realism and naivety as a landscape painter, or Johan Maurits' scientific interest as a humanist prince'.[3] Post's *Itamaracá* was reinterpreted as a colonial landscape. It documents the newly conquered territory of the Dutch Republic in all its forms: the small village with its Portuguese buildings and Catholic church; Fort Orange representing Dutch military power; and in the foreground the racial hierarchy of the plantation system in daily life – European masters and black, enslaved African servants. Post's great oeuvre of 'Brazilian' paintings produced for a specific market after his years in Brazil shows the European desire to consume representations of the New World. Later on, Dutch museums started acquiring these works for their 'historical value'. They were also appreciated as testimony to Dutch colonial power overseas, evoking either pride or nostalgia for an idealised worldwide empire.

Notes

1 The original seventeenth-century bust once stood in the garden of the Mauritshuis but was moved to Siegen, Maurits's German town of birth, in 1669; Abaka et al., *Shifting Image*.
2 Monteiro, 'Colonial representations of Brazil'.
3 Monteiro, 'Colonial representations of Brazil', 30.

Bibliography

Abaka, Edmund et al., *Shifting Image: In search of Johan Maurits*. The Hague: 2019. See: https://www.studiolouter.nl/en/mauritshuis-shifting-image-in-search-of-johan-maurits.
Monteiro, Carolina. 'Colonial representations of Brazil and their current display at Western museums: the Mauritshuis case and the Dutch gaze', unpublished MA thesis, University of Leiden, 2019.

Part 4
Imperial houses

12
Cartography, collecting and the construction of empire at Dyrham Park

Rupert Goulding and Louis P. Nelson

In his travels through Britain in the 1720s, Daniel Defoe noted two imposing houses in Gloucestershire: Badminton, the seat of the Duke of Beaufort; and Dyrham Park, the seat of William Blathwayt (?1649–1717). Defoe first caught sight of the house at Dyrham Park from a high hill to the east, a view which sets the house to great advantage nestled into a terraced hillside and just above a broad plain to the west (Figure 12.1). The thirteenth-century parish church stands just behind the house and a greenhouse hides the service wing to the south. The three storeys of the east front are disposed into three parts: ends of three bays each and a seven-bay core. Behind the hooded windows of the first floor ranged the chambers of a lavish state apartment reserved for the reception of royalty. And while Blathwayt never did entertain royalty, this apartment was opened on 'extraordinary occasions' such as a visitation by lesser nobility and foreign envoys in November 1702.[1] The west front of the house boasts lower service wings that bound a raised parterre. Blathwayt's private apartment occupied the grand first floor of this front, with his principal reception chamber opening onto a balcony that provided a glorious prospect of the terraced gardens to the west of the house. Defoe's notice of Dyrham would be entirely unsurprising except that its patron was not of rank; Blathwayt was only a civil servant, though one who served as a leading governmental, military and, critically, colonial administrator from the reign of Charles II (1660–85) to his death in 1717 under the monarchy of George I (1714–27).

Largely built in the 1690s while Blathwayt was England's principal administrator of 'the plantations', Dyrham Park is a microcosm of the emerging empire. As he was working to build the empire before and after the 'Glorious Revolution', Blathwayt was simultaneously building

Figure 12.1 Dyrham Park east front with greenhouse. © Rupert Goulding.

his house. As this chapter will make clear, these two processes were inextricably linked. Largely completed by 1704, the house – in its very fabric, in its capacity to facilitate political and economic manoeuvring, and in its ability to render visible the authority of the British crown and by extension the emerging British Empire – became, we argue, a critical vehicle by which the empire was constructed in the imagination of those familiar with the house. Framed around three rooms in the house as three acts – Blathwayt's staircase, his private chamber and his greenhouse – the chapter explores the ways in which this colonial official used his administrative privilege to collect colonial assemblages – evidence of empire – and build a house like none other in England.

William Blathwayt

But first, an introduction to the man. William Blathwayt, descended from London's merchant class, made his career as a civil servant deeply involved in the administration of Britain's plantations. His father was a senior barrister who died at the time of his birth, leaving the widow Anne Povey and three young children in financial troubles. Anne's brother, colonial administrator Thomas Povey (?1613–?1705), settled their debts and in due course raised his nephew to follow in a career established by Justinian Povey (d. c. 1652), father of Thomas and Anne, an exchequer auditor and accountant-general to Queen Anne of Denmark and, perhaps of most significance, commissioner of the Caribbee Islands in 1637. After his education and three years at the English embassy to The Hague, Blathwayt began a long career as an administrator over the colonies, entering the plantation office in 1675 as a clerk, and in 1679 becoming Secretary of the Committee on Trade and Foreign Plantations. Ever the pluralist, in 1678 he was appointed clerk of the Privy Council, and in 1680 he became England's first Surveyor and Auditor-General over plantation revenues. These posts effectively positioned him as the leading English official involved in colonial administration. In 1683, he added to these roles the responsibilities of Secretary at War, followed in 1685 by election to the House of Commons for Newtown on the Isle of Wight. In 1692, Blathwayt was granted £1,000 by the king to establish and properly equip his war office, complete with horses and carriages to make it mobile when in Flanders. While abroad with the king, he was appointed acting Secretary of State. Soon thereafter, he represented the city of Bath in Parliament and became a member of the Board of Trade. So, in sum, by 1696, Blathwayt was the leading administrator for the king's Privy Council, overseer of all colonial revenues and all acts of war, and was a leading member of the board overseeing all foreign trade.[2]

In the midst of this rapidly growing bureaucratic portfolio, Blathwayt married Mary Wynter (1650–91), the heiress to the Dyrham estate, then settled with a decrepit Tudor house, about which he remarked 'I am afraid there will be a necessity of building a new house at Dirham or being at a very great expense in repairing this'.[3] Mary brought both wealth and land to their union and, we can surmise, an opportunity for architectural expression. It is also possible that Dyrham offered Blathwayt some residual if intangible markers of status, for it was purchased in 1571 by brothers Sir William (c. 1525–89) and George Wynter (d. 1581) on the proceeds of their naval administration and ship-owning career – ships used for trading, exploration and privateering, including investing in their colleague Sir John Hawkins's slave-trading voyages. Mary was directly descended from George, who invested £400 in Sir Francis Drake's project to circumnavigate the globe in 1577, and whose son John sailed as Vice-Admiral.[4] Blathwayt's building works began in early 1692 on an expansive reconstruction of the house into the double-flanked mansion as it stands today, uninterrupted by Mary's premature death the preceding November after the birth of their daughter Anne (1691–1717). Described by John Evelyn as 'having raised himselfe by his Industry, from very moderate Circumstances', Blathwayt was an early beneficiary of the emerging state bureaucracy, where administrative endeavours could be quite lucrative, even for colonial officials who never travelled to the colonies, and all was expressed in the Dyrham Park he created.[5]

Blathwayt came into office after the rapid expansion of English colonies through the seventeenth century. England's oldest colonies were Munster and Ulster in Ireland. By 1686, however, English colonies on the American mainland included Maine, Massachusetts, New Hampshire, Rhode Island, Connecticut, New York, New Jersey, Pennsylvania, Delaware, Maryland, Virginia and Carolina. Atlantic and Caribbean holdings included Bermuda, Barbados, St Christopher, Montserrat, Nevis, Antigua, Jamaica and the Cayman Islands. Factories in the East Indies could be found at Bantam, Bengal, Surat, Madras, Bombay, Calcutta and Canton in China; others were dotted along the Atlantic coast of Africa, including the Gambia River, Komenda, Accra and Cape Coast. While the East India Company and the Royal African Company were structurally independent of the crown, Blathwayt was interested in and aware of their activities through his roles in colonial auditing and committee membership.

Blathwayt served as principal bureaucrat through a time of extraordinary structural change in England's colonial project. By 1680 Charles II had already granted the East India Company the rights to autonomous territorial acquisitions, to mint money, to command fortresses and troops and form alliances, to make war and peace, and to exercise both civil and criminal jurisdiction over the acquired areas. By 1680, the Hudson Bay Company was ten years old and the Royal African Company had for eight years enjoyed their exclusive license to trade along the African coast.[6] Soon thereafter, the company was exporting 5,000 enslaved people per year. These were also the years that saw the gradual increase in dependence on colonial monocrops. Tobacco in Virginia was a half-century old, and Blathwayt would witness the birth of rice culture in South Carolina; but the greatest transformation would be in sugar cane. By the 1680s, Blathwayt would see the skyrocketing demand for sugar and the equally dramatic attempt to meet that demand, forces which would radically alter the economic and cultural landscapes of both Africa and the Caribbean. All the while he was building his house. While traditional interpretations of the house and its contents focus on the importance of the large collection of Dutch art and European ceramics, this chapter turns its gaze to Blathwayt's enduring interest: the colonies and settlements of the Atlantic.

Act I: building empire

In March 1692, King William III (1650–1702) sailed from Harwich to the Netherlands to lead an army against his French counterpart Louis XIV (1638–1715), attended for the first time by his versatile secretary William Blathwayt. Each subsequent year until 1701 Blathwayt accompanied the king on spring to autumn military campaigns, and throughout he rebuilt Dyrham Park via correspondence.[7] One of the first concerns for Blathwayt was securing building materials, a particular challenge because he wanted specifically to exhibit exotic colonial woods.

As Blathwayt travelled east to Flanders, sailing westward was Edward Randolph (1632–1703), Blathwayt's deputy Auditor-General of Plantation Revenues and newly appointed Surveyor-General of Customs. Randolph was officially starting a three-year inspection of every port between Maine and Carolina, but also on his mind were private instructions from Blathwayt to secure timber.[8] Years earlier Randolph had written to Blathwayt, 'Sir, I owe to you the bread I eat', which he acknowledged through 'handsome presents' for his patron.[9] This trip proved no different, with Randolph writing in April soon after reaching 'James Citty in Virginnia … my arrival so late in ye year will not suffer me to provide so much black walnut wood as I intended to have done … Capt. Nicholson … will send you some black Walnutt to Bristol.'[10] In June he wrote to confirm Nicholson's supply was shipping to Bristol on the *Sarah* captained by Joseph Leech, while he had acquired 10,000 foot of pine boards and 'walnut plank, but very scarce in Virginia: it will be ready next spring … I have bespoak some cedar & will make it my business to gett what I can to adorn yr House at Durham.' The timber came from Thomas Evernden at Little Annamesseck (near Crisfield, Maryland) in Chesapeake Bay, later sailing with Captain Thomas Warner of the *Hopewell* of Bristol.[11]

The following year, in July 1693, Randolph sourced 5,000 foot of pine planks 'ready to be shipp'd off … but one ship will not take them all aboard because they will take up too much Room. the Black walnutt plank is in Potomack River.'[12] By November he complained, 'I cannot looke Mr Blathwayt … in the face till I have shipd off their Tymber', having acquired red cedar from North Carolina, and with pine stored 'at the Eastern shore, at Col Scarburgh's landing'.[13] Arranging shipping consistently proved difficult: 'I hope the Black walnut & ye Cedar are shippd off from James River: Scott of Bristol was this spring in Potomack my friend would have Engaged him … but he refused to do it unless he were paid twice the value of it for freight.'[14] Eventually and with consistent effort the timber crossed the Atlantic – imported colonial woods intended for display in Blathwayt's house.

In his substantial reconstruction of the house, Blathwayt installed two very grand staircases, each rising within one of the two major flanks of the house. The so-called Old Stair Case of American black walnut belongs to the first phase (1692–4) of development, while the Best Stair Case of red cedar was part of William Talman's (1650–1719) additions of 1700–4 (Figure 12.2). The first phase created a new west front designed by the little-known Huguenot Samuel Hauduroy. Surviving drawings include designs for the staircase, alongside one of Blathwayt's preferred question and answer letter-sheets, with his Flanders-penned responses provided in a wide margin left blank for the purpose. They show the extraordinary level of detail Blathwayt demanded. The showcasing of imported walnut was evidently central to the stairs' purpose. Blathwayt offered his agents this general guidance: 'What is wainscoted (so called) must be done with walnut throughout the whole area of the staircase Room but only Rail high, Except the door cases which are to be of Walnutt towards the Staires.' Asked 'Whether the Rail is to be fineered [veneered] Crossways of the wood which is the finest or to be workd straight', he responded 'I did not think there was to be any faneerng, but if there be the best way is to be used'. When considering the stair spandrels, Blathwayt requested 'Plain but of the best Walnut, as good as faneiring, or faneiring if it be thought advisable'.[15]

Figure 12.2 The Old [walnut] Stair Case, Dyrham Park. © Rupert Goulding.

Stair construction was contracted to a London joiner, Robert Barker of St Martin-in-the-Fields, in June 1693.[16] Barker's team used salvaged oak timbers, likely from the demolished parts of the house, for reuse as the principal structural members; to this was applied a soft-wood carcass clad with walnut veneer, and the balusters were made from turned walnut.[17] Elements of the room that were not finished in varnished walnut, notably the soffits of the stairs, were grained. A Mr Hauduroy, either the same architect or another of his family, who were known decorators, billed £2 12s. 4d. for 44 yards and eight foot of 'Wallnutt colour' for the room.[18] By 1694 the new west front was complete, decorated and furnished. Blathwayt had recently purchased his uncle Thomas Povey's collection of paintings, and by c. 1701 Samuel van Hoogstraten's *Great Perspective* had been hung on the 'Noble Stair Case one of Walnut'.[19] Had Blathwayt followed typical protocol for grand mansion staircases, these would have been built out of English oak. While grand staircases and wainscotting had been incorporated into British country houses for decades, those in Dyrham Park are among the earliest to intentionally utilise exotic woods.

Even more interesting than the *fact* of these woods is the *manner* by which they were procured. The emergence of a singular colonial administrator meant that the scope of Blathwayt's responsibilities and the means of his compensation were open for negotiation. Furthermore, he had authority to represent any colony's interests in court, a position of power clearly understood by governors and other colonial officials who worked hard to curry his favour. One leading colonist wrote: 'It may *make him* willing, who we know, is in the way of doing more service to these parts than any other can' [emphasis added].[20] But simple gifts were sometimes insufficient: Blathwayt went so far as to communicate to officials that he expected to be paid by them for the service of representing their interests to the king or in the Privy Council or to the various boards. Blathwayt, for example, demanded of Virginia Governor Andros 400 nightingales and a wide range of Virginia fauna in exchange for his efforts to enhance Virginia's standing with the king.[21]

Some of the supply of exotic timbers was evidently the result of Blathwayt's direct commission via his most loyal associates in the Americas. As we have seen above, his deputy Randolph was particularly active, as was Captain Francis Nicholson, who wrote in 1694: 'If you want any more Black Walnut or Cedar upon notice I hope I shall be able to send you'. Eight years later, he remained committed to the endeavour:

> I am very glad that the Cedar &c which I did myself the honor to send you, proved to yor satisfaction, and have spoke to Collo Quary

to wait upon you concerning some more, as likewise black walnut for a summer House at ye end of yor extraordinary Pile and noble upper Terras walk: and I am very ambitious of having the Stairs, wainscot &c sent you by him who begs leave to subscribe himself.

It is interesting to note here the architectural specificity, which suggests Nicholson either knew Blathwayt's designs or more likely had personally visited Dyrham. Nicholson had both opportunity and ability, as he was resident in England in the early 1690s between postings and was particularly skilled in urban planning, laying out Annapolis, Maryland and Williamsburg, Virginia.[22]

Blathwayt exploited the pressure felt by many colonial officials to ensure his good graces to collect exotic building materials for his new house. Joseph Blake (1663–1700), Governor of Carolina, sent him cypress and cedar; Samuel Day (d. c. 1704), Governor of Bermuda, sent cedar planks and wainscot boards; while a Maryland correspondent sent him black walnut.[23] Even before he began construction on Dyrham, Blathwayt made requests for colonial timber. His request for cedar from Bermuda sent Chief Justice Henry Hordesnell scouring the island for a tree of sufficient girth to meet Blathwayt's request. Failing the request, he shipped a large oval table of local cedar which he hoped Blathwayt might be able to alter to suit his needs.[24] The building of the house at Dyrham Park was quite literally an international endeavour. Bound up in the requests for and supply of exotic woods for the construction of staircases and wainscoting were the very stuff of colonial negotiations, the currying of favours and the everyday business of building of an empire. Through these transactions, Blathwayt's audience was one which would – with very few exceptions – never even see his house: colonial officials an ocean away who might only imagine the beauties of his grandest spaces.

The cultural currency of exotic American walnut and cedar, however, would not last long. By the 1720s, Jamaican mahogany became the exotic wood of choice. This rapid transformation was a result of both supply and demand. As Jennifer Anderson has so deftly demonstrated, the early eighteenth-century abundance of Jamaican mahogany was in part the result of the rapid clearing of land in those same decades for the planting of sugar cane. In 1721 the Board of Trade lifted all duties on the importation of timber from British holdings in America, including the Caribbean. This customs change opened the floodgates for the introduction of Caribbean mahogany into the English market and, as a result, the lavish use of mahogany.[25] What in the 1710s was a largely unknown material became by the 1730s the wood of choice among both British and American elites. Spurred by both supply and demand, mahogany exports from Jamaica climbed steadily from the 1720s through the 1760s. As Anderson makes clear, the great size of mahogany trees felled through these decades – the result of the clearing of virgin forests for sugar cane fields – produced an extraordinarily rich and sophisticated finish.[26]

If Dyrham Park was largely completed before the 1720s appearance of mahogany, the embrace of the darker Caribbean wood as a building material is nowhere better demonstrated than in Marble Hill House, under construction through the late 1720s in the suburbs west of London. One of the most striking characteristics of the house is the very extensive use of mahogany, especially the mahogany floors of the great room and the unpainted mahogany of the staircase. Furthermore, Lawrence Brown's recent research on Marble Hill House makes clear that the patron, Henrietta Howard, depended on investments in both the South Sea Company and other slaving ventures to fund the construction of her new house.[27] While Howard was not herself a Jamaican, the construction of her house depended heavily on a financing scheme that profited from the Atlantic trade. Her novel and conspicuous use of mahogany – likely from Jamaica – not only for doors but also for the floors and the staircase, sent a very clear signal of her connections to the expanding British Empire. And her connections to enslaved Africans who laboured to fell the trees was made personal through her familiarity with Scipio Africanus, an enslaved African manservant owned by her nephew, Charles William Howard.[28] From her Caribbean mahogany floors to the black manservant of her nephew, Howard's material world was profoundly shaped by the African and Caribbean trade. But what had been a conspicuous and exotic display of mahogany in the 1720s would quickly become pervasive among the elite as the consumption practices made possible by colonialism quickly reshaped normative fashion among those benefiting from the power of empire.

This proclivity to collect exotica as evidence of an elite's global reach was not, of course, a new phenomenon. In her important essay on the *Wunderkammer*, Joy Kenseth makes clear that the collection of natural marvels through the early modern period was closely connected to the exploration of the Americas, Africa and the Orient.[29] The *Wunderkammer* was a cabinet of curiosities, a room of collection. Where most scholars see the decline of such rooms by the long eighteenth century, it is possible to see the shifting interest in the exotic from the curious and collectible to the conspicuous and consumable as different historically situated expressions of the same impulse. The demise of the singular cabinet serving this purpose might well have happened through the seventeenth century, but the impulse to collect and display exotica certainly did not disappear. It simply bled beyond the single dedicated chamber. John Evelyn, for example, noted on a 1671 visit to the house of Thomas Browne that 'His whole house and garden is a paradise and Cabinet of rarities and that of the best collection, amongst Medails, books, Plants, natural things'.[30] But if Brown's display was still in the vein of the *Wunderkammer*, Blathwayt's choice pivoted from the display of discrete objects to the integration of the exotic into the very construction of the house. In this way, exotica on display and the spaces of its containment became one and the same.

Act II: capitalising the empire

Hanging in a parlour at Dyrham, part of an enfilade of private chambers, is a vertical painting of a cocoa tree, barbeques and a drying hut, exhibiting not only the plant and its seeds but also the mechanisms necessary to dry them in the preparation of cocoa (Figure 12.3). Cocoa, whose primary form of consumption was as a warm drink, was Mexican in origin and first found popularity among Spanish colonials. But cocoa came easily into the English market with the seizure of Jamaica from the Spanish in 1655 and the costly drink was available in London coffee houses by the 1660s. By the later seventeenth century, cocoa was being grown experimentally throughout the Caribbean, in Africa and even in the Philippines, and it was consumed by the Spanish, English, Dutch and others.[31] After harvesting, the pods of the cacao tree were opened and the seeds and their pulp fermented for several days in the Jamaica sun. Then enslaved labourers separated the seeds and air dried them upon trays for weeks or heated over fires. At this point the seeds were 'cured' and ready for export, where local roasting and processing made a drink of many flavours.[32] As with tea and coffee, chocolate's popularity amongst Europeans was directly tied to its sweetening with sugar.

The painting now hanging in Dyrham is a copy of an original painted in 1672 of a specific specimen then growing on the Jamaica plantation of Governor Sir Thomas Modyford (1620–79).[33] The original accompanied a letter sent by Sir Thomas Lynch (d. 1684) to Sir Robert Moray (1608/9–73) describing the plant and its harvesting. A recent investigation of the painting by Philip Emanuel and Rupert Goulding has made clear that the Dyrham copy of the original now in the Royal

Figure 12.3 *A Cocoa Tree and Roasting Hut*, unknown artist, *c.* 1672. © Rupert Goulding.

Collection was likely commissioned soon after its arrival in London by Thomas Povey, a close associate of Moray and Lynch and a fellow member of the Royal Society. In 1682, William Blathwayt pursued a partnership with Lynch, then Lieutenant-Governor of Jamaica, to jointly purchase a 1,000-acre cocoa plantation on that island, one of only 32 such plantations on the island compared with 246 sugar cane plantations.[34] Surely aware of the economic potential of the crop, Blathwayt explored the possibilities of capitalising on this colonial opportunity, but soon thereafter a blight on cacao and delays in the purchase of the land meant he abandoned the plan. Nearly a decade later, after his reconstruction of Dyrham was underway, Blathwayt purchased dozens of paintings from Thomas Povey, his uncle, presumably including the *Cocoa Tree*. While Blathwayt's intent in this purchase is far from clear, the hanging of this painting in Dyrham might well have served as a visual reminder for Blathwayt and others that his colonial entanglements were inextricably linked to plantations, their products, and the labour – invisible in the painting – that was necessary for their operation. Passing from his bedchamber into his richly appointed state chamber – originally painted to emulate three kinds of marble – he could daily set his gaze on another reminder of his participation in colonial economies: two figures that stood 'in one of the Best Rooms', a principal reception chamber for receiving visitors, a room he called the Balcony Room (Figure 12.4).[35]

The three earliest archival descriptions of the interior of Dyrham Park all reference the same arrangement of furniture within the Balcony Room. The previously quoted letter of *c.* 1700 notes that 'two Black Boys have a Proper Place on Each side of an Indian Tambour', which is corroborated by two household inventories of 1703 and 1710, which list 'a Large Tea Table & Two Blacks' and 'a large black Japan Tea Table & 2: Blacks'.[36] The tea table also remains at Dyrham and is likely Javanese or possibly from Vietnam; along with the stands, they were once the property of Blathwayt's uncle Thomas Povey. The room contained another trio of lacquered tea tables with flanking stands for candles; chairs upholstered in silk; silk curtains and valances; a large Dutch delftware flowerpot in

Figure 12.4 Stand, formed from enslaved African figure, late seventeenth century, English. © Rupert Goulding.

the chimney place, itself with designs influenced by imported Chinese porcelain; and very likely the surviving inset painting by Melchior de Hondecoeter (1636–95) featuring ornamental birds: pelican, flamingo, peacock and African crowned crane. This assemblage was overtly global, including the clear influence of the Dutch East India Company (VOC) through its supply of lacquered items, decorative textiles and exotic birds.[37] Affirming this association are the pair of delftware plaques, elsewhere in the house, which depict China as shown in book illustrations published for VOC emissary Johan Nieuhof in 1665.[38]

The Balcony Room was not an isolated space. For Blathwayt's visitors, their approach necessitated climbing the aforementioned Old Stair Case of imported walnut and absorbing all the global resonances its uncommon use sought to express. But between this and Blathwayt's bedchamber lay several other rooms, including the now lost Japan Closet. A small place for private work or intimate conversation, it was entirely decorated in a combination of imported lacquer or imitation 'japanned' panelling, alongside imported painted satin wall hangings and curtains.[39] This room conformed with the court style of William III and Mary II, a French Baroque style heavily influenced by their leading designer, Huguenot émigré Daniel Marot (1663–1752). Marot, an early proponent of a unified design philosophy across architecture, furniture and ornaments, published a similar room design, featuring multiple shelves for the display of Chinese and delftware ceramics, based on his work for the queen at Het Loo in the Netherlands and English palaces Kensington and Hampton Court.[40]

Returning to the Balcony Room, the 'two black boys' are enslaved Africans wearing red tunics, their bondage made explicitly clear by the shackles around their ankles, chains, and the metal bands around their necks.[41] Like similar figures from this period, these two examples wear red tunics, suggesting their identity as 'moors', a stereotype for an African Muslim that would have been familiar not just in early modern England but also across Europe and the Mediterranean. The so-called blackamoor as a type was multivalent, associated not only with North African 'moors', but also with enslaved West Africans.[42] The location of these figures in this room is also significant. This chamber was his private reception room, a critical space available for important transactions of business. The stands, often described as torchieres for holding candles, ignore the impracticality of a naked flame within the dished and ribbed scallop-shell bowl each figure holds aloft. Their design suggests a liquid receptacle for scented water or to contain an offering of sweetmeats or fruits. Of little doubt is how the stands were functional in support of the conspicuous consumption of the luxurious commodities tea, coffee and chocolate, as shown in contemporary illustrations featuring the same tea table form (Figure 12.5).[43] Blathwayt owned an array of ceramics – Chinese, Dutch delftware and domestically produced – for these drinks' dedicated consumption. He also owned an instructional copy of *The Indian Nectar, Or a Discourse Concerning Chocolata* (1662), purchased again from his influential uncle Thomas Povey.[44]

The two enslaved figures, silenced and subservient black bodies, have knelt in this room for more than 300 years. For Blathwayt, however, these were not just objects of general curiosity but also evidence of the benefits of his post; one of Blathwayt's primary and more lucrative activities was the implicit promotion of the African slave trade. In the 1690s the trade grew to an exportation of 5,000 Africans per year, most bound for Brazil, Barbados or Jamaica. As Jamaican Edward Long argued a century later, 'the sovereign of Great Britain holds an interest in Negroes … for his revenue is very greatly benefited and supported by the

Figure 12.5 Portrait of a family drinking tea in an interior, attributed to Roelof Koets (II), *c.* 1680. Reproduced courtesy of RKD: Netherlands Institute for Art History.

produce of their personal labour'.[45] These two stands with their enslaved figures raise important questions about the place of the black body in the British imagination through the eighteenth century.

Blathwayt's blackamoor figures correlate closely with the late seventeenth-century portrait practice of including black servants, often identified as slaves by silver collars, as anonymous attributes of the sitter.[46] However, as Susan Amussen has argued, the appearance of these figures was not random. Enslaved Africans appeared as servants first in the portraits of British royalty and military leaders, demonstrating the direct connections between the representation of anonymous Africans and the expanding empire in the English visual imagination.[47] As David Bindman points out, the increasing presence of black individuals in later seventeenth-century portraits was likely a result of the 1663 charter of the Company of Royal Adventurers to Africa (RAC), the rise of Charles II, and the return of courtly culture and its association with black pages.[48] Given that Thomas Povey was a member of the RAC, their three-dimensional presence can be seen as an extension of that idea. The frequency of such individuals in portraits demonstrates that the ownership of an African generated little moral anxiety in the minds of Englishmen and women well into the next century.

If more common in painted depictions, the realisation of the black body in sculptural form was more distinctive, surviving in only a few instances in late seventeenth-century and early eighteenth-century houses and gardens.[49] The most popular manifestation of this form by the middle of the eighteenth century was decorative objects for table and mantle; the Bow porcelain manufactory and Chelsea porcelain manufactory were both producing such figures by the 1760s. In 1765 Bow produced a pair of figures – one male and one female – who were cast with upraised arms supporting a pierced porcelain basket over their heads, often intended to hold sweetmeats during the dessert course of a meal.[50] These black bodies were simultaneously exotic, collectible and – as with Blathwayt's figures – working. In all manifestations – live bodies, portrait attributes and sculptural figures – the black body in late seventeenth-century and eighteenth-century Britain represented simultaneously exotic wonder and imperial aspiration. They also served to reinforce through contrast the whiteness, and by implication the power, of the British elite.

It seems not coincidental that the appearance of porcelain collectible versions of black bodies began to appear in the middle decades of the century, just as racist sentiments increased in the public sphere, the fashion for liveried black servants declined and the numbers of black persons in British port cities began to rapidly increase. In the 1760s, newspapers in Bristol, Liverpool and other port cities regularly printed advertisements for the sale of slaves or requesting the recovery of a runaway, closely linking the public spaces of Britain with those of the British Caribbean, at least until the Somerset Act of 1772, which hindered legal slavery in England and raised the spectre of moral shame associated with the trade.[51] The close visual proximity of the kneeling 'blackamoor' and the final version of the famous Wedgwood image of the kneeling slave surrounded by the text 'Am I Not a Man and Brother?' seems not accidental. Wedgwood and others working to end the African slave trade would surely have known kneeling forms similar to those in Dyrham Park. Blathwayt's, at half-scale, stand – or, more precisely, kneel – at an extraordinary threshold. The imperial project commodified the black body, and as consuming patterns evolved, the black body shifted from real to represented to mass-produced. In the late seventeenth century, though, the 'blackamoor' was still an exotic collectible, and William Blathwayt had two in his principal business chamber, a reminder of the increasing centrality of African slavery to the financial stability of the tobacco plantations of Virginia and the sugar cane plantations of the Caribbean.

Act III: sensing the empire

An evocative articulation of Blathwayt's colonial entanglements at Dyrham Park was surely his greenhouse, which he began in 1701 as the final act of construction on his house. Described as 'one of the most beautiful and commodious Piles for its Purpose' by Stephen Switzer, in winter the building was 'replete with all Manner of fine Greens, as Oranges, Lemons, Mirtles, etc. set in the most beautiful order'.[52] The greenhouse was – and remains – one of the largest and most spectacular of its type in late seventeenth- and early eighteenth-century England. The building was specifically designed to sustain large quantities of non-native plants susceptible to an English winter. It is more than 100 feet long and tall enough to accommodate 'several Rose of Scaffolds one above another ... on the Topmost whereof are plac'd the most tender, but largest Plants; and the Shrubs, Flowers, etc. below ... with Walks between the whole Length, for the Gardener to examine the Health and State of his numerous Vegetables'.[53] Once packed with plants for the winter months, the interior was heated via 'several Stoves underneath at convenient distances for Firing, whereby a regular Heat is diffus'd over the whole House, and the Outside is so well guarded with Shutters in the Winter, as to distain the Fury of the most penetrating Winds'.[54] By the end of the seventeenth century, English plant collections included specimens from Africa, Persia, India and the Caribbean, most delivered via merchant traders and sea captains.[55] Blathwayt's appetite for exotic produce had likely been piqued by his regular receipt of various dried fruits, casks of preserved ginger and even pickled peppers from West Indians hoping to earn his favour.[56] While greenhouses were fairly common among royalty and the nobility by the end of the seventeenth century, such a feature at a country house of the gentry was quite unusual. Even more, Blathwayt's was far finer than most, signalling his particular interest in floral exotica.

Nothing more clearly communicated this commitment than the 'two prodigious large and fine Aloes, which with their prickly, bulky Arms, high extended, appear like Giants to defend the Entrance of the Conservatory'.[57] These two aloe plants – native to Mexico but naturalised to the West Indies in the seventeenth century – framed the transition from the greenhouse into the eastern garden which climbed away from the house (Figure 12.6). Blathwayt's correspondence

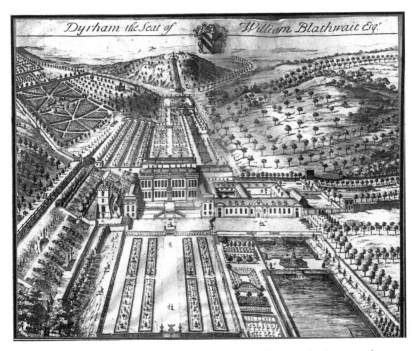

Figure 12.6 Johannes Kip, *Dyrham Park* (1712), showing the house and garden. © Rupert Goulding.

offers further evidence that he had ambitions for displaying exotic North American plants. Edward Randolph, for example, provided him specimens from Virginia that might 'grow in your parke' in one shipment, while Captain Nicholson sent a large consignment in 1691 collected by the eminent colonial naturalist John Banister (1654–1692), though they were spoilt on arrival. Some years later Nicholson mentions the assistance of a new botanist clergyman, recommended by Dyrham's garden designer George London (c. 1640–1714), who would help 'add to ye beauty of yor paradise at Dirham'.[58] Virginia Auditor William Byrd (1652–1704) sent in 1693 an array of plants, seeds and nuts, including peach stones, walnuts, tulip tree cones, sassafras berries, *Magnolia virginiana* and even two live rattlesnakes in a cage.[59] Virginia Governor Sir Edmund Andros (1637–1714) sent a substantial consignment in 1694, containing multiple live plant specimens including myrtles, maples, gourds, 'Guiney corn', 'Indian Corn' and again an item of North American exotica, a 'Tomahawk an Indian weapon'. Also in the chests and barrels of plants were kalmia (*Kalmia angustifolia*) and black haw (*Vibernum prunifolium*) in some of their first British introductions.[60]

Blathwayt's greenhouse was not simply a conservatory to support non-native flora; it was also a critical site for the imagination of empire. In the summer, when many of the heartiest plants were moved into the gardens, the greenhouse retained 'two or three rows of Oranges &, the Length of the House, which make the most beautiful and fragrant Walks within Doors; and the whole house is whitewash'd, and hung round with the most entertaining Maps, Sculptures, & And furnished with fine Chairs of Cane'.[61] Cross-referencing Switzer's description with household inventories of 1710 and 1742, after the death of William Blathwayt's son William (1688–1742), reveals that there were 88 maps and prints on the walls.[62] Previous analysis of Blathwayt's print collection by Rupert Goulding has highlighted the large quantity of sculptural illustrations Blathwayt owned, while maps were once a significant part of Blathwayt's working library – notably the volume of some 48 print and manuscript maps of the Americas, Africa, Asia and the Caribbean, assembled by Blathwayt in the 1680s.[63] It is therefore entirely likely that Blathwayt displayed a blended assemblage of classical statuary, containing characters from both ancient mythology and Roman imperium, alongside a selection of cartographical views depicting places within his purview and interests: primarily the Netherlands, military scenes and English colonies. This approach is consistent with pictorial display within the house proper, which contained many painted views of Amsterdam and Antwerp, multiple English naval ports, and views of Tangier and Barbados.[64]

One final ingredient in Blathwayt's greenhouse and gardens was the specific allusions to King William III.[65] Running along a frieze the length of the façade is a Latin moto, drawn from the Roman poet Lucan but adopted as the personal moto of Sir William Temple (1628–99), which features in his printed portrait and is explained in his essay *Upon the Gardens of Epicurus*: 'I know not three wiser precepts for the conduct either of princes or private men, than – Servare modum, finempue tueri, Naturamque sequi'.[66] This good advice had multiple meanings for Blathwayt. Temple was his first employer when clerk in the Embassy at The Hague between 1668 to 1672, and its use clearly paid homage to his personal influence. But it had deep Williamite resonances, for Temple was King William's favourite statesman, despite his long retirement from public life. Directly opposite the greenhouse, itself replete with the overt symbolism of orange trees, lay a long canal which met a lofty and celebrated cascade, its summit commanded by a statue of Neptune – an overtly allegorical symbol of William's kingship.[67] Therefore, the quote upon the greenhouse was an affirmation of Blathwayt's affinity with the monarch. Yet while these messages can be read as dynastic or domestic, they were also inherently global. Blathwayt wrote very little to articulate his professional philosophy, but one statement stands out: colonies were 'necessary and important because they enlarge His [Majesty's] Empire & Revenue very considerably'.[68] Clear in this statement is an imperial prerogative. Remembering that Blathwayt's other significant role was as Secretary at War throughout the Nine Years' War (1688–97), this too included a North American theatre of conflict (King William's War). Therefore, the greenhouse at Dyrham was able to fold into its Williamite narrative articulation of its global imperative and vice versa.

This combination of architectural setting, plants, prints and maps conspired to create a space of extraordinary imperial vision, expressed not through fortifications but through iconography, cartography and consumption. An example of the maps that may have hung in the greenhouse is Joel Gascoyne's 1682 *New Map of the Country of Carolina*, part of the *Blathwayt Atlas*.[69] This image was published together with a promotional tract that praised Carolina's temperate nature and productive potential. The map made clear that individual settlements in Carolina clung closely to the riverfronts and those closest to the shoreline. And at the time of its production the map shows only 33 such settlements. In the era of timber and ranching, before the onset of rice as Carolina gold, the map made clear the abundant and available land of this new colony, all easily connected to the port city of Charles Town through the network of waterways that made Carolina easily navigable.

In the opening years of the eighteenth century, one of the best introductions to the nascent British empire was to enter Blathwayt's greenhouse, where lands, oceans, aloe plants and other flowering flora, orange trees and fruit from around the empire came together in a single afternoon stroll. Rain or shine, in perpetual warmth, it encouraged a moment of repose at tables and chairs for that very purpose, perhaps sampling the latest delicacies sent from afar: Jamaican sweetmeats and tobacco or citron water from Barbados. To wander through Blathwayt's greenhouse was not only to see the empire but also to smell it, touch it, even to taste it – and, when the doors between the greenhouse and the rooms of the main house were open, to hear the unfamiliar song of the Virginian red cardinal emanating from the birdcages Blathwayt kept around his house.[70]

Recent scholarship has explored the attempts by early eighteenth-century Jamaicans to transform their tropical environs into picturesque landscapes; the gardens of Charles Price were among the most spectacular attempts.[71] In a remarkable move that Jill Casid has called the colonial intermixing of landscapes that fuelled the production of empire, tropical exotica also transformed British landscapes, in and outside of greenhouses.[72] While the significance of the imperial gardens at Kew are well understood, the cultivation of colonial varieties reached well beyond.[73] Blathwayt's earlier proclivity for collecting objects of empire – from 'blackamoors' to colonial hardwoods to North American and other plants and foodstuffs – is just an early example of a practice of collection from the colonies that profoundly reshaped spaces in Britain.

Conclusion

While this discussion just begins to cut the surface, the architecture and material worlds of colonial bureaucrats such as William Blathwayt are likely to prove rich fodder for the examination of the impact of the colonies on the spaces, objects and lives of the motherland. The empire was a complex web of flows and networks that certainly had a profound impact on the places colonised, but this brief assessment of Dyrham Park reminds us that the empire also reshaped Britain in explicit and nuanced ways. Each of these three examples evidences a different strategy for signalling the colonial authority of the house's patron. The use of exotic hardwoods in the two Dyrham Park staircases reminds us that the British Empire was (and empires are) fundamentally extractive: they literally consume the resources of their colonial holdings. While Blathwayt could have had them built from English oak, he was insistent that the visible surfaces of his stairs – a sight of social spectacle and often one of the most spectacular components of an early modern English house – conveyed through their visual difference his power to shape the material flows of a growing Atlantic empire. The images and object associated with his private suite, and especially the Balcony Room, even more explicitly visualised his colonial entanglements and their personal benefits. These spaces make clear not only that the empire rested on the exploitation of colonial others for personal gain but also that these conditions were not a source of moral anxiety but simply an expression of an assumed natural order of things.[74] Lastly, his greenhouse was literally a microcosm of empire, one designed to enlist all five senses to entice visitors with the richness and wonders of exotic places, all collected under the careful control and management of the empire. These spaces invited viewers into the 'delights' of collecting places, people and things, all the while reminding them through intrigue of the coloniser's power over far-flung dominions.

Furthermore, each space had its own audience. The staircases and cedar-lined walls of the entrance hall mattered enormously to the body of colonial dignitaries who provided the materials in order to curry the favour of an important official. These rooms lived only in their imaginations; most would visualise these rooms but would never have seen them. The spaces of Blathwayt's private chambers were intimate, reserved for himself and his closest associates. In these spaces the empire became personally commodified in the images of cocoa and bodies of Africans, both capitalised to fuel his transition from low-level bureaucrat to colonial advisor to the crown. The more public greenhouse was a place where the empire was magically transformed from idea to images and things. In this space curious visitors could literally consume the empire. All three places enlisted the visceral power of the senses towards the project of imagining the empire. While imperial power is commonly read through military fortifications or other manifestations of royal authority, in the combination of a Virginia walnut staircase, enslaved 'blackamoor' figures and maps of the expanding empire, Dyrham Park offers an alternative, domesticated manifestation of empire, an empire claimed, controlled and contained in the rooms of a house.

Notes

1. Gloucester Archives (GA), D1799/E240; The James Marshall and Marie-Louise Osborn Collection, Beinecke Rare Book and Manuscript Library, Yale University, OSB MMS 2, 6 November 1702, Blathwayt to Stepney: 'I had the second order of the court with me. Lord treasurer D of Somerset with his Duchess, lady Marlborough ... I did the honour to all the foreign ministries at the bath ...'.
2. Jacobsen, *William Blathwayt*.
3. GA, D1799/C8, 25 September 1686, Blathwayt to Sir Robert Southwell.
4. Goulding, *Dyrham Park*, 18–19.
5. Webb, 'William Blathwayt: muddling through empire', 3.
6. For an excellent introduction of the Royal African Company see Pettigrew, *Freedom's Debt*.
7. Mackley, 'Building management at Dyrham', 107–16.
8. Johnson, *Edward Randolph*.
9. Jacobsen, *William Blathwayt*, 122.
10. Francis Nicholson (1655–1728) was then Lieutenant-Governor of Virginia and a close friend of William Blathwayt; Goodrick, *Edward Randolph*, 352.
11. Goodrick, *Edward Randolph*, 382–3, 390, 394.
12. Goodrick, *Edward Randolph*, 446–7.
13. Colonel Charles Scarburgh (c. 1643–1702) was a substantial landowner, based at Pungoteague, Accomack County, who in 1680 sold land to create Port Scarburgh, soon renamed Onancock. He was an officer in the militia, member of the House of Burgesses and recently appointed to the Virginia Council. Goodrick, *Edward Randolph*, 453; 'The Randolph Manuscript', 2; Whitelaw, *Virginia's Eastern Shore*.
14. Goodrick, *Edward Randolph*, 466: Randolph to Blathwayt, 22 August 1694.
15. GA, D1799/E236, Queries relating to the Draughts for the Stairs at Dirham.
16. GA, D1799/E236.
17. Heaton, *Walnut Stairs*.
18. GA, D1799/E234.
19. GA, D1799/E247; D1799/E240.
20. Webb, 'William Blathwayt: muddling through empire', 8.
21. Webb, 'William Blathwayt: Glorious Revolution', 401 (see also 405, 410).
22. The Huntington Library, San Marino, California, Blathwayt Papers MSS BL63; Rockefeller Library, Colonial Williamsburg (CW), Blathwayt Papers, XV f2, 2 December 1702, Nicholson to Blathwayt; Hardwick, 'Francis Nicholson'
23. CW, Blathwayt Papers, XIII f7, 11 June 1700, Nicholson to Blathwayt; XXXVI f5, 4 May 1699, Day to Blathwayt; Webb, 'William Blathwayt: muddling through empire', 9.
24. See CW, Blathwayt Papers, XXXVI f2.
25. Bowett, 'Commercial introduction of mahogany', 42–56; Bowett, 'English mahogany.'
26. Anderson, *Mahogany*, 65.
27. Brown, 'Atlantic slavery', 91–101.
28. Brown, *Slavery Connections*, 17.
29. Kenseth, *Age of the Marvelous*, 29–36. On the 'naturalness' of Africans see Jordan, *White over Black*, 3–44.
30. Evelyn, *Diary of John Evelyn*, 186: 17 October 1671.
31. Walvin, *Fruits of Empire*, 89–101.
32. Coe and Coe, *True History of Chocolate*, 22; Buisseret, *Jamaica in 1687*, 207–8.
33. For a full account of this painting see Emanuel and Goulding, '"Whole story of cocoa"'.
34. Walvin, *Fruits of Empire*, 96.
35. GA, D1799/E240, 5 December ?1700, John Povey to Thomas Povey.
36. GA, D1799/E240; D1799/ E254; see Walton, 'Inventory of 1710'.
37. National Trust Collections (NTC) 453774 (see https://www.nationaltrustcollections.org.uk/object/453774); Gàldy and Heudecker, *Collecting Nature*, 70–1.
38. NTC 452247 & 452248 (see https://www.nationaltrustcollections.org.uk/object/452247).
39. See Walton, *Fruits of Empire*.
40. See https://collections.vam.ac.uk/item/O111909/nouvelles-cheminée-faitte-en-plusier-etching-marot-daniel/; Jackson-Stops, 'Court style in Britain'.

41 NTC 452977 (see https://www.nationaltrustcollections.org.uk/object/452977); Goulding, *Dyrham Park*, 43.
42 Molineux, *Faces of Perfect Ebony*.
43 Such as *Portrait of a Family Drinking Tea in an Interior*, c. 1680, attributed to Roelof Koets (see https://rkd.nl/explore/images/116428).
44 See Walton, *Fruits of Empire*; GA, D1799/E247.
45 Long, *History of Jamaica*, vol. 2, 87.
46 An excellent and sophisticated discussion of this subject appears in Molineux, *Faces of Perfect Ebony*. See Bindman, 'Black presence in British art', 253–70. See also Massing, *Image of the Black*, vol. 3, pt. 2, 225–60. On African slaves as exotics see Walvin, *Making the Black Atlantic*, 105–7.
47 Amussen, *Caribbean Exchanges*, 191–217.
48 Bindman, 'Black presence in British art', 255–6.
49 Lee, 'Serving as ornament'.
50 Bradshaw, *Bow Porcelain Figures*, figure 216.
51 Walvin, *Making the Black Atlantic*, 107–12.
52 Switzer, *Ichnographia Rustica*, vol. 3, 115–16.
53 Switzer, *Ichnographia Rustica*, vol. 3, 116.
54 Switzer, *Ichnographia Rustica*, vol. 3, 117. See also Jeffery, 'Flower of all the Private Gentlemen's Palaces', 14–15. On Dyrham Park and early modern greenhouses see Woods and Warren, *Glass Houses*, 43–6.
55 Casid, *Sowing Empire*, 45–94; Woods and Warren, *Glass Houses*, 34.
56 Dunn, *Sugar and Slaves*, 278.
57 Switzer, *Ichnographia Rustica*, vol. 3, 117.
58 CW, Blathwayt Papers XV. 2 10 June 1691, Nicholson to Blathwayt; 5 December 1691, Blathwayt to Nicholson; XV. 3. 30 March 1697, Nicholson to Blathwayt.
59 GA, D1799/E234/19.
60 GA, D1799/X5.
61 Switzer, *Ichnographia Rustica*, vol. 3, 117; Woods and Warren, *Glass Houses*, 46.
62 Walton, 'Inventory of 1710'; GA, D1799/E256.
63 Goulding, 'A tutored eye', 29–37; Black, *The Blathwayt Atlas*.
64 Details of Blathwayt's paintings are best understood from a sale catalogue of 18–21 November 1765: British Library S.C. 1360.
65 Goulding, *Dyrham Park*, 56–7.
66 Translated as: preserve a sense of limit, stay on course towards a goal, and follow nature; Temple, *Miscellanea*, 127–8.
67 Goulding, *Dyrham Park*, 56–7: for example see Hughes, *Court of Neptune*.
68 Quoted in Jacobsen, *William Blathwayt*, 96; original: Huntington, Blathwayt Papers, Box II, BL416.
69 John Carter Brown Library, Cabinet Blathwayt 23.
70 Walton, *Fruits of Empire*; CW, Blathwayt Papers XV. 2, 10 June 1691, Nicholson to Blathwayt.
71 Nelson, *Architecture and Empire*.
72 Casid, *Sowing Empire*.
73 Brockway, *Science and Colonial Expansion*. See also Katie Donington, Chapter 13, this volume.
74 For an excellent discussion of the shift in these considerations over the course of the eighteenth century see Gikandi, *Slavery and the Culture of Taste*.

Bibliography

Amussen, Susan Dwyer. *Caribbean Exchanges: Slavery and the transformation of English society, 1640–1700*. Chapel Hill: University of North Carolina Press, 2007.
Anderson, Jennifer. *Mahogany: The costs of luxury in early America*. Cambridge: Harvard University Press, 2015.
Bindman, David. 'The Black presence in British art: sixteenth and seventeenth centuries'. In *The Image of the Black in Western Art*, 5 vols, edited by David Bindman and Henry Louis Gates, Jr, vol. 3, part 1, 235–70, 5 vols. Cambridge: Harvard University Press, 2011.

Black, Jeannette D. *The Blathwayt Atlas: Commentary*. Providence: Brown University Press 1970.
Bowett, Adam. 'The commercial introduction of mahogany and the Naval Stores Act of 1721', *Furniture History*, 30 (1994): 43–56.
Bowett, Adam. 'The English mahogany trade, 1700–1793', PhD thesis, Brunel University, 1996.
Bradshaw, Peter. *Bow Porcelain Figures, 1748–1774*. London: Barrie and Jenkins, 1992.
Brockway, Lucile. *Science and Colonial Expansion: The Role of the British Royal Botanic Garden: The Role of the British Royal Botanic Gardens*. New York and London: Academic Press, 1979.
Brown, Laurence. *The Slavery Connections of Marble Hill House*. Swindon: Historic England, 2010.
Brown, Laurence. 'Atlantic slavery and classical culture at Marble Hill and Northington Grange'. In *Slavery and the British Country House*, edited by Madge Dresser and Andrew Hamm, 89–97. Swindon: English Heritage, 2013.
Buisseret, David. *Jamaica in 1687: The Taylor Manuscript at the National Library of Jamaica*. Kingston: University of West Indies Press, 2008.
Casid, Jill. *Sowing Empire: Landscape and Colonization*. Minneapolis: University of Minnesota Press, 2004.
Coe, Sophie, and Michael Coe. *The True History of Chocolate*. London: Thames & Hudson, 2013.
Dunn, Richard. *Sugar and Slaves: The rise of the planter class in the English West Indies, 1624–1713*. Chapel Hill: University of North Carolina Press for the Omohundro Institute of Early American History and Culture, 1972; reprinted 2000.
Emanuel, Philip, and Rupert Goulding. '"The whole story of cocoa", Dyrham Park and the painting and planting of chocolate in Jamaica'. In *National Trust ABC Bulletin Autumn 2021*, edited by David Boulting, 5–9. https://nt.global.ssl.fastly.net/documents/abc-bulletin-autumn-2021.pdf.
Evelyn, John. *The Diary of John Evelyn*. Edited by Guy de la Bédoyére. Woodbridge: The Boydell Press, 1995.
Gàldy, Andrea and Sylvia Heudecker, *Collecting Nature*. Cambridge: Cambridge Scholars Publishing, 2015.
Gikandi, Simon. *Slavery and the Culture of Taste*. Princeton: Princeton University Press, 2011.
Goodrick, Alfred, ed. *Edward Randolph*, vol. 7. Boston: The Prince Society, 1898.
Goulding, Rupert. 'A tutored eye', In *National Trust Historic Houses & Collections Annual 2013*, 29–37. London: Apollo, 2013.
Goulding, Rupert. *Dyrham Park and William Blathwayt*. Swindon: National Trust, 2017.
Hardwick, Kevin. 'Francis Nicholson (1655–1728)'. In *Oxford Dictionary of National Biography*, 23 September 2004; accessed 12 March 2020, https://doi.org/10.1093/ref:odnb/20130.
Heaton, Michael. *The Walnut Stairs: Assessment of historical significance*. Unpublished National Trust Report, 2018.
Hughes, John. *The Court of Neptune*. London, 1700.
Jackson-Stops, Gervase. 'The court style in Britain'. In *Courts and Colonies: The William and Mary style in Holland, England, and America*. New York: The Smithsonian Institution, 1988.
Jacobsen, Gertrude. *William Blathwayt: A late 17th century English administrator*. New Haven: Yale University Press, 1932.
Jeffrey, Sally. '"The Flower of All the Private Gentlemens Palaces in England": Sir Stephen Fox's "Extraordinarily Fine" Garden at Chiswick', *Garden History* 32, no.1 (2004): 1–19.
Johnson, Richard. 'Edward Randolph (1632–1703)'. In *Oxford Dictionary of National Biography*, 23 September 2004; accessed 5 August 2021, https://doi.org/10.1093/ref:odnb/23117.
Jordan, Winthrop. *White over Black: American attitudes towards the Negro*. 2nd edition. Chapel Hill: University of North Carolina Press, 2012.
Kenseth, Joy, ed. *The Age of the Marvelous*. Hanover: Hood Museum of Art, 1991.
Lee, Hannah. 'Serving as ornament: the representation of African people in early modern British interiors and gardens', *British Art Studies* 21 (2021), https://doi.org/10.17658/issn.2058-5462/issue-21/hlee.
Long, Edward. *The History of Jamaica*. London: T. Lowndes, 1774.
Mackley, Alan. 'Building management at Dyrham', *The Georgian Group Journal* 7 (1997): 107–16.
Massing, Jean Michel. *The Image of the Black in Western Art. Vol. 3, pt. 2: From the "Age of Discovery" to the Age of Abolition. Europe and the World Beyond*. Cambridge: Harvard University Press, 2011.

Molineux, Catherine. *Faces of Perfect Ebony: Encountering Atlantic slavery in imperial Britain*. Cambridge: Harvard University Press, 2012.

Nelson, Louis. *Architecture and Empire in Jamaica*. New Haven: Yale University Press, 2016.

Pettigrew, William. *Freedom's Debt: The Royal African Company and the politics of the Atlantic slave trade, 1672–1752*. Chapel Hill: University of North Carolina Press, 2013.

Stubbe, Henry. *The Indian Nectar, Or a Discourse Concerning Chocolata*. London, 1662.

Switzer, Stephen. *Ichnographia Rustica: or, the Nobleman, Gentleman, and Gardener's Recreation ...*, vol. 3. London, 1718.

Temple, William. *Miscellanea. The second part in four essays*. London: 1690.

'The Randolph Manuscript'. Virginia Seventeenth Century Records (Continued), *The Virginia Magazine of History and Biography* 20, no. 1 (1912). Accessed 3 August 2021, http://www.jstor.org/stable/4243174

Walton, Karin-M. 'An inventory of 1710 from Dyrham Park', *Furniture History* 22 (1986): 25–80.

Walvin, James. *Fruits of Empire: Exotic produce and British taste, 1660–1800*. New York: New York University Press, 1997.

Walvin, James. *Making the Black Atlantic: Britain and the African diaspora*. London: Cassell, 2000.

Webb, Stephen Saunders. 'William Blathwayt, imperial fixer: from Popish Plot to Glorious Revolution', *William and Mary Quarterly* 25, no. 1 (1968): 3–21.

Webb, Stephen Saunders. 'William Blathwayt, imperial fixer: muddling through to empire, 1689–1717', *William and Mary Quarterly* 26, no. 3 (1969): 373–415.

Whitelaw, Ralph. *Virginia's Eastern Shore: A history of Northampton and Accomack counties*, vol. 2. Gloucester: P. Smith, 1968.

Woods, Mary, and Arete Swartz Warren. *Glass Houses: A history of greenhouses, orangeries and conservatories*. London: Aurum Press, 1990.

13
Cultivating the world: English country house gardens, 'exotic' plants and elite women collectors, c. 1690–1800

Katie Donington

The National Trust report into the links between the properties in its care, slavery and colonialism, published in September 2020,[1] garnered extensive public interest and became the subject of 'culture war' (see Introduction).[2] Its remit included country house gardens, noting that 'a significant number of ... gardens and parklands in our care were created or remodelled as expressions of the taste and wealth, as well as power and privilege, that derived from colonial connections'.[3] It highlighted the 'complex sets of transnational influences that lay behind the design of buildings, gardens and parklands, and so many of the plants and collections that filled them'.[4] However, the report did not engage in any detail with the materiality of the garden, concentrating instead on the colonial finances used to transform these landscapes. Outside the report's scope, the global story of the country house garden reached beyond the formal borders of the British Empire, encompassing people and places which spanned the world.

    The country house and garden occupy a sacred position in popular constructions of Englishness. As Peter Mandler has argued, '[t]he stately homes of England, it is often now claimed, are that country's greatest contribution to Western civilisation. They are the quintessence of Englishness; they epitomise the English love of domesticity, of the countryside, of hierarchy, continuity and tradition.'[5] In his poem 'The Glory of the Garden' (1911), Rudyard Kipling proclaimed that 'Our England is a garden'. The garden he chose as his metaphor for the nation – with terraces, 'stately views', border, beds and avenues – was no urban backyard but rather a country house garden. The text referenced peacocks, begonias and hot houses, gesturing towards England's commercial and cultural global interactions as well as its history of empire. The inclusion of these symbols of the 'exotic' recall what Stuart Hall has described as the 'outside history that is inside the history of the English'.[6] Imperial and global perspectives on the country estate offer new ways of thinking about domesticity and consumption, gender and empire, home and identity, heritage and belonging. They demand attention to how the local interacted with the wider world to create dynamic living spaces whose networks of supply, influence and identification reached far beyond their own boundaries.

Women played an active role in shaping these spaces and networks. They acted as conduits for property and capital, and their personal experiences and family ties linked the country estates they inhabited to other parts of the globe. As household managers, they were involved in the purchase of goods for the home and garden. While most branches of the sciences were considered masculine spheres of interest, botany and horticulture became increasingly feminised practices by the late eighteenth century.[7] Although intimately tied to the home, plant culture provided a means by which women could transcend the domestic sphere through involvement in networks of international commerce and scientific knowledge. In exploring the gardens and hot houses these elite women created, it is possible to understand more about how the materiality of the country estate was shaped by their participation in imperial and global forms of consumption.

This chapter considers the country house gardens of two elite women plant collectors: Mary Somerset, Duchess of Beaufort (1630–1715) and Margaret Cavendish Harley Bentinck, Duchess of Portland (1715–85). It charts the metropolitan and colonial networks of collaboration that enabled these women to build their collections. The movement of 'exotic' plant species into the country house garden impacted on its design through the incorporation of new technologies and forms of display. The chapter explores how the presence of 'exotic' plants reshaped the visual and material landscape. It also looks at how they inspired botanical art, creating a distinctive legacy and record of the ephemeral garden or live plant collection. In taking the garden as the primary focus for analysis, the chapter addresses an area of country house culture that has received less attention within public history as a site which bears the traces of imperial and transnational connections. In doing so it highlights the potential of the garden as a space to facilitate dialogue about the global dimensions of country house culture and national heritage.

Enlightenment, empire and botany

Botanical gardens were established in Padua and Pisa in 1543, Bologna in 1567, Leiden in 1587, Heidelberg and Montpellier in 1593 and Oxford in 1621.[8] Historians have written extensively about the explosion of interest in botany aided by the confluence of Enlightenment and empire in the eighteenth century.[9] With the 'Age of Discovery', Europeans sailed to the Americas, Africa and Asia, establishing fledgling colonies and new trading routes which increased the flow of 'exotic' imports into Europe. Private and institutional collectors funded botanists to participate in exploratory voyages with the purpose of returning with rare specimens.[10] The impact of imperial expansion was reflected in the scope of the royal collection at Kew Gardens: 'In 1770 fewer than 3,400 exotic introductions were housed in the royal collection at Kew. By 1813 that collection alone contained over 11,000 exotic species.'[11]

The natural sciences were not simply an adjunct to empire; colonial bioprospecting led to the establishment of plantation societies in the Americas and the transformation of habits and taste in the metropole.[12] Empire enabled the cultivation of 'exotic' plants for European mass consumption on an industrial scale using plantation agriculture and forced labour. For elite collectors, empire also provided access to an expanded market in 'exotic' plants. The ability to locate and collect these precious items required agents on the ground in the form of both 'plant hunters' and indigenous and enslaved people whose knowledge and skills were drawn upon in the process of accrual.[13] Networks of ship captains, naval officers, merchants and nurserymen formed part of the 'cycle of accumulation' that moved tropical plants into the country house gardens of the elites.[14]

Developments in science and technology brought an intensification of interest in the natural world. The capacity for successful cultivation rested on innovations to transport specimens and create artificial climates to sustain them.[15] The natural world's commercial potential created close links between learned societies, trading companies, merchants, colonists and collectors.[16] Knowledge generated in the colonies was circulated into the metropole through correspondence, scientific reports, exhibitions, lectures and public experiments. Visiting gardens provided the curious with instruction and aesthetic delight; physic gardens, pleasure gardens, nursery gardens, botanical gardens and country house gardens allowed audiences a glimpse of the flora and fauna of the world.[17] Private collectors could stake a claim to scientific participation through the acquisition and cultivation of botanical specimens, some of which were only accessible in their gardens. This transformed their hothouses into 'both a museum and laboratory' and their homes into places of learning.[18] As visitors came to observe, draw and converse about their collections, the distinction between the private domestic and public spheres became less marked.

'The female province': gender, botany and the garden

A growing body of work has highlighted the contribution of women to the natural sciences.[19] Studies of individual women in the early modern period provide insight into the gendered dynamics of botanical culture.[20] Evidence of horticultural and botanical activities can be found in women's magazines, letters, diaries, notebooks, travel writing and needlework. For some elite collectors their practice was recorded in the published works of male scientists and naturalists. Suzanne Moss has argued that the problem of preserving live botanical collections could mean that this practice was more widespread than the surviving evidence suggests.[21] While the gardens they tended proved to be more transient, other forms of material culture associated with the garden including infrastructure, libraries, artwork and herbariums have been conserved in museums and country houses.

The ways that women's interest in botany was framed was gendered and classed. Ann Shteir has argued that by the latter part of the eighteenth century botany had 'become part of the social construction of femininity for girls across the middle and upper ranks of society'.[22] Botanical reading, drawing and conversation were viewed as polite pastimes for young women. In a passage in the *Gentleman's Magazine*, cultivating 'exotics' was specifically recommended as the 'female province':

> The nurture of exotics not only belongs more particularly to the female province, on account of it being an elegant home amusement, but because of there being much delicate work, essential to the welfare of plants, that is more dexterously performed by the pliant fingers of women. Ladies can also more conveniently attend the regulation of the green-house sashes, which require closer attention than the ordinary concerns of gentlemen will allow them to pay.[23]

Tending to these delicate plants within the confines of the domestic sphere suited women's physical attributes, ample leisure time and motherly instincts. This construction of women's skill divorced it from their botanical knowledge. This reductive attitude could be subverted by elite women who were able to leverage their 'class privilege' to transgress 'emerging beliefs about women's capacities and actively contribute to the collaborative advancement of knowledge of the natural world'.[24] Influential figures such as Queen Charlotte (1744–1818) fostered a scholarly botanical culture that centred networks of women as well as men.[25] The scientific and botanical patronage of royal and aristocratic women allowed the garden to become 'an environment in which women could learn and exhibit that learning'.[26]

Increased attention has been paid to how women's botanical activities intersected with empire.[27] Research into women as active imperial agents demonstrates how their colonial wealth supported their lifestyles.[28] Women also participated in the economy of empire through their consumer habits, including the purchase of plants. Hong has described this process as the 'domestication of colonial botany'.[29] While some elite women travelled out into empire, most experienced it at a distance. The cultivation of, or visit to, a country house garden created a space for women to 'explore ... travelling in their minds to distant places through interaction with the materials of foreign cultures'.[30] As Jael Henrietta Pye (1737–82) remarked on attending the gardens at Twickenham in 1775, 'I have observed that ladies in general visit these places, as our young gentleman do foreign parts. ... These little excursions being commonly the only travels permitted to our sex.'[31] Fowkes Tobin has analysed how collecting, growing and displaying 'exotic' specimens was part of constructing the self. She suggests that plant cultivation projected a sense of 'one's sophistication and worldliness' and offered 'educational, emotional and spiritual benefits'.[32] She also outlines the colonial dimension of 'exotic' plants as a signifier of the nation's 'mastery over the globe's natural resources'.[33] The uprooting and movement of plants was an expression of Britain's position as a colonial commercial power.

Domesticating the 'exotic': the country house gardens of Badminton and Bulstrode Park

Mary Somerset (1630–1715) became mistress of Badminton, Gloucestershire, following her second marriage to Henry Somerset (1629–1700), Duke of Beaufort, in 1657 (Figure 13.1). The couple set about renovating the 'solid, if unattractive, house ... situated in fine woodland

Figure 13.1 *Mary Capel (1630–1715), Later Duchess of Beaufort, and Her Sister Elizabeth (1633–1678), Countess of Carnarvon* by Sir Peter Lely. Oil on canvas. Accession number 39.65.3. Bequest of Jacob Ruppert, 1939. © Metropolitan Museum of Art.

and hill country'.[34] By 1690 they had spent £29,760 on improvements, including considerable sums on the garden.[35] Mary's botanical vision reflected the taste of a cultural elite whose outlook was increasingly global as trade and empire expanded the nation's vistas. With her husband away from the home, Mary controlled domestic finances and kept the account books. She spared no expense, amassing one of the 'largest collection[s] of exotic plants in England'.[36]

Mary was 'born into a family renowned for its horticultural achievements' including the cultivation of gardens at Kew, Cassiobury Park and Little Hadham.[37] Following her several bouts of melancholy in the 1660s and 1670s, Mary's garden took on an intensified meaning, providing 'personal salvation through knowledge and contemplation of the natural world'.[38] Molly McClain has argued that there was a religious dimension to Mary's collecting practices – that in assembling plants from across the world, she tried to 'recreate Paradise'.[39] This related to a Renaissance idea that the Garden of Eden might be made anew on English soil through the transfer of botanical specimens from Asia and the New World.[40] Mary's consumption of travelogues, natural histories and catalogues of 'exotic' plants offered her respite from her emotional distress. Writing in 1694 to Sir Robert Southwell (1635–1702), president of the Royal Society, Mary described her botanical practice as 'my innocent diversion of gardening'.[41] Immersing herself in the natural world provided an all-consuming distraction, as she confided to Sir Hans Sloane (1660–1753): 'When I get into storys of plants I know not how to get out.'[42] Perhaps she also experienced comfort in the sense of order which collecting and cultivation offered. Writing in 1715, the garden designer Stephen Switzer (1682–1745) commended the 'progress' Mary had made with her 'exotics', enthusing about 'the "Thousands" of those foreign Plants (by her as it were made familiar to this Clime) regimented together, and kept in a wonderful deal of Health, Order and Decency'.[43] Switzer's comment is indicative of the process of domestication which took place as 'exotic' plants were removed from their countries of origin and recontextualised in the country house garden. Here they became symbolic of orderliness and decency, a marker of the duchess's power to regiment unruly nature and render the 'foreign' as 'familiar'.

Mary's status as an aristocratic woman gave her access to influential networks. The position of her townhouse – Beaufort House in Chelsea – meant her garden was 'closely allied to the collection at the nearby Chelsea Physic Garden'.[44] Jacob Bobart (1641–1719), superintendent of the Physic Garden, regularly corresponded with Mary and her staff at Badminton. She also had 'working relationships' with leading botanists, naturalists and members of the Royal Society, including James Petiver (c. 1665–1718), Samuel Doody (1656–1706), William Sherard (1659–1728) and John Ray (1627–1705).[45] Sherard served as her gardener at Badminton for 18 months, helping her with collecting and cataloguing. He used his own networks to source specimens for her, writing in 1700 that he had sent 'requests to all my Botanick friends for seads … for her Graces garden'.[46] Research into the networks that facilitated the exchange of seeds and plants evidences intersections with the slave trade and other commercial routes. Kathleen Murphy's work on James Petiver's collecting practices documented the involvement of merchants, slave ship captains and enslaved people.[47] She has shown how enslaved and indigenous knowledge and practice were used to find, identify and procure botanical and entomological specimens. Petiver's networks stretched beyond Britain's Atlantic empire, as Richard Coulton has documented in his analysis of *Musei Petiveriani*:

> 24% (101) name 19 different contributors from the East Indies; 21% (87) concern 38 contacts in Britain; 20% (81) are for 20 collectors

in southern or western Africa; 18% (73) relate to 34 donors from the Americas (from Newfoundland in the north to the coast of Brazil in the south); and 15% (64) name 22 individuals across the rest of Europe.[48]

Other correspondents hailed from the Levant and the islands of the South and mid-Atlantic. Petiver exchanged letters and specimens with Mary and visited her garden at Badminton, describing it as 'a Paradise'.[49]

Like Petiver's, Mary's networks followed both imperial and global trade routes. She was a recipient of plants brought from Jamaica by Hans Sloane following his time there as physician to the governor.[50] Her brother Henry Capell, baron of Tewkesbury, raised plants from North America and the Far East, and among Mary's papers was a 'Catalogue of seeds from the East Indies sent by my brother Harry April 1 1693'.[51] She commissioned colonial agents to track down specimens. Reverend James Weir wrote in 1696 that Mary had a vast shipment of goods transported from Barbados including cuttings, saplings and mature trees. The 'consignment was so large that the first 11 tubs were split between five ships, with eight more promised in the next fleet'.[52] The garden designer and nurseryman George London (c. 1640–1714) sent her plants and seeds from Portugal, the Canaries, Africa and China.[53]

Mary was credited with the introduction of 87 new plants from around the world in *Hortus Kewensis* (1789). A selection of the entries gives an impression of the geographic range of her collection: Virginian blush flowered speedwell, Malabar nut from Ceylon, Jamaica vervain, Canary sage, purple panic grass from the East Indies, thick spiked dog-tail grass from India, dwarf bindweed from Spain and France, red spined nightshade from South America, African and Asian box thorn, argan from Morocco, twinning Rhamnus from Carolina, wild cumin from the Levant, silvery spiked Celosia from China and bell flowered gigantic swallow wort from Persia. Mary asked her agents for contextual information about the plants. Weir wrote to her lamenting that 'You desire to know the Authors of the plants but I can find none but names which the common people have'.[54] The annotations in Mary's catalogues demonstrated her absorption of indigenous forms of knowledge. For one entry she wrote 'All sow'd 9 – Some will have this to be Jallap, others Mechocan, but it agrees not with ye description of either, the Indians call it poke'.[55] She struggled with names from China, noting down 'names gues's at mark't only wth figures' on her list.[56]

The cultivation of 'exotics' required specialist buildings and equipment to accommodate plants outside their natural climate.

This made a lasting imprint on the landscape of the English country house garden. As Philip Miller (1661–1791), chief gardener at the Chelsea Physic Garden, wrote in 1768:

> As of late years there have been great quantities of curious exotic plants introduced into the English gardens, so the number of Green-houses, or Conservatories, have increased; and not only a greater skill in the management and ordering of these plants has increased, but also greater knowledge of the structure and contrivance of these places, so as to render them both useful and ornamental.[57]

Mary raised 'exotics' without the use of a hothouse at Beaufort House using hotbeds and pots, but her plans for Badminton were more ambitious.[58] She already had substantive greenhouses, as noted by Cassandra Willoughby when she visited in 1697: 'All the Gardens &c they reckon to be 50 Acres, I mean the courts and all the nurseries for plants &c which with the Green Houses are very neat and very fine.'[59] Whilst orangeries were in use for growing citrus fruits, hothouses first appeared in Amsterdam in the early 1680s. They were heated 'from subterranean ovens fed with coal or oak billets'.[60] By about 1690 this innovation was used by Magdalena Pouelle at her country estate Gunterstein. The technique was adopted in Chelsea by a Mr Watt in 1685, and by 1689 'glass cases' were built at Hampton Court for Queen Mary.[61] The duchess visited both English sites in preparation for her own installation. Having examined Badminton's 'cash books', Mark Laird noted a significant 'flurry of activity in her "Orringere" from September 1698 onwards' as Mary transformed her greenhouse into a tropical hothouse.[62] In February 1699 work began 'on a chimney and on plastering and glazing', with construction ongoing in March on 'ye New Stove'.[63]

A painting attributed to Thomas Smith of Derby captured the extent of the hothouses (Figure 13.2). Located on the right-hand side of the painting adjacent to the cylindrical building, the structure was 110 feet long and 18 feet high. Not entirely constructed from glass, 'the south facade had eight windows divided by three doors into four pairs. Five dormer windows surmounted the roof.'[64] Mary wrote to Sloane in 1799 declaring her hothouse as 'made for all Curiosities',[65] including an Indian laurel which 'attained the height of an 18-foot wall at the rear of the structure' and a 17-foot guava plant, custard apples and banana trees.[66] Outside to the left of the structure was a melon garden.[67] The stove enabled Mary to grow succulents 'which could be overwintered in

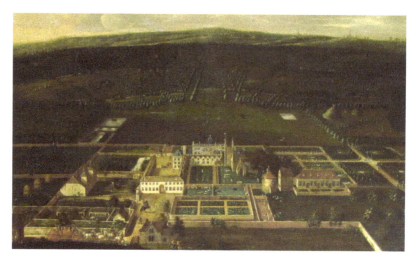

Figure 13.2 Badminton from the south, attributed to Thomas Smith (c. 1708–10)

the Orangery' and 'displayed outdoors in tubs and pots each summer'.[68] This allowed her to create an 'aesthetic of exoticism' which linked the practical internal workings of the hothouse to the ornamental exhibition of her labours in the external garden space.[69]

Badminton was acknowledged as a centre of botanical excellence in Miller's *Catalogus Plantarum* (1730). He noted that 'the Duchess of Beaufort did also collect a numerous Quantity of rare Plants into those famous Gardens of Badminton, where she preserved and maintained them with great Care'.[70] Petiver recognised her skills working with 'specimens from the most Distant climates', which enabled him to study 'many New, Rare and very curious Plants, most of them raised to that Perfection I never saw before'.[71] Both Sloane and Petiver described Mary's activities in gendered language, the former referring to her hothouse as her 'Infirmary' and the latter to her 'Nursing Care'.[72] While her knowledge and practice were respected, they were still shaped by her position as a woman. Sloane sent Mary copies of the Royal Society's *Philosophical Transactions*, which featured reports on botanical projects at Badminton, but she was unable to become a fellow of the Society or publish work. Despite this Mary left a significant material legacy. She created a 12-volume herbarium and commissioned a two-album florilegium of 178 images by the Dutch artist Everhard Kick (1636–1701) and others. The individual plant portraits offer a partial view of the botanical spectacle of Mary's garden. The volumes are preserved by her descendants at Badminton and have been described as 'the most

Figure 13.3 Beaufortia Decussata, Splendid Beaufortia in *Curtis's Botanical Magazine* 42.1726–1770 (1815): 1733. Image © Biodiversity Heritage Library. Public domain, available at https://www.biodiversitylibrary.org/bibliography/706.

evocative relic of the duchess's gardening'.[73] Her herbarium stood as testament to the years of reading, learning and applied practice necessary to create such a significant compendium. On Mary's death in 1715, she bequeathed it to Sloane, who incorporated it into his collection. It is now housed at the Natural History Museum, London. Nearly one hundred years after her death, the botanist Robert Browne (1773–1858) named an Australian specimen after Mary (Figure 13.3), honouring her as 'an early encourager of the science of Botany'.[74]

Born the year of Mary's death in 1715, Margaret Cavendish Harley Bentinck, Duchess of Portland (1715–85), was a botanical and natural history collector. In 1734 she married William Bentinck, second Duke of Portland (1709–62), and became mistress of Bulstrode Park, Buckinghamshire (Figure 13.4). On marriage, Margaret turned her attention to her husband's country estate. She redesigned the grounds, adding 'sweeping lawns, flower gardens, and wooded groves' so that

BULSTRODE, Buckinghamshire.

Figure 13.4 'Bulstrode, Buckinghamshire' engraved by Walker after a picture by Corbould, published in *The Copper Plate Magazine*, 1794. Image the Trustees of the British Museum. Available at https://www.britishmuseum.org/collection/image/473982001 and reproduced under the Creative Commons licence, CC BY-NC-SA 4.0.

by 1753 a visitor described the 'works and improvements' there as 'innumerable'.[75] Horace Walpole estimated that the duchess spent 'not less than three score thousand pounds' on alterations and her collection.[76] Fowkes Tobin argued that the duchess's natural history collection marked her as 'a dedicated naturalist engaged in the Enlightenment project of collecting and classifying the natural world'.[77] David Elliston Allen suggested that the collection made Bulstrode 'even more important than the British Museum' to the study of natural history in Britain.[78] Margaret cultivated a scholarly environment at her home, welcoming literary, artistic, scientific and botanical experts and practitioners. This learned traffic transformed Bulstrode from a private residence into 'something between a museum and a university'.[79] It was this reputation for intellectual labour which saw Bulstrode given the epithet 'The Hive'.[80]

The duchess's collection has been compared to both an earlier aristocratic tradition of the *Kunst und Wunderkammern* and an Enlightenment museum. Fowkes Tobin theorised the former as a practice by which 'the collected object, a rarity, represented a region or a people and displayed the owner's global reach and figurative dominion over the world's resources'.[81] The gathered objects conveyed a sense of wonderment and intrigue, sparking conversation or providing an impetus for thought and reflection. The latter placed emphasis on the categorisation and ordering of the collection to produce useful knowledge.[82] The grounds at Bulstrode certainly lent themselves to a sense of awe; they included a botanical garden, hothouse, menagerie and aviary as well as the Portland Museum. While Badminton was home to some 'exotic' animals including species of deer from India and America, Bulstrode's grounds had a large collection of rare beasts and birds. Writing in 1768, Mary Delany (1700–88), a botanical artist and close friend of Margaret's, captured the impact that the landscape, house and collection made upon the visitor:

> Surely an application to natural beauties must enlarge the mind? Can we view the wonderful texture of every leaf and flower, the dazzling and varied plumage of birds, the glowing colour of flies, &c. &c., and their infinite variety, without saying *'Wonderful and marvellous art thou in all thy works!'* And this house, with all belonging to it, is a *noble school* for such contemplations![83]

Ten years later Bulstrode still elicited an almost religious fervour in Delany. Writing again in 1778, she described it as 'Paradise', proclaiming that 'A curious and enquiring mind can't fail of being gratified'.[84] Her use of the term 'Paradise' calls to mind the earlier Renaissance preoccupation with reconstructing an Edenic totality of all the world's plant life. In another biblical reference, Elizabeth Montagu (1718–1800), founder of the Bluestocking Society, wryly noted that it seemed that Margaret 'is as eager in collecting animals, as if she foresaw another deluge, and was assembling every creature after its kind, to preserve the species'.[85] An auction catalogue of Margaret's collection complied after her death opined that 'It was indeed the intention of the Enlightened Possessor [the duchess] to have had every unknown Species described and published to the world'.[86] The description recognised Margaret as both a collector and a producer of knowledge – she wanted not only to possess these objects but also to increase public understanding by cataloguing and disseminating her findings.

Margaret's scientific and botanical networks included both men and women. One of the most productive relationships that Margaret fostered was through her patronage of Mary Delany. Delany's second husband died in 1768, whereupon she was invited by the duchess to take up long periods of residence at her country estate. Delany's art blurred the boundaries between the internal and external at Bulstrode.

Inspired by the garden and the animals it housed, she created pieces which drew on the world in microcosm that the duchess had assembled. On observing a 'little Jonquil parrot' which 'breakfasted' with the household, Delany made a 'seat back' for a chair in chenille inspired by the bird.[87] Her most celebrated works were paper mosaics of botanical specimens, many of them based on Margaret's collection (Figure 13.5).[88] Stacey Sloboda has commented that Delany's ten-volume *Flora Delanica* functioned as 'a paper museum that complemented Portland's physical one'.[89] Delany was not the only artist working at Bulstrode. The duchess employed Georg Ehret (1708–70), a friend of Linnaeus and botanical draughtsman, to teach her daughters the art of botany. His work as tutor linked Ehret to both Bulstrode and Badminton, where he had been employed teaching Henrietta Somerset, the daughter of the fourth Duke of Beaufort. At Bulstrode, Ehret painted 300 'exotic' plants and 500 domestic varieties for Margaret's collection.[90]

Figure 13.5 'Portlandia Grandiflora' by Mary Delany from an album Vol. VII, 91 (1782). Collage of coloured papers, with bodycolour and watercolour, on black ink background. Composition made at Bulstrode Park. Image © British Museum.

Margaret traded letters and specimens with leading Enlightenment figures. She corresponded and exchanged gifts with Jean Jacques Rousseau.[91] John Lightfoot (1735–88), a founding member of the Linnean Society and fellow of the Royal Society, was her chaplain and librarian, and he helped to curate and inventory her collection. She received cataloguing assistance from Daniel Solander (1733–82), a student of Linnaeus who went with Sir Joseph Banks on Captain Cook's first *Endeavour* voyage and became keeper of the natural history collection at the British Museum. In 1771, following Cook's Pacific travels, he, Banks and Solander visited Bulstrode, bringing material for Margaret's perusal. Audrey Baker has speculated that 'it is possible that some of these were grown at Bulstrode, for an old map marks an area called "Botany Bay field"'.[92] The duchess was in contact with 'naval officers and commercial captains who sailed to the East and West Indies'.[93] In 1761, when Solander went down to the Thames to visit the returning West India fleet to enquire about 'natural curiosities', he was disappointed to find 'They are destined for the Duchess of Portland'.[94] Margaret also used her personal ties to ensure her supplies. Her friend Frances Boscawen (1719–1805) was married to Admiral Edward Boscawen (1711–61), whose service took him to Europe, the Americas and India, where he acquired material on Margaret's behalf.[95]

Margaret amassed a vast collection of shells which were sourced both locally and internationally. She commissioned agents to collect on her behalf, contributing £100 in 1771 to fund Henry Smeathman in his work on the west coast of Africa.[96] When her collection was auctioned off in 1786, the catalogue listed shells from Australia, New Zealand, Tahiti, New Caledonia, Tonga and North America. Shell grottoes became a fashionable garden feature, with some using material from Africa and the East and West Indies.[97] Construction of a shell grotto at Bulstrode began in 1743 and was nearing completion by 1770. Many of the grotto shells were sourced from the estate itself, including snail shells. The exact location of the grotto is unclear, although it has been speculated it was close to the menagerie which housed the duchess's 'exotic' animals.[98]

The transformation of the landscape can be traced in visitor commentary. In 1748 Lady Sophia Newdigate (d. 1774) described a garden in the Dutch style with orange trees as a notable feature:

> The gardens are 70 acres laid out by ye Earl of Portland Grandfather to ye present Duke who came over with King William & brought ye dutch taste along with him in which they still continue. I was extreamly pleas'd wth a myrtle hedge that grows ye whole length

of ye house wch is sixteen windows in front, at seven foot asunder stand Orange trees nail'd against it full of fine fruit.[99]

By 1754, Delany's account prioritised the hothouse, offering a glimpse inside the structure: 'The hot-house is very full; the coffee tree loaded with berries: do you know the Ipecacuanha plant? It is very pretty.'[100] The travel writer Richard Pococke (1704–65) visited in 1757, describing the location of the menagerie next to the dairy and noting a fusion of aesthetics between the building and the birds in his recollection that the dairy was 'adorn'd with a Chinese front' and that 'Chinese Pheasants' were bred in the menagerie.[101] The greenhouses formed a wing of Bulstrode, and Laird has speculated that an enclosure for 'exotic' birds must have been close by given they were 'routinely fed on short garden walks'.[102] The house and the garden were in dialogue, shaping the meaning of the space for visitors. The diarist and country house tourist Mrs Philip Lybbe Powys (1756–1808) documented her excursion to Bulstrode in 1769. Her writing articulated how the symbols of European civilisation – high art – were juxtaposed with those which signified the 'exotic' unruliness of the 'other':

> This place is well worth seeing, a most capital collection of pictures, numberless other curiosities, and works of taste in which the Duchess has displayed her well-known ingenuity ... The menagerie ... contains, of which there was great variety, as a curassoa, goon, crown-bird, stork, black and red game, bustards, red-legg'd partridges, silver, gold, pied pheasants, one, what is reckoned exceedingly curious, the peacock-pheasant. The aviary, too, is a most beautiful collection of smaller birds tumblers, waxbills, yellow and bloom paraquets, Java sparrows, Loretta blue birds, Virginia nightingales, and two widow-birds, or, as Edward calls them, red-breasted long-twit'd finches. Besides all above mention'd, her Grace is exceedingly fond of gardening, is a very learned botanist, and has every English plant in a separate garden by themselves.[103]

The riotous assemblage of 'curious' birds contrasted with the order imposed by the duchess in her separation of 'native' English plants. Her description of the cornucopia of 'exotic' goods on display is suggestive of the ways that these collections helped domestic audiences to imagine a world beyond their own.

In 1759, the botanist John Ellis (1710–76) wrote to the 'father of taxonomy' Carl Linnaeus (1707–78) asking to name a specimen after

Margaret. The plant, originally from Jamaica, became known as the 'great flowered Portlandia' in honour of the 'eminent patroness of botany and natural history, the Duchess of Portland'.[104] Although few records have survived that document her plant collection, Margaret continues to be recognised as an important botanical figure.

Mary and Margaret were exceptional women owing to the breadth of their collections, but they were not unique in their embrace of the global culture of botany. In their country house gardens Mary Watson-Wentworth, marchioness of Rockingham (c. 1735–1804), Jane Barrington (1733–1807), the dowager lady de Clifford (1743–1828), Mary Eleanor Bowes, countess of Strathmore (1749–1800), Lady Amelia Hume (1751–1809) and Lady Shelburne 'collected exotic plants to grow in their hothouses and "stoves"'.[105] Their activities are indicative of the ways that women engaged with the imperial and global economy within the domestic realm, giving new meaning to these symbolic landscapes.

Decolonising country house gardens?

Calls for 'decolonising garden history' within academia are not new, but the research produced has been slow to translate into public histories of natural science, collecting and the country house garden.[106] In 2020, following worldwide Black Lives Matter anti-racist demonstrations, heritage sites and museums committed to exploring their connections to slavery and empire. The director of science at Royal Botanic Gardens, Kew declared that 'it's time to decolonise botanical collections'.[107] The Natural History Museum launched the research project 'Decolonising the Sloane Herbarium'. The Garden Museum curated 'Sowing Roots: Caribbean Garden Heritage in South London'. These initiatives were met with resistance from the right-wing press and politicians. The conservative think tank Policy Exchange published the report 'Politicising Plants', which claimed that '[p]olitics has nothing to do with the science of plants and Kew has no business providing a platform for political views'.[108] There are indications that this backlash has caused a retreat from explicitly addressing these histories in public. In 2022, the National Trust curated the 'Plant Hunters' exhibition at Leith Hill Place. The exhibition blurb made oblique mention of 'exploration' and 'expansion' but the terms 'empire' and 'colonialism' were absent.[109]

While critiques of efforts to decolonise botany have focused on accusations of 'presenteeism', an examination of English country house garden history reveals a culture entirely comfortable with identifying its imperial and global connections. As Philip Miller noted in 1730:

> The Way being thus pav'd for the Improvement of Gardening, the Profits that do accrue, and the innocent Delights to be enjoyed in a well dispos'd and artfully manag'd Fruit, Kitchen and Pleasure-Garden, have allured many curious Persons, Nobility and Gentry, to encourage this profitable and delightful Art, and these have not contented themselves with the narrow compass, and mean Stock of our former poorly-furnish'd Gardens; but they have industriously procured from abroad Trees, Plants, Flowers, and Fruits, not only from our own Plantations in America, but those also of other parts of Europe, nay even Asia and Africa.[110]

For Miller and his contemporaries there was nothing controversial about acknowledging how these external interactions shaped the English garden. Instead, he suggested that this intermingling led to aesthetic, commercial and intellectual 'Improvement'. Inscribed in the catalogue entries and proudly proclaimed in letters, the origins of plants and seeds from around the world were documented for posterity. Their provenance traces how the country house garden connected to land and people across time and space. Country house gardens have enormous potential as public sites to explore the cultural exchanges, forced and voluntary, that came about through empire and trade. In acknowledging the routes by which 'exotic' plants became domesticated, the garden can become a place where diverse peoples can see themselves reflected in the narrative of the home and by extension the heritage of the nation.

Notes

1 Huxtable et al., *Interim Report*.
2 Finn, 'Material turns in British history', 1–21.
3 Huxtable et al., *Interim Report*, 5.
4 Huxtable et al., *Interim Report*, 7.
5 Mandler, *Fall and Rise of the Stately Home*, 1.
6 Hall, 'Old and new identities', 48–9.
7 LaBouff, 'Public science', 228.
8 Tigner, *Literature and the Renaissance Garden*, 162.
9 Drayton, *Nature's Government*; Fara, *Sex, Botany, and Empire*; Schiebinger and Swan, *Colonial Botany*; Wulf, *Brother Gardeners*; Miller and Hanns Reill, *Visions of Empire*; Bleichmar, *Visible Empire*; Batsaki et al., *Botany of Empire*; Easterby-Smith, *Cultivating Commerce*.

10 Saltmarsh, 'Francis Masson', 225–44.
11 Alcorn, '"His utter unfitness"', 2.
12 Schiebinger, *Plants and Empire*.
13 Grimé, *Botany of the Black Americans*; Delbourgo, 'Gardens of life and death', 113–18; Ogborn, 'Talking plants', 251–82; Voeks and Rashford, *African Ethnobotany*; Brixius, 'From ethnobotany to emancipation', 51–75; Williams, 'Plantation botany', 137–58.
14 Batsaki et al., *Botany of Empire*, 9.
15 For a discussion on the development of the hothouse see Arens, 'Flowerbeds and hothouses', 276–8.
16 For examples of the Royal Society's connections see Govier, 'Royal Society, slavery and the island of Jamaica', 203–17; and Winterbottom, 'An experimental community', 323–43.
17 Hickman, 'Curiosity and instruction', 59–80.
18 LaBouff, 'Public science', 226.
19 Schiebinger, *The Mind Has No Sex*; Shteir, *Cultivating Women*; George, *Botany, Sexuality, and Women's Writing*.
20 Zemon Davis, *Women on the Margins*; Zwaan, 'Magdalena Poulle', 206–20: Powell, 'Locating early modern women's participation', 234–58.
21 Moss, 'Cultivating curiosities', 221.
22 Shteir, *Cultivating Women*, 36.
23 A Southern Faunist, 'Letter to the editor', *Gentleman's Magazine* 71.1 (1801): 198–200.
24 Davies, 'Botanizing at Badminton', 21–2.
25 Hansen, 'Queen Charlotte's scientific collections'.
26 Pelling, 'Collecting the world', 102.
27 Schiebinger, 'Feminist history of colonial science', 233–54, Pelling, 'Collecting the world', 101–20; Shteir and Cayouette, 'Collecting with "botanical friends"', 1–30; Taylor-Leduc, 'Joséphine at Malmaisson'; Hong, 'Angel in the house', 415–38.
28 For a case study of Anna Eliza Elletson (1737–1813), duchess of Chandos, Jamaican slaveowner and mistress of Stowe, Buckinghamshire, see Young, 'Gender and absentee slaveownership'.
29 Hong, 'Angel in the house', 419.
30 Pelling, 'Collecting the world', 102–3.
31 Jael Henrietta Pye quoted in Bell, 'Women create gardens', 472–3.
32 Fowkes Tobin, *Colonizing Nature*, 172, 175.
33 Fowkes Tobin, *Colonizing Nature*, 171.
34 McClain, *Beaufort*, 26.
35 Davies, 'Botanizing at Badminton', 22.
36 McClain, *Beaufort*, 120.
37 Laird, *Natural History*, 77–8.
38 McClain, *Beaufort*, 119.
39 McClain, *Beaufort*, 120.
40 Tigner, *Literature and the Renaissance Garden*, 160–5.
41 Somerset quoted in Munroe, '"My innocent diversion of gardening"', 111.
42 Somerset quoted in Chamber, '"Storys of plants"', 49.
43 Switzer quoted in Chamber, '"Storys of plants"', 49.
44 Chamber, '"Storys of plants"', 51.
45 Davies, 'Botanizing at Badminton', 22.
46 Bobart quoted in Davies, 'Botanizing at Badminton', 22.
47 Murphy, 'Collecting slave traders', 637–70.
48 Coulton, '"What he hath gather'd together"', 202–3.
49 Petiver quoted in Davies, 'Botanizing at Badminton', 27.
50 Morris, 'Legacy of a bishop', 16.
51 Chamber, '"Storys of plants"', 50.
52 Davies, 'Botanizing at Badminton', 19.
53 Laird, *Natural History*, 86.
54 Munroe, 'Mary Somerset and colonial botany', 106.
55 Mary Somerset, 'Seeds Recd. From New England An. 1696/7', Sloane MS 3343 fol. 56, British Library.
56 Laird, *Natural History*, 87.

57   Miller, *The Gardeners Dictionary*.
58   Laird, *Natural History*, 79.
59   Cassandra Willoughby quoted in Hagglund, 'Cassandra Willoughby's visits', 196.
60   Laird, *Natural History*, 66.
61   Laird, '"Perpetual Spring"', 158.
62   Laird, '"Perpetual Spring"', 164.
63   Laird, *Natural History*, 86.
64   Laird, '"Perpetual Spring"', 164.
65   Somerset quoted in Laird, *Natural History*, 103.
66   Somerset quoted in Laird, '"Perpetual Spring"', 2006, 165.
67   Laird, *Natural History*, 102–3.
68   Laird, *Natural History*, 97. For more on Mary's expertise with succulents see Rowley, 'Duchess of Beaufort's succulent plants', 1–16.
69   Laird, *Natural History*, 97.
70   Miller, *Catalogus Plantarum*, vii.
71   Petiver quoted in Davies, 'Botanizing at Badminton', 27.
72   Sloane and Petiver quoted in Laird, '"Perpetual Spring"', 165.
73   Laird, *Natural History*, 67.
74   *Curtis's Botanical Magazine* 42.1726–1770 (1815): 1733.
75   Fowkes Tobin, *Duchess's Shells*, 28.
76   Walpole quoted in Fowkes Tobin, *Duchess's Shells*, 28.
77   https://www.wondersandmarvels.com/2014/08/the-duchesss-shells.html, accessed 3 February 2021.
78   Ellitson Allen, *Naturalist in Britain*, 25.
79   Vickery, *Behind Closed Doors*, 152.
80   For a discussion of Bulstrode in relation to productive intellectual work see Clayton, '"For the love of ink"', 176–232.
81   Fowkes Tobin, *The Duchess's Shells*, 46.
82   Sloboda, 'Displaying materials', 459.
83   Laird, *Natural History*, 277.
84   Delany quoted in Fowkes Tobin, *The Duchess's Shells*, 48.
85   Montagu quoted in Fowkes Tobin, *The Duchess's Shells*, 50.
86   Thomas Skinner quoted in Eger, 'Collecting people', 497.
87   Laird, *Natural History*, 275.
88   Martin, 'Society, creativity, and science', 102–7; Babilas, 'From female accomplishment to botanical science', 631–42.
89   Sloboda, 'Displaying materials', 464.
90   Llanover, *Autobiography and Correspondence of Mary Granville*, 255.
91   Cook, 'Botanical exchanges', 142–56. For more on women and botanical letter writing more generally see George, 'Epistolary exchange', 12–29.
92   Baker, 'Bulstrode Park and the Bentinck family', 170.
93   Fowkes Tobin, *The Duchess's Shells*, 134.
94   Solander quoted in Fowkes Tobin, *The Duchess's Shells*, 135.
95   Fowkes Tobin, *The Duchess's Shells*, 135.
96   Fowkes Tobin, *The Duchess's Shells*, 73–4.
97   Fowler, *Green Unpleasant Land*, 232; Hicks, '"Places for thinking"', 382.
98   Laird, *Natural History*, 282–3.
99   Newdigate quoted in Cox, 'From power to enslavement'.
100 Mrs Delany to Mrs Dewes, 25 October 1754, Llandover, *Autobiography and Correspondence of Mary Granville*, 293.
101 Pococke quoted in Laird, *Natural History*, 281–2.
102 Laird, *Natural History*, 282–3.
103 Climenson, *Passages from the Diaries of Mrs. Philip Lybbe Powys*, 120–1.
104 John Ellis to Carl Linnaeus, 2 March 1759, quoted in Smith, *A selection of the correspondence of Linnaeus, and other naturalists from the original manuscripts*, 122.
105 Fowkes Tobin, *The Duchess's Shells*, 48. For a more in-depth analysis of these women's botanical work see LaBouff, 'Public science', 223–55.
106 Fowkes Tobin, *Colonizing Nature*, 215–19.

107 Antonelli, 'It's time to decolonise botanical collections', *The Conversation*, 19 June 2020, https://theconversation.com/director-of-science-at-kew-its-time-to-decolonise-botanical-collections-141070, accessed 17 August 2022.
108 Buchan et al., 'Politicising plants', 12. https://policyexchange.org.uk/publication/politicising-plants/, accessed 17 August 2022.
109 https://www.nationaltrust.org.uk/leith-hill-place/features/the-plant-hunters-an-exhibition, accessed 17 August 2022.
110 Miller, *Catalogus Plantarum*, vi.

Bibliography

Alcorn, Keith. '"His utter unfitness for a commercial collector": sponsorship of exotic plant collecting in early nineteenth-century Britain', *Journal of the History of Collections* (2022): 1–15.
Arens, Esther Helena, 'Flowerbeds and hothouses: botany, gardens, and the circulation of knowledge in things', *Historical Social Research* 40, no. 1 (2015): 265–83.
Babilas, Dorota. 'From female accomplishment to botanical science: Mary Delany's 'Paper Mosaicks', *Literature Compass* 10, no. 8 (2013): 631–42.
Baker, Audrey. 'The Portland family and Bulstrode Park'. *Beaconsfield Historical Society* (2002): 159–78.
Batsaki, Yota, Sarah Burke Cahalan and Anatole Tchikine, eds. *The Botany of Empire in the Long Eighteenth Century*. Washington, DC: Dumbarton Oaks Research Library and Collection, 2017.
Bell, S.G. 'Women create gardens in male landscapes: a revisionist approach to eighteenth-century English garden history', *Feminist Studies* 16, no. 3 (1990): 471–91.
Bleichmar, Daniela. *Visible Empire: Botanical expeditions and visual culture in the Hispanic Enlightenment*. Chicago: University of Chicago Press, 2012.
Brixius, Dorit. 'From ethnobotany to emancipation: slaves, plant knowledge, and gardens on eighteenth-century Isle De France', *History of Science* 58, no. 1 (2020): 51–75.
Buchan, Ursula, Christopher Forsyth and Zewdita Gebreyohanes, *Politiciing Plants*. London: Policy Exchange, 2021.
Chamber, D. '"Storys of plants": the assembling of Mary Capel Somerset's botanical collection at Badminton', *Journal of the History of Collections* 9, no. 1 (1997): 49–60.
Clayton, Stephanie. '"For the love of ink": patronage and performance in the eighteenth century', PhD dissertation, University of Cardiff, 2019.
Climenson, Emily J., ed. *Passages from the Diaries of Mrs. Philip Lybbe Powys of Hardwick House, Oxon, 1756–1808*. London: Longmans, Green & Co., 1899.
Cook, Alexandra. 'Botanical exchanges: Jean-Jacques Rousseau and the Duchess of Portland', *History of European Ideas* 33, no. 2 (2007): 142–16.
Coulton, Richard. '"What he hath gather'd together shall not be lost": remembering James Petiver', *Notes and Records of the Royal Society* 74 (2020): 189–211.
Cox, Oliver. 'From power to enslavement: recent perspectives on the politics of art patronage and display in the country house', *Art and the Country House* (2020). https://artandthecountryhouse.com/essays/essays-index/from-power-to-enslavement-recent-perspectives-on-the-politics-of-art-patronage-and-display-in-the-country-house.
Davies, Julie. 'Botanizing at Badminton: the botanical pursuits of Mary Somerset, First Duchess of Beaufort'. In *Domesticity in the Making of Modern Science*, edited by Donald L. Opitz, Staffan Bergwik and Brigitte Van Tiggelen, 19–40. New York: Palgrave Macmillan, 2016.
Delbourgo, James. 'Gardens of life and death', *British Journal for the History of Science* 43, no. 1 (2010): 113–18.
Drayton, Richard, *Nature's Government: Science, imperial Britain, and the 'Improvement' of the world*. London: Yale University Press, 2000.
Easterby-Smith, Sarah. 'Botanical collecting in eighteenth-century London', *Curtis's Botanical Magazine* 34, no. 4 (2017): 279–97.
Easterby-Smith, Sarah. *Cultivating Commerce: Cultures of botany in Britain and France, 1760–1815*. Cambridge: Cambridge University Press, 2017.
Eger, Elizabeth. 'Collecting people: Bluestocking sociability and the assembling of knowledge', *Journal of the History of Collections* 33, no. 3 (2021): 493–503.

Ellitson Allen, David. *The Naturalist in Britain: A social history*. Princeton: Princeton University Press, 1994.

Fara, Patricia. *Sex, Botany, and Empire: The story of Carl Linnaeus and Joseph Banks*. Cambridge: Icon, 2003.

Finn, Margot. 'Material turns in British history: IV. Empire in India, cancel cultures and the country house', *Transactions of the Royal Historical Society* 31 (2021): 1–21.

Fowkes Tobin, Beth. *Colonizing Nature: The tropics in British arts and letters, 1760–1820*. Philadelphia: University of Pennsylvania Press, 2005.

Fowkes Tobin, Beth. *The Duchess's Shells: Natural history collecting in the age of Cook's voyages*. New Haven: Yale University Press, 2018.

Fowler, Corinne. *Green Unpleasant Land: Creative responses to rural England's colonial connections*. Leeds: Peepal Tree Press, 2020.

George, Sam. *Botany, Sexuality, and Women's Writing 1760–1830*. Manchester: Manchester University Press, 2007.

George, Sam. 'Epistolary exchange: the familiar letter and the female botanist, 1760–1820', *Journal of Literature and Science* 4, no. 1 (2011): 12–29.

Govier, Mark. 'The Royal Society, slavery and the island of Jamaica: 1660–1700', *Notes and Records of the Royal Society of London* 53, no. 2 (1999): 203–17.

Grimé, William Ed. *Botany of the Black Americans*. St. Clair Shores: Scholarly Press, 1975.

Hagglund, Elizabeth. 'Cassandra Willoughby's visits to country houses', *The Georgian Group Journal* 11 (2001): 185–202.

Hall, Stuart. 'Old and new identities, old and new ethnicities'. In *Culture, Globalization, and the World-System: Contemporary conditions for the representation of identity*, edited by Anthony D. King, 41–68. Minneapolis: University of Minnesota Press, 1997.

Hansen, Mascha. 'Queen Charlotte's scientific collections and natural history networks', *Notes and Records: Royal Society Journal of the History of Science* 77, no. 2 (2022): 323–36.

Hickman, Clare. 'Curiosity and instruction: British and Irish botanic gardens and their audiences, 1760–1800', *Environment and History* 24, no. 1 (2018): 59–80.

Hicks, Dan. '"Places for thinking" from Annapolis to Bristol: situations and symmetries in "world historical archaeologies"', *World Archaeology* 37, no. 3 (2005): 373–91.

Hong, Jiang. 'Angel in the house, angel in the scientific empire: women and colonial botany during the eighteenth and nineteenth centuries', *Notes and Records of the Royal Society of London* 75, no. 3 (2021): 415–38.

Huxtable, Sally, Corinne Fowler, Christo Kefalas and Emma Slocombe, eds. *Interim Report on the Connections between Colonialism and Properties Now in the Care of the National Trust, Including Links with Historic Slavery*. Swindon: National Trust, 2020. Available at: https://nt.global.ssl.fastly.net/documents/colionialism-and-historic-slavery-report.pdf, accessed 2 September 2022.

LaBouff, Nicole. 'Public science in the private garden: noblewomen horticulturalists and the making of British botany c. 1785–1810', *History of Science* 59, no. 3 (2021): 223–55.

Laird, Mark. '"Perpetual Spring" or tempestuous fall: the greenhouse and the Great Storm of 1703 in the life of John Evelyn and his contemporaries', *Garden History* 34, no. 2 (2006): 153–73.

Laird, Mark. *A Natural History of English Gardening, 1650–1800*. New Haven and London: Yale University Press, 2015.

Llanover, Lady, ed. *The Autobiography and Correspondence of Mary Granville, Mrs. Delany*, vol. 3. London: Richard Bentley, 1861.

Mandler, Peter. *Fall and Rise of the Stately Home*. New Haven and London: Yale University Press, 1997.

Martin, Alison E. 'Society, creativity, and science: Mrs. Delany and the art of botany', *Eighteenth-Century Life* 35, no. 2 (2011): 102–7.

McClain, Molly. *Beaufort: The duke and his duchess, 1657–1715*. London: Yale University Press, 2001.

Miller, David Philip, and Peter Hanns Reill, eds. *Visions of Empire: Voyages, botany and the representations of nature*. Cambridge: Cambridge University Press, 2010.

Miller, Philip. *Catalogus Plantarum*. London: Society of Gardeners, 1730.

Miller, Phillip. *The Gardeners Dictionary*. London: John and Francis Rivington, 1768.

Morris, Sandra. 'Legacy of a bishop (Part 2): the flowers of Fulham Palace gardens introduced, 1675–1713', *Garden History* 21, no. 1 (1993): 14–23.

Moss, Suzanne. 'Cultivating curiosities: plants as collections in the eighteenth century', PhD dissertation, University of York, 2018.

Munroe, Jennifer. '"My innocent diversion of gardening": Mary Somerset's plants', *Renaissance Studies* 25, no. 1 (2011): 111–23.

Munroe, Jennifer. 'Mary Somerset and colonial botany: reading between the ecofeminist lines', *Journal of Early Modern Studies* 6 (2014): 100–28.

Murphy, Kathleen S. 'Collecting slave traders: James Petiver, natural history, and the British slave trade', *William and Mary Quarterly* 70, no. 4 (2013): 637–70.

Ogborn, Miles. 'Talking plants: botany and speech in eighteenth-century Jamaica', *History of Science* 51, no. 3 (2013): 251–82.

Pelling, Madeleine. 'Collecting the world: female friendship and domestic craft at Bulstrode Park', *Journal for Eighteenth-Century Studies* 41, no. 1 (2018): 101–20.

Powell, Catherine. 'Locating early modern women's participation in the public sphere of botany', *Early Modern Low Countries* 4, no. 2 (2020): 234–58.

Rowley, Gordon D. 'The duchess of Beaufort's succulent plants', *Bradleya* 5 (1987): 1–16.

Saltmarsh, A.C. 'Francis Masson: collecting plants for king and country', *Curtis's Botanical Magazine* 20, no. 4 (2003): 225–44.

Schiebinger, Londa L. *The Mind Has No Sex? Women in the origins of modern science.* Cambridge: Harvard University Press, 1989.

Schiebinger, Londa. 'Feminist history of colonial science', *Hypatia* 19, no. 1 (2004): 233–54.

Schiebinger, Londa L. *Plants and Empire: Colonial bioprospecting in the Atlantic World.* Cambridge: Harvard University Press, 2004.

Schiebinger, Londa L., and Claudia Swan, eds. *Colonial Botany: Science, commerce, and politics in the early modern world.* Philadelphia: University of Pennsylvania Press, 2005.

Schurch, Millie. '"All the productions of that nature": ephemera, mycology and sexual classification at the Bulstrode estate', *Journal for Eighteenth-Century Studies* 42, no. 4 (2019): 519–39.

Shteir, Ann. *Cultivating Women, Cultivating Science: Flora's daughters and botany in England, 1760–1860.* Baltimore: Johns Hopkins University Press, 1996.

Shteir, Ann, and Jacques Cayouette. 'Collecting with "botanical friends": four women in colonial Quebec and Newfoundland', *Scientia Canadensis* 41, no. 1 (2019): 1–30.

Sloboda, Stacey. 'Displaying materials: porcelain and natural history in the duchess of Portland's museum', *Eighteenth-Century Studies* 43, no. 4 (2010): 455–72.

Smith, Sir James Edward, ed. *A selection of the correspondence of Linnaeus, and other naturalists from the original manuscripts*, vol. 1. London: Longman, Hurst, Rees, Orme and Brown, 1821.

Taylor-Leduc, Susan. 'Joséphine at Malmaison: acclimatizing self and other in the garden', *Journal18*, 8 (2019). https://www.journal18.org/issue8/josephine-at-malmaison-acclimatizing-self-and-other-in-the-garden/.

Tigner, A.L. *Literature and the Renaissance Garden from Elizabeth I to Charles II: England's paradise.* London: Routledge, 2012.

Vickery, Amada. *Behind Closed Doors: At home in Georgian England.* New Haven: Yale University Press, 1997.

Voeks, Robert, and John Rashford, eds. *African Ethnobotany in the Americas.* New York: Springer, 2013.

Williams, J'Nese. 'Plantation botany: slavery and the infrastructure of government science in the St. Vincent Botanic Garden, 1765–1820s', *Berichte Zur Wissenschaftsgeschichte* 44, no. 2 (2021): 137–58.

Winterbottom, Anna. 'An experimental community: the East India Company in London, 1600–1800', *British Journal for the History of Science* 52, no. 2 (2019): 323–43.

Wulf, Andrea. *The Brother Gardeners: Botany, empire and the birth of an obsession.* London: Windmill Books, 2009.

Young, Hannah, 'Gender and absentee slave-ownership in late eighteenth- and early nineteenth-century Britain', PhD dissertation, University College London, 2017.

Zemon Davis, Natalie. *Women on the Margins: Three seventeenth-century lives.* Cambridge: Harvard University Press, 1997.

Zwaan, Marisca Sikkens-De. 'Magdalena Poulle (1632–99): a Dutch lady in a circle of botanical collectors', *Garden History* 30, no.2 (2002): 206–20.

14
Colonial power and global gifts: the governorship of Johan Maurits, Count of Nassau-Siegen in Dutch Brazil (1637-44)

Yme Kuiper

Generations of historians considered the rise of the Dutch Republic to the leading position in seventeenth-century world trade as a miracle. Thanks to the standard works of Charles Boxer and Jonathan Israel, we understand this remarkable phenomenon much better now.[1] Both authors also share a great interest in the short existence of 'New Holland', the colony Dutch Brazil (1624–54).[2] Even before the West India Company (WIC) had been founded in 1621, direct Dutch trade to Brazil already existed. The States-General of the Dutch Republic had given the WIC a monopoly of all Dutch trade with America and West Africa; likewise it was authorised to make peace and war with indigenous powers. The WIC was founded with an eye on the silver of Spanish America, but soon it actually concentrated on the sugar production and trade of Portuguese Brazil and on the gold, ivory and enslaved people of Portuguese West Africa.[3]

In the summer of 1636 the Board of Nineteen Directors (the Heeren XIX) of the WIC appointed Johan Maurits, Count of Nassau-Siegen (1604–79), as their governor-general of the colony New Holland. The board gave him the illustrious titles of Captain-General and Admiral General. Especially his relative stadtholder Frederick Henry, Prince of Orange, pushed his nomination. The contract was for five years. Johan Maurits – the first but also the last governor of New Holland – had to work within the guidelines of the Heeren XIX. The WIC functioned as a joint-stock commercial enterprise, but also as a political and military organisation, loosely supervised by the States-General in The Hague. According to Boxer, the WIC made a good choice in appointing him governor-general of Dutch Brazil.[4] He had no colonial experience at all but had received a solid intellectual education and military training. Maurits was from high noble birth (the House of Orange-Nassau) and a convinced Calvinist. Israel points to the particular courtly Neo-Stoic values cultivated in Maurits's own personal circle.[5] During his governorship, a remarkable degree of religious tolerance was practised in New Holland – a political concession of the WIC to two particular groups: sugar plantation owners and tradesmen.[6] In his 1957 *The Dutch in Brazil 1624–1654* Boxer wrote two long chapters about Johan Maurits's Brazilian adventures and legacy. As a young man Maurits had great career ambitions; living in The Hague, he threw himself into court life and, in close cooperation with his friend Constantijn Huygens, he made plans for the building of a superb town residence in the city. To finance this project, the invitation of the Heeren XIX was welcome and timely.

This chapter we will focus on Johan Maurits's lifestyle as a governor in the tropics and his cultural entrepreneurship in Brazil. His interest in power and science was entangled with the colonial and capitalist aspirations of the WIC. Colonialism and imperialism are crucial aspects of his Brazilian period, and the same is true for his military adventures and his involvement with the slave trade. From a biographical point of view Maurits's career in Brazil ('the sugar colony') was strongly motivated by his thirst for glory, his desire for power and cultural prestige and, alas, his lust for gain. As we will see, he initiated many building activities in Brazil and was the founder of the new capital, Mauritsstad (Maurice's Town), of the colony Dutch Brazil of the WIC on the island Antonio Vaz. This location is part of the present-day city of Recife in the state of Pernambuco (Figure 14.1).

It is against this background that we will pay much attention to his two country residences in colonial Brazil – the palace Vrijburg and the villa Boa Vista – with their impressive utility and pleasure gardens (Figures 14.2 and 14.3). As his Dutch contemporary Caspar Barlaeus wrote in a hagiographic study on his governorship in Brazil, Johan Maurits felt inspired by the Roman emperor Diocletian, 'who personally saw to the arrangement of his garden and to the cultivation and planting of trees'.[7] Like many Roman rulers, Maurits's self-image was firmly based on military glory.[8] The key questions of our chapter are firstly biographical and personal – what drove Maurits to erect new buildings? – and secondly refer to cultural exchange: which goods and practices did he introduce into the New World, and what happened to the cultural treasures from Brazil that he brought back to Europe?

As Jacob Burckhardt, the founding father of European cultural history, once observed, from time to time history takes pleasure in

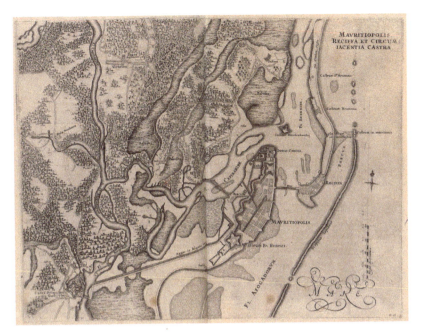

Figure 14.1 Map of Mauritsstad and Recife, c. 1645–47. Reproduced courtesy of Rijksmuseum. Public domain. Available at https://commons.wikimedia.org/wiki/File:Kaart_met_Mauritsstad_en_Recife,_ca._1636-1644_Mauritiopolis,_Recifa,_et_circumiacentia_castra_(titel_op_object),_BI-1892-3415-43.jpg.

converging itself in one person. Was Johan Maurits such a man? Perhaps. No doubt, he was the most prominent person in the history of the Dutch colony in Brazil. Over the last century his governorship has been described in numerous studies as part of a history of colonial expansion, military conflicts, sugar industry and trade, scientific progress, cultural patronage, artistic collectorship and religious toleration.[9] In our analysis of Maurits's governorship we will limit ourselves mainly to his building projects and cultural entrepreneurship in Brazil. Eye-catching architectural creations characterised him during his whole life. The Dutch architectural historian J.J. Terwen rightly observes that Maurits was a patron in the field of Dutch seventeenth-century architecture. 'His Brazilian creations', Terwen wrote, 'will have been largely the result of his own inventions'.[10]

Education and court life in The Hague

Johan Maurits was a German nobleman, born at Dillenburg Castle, the ancestral seat of the Nassau family, in the county of Nassau-Dillenburg,

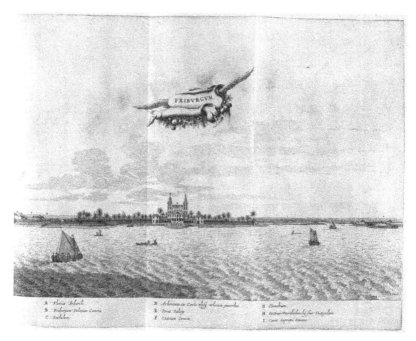

Figure 14.2   Jan van Brosterhuyzen, after Frans Post, *Vrijburg*, c. 1645–7. Reproduced courtesy of Rijksmuseum, FMH 1822–38.

now in Hesse, in 1604. His father, John VII the Middle of Nassau-Siegen (1561–1623), was a convinced Calvinist and was involved with the Nassau stadtholders in the Dutch Republic, the full cousins Maurice and William Louis, respectively prince of Orange and count of Nassau-Dillenburg, in their far-reaching military innovations around 1600. The young Maurits stayed for some time at the court of Landgrave Maurice the Learned of Hesse-Kassel, which had an additional advantage: the Collegium Mauritianum. The curriculum included theology, philosophy, history, medicine, astronomy, rhetoric, as well as Latin, Greek, French, English, Italian and Spanish. Typical courtly training was, of course, no less important, including dancing, music, drawing, riding, fencing and other forms of combat. Here we find a perfect match of older, courtly and newer, humanist principles of education.[11]

In 1618 Johan Maurits was sent to his uncle William Louis, stadtholder of the northern provinces of the Dutch Republic, who held a court in Leeuwarden. Two years later he received a position in a cavalry regiment commended by Frederick Henry (1584–1647), younger brother of Prince Maurice. Maurits moved from Leeuwarden to The Hague. Here he also met the deposed winter king of Bohemia,

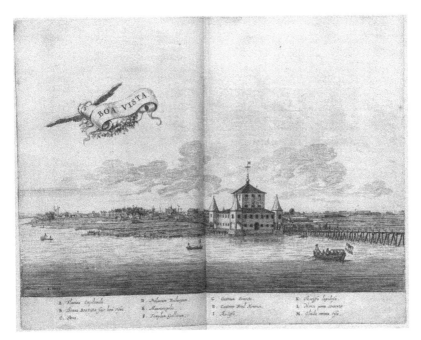

Figure 14.3 Anon., *Boa Vista*, c. 1671. Reproduced courtesy of Rijksmuseum. Public domain. Available at https://www.rijksmuseum.nl/nl/zoeken/objecten?q=boa+vista&p=1&ps=12&st=Objects&ii=8#/BI-1892-3415-44,8.

Frederick V of the Palatinate, and his wife Elizabeth Stuart, daughter of James I of England, who had, since spring 1621, his own court next to that of Maurice and Frederick Henry. In the summer of 1620 Maurits experienced his first campaign. As an officer in Frederick Henry's cavalry he was sent to Germany to defend the Palatine. In Nassau territory near Wiesbaden he witnessed much destruction by the Spanish army, commanded by the famous Italian *condottiero* Ambrogio Spinola. After Maurice's death in 1625 his successor, Frederick Henry, switched to a much more offensive war strategy. His finest hour as chief commander of the army of the Dutch Republic came in September 1629 with the siege of 's-Hertogenbosch. Maurits played a prominent role in this victory and even more in the siege of Maastricht in August 1632.

In March 1632 Johan Maurits had bought a plot of land close to the east entrance to the stadtholder Frederick Henry's residence in The Hague. He had plans to erect a town palace on this spot. The same year saw the start of Maurits's friendship with the poet and composer Constantijn Huygens (1596–1687), the secretary of Prince Frederick Henry. Both men had a great interest in architecture, especially Palladio's classicism.

In the early 1620s Huygens had visited Venice and London, participating in delegations to represent the interests of the Dutch Republic. In March 1634 Frederick Henry offered Huygens a piece of land adjoining the land where Maurits planned to build. Maurits wrote to Huygens on April 4, 'I would like to tell you that we are neighbours from now on'.[12] In the same letter he remarked that he had become a sort of 'merchant in wood and iron', being aware that Huygens was also planning to build a house on his newly acquired ground. Both men were friends with Jacob Van Campen (1596–1657), architect and painter, who was strongly influenced by the Italian architects Palladio and Scamozzi and even by the classical architecture of Vitruvius. After a stay in Italy between 1617 and 1624 Van Campen introduced so-called Dutch classicism in the Northern Netherlands, a new style in Baroque architecture, which also enjoyed international influence.[13] Both friends asked Van Campen to design their new houses. The count and the secretary stimulated each other's building projects in The Hague and together ordered building materials from Germany (oak and sandstone), Luxembourg (chalk and paving stone) and the Southern Netherlands (iron and nails). When Maurits got ready to sail to Brazil, the building of Huygens's residence was nearly completed. Huygens made his friend an offer he could not refuse: he himself was willing to monitor Johan Maurits's building project during the latter's stay in Brazil. Huygens would do that in due cooperation with the young architect Pieter Post (1608–69), the talented assistant of Van Campen.[14]

After Prince Maurice's death in 1625, the court culture of the House Orange-Nassau under his brother Frederick Henry became much more prominent in the Dutch Republic.[15] In April 1625, Frederick Henry married Amalia von Solms-Braunfels, an attractive, noble court lady of Elizabeth Stuart, the wife of the winter king; she was a distant cousin of Frederick Henry. Following their marriage Frederick Henry and Amalia made court culture in The Hague, including theatrical performances and masquerade balls, much more glittering for nobles, diplomats and military officers. At that time, it was common for reigning monarchs of England, Germany, Denmark and Sweden to send their children to The Hague as a kind of finishing school. Living among such company must have impressed Johan Maurits. Moreover, his own architectural ambitions matched perfectly with those of Frederick Henry, who also made use of the talents of Van Campen and Post for his own building projects of palaces in and around The Hague from the 1620s. Frederick Henry and Maurits did not bother about the costs of their building projects, so Maurits's cosmopolitan motto 'As far as the world reaches' (*Qua patet orbis*, taken from Ovid's *Tristia*) also fits perfectly his financial habitus.

The Brazil expedition

Right from the start the relationship between the Heeren XIX and Johan Maurits was uneasy. Initially, the directors talked about a fleet of 32 ships and an army of 7,000–8,000 men; later on, they promised him 12 ships with 2,700 men, but in October 1636 he sailed to Brazil with four ships and 350 men.[16] After three months, two ships of this small fleet arrived at the port of Recife. On board Maurits's ship was a whole group of scholars, artists and pastors. One of the first problems that the new governor had to deal with in Brazil was the existing monopoly policy of the WIC. In a letter to the Heeren XIX (written in January 1638) Maurits made a plea for free trade of sugar and other merchandise as he felt that this would contribute to the flourishing of the colony and stimulate the arrival of new colonists.[17] Shortly afterwards the States-General decided that free trade would be allowed, with three exceptions: the import of enslaved Africans and war materials and the export of brazilwood, used by the dye industry. During the whole period of his governorship Maurits's greatest handicap was that the WIC always thought in terms of profit and had no real aspirations to build up a strong colony with a vibrant community life. Time after time he wrote letters to his superiors in the Republic to send more troops to the tropics, but always in vain.[18]

From 1637 to 1644 Johan Maurits reigned over his colony in the region of Pernambuco, with its capital Recife, as a 'humanist Prince', as Boxer calls him.[19] This small, crowded town had about 2,000 inhabitants when the new governor arrived but would grow to 6,000 persons during his reign. Originally, Recife was just a harbour village of sailors and prostitutes, while the nearby town Olinda was the main urban centre for Portuguese settlers as it had churches and stone houses. But the Dutch army had sacked Olinda in 1631, preferring Recife as it had a more strategic location: easier to defend and close to the area richest in plantations and sugar mills. These properties were concentrated in the hands of relatives of the settlers, who mostly belonged to well-to-do families of the Portuguese lower nobility or bourgeoisie. During the Portuguese–Dutch conflict, many planters fled from this area and destroyed their possessions, consisting of the sugar mill, the *casa grande* of the plantation owner and the lodgings of his servants and enslaved families (Figure 14.3).

During his governorship, Johan Maurits was eager to restore and improve relations with Portuguese landowners. Olinda was rebuilt and many of the original plantation owners returned to the area around

Recife. The governor promised them free trade and, very important in this context, he took care of a massive influx of enforced labour from Africa to his colony. Without the enslaved Africans, the sugar mills could not operate since the enslaved indigenous people were far less numerous. The lack of manpower was so severe that the governor himself ordered excursions by the WIC to the African coast. This led to the conquest of the main slave trading ports of 'the Gold Coast', now Ghana (1637, Fort Elmina) and Angola (1641, Loanda). During Maurits's governorship, about 23,000 enslaved Africans were sold by auction in his colony. At first Maurits toyed with the idea of using hard-working German emigrants in the sugar mills, but he soon changed his view and argued: 'it is not possible to effect anything in Brazil without slaves ... if anyone feels that this is wrong, it is a futile scruple'.[20] The slave trade would become one of the WIC's main sources of profit.[21]

By a series of successful expeditions, Johan Maurits gradually extended the Dutch possessions in Brazil. Just one month after his arrival he conquered the town of Porto Calvo. In this battle his relative Charles of Nassau lost his life; he was 25 and an illegitimate son of the aforementioned stadtholder Prince Maurice. In his first fights against the Portuguese Maurits commanded an international army of more than 6,000 men – not only Dutchmen and Germans but also French, Scots, English, Danes and Swedes. Sometimes his troops were supported by the Tapuyas, an indigenous tribe, and by enslaved men from Africa.[22]

Building projects in Brazil

From the beginning of his Brazilian adventure, Johan Maurits had great plans to build a new city on the island of Antonio Vaz. He decided to extend Recife beyond the peninsula onto this swampy island that already contained a convent, some houses and two Dutch fortresses (Frederick Henry and Ernestus).[23] On the north side, Antonio Vaz was protected by a fortress island, Waerdenburgh. The young governor immediately identified suitable terrain for erecting a new palace: the northern end of the island, where the Beberibe and Capibaribe rivers meet, and overlooking the sea and the port of Recife. Around this palace, to which he gave the Dutch name Vrijburg, a new city was built: Mauritsstad (Maurice's town). The layout of this new city had a geometrical design with streets running north–south and east–west. Perhaps we might attribute this master plan to Pieter Post, but it is almost certain that he did not travel with Johan Maurits to Brazil. The most important challenge was to connect Mauritsstad to the old, built-up area of Recife by a long bridge, while another bridge connected it to the hinterland. Mauritsstad must have been built in a relatively short time by a skilled technical staff, consisting of surveyors who made the plans and staked out the plots, in close cooperation with fortress engineers supervising the construction of strongholds, bastions, ravelins and canals. The governor himself took great interest in the town plan (which shows parallels with the plan for Harlem in the Dutch Republic) and undertook his own land surveys.[24] Indeed, it is plausible that Maurits's part in the construction of the palace Vrijburg was substantial. The transport of building material, particularly bricks and tiles, to Brazil was not difficult to organise. Ships were laden with sugar and brazilwood and sent to Amsterdam; here the same ships, sailing back to Brazil, were loaded with brick and tiles, which formed an ideal ballast.

There was only one obstacle, or perhaps two: the cost of this whole project and, at a distance, the critical eyes of the board of the WIC. The governor defended himself with the argument that he would pay part of the costs for the palace and its garden from his own funds. The total costs were about 600,000 guilders.[25] Barlaeus defended his hero against the reprimands of the directors of the WIC: 'It did not matter if his [Maurits] dignity was enhanced by the pomp of his residence, provided that not all his dignity stemmed from the building, and provided the residence derived more glory from its owner than he from his residence.'[26] J.J. Terwen made (in 1979) a convincing reconstruction of the palace. His concluding remarks are worth quoting at length:

> It was a typical example of a building created to meet tropical need, with a high central hall, which was therefore cool ... Moreover it had the hallmark of a distinguished country seat; a villa in the classical and humanistic sense of the word. ... The complex comprising the main building and the side wings clearly had the structure of a North Italian villa of the type so often designed by Palladio and his colleagues, although they did not have any towers higher than the pigeon-lofts.[27]

Terwen points to many similarities between Johan Maurits's palace and the Villa Pisani at Bagnolo, designed by Palladio, with its twin pigeon lofts. Perhaps Scamozzi's *Idea dell'Architettura* also provided inspiration. One of the towers of Vrijburg served as a lighthouse for guiding ships at night; in the other tower was an observatory. Thus, in this palace we meet sixteenth-century Italian, classical architecture transplanted to the New World via its seventeenth-century Dutch appropriated form.

Next to the palace a large area was intended for plantations of different types, for example one with about 2,000 adult coconut trees (more than 25 years old and 10–15 metres high), which were carefully transplanted by the governor's staff of soldiers and slaves, and 252 orange trees (introduced to Brazil by the Portuguese around 1530) and numerous other exotic plants for utility, medical study and embellishment. According to Boxer, the local population of Pernambuco (the *moradores*) were willing to support the governor in all his building and collecting projects. His tolerance, courtesy and policy of reducing taxes made him popular.[28] They offered him trees (including the coconut and orange trees, transported from miles away by ox cart), stones, weapons, feathers, jewellery, plants, birds and animals. In the governor's zoological garden we find not only famous Brazilian animals such as normal and black jaguars, pumas, anteaters, apes, coatis and squirrel monkeys but also goats from Cabo Verde, sheep from Angola, Asian snow leopards and bears from India. Friar Manuel Calado saw Johan Maurits's zoological garden and wrote: 'In short there was nothing rare in Brazil that he did not have.'[29] Stadtholder Frederick Henry had a menagerie near The Hague. In 1636 he gave Maurits an elephant (called Hansken) from Sri Lanka as a gift. Hansken was transported by the East India Company to Amsterdam (together with a leopard and cassowary) where they were drawn by Rembrandt. Probably, Maurits's Brazilian collection of exotic animals from different continents was a zoological garden, primarily founded out of scientific and educational interest and not only as a place for aristocratic display.[30] The *moradores* knew the governor's taste and preferences for his botanical garden, zoo and museum at the estate Vrijburg. At the end of his life Johan Maurits still boasted about his huge botanical achievement in a letter to a French diplomat and high nobleman, who visited the Treaties of Peace of Nijmegen in 1679: 'coconut trees, weighing a ton, with leaves and fruit, without a single tree dying. This elicited the general admiration and astonishment of the Brazilians, who had never seen trees of this type and size transplanted before.'[31] On the northern side of the palace we find, as Barlaeus described, 'all kinds of herbs and fruit bushes, all sorts of fruit growing on the ground, and many other garden plants used in medicine and surgery, as well as in the kitchen'.[32] Behind the palace were three fish ponds; in the centre of the larger one was a rectangular island, with another smaller pond of an irregular shape. All the ponds contained different kinds of fish to be served at the governor's table.[33]

Barlaeus wrote that the work of planting and landscaping started in 1639. Palace and garden formed a unified concept, so the two towers were crucial for the garden design in that each of them formed the viewpoint of a double row of tall coconut palms. The surrounding plantations with figs and bananas, lemon trees, pergolas of vines, deer parks, fishponds and a handful of palm avenues gave splendour to the palace in European style. 'These four lines of trees, running from west to east, i.e. from the Capibaribe to the centre of the palace, formed the main axis of the garden and the building', Diedenhofen wrote in his 1979 reconstruction of the governor's utility and pleasure garden. He was able to do so on the basis of the map of Vrijburg and gardens that he found in Barlaeus's book. The map was made by Georg Markgraf (1610–1644), a young astronomer and naturalist, and a member of the group of scholars which surrounded the governor.[34] Johan Maurits's patronage made it possible for Markgraf to undertake several zoological, botanical and astronomical expeditions in the colony, studying its natural history and geography. With Willem Piso, Maurits's court physician, Markgraf was the author of *Historia Naturalis Brasiliae* (1648), a work that remains famous today, on the botany and zoology of Brazil. During an expedition to Dutch Guinea in 1644 he fell victim to the climate there. His large map of Brazil was posthumously published three years later.

In 1643 Johan Maurits created a villa on his island Antonio Vaz, near the Capibaribe Bridge that connected the island with the mainland. Barlaeus gave the following description of this much smaller building: 'In front of the bridge ... there was the fine pleasure house "Boa Vista" built by the prince on his own ground, with his own money, and decorated with beautiful gardens and fishponds' (Figure 14.3).[35] This project is reminiscent of practices in ancient Rome and is another clear example of moving European culture to the New World. Unfortunately, we cannot see the gardens and ponds around the villa on Frans Post's drawing of the villa, the square form and elevated *sala centrale* of which follows the tradition of European styles. Barlaeus made a comparison with the famous ancient villas of the town of Baiae and of the Roman magnate Lucullus. Like the Roman elite, Maurits spent his leisure hours in Boa Vista (from the Italian Belvedere). 'Here it was that he could live for his pleasures when he has the time or sometimes made the time, and it was also here that he made wide-ranging plans', as Barlaeus wrote.[36] The governor's imprint on the villa is very clear: below the upper windows we see his coat of arms and coronet bearing the date ANNO 1643.[37]

Boa Vista was a strictly symmetrical, square building with four towers at the corners. These were entirely open on the ground floor and capped by archaic turrets so that, in case of attack by the enemy, they could be used as bastions in the defence of the whole complex. The central structure of the building was of brick and continued downwards to the ground floor in the form of a *salle à l'italienne*, as at the palace Vrijburg. In this detail, Terwen argues, Boa Vista also resembled Scamozzi's Villa Molin near Padua, 'but here the similarity ends. As for the designer of Boa Vista, we can only suggest the Governor himself.'[38]

The engraving after Frans Post's drawing of the villa (printed in Barlaeus's book) gives us a good impression of Mauritsstad. On the far left we see the towers of Vrijburg and just to the right of it is Fort Ernestus. The town itself is located just past the trees and in its centre stood the Walloon Reformed Church, a cross-shaped building that resembles churches in Amsterdam at the time. On the far right lies Fort Frederick Henry, recognisable from the long, tall barracks. In front of the villa, on the water, we see a pleasure yacht and two canoes being paddled by black people, apparently town slaves doing jobs for Maurits or other masters in Recife or Mauritsstad.

Court society in Brazil

Gilberto de Mello Freyre (1900–1987) was a Brazilian sociologist, anthropologist and historian, born in Recife. He was also the author of a famous book on slavery, published in 1933: *Casa-Grande and Senzala* (literally: 'The main house and the slave quarters'). In a later article, he argues that Johan Maurits 'was anxious to behave like a prince, to exercise political power as Governor counter to the solely mercantile interests of the Company which had charged him to represent it'.[39] Not that Maurits himself despised profit and business; we know that this was not the case given his involvement with the transatlantic slave trade. 'Although such a possibility was never clearly foreseen by Maurits he was in fact an imperialist favouring the emergence of a new nation.'[40] Maurits's cultural legacy is very clear in Freyre's eyes. It involved, in his words, 'cartography, anthropological research, medical studies, town planning for Recife, together with the social studies and humanities – the literature and historiography of Van Baerle [Barlaeus], the paintings and drawings of Frans Post, Eckhout, Wagner and research in the natural and biological sciences' (Figure 14.4).[41] So far as Brazil is concerned, these represented the road to self-knowledge. Seen in the rear-view mirror, this is the crux of the career of a German nobleman serving a Dutch trade company: 'Brazilians were empowered to analyze and interpret their

Figure 14.4 Frans Post, *Landscape in Brazil*, 1652, showing sugar plantation. Reproduced courtesy of Rijksmuseum. Public domain. Available at https://commons.wikimedia.org/wiki/File:Landschap_in_Brazili%C3%AB_Rijksmuseum_SK-A-3224.jpeg.

country and to write its own collective autobiography in a process in which paradoxically an imperialist was involved.'[42]

Freyre points to another remarkable aspect of Johan Maurits's governorship: his tolerance in religious matters. Especially Jews of Portuguese origin who had migrated from Amsterdam to Brazil enjoyed complete freedom. In turn, these Jews praised the governor for his religious policy and were willing to do him favours. We have two contemporary witnesses to confirm this policy of toleration. The minister of the French Protestant Reformed community in Dutch Brazil, Vincent Soler, was a former Augustinian monk born in Valencia who became a Calvinist pastor in France. His wife Maria and his son and daughter followed him to the tropics. The son lived for a time in Maurits's house and his sister Margarita had a short liaison with the governor. She was married to the owner of a sugar mill who lived in the interior, but the couple divorced after some years. She then started a relationship with Johan Maurits but it soon ended in tears. Margarita returned to Europe, where she died in 1643. Nevertheless, Soler praises the governor for his kind treatment of subjugated Luso-Brazilians and indigenous people: the first saw in him as a kind of St Anthony and the second called him 'brother'.[43]

This friendliness is confirmed by various other sources. We possess the testimony of a Portuguese friar, Frei Manuel Calado do Salvador, about Johan Maurits's relations with the Luso-Brazilian population in Recife. In the memoirs of his Brazilian period of more than 20 years, Calado gives a vivid impression of the governor's political treatment of the people under his rule, including his eagerness to receive gifts of chests of sugar from sugar mill owners. Generally speaking, Calado's testimony is quite favourable to the governor; he 'was of a naturally good disposition and the royal blood from which he sprang disposed him towards good'. Most Luso-Brazilians called him 'Prince or Excellency'. Maurits offered the friar hospitality in his first house near the harbour of Recife (before he moved to Vrijburg). Calado refused the offer but was willing to settle in Mauritsstad. The governor helped him to build a house with his own money. Later he gave the friar permission to hold a mass in his palace 'behind closed doors for his consolation and that of some Catholic friends of his'.[44]

Although Barlaeus does not tell us anything about daily life at the Brazilian court of the governor, there is a surviving document that can tell us something. It concerns a list of people who had free table at the governor's palace Vrijburg. The list of 'domestics' (written in Dutch) was made on 1 March 1643 and signed by Johan Maurits himself (in French).[45] It mentions 46 people, of whom the most important guests were accompanied by a young servant. Added to this list is another large group, also fed by the court kitchen: ten stable boys, six sailors of the governor's sloop, 12 halberdiers of the daily guard, 80 African men and women (owned by 'the Company and his Excellency'), ten Turks, two bookkeepers, a Brazilian from Marahoan and the sentry of the palace's entrance – in total almost 200 persons. From the group of 46, some are explicitly mentioned by name, including Frans Plante (minister), the doctor Piso (personal physician), three noblemen (Steenborn, Uttenhoven and Stamnia), the painters Albert Eckhout and Frans Post, and the cartographer Georg Markgraf. At the end of the list we find an enumeration of foods that were needed in the court kitchen, so we know that the main parts of the meals at Vrijburg were meat, bacon, fowl and poultry, and much less fish. The period just before the event captured in this document, 1636–40, had been devastating for livestock in Pernambuco, and meat, butter and cheese, and also flour, textiles and wine, had to be transported from the Dutch Republic to the palace in Mauritsstad. Of all Dutch colonies in the world, New Holland was the most expensive in which to live.

Whom do we find at His Excellency's high table at noon? This is a select group, comprising the governor himself, the chief of the guard, the secretary, the minister (Franciscus Plante), the counsellor (Pfilts), the stable master (Christof Lindenau), the physician (Willem Piso) and 'the old' Perceyn. The painters and the cartographer had seats at the second table, together with the chief steward, the superintendent, the three nobles and two page boys. Thus, the two guards of the governor's spiritual and physical well-being, the minister and the physician, stood one step higher in the official court hierarchy than the two artists and the scientist. The same is true for the stable master in comparison with the chief steward and the superintendent. At the third table we find, amongst others, three gardeners of the court, his silver keeper, two of his cooks and the cantor. Persons at the high table had permission to order as much bread and (Spanish or French) wine as they wanted. Their table was placed on a platform in the dining room. In the evening, most of the table companions of the noon high table joined those of the second table for dinner. Plante, Piso, Eckhout, Post and Markgraf, the core group of Johan Maurits's scientific and artistic staff, were now united around the evening table. Apparently, the count dined alone or in private company in the evening. Of course, this document shows us only one side of court life: the front stage, so to speak. We can only guess about what happened back stage. For example: how did the governor treat his enslaved servants?[46] Was there a rivalry between the scholars? We suspect some tension between Piso and Markgraf. The German cartographer and astronomer had broad interests and was also busy with research on animals, insects and plants – more the research area of the physician Willem Piso. Perhaps this is why Markgraf made his notes in secret code at one point. The work of Post and Eckhout appears to have been complementary: Post ('the Canaletto of Brazil') is the landscape painter, also showing the plantations with the sugar mills and the enslaved workers, and Eckhout painted still lifes with plants and fruits and made life-size portraits of black, enslaved men and women, and of people from different indigenous tribes (Tupi and Tapuya).

Seven years had passed since most of these young men left the Dutch Republic and followed Johan Maurits to Brazil. The latter had always shown great passion to stimulate their art, research and writings. He made comments on the drawings of Eckhout and Post and read the notes of Piso and Markgraf. He was present when Markgraf studied the evening skies in the observatory and walked with Piso through the gardens to study plants and trees. The governor asked Plante for ethnographic research, but the minister was too busy with his pastoral tasks, so he made use of the fruits of the ethnographic explorations of Elias Herckmans – seaman, writer-poet and governor of Paraiba – who sailed to Brazil in 1634 and died ten years later in Recife. With a Portuguese guide, he wandered through the tropical jungle exploring the country and indigenous peoples. A young German soldier of the WIC, Zacharias Wagener, probably arrived in Brazil with Herckmans. Some years later, in 1637, Maurits offered him a job as kitchen secretary and in this function he followed his superior on many expeditions. As an amateur painter Wagener worked in close cooperation with Albert Eckhout for his ethnographic portraits. After leaving Brazil in 1641, this genuine adventurer made an astonishing career in the East Indies, in Java, and thereafter in China, Japan and the Cape Colony (as governor).[47]

When the core group of scholars dined together in March 1643, did they know that Johan Maurits had been asked for his resignation? Inhabitants of Recife and Mauritsstad wrote petitions to the WIC in Amsterdam and pleaded for an extension of 'their' governor's contract, but in vain. The board of directors did not hesitate to break the relationship with Maurits. On 6 May 1644, the governor pronounced his political testimony in the great hall of the High Council, where he had presided for seven years. All Mauritsstad and Recife was present. Bouman characterised the speech as the self-presentation of an enlightened sovereign *avant la lettre* (aristocratic, tolerant and decisive), but this glosses over the repressive dimensions of the reign of Maurits in Brazil (extreme forms of racism, enslavement, forced labour and brutish military combat).[48] Five days later, Maurits left Mauritsstad and via Olinda arrived in the harbour of Paraiba. From near and far, Amerindians, Mulattos, Portuguese and Jewish merchants, Dutch planters, officers and soldiers showed up for a final farewell. Three sons of the Tapuya king Jandovi wanted to travel with the prince to The Hague and took with them eight other Tapuyas. The governor himself was deeply moved by the loyalty of his Brazilian subjects. When embarkation was near, a group of indigenous people lifted the governor from his seat in his sloop, put the prince on their shoulders and brought him on board the flagship. Soldiers played the Dutch national hymn, the Wilhelmus (also symbolising the House Orange-Nassau), and the guns of the Dutch fortresses fired salutes.[49] To what extent was it an orchestrated farewell ceremony? The richly loaded return fleet comprised 13 ships; it transported 1,400 people, sugar, brazilwood and, of course, the governor's Brazilian treasures. Three years later, the WIC approached Maurits with an offer for a new term as governor-general in Brazil but he declined. He had found a new challenge in 1646, when he was present at the wedding party in The Hague of Frederic William of Brandenburg and Louise Henriette of Nassau, daughter of stadtholder Frederick Henry. The elector needed a new stadtholder for his Duchy of Cleves; Maurits felt honoured and immediately accepted this new, well-paid function.

The culture of gift exchange

Back home in The Hague, Johan Maurits could ascertain that the job – the Mauritshuis – was done. 'La belle, très belle et bellissime maison', as his friend Huygens wrote, was ready.[50] It was August 1644, and even before Maurits had his first meeting with the Heeren XIX of the WIC in Amsterdam he organised a reception. The nearly naked Tapuya Indians performed their war dances, but many of his guests, especially the ministers and their ladies, were not amused. The host was too busy showing his social equals the treasures that he had brought with him: tropical plants, stuffed animals, paintings of Brazilian landscapes and people, Indian feathers and weapons, and replicas of sugar mills. Only a few of the guests could appreciate the Brazilian pepper-spiced drink that was served. The reception was the talk of the town. The Leiden professor Adolph Vorstius, who visited the Mauritshuis in December 1644, was very impressed and wrote about it in a letter to Huygens, praising Johan Maurits's extraordinary interest in scholars, science and art.[51]

Eight years later, in May 1652, at the wedding of the Frisian stadtholder William Frederic, count of Nassau (1613–64) to Albertine Agnes (1634–96), princess of Orange and daughter of Frederic Henry's widow Amalia van Solms, 24 representatives of African and Indian tribes were part of a re-enactment of the Battle of Zama (202 BCE). The classical heroes Scipio and Hannibal were played by the elector of Brandeburg and the count of Waldeck respectively, while the African participants and the Tapuyas formed part of Hannibal's Carthaginian army.[52] The wedding took place at Maurits's castle Zwanenburg at Cleves, where he had lived since his appointment as stadtholder there. A black African king was carried around in a litter, surrounded by 12 'morish servants' in chains; about ten Tapuya Indians were also chained and adorned with feathers; they carried with them bowls and barrels filled with lemons, sugar, apples and exotic fruits. Some of the Indians showed the guests woven baskets full of human meat, including arms and legs, everything 'prepared in the barbaric way at its best'.[53] The Tapuya were cannibals and ate their own dead, old and young, as Johan Maurits's informants had observed in Brazil. The whole performance was a complex comparison over time and space: the glory of the Roman empire mirrored that of the House of Orange-Nassau, while the otherness of African people and Amerindians refers to and reaffirms Maurits's colonial world, including its brutal social order with enslaved people (Figure 14.5).

The elector of Brandenburg was probably the first reigning monarch to show interest in Maurits's collection of Brazilian trophies. In The Hague, he had already admired the Brazilian legacy of Johan Maurits in the so-called Orange Room of the stadtholder's summer residence Huis ten Bosch (House in the Forest). Selected by Frederic Henry's widow Amalia and the architect Jacob van Campen, artists had worked on panels and vault paintings, including contributions by Frans Post (for example, a portrait of Johan Maurits and a view of Vrijburg) and Albert Eckhout.[54] The elector exchanged some plots of land near Cleves for a part of his stadtholder's collection of paintings and drawings depicting Brazil. As an admirer of the world trade of the Dutch, the elector also had aspirations to found colonies for himself. In autumn 1652, Brazilian and African objects, including ivory furniture, brazilwood, animal skins and many works of art, were moved from the Mauritshuis in The Hague to the elector's court in Berlin.[55] From Maurits's point of view, this gift exchange was part of his strategy to climb one step higher in the status hierarchy of the European high nobility. He aspired to the ranks of imperial prince and master of the Order of St John, which he duly became on the instigation of the elector. Johan Maurits knew of his own

Figure 14.5 Albert Eckhout, *Dancing Tupuyas*, 1643. National Museum of Denmark.

blood relationship with the Danish royal family and in 1654 he offered the Danish king Fredrick III an entire collection of 'Brazilian' paintings by Albert Eckhout. These comprised 12 still lifes (mostly of tropical fruits), eight life-size portraits of different ethnic groups, a large painting of Tapuya men dancing while two women look on, a portrait of Johan Maurits surrounded by Tapuyas and another portrait showing only him. Some portraits show black men from the Congo, referring to his exchange of gifts with African rulers.[56] Since the exchange of gifts was closely connected with court society and diplomatic relationships, some reciprocity was required and the Danish king rewarded Maurits with the very exclusive Order of the White Elephant. During his stadtholdership in Germany, Maurits had initiated the construction of residences with impressive gardens in the towns of Cleves and Siegen. Near Küstrin, in present-day Poland, he built Sonnenburg Castle of the Order of Saint John (Bailiwick of Brandenburg).

Near the end of his life Johan Maurits approached the most powerful ruler in Europe at that time, the French king Louis XIV, with the offer of a 'Brazilian' gift.[57] He exchanged letters about his offer with the French secretary of state and with Louis XIV himself. 'The Brazilian' refers to the beauty of his country in the New World, 'that has no equal under heaven'. If the king could send an artist to Cleves, Maurits was willing to give him access to his drawings of Brazil; the king could use these drawings as models for tapestries. We do not know how many paintings by Post and Eckhout were sent to Versailles at a later time.

Conclusions

The message behind Johan Maurits's efforts in light of his impending death seems quite clear: he used his Brazilian cultural capital to strengthen his reputation as a man of glory, power, honour and generosity. But perhaps this conclusion is too simple and one-sided for such a complex and adventurous man. Of course, his building activities are representations of colonial power and imperialism. Vrijburg and Boa Vista are definitely 'power houses', to borrow Mark Girouard's famous characterisation of England's stately homes. As a humanist collector, Maurits was also motivated in the first place to show his social equals – the born rulers, the aristocrats striving for knowledge – the beauty and uniqueness of the New World. Looking back on his life, he felt satisfied that he had inspired a whole group of talented men to discover new things. In all his later building activities and his carefully planned parks and gardens, we can recognise his experiences in Brazil.[58] As a *dilettante* and *honnête homme* in the true sense of the word, he had enjoyed all his architectural activities – ranging from designing palaces to creating complementary utility and pleasure gardens. Certainly, he was outstanding and exceptional among his aristocratic peer group in Northwest Europe. And he was the first European ruler, identifying himself with legendary Roman generals, to introduce such cultural institutions as a botanical garden, a zoo and a museum of natural history and art (a sort of *Kunstkammer*) in the New World (Figure 14.6).

At Bergenthal, near Cleves, Johan Maurits retired from the world. In a 1678 letter to minister Frans Plante he looked back on their lasting friendship of more than 40 years, including the eight years in Brazil. Maurits thanked God for acknowledging and forgiving his sins and granting him a long life to gain honour and glory and, especially, a farewell to arms. His own sepulchral monument at Bergenthal was part of an open-air museum. In combination with the surrounding 21 altars and

Figure 14.6 Pieter Nason, *Johan Maurits, Count of Nassau-Siegen*, 1675. Photograph Geheugen van Nederland, Reproduced courtesy of Rijksmuseum. Public domain. Available at https://commons.wikimedia.org/wiki/File:Johan_Maurits_(1604-1679)_by_Pieter_Nason.jpg.

tombstones, it also suggests the Roman origin of the Nassau family. Amid Roman soldiers, emperors and deities, 'the Brazilian' figures as the main character in this amphitheatre. A two-line inscription running all around the tomb invites the visitor to walk around it and read the text: 'Wanderer, look at Death's iron monument!; Learn from Maurits how to live and die.'[59]

Acknowledgements

I thank my colleagues Jan Bremmer and Auke van der Woud for comments on an earlier version of this chapter.

Notes

1. Boxer, *Dutch Seaborne Empire*; Israel, *Dutch Primacy in World Trade*.
2. Boxer, *Dutch in Brazil*; Israel, 'Religious toleration', 13–32.
3. Mintz, *Sweetness and Power*; Wolf, *Europe and the People without History*, 197.
4. Boxer, *Dutch in Brazil*, 12–13 and 67.
5. Israel, 'Religious toleration', 14.
6. Israel, 'Religious toleration', 18–19.
7. Barlaeus, *Rerum per octennium in Brasilia*, 202.
8. Hoetink, 'Some remarks', 8–9.
9. Hoetink, 'Some remarks', 7–11.
10. Terwen, 'Buildings of Johan Maurits', 139.
11. Mout, 'Youth of Johan Maurits', 23.
12. Bouman, *Johan Maurits van Nassau*, 20.
13. Some historians of architecture assume that Van Campen did not visit Italy but worked with architectural treatises of Palladio (1570) and Scamozzi (1615). Cf. Terwen, 'Buildings of Johan Maurits', 59.
14. Terwen and Ottenheym, *Pieter Post*.
15. Cf. Mout, 'Youth of Johan Maurits', 36.
16. Most of the information in this paragraph and the following two comes from Boxer, *Dutch in Brazil*, 77–111.
17. Boxer, *Dutch in Brazil*, 75–7.
18. Boxer, *Dutch in Brazil*, 87.
19. Boxer's chapter 'A humanist Prince in the New World' paints Johan Maurits in a very positive light, praising his effort to develop the colony and his cultural and scientific legacy; *Dutch in Brazil*, 112.
20. Boxer, *Dutch in Brazil*, 83–4.
21. Boxer, *Dutch in Brazil*, 138.
22. Van den Boogaart, 'Infernal allies', 527.
23. Fort Ernestus was named after John Maurice's youngest brother John Ernest, who died in Brazil in 1639; Bouman, *Johan Maurits van Nassau*, 66.
24. Terwen, 'Buildings of Johan Maurits', 88.
25. Terwen, 'Buildings of Johan Maurits', 89; in comparison, the Mauritshuis in The Hague was mortgaged for 160,000 guilders in 1660.
26. Barlaeus, *Nederlandsch Brazilië*, 201. Also cited in Terwen, 'Buildings of Johan Maurits', 89.
27. Terwen, 'Buildings of Johan Maurits', 96.
28. Boxer, *Dutch in Brazil*, 114.
29. Whitehead, 'Georg Markgraf and Brazilian zoology', 428–9.
30. Roscam Abbing, *Rembrandt's Elephant*.

31 Diedenhofen, 'Johan Maurits and his gardens', 197.
32 Barlaeus, *Nederlandsch Brazilië*, 202. Also cited in Diedenhofen, 'Johan Maurits and his gardens', 199.
33 Barlaeus, *Nederlandsch Brazilië*, 203.
34 For the scholars that Johan Maurits gathered around him in Brazil see Boxer, *Dutch in Brazil*, 112–13 and Joppien, 'Dutch vision of Brazil', 299 and following. Not all of them sailed with him to Brazil. For example, Zacharias Wagner (1614–68) came to Recife in 1634. Wagner left Brazil in 1641 and took with him his illustrated manuscript *Thierbuch*, preserved in the *Kupferstichkabinett* in Dresden; Joppien, 'Dutch vision of Brazil', 319.
35 Barlaeus, *Nederlandsch Brazilië*, 210.
36 Barlaeus, *Nederlandsch Brazilië*, 205.
37 Diedenhofen, '"Belvedere"', 49–51.
38 Terwen, 'Buildings of Johan Maurits', 98.
39 Freyre, 'Johan Maurits from a Brazilian viewpoint'; Boogaart, et al., *A Humanist Prince*, 243.
40 Boogaart, et al., *A Humanist Prince*, 243.
41 Boogaart, et al., *A Humanist Prince*, 243.
42 Boogaart, et al., *A Humanist Prince*, 243.
43 This paragraph is based on Gonsalves de Mello, 'Vincent Joachim Soler', 247–8 and 251–2.
44 Gonsalves de Mello, 'Vincent Joachim Soler', 254–5.
45 Caland, 'Hofhouding', 557–61.
46 Monteiro and Odegard, 'Slavery at the court'.
47 Thomsen, *Albert Eckhout*, 66.
48 Bouman, *Johan Maurits van Nassau*, 78.
49 Bouman, *Johan Maurits van Nassau*, 81–3.
50 Bouman, *Johan Maurits van Nassau*, 85.
51 Buvelot, *Albert Eckhout*, 141.
52 Françozo, 'Global connections', 105–23.
53 Joppien, 'Dutch vision of Brazil', 322 (notes 138 and 139).
54 Cf. Broomhall and van Gent, *Dynastic Colonialism*.
55 Joppien, 'Dutch vision of Brazil', 322–3.
56 Joppien, 'Dutch vision of Brazil', 322. See also Thomsen, *Albert Eckhout*. On the recommendation of his patron Johan Maurits, Eckhout was court painter in Dresden for a period of ten years.
57 Thomsen, *Albert Eckhout*, 126–56.
58 Terwen, 'Buildings of Johan Maurits'; Diedenhofen, 'Johan Maurits and his gardens'.
59 Diedenhofen, '"Belvedere"', 76.

Bibliography

Barlaeus, Caspar, *Nederlandsch Brazilië onder het bewind van Johan Maurits Grave van Nassau 1637–1644. Historisch-Geographisch-Ethnographisch* (1647), edited and translated by S.P. L'Honoré Naber. The Hague: Martinus Nijhoff, 1923.

Boogaart, Ernst van den. 'Infernal allies: the Dutch West India Company and the Tarairu 1630–1654'. In *Johan Maurits van Nassau-Siegen 1604–1679: A humanist prince in Europe and Brazil*, edited by Ernst van den Boogaart, 519–38. The Hague: the Johan Maurits van Nassau Stichting, 1979.

Boogaart, Ernst van den, R. Hoetink and P.J.P. Whitehead, eds. *Johan Maurits van Nassau-Siegen 1604–1679: A humanist prince in Europe and Brazil*. The Hague: the Johan Maurits van Nassau Stichting, 1979.

Bouman, Pieter J. *Johan Maurits van Nassau: de Braziliaan*. Utrecht: Oosthoek, 1947.

Boxer, Charles. *The Dutch in Brazil 1624–1654*. Oxford: Clarendon, 1957.

Boxer, Charles. *The Dutch Seaborne Empire 1600–1800*. London: Hutchinson, 1965.

Broomhall, Susan, and Jacqueline van Gent. *Dynastic Colonialism: Gender, materiality and the early modern house of Orange Nassau*. New York: Routledge, 2016.

Buvelot, Quentin, ed. *Albert Eckhout: Een Hollandse kunstenaar in Brazilië*. Zwolle: Waanders Uitgevers, 2004.

Caland, Fred. 'Hofhouding van Johan Maurits Graaf van Nassau in Brazilië', *De Navorscher* 48 (1898): 557–61.

Diedenhofen, Wilhelm. 'Johan Maurits and his gardens'. In *Johan Maurits van Nassau-Siegen 1604–1679: A humanist prince in Europe and Brazil*, edited by Ernst van den Boogaart, 197–236. The Hague: the Johan Maurits van Nassau Stichting, 1979.

Diedenhofen, Wilhelm. '"Belvedere", or the principle of seeing and looking in the gardens of Johan Maurits van Nassau Siegen at Cleves'. In *The Dutch Garden in the Seventeenth Century*, edited by John Dixon Hunt, 49–80. Washington, DC: Dumbarton Oaks, 1990.

Françozo, Mariano, 'Global connections: Johan Maurits of Nassau-Siegen's collection of curiosities'. In *The Legacy of Dutch Brazil*, edited by Michiel van Groesen, 105–23. Cambridge: Cambridge University Press, 2014.

Freyre, Gilberto. 'Johan Maurits van Nassau-Siegen from a Brazilian viewpoint'. In *Johan Maurits van Nassau-Siegen 1604–1679: A humanist prince in Europe and Brazil*, edited by Ernst van den Boogaart, 237–46. The Hague: the Johan Maurits van Nassau Stichting, 1979.

Gonsalves de Mello, Jose Antonio. 'Vincent Joachim Soler in Dutch Brazil'. In *Johan Maurits van Nassau-Siegen 1604–1679: A humanist prince in Europe and Brazil*, edited by Ernst van den Boogaart, 247–55. The Hague: the Johan Maurits van Nassau Stichting, 1979.

Hoetink, H.R. (Hans). 'Some remarks on the modernity of Johan Maurits'. In *Johan Maurits van Nassau-Siegen 1604–1679: A humanist prince in Europe and Brazil*, edited by Ernst van den Boogaart, 7–11. The Hague: the Johan Maurits van Nassau Stichting, 1979.

Israel, Jonathan. *The Dutch Primacy in World Trade 1585–1740*. Oxford: Oxford University Press, 1989.

Israel, Jonathan. 'Religious toleration in Dutch Brazil'. In *The Expansion of Tolerance: Religion in Dutch Brazil (1624–1654)*, edited by Jonathan Israel and Stuart B. Schwartz, 13–32. Amsterdam: Amsterdam University Press, 2007.

Joppien, Rüdiger. 'The Dutch vision of Brazil'. In *Johan Maurits van Nassau-Siegen 1604–1679: A humanist prince in Europe and Brazil*, edited by Ernst van den Boogaart, 297–377. The Hague: the Johan Maurits van Nassau Stichting, 1979.

Mintz, Sidney. *Sweetness and Power: The place of sugar in modern history*. New York: Viking, 1985.

Monteiro, Carolina, and Erik Odegard. 'Slavery at the court of the "humanist prince": reexamining Johan Maurits van Nassau-Siegen and his role in slavery, slave trade and slave-smuggling in Dutch Brazil', *Journal of Early American History* 10 (2020): 3–32.

Mout, M.E.H.N. (Nicolette). 'The youth of Johan Maurits and aristocratic culture in the early seventeenth century'. In *Johan Maurits van Nassau-Siegen 1604–1679: A humanist prince in Europe and Brazil*, edited by Ernst van den Boogaart, 12–38. The Hague: the Johan Maurits van Nassau Stichting, 1979.

Odegard, Erik, *Graaf en gouverneur. Nederlands-Brazilië onder het bewind van Johan Maurits van Nassau-Siegen, 1636–1644*. Zutphen: Walburg Pers, 2022.

Roscam Abbing, Michiel. *Rembrandt's Elephant: Following in Hansken's footsteps*. Amstelveen: Leporello, 2021.

Terwen, J.J. (Jan). 'The buildings of Johan Maurits'. In *Johan Maurits van Nassau-Siegen 1604–1679: A humanist prince in Europe and Brazil*, edited by Ernst van den Boogaart, 54–141. The Hague: the Johan Maurits van Nassau Stichting, 1979.

Terwen, J.J., and K.A. (Koen) Ottenheym. *Pieter Post (1608–1669): Architect*. Zutphen: Walburg Pers, 1993.

Thomsen, Thomas. *Albert Eckhout. Ein Niederländischer Maler und sein Gönner Moritz der Brasilianer. Ein Kulturbild aus dem 17. Jahrhundert*. Copenhagen: Einar Munksgaards Forlag, 1938.

Whitehead, Peter J.P. 'Georg Markgraf and Brazilian zoology'. In *Johan Maurits van Nassau-Siegen 1604–1679: A humanist prince in Europe and Brazil*, edited by Ernst van den Boogaart, 424–71. The Hague: the Johan Maurits van Nassau Stichting, 1979.

Wolf, Eric. *Europe and the People without History*. Berkeley: University of California Press, 1982.

Conclusions
Jon Stobart

Country houses have long been lauded as centres of economic, social and political power, the physical manifestation of personal and familial status. Their role as powerhouses owed as much to their contents as to their monumental use of bricks and mortar – plus stone, timber, tiles, lead, glass, marble and so on. Yet these have all too often been viewed in terms of artistic treasure rather than statements of power that underpinned the economic and cultural reach of the landowning elites, who were both able and willing to draw in goods from across the globe to make their houses magnificent, luxurious, cosmopolitan and sometimes imperial. There is growing awareness of the global connectivity of the elite and their houses in Britain and elsewhere in Europe, but this was equally true of samurai castles in Japan, Rajput palaces in Rajasthan and the houses of the Efik elite in West Africa – among many others. The broader geographical perspective adopted in this volume is vital in allowing us to uncover these commonalities and explore the extent to which common values and motivations lay behind the accumulation of global goods in such diverse settings. Widening our horizons, and thus decentring our analysis, also helps us to avoid a preoccupation with the terminology of country house, palace, manor, castle, mansion and plantation house and focus on their equivalence as the houses of the political, social and cultural elite.

Most importantly, the analyses of global goods offered in individual chapters and object lessons, and in the collection as a whole, have served to place collections and commodities into their global context. At the same time, they have been attentive to the ways in which the global and local were mutually constitutive. *Global Goods in the Country House* connects all manner of country houses to wider economic, cultural and political systems and emphasises the importance of the local in understanding the differential impact of global and globalising processes. Global goods were present in country houses across Europe and the wider world, both within and beyond the formal bounds of empire. However, the nature and meaning of the global and of global goods varied over space and time. What constituted 'global' in terms of material culture depended on relative geopolitical location. For the Efik, the new political elite in early nineteenth-century Wallachia and the samurai of early modern Japan, it generally meant European goods; for European landowners, it was primarily associated with Eastern and Atlantic goods; for merchants in North America, slaveowners in Jamaica and the maharani in India, it was a mixture of the two. Global was thus a matter of perspective and politics as much as geographical scale.

Recognising these distinctions is vital in decentring our perspective on global integration. Across the world, the houses of the elite were nodes in global webs of material and cultural exchange. For some, this position was maintained and sometimes enhanced by the expansion of European empires, but these are all too easily read as the driving force of globalisation and obscure other global dynamics. Equally important is the need to acknowledge the common and distinct meanings attached to these various global goods in different geographical, cultural and political contexts. Recent analyses and public initiatives by the National Trust and other heritage organisations have rightly emphasised the political significance of global goods – part of the broader move to rewrite histories of slavery. This is underscored in an English and imperial context in the analyses of William Blathwayt's development of Dyrham Park, the botanical collections in English country house gardens and Johan Maurits's exploits in Dutch Brazil. In these places, and many others besides, country houses are seen as overt and conscious statements of empire: assemblages of goods that spoke of the ability of the individual and nation to exert power in distant lands. Elsewhere, however, global goods communicated different forms of power and influence, including the explicit embodiment of modernisation in Western goods in early nineteenth-century Wallachia, their softer cultural influence in Japan (not least through the media and representation of knowledge in the form of European books) and their emphasis of cosmopolitanism in Rajasthan palaces. Conversely, Eastern goods were used to underpin noble and cosmopolitan status in eighteenth-century Naples, more importance being given to their status as royal gifts than as exotic or imperial objects. The extent to which this was true of all 'non-imperial' nations merits further investigation, but German and Swedish nobles valued global goods for similar reasons. In colonial spaces, where the influence of empire might be expected to be greatest, global goods could speak of both empire (by representing and strengthening ties to the imperial metropolis, and cementing ideas of status and racial distinction) and cultural refinement in the form of learning and good taste.

The hybrid nature of colonial cultures is well established and often marked out their distinction from metropolitan norms, as with the centrality of punch drinking to Jamaican heterosocial entertaining. However, hybridity is also apparent in European country houses. Global goods from tea and coffee to mahogany were thoroughly naturalised and domesticated within Western domestic routines, yet this process in itself created hybridity. The obvious example is tea-drinking: a genuinely new performance created through melding social practices, material cultures and commodities from China and Europe. But there were others: 'English' mahogany furniture arose from the new woodworking and aesthetic possibilities offered by tropical hardwoods. Hybridity in specific objects is more elusive. Punch bowls, tea cups and sugar bowls might be viewed in this light; so too could the content and form of tobacco rolls, and the porcelain rooms of Rajasthan. However, blending is more apparent in many of the things discussed in the object lessons, including European yarns being woven into traditional Japanese *jinbaori*, the assemblage of fabrics and shells in miniature grottoes crafted in colonial Pennsylvania, and the addition of domestic embroidery as upholstery on ebony chairs made in Visakhapatnam. More generally, these object lessons have brought home the power of material things to illustrate connections and to carry layered meanings, both in the past and in the present.

Some of these objects came from or went to places beyond the formal bounds of empires, complicating narratives of power and sociocultural influence. This again underlines the fresh insights offered by taking the broad geographical and decentred perspective adopted in this volume: one that has placed empire centre stage but also recognises that other motivations and meanings were critical in different times and places. Indeed, further research is needed to expand the range of places and create a truly global perspective: analyses of elite consumption and houses in Spanish colonies, the Islamic world and Imperial China, for instance, would provide further insights into the role of culture, religion, politics, commerce and geography in shaping engagement with global goods. Further, analyses taking a more explicitly decolonialising approach to country houses both within and beyond imperial powers would add further variety and nuance to the subaltern voices that can speak to us through the global goods found within them. One book cannot achieve everything: *Global Goods in the Country House* has served to open up exciting new perspectives and approaches that provide a much richer history of houses and their owners but also of material objects, international exchange and, above all, the contingent nature of globalisation.

Index

Note: Page numbers in italics are figures. Page numbers in bold are tables.

Abbas, Shah, 308–9
abolitionists, 8
   See also slavery; slave trade
Aburaya Katatsuki tea caddy, 92
accounts, household, 29–30
Adam, Robert, 1
Adelmann, Joseph Anselm von, 66, 68–9
Adelmann family, 68–9
Adrianople, Treaty of, 138, 194
advertisements for osnaburgs, *129*
Africa, West, 5, 285–301
African elites, 285, 287, 288–9, 291, 292–4, 300
   benefited from slave trade, 297
Ahlefeldt, Count, 175
Ahlefeldt, Countess Marie Elisabeth, née Leiningen-Dachsburg-Hartenburg, 175, 187
Aitken, Molly Emma, 319
Aiton, William Townsend, 342
'Akai Jinbaori', 250
Akbar, Mughal Emperor, 309
Albertine Agnes, princess of Orange, 422
alcove (*tokonoma*), 81, 92–3
Ali Qapu palace, 309
Allen, David Elliston, 392
aloeswood, 92
Alrichs, Jacob, 129
America, North, 215–32
Amussen, Susan, 369
anchovies, 65
Anderson, Jennifer, 362, 363
Andros, Sir Edmund, 372
Angola, 412
animal products, 33, **266**, 269
   See also ivory

animals, exotic, 151, 153–5, 393, 414
animal skins, 225, 270, 271, 277–8, 281
Anna, Princess, 160
Anson, Admiral George, 13
Antigua, 101, 102, 109
antiquarian paintings, 85
Antonio Vaz (island), 412, 415
Ardebil Shrine, 308–9
Ari Sing, Maharana, 318, *319*, 320
armorial china, 158–9
armorial dinner services, 12–13
armour, suits of, 85
Arundel, Countess, 309
Ashikaga Yoshimitsu, 88
Asian porcelain, 12, 59, 67, 180–1, 273
   See also Chinese porcelain
auctions, 263–81, **266**
Audley End, 338, 339
Augusta, Dowager Princess of Wales, 242
Augusta, Duchess, 175–9
Augustenborg Castle, 172, 174–9, 183, 187, 188
Augustenborg, Duke Frederik Vilhelm, 175, 176
Augustenborg, Dukes of, 174–5
August the Strong, 309
Avrig, Transylvania, 200
Azuchi Castle, 79–80, *80*

Babur, emperor, 308
Baburnama, 308
Badal Mahal (Cloud Palace), Junagarh Fort, Bikaner, 321
Badminton, Gloucestershire, 355, 385–91, *390*, 394

INDEX   **433**

Bahadur Shah I, Mughal Emperor, 314
Baker, Audrey, 395
Bakhta, Maharana Ari Singh II in durbar, 319
Balcony Room, Dyrham Park, 366–7, 375
ball-headed war clubs, *337*, 338
Balls Park, 135
Banister, John, 372
Banks, Lady Dorothea, 342, 343
Banks, Sir Joseph, 342, 343, 395
Barbadian Monkey Jar, *245*, 246–7
Barbados, 246, 388
Barczewski, Stephanie, 6, 265
Bari Chitrasali, 318–19
Barker, Robert, 361
Barlaeus, Caspar, 406, 413, 414–15, 418
Barra villa, 150, 151–2, 153, 155–6
Barrington, Jane, 397
Barton Hall, 270
Beach, Rachel, 107, 110, 111
bear skin, 271
Beaufort, Duke, 355
Beaufort, Mary Somerset Duchess of, 382, 385–91, *386*, 397
Beaufortia Decussata, Splendid Beaufortia, *391*
Beckford, William, 8, 263
Beckmann, Jacob, 126–7
  statuette of, *125*
bed chamber at Brede House, 185, *186*
Bedford, Duke of, 342
Bell & Anderson, 194–5
The Belvedere Mansion (painting), 206
Bennett, Ann, 108
Bentinck, Margaret Cavendish Harley, Duchess of Portland, 382, 391–7
Bentinck, William, second Duke of Portland, 391
Berg, Maxine, 107
Berlin, Castle Charlottenburg, 309

Best Stair Case of red cedar, 360
beverages
  and the Imperial Knights, 58, 59, 61–2, 63, 66
  in Jamaica, 107, 108, 113, 114, 118
  and Samuel Martin, 101
  and Spens family, 37, 39, 42
  See also chocolate; coffee; tea
Beverley, Robert, 130
Bhim Singh, Maharana, 316, *317*
biblical scenes on tiles, 313
Bibliotheca Graeca (Fabricius), 228–9
Bight of Biafra, 289–90
Bindman, David, 369
bird cages, 181
birds
  exotic, 153–4, 367, 396
  silver, chiselled on silvers, *154*
Bischoff, Cordula, 313
Bishop, Elizabeth, 104
'blackamoor', 367, 369, 370
black individuals, in portraits and figures, *366*, 367–70
black walnut, 362
Blake, Joseph, 362
Blandford, Marquis, 342
Blathwayt, Anne, 357
Blathwayt, William, 355–8, 364, 368, 370, 373
  and cocoa, 365
  and colonial timber, 359–60, 361–2, 375
  and greenhouse at Dyrham Park, 371–2
Blathwayt, William (son), 372
Blickling Hall, Norfolk, 242
Blondel, Jacques-François, 4
blue and white Chinese tiles, 311–13, 321
blue and white Dutch tiles, 307
blue and white porcelain, 308
Blue Willow Pattern plates, Staffordshire, 321, 322, *322*, 323–4
  detail of the *Chini Gokhada*, Juna Mahal, Dungarpur, *323*

Blue Willow Pattern porcelain tiles, 321
Boa Vista, 415–16, 423
   c. 1671, *409*
Bobart, Jacob, 387
books
   in the Caribbean, 111–12
   and James Logan, 227, 228, 231
   of Matsura Seizan, 93
Boscawen, Admiral Edward, 273, 395
Boscawen, Frances, 395
botanical gardens, 383–4
botany, and women, 384–97
Bourdieu, Pierre, 85
Bowes, Mary Eleanor, countess of Strathmore, 397
Bow porcelain manufactory, 369
Boxer, Charles, 405–6, 411, 414
boyar interior, 205, *210*
boyars, 197–8, 204, 206–10, 211
Brâncoveanu, Constantin, 196
Brandenburg, elector, 422
brass, 58, 64, 292, 299
   kettles, 178
   teapots, 185
   tea urns, 66, 69
Brătuleanu, Anca, 196
Brazil, 349, 350–1, 405–6, 410–20
brazilwood, 267
Brede House, 172, 183–8
Breen, Timothy, 227
Bristol, Kerry, 275
Britain, and Romania, 194–5
Brixworth Hall, 266
Brodsworth estate, 142
Brodsworth Hall, 141, 143
Broughton rectory, 269, 271, 274
Brown, Lawrence, 363
Browne, Robert, 391
Browne, Thomas, 364
Brukenthal, Baron Samuel, 200
Buchanan, William, 134, 135
Bucharest, 139
Builder magazine, 289
Bulstrode Park, Buckinghamshire, 391–6, *392*
Burckhardt, Jacob, 406–7
Burke, Peter, 173

Burney, Fanny, 263
buttered bread, with tea and coffee, 62
Byrd, William, 372

Cadogan, Elizabeth, 110–11, 112
caffeine drinks, 4, 64
   See also coffee; tea
Calabar, West Africa, 285–6, 289, 291, 300, 301
Calado, Friar Manuel, 414, 418
calico, 110, 130, 269
camlet, 39
Campen, Jacob van, 409, 410, 422
Capel, Elizabeth, *386*
Capell, Henry, baron of Tewkesbury, 388
capers, 64–5
Capodimonte workshop, 158
the Caribbean, 101–19, 169
Caribbean mahogany, 1, 107–8
Carletti, Francesco, 91
Caroline, Queen, 342
Carson, Cary, 219
Casa-Grande and Senzala (Freyre), 417
Casid, Jill, 374
Castle Ashby, 271
Castle Charlottenburg, Berlin, 309
castles
   in Japan, 78–84, 96
   in Monteleone, 150
Catalogus Plantarum (Miller), 390
cat with kitten, China, *159*
Cecil, Lady Anne, 115–16
cedar, 84, 362
ceramics
   at Stenton, *221*
   in India, 308
   manufacture/place of origin of, **60**
   in porcelain rooms, 307
   for tea, 90–1
chairs
   chinoiserie, *13*
   ebony inlaid with engraved ivory, *133*
   mahogany, *6*

chamber pots, 180
Chambers, William, 242
chanoyu (tea ceremony), 89–93
Charlecote Park, 134, 135
Charles II, 355, 358
Charles of Nassau, 412
Charlotte, Queen, 385
Chelsea Physic Garden, 387
Chelsea porcelain manufactory, 369
chestnut bookcase with the Pignatelli coat of arms, and chinaware, *158*, 159
chests of drawers, 84
Chida-Razvi, Mehreen, 308
chigaidana, 81
china
    armorial, 158–9
    Imperial Knights, 67–8
    in Jamaica, 107, 108
    nankeen, 272, 279
chinaware, 4, 110, 156–7, 160, 230
    on top of Chestnut bookcase with the Pignatelli coat of arms, *158*, 159
Chinese calligraphy, 85
Chinese cups with a handle, 181
Chinese furniture, 159–60, 271
Chinese objects, 151, 155–6, 156
Chinese pagoda, model of, *241*, 242–3
Chinese paintings, 85
Chinese porcelain, 12, 272, 273, 307, 308, 309
    in Lille Hesbjerg Manor, 180–1
    in the Pignatelli Museum, 158
    teapot, 221, *221*
Chinese tea, 101
Chinese tiles, 308, 313, 319, 321
Chinese vases, 157
Chinese wallpapers, 1, 12, 156, 182
Chini Gokhada, detail of, Juna Mahal, Dungarpur, *323*
Chini khana, 307, 308
Chini-ki-Chitrashali with *jharokha* overlooking Manek Chowk, City Palace Udaipur, *312*

chinoiserie, 108, 109, 325
    chair, *13*
    designs, 6
    furniture, 12
chintz, 11, 39, 268–9, 272
Chippendale furniture, 1, 268
Chippendale, Thomas, 4, 12, 13
Chitrashala, 311
chocolate, 39, 44, 45, 55, 61–2, 178
    paraphernalia, **60**, 61
chocolate cups, 61, 67–8, *173*
chocolate sets, 178
Christie's Auction Room, *264*
City Palace of Udaipur, 307, 309–17, 322, 323
classicism, 227–32
Clifford, Helen, 156
Clive, Robert, 7, 8
cloth, imported to America, 225
clothing, Spens family, 37, 39, 45
Cloud Palace (Badal Mahal), Junagarh Fort, Bikaner, 321
coat of arms, 158–9, 160, 162
cocoa, 107, 364–5
A Cocoa Tree and Roasting Hut (painting), 364–5, *365*
coffee, 4, 55, 63–4, 181
    ceramics paraphernalia, **60**
    Chinese cups with a handle, 181
    copper set, 66
    and Imperial Knights, 57, 58
    and silver, 59
    with slices of buttered bread, 62
    in south-western German country houses, 71
    and the Spens family, 44, 45
coffee beans, 39
'coffee cake', 63
coffee cups, 67–8, *69*
coffee pots, 57, 58, 59, 69, 172
coffee sets, 64, 178
coffee spoons, 59
coffee trays, 59, 62
coin collection, 95
Collinson, Peter, 229–30
Cologne stoneware, 59
colonial groceries, 37, 39, 42, 44
colonialism, 8, 223, 267

Company of Royal Adventurers to Africa (RAC), 369
concubines, 82–3, *82*
conservatories, 342
conspicuous consumption, 56, 173, 368
Cook, Captain James, 270, 395
cookbooks, 62–3, 64
Copenhagen porcelain, 180, 181
copper, 58–9
    coffee set, 66
Cornwallis, Charles,1st Marquess, 338–9
Cornwallis, Lady Jane, 338
Corrantee, John, 290, 291, 293
Cortés, Hernán, 147, 160, 162
    golden bronze on granite column and marble base, 160–1, *161*, 162
Cosimo I Medici, 334
Cottingham, 274–5, 276
cotton linens, 10
cotton textiles, 4, 182
Coulton, Richard, 387–8
Courtenay, Lord Viscount, 342
Crewe, Louise, 274
Crick rectory, 266, 267, 268, 269
Crimean War, 339
crockery, Spens family's, 40
cultural capital, 69, 71
cups, 158, 172, *173*
cypress, 362

da Costa, Donna Juliana Dias, 315
daimyo, 77, 78, 79, 81, 85
    collections, 95–6
    and concubines, 82–3, *82*
    and falconry, 87
    and libraries, 93
    patronised noh, 89
    and *ranpeki*, 94–5
    and swords, 86
    and tea ceremony, 92
daimyo tea schools, 89–90, 91
damask, 39, 222
Dancing Tupuyas (painting), *422*
darshan, 312
Day, Samuel, 362

Daylesford, 135
de Clifford, dowager lady, 397
'Decolonising the Sloane Herbarium', 397
Defoe, Daniel, 269, 355
déjeuner set, eight-piece, with rococo decorations, *67*
Delany, Mary, 393–4, 396
Delaware nation, 225
Delft tiles, 222, *223*
delftware, 59, 309
Denmark, 169–70, 172, 174–88
'Design for a House in a Tropical Climate', *297*
Designs of Chinese Buildings (Chambers), 242
desk and bookcase in Stenton's parlour with the Greek wine cup, or skyphos, and marble sample, *231*
de Toledo, Eleonora, 334
di Amalfi, Princess Anna Maria, 149
di Amalfi, Princess Rosa Fici, 148–9
di Borbone, Carlo, 157
Dickens, Charles, 322
Diderot effect, 12
Diedenhofen, Wilhelm, 415
dinner services, 12–13, 40
di Noja, Duke Giovanni Carafa, 152
Diwan Dewdi at Hyderabad in the Deccan, 307
Doody, Samuel, 387
Dornbach, 200
Drake, Sir Francis, 357
Dresden porcelain, 66, 67
dress in late empire style, of Indian cotton with silver embroidery in *boteh* pattern, *171*
drinks. *See* caffeine drinks; coffee; exotic drinks; tea
Duke, Antera, 299
Duke Town, Old Calabar, 285–6, 288, 291, 299
DuPlessis, Robert, 6
Dutch blue and white ceramic tiles, 313
Dutch Brazil, 349, 350–1, 405–6, 410–20

INDEX   437

Dutch East India Company (VOC), 94, 134, 314, 367
The Dutch in Brazil 1624–1654 (Boxer), 406
'Dutch Pranketing Room' at Tart Hall, 309
Dutch Republic, 405
Dutch tiles, 222, *223*, 307, 313, *314*, 319
Dyrham Park, 355–6, *356*, 357, 359–75, *371*

Eacott, Jonathan, 6, 9, 12
Earle, Thomas, 300
earthenware jars, 160, 162
East India Company (EIC), 3, 6–7, 160, 358
ebony, 159, 269–70
ebony chairs inlaid with engraved ivory, *133*
ebony furniture, 134, 135
Eckhout, Albert, 350, 419, 420, 421, 422, 423
Ecton rectory, 268, *268*, 271, 272, 273, 276, 278
Edo period, 77, 89
Efik king, 285
Efik traders, 288–9, 291–4, 295, 299, 300
  households, 296–7
Egbo Young Eyambo, 290
E. Grant & Comp., *137*, 138–9, 203
Ehret, Georg, 394
Eisei Bunko Museum, 96
Elias, Norbert, 172
elite. *See* African elites; boyars; Romanian elite
elite self-fashioning, 293–4
Ellis, John, 396–7
Ellwangen, 68, 69
Elm House, 300
Emanuel, Philip, 364–5
Emlen, Anne, 254, 255
Emmer, Pieter, 3
English Depot. E. Grant & Comp., advertisement in *Românul. Diariu politic, comercial, literar*, *137*, 138–9

enslaved African figure, stand formed from, *366*, 367–9
enslavement, 142, 143
  See also slavery; slave trade
Ephraim, Duke, 294
Ephraim, Otto, 291
Epke Society, 295
Erddig, 242
erotic paintings, 316
Ertingen, Ludwig Christoph Leutrum von, 59, 61
Europeanisation, 207, 210, 211
Europeanness, 204, 205
Evelyn, John, 357–8, 364
the exotic
  in Indian art works, 315
  porcelain, 180–1
  silks and chintzes, 11
exotic animals, 85, 86, 151, 153–5, 393, 414
exotic birds, 153–4, 367, 396
exotic drinks, 59, 172, 183, 184
  See also coffee; tea
exoticism, 153–5, 157, 269–71, 272, 273, 277
  and Dutch and Chinese tiles, 313
  and murals, 315–17
  and pineapples, 335
exoticness, and porcelain rooms, 311, 325, 367
exotic objects
  appeal of at auction sales, 277
  in the Pignatelli houses, 151, **151**, 158, 160, 161, 162
exotic other, 6
exotic plants, 383, 387, 398
  at La Floridiana, 333, 334
  and Blathwayt, 372
  and Margaret, Duchess of Portland, 394, 397
  and Mary, Duchess of Beaufort, 388–91
  and Sir Joseph Banks, 342
exotic wood, 29, 84, 174
  and Blathwayt, 359, 361, 362–3, 375
  See also mahogany

expenditure on silver, Spens family, 33
Eyemba, Obong (King), 286–7, 289, 290–1, 298–9, 300
Eyo Honesty, Obong (King), 298

Fabricius, Johann Albrecht, 228–9
Fabricius, Johann Christian, 342–3
faience, 180, 181
falconry, 87
farangi, 307–8, 315–16, 317
    ornamental interior detail, *316*
Fateh Prakash Palace, 321
Ferdinando I Borbone, King, 333
Fersen, Axel von, 45
Finch House, 300
Finn, Margot, 6, 9
fireplace wall of the 'Yellow Lodging Room', Stenton, *223*
The First Day of the Yam Custom (painting), *298*
Firuz Shah, 308
Fisher, William, 130
Flora Delanica (Delany), 394
La Floridiana, 333–4, *333*
flowerpots, 180
Fonthill, 275, 277
foodstuffs, Spens family, 37, 39, 42
foreign consumer goods, Spens family, 39–40, 42
Fotino, George, 201
The Four Books of Architecture (Palladio), 196
Franklin, Benjamin, 215, 217, 228, 229
Frederick Henry, Prince of Orange, 405, 408, 409, 410, 414
Frederic William of Brandenburg, 421
Frederiksnagore, 169
Fredrick III, 423
Free Ports Act, 267
French-Mediterranean culinary influences, 65, 71
Freyberg, Anton Fidel von, 59
Freyre, Gilberto de Mello, 417
Frogmore in Berkshire, 342

Fróis, Luis, 79, 80
The Frontier Lands of the Christian and the Turk (Skene), 193
Fryer, Henry, 277
Fumai, Matsudaira, 92
furnishings, Spens family, 36, 44
furniture
    chestnut bookcase with the Pignatelli coat of arms, and chinaware, *158*, 159
    Chinese style, 159–60
    Indian, 134, 135, 271
    japanned, 222
    kingwood, 267, 268, 276
    See also chairs; ivory
fur trade, 215, 225
Furuta Oribe, 89–90, 92

game recipes, 64
Garden Museum, 397
gardens, 83, 383–4
    of Margaret, Duchess of Portland, 391–7
    of Mary, Duchess of Beaufort, 386–91
Garvin, James, 296
Gascoyne, Joel, 373–4
gate, iron, 334, 335
Geddington House, 266, 267, 269, 277
    catalogue for the sale at, *277*
Gentleman's Magazine, 384
geo-cultural landscape, 65, 71
George I, 355
Germany, 53–4, 55, 57, 61, 64, 71
    and tobacco rolls, 257–9
Gerritsen, Anne, 160
gin bottles, 317
Girouard, Mark, 3, 78, 423
glassware, 34, 36, 39, 40, 94, 95
'The Glory of the Garden' (Kipling), 381–2
Godsey, William D., 65, 71
Goetz, Hermann, 311
Gold Coast, 169, 289, 412
Golding, Sarah, 103–4
Golescu, Constantin (Dinicu), 199–201, 202

Golescu family, 197, 199–200, 204, 206, 207, 210
  and Effingham Grant, 202–3
Golescu, Nicolae, 204, *205*
Golescu, Zinca, 201, 202, 203, 204
Goleşti, 198–9, 201–2, 207, 211
Goleşti Konak (painting), *207*
Gomm, William, 6, 276
goshawk, 87
Göthe, Johann Friedrich Eosander von, 309
Goulding, Rupert, 364–5, 372
grain, 30, 33, 37, 225
Grand Tour, 4–5
Grant, Eduard, 206
Grant, Effingham, 138, 139, 195, 202–3, 206
Grant, Marie, 206
Grant, Nicolae, 206–10
Grant-Rosetti, Marie, 206
grape shot, 64
Gråsten Castle, 175
Great Perspective (painting), 361
Greek classics, 228
Greek wine cup, *231*
greenhouses, 342, 370–4, 375, 389, 396
Gregson, Nicola, 274
Greig, Hannah, 263
Griffin, Sir John Griffin, 339
grinders, 4, 58
groceries, colonial, 37, 39, 42, 44
Grosser Atlas über Die Gantze Welt (Homann), *345*, 346, 347

Habsburg dynasty, 157, 162
Hague, Stephen, 273
Halifax, Earl of, 277
Hall, Stuart, 382
Hallweyl, Ludwig Friedrich von, 57
Hampton Court, 389
Hancock, David, 231
Handbook of Mewar, 310
Hanley, Ryan, 8
Hanseatic merchants, 3
Hatton, Sir Christopher, 277
Haudenosaunee people, 337, 338, 339

Hauduroy, Samuel, 360
Hawke, Lord, 273
hawking, 87–8
Hawkins, Sir John, 357
Hazlebeach Hall, 267, 270, 273
heating stoves, 181
Heeren XIX, 405, 406, 411
Hemert, Miss Justine van, 185, 186
Hemert, Peter van, 183–4, 187
Henshaw Town, 291
Herckmans, Elias, 420
Hernandez, Francisco, 334
Hidetada, Tokugawa, 87
Hindu households, 308
Histoire des deux Indes (Raynal), 141–2, *141*, 143
Historia Naturalis Brasiliae (Markgraf), 415
The History of England (de Rapin), 112
History of Japan (Kaempfer), 93
Hodgson's (or mountain) hawk eagle, 87
Hogarth, William, 114–15
Hohenzollern-Sigmaringen rule, 195
Höja estate, 32, 33
Holberg, Baron Ludvig, 172
'Holland' linen, 225
Hollandse tegelkamers, 313
Holtz, Eberhard Maximilian vom, 59, 67–8
Holtz, Gottfried vom, 66
Homann, Johann Baptist, 345
Hondecoeter, Melchior de, 367
Hong, Jiang, 385
Hooglandt, Agatha, 184
Hoogstraten, Samuel van, 361
hookahs, 12
Hordesnell, Chief Justice Henry, 362
Horemans, Peter Jakob, 70
Horton, 270, 272–3, 277, 279
  catalogue for the sale at, *280*
Hortus Kewensis, 388
hot drinks, 39, 44, 63, 178
  See also chocolate; coffee; tea
hothouses, 342, 384, 389–90, 396

house contents, Spens family, **35**, **41**
household accounts, 29–30
household possessions, Spens family, 40
houses, prefabricated, 295–7, 299
Howard, Charles William, 363
Howard, Harriett, 363
Howard, Henrietta, Countess of Suffolk, 242
Hudson Bay Company, 358
Huis ten Bosch, 422
Hume, Lady Amelia, 397
Humphreys, Elizabeth, 130
hunting, 86–7, 153, 203, 204
Hutchinson, Mary, 107, 111–12
Huygens, Constantijn, 406, 409, 421

identity, personal, and second-hand goods, 276–7
Ieharu, Tokugawa, 95
Ieyasu, Shogun Tokugawa, 77, 79, 87, 88–9, 94
illicit trade, in the Caribbean, 109–10
Ilmakunnas, Johanna, 45
Imbua, David, 289, 295
imitation, 3–4, 46, 59, 67, 157, 222, 269
imperialism, 5, 6, 135, 161, 218
 and Maurits, 406, 423
Imperial Knights, 11, 53–71
import-substitution, 3–4, 10, 157, 269
incense, 92
income, Spens family, 32–3
India, 307–25
Indian chintz, 272
Indian earthenware jars, 160, 162
Indian furniture, 134, 135, 271
The Indian Nectar, Or a Discourse Concerning Chocolata, 368
Indian pieces, 151
Indian porcelain, 273
Indian textiles, 110, 272
India prints, 110–11
indigenous people, 223–5
interior (painting), *208*, *209*

interior boieresc, 205
Interior with Lamplight Effect (painting), 206
inventories, probate. *See* probate inventories
'Irish' linen, 225
iron gate, 334, 335
iron manillas, 292
iron palace, 285–7, 289, 298, 300
 of King Eyembo, plans and view, *286*
Iroquois people, 337, 338, 339
Isaacs, Samuel, 134, 135
Islamic courts, 308
Israel, Jonathan, 405, 406
Itamaracá Island, view of (painting), *349*, 351
ivory, 84, 92, 135, 269–70, 277, 281
 handles on cutlery, 279

Jagat Singh II, Maharana, 318
Jahangir, Mughal Emperor, 308, 309
Jaipur, 345–6
Jaipur observatory, 346
Jaisalmer Fort in Kishangarh, 307, 311
Jamaica, 102, 110, 111, 112–14, 117–18, 388
 and Spanish merchants, 109
 and tea, 106–8
Jamaica Ladies: Female slaveholders and the creation of Britain's Atlantic empire (Walker), 111–12
Jamaican mahogany, 362–3
James, Abraham, 116–17, 118
Jantar Mantar, 346
Japan, 77–96, 249–1
Japan Closet, Dyrham Park, 367
Japanese cups, 158
The Japanese Discovery of Europe (Keene), 96
Japanese paintings, 85
Japanese porcelain, 12, 180–1
Japanese tea ceremony: utensils, *91*
Japanisches Palais, 309
japanned furniture, 222

Jesuits, 346
jewellery, Spens family, 34, 36, 40
Jianu, Angela, 201
jinbaori, *249*, 249–1
Johan Maurits, Count of Nassau-Siegen, *424*
John, Robin, 292–3
Johnson, Laura, 225
John VII the Middle of Nassau-Siegen, 408
Junagarh Fort in Bikaner, 307
Juna Mahal in Dungarpur, 307, 323–4

Kaempfer, Engelbert, 93
Kalenberg, 200
Kan'ami, 88
Kanazawa Castle, 80
Kangxi porcelain tiles, 311–13, 321
Kangxi vases, *181*
Kanō Eitoku, 80
karamonoya, 95
Karan Singh I, Maharana, 312
Karl Philipp of Schwarzenberg, Prince, 200
Kasaba, Reşat, 194
Katagiri Sadamasa, 90
Keene, Donald, 96
Kenseth, Joy, 363
Ketelaar, Johan Josua, 314–15
kettles, 4, 58, 104, 107, 110, 178, 246
    silver, 59, 115
Kew Gardens, 242, 383
Kick, Everhard, 390
in-kind economy, 31
kingwood, 267, 268, 276
Kinoshita Junji, 250
Kipling, Rudyard, 381–2
Kirby Hall, 272, 277
Kizaemon tea bowl, 92
knife handles, 270
Knights, Imperial, 11, 53–71
konak, 196, 198, 199, 201, 202, 203, 207–8
Kongen af Danmark (ship), 127
Korea, 87
Korean tea bowls, 92

Kragsbjerg Manor, 179–80
Krünitz, Georg, 64
Kunst und Wunderkammern, 392–3
Kutsuki Masatsuna, 95
Kyōhō meibutsuchō, *86*

Labrot, Gerard, 148
Lace, Ambrose, 292, 293
lacquer *inrō* with hawk, *88*
lacquer panelling *à la chinoise*, *177*
Laguerre, Louis, 4
Laird, Mark, 389, 396
laken, 250
lake palace (Udaipur City Palace), 309–17
Lamoral, Charles-Joseph, Prince de Ligne and Marshal of the Holy Roman Empire, 200
Landscape in Brazil (drawing), 416–17, *417*
Laxton Hall, 266
Leigh, Lord, 276
Leith Hill Place, 'Plant Hunters' exhibition, 397
lemons, 39, 42
Lenape nation, 225
leopard skin, 271
Leopoldberg, 200
Levi, Giovanni, 174
Lewis, Anna, 110
libraries, 93, 228, 229, 231
Liebenstein, Maria Frederica von, 64
Life in the English Country House (Girouard), 78
Lightfoot, John, 395
Lilje, Joseph Christian, 184, 185
Lille Hesbjerg Manor, Funen, 172, 179–83, 187, 188
linen, 39, 42, 180, 225
linen bounty, 130
Linnaeus, Carl, 396–7
lions, 153, 251
Lisbon, Santos Palace, 309
Liverpool, 285, 288, 289, 291, 296–7, 300
Liverpool Hall, 288
loaf sugar, 39
localism, 11–12

Logan, James, 129, 215, 216, 217, 218–19, 222
  and books, 227, 228–9, 231–2
  brought family tea service from England, 220
  and political and economic involvement with Native inhabitants, 223–7
Logan family, 232
London, George, 372, 388
London-made Logan family tea service, *220*
Long, Edward, 368–9
Longmore, Jane, 300
Louise Henriette of Nassau, 421
Louis XIV, 423
Lucy, George Hammond, 134, 135
Ludwigsburg factory, 59–60
Luso-Brazilian population, 418
luxury goods
  and daimyo, 78
  and Efik traders, 292–3, 294, 295
  in Golescu family, 202
  in India, 308, 315
  in Pignatelli houses, 151, 160
Lynch, Sir Thomas, 364

Madonna di Piedigrotta, 150
Maeda family of Kaga-han, 77
Maeda Toshitsune, 94
Maeda Tsunanori, 93
Magasin Anglais E. Grant & Comp., 203
Maharaja Sawai Man Singh II Museum, 345
mahogany, 12, 267
  Caribbean, 1, 107–8
  chair by William Gomm, *6*
  Jamaican, 362–3
  in Lille Hesbjerg Manor, Funen, 182
  Spanish, 267, 276, 279
  and Spens family, 40, 44, 45
mahogany furniture, 12, 431
  in Northamptonshire auctions, 265–6, 268, 273, 276, 277, 281

mahogany tea chests, 108
Maids Moreton, 275, 277
maisons de plaisance, 183, 188
maladie de porcelaine, 309
Malwa Sultanate, 308
Mandler, Peter, 381
Man in Oriental Clothing (painting), 315
Man Singh Mahal, 313
map collection, of William Blathwayt, 372, 373–4
Marble Hill House, 363
marbles, 230
Maria Teresa of Austria, Empress, 147, 156–7
Markgraf, Georg, 415, 419
Marot, Danial, 367
Martin, Benjamin, 93
Martin, Josiah, 104, 105–6, 109, 112
Martin, Mary, 105–6, 112
Martin, Samuel, 101, 104–5, 107, 109, 113
Martin, Samuel Junior, 108–9
Marybone House, Gloucester, 242
Mary Capel (1630–1715), Later Duchess of Beaufort, and Her Sister Elizabeth (1633–1678), Countess of Carnarvon, 386
Mashiyama Sessai, 85
Masuda Takeshi, 95–6
Matson, Dorothy, 107
Matsudaira Fumai, 92
Matsudaira Sadanobu, 95
Matsudaira Tadami, 94
Matsudaira Yorishige, 81
Matsura Sanenobu, 94
Matsura Seizan, 93
Maurits, Johan, Count of Nassau-Siegen, 349, 350, 405–6, 407–25, *424*
Mauritshuis, 349–51, 421
Mauritsstad, 412–13
  and Recife, map, *407*
McCants, Anne, 4, 55
McClain, Molly, 386
medicinal gardens, 83
Mehta, Fateh Lal, 319

meibutsugari, 91
Meibutsuki (record of famous objects), 90
Meissen factories, 157
Meissen porcelain, 59, 178, 181
Mewar kingdom, 309
Mexican Treasure, 334
Mexico, 160, 161
Michelet, Jules, 201
A Midnight Modern Conversation (painting), 114–15, *115*
Migliaccio, Lucia, Duchess of Floridia, 333
military gear, 85–6
milk, 63, 64, 71
milk jug, 64
milk pitcher, 107
milk pot, 104
Miller, Philip, 389, 390, 398
Mimizuka (Ear Mound), 84
Ming celadon vase, 92
Ming porcelain, 309
miniature paintings, and porcelain cabinets, 317–21
Modyford, Governor Sir Thomas, 364, 365
moiré silk, 177
Moldavia, 138, 193, 194
Monkey Jar, *245*, 246–7
monsoons, 320–1
Montagu, Elizabeth, 393
Monteiro, Carolina, 351
Monteleone Castle, 150, **151**
Moray, Sir Robert, 364, 365
Morse, Edward S., 83–4, 96
Moss, Suzanne, 384
murals
  in the *Chitram ki Burj*, City Palace Udaipur, *317*
  and exoticism, 315–18
Murphy, Kathleen, 387
Murray, John, 298
Musei Petiveriani, 387–8

Nabeshima Naomasa, 94
nankeen china, 272, 279
Naples, Kingdom of, 147, 148, 149, 154, 157, 162

Naples palace, 150–1, 155, 156–7, 159–60
National Trust report on colonialism, slavery and English country houses, 8, 381
Native Americans, 223–5
Natural History Museum, London, 391, 397
Neapolitan aristocrats, 147, 148, 152, 158, 162
  See also Pignatelli family
Nederlandsche Handel Maatschappij, 94
'negro cloth', 130
Nenadic, Stana, 274
Netherlands, 4, 5, 78, 157, 160, 350
  and Blathwayt's cartographical views of, 372
  Het Loo, 367
  porcelain cabinet, 309
  tiles, 313
  Van Campen introduced Dutch classicism to, 409
Neuhausen, Philipp Wilhelm von, 55
Neville, Grey, 339
Neville, Henry, 339
Neville, Richard, 338
Newdigate, Lady Sophia, 395–6
New Holland, 405–6, 410–20
New Map of the Country of Carolina, part of the *Blathwayt Atlas* (Gascoyne), 373–4
Niccolini, Antonio, 334
Nicholls, Henry, 288, 290, 291, 298
Nicholson, Captain Francis, 361–2, 372
Nicolae Golescu, *205*
Niels Krag Levetzau, Count, 179
Nieuhof, Johan, 242, 367
Nijo Castle, 89
Ni'matnama, 308
noh theatre, 88–9
Norris, Jr, Isaac, 231
North America, 215–32
Northamptonshire house sales, 263–81, **266**
Nostell Priory, Yorkshire, 1–2, 12

oak, 266
Octavian, Tudor, 209–10
Oda Nobunaga, 79, 80, 87, 89, 90–1, 94
Oeconomische Encyclopädie (Krünitz), 64
Ogasawara etiquette rule book for the military classes, 89, 90
Ogilvie, Shelagh, 4
Ökna estate, 32, 33
The Old [walnut] Staircase, Dyrham Park, *360*
Old Calabar, West Africa, 285–6
Old Staircase of American black walnut, 360
Old Town, Old Calabar, 291
Olinda, 411
olive oil, 65
olives, 65
Olusoga, David, 8
Ōmura Sumihisa, 94
orientalism, 242–3
oriental porcelain, 7, 45, 158
　See also Chinese porcelain; Japanese porcelain
ornamental interior detail showing the *farangi* theme, *316*
Osnabrück, 129
osnaburgs, 129–30
　advertisements for, *129*
ostriches, 153
ostrich feathers, 295
Otele, Olive, 8
'other', 11
Ottoman Porte, 194, 195
Overton, Mark, 69
Owari Tokugawa, 96
Owen, Nicholas, 294
oznabrigs, 225

pagodas, 242–3
　Chinese, model of, *241*, 242–3
Paine, James, 1
paintings
　Chinese and Japanese, 85
　miniature, and porcelain cabinets, 317–21

Palace of the Marquess de Fronteira in Lisbon, 313
Palladio, Andrea, 196
Paris, Treaty of, 296
Parr family, 300–1
pastries, 62–3
Patta Palace, 313
Paul of Aleppo, 198
Paulownia, 84
peacocks, 153–4
Penn, Sir W., 273
Pennsylvania, 215, 218–19
peregrine falcon, 87
Persia, 308–9
personal identity, and second-hand goods, 276–7
Petiver, James, 387, 390
pewter, 58–9, 64
　coffee pots, 58, 69
　plates, 220
　serving dishes, 220
　teapots, 58, 59, 68
Philips, Harry, 263
Philosophical Grammar: Being a View of the Present State of Experimented Physiology or Natural Philosophy (Martin), 93
Philosophical Transactions (Royal Society), 390
pianos, 269, 270
Pignatelli, Duchess Margherita, 147, 156–7
Pignatelli, Duke Nicolò, 150, 157
Pignatelli Aragona Cortés, Duke Diego, ninth Duke of Monteleone and Terranova, prince of Castelvetrano, Duke of Bellosguardo, prince of the Holy Roman Empire, marquis of the Oaxaca Valley, knight of the Toson d'or, 148, 149, 150, 152, 154, 157
Pignatelli family, 148, 149–51, 152, 157, 159–60, 162
Pignatelli houses, **151**, 161
　See also Naples palace; villa Pignatelli
Pignatelli Museum, 158

pineapples, 11–12, 334–5, 342, 343
pinery, *341*, 342–3
Piso, Willem, 415, 419–20
Pitam Niwas Apartments, 319
placenames, and provenance, 271–3, 277, 281
Plans, elevations and sections, of hot-houses, green-houses, an aquarium, conservatories (Tod), 342
Plante, Franciscus, 420, 424
'Plant Hunters' exhibition at Leith Hill Place, 397
plants, exotic. *See* exotic plants
'A Plated Article' (Dickens), 322
plates
    Blue Willow Pattern, Staffordshire, 321, 322, *322*, 323–4
    pewter, 220
Plumstead, Clement, 226
Pococke, Richard, 396
'Politicising Plants' (Buchan et al.), 397
Pope, David, 300
porcelain
    at auctions, 274
    in the Caribbean, 108
    Copenhagen, 180, 181
    Duchess Augusta's, 178
    Imperial Knights, 59–61, 62, 66–9
    Japanese, 12, 180–1
    Meissen, 59, 178, 181
    Ming, 309
    oriental, 7, 45, 158
    Pignatelli family's, 156–61
    and provenance, 272
    Spens family's, 45
    teapot with lid, Ludwigsburg, *60*
    tea sets, 114
    tiles, 321
    of Ulugh Beg, 308
    vases in Kangxi style, *181*
    Yuan, 308–9
    See also Chinese porcelain
porcelain cabinets, 309, 311–21, 323, 325
Porcelain Pagoda of Nanjing, 242
porcelain rooms, 307, 324–5, 367
    City Palace of Udaipur, 311–17
    contemporary use, 317–21
    furnished with Staffordshire Blue Willow Pattern plates, *322*
    transformation of in the nineteenth century, 321–4
porcupine ray skins, 86
Portici, Royal Palace, 152
Portland, Margaret Cavendish Harley Bentinck Duchess of, 382, 391–7
'Portlandia Grandiflora' (painting), *394*
Portrait of William Ansah Sessarakoo, son of Eno Baisie Kurentsi (John Currantee) of Anomabu, 293
Post, Frans, 349, 350, 351, 416, 419, 422
Post, Pieter, 409, 410
pottery manufacturing, in Barbados, 246–7
Pouelle, Magdalena, 389
Poukens, Jan, 4
Povey, Anne, 356, 357
Povey, Justinian, 356–7
Povey, Thomas, 356, 361, 365, 366, 368, 369
Powderham Castle, Devon, 342
Powys, Mrs Philip Lybbe, 396
Powys Castle, *7*, 135
prefabricated houses, 295–7, 299
Price, Charles, 374
Principe Diego Aragona Pignatelli Cortes Museum, Naples, 149
probate inventories, 103, 148
    of Imperial Knights, 55, 65
    of Spens family, 27, 29, 31, 45
provenance, 271–3, 277
Prown, Jules, 148
punch bowls, 114, 118, 180
punch ladles, 112, 114, 118
Purefoy, Elizabeth, 263, 264, 275
Purefoy, Henry, 277
Pye, Jael Henrietta, 385

Quinet, Edgar, 201

Racoviță, Zoe, 206
Rajasthan, 309–17
Rajput palaces, 307, 308, 324–5
  City Palace of Udaipur, 307,
    309–17, 322, 323
raku, 90
Rakusaidō, 93
Randolph, Edward, 359–60, 372
ranpeki, 94–5
Rantzau, Countess Birgitte
    Eleonora, 179, 180, 181–2,
    183, 187
Rapin, Paul de, 112
Ratcliffe, Elizabeth, 242–3
Ray, John, 387
Raynal, Guillaume Thomas
    François, 141–3
ray skins, 86
Read, Charles, 226
Recchi, Nardo Antonio, 334
Recife, 411–12, 413
  and Mauritsstad, map, *407*
recipe collections, 62–3
red deer roast, 64
redware bowl with a slip-figure of a
    Native American, 224, *224*
Rembrandt, 315
Revolutionary Romania (painting),
    206
Ricci, Matteo, 94
rice, 77, 78
Rice, Charles, 207
Riello, Giorgio, 6, 103
Robins, Willy Tom, 294–5
Rollaston Hall, 266, 269
roller blinds, 180, 182
Roman classics, 228
Romania, 138–9, 193–211
The Romanian (Românul), 202,
    204
Romanian elite, 196, 200, 205, 206,
    210, 211
  and Effingham Grant's shop, 203
  subscribed to foreign newspapers,
    202
Rose, Martha, 112–13

Rosetti, Constantin A., 139, 206
rosewood, 267, 268, 281
Rost Pfiff, 65
Rothery, Mark, 68
Rousseau, Jean Jacques, 395
Rowland, Thomas, 264
Royal African Company, 358
Royal Cabinet of Paintings, 349
Royal Chartered Danish Asiatic
    Company, 125–6, 127, 169,
    188
Royal Palace, Portici, 152
Rückerschöld, Anna Maria, 44
rum, 112, 113, 118
rum punch, 114
  bowls, 112, 114
  wares, 112, 113
Rushton Hall, 271

Sadanobu, Matsudaira, 95
Said, Edward, 11
Saint-Barthélemy, 28
Saint-Fond, Barthélemy Faujas de,
    343
Sala dos Paineis, Palace of the
    Marquess de Fronteira, Lisbon,
    313
salt-glazed stoneware teapot, 221
sandalwood, 92
Sanenobu, Matsura, 94
Sangram Singh, Maharana, 310,
    315
sankin kōtai (alternate attendance),
    78
Santos Palace, Lisbon, 309
Satake Shozan, 85
satinwood, 267, 268
  table, 276
saucers, 104, 107, 108, 109, 172,
    173
Sawai Jai Singh II, Maharaja,
    346–7
Schimmelmann, Baron von, 7
Schloss Hohenstadt, 68, 69
Schloss Schechingen, 68
Scipio Africanus, 363
'Seaweed Castle' (*Tamamo-jō*), *81*
Sebastopol campaign, 339

INDEX   447

second-hand goods, 274–80, 281
Segar Smoking Society in Jamaica (satirical print), 116–17, *117*, 118
Seizan, Matsura, 93
Sekishū, 90
self-fashioning, 293–4
self-orientalism, 243
Sen no Rikyū, 92
serving dishes, pewter, 220
Sessarakoo, William Ansah, portrait, *293*
Seven Years War, 339
shachihoko, 79
Sharpe, Katherine, 270
sheesh mahal, 310
Sheffield, Lord, 130
Shelburne, Lady, 397
shell grottoes, 395
shells, 254–5, 270, 277, 395
shellwork shadowbox grotto, *253*, 254–5
Sherard, William, 387
Shiba Kōkan, 93
Shimazu Shigehide, 94
Shiva, 318
Shiva, Maharana Ari Singh seated at night. On the terrace of the *Chini ki Chitrashali*, *318*
shoin-zukuri, 81
Shteir, Ann, 384
Shugborough Hall, Staffordshire, 13, 242
Sichterman, Jan Albert, 7
Sierra Leone Company, 296
silk, 11, 37, 39, 42, 105–6, 177
  furniture upholstered with, 182
silver
  birds chiselled on silvers, *154*
  for chocolate, 61
  coffee spoons, 59
  coffee trays, 59, 62
  cutlery with ivory handles, 269
  kettles, 59, 115
  snuff boxes, 55
  Spens family's, 34, 40
  for tea and coffee, 59
  tea urns, 62

Skene, James Henry, 193, 194, 195, 196–7, 201, 203
skins, animal, 225, 270, 271, 277–8, 281
Skipp, Mary, 111
skyphos, 230–1, *231*
slavery, 118, 119, 223, 370
  in Dutch Brazil, 351
  and silk, 103–5, 106
slave trade, 8, 142, 143, 226, 232, 367–9
  in Brazil, 412
  and elite Africans, 297
  and Johan Maurits, 350
  and Liverpool, 300–1
  and Marble Hill House, 363
  and Royal African Company, 358
  and West African traders, 290, 291–3
Slesvig-Holsten-Sønderborg, Duke of, 174
Sloane, Sir Hans, 229, 387, 388, 389, 390, 391
Sloboda, Stacey, 394
Smeathman, Henry, 395
Smith, George, 269
Smith, John, 219, 222, 224, 226, 227, 228
  on Logan's library, 229
Smith, Kate, 6, 158–9, 160, 269
Smith, Thomas, 389
Smith, Woodruff, 56
snuff, 55
snuff boxes, 55–6
social capital, 71, 277
Solander, Daniel, 395
Soler, Margarita, 417–18
Soler, Vincent, 417
Solms-Braunfels, Amalia von, 309, 410
Somerset, Henrietta, 394
Somerset, Henry, Duke of Beaufort, 385
Somerset, Mary, Duchess of Beaufort, 382, 385–91, *386*, 397
Somerset Act, 370
Sonnenburg Castle of the Order of Saint John, 423

Sotheby, John, 263
South Sea Company, 363
Southwell, Sir Robert, 387
south-west Germany, 53–4, 55, 57, 61, 62, 64, 66, 71
'Sowing Roots: Caribbean Garden Heritage in South London', 397
Spain, and the Caribbean, 109, 110
Spanish chairs, 110
Spanish chests, 110
Spanish mahogany, 267, 276, 279
Sparks, Randy, 290
sparrowhawk, 87
Spekelands, 300
spending, Spens family, 40, 42–4
Spens, Count Carl Gustaf, 27, 29, 31
Spens, Countess Beata née Oxenstierna af Croneborg, 29, 30, 34, 36, 37, 39, 44
Spens, Countess Ulrika Eleonora née Falkenberg af Bålby, 27, 29, 30, 31, 34, 44
Spens family, 29–30, 31–46, 47–9
  annual income and expenditure, **32**
  assets, **31**
spices, Spens family, 39, 44
'Spring (Johanna de Lasence Drinking Coffee in the Garden)', *70*
Spring Grove, Middlesex, 342–3
staircases, 360–1, *360*, 362, 375
Stanford Hall, 267, 274, 275, 276
Stanwick, 272
statues, Chinese, 157
statuette of Jacob Beckmann, *125*, 126
St Croix (island), 169
Steers, John, 225
Stenton, 215, 216–18, *216*, 219–22, *221*, 225–32
  desk and bookcase in the parlour with the Greek wine cup, or skyphos, and marble sample, *231*
St John (island), 169

St Martin's, Northamptonshire, 268, 269, 270
Stobart, Jon, 68, 148
Stoneleigh Abbey, 276
stones to ignite gunpowder, 64
stoneware, 59, 180, 221
Strode, William, 115
The Strode Family (painting), 115–16, *116*
Stroud cloth, 225
St Thomas (island), 169
Sudborough House, 273
sugar, 4, 8, 63, 64, 358
  mills, 412
  and pottery manufacturing, 246
  and Spens family, 44, 45
  tongs, 172
'the Sugar House', 350
Swarup Singh, Maharana, 321
Sweden, 5, 28, 34, 44, 46
Swedish East India Company (SOIC), 28
swings, 316
Switzer, Stephen, 370, 387
sword furniture, 86
swords, 86
symbolic capital, 85

tableware, 40, 180–1, 274
Tadami, Matsudaira, 94
Talman, William, 360
tansu, 84
Tanuma Okitsugu, 95
Tapuya Indians, 421, 422
Tarleton, John, 300
Tart Hall, 309
tea, 4, 55, **58**, 63–4, 101–2
  in the Caribbean, 106–11, 113–14
  ceramics paraphernalia, **60**
  and Imperial Knights, 57
  and Royal Chartered Danish Asiatic Company, 125
  and Samuel Martin, 104
  and silver, 59
  with slices of buttered bread, 62
  in south-western German country houses, 71
  and Spens family, 44

tea bowls, 92
'tea bread', 63
tea caddies, 58, 59, 92
tea ceremony (*chanoyu*), 89–93
Tea Ceremony Ogasawara shorei taizen, in *The Complete Ogasawara Etiquette*, 90
tea chests, 108
tea cups, 67–8
tea-drinking, 115, 220, 431
   portrait of a family, in an interior, *368*
   'Two Ladies Drinking Tea', *63*
teapots
   Chinese porcelain, 221, *221*
   in Denmark, 172, 181
   Imperial Knights, 57, 58, 59, 68
   salt-glazed stoneware, 221
   at Stenton, 221, *221*
tea service, Logan family London-made, 220, *220*
tea sets, 64, 114, 178
tea tables, 107–8
tea urns, 58, 59, 62, 66, 69
Temple, Sir William, 373
Temple of the Sun at Palmyra, 243
tempura, 94
tenshu, 79, 82
Terwen, J.J., 407, 413, 416
Tessin, Anna Elisabetha Philippina von, 66
Tessin family, 68
textiles
   furnishing, 268–9
   Indian, 110, 272
   key good of exchange, 225, 226
   osnaburgs, 129–30
   Spens family's, 37, 39, 40, 42, 45
Thellusson, Peter, 141, 142, 143
Third Anglo-Mysore War, 339
Thomas Parr House, *301*
Thorp Malsor, 267, 277
tiger skins, 271, 278, 281
tiles
   Blue Willow Pattern porcelain, 321

   Chinese, 308, 319, 321
   Dutch, 222, *223*, 307, 313, *314*, 319
   Kangxi, 311–13, 321
timber, 77, 265, 277, 359–60, 361–2
Timur, 308
tin, 58–9, 64
Tipu Sultan, 339
Titsingh, Isaac, 95
tobacco, 55, **56**, 257–8
tobacco pipes, 55
tobacco rolls, *257*, 258
Tobin, Fowkes, 385, 392–3
Tod, George, 342
Tod, James, 310
tokonoma, 81
Tokugawa Art Museum, 96
Tokugawa Hidetada, 87
Tokugawa Ieharu, 95
Tokugawa Ieyasu, Shogun, 77, 79, 87, 88–9, 94
Tokugawa Yoshimune, 86, 94
Tokugawa Yoshinao, 86
Tolsà, Manuel, 161
tombac, 56
tomoe, 251
Topkapi Palace, 308
Topkapi Palace Museum, 311
Toshitsune, Maeda, 94
Toson d'Or, 149, 157
townhouses, 68, 69
Toyotomi Hideyoshi, 79, 87, 88, 89, 94
tozama, 81
Tranquebar, 169
Treaty of Adrianople, 138, 194
Treaty of Paris, 296
trophies, 84–5
tropical plants, 383, 421
   See also exotic plants
tropical woods, 4, **266**, 267
   See also individual woods
Tsunanori, Maeda, 93
Tughlaq palace of Firuz Shah, 308
Tughlaq Sultanate, 308
Twining, Daniel, 108–9
'Two Ladies Drinking Tea', *63*

Udaipur City Palace, 309–17
Udaipur, Rajasthan, 309–17
Udai Singh II, Maharana, 309, 323, 324
Ulugh Beg, 308
umbrellas, 298, 299
Union of the Romanian Principalities, 195
Upon the Gardens of Epicurus (Temple), 373
utensils, Japanese Tea Ceremony, *91*
Uya, Okon Edet, 296

vases
   Chinese, 157
   porcelain, in Kangxi style, *181*
Veblen, Thorstein, 173
View of Itamaracá Island (painting), *349*, 351
villa Pignatelli, 150, 151–2, 153, 155–6
Virginia walnut, 267, 359–60, 361, 375
Vizagapatam, India, 134, 135
Vorstius, Adolph, 421
Vrijburg, c. 1645–7, *408*
Vrijburg palace, 412, 413–15, 423

Waddell, Hope Masterton, 285–7, 291, 294, 295, 298–9, 300
Wadström, Carl Bernard, 296, 297
Wagener, Zacharias, 420
wainscoting, 362
'Walking Purchase', 224–5
Wall, Cynthia, 277
Wallachia, 138, 193, 194–5, 203
wallpapers, Chinese, 1, 12, 156, 182
walnut, 266–7, 359–60, 361, 362
Walpole, Horace, 392
war clubs, 337–9, *337*
Warg, Kajsa, 44
Washington, George, 130
washstands, 180
water pitchers, 245–7
Watson-Wentworth, Mary, marchioness of Rockingham, 397
Weatherill, Lorna, 55

Wedgwood, Josiah, 12, 157
Weiler, Eberhardine von, 64
Weir, Reverend James, 388
Wendell, Evert, 129
West, Benjamin, 339
West Africa, 285–301
West India Company (WIC), 405–6, 410, 412, 420–1
Whiteknights, Berkshire, 342
Wilanow Palace, Poland, 313
Willement, Thomas, 134
William Frederic, count of Nassau, 421
William III, King, 359, 373
Williams, Winn, 275
Willoughby, Cassandra, 389
Wilton House, Virginia, *10*
wine
   in Jamaica, 113
   and Spens family, 36, 37, 39, 42, 45
Winn, Sabine, 1
Winn, Sir Rowland, 1
Winterer, Caroline, 227
Woburn Abbey, 342
Woellwarth, Wilhelmine von, 64
'wokism', 8
Wollaston Hall, 271
women, and botany, 384–97
wood
   aloeswood, 92
   brazilwood, 267
   kingwood, 267, 268, 276
   oak, 266
   rosewood, 267, 268, 281
   sandalwood, 92
   satinwood, 267, 268, 276
   walnut, 266–7, 359–60, 361, 362
   zebrawood, 267
   See also exotic wood; mahogany; tropical woods
Woodforde, Parson, 275, 280
wool, 250
the *Wunderkammer*, 363–4, 392–3
Wynter, George, 357
Wynter, John, 357
Wynter, Mary, 357
Wynter, Sir William, 357

Yam Custom, 298
Yorishige, Matsudaira, 81
Yoshimune, Tokugawa, 86, 94
Yoshinao, Tokugawa, 86
Young, Ebo, 288
Yuan porcelain, 308–9

Ze'ami, 88
zebrawood, 267
Zij-i-Muhammad Shahi, 346
Zucchi, Antonio, 1

www.ingramcontent.com/pod-product-compliance
Lightning Source LLC
Chambersburg PA
CBHW042258240125
20677CB00034B/16